W9-BDS-384

GOD'S

Almost

CHOSEN

PEOPLES

I shall be an humble instrument in the

hands of the Almighty, and of this, his

almost chosen people.

— *Abraham Lincoln, Address to the*

 New Jersey Senate, February 21, 1861

THE LITTLEFIELD HISTORY

OF THE CIVIL WAR ERA

Gary W. Gallagher and T. Michael Parrish, editors

Supported by the Littlefield Fund for

Southern History, University of Texas Libraries

GOD'S

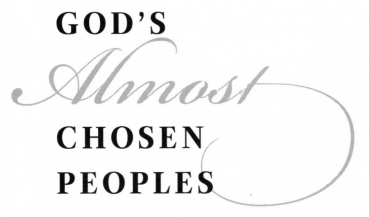

CHOSEN

PEOPLES

A RELIGIOUS HISTORY OF

THE AMERICAN CIVIL WAR

GEORGE C. RABLE

THE UNIVERSITY OF NORTH CAROLINA PRESS

Chapel Hill

© 2010 The University of North Carolina Press
All rights reserved

Set in Arnhem, TheSerif and Bickham types
by Tseng Information Systems, Inc.
Manufactured in the United States of America

The paper in this book meets the guidelines for
permanence and durability of the Committee on
Production Guidelines for Book Longevity of the
Council on Library Resources.

The University of North Carolina Press has been
a member of the Green Press Initiative since 2003.

Library of Congress Cataloging-in-Publication Data
Rable, George C.
God's almost chosen peoples : a religious history of the
American Civil War / George C. Rable. — 1st ed.
    p. cm. — (The Littlefield history of the Civil War era)
Includes bibliographical references (p.) and index.
ISBN 978-0-8078-3426-8 (cloth : alk. paper)
1. United States—History—Civil War, 1861–1865—Religious
aspects. 2. United States—Religion—19th century. I. Title.
E635.R33 2010
973.7′78—dc22   2010023646

14 13 12 11 10 5 4 3 2 1

For

Kay, Anne, Katie, and Dave

And to my teachers:

Robert Robinson,

John D. Unruh Jr.,

William J. Cooper Jr., and

T. Harry Williams

CONTENTS

ILLUSTRATIONS

GOD'S Almost CHOSEN PEOPLES

PROLOGUE

In August 1864, Presbyterian editor Amasa Converse concluded that the past three years of war had clearly demonstrated the power of prayer. The first great Confederate victory at Manassas in July 1861 had followed an official day of prayer. But then a period of spiritual indifference during the fall and winter had preceded disastrous losses in Tennessee. The southern people again fell to their knees during the spring of 1862, and Richmond had been delivered from General George B. McClellan's mighty hosts. Other victories had followed, but too much faith had been placed in generals and armies, and so once again God's favor had temporarily departed, and General Robert E. Lee had retreated from the bloody Antietam battlefield. March 27, 1863, had been another day of fasting, humiliation, and prayer, and a little over a month later came the dramatic triumph at Chancellorsville. Yet, once more, people had relied on human strength, neglected prayer, and received their just punishment at Gettysburg and Vicksburg. But after a fast day in August 1863, southern arms enjoyed a glorious victory at Chickamauga, thus sparking a season of intense revivalism in the Confederate armies. And following a fast day on April 8, 1864, southern armies had enjoyed a nearly "unbroken" string of successes that had stymied both Ulysses S. Grant and William T. Sherman.[1]

One could easily object to Converse's chronology and theology, but his long editorial exemplified a pervasive, providential interpretation of the Civil War. Men, women, and children, free and slave, Protestants, a growing number of Catholics, Mormons, and even the small number of Jews formed a complex cultural mosaic, but one that nevertheless shared a providential outlook on life. Historians have yet to write a religious history of the Civil War, but many Americans living during the era saw God's hand in the war's origins, course, and outcome. Prominent Methodist divine Daniel S. Doggett recognized how reluctant historians might be to acknowledge the Almighty's role in human history. "It has become customary for history to ignore God," he lamented in an 1862 Thanksgiving sermon. "The pride of the human heart is intolerant of God, and historians are too obsequious to its dictates. They collect and arrange their materials; they philosophize upon them. But their philosophy knows not God." Ministers often excoriated both individuals and nations for a variety of sins, but Doggett feared that historians failed to recognize, much less understand, how the war marked the unfolding of divine purpose. "Those who undertake the task of committing to posterity the record of our times, will be guilty of startling dereliction, if the manifest and acknowledged hand of God be discarded from their pages."[2]

Doggett was largely right about the historians, but many of his contemporaries embraced a providential understanding of not only the war but also everyday life.[3] Everything—storms, harvests, illnesses, deaths—unfolded according to God's will. Popular understandings of how the Almighty shaped the destinies of individuals and nations may not have been profound, but such beliefs were pervasive. Northerners and southerners, blacks and whites often spoke in remarkably similar ways. References to God's will filled diaries, letters, conversations, and presumably many people's thoughts. For some folks, explaining fortune in terms of divine favor or calamities as signs of divine judgment might have been simply customary or habitual, verbal ticks that hardly bespoke deep piety. And those hostile or indifferent to any religious world view hardly thought in such terms. But even taking such people into account, a good number of Americans sincerely believed that the Almighty ruled over affairs large and small. So it was hardly surprising when they saw the anguish of sectional strife and civil war reflecting a providential design.

In what remained a largely pre-Darwinian world, countless Americans would have agreed that the Lord's will governed all operations in the universe. Presbyterian Robert Lewis Dabney, eulogizing another stern Presbyterian, Thomas J. Jackson (struck down in the hour of victory at Chancellorsville by friendly fire), clung to the strictest Calvinist precepts: "God's special providence is over all his creatures, and all their actions; it is them that fear Him; for their good only. By that almighty and omniscient providence, all events are either produced; or at least permitted, limited, and overruled." In battle, the smallest actions conformed to the divine will. "Even when the thousand missiles of death, invisible to mortal sight, and sent forth aimless by those who launched them, shoot in inexplicable confusion over the battle-field, His eye gives each one an aim and a purpose according to the plan of his wisdom."[4]

Dabney's view reflected a belief in divine sovereignty firmly rooted in the Protestant Reformation, English Puritanism, and the Great Awakening. Despite the emphasis on human agency in the Second Great Awakening, the spread of Arminianism, Charles G. Finney's "new measures" revivalism, and the fracturing of Calvinism, traditional notions of providence held sway among clergy and laity alike. The laws of God still determined the course of human history. Even as the sectional conflict reached a crisis point in the wake of Abraham Lincoln's election, any resolution remained outside human control. A New School Presbyterian editor warned that "there is a Third Party, higher than both—the great Judge of all the Earth, the Governor among the nations, who has a controversy with the whole people, not so much for their sectional injuries to each other as for their common and united offenses against Him." But it was not only Calvin's heirs who made such statements. Methodists, Episcopalians, and many others believed in a sovereign God who decreed the fate of nations.[5]

Many pious folk surely missed the irony of citizens in a republic affirming the unlimited sovereignty of God. There was after all a certain tension between divine authority and popular democracy, but to most Americans faith and freedom went hand in hand. Indeed, freedom and voluntarism had become hallmarks of religious practice in the United States, and most people did not even notice any contradictions between civil and biblical religion. Civil religion in America developed as a set of beliefs about the relationship between God and the nation that emphasized national virtue, national purpose, and national destiny. A general faith in the work of divine providence in human history grew into a more specific conviction that Americans were a people chosen by God to carry out his mission in the world. The creation and growth of the American republic therefore acquired transcendent meaning and signified the Lord's direct intervention in human history. Religious faith and civic belief reinforced each other as the nation's unfolding history and democratic institution became expressions of God's will.[6]

Puritans, Quakers, and Baptists among other groups had long described God as an absolute monarch. From an orthodox perspective, all human institutions, including churches, had limited authority, an assertion that ironically gave Americans increasing freedom to decide the most fundamental religious questions for themselves. In stressing both divine sovereignty and human means to advance the Lord's kingdom in America, Finney and other revivalists squared a changeless God with an ever-changing society. As millennial optimism followed in the wake of revivalism, many of the devout no longer viewed God's kingdom as otherworldly but rather expected the reign of a triumphant Christ to begin soon (if it had not already begun) on earth—and specifically in America. Relying on tortured readings of Revelation and other prophetic scriptures, Americans tied messianic hope to national destiny. Of course, premillennialists still anticipated a fiery judgment before Christ's return, but many Americans exuded a far more optimistic faith. This kind of reasoning produced one notably striking conclusion: a host of social problems ranging from materialism to alcoholism to slavery could and would be alleviated, if not eradicated altogether.[7] But despite such optimistic expectations, sectional tensions mounted, and the war came.

So did millennial hopes then give way to apocalyptic fears? In the war's first years not at all, and only rarely in the war's later years, even as Confederates watched their dream of separate nationhood collapse. Apocalyptic imagery acquired a certain currency, but rebel and Yankee alike saw themselves as part of a righteous, redeemer nation. Even warnings about divine judgment became justifications for patriotic sacrifice, a call to action rather than a surrender to despair. As Abraham Lincoln would eloquently observe toward the war's end, both sides not only prayed to the same God but also read the same Bibles. And whatever their differences over such matters as slavery and political preaching, both sides read their Bibles in remarkably similar ways. Ministers had long seen the American republic as a new Israel, and Confederate preachers viewed the southern nation in roughly the same light.[8] The relentless, often careless application of biblical typologies to national problems, the ransacking of scripture for parallels between ancient and modern events produced a nationalistic theology at once bizarre, inspiring, and dangerous. Favorite scripture passages offered meaning and hope to a people in the darkest hours and, at the same time, justified remorseless bloodshed.

Complex rationalizations and special pleading reflected more than simply the process of patriotic nationalism corrupting religious faith. A great crisis compounded life's normal uncertainties, especially over questions of ultimate meaning. When war breaks out, people often sacrifice religious to patriotic principles, but theological inconsistencies reflected more than intellectual dishonesty or even a failure of moral imagination. It was one thing to believe that divine providence governed human history, quite another to discern the Lord's purpose with any degree of clarity and certainty. Dabney readily admitted—as any good Calvinist would—that human minds were too "puny" to comprehend the ways of God. Ultimately, faith could not be separated from the irreducible mystery that human beings saw, at best, through a glass darkly. Given the confusion of ideas and purposes in the war itself, Nathaniel Hawthorne wondered if the "Great Arbiter to whom they [northerners and southerners] so piously and solemnly appeal must be sorely puzzled to decide." Few Americans, however, would have expressed such doubts. Despite the temptation to view calamities as punishment for sin, whether such a simple relationship actually reflected the Lord's immediate purpose—much less some larger plan—remained to be seen. A Unitarian and former Harvard president made this very point in an election sermon before the Massachusetts legislature. His censure of self-righteous busybodies who seemed to delight in human suffering was a point well taken, but many people longed to find some larger significance in all the sacrifice and bloodshed. Satisfactory answers were not forthcoming, not even from experts. Correspondents asked the editor of the nation's leading religious weekly, the *Independent*, to explain how the war's course fulfilled prophecies in Revelation: he demurred except to argue that God surely willed the death of slavery.[9]

_____

However much the problems and contradictions might weigh on historians studying wartime religion, many people of the Civil War generation simply looked to their religious faith for consolation, if not understanding. To ask whether the war shattered millennial hopes or even weakened religious faith is to pose the wrong question. Both in the short term and even by the end of the war, a providential interpretation of events with millennial overtones showed remarkable staying power. Religious faith itself became a key part of the war's unfolding story for countless Americans, and historians must address that reality.

I have chosen to subtitle this work "a religious history of the American Civil War." The grand and sweeping narratives of the sectional crisis and Civil War from James Ford Rhodes to Bruce Catton to Shelby Foote and beyond have seldom paid attention to religion much less tried to create a religious narrative of the conflict.[10] Yet many devout people of the time would have considered this a curious omission. Likewise, the easily overlooked article "a" is important here. There could well be many different religious histories of the Civil War written, and in these pages I am presenting merely one. Given the richness of the sources, the importance of the subject, and the complexity of the questions involved, there will be plenty of room left for other religious histories of the conflict.

In fact, the sources themselves require some comment. Not surprisingly, members of the clergy often have prominent speaking roles in this narrative. Ministers of various stripes held forth often and at length on the ripening sectional conflict and war. The published sermons alone are staggering in quantity and diversity, if not always profundity. One friend sarcastically asked how I could stand to read "all those sermons." One obvious answer was in small doses over time, but despite their arid and repetitive nature, the sermons are vitally important, often revealing, and occasionally even stimulating sources for understanding how Americans interpreted the war through a religious lens. Some readers might prefer a more exegetical and extended treatment of major statements on religion (including famous sermons), but I decided not to take this approach because it would have involved hauling out the usual suspects when the point was that many of the ideas discussed in these pages extended beyond the nation's leading pulpits not only into the pews but out into the wider world.[11] Civilians and soldiers alike echoed many of the central themes as they struggled to understand what was happening to themselves, their families, their communities, and their nation. The sheer diversity of perspectives in the midst of certain common assumptions and ideas poses a continuing but worthwhile challenge to anyone tackling this endlessly intriguing topic.

That being said, the purpose here is not primarily to explore the role of the clergy or even the churches. This work is not "church history" in the usual definition of that term, but obviously the history of the churches is an important part of the story. The various synods, conferences, associations, and other ecclesiastical bodies often made official statements about the war, and their records contain important material on a variety of questions.[12] Denominational papers and periodicals proved equally valuable. The three largest Protestant denominations, the Methodists, Baptists, and Presbyterians, all published newspapers that carried voluminous material on any number of subjects. Then too the Catholic press expressed a range of opinion often ignored by students of Civil War religion who have focused almost exclusively on Protestants.[13]

In a still broader sense, Americans who commented on the war whether in newspaper editorials, diaries, or letters to friends and family often remarked about how religious beliefs shaped their views of passing events and larger questions. Here too there are problems of representativeness, and any attempt to comprehensively examine the available material would be more than a lifetime's work. Whatever their limitations, the sources on the topic are rich and virtually endless; for each citation in the notes, five or six were cast aside. I have endeavored throughout the manuscript to include a cross section of denominational and theological perspectives (including the nonreligious), but this was not possible on every issue, especially as I trimmed the documentation from two earlier and considerably longer drafts.

Although this is not a thesis-driven work, it does address important questions about the war's origins, course, and meaning. It is not a history of theology, yet theologians make an occasional appearance, and certainly theological questions receive considerable attention.[14] Nor is the book primarily concerned with the relationship between religious values and the war's conduct. Harry Stout has already offered a searing critique of how civil religion helped justify and sustain an increasingly brutal conflict in his "moral history" of the Civil War.[15] And however pervasive civil religion proved to be in both the Union and the Confederacy, it is far from being the entire story. Instead, what follows is a broad narrative that shows how all sorts of people used faith to interpret the course of the Civil War and its impact on their lives, families, churches, communities, and "nations."

This is by no means a straightforward story, and the narrative has to zigzag and even backtrack to do justice to the struggles of the Civil War generation. For example, emphasizing an all-encompassing civil religion would present a much simpler tale but would miss important exceptions, ignore significant dissenters, and overlook paths not taken. Whatever the obvious pitfalls involved in a more comprehensive and complex religious narrative, it has the advantage of dealing with the many ways in which religious values touched people during the war.

Religious faith had long shaped political attitudes and behavior, not only in the obvious tensions between Protestants and Catholics but also as a reaction to sectional conflict in the 1850s. Not surprisingly, many Americans viewed the secession crisis from a religious perspective.[16] Providence, sin, and judgment became powerful themes in both public and private discourse, and wartime jeremiads—complete with castigation of sinners and warnings of impending judgment—began to appear even before the first shots were fired.[17] From April 1861 on, many northerners and southerners tried to make sense of a brutal war by thumbing through their Bibles, listening to their preachers, and even interpreting battles as a fulfillment of a mysterious, divine plan. Few churchgoers hesitated to hitch their faith to patriotism, and the pious sent off young men to war with remarkable unity and enthusiasm. For clergy and laity alike, the war became a holy crusade.

But how was its course and conduct to be interpreted? Sacrifice and bloodshed tested faith and produced wildly divergent assessments of divine intent. What sins had merited God's wrath? Would the war itself, and especially the evils of camp life, destroy faith, weaken the churches, and delay the coming of God's kingdom?

Folks at home might pray for the soldiers, and chaplains struggled to meet their spiritual needs. Yet, ironically, neither government did much to support those chaplains, and there were never enough good ones.[18] The strain on families and indeed on the churches themselves became a constant, everyday reality. Religious consolation often proved elusive because the war spun out of control and God seemed so far away. Religious beliefs shaped popular thinking on the conflict, but then the war buffeted not only clergy and the laity but also the indifferent and skeptical. Religious faith could be both wind and weathervane—a driving force and a sensitive gauge—but what was perhaps most striking was its flexibility and resilience in the face of political and military storms such as Americans had never before endured.

With remarkable consistency, large numbers of believers persisted in taking a providential view of both daily life and wartime events. Indeed, the idea of divine judgment on various personal and national transgressions became a standard response to any major or minor trial. Many believers held that the Lord kept track of individual and collective sins, doling out victories and defeats according to a precisely calculated evaluation of the contending sides. Days of fasting, humiliation, and prayer, along with days of special thanksgiving, marked such judgments. Amid anguish on the battlefield and home front, many people searched for purpose, justification, and meaning in their religion. Naturally, the staggering numbers of wounded and dead raised doubts and hard questions. Loved ones cherished the dying words of their soldier boys but could not help asking *why*, as the war vastly multiplied the uncertainties of life—why so many missing faces in churches, so much bitter division in the border regions, and so many assaults on faith in the camps, on the marches, in battle.[19]

Explaining human affliction and reckoning with divine judgment became necessary adjuncts to relentless war. Benevolence found outlets in the hospitals and various volunteer organizations, while emancipation kept millennial hopes alive in the North. Then too division, disillusionment, and despair sorely tested faith at home as it did in the armies. By 1863 the devout and skeptical alike wondered if the war might drag on indefinitely. Camp revivals, draft riots, sad holidays, and too many vacant chairs around firesides all whipsawed emotions as casualties mounted on battlefields, in hospitals, and in prisons.

Yet religion undoubtedly helped sustain morale and lengthen the war, a point recognized by even the indifferent and the skeptical. Writing privately for his own family after the war, the Confederate artillerist Edward Porter Alexander scorned religious interpretations of the contest. "Providence did not care a row of pins about it," he commented sharply. "If it did it was a very unintelligent Providence not to bring the business to a close—the close it wanted—in less than four years of most terrible and bloody war." Yet he ironically acknowledged that countless fellow Confederates would have disagreed: "Our president and many of our generals really and actually believed that there *was* this mysterious Providence always hovering over the field and ready to interfere on one side or the other, and that prayers and piety might win its favor from day to day." He considered this a "serious incubus" and thought it a "weakness to imagine that the victory could ever come in even the slightest degree from anything except our own exertions." But, of course, Stonewall Jackson and even George McClellan believed exactly that, as did countless officers, enlisted men, and civilians.[20]

To the pious, the war was always fought for some higher purpose. In fact, even as Alexander was critiquing a providential interpretation of the war, J. William Jones and William W. Bennett were compiling massive volumes emphasizing the piety of Confederate soldiers.[21] Admittedly, the truly devout were a significant though in many ways powerful minority in the Union and Confederate ranks.[22] Yet there is no doubt that religion helped overcome the soldier's natural fear of death and sustained morale. And so, even if the genuinely pious remained a minority, their influence may have well have loomed large in keeping the armies in the field.[23] And one might add, equally large at home.

How then does a religious history of the Civil War change our understanding of the Civil War itself? It should drive home the point that many people on both sides of the conflict turned to religious faith to help explain the war's causes, course, and consequences. In short, religious conviction produced a providential narrative of the war. These religious convictions created a fatalism grounded not in deism but in providence. Many Americans believed in a providential God who was also a personal God, a God deeply invested in the fate of nations and individuals. This is precisely the view Abraham Lincoln adopted in his Second Inaugural: if God wills that the war continue "until every drop of blood drawn with the lash, shall be paid by another drawn with the sword," then so be it, for "the judgments of the Lord, are true and righteous altogether." Faith not only buttressed morale in the armies and at home but offered ways to give all the bloodshed some higher and presumably nobler purpose. Many Americans found in their Bibles, their churches, and their families, and even in the armies, answers to some of the most pressing questions raised by the war. Suffering and sacrifice, anguish and bloodshed certainly brought despair and disillusionment, and even a certain loss of faith.[24] But the attributes most remarkable and most revealing about countless believers of the Civil War generation were their persistence and endurance in viewing their lives and the war itself as part of an unfolding providential story.

CRISES OF FAITH

As the Lord commanded Moses, so he numbered
them in the wilderness of Sinai.
— Numbers 1:19

Therefore all things whatsoever ye would that men should do to you,
do ye even so to them: for this is the law and the prophets.
— Matthew 7:12

Righteousness exalteth a nation: but sin is a reproach to any people.
— Proverbs 14:34

Émigré theologian and church historian Philip Schaff returned to Berlin in September 1854 to deliver two important lectures on the state of religion in his adopted country. Schaff's European background, American experiences, and ecumenical theology made him acutely sensitive to the relationship between religious practices and national character. Be it Sabbath observance, church schools, Bible societies, foreign missions, or worship attendance, he found Americans "already in advance of the old Christian nations of Europe." In the United States, there were "probably more awakened souls, and more individual efforts and self-sacrifice for religious purposes . . . than in any other country in the world."[1]

Such a comparison sounded more quantitative than qualitative, and that was no accident because Americans increasingly calculated ways to improve their lives and tried to measure such improvement precisely. This attribute had developed slowly, but even in matters of faith, what counted was often defined as what could be counted.[2] Yet it was not until 1850 that the census offered the first crude numerical assessment of religion's central place in the United States. By then an estimated one in seven Americans was a church member; fifty years earlier it had been no more than one in fifteen. Some four to five million Americans adhered to some form of evangelical Protestantism, and if one counts children and adults who attended a church without joining, those numbers jump much higher.[3] The religious mix of the population had changed radically. Congregationalists and Episcopalians had lost ground, and Presbyterians had more or less held their own. Baptists and especially Methodists had enjoyed explosive growth, and Catholics had steadily gained adherents in both eastern cities and the Midwest. During the final decade before the Civil War, the number of Jews roughly tripled.[4]

And any such estimates undercounted religious strength. Especially in the more evangelical groups, people who either doubted they had experienced a "second birth" or hesitated to proclaim it in front of a congregation nevertheless attended services. Without joining a church, thousands of Americans remained religious. During the Civil War, English journalist Edward Dicey reported that in New York the number of "churchgoers" is "larger in the proportion to the population than it would be in London."[5] All such generalizations revealed nothing about the depth of individual faith, the vitality of the churches, or the meaning of all this apparent spirituality for the wider society. And Dicey's statement paid no attention to the substantial number of Americans who remained outside any religious tradition.

The numbers of the faithful, however, were both striking and ironic. The steady erosion of established religion during the eighteenth century and the birth of an American republic conceived during the Enlightenment's heyday had launched an experiment in religious voluntarism. There may not have been a "wall" separating church and state under the Constitution but there was at least a fairly sturdy fence roping off public life from religious control. Yet at the same time, and especially with the revivalism of the so-called Second Great Awakening during the early decades of the nineteenth century, religion deeply influenced American society and culture. Religious and social life became intertwined for many Americans, and so even overblown estimates of conversions show how churches enticed the indifferent or merely curious into their orbit at least for a time.[6]

The growing power of organized and barely organized religion in American life extended well beyond the churches as cooperation in benevolent enterprises created any number of mission groups and reform societies. Campaigns against various sins, the desire to build holy communities, and a sense of God's presence in daily life produced not only a willingness to tackle social problems such as alcoholism and poverty but a conviction that such problems could ultimately be solved by human efforts aided by divine grace.[7] Missionary, Bible, tract, and Sunday school societies embodied this organized benevolence: forming committees, raising money, and proselytizing across the nation. Much of this activity reflected expectations about an advancing Kingdom of God in America, a millennial optimism that became ever more prominent as religion assumed a larger role in American society and culture.[8]

———

Only one thing appeared to stand in the way of a glorious future: slavery. By the 1830s, equivocation and conservatism on the issue seemed utterly spineless to antislavery ministers and many of the laity for that matter. Abolitionists declared slavery a sin against God and man that demanded immediate action. In renouncing gradualism, colonization, and other halfway measures, abolitionists embraced a vision of America, its people, and its churches reborn free of sin. Whatever their differences over the legitimacy and efficacy of political action, William Lloyd Garrison and his fellow abolitionists believed the nation faced a clear choice between damnation and salvation. For some abolitionists, especially those who had lost their youthful spiritual fervor, the crusade against slavery became a substitute for religion. And in the calls for immediate emancipation, one could hear echoes of perfectionism and millennialism.[9] Then, too, abolitionists took aim at southern churches that buttressed an unjust social order; what passed for religion there only mocked genuine Christianity. In the view of Garrison and countless others, southern ministers had become pawns of wealthy slaveholders and southern theologians apologists for oppression.[10]

The targets of such attacks responded swiftly and unequivocally. So far as defenders of slavery were concerned, the abolitionists assailed religion itself. The "parties in the conflict are not merely abolitionists and slaveholders," declared James Henley Thornwell. "They are atheists, socialists, communists, red republicans, jacobins, on the one side, and friends of order and regulated freedom on the other. In one word, the world is the battle ground—Christianity and Atheism the combatants; and the progress of humanity at stake."[11] That this son of a poor overseer growing up without a father but also experiencing the nurturing kindness of a cousin and a teacher should view the conflict in such Manichaean terms and long for the protection of family and hierarchy in a cruel world is hardly surprising. His linking of slavery to human progress jars the modern reader but became common enough as southern intellectuals and politicians shifted from necessary evil to positive good arguments.

Stoop-shouldered and hollow-chested, the diminutive Thornwell sometimes seemed to be all intellect. He could lecture students on moral character, condemn novel reading, and declare social dancing immoral as readily as he could debate fine points of reformed doctrine. Wedded to theological abstractions but also drawn to creature comforts, Thornwell defended slavery as the linchpin of the southern social order. Many of his fellow Presbyterians owned human property, and like most apologists for slavery, Thornwell never commented much on particular slaveholders or slaves. Although readily acknowledging abuses in the master-slave relationship, Thornwell adopted an idealist approach to social problems that seldom examined the messiness, the conflicts, the fears, or the violence that were part and parcel of slave society.

For example, he argued that slavery was not in fact property in man because slaveholders owned only the slaves' labor and therefore slaveholder and slave could live harmoniously. Like John C. Calhoun, Thornwell reveled in such philosophical propositions without bothering to address the practical difficulties, much less the injustices inherent in a system of class and racial domination.[12]

Thornwell's literal reading of the scriptures turned into an intellectual trap, but then that was true for southerners and northerners of various theological stripes. Americans favored a commonsense understanding of the Bible that ripped passages out of context and applied them to all people at all times. *Sola scriptura* both set and limited the terms for discussing slavery and gave apologists for the institution great advantages. The patriarchs of the Old Testament had owned slaves, Mosaic Law had upheld slavery, Jesus had not condemned slavery, and the apostles had advised slaves to obey their masters — these points both summed up and closed the case for many southerners and no small number of northerners. Catholics, Episcopalians, Lutherans, African Americans, and even some Presbyterians might offer alternative ways of reading and applying scriptures to the slavery question, but none were convincing or influential enough to force the debate out of the rut of an often slavish (pun intended) literalism. Abolitionists vainly appealed to the spirit of the Gospel in an age that preferred citations to chapter and verse, and because they seemed to be losing the biblical argument, some decided to abandon religious appeals altogether.[13]

So long as the controversy centered on the Bible and slavery in the abstract as opposed to religion and slavery in practice, southern defenders of the institution felt confident. According to Robert Lewis Dabney, the "masses" plainly understood the matter — that "we must go before the nation with the Bible as the text, and 'Thus saith the Lord' as the answer. . . . we know that on the Bible argument the abolition party will be driven to unveil their true infidel tendencies. The Bible being bound to stand on our side, they have to come out and array themselves against the Bible. And then the whole body of sincere believers at the North will have to array themselves, though unwillingly, on our side. They will prefer the Bible to abolitionism." The appeal of such reasoning extended well beyond Presbyterian theologians such as Dabney and Thornwell. On the basis of their reading of the Hebrew scriptures, some American Jews found the case for slavery persuasive and suspected New England abolitionists of being anti-Semitic.[14]

Racial considerations underlay some religious arguments and certainly shaped popular thinking. Those church leaders who emphasized the biblical foundations for servitude often added that slavery was necessary to govern supposedly primitive Africans and was well adapted to their character. Even northern Episcopalians doubted that darker-skinned people would ever be capable of self-government, and one of their leading church papers declared that the Caucasian was "morally and intellectually superior to all other races, black, brown, red, or yellow." The biblical curse of Ham that consigned Africans to permanent inferiority—an idea that could be traced back not only to rabbinical teachings but to the early church fathers—rested on thin textual evidence and required a great leap of logic to tie the incident involving Noah's son to any race at all, but that hardly prevented everyone from Brigham Young to conservative Presbyterians from trotting it out when needed.[15]

The absence of any consensus on slavery mirrored the country's religious diversity, despite the great success of evangelical revivals. Disagreements grew out of particular religious traditions or denominational divisions. Most notably, the "confessional" or "liturgical" churches were often more cautious and reticent in dealing with slavery, especially in contrast to evangelicals. Lutherans, for instance, often fought over doctrinal issues but avoided taking stands on political questions, though largely independent synods could chart their own course.[16] Unitarians devoted far more energy to promoting liberal theology, genteel reform, and social respectability than to worrying about slavery. Their clergy—with some notable exceptions such as William Ellery Channing and Theodore Parker—had little stomach for angry confrontations with slaveholding southerners, and their churches depended on wealthy, conservative supporters who deplored political agitation.[17]

In Hartford, Connecticut, with its strong economic ties to the South, Congregationalist Horace Bushnell sounded a similar note. He tempered opposition to slavery and his own romantic idealism with concern for social stability. His evolving idea of Christian nurture stemmed from a belief in the organic but increasingly fragile unity of church and family. To Bushnell, the debates over slavery above all else threatened to destroy the sacred Union. As for slaveholders, he advised them to prevent the breakup of slave families, hoping they would ultimately see the wisdom of emancipation. Like all too many moderates, Bushnell saw little future for freed blacks in the United States, though the whole question of territorial expansion eventually pushed him into declaring slavery a national curse. Even then, however, he never gave up searching for an ever more elusive middle ground.[18]

In many ways the most agonizing quest for answers to the slavery question occurred among the already fractured Presbyterians. The 1801 Plan of Union between the Presbyterians and Congregationalists had marked an alliance between evangelical religion and moral reform, but theological fissures soon appeared. The "Old School" Presbyterians remained staunch Calvinists, skeptical about the younger revivalists and reformers. The slowly developing and theologically heterodox "New School" faction espoused cooperation with Congregationalists and interdenominational societies. By 1838 the New School forces had been driven out or withdrawn (depending on one's theological perspective) from the General Assembly and, in effect, formed their own denomination.[19]

The Presbyterian schism did not grow directly out of divisions over slavery, though southerners went largely with the Old School faction. Like many religious conservatives and moderates, Presbyterian leaders struggled mightily to prevent the slavery question from disturbing their churches. A faculty member at Princeton Theological Seminary for more than half a century, editor and theologian Charles Hodge rejected Thornwell's biblical defense of slavery but denied that slavery was a sin in itself. In 1844 he wrote to a British friend deploring recent criticism of American churches. Pilate-like, he absolved them of any responsibility for the evils of slavery: "It cannot do us any good to tell us that it is wrong to be cruel, to be unjust, to separate husbands and wives, parents and children, or to keep servants in ignorance. Our churches do not sanction any of these things, though our laws often do." Kentuckian Robert J. Breckinridge partly agreed with Hodge but had freed his own slaves and denied that slavery as practiced in the southern states was sanctioned by the Bible. Indeed, he believed that God had created everyone free (though hardly equal). Ironically, his antislavery convictions waned after the 1830s, even though he remained a staunch and prickly Unionist.[20]

The desire for peace and order (and not solely among Presbyterians) ran deep and grew out of real concern for the churches' mission in the world. Keeping mum about slavery often became the price for evangelical success, especially for interdenominational organizations. The American Bible Society, the American Tract Society, and the American Sunday School Union had all thrived by steering clear of sectional questions.

Yet increasingly charge and countercharge became the pattern as churches, ministers, and the laity battled over slavery. Disputes over the Bible divided the clergy and sometimes denominations, but there was very little real discussion and hardly any give-and-take. Abolitionists and proslavery ideologues staked out uncompromising positions, though moderates could be equally dogmatic. Almost everyone talked past one another. People tossed around terms such as infidelity, corruption, and sin carelessly and self-righteously. Some cast themselves with the apostles in the book of Acts, preaching divine truth and letting the consequences take care of themselves. Those seeking peaceful accommodation faced great difficulties but always placed a premium on order and especially on union in church and state. At stake was the mission of the churches and seemingly their very souls.

——

The steady decline of antislavery sentiment in southern churches, most dramatically among the Methodists and Baptists, helped solidify the position of clergymen and their flocks in the southern social order. Patriarchy, hierarchy, and subordination in household, congregation, and community all exalted the authority of Christian masters and not coincidentally their clerical allies. Therefore, it was easy for proslavery clergy to spurn the Enlightenment legacy of equality and natural rights. Responding to abolitionist charges that slaveholding violated the golden rule, leading southern Baptist Richard Furman maintained that this law of love did not overturn the "order of things, which the divine government has established." A father wished his son to obey his instructions, but that hardly meant that the father should also obey the son. Creditors could not simply forgive debtors, nor would rich men distribute property to their poor neighbors. Rather all people must be treated under the law of the Gospel according to their station in life. Fellow Baptist Basil Manly agreed that the master-slave relationship entailed mutual obligations with the full realization that both served a greater master in heaven.[21]

The idealization of slaveholding society went beyond a literal biblicism, abstract theories, or special pleading. As Dabney pointed out in a series of articles published in the *Richmond Enquirer*, "slaveholders will have to pay a price" to enjoy the sanction of the Holy Scriptures. They "must be willing to recognize and grant in slaves those rights which are a part of our essential humanity, some of which are left without recognition or guarantee by law, and some infringed by law." He would never defend separating families or "violat-[ing] chastity of the female by forcible means." This seemingly hard-hitting commentary aimed at amelioration and reform, not abolition. Nor could Dabney explain how owning human beings had become "part of our essential humanity," though like many other conservatives he drew a sharp distinction between slavery as a social evil and slavery as a moral evil.[22]

For their part, ministers preached about masters' obligations to slaves and likely with greater success than their sermons about slaves' duties to masters. Prominent religious leaders supported legal recognition of slave marriages, and a few favored laws to prevent the separation of families. Deeds unfortunately never matched words. In practice, churches could not protect slave marriages and had to be flexible about allowing couples separated by sale to remarry. Ministers harangued slaves about the sanctity of marriage, and church discipline cases regularly dealt with adultery and other family problems in the quarters, but slaveholders need not have worried about interference with their prerogatives. After explaining how masters should hold wedding ceremonies for their slaves, one Episcopalian layman quickly added, "I of course do not advocate legal interference to prevent the master from exercising sole and unfettered control over his servants as property."[23]

When slaveholders provided religious instruction for slaves, they faced an equally stunning paradox. States often forbade teaching slaves to read, but churches insisted on the centrality of the Bible; indeed, many pious folk held that the slaves' religious conversion became the final sign that the Lord approved their work. But all this was a decidedly uphill struggle. Despite a genuine affection for his slaves and an idealistic vision of a biracial Christian community, Reverend Charles Colcock Jones could never convince enough ministers or slaveholders to develop an effective program for religious instruction. Jones labored year after year but with increasingly little success as slaves evidently did not find his Presbyterian preaching all that appealing. For their part, too many slaveholders seemed content to go through the motions, showing little genuine or at least consistent interest in their slaves' spiritual welfare. In 1851 a Baptist association in Hancock County, Georgia, pointedly asked "Who, among us, who is a slave-holder can with a clear conscience say or feel he has as a Christian discharged his duty to these [the colored] people?" Other evangelicals admitted there were many slaves who had never heard even a small part of the gospel message.[24]

To calm nervous masters, Texas Baptists promised to "employ none but discreet, pious and tried men, men who will instruct and not merely excite the emotions of this excitable people." Put most simply, in the words of one Baptist association, religion made for "good masters and good slaves."[25] Such reassurance must have been necessary. Patriarchal planters had traditionally proved resistant to preaching that struck at their pride or authority. The whole idea of repentance and submission had cut against their grain, not to mention clashing with antique notions of honor. To be on equal footing with women and children before God presented enough of a problem, so it is hardly surprising that to think of slaves as brothers and sisters in Christ aroused skepticism and apprehension. Whatever might be the case in the world to come, temporal distinctions remained, and the churches had to work within the social structure, not against it. Therefore religious instruction and even separate black churches were perfectly safe so long as white paternalists remained firmly in control.[26]

Regardless of such limitations, the flowering of African American Christianity in the slaveholding states had been remarkable. One contemporary estimate placed slave members in all southern churches on the eve of the

Civil War at nearly 450,000. Blacks made up anywhere from 30 to 40 percent of Georgia Baptists and Methodists.[27] The churches scrambled to accommodate black members, who in turn carved out a place for themselves both in their churches and in God's kingdom.

Jerusalem Methodist Church in Green County, North Carolina, was a rough, frame building standing in the woods. At monthly services, a crowd equally divided between blacks and whites gathered to hear three uneducated "exhorters," who each preached long enough "for any common sermon," or so a visiting New York woman complained. Even if blacks had to sit in the back of the church, both races heard the same scriptures and the same sermon. But in larger churches, and especially in towns and cities, there was separate worship for slaves in the afternoon. A Virginia Baptist association explained that the "colored members" needed special services because they were not "receptive" to sermons heard by white congregations.[28]

Devout masters insisted slaves attend church, though with what result is difficult to say. Some blacks worshiped with great enthusiasm, others appeared stolidly indifferent, and still others simply enjoyed the opportunity to rest. Perhaps many slaves did become good Christians, but there remained a strong suspicion among pious whites that the blacks simply put on a good show. Slave recollections illustrated how much racial perspectives diverged. Some recalled sermons emphasizing obedience to the masters with the usual proslavery passages from Paul's epistles and little else. Slaves heard messages that stated the obvious: the world was a place of toil, trouble, sickness, and death. Ministers might offer hope for happiness in the world to come, but some slaves claimed they never learned a thing about Jesus or salvation or heaven.[29]

Church services and plantation missions could never satisfy the hunger for more genuine religious experience. On a few plantations, slaves conducted their own preaching and prayer meetings each week, but more commonly these gatherings were less regular and more furtive. Whites on occasion visited the prayer meetings and were delighted to hear slaves blessing their masters and mistresses; one slave thanked the men "who come here to read the Bible to us, and pay so much attention to us, though we ain't the sort of people as can enterpret thy word in all its colors and forms."[30]

Such performances proved that the slaves were the "sort of people" who could fool gullible slaveholders. Though wary of slave patrols, blacks more freely expressed their faith at secret meetings in the woods. Some prayed for deliverance not only from sin but from slavery, and the earthly implications of spiritual equality became much more explicit. Here slaves could sing the spirituals that spoke of sorrow and salvation, they could talk of the Exodus, and they could compare themselves to the children of Israel. For slaveholders, this underground religion aroused fears about losing control of "their people." A Mississippi master warned his slaves Rich and Viney that he would whip them whenever he heard any praying. "Yessir," they replied, "but you can whup us ever' day, but you can't make us stop prayin' to my Jesus."[31] It must have stunned this slaveholder to meet such defiance and, worse, to hear slaves lay claim to "my Jesus."

In cities and especially in the Border South, "mission" churches evolved into separate congregations. From Richmond, to Macon, to Mobile, to Houston, African American churches sprang up as population pressures, black preferences, and white inclination converged.[32] Most black congregations had white pastors and were less than independent. At Calvary Episcopal Church in Charleston, there were fifty raised seats for white supervisors so the worshipers would have "a sensible eye image of the subordination that is due those to whom, by the course of Providence, they are to look upon as rulers." Slaves, however, had good reason for associating cities with greater freedom, and white control of black churches remained tenuous. This fact was all too evident during the 1850s as sectional alarms kept slaveholders on tenterhooks. A scene described by a northern visitor illustrated what most worried southern whites. During a service at the African Baptist Church in Charleston, one woman affirmed that the Son of God had made her free, and another declared, "Stand fast, therefore, in the liberty wherewith God shall make you free."[33] She dared not say whether this meant spiritual freedom or some other kind but did not need to.

On a more fundamental level, religion provided the wherewithal for surviving slavery. Black preachers challenged the white monopoly on religious faith, speaking to their people's misery and to their hope. They might craftily preach the master's Gospel but could not become too closely tied to whites or grow too aloof from their fellow slaves. Nor could they go too far in pushing a message of spiritual liberation that might stir their listeners to physical resistance or trigger white repression. Earthly deliverance would be a far too dangerous message, despite occasional apocalyptic visions of masters being whipped for their sins or armed black rebels loosening the shackles of slavery. Accommodation (often accompanied by day-to-day resistance) became a costly compromise between docility and defiance.[34]

Nor was this a purely southern phenomenon. Tired of discrimination and segregation in white Methodist churches, former slave Richard Allen had founded the African Methodist Episcopal (AME) Church in Philadelphia. By the 1850s the church had grown to some twenty thousand members. Fighting against slavery and prejudice, northern black preachers taught that the

Almighty was no respecter of persons. "I owe my freedom to the God who made me," declared fugitive slave and minister Jermain Wesley Loguen. "I will not, nor will I consent that anybody else shall countenance the claims of a vulgar despot to my soul and body." Such messages anticipated wartime calls for general emancipation. Although in 1851 AME bishop William Paul Quinn asserted, "Nine times out of ten when we look in the face of a white man we see our enemy," most black preachers offered a less militant message of moral improvement and racial uplift. Like white ministers who linked faith in progress to biblical prophecies, black ministers sometimes dreamed of a grand mission to Africa to regenerate that continent.[35]

As slavery threatened to tear apart the churches and set believer against believer, such hopes might have seemed out of place. But millennial expectations had flourished during the heyday of the Second Great Awakening and continued to shape theological and even political debate. The connections between social reform, mass revivalism, and popular politics might not be obvious, but for many Americans both religious enthusiasm and a vital democracy seemed a providential blessing. An evolving civil religion reflected an optimistic faith in the United States as a reforming and ultimately transforming force in the world. The intermingling of secular and religious hope was typically American, but so were nagging doubts about the future.[36]

Pious antislavery advocates presented a beatific vision of a nation purged of that great iniquity, yet proslavery ministers often proved equally idealistic as they looked for some glorious future state. South Carolinian John Adger, who served as a missionary to slaves, even maintained that bondage could be perpetual once abolitionists admitted their errors and embraced theological and social orthodoxy. As late as 1860, in the midst of the most heated and perilous presidential election campaign in American history, discussion of religious instruction for slaves led a North Carolina editor to welcome the "signs of progress in our Southern Zion." Americans, as Abraham Lincoln later observed with such poignant irony, prayed to the same God and read the same Bible. They also spoke a common religious language, and Christianity proved both appealing and ambivalent enough to accommodate slaves, slaveholders, abolitionists, and those who cared little about slavery one way or another.[37]

That was the problem. Religious faith offered no solution to these issues, or at least no solution that could win support across racial and sectional lines. Everyone seemed to agree that the souls of the churches (and their parishioners) were in mortal danger whether from slaveholders, abolitionists, or the morally indifferent. But saving the churches or the nation for that matter required more than heated debate in which people talked past each other.

Rather than the word becoming flesh, it seemed as if the flesh—of northerners and southerners, of blacks and whites—had become words, an endless stream of words. There was in this flood of rhetoric a failure of moral imagination all around. Slaveholders could not put themselves in their slaves' ragged shoes; abolitionists could not imagine themselves as slaveholders, or as slaves for that matter. The morally indifferent could not understand the morally committed and vice versa. African American religion developed a language of freedom yet could not point the way for the nation to escape the twin curses of slavery and caste.

Abraham Lincoln perhaps came closest to overcoming his contemporaries' all too narrow vision. During a speech at Peoria, Illinois, in the aftermath of the political firestorm over the notorious Kansas-Nebraska Act, he somehow rose above the passions and the self-righteousness that afflicted so many Americans. "I have no prejudice against the southern people," he declared. "They are just what we would be in their situation. If slavery did not now exist amongst them, they would not introduce it. If it did now exist amongst us, we should not instantly give it up." Lincoln could almost allow that in similar circumstances he might have owned slaves. He conceded that slavery would be difficult to abolish and refused to criticize southerners for "not doing what I should not know how to do myself." But here his moral imagination faltered because Lincoln paid much more attention to the effects of slavery on white people and on free labor than to the injustices suffered by the slaves. He dreamed of freeing all the slaves and sending them to Liberia because he did not see how blacks could live among whites as political and social equals.[38] Lincoln himself had never joined a church and professed no creeds aside from love of God and love of neighbor, though he surely realized that his Christian neighbors, not to mention devout Americans of various faiths, had failed to live up to the standards of the golden rule. The churches and the ministers could not escape their fathers' sins or their own. Slavery and racism appeared to be irreducible realities and insoluble problems; ultimately the entire nation would have to pay the wages of sin.

———

Although John Wesley had decried slavery as evil and Thomas Coke had favored denying communion to slaveholders, American Methodists had steadily diluted their antislavery witness. Yet, by the 1840s, the departure of outraged abolitionists from northern Methodist churches made many ministers and congregations reluctant to make further concessions to slavery. New Englanders grew bolder in denouncing slavery, and there was even talk of expelling slaveholders from the church.[39]

What in hindsight appeared to be an inevitable explosion occurred at the 1844 General Conference. Crowding into New York's Green Street Church on May 1, the delegates could no longer evade the question that threatened to tear the evangelical churches and the political parties, if not the nation, apart. Since 1832 James Osgood Andrew had been a Methodist bishop. He had recently married a widow who owned several slaves, though he hardly expected that to become a problem, especially because he could not emancipate them under Georgia law. However, a resolution was introduced calling on Andrew to resign from the episcopacy, and the Georgian was inclined to do so because he had little stomach for controversy, but his fellow southerners would not hear of it. After a heated debate, and by a vote of 111–69, the conference adopted a motion calling for Andrew to "desist from the exercise of his office so long as the impediment [ownership of slaves] remains."[40]

In the end, the General Conference voted overwhelmingly to separate the church into two general conferences and to divide the proceeds of the publishing house. Both sides pretended that the divorce was amicable. Ironically, the next two General Conferences of the northern church paid little attention to slavery and the Methodist press also fell silent. Engaging in his usual invective, William Lloyd Garrison blasted the church for attempting "so to serve God as not to offend the devil." The abolitionist firebrand had a point because whatever their personal abhorrence of slavery, all too often northern clergy and laity sought peace above all else.[41]

With three bishops present and thirteen annual conferences represented at Louisville in May 1845, the Methodist Episcopal Church, South, was born. The following year southern Methodists resolved that slavery "is not a proper subject of ecclesiastical legislation." The real battle was joined in the border states where it was easy to brand northern Methodists abolitionist incendiaries; the all too predictable countercharge was that the southern church had become a tool of slaveholders. Attempts to maintain what was euphemistically termed "fraternal relations" between the two branches of Methodism foundered.[42] Southern Methodists largely won the contest for the border conferences without ever quite vanquishing the northern branch.

Despite their congregational polity and traditional commitment to liberty of conscience, Baptists followed a similar path to disunion. Indeed, northern Baptists proved no more eager than northern Methodists to tackle the slavery question. At Brown University in 1835, President Francis Wayland barred any discussion of the subject in the classroom. Wayland himself was moderately antislavery and considered the institution sinful but always thought that saving souls took precedence over saving society. Like an erudite Presbyterian, Wayland condemned slavery as a moral evil and violation of human rights while maintaining that the mere holding of slaves—so long as they received religious instruction—did not necessarily entail moral guilt.[43]

Yet even the cautious Wayland would not concede the right of slaveholders to receive assignments from national mission boards, and though the Home Missionary Society in 1844 still declared itself neutral on slavery, papering over sectional differences had become impossible. The middle ground was disappearing even in the nation's most highly decentralized religious body. In late 1844 the Home Missionary Society and the Foreign Missionary Board refused to appoint slaveholders as missionaries. In May 1845, 293 delegates met in Augusta, Georgia, to form the Southern Baptist Convention.[44]

Like their Methodist brethren, southern Baptists might not embrace positive good arguments for slavery and might even favor mild reforms, but any serious discussion with northern religious bodies and leaders had largely been cut off. According to John C. Calhoun, "ecclesiastical" ties had been the strongest cord binding the Union, and that cord had been snapped. Henry Clay, who had clashed with his Senate colleague on so many issues, agreed that this "sundering of religious ties" was the "greatest source of danger to our country." As it turned out, the painful ruptures in the churches, much like the growing fissures in the political parties, undercut moderation. This is not to say that moderate Methodists, Baptists, or Presbyterians for that matter might have forged some workable solution. Most never tried, and for all the rhetoric on both sides of the question, the typical pastor delivered few if any sermons on slavery, and most of the laity preferred gospel preaching to political preaching.[45]

———

And in any case, the slavery question like all other matters remained in the Lord's hands. Believers' powerful and sustained faith in divine providence could at times become a fatalistic attitude toward both ordinary and extraordinary events. "It was God who sent you children, made the potatoes turn out well, put the blight on the orchard trees, and caused the roan mare to sicken and die," ran one representative description of popular belief. God remained in control of human life down to the smallest details. Providence could be benevolent or destructive, but human beings still had to take responsibility for their actions and muddle through life. In the end, all people died, so resignation and submission seemed advisable.[46]

Such attitudes would encourage people to avoid wrestling with slavery altogether—at least for a time. Ignoring such a vital moral and political question came at a price, but for those who believed that the church's mission was strictly evangelical, that price seemed reasonable. Such an evasion, however, proved both elusive and short-lived. The vision of religion transforming society might at times fall into abeyance, yet the slavery question itself would not go away. And to bring the argument back full circle, for those with a providential turn of mind, this too represented God's will.

So however hard they might try, pious Americans could not escape the political turmoil of the 1840s and 1850s. In terms of sheer numbers, believers were bound to wield enormous influence in public life. In point of fact, the public obsession with politics in the United States, especially during the heyday of the second American party system, inevitably drew the devout into the fray.[47] As Alexis de Tocqueville observed, Christianity in America (and Judaism for that matter) often embodied a fervent faith in republican government. Religious ferment, if anything, reinforced a democratic belief in the wisdom and judgment of everyday people. For their part, theologians, ministers, and many ordinary believers often spoke in the language of republicanism.[48]

From at least the late eighteenth century on, religious life had become increasingly entwined with soaring hopes for the United States. Religion provided moral standards and a social structure that might otherwise have been lacking in a democratic era. Religion served as a counterweight in an ever-changing political environment. But in the absence of any central religious authority, the churches themselves became part of the great American experiment in representative government, and they certainly had to compete in the marketplace of ideas. A republican government placed considerable responsibility on its citizens and at the same time subtly undermined belief in human depravity and divine sovereignty. Yet this did not necessarily bring about a clash between democratic and religious impulses. According to Tocqueville, a human mind naturally tried to "harmonize the state in which he lives upon earth, with the state which he believes to await him in heaven." In the early American republic, political and religious freedom had fit together as easily as a tongue and groove joint, though how long they would stay in place remained doubtful. The overlapping of faith and polity usually held up despite lesser or greater amounts of theological, denominational, and sectional stress. The millennial hopes that had become so commonplace in American religious life made this entire structure of spiritual and political liberty quite appealing, at least until slavery literally threatened to pull apart the republican house.[49]

Believers naturally could not place too much faith in human wisdom and institutions. Indeed, the absence of clear-cut religious patterns in voting reflected a welter of factors that shaped political behavior and revealed great ambivalence about political parties and the political process itself. Prominent ministers such as Charles G. Finney and Henry Ward Beecher defended their interest in politics and the introduction of political topics in the pulpit, but other preachers roundly condemned any discussion of secular matters in a sacred setting. That exemplar of conservative Presbyterianism, Charles Hodge pointedly observed that Christianity offered "not worldly prosperity . . . not dominion over nations, but the forgiveness of sin, the renewal of the heart, reconciliation with God, and eternal life." Some ministers even doubted whether God showed any special favor toward America or toward democracy. And many clergy drew a sharp line between preaching on public questions and involvement in partisan politics, worrying that raucous campaigns and close elections were becoming dangerous distractions.[50]

Such theological reservations were both philosophical and practical. The rise of political parties had helped reduce clerical influence in public life, and it became increasingly difficult to fix one's attention on saving souls amid the political excitement that periodically gripped communities, states, and nation. Not surprisingly, evangelical ministers solemnly warned against partisanship and corruption, not to mention the drinking and gambling that accompanied many a hot canvass.[51] Whatever the ministers thought about the politicians, the politicians understood that many of their constituents were deeply religious people who voted accordingly.

By the 1840s, the slavery question intensified partisan jockeying for religious voters. As a result of the Mexican War, the possible expansion of slavery became *the* issue in American politics for more than a decade, severely testing the political parties and polarizing the country. For a time, the so-called Compromise of 1850 calmed the waters, but the question then became whether the moral price—especially the enactment of a tougher fugitive slave law—was too high. To Christian abolitionists, it was. Theodore Parker, George Cheever, James Freeman Clarke, the once moderate Leonard Bacon, and black ministers such as Robert Purvis and Alexander Crummell called on Americans to obey God's "higher law" by disobeying an unjust human law. By aiding and, if necessary, rescuing fugitive slaves from pursuing slaveholders and federal marshals, Christians could truly love their neighbors as themselves.[52] To devout Unionists, however, "higher law" doctrine simply meant anarchy and ultimately civil war. In a sermon printed as a Whig campaign document, Presbyterian John C. Lord began with the famous "render unto Caesar" text from Matthew to emphasize the Christian's duty to obey the powers that be.[53]

Southern ministers repeatedly exposed their own ambivalence and confusion by hewing to familiar arguments and presenting no real solutions. After calling John C. Calhoun "our Moses," South Carolina Methodist Whitefoord

Smith charged that abolitionists who had abandoned the Bible for a higher law "fight not against us but against God." At the same time southern clergy remained staunchly Unionist, and a prominent Virginia Presbyterian wrote to a friend, "I just wish Old Hickory was alive." Few ministers joined Southern Rights politicians in condemning the Compromise of 1850; in fact, echoing the fears of northern conservatives, Thornwell and others deplored talk of disunion.[54] The division of the churches, however, had encouraged southern Christians to more closely identify with their section, so religious opinion was still up for grabs.

In the northern states, the picture was even more mixed. Just as Democrats and Whigs generally supported the Compromise of 1850, so many northern church leaders sought to defuse the slavery debate. At the Methodist General Conference in 1852, where there was little discussion of slavery, one delegate blandly remarked that the northern church welcomed slaveholders and slaves alike. With great force but less logic, Matthew Simpson maintained that Methodists had always been both an antislavery and a slaveholding church. Even the New School Presbyterians—supposedly more antislavery than their Old School brethren—nimbly dodged the question. Their General Assembly broadly condemned slavery but allowed lower judicatory bodies to deal with stickier specific issues. Old School Presbyterians along with Catholics, Episcopalians, Unitarians, Lutherans, and the Disciples of Christ proved equally reticent.[55]

For the churches as for the politicians, the Kansas-Nebraska bill marked a sea change. Potentially opening a large area of the old Louisiana Purchase to slavery on the basis of popular sovereignty not only enraged many northern politicians and voters but also riled clergy from Maine to the Midwest. Congregationalist editor Joseph Thompson subtitled his published sermon *The Voice of God against National Crime*. More than three thousand New England ministers petitioned Congress to reject the measure, and its sponsor, Stephen A. Douglas, furiously condemned clerical meddling in politics. Douglas had good reason to worry because the protest reflected widespread outrage, and this was only the beginning. Indeed, Douglas's criticism only rekindled the preachers' fury and led to charges that the "slave power" was trying to silence the churches.[56]

Even as the Kansas-Nebraska Act shocked Abraham Lincoln out of his political doldrums, so too it stirred up ministers who had once expressed only the mildest antislavery sentiments. Francis Wayland still refused to denounce southern slaveholders but believed that this legislation would inevitably lead to the expansion of slavery. When this essentially moderate Baptist spoke about proclaiming liberty to the captives and declared both Africans and Indians to be Christian brothers, it did indeed seem that a great shift in opinion was taking place. Horace Bushnell, who had long steered a moderate course, now decided that the slave power posed a far greater danger to the nation than the abolitionists. Leading Unitarian Ezra Stiles Gannett hesitated to condemn southerners, considered Harriet Beecher Stowe's *Uncle Tom's Cabin* a "narrative of exceptional cases," and doubted the government's constitutional authority to interfere with slavery in the states. But for Gannett the time for compromise had passed; he now opposed any extension of slavery and decided that preserving the Union "may cost us too much."[57] Such strong statements from such unexpected sources should have worried Douglas, who faced both a political and a religious firestorm.

In all the uproar over the Kansas-Nebraska Act, a growing number of Protestants identified another familiar threat to religious liberty. Congregationalist Eden Burroughs Foster wildly charged that slaveholders had allied themselves with the Catholic Church.[58] This accusation seemed especially ironic because, despite dramatic growth (the number of Catholics in the United States was nearing the two million mark), priests seldom engaged the issues of the day, and the slavery question was a case in point. Like conservative Presbyterians, Catholics did not believe that the Bible condemned slavery and accepted it as part of man's fallen nature. Even Archbishop John Hughes, who went as far as any leading Catholic during the 1850s in criticizing slavery as an "evil," denied that the institution was "an absolute or unmitigated evil." Having little faith in any reform outside the church, Catholic leaders viewed emancipation as a dangerously utopian idea. Catholic thinkers readily linked abolitionism to rationalism and humanism, and of course to anti-Catholicism.[59]

Nor could anyone accuse Catholics of fanning the flames of sectional hatred. Their priests did not petition Congress or deliver political sermons; nor did they declare God's hand at work in all the bitter disputes over slavery. "Every Catholic has a right to be Abolitionist, Republican, Freesoiler or Democrat," a Pittsburgh editor declared, "but not to make his opinion to be the opinion and teaching of the church." And if Protestant ministers sometimes linked the Catholic Church to the slave power, Catholics in turn criticized the supposed alliance between radical abolitionists and religious bigots. Above all else, the Catholic hierarchy—North and South—strove to avoid divisions that would weaken the church when it was both prospering and facing ever more intense Protestant hostility. As the political skies darkened, American Catholics took comfort and no little pride in their own unity.[60]

When the anti-Catholic and anti-immigrant American (Know Nothing)

Party burst upon the political scene and vied to replace the dying Whigs, many evangelicals remained attached to the Democrats or would have nothing to do with this new party's secrecy, violence, and bigotry. In the summer of 1854, Archbishop Hughes predicted that political nativism would not last, and the sudden collapse of the Know Nothings proved him at least partly right.[61] The crosscurrents of opinion bespoke confusion and reflected the political turmoil coming in the wake of the Kansas-Nebraska Act and the violent struggles along the Kansas-Missouri border.

After South Carolina fire-eater Preston Brooks caned Massachusetts radical Charles Sumner on the Senate floor, bleeding Kansas and bleeding Sumner became religious as well as political rallying cries. Preaching from Genesis 4:10, New Jersey Baptist Henry Clay Fish declared that the blood of the fallen brother cried out for justice. The attack on Sumner marked the "beginning of the code of blood and the reign of brute force," a part of a great "conspiracy" to protect and expand slavery. The problem was not simply sectional, one Massachusetts Unitarian asserted, but rather "a question between civilization and barbarism; between Christianity and heathenism; between light and darkness." To portray the conflict in such stark terms placed a premium on demonizing the other side. Methodist Gilbert Haven even compared the caning of Sumner to the flailing of Jesus, and bloodguilt became a powerful theme in his preaching.[62]

Harsh denunciations and apocalyptic images especially alarmed northern moderates, who shrank from joining the sectional fray. Despite his growing antislavery convictions, Unitarian Ezra Stiles Gannett dreaded dissolution of the Union and especially regretted seeing religious people drawn into the conflict: "I read with sadness the language of Christian men and Christian ministers, whose brave words, if they be well considered, are bloody words. To me the musket and the Bible do not seem twin implements of civilization." This unmistakable swipe at Henry Ward Beecher reflected a great fear among men who still hoped that reasonable Christians could find a peaceable solution to sectional troubles.[63]

Such an outcome became increasingly unlikely as many northern Presbyterians along with Congregationalists (including Beecher) and significant numbers of Methodists and Baptists flocked to the new antislavery Republican Party. Although some evangelicals preferred the Know Nothings, supposed connections between the slave power, the Catholic Church, and the liquor interests drew others to the Republicans. In response, Catholic priests predicted that the new party would inevitably turn to anti-Catholicism once the slavery controversy had subsided. Not surprisingly, leading Democrats and their clerical allies defended religious liberty, or what conservative Pennsylvania jurist Jeremiah Black termed a "state without religion, and a Church without politics."[64] These words showed how Jeffersonian attitudes survived even as religious expansion and the sectional conflict itself had at times lowered the barriers between church and state.

———

That slavery roiled the religious and political waters should have caused no great surprise, but there were several ironies. Northerners portrayed the slave power as an aggressive force hell-bent on stamping out civil and religious liberty—a mirror image of southern diatribes against Yankee political preachers. Extremism quite literally bred extremism, even though southern believers were largely Unionist albeit proslavery, while many of their northern brethren were at least mildly antislavery but remained skeptical of abolitionists and equally Unionist.[65]

Congressional debates—and even the violence on the Kansas frontier—all had abstract and philosophical qualities that aroused passions and unleashed recrimination but somehow seemed remote from daily life. But then, in October 1859, John Brown's raid on the federal arsenal at Harpers Ferry and apparent attempt to spark a slave insurrection suddenly made the whole sectional controversy much more tangible. The threat to southern homes and the emotional reaction to Brown's execution in many northern households created a whirlwind of fear, outrage, and admiration. To Christian abolitionist George Cheever, God's word had forced Brown to strike a blow against slavery. Brown would have been everywhere lauded as a hero, the *Independent* tartly noted, had he set out to liberate white men.[66]

At the same time, John Brown's apocalyptic visions and muddled plans placed many northern ministers and their congregations in a dicey position. Their antislavery words seemed to pale beside Brown's antislavery deeds. Henry Ward Beecher had been a leading, indeed notorious supporter of the Free State Party in Kansas, but Harpers Ferry clearly frightened him. "I disapprove of his mad and feeble schemes," Beecher informed his Brooklyn flock two weeks after Brown's capture. The most famous clergyman of his day would not shed blood to free slaves, or incite them to insurrection, or even encourage them to run away.[67]

To many northerners John Brown embodied the dangers of "higher law" fanaticism. For New Yorker George Templeton Strong, an eminently respectable Episcopalian, it was time to "assert the claims of the church as a conservative, law-abiding institution against Calvinism and the ultra Protestantism that it has produced." Union men must rally around a faith that would "define the limits of authority and private judgment in political ethics." Catholic editors agreed that Brown and his supporters embodied "irrepressible conflict" radicalism, and they typically denounced extremists North and South.[68]

Southern ministers might boldly assert that John Brown represented the logical culmination of northern infidelity, but they were truly stunned when so many pious northerners appeared sympathetic to Brown and positively apoplectic when some ministers compared him to Jesus Christ. Writing to a northern colleague, Episcopal rector William Nelson Pendleton of Virginia insisted that Yankee preachers offer reassurances to their southern brethren or face disunion and war. Nearly three months after Brown's execution, a Virginia Presbyterian editor surveyed the religious landscape and assessed the damage. He concluded that the promise of an American republic founded on religious liberty had not been fulfilled. Even the building of railroads and other sweeping economic changes had failed to bind the nation together. Harsh attacks on southern institutions and on southerners rang out from northern pulpits, and now antislavery zealots were inciting slaves to bloody revolution.[69]

Aside from the sectional special pleading, this editorial offered a fair summary of how religion had become intricately connected to the greatest crisis in American history. Having failed to find a solution to the slavery question and having made far too many statements about how divine providence would make all things right, the churches could not tamp down the fires of sectionalism. Political preaching had raised a good deal of heat, but those Americans embracing a religious faith presumably divorced from politics had proved just as ineffectual. Disputes over slavery expansion had weakened the political system and now threatened to further divide the churches and tear the nation apart. From northern abolitionists to southern fire-eaters, the attempts to score debating points had loomed more important than efforts to find a resolution to a deepening crisis. For their part, moderates had shown neither much courage nor judgment; the middle ground remained elusive and all other ground fraught with peril. A vast outpouring of political sermons and religious editorials had been just so many words—but words that in some cases only made matters worse. Moral posturing, along with a large dose of millennialism, made any possible compromises all that much harder to swallow.

Territorial expansion, partisan politics, and political nativism had all tugged the faithful this way and that, inevitably raising questions about the proper role of clergy and laity alike. Each new flash point from the Compromise of 1850 to Kansas-Nebraska to John Brown had shaken the churches, while producing new fissures along sectional, party, racial, and theological lines. Pious folk had struggled to escape the tremors convulsing both church and state, but there were few safe havens. The danger was that "irrepressible conflict" would no longer simply be a political catchphrase but instead would become an all too accurate description of the looming disasters facing what Lincoln would famously term an "almost chosen people."[70]

REAPING THE WHIRLWIND

Therefore hath the Lord watched upon the evil, and brought it upon us: for the Lord our God is righteous in all his works which he doeth: for we obeyed not his voice.
— Daniel 9:14

On March 11, 1859, near Bonham, Texas, during a meeting of the Arkansas Conference of the Methodist Church, a northern preacher made inflammatory remarks about slavery—at least according to two southern Methodist ministers sent to spy on the proceedings. After a hurriedly assembled mass meeting, a mob estimated at between fifty and two hundred men marched into the church where the conference was being held and accused several northern men of being abolitionist emissaries. Adjournment quickly followed. Later in the year two northern Methodist ministers were forced to leave Dallas, Texas, and one received seventy lashes.

These reactions were hardly proportional to the threat. In 1859 the northern Methodists in Texas could claim only 232 members, but that did not seem to allay local fears. Take the case of the Reverend Anthony Bewley, a Tennessean sent to Texas as a missionary. Bewley doubted he could accomplish much except perhaps among the Germans but immediately came under suspicion, especially after a series of mysterious fires, known as the "Texas Troubles." Bewley fled with his family to Missouri but was hauled back by a Fort Worth vigilance committee and on September 13, 1860, lynched. It hardly mattered that the charges against him were flimsy at best. In this superheated atmosphere, southern editors either ignored or defended the treatment of Bewley, who in the North became another martyr to the slave power.[1]

Perhaps none of this should have been surprising in the midst of the most divisive election campaign in American history, yet to focus on a supposedly dangerous Methodist minister in rural Texas carried its own ironies. "The anti-slavery column stands strong and united," the Reverend Alfred Cookman reported to his wife on the eve of the 1860 General Conference in Buffalo, but his statement was more hopeful than accurate. Antislavery editors had steadily agitated for excluding slaveholders from fellowship, but moderates feared that changing the General Rule on slavery would further alienate the border conferences and divide the church. As it turned out, the General Conference pleased no one. A watered-down resolution that condemned slavery for violating the golden rule irritated the border state conferences and disappointed the antislavery faction.[2]

Only a little more than two weeks after the Methodists had convened, the Republican Party meeting in Chicago nominated Abraham Lincoln for the presidency. Lincoln would later warmly praise these same Methodists—who seemed so timid in 1860—for staunchly supporting the Union war effort. After the northern faction of an irrevocably divided Democratic Party nominated Stephen A. Douglas, Republicans not only tried to beef up Lincoln's spiritual credentials but also plied evangelical voters with tales of the Little Giant's drinking and ties to Catholicism. In fact, Catholic support for the Democrats seemed more sustained and public than in any previous election campaign. Yet Catholic confidence in both Democrats and Douglas wavered during the summer—in part owing to reports that supporters of southern Democratic candidate John C. Breckinridge were attacking Douglas, Archbishop John Hughes, and the pope to woo anti-Catholic voters.[3]

This is not to say that Catholic clergy (or most Protestants for that matter) suddenly entered the lists as "political preachers." Although moral rhetoric suffused stump speeches, and politicians were well attuned to the sensitivities of religious voters, the connection between church affiliation and voting behavior was by no means simple or direct. Disagreements over the relationship between faith and public affairs persisted; neither members of the clergy nor their congregations seemed ready to weld religious faith to partisan politics. Although the *Independent* urged the "Christian men of the nation" to "show their patriotism by carrying their religion into their politics," Washington Gladden recalled that for the most part churches stayed out of the canvass. Comments on the campaign in the religious press were surprisingly spotty.[4] The Augustinian distinction between the City of God and the City of Man made sense even in a largely Protestant nation during a period of growing disillusionment with politics.

On the eve of the election, South Carolina widow Keziah Brevard pointedly observed, "I expect nothing from man—all good must come from *God*." She could not help but wonder if "our dear country" will be "torn asunder." Praying that her slaves would find "true religion," Brevard dreaded the days ahead yet still hoped people would bend their stiff necks to the will of an inscrutable God. In any event, it seemed impossible that the unbearable tension could last much longer. When it appeared that Lincoln would be elected, one Presbyterian editor still recommended prayer but added ominously: "An agitation that perpetually sends dread and disturbance to every hamlet, and to every home and fireside in the land is intolerable. No people can abide it long. They will prefer the hazard of any convulsion, the perils of any terrible adventure, to a life of perpetual anxiety and disquiet. The instincts of nature will drive them to seek relief by any, even the most dangerous means."[5]

Whether Lincoln's election would bring on the inevitable explosion alarmed and baffled leading ministers throughout the country. The temptation to defend one's section against the "enemy" was strong, but so were clerical instincts for peace, safety, and accommodation. "From pure motives I have ignored politics, so far as parties are concerned," veteran Methodist preacher Heman Bangs wrote proudly on election day. "Since I became a minister of Christ, my only business has been to save souls."[6] But could he continue to seal off his professional life from the public turmoil? In the North, Thanksgiving Day 1860 took on special meaning for conservatives who hoped against hope that God would answer prayers for peace and instill a true sense of patriotism in a people distracted by political agitation. All too often the devout now sounded like the politicians. In both sections, religious arguments at times shaped the debates over secession, but more often clerical and lay opinion lagged a bit behind. The preachers might beat the political drums but did so hesitantly, often striking uncertain notes.

With storm clouds darkening the political skies, the religious chasm between the sections had become much wider. Southerners might not succumb to apocalyptic nightmares, but rising above the political fray hardly seemed possible. White clergy had often enjoyed the benefits of living in a slaveholding society with few if any moral qualms. Compared to the general southern population, some ministers accumulated a respectable worldly estate, including land and slaves along with a paternalistic self-image. Whether they merely aped the opinions of their most wealthy and powerful patrons or actually shaped the attitudes of their congregations and communities, they became bulwarks of the southern social order.[7]

Prominent Presbyterian Benjamin Morgan Palmer was a prime example. In New Orleans, on November 29, 1860, the small and slender Palmer delivered a powerful sermon that reverberated well beyond the walls of First Presbyterian Church, an imposing Gothic structure on Lafayette Square, which could hold nearly two thousand people. Every seat was needed that day. Reading slowly from a carefully prepared text, Palmer defended slavery as a biblically sanctioned, economically vital, and socially necessary institution. Millennial themes became entwined with southern honor as Palmer warned against the "degradation" of submitting to the election of a black Republican. He mourned the passing of "our once happy and united confederacy" but urged southerners to take up the fight because "the abolition spirit is undeniably atheistic."

He sadly concluded, "Nothing is now left us but secession." This seemed especially telling because there was still significant Unionist sentiment in the state and city. The response was electrifying. A pamphlet edition of the sermon was immediately printed, with perhaps as many as ninety thousand copies eventually in circulation. Full texts appeared in southern newspapers, and in the North, Palmer's words were widely discussed and denounced.[8]

And now even Thornwell sounded like one of those hated Yankee political preachers. Although proudly claiming that in twenty-five years of ministry he had never spoken of secular politics from the pulpit, now he was surely doing so. He would uphold slavery against northern attack and still chide southerners for not living up to their obligations as Christian masters, but his preaching acquired a new edge and certainly his ringing endorsement of "state sovereignty" came perilously close to endorsing secession. Privately, he maintained that submission to Lincoln's election would be dishonorable and disunion had become inevitable.[9]

Ironically the northern pulpit rang out with the very kind of assurances that southerners such as Thornwell had once demanded. Addressing his Detroit congregation, Presbyterian George Duffield seemed far more worried about the influence of theaters, saloons, and even musical performances than about slavery, or abolitionists, or fire-eaters. He chastised the churches for harboring "pride, vanity, boasting, ostentation, self-righteousness, luxury, covetousness ambition, sensuality . . ."—his list of vices went on and on. Duffield did suggest a need for sectional compromise but devoted much more attention to Sabbath breaking and liquor traffic. In Philadelphia, Baptist William T. Brantly, who had divided his ministerial career between northern and southern congregations, maintained that love of country should never degenerate into idolatry but blamed the political crisis on partisanship and the press. At the request of several prominent local Baptists, Brantly's sermon appeared as a pamphlet that circulated right alongside what he denounced as "sensation newspapers."[10]

Brantly had a point. Many northern preachers expressed a strong (if not idolatrous) faith in the United States even as their southern counterparts were wondering if the nation's experiment in republicanism had at last failed. Despite disdaining politics, Alabama Baptists declared that the once great American Union no longer protected persons or property. Devout southerners poured through their Bibles reading about Lot's departure from Sodom, the revolt against Jeroboam, and other sacred precedents for secession. South Carolina Presbyterians piously resolved to remain silent on political questions but then quickly added that "the people of South Carolina are now called on to imitate their revolutionary forefathers and stand up for their rights."[11] Condemning northern fanatics in one breath and suggesting revolutionary measures in the next showed how a vaunted religious conservatism had morphed into something entirely different.

But then Lincoln's election had done more than unsettle the political universe; talk of disunion flummoxed religious leaders of all persuasions. A cacophony of warring tongues undoubtedly added to the sense of crisis in both sections. Arch conservatives such as Brooklyn Presbyterian Henry J. Van Dyke echoed southern divines in condemning abolitionists as infidels whose clerical allies "would utterly reject and destroy the authority of God's word." Other clergy, however, tried to be more evenhanded in denouncing sectional extremism and indeed hoped that leaders of goodwill and good sense would somehow prevent disunion. A formulaic faith in divine providence and human reason bespoke a naive optimism that especially affected Old School Presbyterians (and to some degree Unitarians and Episcopalians), who still hoped that, if they ignored slavery and avoided political preaching, the crisis would pass. As one Catholic editor calmly observed, Lincoln had won the election fairly and could be expected to abide by the oath of office.[12]

This last comment hinted at the development of a Catholic counternarrative on the entire sectional crisis. Sounding like an Old School Presbyterian in the midst of the 1860 campaign, Orestes Brownson had warned that a Catholic periodical engaging in "party politics" would seriously weaken its religious influence because in a democracy people made up their own minds on public issues. But this ostensible political neutrality carried with it a good deal of sectarian chauvinism. After Lincoln's election, editor James A. McMaster noted how the main Protestant churches had all divided over slavery in striking contrast to the "universal" Catholic church that welcomed all people, bond and free, North and South. Therefore, Catholicism became the model for holding the Union together.[13]

McMaster's rather narrow views no doubt offended many Protestants, who had their own blinds spots, but such calls for unity and restraint were commonplace among northern moderates of various religious persuasions. Was not compromise, a leading Presbyterian editor asked, part of the genius of the United States Constitution itself? According to a prominent Episcopalian rector who developed a sermon around the story of ancient Israel dividing into two kingdoms, the pulpit should always present "lessons of moderation, conciliation, and love." Other ministers praised the republic's religious pluralism and its shining example to oppressed peoples around the world. More specifically, a Baltimore Presbyterian pointed to the common blessings of "a free Bible; a Protestant Sabbath, and an unsecularized, untrammeled and pure Church."[14]

Southern ministers seeking an escape from secession and possible war often parroted these Unionist sentiments. Church papers warned against any hasty endorsement of secession and still urged ministers to avoid politics; tactically, some editors rejected immediate secession and sided with the so-called cooperationists, who favored holding a convention of the southern states to seek a redress of grievances. Denying that either abolitionists or Republicans yet controlled the northern states, Robert Lewis Dabney insisted that southern rights could best be preserved in the Union. Like northern moderates, some southerners still could not imagine the breakup of the American republic. "I believe there have been too many Christians both North and South praying for the preservation of our National Union," one Virginian hoped, "for the combined efforts of the fanatics of the North and the fire-eaters of the South to prevail against our prayers."[15]

Such calm assurances belied deep sectional divisions yet reflected fundamental theological assumptions about the providential nature of human history. "We do not believe Providence has done with the American people," a Methodist editor wrote. The judgments of God, according to common understandings of Old Testament texts, were designed to chasten a wayward but still presumably chosen people. Northerners and southerners who self-righteously blamed each other for the sectional troubles, one North Carolinian feared, were acting in "the spirit of the world and not of Christ." It all came down to believing that what a Virginia doctor termed an "over-ruling Providence" would yet save the country from the "horrors of dissolution." The prayers of the righteous could redeem the nation, many believers maintained, and in any case, God remained sovereign. After listening to a minister in Lexington, Virginia, preach a sermon lamenting the nation's troubles, that model Calvinist Thomas J. Jackson gave the orthodox response: "Why should Christians be at all disturbed about the dissolution of the Union? It can only come by God's permission, and will only be permitted, if for his people's good, for does he not say that all things shall work together for good to them that love God?"[16]

Pious secessionists, however, hardly felt like leaving matters entirely in the Almighty's hands. "Turn your paper politician in some degree," one Alabamian advised the editor of the *South-Western Baptist*. "Not one in fifty cares to read about revivals now. I want to hear you talk coolly about our governmental affairs." Whether "coolly" any longer suited readers' tastes seemed doubtful as Deep South Baptists openly expressed their secessionist sentiments, often mirroring opinion in their states.[17] Methodists joined in raising the predictable alarms about a Union dominated by abolitionists as they called on the Lord for deliverance from the northern "Egypt." The division of Israel and Judah (not to mention the nation's already fractured churches) became typologies for the American crisis. Just as southern Methodists had once "seceded from a corrupt church," a Mississippi politician declared, "We must secede from a corrupt nation." To drive the point home, Georgia Methodist ministers endorsed disunion by an overwhelming 87–9 vote.[18]

Some southerners and many more northerners—despite considerable signs of reluctance and hesitation—believed that the clergy had helped push the Deep South states into disunion. Secession "has been accomplished mainly by the Churches," declared the devout lawyer Thomas R. R. Cobb.[19] This pious Georgian exaggerated, but his claim showed how the most determined clerical voices usually received the most attention. In all the heated rhetoric, few people at the time or later paid much attention to how divided clerical and lay opinion for that matter remained in both sections.

Secessionists, for example, tried to reassure everyone that their crusade was a holy one. Not surprisingly biblical passages and religious themes were often emblazoned on secession banners even as Unionists faced accusations of worshiping the American flag rather than Jesus Christ. Normally moderate men such as Mississippi Episcopal bishop William Mercer Green spoke in the language of cultural warfare, denouncing the "restless, insubordinate, and overbearing spirit of Puritanism" that was destroying the nation. A few ministers became active in politics. Nearly twenty served as delegates to the secession conventions in the Lower South, divided about evenly between proponents of immediate, individual state secession and cooperationists who favored waiting for consultation between the states.[20]

"What do women and preachers have to with succession [sic] and war?" one young Virginia minister asked his fiancée. Despite a fiery editorial here and there along with the wide reprinting of a few secessionist sermons, southern church publications still filled their columns with the usual reports of meetings and revivals. At the same time, editors blamed northern denominational papers for stirring up sectional tensions.[21] That charge was hardly fair because in the northern states too there remained a considerable aversion to church entanglement with political disputes along with a commitment to the Union that covered a wide ideological spectrum. On the more cautious end, Old School Presbyterians proudly pointed to their own unity and argued that the vast majority of Americans had no sympathy with northern abolitionists or southern fire-eaters. Secession itself marked a sinful uprising against God that could lead only to anarchy and war. Citing Absalom, Jeroboam, and Judas along with lesser examples of rebellion from the Bible, a Cincinnati minister used the title of his patriotic sermon to argue that the "Cause of the United States" and the "Cause of Jehovah" were identical. Yet a traditional nationalism could veer off in more radical directions. Months before a single shot had been fired, this same minister insisted that "a just defensive war" against southern secessionists is "one of the prominent ways by which the Lord will introduce the Millennial Day." And even secular editors talked of bringing government into line with divine principles.[22]

Given this lofty sense of mission, compromise with secessionists would be not only impolitic but also immoral, though such points would not go undisputed. Indeed, opinion of both clerics and their congregations remained much in flux. Especially for anyone with strong antislavery commitments, compromise posed a greater danger than disunion because it meant sacrificing religious principles and slowing the progress of Christian civilization. The appeal of such moral clarity was powerful—especially because previous compromises had failed to resolve sectional disputes. At the same time, however, conservative Unionists countered these arguments with warnings about self-righteousness. Northerners must understand the deep southern interest in slavery, Unitarian Henry W. Bellows advised, just as southerners must acknowledge the sincerity of northern antislavery convictions. Therefore, preachers in both sections should promote peaceful settlement rather than martial preparation. Leading Presbyterian theologian Charles Hodge naively expected appeals to conservative southerners and moderate Republicans to somehow stem the secession tide. But his long essay in the *Princeton Review* calling for men of reason to preserve the Union was harshly criticized in the South and failed to make Republicans more amenable to compromise. As leading Kentucky Presbyterian and Unionist Robert J. Breckinridge informed Hodge, southern secessionists were more united than their opponents, and Republicans seemingly preferred disunion to giving up any of their newly won political power.[23]

A faith that compromise could somehow ease the crisis persisted, especially in denominations that had avoided sectional schisms. Unitarians trusted in the wisdom and goodness of men who with God's help could prevent a disunion brought on by extremist agitation and abetted by corrupt politicians. "I am sorry to see the pulpit and religious press, North and South fanning the flame of discord," a Cincinnati minister complained, but he still hoped that the churches could set an example of Christian forbearance. Southern Episcopalians deplored what one bishop termed the "passion and prejudice, arrogance and defiance" that seemed "to rule the hour." Pastoral letters advised moderation but, beyond calls for prayer and appeals for patience, offered no way out of the sectional impasse.[24]

For some northerners secession itself was no longer unthinkable. A New England Baptist editor speculated that losing several southern states might simply relieve the nation of a moral burden. The bloody rebellions recounted in the Bible convinced a Cincinnati Presbyterian that forcing the seceding states back into the Union would be impossible. For anyone with strong anti-slavery convictions, further compromise and even remaining in the same Union with slaveholders seemed neither possible nor desirable. Some ministers would no longer pray for the American nation.[25]

By the end of 1860, the election of Lincoln and the secession of South Carolina on December 20 had pushed the nation to the brink of its greatest political crisis since the Revolution. Neither the clergy, the churches, nor millions of believers could escape the consequences as confusion and desperation spread. How pious folk and the churches should respond, what they should say and do, became the great question of the hour. Inside and outside the churches, fire-eaters and abolitionists sounded the tocsin. As the devout leafed through the scriptures seeking guidance and prayed for illumination, members of the clergy struggled to define their own role. Strident voices echoed from the pulpits in both sections, but more tempered ones could also be heard explaining how explosive sectional tensions fit into the course of providential history.

Less than a week before South Carolina seceded, President James Buchanan had issued a proclamation calling for the observance of January 4, 1861, as a "day of humiliation, fasting and prayer." Perhaps Buchanan's own failed leadership led him to conclude that only an appeal to the Almighty could save the nation. Abolitionists sarcastically remarked that Buchanan preferred to pray for the Union rather than act against secession, and a doughface's call for repentance naturally elicited derisive comments. The day should be observed, sniffed the *Independent*, even if the president was "a dotard, a hypocrite, a traitor."[26] Especially for Upper South moderates, however, Buchanan's proclamation appeared to be a godsend. Here was another chance—perhaps the last—to save the Union created by the revolutionary fathers. In many communities, the observance was a solemn one, though some ruefully admitted that they had not held strictly to the "fasting" part of the president's proclamation.[27]

Maybe it was in fact too late, and in any case the southern clergy never quite rose to the challenge. Few sermons were published, and those that were seemed jejune if not purblind. North Carolina Episcopalian Thomas Atkinson called on those in his congregation to confess their sins but emphasized the corruption of society exemplified by religious declension and commercial dishonesty. Rather than addressing the current crisis, Augustin Verot, the Catholic bishop of Florida, delivered a conventional proslavery discourse that tediously reviewed biblical texts and blasted the abolitionists as infidels. More ominously, Kentucky Presbyterian Thomas A. Hoyt maintained that the national government had no right to coerce a sovereign state but then weakly added that he would not address political questions from the pulpit.[28]

Many more northern ministers had their fast-day sermons published but that hardly proved more edifying for the county. Eminent New York Congregationalist Joseph Parrish Thompson began by sharply reviewing Buchanan's proslavery policies that had already brought down divine judgment on the nation. In many ways, Thompson repudiated the very purpose of the president's proclamation by chastising the American people for worshiping the false idol of Union. He firmly believed that Almighty God would condemn any man-made compromises with wrong and injustice.[29] Not surprisingly, slavery received considerable attention in fast-day sermons, but northern ministers offered little more original, enlightening, or helpful expositions than had their southern brethren. "In the Union or out of it," declared one New York Presbyterian. "Slavery must die. God has written upon it its inevitable doom; and universal civilization has pronounced against it."[30]

It was just such statements that alarmed northern conservatives. One Congregationalist discerned "far more danger" to the country from "unscriptural" attacks on slavery than from slavery itself. A small-town editor in New York sarcastically noted how "clerical agitators" had recently discovered the "sin" of slavery. Even ministers who made a point of condemning extremists in both sections often came down much harder on abolitionists. How could God suddenly decide to punish the nation for slaveholding when the practice had flourished in America for more than two centuries? That rhetorical question allowed conservative Presbyterian Charles Wadsworth to literally wash his hands of the entire issue and claim to "have no more concern with Southern slavery than with Russian serfdom."[31] Wadsworth went much too far for moderates who might spurn abolitionism but still considered slavery a moral evil. Such a middle ground, however, was becoming treacherous as southern states prepared to the leave the Union. It was easy enough to condemn northern and southern extremists, but most clergymen had surprisingly little to say about compromise measures already on the table.[32]

Falling back on divine sovereignty made some theological sense, but years of sectional tension and now real threats of secession deeply divided clerics and their congregations. Stealing a line from Thomas Jefferson, the aged New England Congregationalist Heman Humphrey begged Americans to remember that "we are all Democrats and all Republicans." Such desperate pleas for national unity met with a tepid response. A blind inmate preaching in a New York almshouse urged northern Christians to prevent misguided southerners from destroying the Union—by force if necessary. That last proviso was the problem: the willingness of people to push their particular positions to the point of war. Episcopalian Charles H. Hall, a Democrat who was ironically a close friend of Henry Ward Beecher, urged his Washington congregation (with President Buchanan in attendance) to abandon any "false pride of opinion." He prayed for the "triumph of good order, and piety over misrule and fanaticism, the restoration of charity and kindliness instead of hate and passion, the real practical law abiding service of every one of us, in the place of prejudice, pride, and folly."[33] But too many northerners and southerners had abandoned moderation, and so condemnations of sectional fanaticism solved nothing.

For the orthodox, all of these problems—from slavery, to divided councils, to political and religious polarization—grew out of human sin. The key point, and one that would echo throughout the war years, was made by a Presbyterian minister in Jacksonville, Illinois: "The law of retribution pertains to nations as well as individuals. God's providence is against the people that do iniquity as truly as against the individual transgressor of his holy commandments." In short, divine judgment fell on nations as well as on individuals. A Philadelphia Lutheran pastor agreed that all political and ecclesiastical structures must eventually collapse and that no nation was immune from inexorable decay. Anyone who believed that Americans might somehow be exempt from the workings of divine providence stood condemned for a boastful pride that would only further provoke the Lord's wrath.[34]

The list of national sins grew long: pride, vanity, ingratitude, materialism, infidelity, drunkenness, licentiousness, divorce, polygamy, corruption, and bribery. Each minister emphasized particular favorites. The distinguished Princeton seminary professor Alexander T. McGill argued that transportation networks binding the nation together had been used to "profane" the Sabbath, "cheat each other," and "rob the country at large" through fraudulent investment schemes. He lamented how once pious topics of family conversation had been supplanted by sensational newspaper reports and political alarms. Even Beecher, who predictably pointed to slavery as the nation's great sin, railed against the lax morals associated with burgeoning cities and unrelenting commerce.[35]

In a more general sense, clergymen who envisioned the United States as a Christian republic concluded that the nation suffered from failing to acknowledge God in the Constitution. Apparently, Americans neither feared God nor followed his will. Instead, they worshiped a gaudy idol: popular will. If government were a mere expression of human will, a Philadelphia Episcopalian pointedly remarked, secession could readily and legitimately dissolve it. But if civil magistrates were indeed ministers of God, rebellion became the ultimate sin. In stressing the divine origins of civil government, a covenant between rulers and ruled, and the consequences of arousing the Lord's wrath, such preaching seemed a throwback to the old Puritan election sermons. The central arguments rested on a commitment to political and religious order that resonated with conservatives and moderates.[36]

The hope remained, as one Methodist minister wrote in his diary, that "a universal and hearty National repentance . . . may turn away the wrath of God." But whether all the passionate preaching and fervid prayer could accomplish such a lofty purpose stood very much in doubt. According to a German Reformed editor, fast-day sermons too often became "political harangues." And it was not only conservatives who sounded skeptical. Unitarian Henry W. Bellows, who insisted that the only real issue facing the nation was slavery, refused to "believe that vague confessions of a guilt we do not feel, and formal prayers for an interposition we do not expect, are likely to produce anything but the ordinary fruits of hypocrisy."[37]

It might be tempting to criticize or even dismiss much of the preaching and praying as empty exercises. But whatever the weaknesses of the fast-day sermons—and they were significant—the preachers had offered some prodding, comfort, and a bit of guidance to people beset by doubts, anxieties, and fears. That their messages contained an often perplexing mix of sectional chauvinism, sterile dogma, and doubtful theology sprinkled with occasional insight was perhaps inevitable. As human beings they could hardly escape the prejudices of place and time; few could transcend parochial viewpoints, regional interests, denominational blinders, or their own political views. At the same time, a literal and by definition quite limiting reading of scripture may well have compounded these problems for both ministers and their flocks. Like Americans more generally, the devout stumbled forward with little hope that the crisis might ease.

———

Less than a week after the national fast day, the Mississippi convention voted to secede; Florida and Alabama quickly followed suit. By January 19, Georgia had joined them though the decision there had been touch-and-go; by the end of the month, Louisiana had left the Union, and Texas was on the verge. Across the Deep South, Baptists and Methodists were often divided over the question of *immediate* secession, if not over the legitimacy of secession itself. At the opening session of the Mississippi secession convention, a Methodist minister had invoked the Lord's aid against hostile northerners and any who would touch the institution of slavery, "which thy Providence has solemnly bound us to uphold, defend, and protect." In Georgia, however, Bishop Andrew sounded doubtful and Augustus Baldwin Longstreet warned against precipitous action. Yet, as the conventions deliberated, the political and social pressure against clerical dissenters mounted, and some were forced to abandon their pulpits.[38]

In January, Thornwell published a long article in the *Southern Presbyterian Review* (soon issued as a pamphlet) that defended the secession of South Carolina. He rejoiced over other states moving in the same direction, reviewed the constitutional status of slavery, explained how Lincoln's election threatened the institution, and declared that the question of peace or war rested entirely with the northern people. Here was a purely political essay written for a religious periodical by the leading advocate for the church as an exclusively spiritual body. But the South's greatest theologian had now become a secession torchbearer whose writings were widely read and applauded. Privately, he exulted over South Carolina's unity, rejoicing at "how thoroughly law and order reign in the midst of an intense and radical revolution."[39]

In a sermon delivered in Brooklyn, Presbyterian Henry J. Van Dyke had blamed abolitionists for driving such good Christians as Thornwell and Benjamin Morgan Palmer out of the Union. His key point that the Bible clearly sanctioned slavery only made his message more inflammatory, as fear of the slave power was reaching a fever pitch. Biblical scholars and even some Old School Presbyterians derided Van Dyke's exegesis; the religious press debated and often reviled the sermon. In Amite, Louisiana, sixteen-year-old Sarah Wadley read it aloud to her best friend and pronounced the sermon a "very able discourse."[40]

——

Wadley could have heard Van Dyke's sentiments echoed much closer to home. Preachers talked about a spiritual and cultural war between true Christianity and Yankee infidelity. Indeed, according to one Georgia Baptist editor, it was northern "opposition to plain Biblical teachings, which has dissolved our once glorious Union." And just as some northern ministers viewed the secession crisis as a millennial opportunity to proclaim liberty to the captives, so southern Christians maintained that the perfection of a slaveholding society would ultimately lead to what a Georgia woman called "the final and universal spread of Gospel civilization."[41]

Such blinkered sectionalism caused considerable unease for Americans belonging to churches that had not divided along sectional lines. Southern Catholics, for instance, remained quite reticent about secession. Patrick Lynch, the bishop of Charleston, who viewed northern threats to southern institutions with alarm, seemed to have a lingering affection for the Union.

In Natchez, Mississippi, Bishop William Henry Elder instructed priests to say nothing about disunion, though privately he observed that Catholic teaching hardly dictated opposition to secession. Such ostensible neutrality could not last. Leading Catholic politicians soon fell into line behind the secession movement, and regardless of any misgivings, the church hierarchy would support the Confederate cause.[42]

The situation in the Border South proved especially delicate. In St. Louis, Archbishop Peter Richard Kenrick urged the faithful to "avoid all occasions of public excitement." The circulars of Kenrick and Bishop Martin John Spalding of Louisville, Kentucky, were welcomed by northern Catholics, who acknowledged that the church had long recognized slavery as a legitimate human relationship even while condemning its abuses. Yet this conservative consensus seemed tenuous as more Deep South states seceded. "Constitution" and "Union" became watchwords for northern Catholic editors, who acknowledged the legitimacy of southern grievances but would not countenance disunion. James McMaster tartly suggested it should be left to southern Baptists, Presbyterians, and Methodists—not to southern Catholics—to promote secession.[43]

Church unity, especially for northern Catholics, became the best hope for preserving national unity. A universal faith and standard liturgy would keep people together without dictating anyone's position on political questions. "The Catholic genius is ever to seek and to promote human concord and union," McMaster wrote in a typical editorial. The secession crisis offered an irresistible temptation to blast the Protestant clergy as an inherently schismatic band whose "religious fanaticism" fomented political disorder. But the plain fact remained that many southern Catholics would support disunion and many northern Catholics would resist it. At best, the shattering of the nation might leave the church undivided—at least theologically. Shortly after Lincoln's inauguration, a Pittsburgh editor drove home this point: "So as we live sinless lives and partake of the same sacraments, North and South, we can still be one in Christ."[44]

For believers to remain of "one accord" (a phrase that occurs repeatedly in the book of Acts) was expecting a great deal because subjection to human and divine authority cut against the grain of American democracy and individualism. During the secession crisis, the duty of Christians to obey "the powers that be" became a common theme among conservatives and moderates, North and South. From a short pastoral message in a rural South Carolina Baptist church, to a Thanksgiving homily by an Episcopalian rector in Washington, to a Presbyterian sermon on the nature of civil government under God delivered in Chillicothe, Ohio, traditional ideas about government as divinely ordained offered the best hope for saving the nation.[45] But whether all the fine words carried much practical import appeared ever more doubtful as states seceded.

———

On departing from his Springfield home for Washington, the president-elect had asked his old neighbors to pray for him, a request that might have been dismissed as a commonplace, meaningless gesture. Yet civil religion was assuming a larger and larger importance. In his inaugural address on March 4, Lincoln weighed in at least briefly about the relationship between divine will and the sectional crisis: "If the Almighty Ruler of nations, with his eternal truth and justice, be on your side of the North, or on yours of the South, that truth, and that justice will surely prevail, by the judgment of his great tribunal, the American people." To those who routinely saw divine providence at work in their own and in the nation's life, Lincoln held out the prospect of restoring sectional concord: "Intelligence, patriotism, Christianity, and a firm reliance on Him, who has never yet forsaken this favored land, are still competent to adjust, in the way, all your present difficulty." But earlier in his speech he had made a simple declarative statement that suggested why compromise might prove difficult, especially for anyone whose political beliefs were shaped by religious faith and moral conviction: "One section of our country believes slavery is *right*, and ought to be extended, while the other believes it is *wrong*, and ought not to be extended."[46]

Whatever the political ramifications of Lincoln's inaugural address, it played well in the northern religious press and began the process of convincing church people that this Illinois politician was a man of faith — however vaguely defined. "The President had devotedly acknowledged his dependence on God," one Baptist editor rejoiced. "With a humility, far too rare among statesmen, he has confessed his need of divine help." According to news reports, the Executive Mansion had become a house of prayer. A Republican editor in Buffalo noted with approval Lincoln's references to both divine will and the moral nature of the slavery question. But even here biblical interpretations of the crisis were at odds. Another New Yorker compared the new president's position to that of King Rehoboam on ascending the throne of Israel. That unwise ruler had immediately adopted a coercive policy toward his opponents with disastrous consequences. Shortly after the inaugural ceremony, however, a Dutch Reformed minister in Brooklyn picked up on this example to make a quite different point, praising Lincoln for not following Rehoboam's foolish course.[47]

The president's soothing phrases won praise from conservative Catholics as well as antislavery Presbyterians, but the southern response was not at all conciliatory. Even Upper South moderates feared Lincoln's words signaled coercion — a policy sure to drive the wavering into the arms of the secessionists.[48]

One problem was that opposition to secession among Upper South clergy hardly signified an unconditional commitment to the Union. As a Virginia Presbyterian editor had pointed out even before South Carolina seceded, there might be division over secession but not on "coercion." Initially, of course, moderates raised all kinds of objections to disunion: secession would only divide southerners; young hotspurs should pause in their revolutionary course; the Upper South would likely become a battleground in any war. Or perhaps the wave of secession in the Deep South would force a sectional compromise in Congress or even in the ill-fated Washington Peace Conference.[49]

In this confusion of voices, a sense of drift was unmistakable. Privately dismissing hotheaded South Carolina as a "little impudent vixen," Robert Lewis Dabney urged southern Christians to "study moderation" and stick with religious subjects on the Sabbath. "The churches seem to be exerting very little influence for good," Dabney confided to his mother, and as one of his friends pointed out, too many southerners thought Christ's "benediction upon the 'peace-makers' was either antiquated, or . . . limited in practice to the discords of individuals."[50] Dabney and other religious leaders would not countenance secession yet would not support forceful measures against it. Nor did they rally around any particular set of compromise proposals; they deplored talk of war but seemed oddly passive.

Religious leaders almost seemed to be giving up on religious leadership. After learning that fellow Episcopal bishops Leonidas Polk and Stephen Elliott "deliberately favor secession," Tennessean James Otey wrote sadly, "It is God alone that can still the madness of the people." In Virginia, Bishop William Meade glumly noted the clergy's utter failure. "If Christian ministers, a body of more intelligence than any in the land, and who may be supposed to excel all others in piety, cannot continue together to consult about the Kingdom of the Prince of Peace, even while civil rulers have preserved their union, can we expect selfish politicians to do it?"[51] The voice of organized religion seemed strident, muted, confused, or powerless.

Appalled by abolitionists and secessionists alike, Kentucky Presbyterian Robert J. Breckinridge accused northern and southern fanatics of ignoring God's purposes for the nation. In a long essay, he bemoaned "the destructive extent to which religious opinion can be made to take the prevailing hue of a fierce enthusiasm, or an intolerant fanaticism, which reigns around it." Yet his Unionist views were treated with dismissive contempt by southern Presbyterians such as Benjamin Morgan Palmer, who replied with a treatise that was pure state sovereignty with no references to scripture, God, or even the church.[52]

The plaintive words of a Dabney, a Meade, or a Breckinridge raised a disturbing question: were religious convictions shaping political convictions, or was it the other way around? As the country drifted toward war, the *Independent* bravely maintained that sectional troubles exposed the differences between those who followed Christ and those "who are simply secular in their plans and hopes." The Christian held fast to a belief in divine providence, therefore avoiding gloom and despair. Did faith then mean simply riding out the secession storm? Warning about the possibility of a long and destructive civil war, New England Congregationalist Zachary Eddy even suggested that disunion "be accepted with pious acquiescence rather than resisted unto blood."[53]

Here was a confession of clerical, if not religious, impotence writ large. The role of religious ideas and leaders in the secession crisis had been decidedly limited; ministers and their congregations had mostly reacted to fast-moving events. Even though a few ministers, such as Thornwell and Palmer, had warmly endorsed disunion, the southern clergy remained both hesitant and divided. For their part, abolitionists and other opponents of sectional compromise might view the secession crisis as a providential opportunity to strike a fatal blow at slavery, but northern churches manifested more confusion than conviction. Moderates continued to search for a way to avoid continued agitation and war but hardly knew how to proceed.[54]

On the eve of the Civil War, religion occupied a powerful if not commanding position in American intellectual, social, and cultural life. It had made incursions and inroads into politics, but here the picture became much messier. Most religious editors and clerics largely confined their attention to spiritual matters and church business, though a significant and growing minority did not. Religious ideas had not driven the sectional conflict or the secession debates yet added a moral and often uncompromising intensity. Heated arguments about "political preaching" had further prevented any kind of consensus on either the role of religion in public life or solutions to the problems threatening to destroy the American republic. Northern and southern preachers struggled to interpret or, just as often, avoid interpreting the crisis for their people.

At the same time, critics could observe with some justice that "civil religion" had trumped "genuine religion." That, of course, oversimplifies the complex debates over the "spiritual nature" of the churches, and intellectual consistency was always at a premium. Sectional and state loyalties along with everything from denominational interests, to theological traditions, to church governance had shaped the reactions of clergy and laity alike. Everyone from Unitarians to Catholics had largely acted in character, and maybe that was the problem. In the secession crisis as in the endless debates over slavery, a failure of moral and political imagination had been apparent across a wide religious spectrum. Maybe there was no way out, maybe there was no reasonable "settlement" of the slavery question, maybe the conflict was irrepressible, but the devout could not avoid being part of the problem. Indeed, even a deep and genuine piety could not prevent people from being buffeted by the political winds. Believers had searched their Bibles for historical analogies and lessons but, as the Deep South states left the Union, could agree only on the fact that all things remained in the hands of providence. That could just as easily spawn a dangerous fatalism; it could also harden into a conviction that God's views on these questions coincided with one's own.

HOLY WAR

Then said he unto them . . . he that hath no sword,
let him sell his garment, and buy one.
— Luke 22:36

This bellicose passage became the sermon text for a northern preacher who quickly threw aside his pacifist principles after hearing that Confederates had fired on Fort Sumter and that the United States flag had been hauled down.[1] War changed everything, or so countless Americans believed. The conflict quickly developed into a religious as well as a political and military contest, a testing ground for spiritual character and theological conviction, including ideas about the relationship between church and state. Countless Americans would view the war—its course, costs, and consequences—through the lens of religious faith, and that process began immediately. Besides raising difficult questions about divine sovereignty and purpose, the war placed immediate strains on those churches that had not yet divided along sectional lines. And these problems were soon eclipsed by the larger one of sending countless young men—many of them devout believers—off to maim and kill each other.

The story began at a small, just-completed fort in Charleston Harbor. Whatever its limited strategic value, Fort Sumter had come to symbolize federal authority in South Carolina, a horrible affront to Confederate claims to being a sovereign nation. To the militarily untutored eye of young Emma Holmes, Sumter had looked "almost impregnable," but she took heart in having "truth, justice and religion on our side." To many ardent Confederates that was the point, and when the fort was surrendered without the loss of a single life, this seemed nothing short of miraculous. And now for the first time but far from the last, southern nationalists would celebrate a military victory that proved the Lord was on their side. "Has not God, by this one token, sufficiently declared his will?" asked a Charleston minister who harbored no doubts about the answer.[2]

The Federals would have to wait longer for a similar sign of divine favor, but for the time being they had something almost as valuable: a Christian hero. The commander at Fort Sumter had been Major Robert Anderson, a slaveholding Kentuckian but a staunch Unionist. The new president would greatly benefit from Anderson's loyalty and judgment; the gallant though hopeless defense of the small garrison won him instant acclaim. As early as January stories about Anderson kneeling in prayer as the American flag was raised over Sumter had appeared in the religious press. He would later tell Sunday school children how he had asked the Lord to bless his men each morning. God had watched over them all at Sumter, Anderson believed, and they had been heartened by the prayers of Christian friends at home.[3] Stories of the major's faith established him as a model Christian soldier in the mold of Oliver Cromwell, defeated but unbowed, and seemingly destined for ultimate victory in this world and the next.

———

News of the fighting in Charleston harbor ended a long period of hesitation and uncertainty. Talk of peaceable secession, of letting the erring brothers go, or of cobbling together a last-minute compromise vanished. In Northampton, Massachusetts, on April 4, Congregationalist Zachary Eddy had preached about the need for peace and conciliation but soon changed his theme. Now the story of King Rehoboam, which he had cited as a warning against a coercive policy, taught a much different lesson. In the end, Rehoboam had gone to war against Jeroboam, who was attempting to destroy the political and religious unity of the Hebrew nation. However reluctant Christians might be to take up arms, there were times when war became unavoidable and even served God's purposes. The Prince of Peace, claimed one Iowa Presbyterian, did not preach peace at any price and had taught his followers to resist evil—with a sword if necessary. If Confederates represented the forces of lawlessness and oppression, not only civil but religious liberty was at stake. Better war than anarchy was the cry in several churches, which hastily sent resolutions of support to Lincoln. The *New York Times* approvingly noted how the city's ministers had with one voice rallied to the side of the government in a "just and holy war." From conservative Catholics to antislavery Baptists came calls for burying partisan differences and crushing a godless rebellion.[4]

The shift in southern sentiments was almost as dramatic. After Lincoln's call for seventy-five thousand militia, denunciations of "coercion" rang from the pulpits, especially in the Upper South. Tennessee Episcopal bishop James Hervey Otey, who had strongly opposed secession, claimed to have "no sympathy with the U.S.—no respect for its rulers—very little regard for the Northern people." Southerners must "repel force by force, and to make every sacrifice rather than submit to an administration that tramples down every barrier raised by our Forefathers for the protection of personal, social, and public rights." In the Confederacy too, secular editors often spoke in religious language; the southern people "could invoke the aid of the God of battles," a

North Carolina newspaper declared, "with a firm faith that he will prosper the Right." That coercion was a wicked policy doomed to failure against a free people became an article of faith.[5]

Even for those who still deplored the necessity for war, the prospect of southern independence seemed glorious. "I look upon the secession of the southern states as the grandest, most noble and chivalrous, patriotic and God-like achievement ever effected by any oppressed people in the world," exulted one Georgia Lutheran. The clergy now embraced the rhetoric of manhood and honor—long a staple appeal of southern politicians. Sermons, editorials in church papers, and denominational resolutions bristled with defiance against Lincoln and the black Republicans along with paeans to King Cotton and calls for resisting oppression.[6] Cries for southern unity carried no particular scriptural or doctrinal justification beyond the general notion that the new nation's strength rested with the Lord.

Of course, northern clergy merely had to cite the thirteenth chapter of Romans to show that the southern people had failed to obey the powers that be. Fighting for constitutional authority meant upholding divine authority—a position that proved equally attractive to conservatives who had previously favored concessions to southern interests and to radicals who had opposed any compromises. Loyalty to nation and loyalty to God became one and the same; patriots need only pray for victory. Upholding the government against traitorous rebels would mean bloody work, as was duly noted in the opening prayer of a New York Methodist conference: "We ask Thee to bring these men [the rebels] to destruction, and wipe them from the face of the country."[7]

Did not the scriptures sanctify fighting in a just cause? Though few Americans cared to delve into the intricacies of just war theory as developed by Aquinas and other theologians,[8] suppressing the southern rebellion seemingly met popular criteria for a just cause. The legitimate election of Lincoln, the attempt of a minority to defy the will of a majority, and the southern attack on the flag all buttressed the idea that the Federal government and the northern people had right on their side. New Hampshire Congregationalist Elias Nason preached about how lawless secessionists were trying to destroy the government; privately he advised Lincoln of his "high mission under God" to save the nation from a "band of desperadoes."[9]

Perhaps it took religious and political outsiders to critique the rhetoric of righteous war. Born in the revivalism of the 1820s, dogged by teachings about polygamy, driven from Missouri and Illinois, their prophet Joseph Smith murdered in 1844, the Mormons (officially the Church of Jesus Christ of Latter Day Saints) had migrated to the Great Salt Lake basin under the leadership of Brigham Young, bringing along their own mythic understandings about the origin of the North American continent and its destiny. Not surprisingly, after an 1857 confrontation with federal troops sent by President Buchanan and commanded by Albert Sidney Johnston, Young and his followers interpreted the mounting sectional conflict as a divine judgment on their enemies. The *Deseret News* predicted that Lincoln's election would mark the end of a republic that had not heeded "the prophetic declarations of the servants of God."

A nation that had shed the innocent blood of Joseph Smith and others would live to see Smith's more terrifying prophecies fulfilled. Brigham Young watched the breakup of the American Union with great interest and no little satisfaction. He coldly noted that the U.S. government had never acknowledged God and wondered whether the Confederates would do any better. Perhaps the Mormons would even inherit the shattered remnants of the American republic. In February 1861 Young rejoiced over signs that the federal union was suffering for the "wicked attempts to root up the Kingdom of God." Divine wrath would fall on the American people and set "State against State, city against city, neighborhood against neighborhood, Methodists against Methodists, and so on." Anticipating Lincoln's second inaugural address, Young noted how both northerners and southerners prayed to the "same God" but added that "if their God should hear and answer them, they would all be utterly annihilated."[10]

Young and his followers echoed many others in believing that the American nation was being punished for a host of sins. Perhaps Americans had been too proud of their wealth and power—some Calvinist pulpits rang with echoes of the old Puritan jeremiads. A Philadelphia Presbyterian declared that the hand of God could always be discerned in the affliction of nations. The Lord might not "crown our armies with instant victory," an Ohio preacher warned. "He may choose to discipline us by disasters and try us by reverses." Yet ultimately the Lord could never allow treason to triumph. "We have too high a civilization and too much Christianity for a protracted war," declared the nation's leading Methodist weekly.[11]

Believers in divine sovereignty held that each twist and turn in the war accorded with a providential plan. A providential view of history carried disturbing ambiguities because mere mortals could hardly discern the Lord's will with any great certainty. How could either side be sure that they had secured God's favor? This tough question received surprisingly little attention at the beginning of the war. "Surely God is on our side," wrote one Baptist minister's daughter, and many southerners would not have made that statement conditional at all. "It would be impiety to doubt our triumph," declared Episcopal theologian James Warley Miles. "We are working out a great thought of GOD—, namely the higher development of Humanity in its capacity for Constitutional

Liberty." There was no way that the Almighty could allow infidel Republicans to prevail. "'In the name of God we set our banners,'" announced one Baptist editor, quoting the twentieth Psalm. "And by the blessing of Him who ruleth in the armies of heaven, the sword will never be sheathed until the last invader shall be driven from our shores." So brave statements about certain victory poured forth from presses and pulpits weeks before a major battle had been fought.[12]

Though discerning historical movement in a much different direction, northern commentators just as readily detected the workings of providence, often from the same biblical texts. On consecutive Sundays after the firing on Sumter, Rhode Island Congregationalist Leonard Swain preached on the theme of God and country. Without actually bothering to examine the proposition, he began by asserting that the Lord justified "national self-defense." Given this assumption, pious young men should go into battle both confidently and cheerfully as Christian soldiers acknowledging their dependence upon the Almighty. The nation is "sent forth to fight the battle of Heaven," Swain avowed. "If there ever was a war undertaken in the name of God in his service, at his command, under his approbation, it is the war to which the whole north has risen as one man." Like his colleagues in the church papers, a Boston editor was sure he had discovered the "hand of God" in the contest. Even a conservative Wisconsin Republican who had favored compromise at the beginning of the secession crisis informed Lincoln that "God the Almighty must be with us" against "rebels and traitors," who would destroy the Constitution that had been created "under the guidance of Almighty God to be the light & glory of the world."[13]

When millennial themes cropped up in private political correspondence, it seemed that religion had moved to center stage. It was just as true, however, that war had moved to center stage. The religious press in both sections became increasingly secular, publishing military news and, almost without exception, supporting either the Union or the Confederacy. Editorials often became indistinguishable from those in regular newspapers, and their main points seldom rested on biblical or theological arguments. Some readers might complain or even cancel subscriptions, but a Methodist editor in Nashville unequivocally defended the change in content and tone: "And it is the part of a religious paper that is not a fossil—a paper that has not and never means to 'dabble in politics'—to treat of these [religious] duties in their season. We must study Joshua and Ezra and Nehemiah, as well as Job and St. John."[14]

Church services, especially those held on the first few Sundays after Sumter, took on a decidedly martial tone. In Savannah, Catholic notices for mass asked that members "offer their fervent prayers for . . . the Southern Confederacy in repelling the aggressive invasions of Northern barbarians." Across the North, the services became more solemn and impressive; some ministers preached two or three times in addition to offering words of encouragement to the Sunday schools or special prayers for Lincoln. In Chicago, a Sunday school superintendent reportedly "preached a war sermon to the children." Flags appeared in Unitarian churches, in Methodist churches, in Catholic churches, almost everywhere. After securing a great twenty by forty foot flag for Trinity Episcopal Church in New York and hearing the chimes ring and seeing crowds gather on Wall Street and Broadway, diarist George Templeton Strong discerned a great change in public life. "The ideas of Church and State, Religion and Politics, have been practically separated so long that people specially delighted with any manifestation of the Church's sympathy with the State." No longer would the church be simply a "private soul-saving society" but instead would occupy a position of importance in the great national crisis. "The Christian church that had grown sleepy," the editor of the *Springfield Republican* rejoiced, "has found something to pray for." The shouting and martial music sometimes drowned out the church bells, but perhaps that was only proper as the Prince of Peace was being supplanted by the God of Battles.[15]

To the millennial optimists, the war would surely advance God's kingdom through a government that Unitarian Henry Bellows believed should blend "civil and spiritual powers." Just "as there are periods of Christian revival in the Church, so there are periods of Christian revival in the State." Bellows did not exactly declare war to be the health of the state and church, but he came perilously close. The contest had become a "holy war"[16] waged for important political principles "in the name of civilization, morality, and religion." Cyrus Bartol expected the war to banish "pride, egotism and class feelings" by promoting self-sacrifice among men and women, soldiers and civilians.[17] The conflation of political crisis, military preparations, divine purpose, and providential history seemed pervasive. Clergymen and their congregations became caught up in the patriotic fervor that swept across the now divided nation. It would not be entirely fair to say that politics rode roughshod over religion, but Americans exhibited much more spiritual hubris than spiritual reflection.

_____

The outbreak of war more seriously tested those churches that had prided themselves on their harmony. The General Assembly of the Old School Presbyterians had steadfastly refused to debate "political" questions, but that seemed no longer possible. Palmer and Thornwell had come out for disunion, and several influential northern Presbyterian ministers, in something of a panic, had signed a circular letter calling for an end to sectional misrepresentations, especially by northern and southern clergy.[18]

In January 1861 Charles Hodge, longtime Princeton professor, editor of the *Princeton Review*, and champion of Calvinist orthodoxy, tried to don the mantle of elder statesman and peacemaker. Concluding that the sectional crisis justified the discussion of secular issues in a religious journal, Hodge appealed to northerners and southerners as fellow Christians with a common and sacred national inheritance. After describing the geographic bonds of Union in language that was at once logical and sentimental, he denied that the supposed grievances of the southern states could justify rebellion. Like many conservatives, Hodge dismissed sectional extremists of various stripes as noisy minorities. He rejected any constitutional or historical arguments for secession and suggested that some slaveholders had become too insistent on the federal government serving their narrow interests. In an essay remarkably devoid of scriptural or religious references, Hodge soberly concluded: "If we are to be plunged into the horrors of civil war and servile insurrections, no tongue can tell how the cause of the Redeemer must suffer throughout our whole land." [19]

Many northerners applauded Hodge's work, but it hardly fostered unity in Presbyterian councils. A staunchly antislavery minister in the Midwest detected "the same old leaven of a temporizing spirit." By his own lights and especially for a minister who had always condemned abolitionists more than slaveholders, Hodge had spoken out boldly against secession but, like other would-be conciliators, kept finding the ground shifting under him and always remained something of a trimmer. Southern Presbyterians accused Hodge of mixing religion and politics, but their largely political responses included a heavy dose of proslavery and sectional polemics. [20]

When the General Assembly convened in Philadelphia on May 16, southern secession already appeared to be an accomplished fact in church as well as state. Only a few presbyteries from southern synods bothered to send commissioners. One South Carolina presbytery offered the excuse that southerners might be "exposed to most embarrassing and vexatious annoyances, and it will be impossible to secure their personal safety." Even many Upper South synods went unrepresented, and three giants of the church, Thornwell, Palmer, and Breckinridge, were absent. To one newspaper correspondent, the delegates looked old and tired as they strove somehow to maintain church harmony. [21]

Even so the policy of silence on sectional and political questions would not survive. Veteran minister Gardiner Spring of Brick Street Presbyterian Church in New York asked that a committee be appointed to draft a statement affirming the church's loyalty to the United States and its government. Conservative in most respects, Spring was nevertheless a devoted Unionist who had been deeply offended by Thornwell's and Palmer's endorsement of secession. Although Spring's motion was tabled without a roll call, he later proposed designating July 1 as a day of prayer to "confess and bewail our nation's sins," standard enough Presbyterian fare. But Spring's second resolution declared that ministers and churches should "do all in their power to promote and perpetuate the integrity of these United States, and to strengthen, uphold and encourage the Federal Government." This ignited a furious five-day debate before the question was finally referred to a committee.

There Hodge helped draft a tepid statement on national loyalty. Those favoring this majority report produced a telegram from the new attorney general and devout Presbyterian Edward Bates advising the church to abstain from any new statement on the nation's troubles, but the other side countered with a dispatch from the equally pious secretary of the treasury, Salmon P. Chase, proclaiming there should be no objection to an official expression "in favor of the Constitution, Union, and freedom." The majority report was defeated, and the minority report, which included the Spring resolutions, was then adopted by a vote of 156–66.[22]

This seemingly decisive result hardly settled matters. It was ironic that Hodge, who had firmly opposed southern secession, now led a protest against the assembly's action. Of course, there was a certain consistency to his deep-dyed conservatism, a conservatism that had always warned about the troublesome influence of abolitionists and fire-eaters and was very protective of both the church and the Princeton Seminary. Hodge and fifty-seven other delegates expressed deep affection for the Union but objected to making political loyalty a test for church membership. The Spring resolutions threatened to divide the Presbyterian church with slaveholders dominating a southern wing and abolitionists controlling the northern branch, or so Hodge feared.[23] Of course, earlier he had argued that such extremists were a minority in each section, but consistency is always one of war's first casualties.

The tide in any case was running against Hodge and other conservatives both inside and outside the General Assembly. Antislavery Presbyterians had cheered the absence of southern delegates and now rallied to the Spring resolutions as a witness to denominational patriotism. Northern presbyteries and synods overwhelmingly endorsed the Spring resolutions and often condemned those commissioners who had voted against them. Presbyterian editors who had once evaded such questions swung into line.[24]

Hodge's protest against the Spring resolutions likely helped keep the border states in the church; the synods there were often hostile both to the General Assembly's actions and to southern threats of division. In Bardstown, Kentucky, Stuart Robinson's *True Presbyterian* stoutly defended traditional ideas about the spiritual nature of the church with a fervor worthy of Thornwell. His attacks on the Old School General Assembly were relentless, and his refusal to editorially support the government or the war naturally led to charges of disloyalty. Breckinridge's more tempered criticism and unswerving Unionism better represented the views of border state Presbyterians.[25]

The political revolution in the seceding states had seemingly produced a theological shift. Southern Presbyterians who had apparently abandoned their views on the exclusively spiritual nature of the church and endorsed secession berated the General Assembly for adopting "political" resolutions that supplanted loyalty to Christ with loyalty to Caesar. In a long essay for the *Southern Presbyterian Review*, John Adger dismissed the majority in Philadelphia as a pack of abolitionists and deplored the "murderous spirit of Northern Ministers, and Churches, and people." With the nation dividing, the Presbyterian Church would have to do likewise. Separate nations dictated separate ecclesiastical organizations; it was as simple as that. From North Carolina to Louisiana to Texas, presbyteries called for abandoning the Old School General Assembly.[26] In December, representatives from forty-seven presbyteries would meet in Augusta, Georgia, to form the Presbyterian Church in the Confederate States of America. According to Thornwell, the Bible would be the constitution of the new church, but in most respects, including doctrine, it resembled the Old School. Thornwell denied that he and the other delegates were schismatics and made sure that everyone understood how the Spring resolutions had made this step necessary.[27]

In their own fashion, southern Episcopalians proved almost as aggressive as southern Presbyterians in pushing for ecclesiastical independence. As the Lower South states seceded, Leonidas Polk consulted with other southern bishops. Once Louisiana had seceded, claimed Polk, his diocese had been effectively cut off from the Protestant Episcopal Church in the United States; in this rather fine distinction, the church was "separated not divided." Although diocesan organization had helped prevent the Episcopalians dividing over slavery before the war, that hardly mattered now. Like the Old School Presbyterians, Episcopalians had prided themselves on avoiding political questions, yet according to Georgia bishop Stephen Elliott, secession forced their hand. Elliott maintained that his state was legitimately exercising its sovereignty, a political statement if there ever was one.[28]

Because American Episcopalians had paid much attention to liturgical details, it was hardly surprising when the forms of prayer for those in authority caused difficulties. Only a short time after the firing on Fort Sumter, an Episcopalian convocation in North Carolina spent much of its time discussing the proper manner for pronouncing major and minor benedictions. Charles Todd Quintard, who would labor tirelessly as a Confederate chaplain, simply could not understand how Christians could live without a prescribed form of prayer. He dismissed the Methodists as a "sect," condemned Baptist "heresy," and ridiculed the divided Presbyterians while extolling the Episcopal liturgy as "so near a resemblance of the perfect form of prayer which our divine master has left us for our use and for our pattern."[29]

Long-standing fears of schism and reverence for ecclesiastical order had prevented northern Episcopalians from speaking out on slavery or other controversial matters, though the more traditionalist Anglo-Catholic group was much more reluctant than the evangelical contingent. But for many northern Episcopalians wishing to support the Union, Bishop Polk became a convenient whipping boy, especially after he joined the Confederate army. Increasingly the issue became one of loyalty. Addressing a Cleveland meeting in June 1861, Ohio bishop Charles McIlvaine, who had turned against slavery and supported Lincoln, was especially adamant: "There is no such thing as being neutral in this controversy." For a more conservative bishop such as Samuel McCoskry of Michigan, whose views resembled those of many northern Catholics, there was still reason to rejoice that the Episcopal Church could not be held responsible for sectional strife.[30]

That could hardly be said of the southern bishops. Polk and Elliott called a meeting of clergy and lay delegates for July in Montgomery, Alabama, but with only six dioceses represented and with signs of hesitation among Upper South Episcopalians, they decided to draft a constitution for a southern church and then meet several months later in Columbia, South Carolina. There the Protestant Episcopal Church in the Confederate States of America was born with only minor changes in the liturgy, though, as good Episcopalians, the delegates debated some of the finer points of church government at length.[31]

The division of the Old School Presbyterians and Episcopalians only reinforced Catholic views of the sectional crisis. The actions of a Gardiner Spring or a Leonidas Polk would have been impossible in the Catholic Church, editor James McMaster crowed. He must have been especially pleased to receive a letter from a Philadelphia Presbyterian who had become so disgusted with the General Assembly's actions that he was attending the Catholic Church where "one can hear the pure Gospel free from politics." Just as northern Catholics had linked the spirit of Protestantism to the spirit of secession, they now offered a similar explanation for the outbreak of war. In March, a Milwaukee priest had warned his parishioners about the danger of Protestant principles "gnawing and corroding the root of society," which inevitably produced a "licentiousness and contempt of all authority, divine and human." Like the Old School Presbyterians and Episcopalians, Catholic leaders proudly claimed that no action or teaching of their church had added to the nation's woes. "While sensation preachers and sectarian papers have been whetting the appetite of the people for discord and war," the *Catholic Mirror* asserted. "Our clergy and papers have endeavored to keep the peace, to allay hostile feelings, and throw oil upon the troubled waters."[32]

Not only had bishops and priests refused to deliver antislavery harangues, as several editors pointed out, but with the outbreak of war Catholics would have to rescue the nation from the effects of Protestant heresies. As a corporal in the famous Irish Brigade explained to his wife, rebellion was not merely a crime but, as described by Saint Paul, a sin that would bring "eternal damnation." Like many other Americans, Catholics viewed the war as just punishment for national sins but associated many of those transgressions with Protestantism. Although admitting that some southern Catholics had followed the mob into rebellion, McMaster argued that Catholic principles alone could save the country from anarchy on the one hand and military despotism on the other. When the "hour of reconciliation" finally arrived, peace could be established on the basis of "Catholic charity and Catholic justice."[33]

However much they might shun Protestant political preaching, after Sumter Catholics in both sections rallied around their governments. In response to Lincoln's call for troops, Cincinnati archbishop John Baptist Purcell advised Catholics to "walk shoulder to shoulder with all our fellow citizens in support of the national honor." Because there could be no justification for rebellion against duly constituted authority, Archbishop John Hughes explained to a southern bishop, Catholics must defend the republic.[34] But then Catholic teaching about loyalty to a legitimate government could just as easily justify southern Catholics in rallying to the Confederacy. In May 1861 Richard V. Whelan, the bishop of Wheeling, Virginia, pressed Hughes to recognize the Confederate States of America because Catholics should not support "the party that contains their most deadly enemies, abolitionists, infidels, and red republicans." Bishop William Henry Elder in Natchez was appalled that northern bishops were advising their people to fight in an unholy war. Regardless of what southern Catholics thought of secession, they should now obey the Confederate government, and southern bishops like their northern counterparts summoned people to do their patriotic duty.[35]

Unlike the Old School Presbyterians and Episcopalians, the Catholics had not officially divided, but war placed immediate strains on the church, produced some harsh exchanges across sectional lines, and raised always difficult questions about the will of God in the midst of war. Churches that had escaped the bitter conflicts of the 1840s and 1850s could not help but be shaken by the outbreak of a civil war that threatened to draw so many Christians into its voracious maw.

The divisions and strains in the churches occurred despite the fact that northerners and southerners had shared a common religious language. A pervasive belief in providence, a firm conviction that God punished nations for their sins, a penchant for drawing comparisons to ancient Israel, and a persistent millennialism remained powerful features of northern and southern religious identity. Civil religion in the new southern nation did not strike off in many new directions. Besides linking public and private life and military and civilian worlds, along with offering men, women, and families anchors in a storm-tossed sea, religion helped legitimate the Confederacy's claims to a superior Christian civilization. In Charleston, young Emma Holmes fulminated about reports of flag-draped altars in northern churches and of congregations singing Yankee Doodle without recognizing how much Confederates melded the secular with the sacred.[36]

Even so Confederates sought to draw a contrast with their enemies and link their own cause to divine purpose. Southerners were in the right because they were fighting a purely defensive war, a fleeting reference to just war theory but also an assertion of righteousness. "Behold, O God, and judge between us and our enemies who have forced upon us this unholy and unnatural war," Rabbi James Gutheim prayed at a synagogue dedication in Montgomery, Alabama. Moreover, Confederates were fighting against infidel abolitionists who rejected the Bible; these vile Yankees embodied the hypocrisy of the Puritans and the fanaticism of Cromwell. For their part, Confederates claimed to be establishing a Christian slaveholders' republic that would fulfill the millennial hopes of proslavery divines.[37]

Anyone doubting this should look no further than the Confederate Constitution "invoking the favor and guidance of Almighty God" in its preamble. This might seem at best a pro forma gesture, a passing bow to religious sensibilities, or meaningless political symbolism, but preachers and politicians drew a sharp contrast between the Confederate Constitution and the godless United States Constitution that failed to acknowledge divine sovereignty. On the first official fast day, Episcopalian O. S. Barten declared the Confederate government a "Christian government" defending "Christian liberty," a liberty resting on a "union of religion and government." Barten confusingly claimed this did not mean an alliance of church and state, although he expected the "votes of Christian men will fill our offices with Christians."[38]

But perhaps the Confederate founders had in fact not gone far enough. Methodist bishop George Foster Pierce believed that by failing to acknowledge

Jesus Christ, the Confederate Constitution became little more than a deists' document. Pierce favored official recognition of the trinity and the establishment of the Bible as the basis for all legislation. Such heavyweights as Thornwell and Palmer agreed that the government should explicitly embrace Christianity.[39]

Presbyterians took the lead in reexamining the whole idea of separating church and state—a "popular fallacy," according to Rev. James A. Lyon. Did such statements mark a hasty retreat from the idea of the church as a purely spiritual body? "Our republic will perish like the pagan republics of Greece and Rome, or the godless republic of the United States, unless we baptize it into the name of Christ," declared the *Southern Presbyterian Review.* The dream of "a truly Christian republic" refused to die. But when Thornwell found that even leading Presbyterians opposed petitioning Congress for official recognition of the Christian religion, he withdrew the proposal. There was no political groundswell on the question, and the churches were divided, so perhaps the Jeffersonian tradition was not dead after all. One irate Baptist warned against reverting to a dangerous establishment of religion that would obliterate the line between church and state, and the whole discussion quickly sputtered out.[40]

This failure marked no great faltering in Confederate civil religion. The circulation of the religious press initially grew, and editors usually supported the government without question. In fact, many southerners expected the war would make people more religious and foster a deeper trust in divine providence. The duties of patriotism and piety were "perfectly compatible," claimed prominent Richmond Baptist Jeremiah Bell Jeter, but "patriotism can be no substitute for piety." The southern people must not simply fight for a "selfish independence," Episcopalian James Warley Miles warned after the war had dragged on for nearly two years. Instead, they must "exhibit to the world that supremest effort of humanity" in building a society that harmonized capital labor through the institution of slavery and was "sanctified by the divine spirit of Christianity."[41]

Yet the danger persisted that these Confederate "rebels" would become religious rebels. The Yankees could kill only their bodies, chaplain Philip Slaughter exhorted members of the 19th Virginia Infantry; the far greater hazard was to their immortal souls. More broadly speaking, human behavior often appeared to deny divine sovereignty. "Loose and licentious notions of liberty are the legitimate out-growth of ignoring the supremacy of God," declared Bishop Pierce in a broad-brush critique of his fellow citizens. Too many vices flourished despite calls for patriotic self-sacrifice. "There is but one way for a nation to have God on their side," a Methodist editor reminded Confederates on

July 4, 1861, "and that is to be on his side." Therefore, much wartime preaching did not dwell on the conflict itself but rather on the usual themes of conviction, repentance, conversion, and the second birth.[42]

Civil religion did not overshadow traditional religion or necessarily co-opt it because, in the midst of war, the great drama of salvation still played itself out. "If we would live by the word of the Lord," Bishop Pierce avowed. "We must no longer compromise our duty to God and the country, by diluting our systems of education to suit carnal taste and worldly wisdom." The young must be enlisted "as conscripts of the Kingdom." There should be "a Bible in every house, an evangelical teacher in every school," so when the war ended "we shall have a state of society so bright, beautiful and blest, that time shall have no emblem of it in the past but Eden, and eternity no type in the future but heaven." Putting the case more simply, a fellow Methodist deemed the Confederate States of America "the last hope of Freedom and the last home of the pure gospel."[43]

The fulfillment of this vision rested with the clergy and with the people, but given the connection between spiritual and national salvation, it also depended on the Confederacy's political leaders. Pious statesmen with the wisdom of Moses should govern the new nation. For a people who believed in the reality of sin and often took a fatalistic view of human prospects, confidence that a Christian president, a Christian cabinet, Christian legislators, and Christian generals could lead them to the promised land of national deliverance might seem misplaced, but in the halcyon days of 1861, everything seemed possible.[44]

The belief that a nation's prosperity and destiny depended on its leaders' virtue harked back to the days of the early republic, if not to the days of New England election sermons. Some Confederates expected their government to end the corruption that had so weakened the old Union, to avoid the pitfalls of partisanship, spoils, and greed. But of course the new nation soon had its share of fallible and venal politicians and generals. Less than a year after the war began, an Alabama soldier complained that the government had become "rotten to the bottom," its strength sapped by office seekers, demagogues, and even traitors. "God has been smiling on us," he believed, "but we have not done our part."[45]

Hopes for a coming age of Christian statesmen were not nearly as pervasive in the North, but religious editors trumpeted loyalty to the Union and sounded ever more belligerent. "Is this a religious war?" asked one Old School Presbyterian; yes was the decided answer in most churches. "He that is not for us is against us," intoned a senior Methodist bishop less than a month into the contest. "There is no middle ground." This was not entirely true, though the middle ground had been shrinking for some time, and even the more conservative churches rallied round the flag. Certainly, ministers worked to convince their congregations that both republican government and revealed religion hung in the balance. "A more unnatural, unreasonable and thoroughly wicked assault upon God's established ordinance has never darkened the pages of history," declared a Connecticut minister who denied that standing against rebellion and treason meant warring against fellow Christians. Like their Confederate brethren, northern ministers maintained that their people fought in self-defense for a righteous cause.[46] Neither side bothered to note the irony of such competing claims.

That organized religion should promote patriotism as armies prepared to take the field was simply a given. Ironically, northern ministers often cited the example of that southern slaveholder George Washington, who had avowed that religion and morality were the foundations of government. Even though admitting there was too much "gasconade" on the Fourth of July, one orator simply asserted that "allegiance to government is a duty of religion." Like the editorials in the denominational papers, northern sermons contained more political arguments than religious ones—despite the expected scripture references that enjoined obedience to government. "We will take our glorious flag," declared Methodist bishop Matthew Simpson, "and nail it *just* below the cross!" His words reportedly had an "electrical" effect on his audience, which may well have preferred placing the flag above the cross.[47]

Such rhetorical flights along with the ever-present flags caused a few second thoughts. "Those of us who profess and call ourselves Christians," a New York editor commented, "used but lately to place the cross of Christ above every thing else." Ministers came under intense pressure to preach patriotism, and those who refused might be forced to resign. Omitting a liturgical prayer for the president or failing to denounce the rebellion spelled trouble. "Patriotic enthusiasm is both natural and right," one conservative religious paper conceded, "but when it attempts to supplant prayer and worship, it needs to be restrained."[48] But by whom? Most of the clergy enthusiastically supported the government, and many believed the war would fulfill a divine mission that, in the human imagination at least, grew ever more expansive.

Here was the promise of emancipation, democracy, and Christianity, with the American republic serving as a shining example to all nations. Even a destructive war became an instrument of progress. Preaching to a newly enlisted Massachusetts regiment, Baptist George Ide extolled northern unity as a sign of divine favor but, more importantly, advised the young men to have faith in the Lord's promises: "Can we fear that He will permit this noble country, the favored child of His Providence, whose planting was superintended by

His agency, whose onward course has been directed by His hand, with whose future weal the highest interests of His Kingdom are identified, to be rent to pieces by a rebellion?" The United States remained a chosen nation, and Americans a chosen people so long as they fought for God and democracy. Indeed, the war itself might atone for previous sins. Americans had conducted a war of aggression in Mexico, and, worse still, many northerners had colluded with southerners in oppressing the African race, declared a leading Quaker weekly. A time for judgment and retribution had come because "national sins, unless repented of, are always punished by national calamities."[49]

Those churches teaching nonresistance *and* condemning slavery faced grave difficulties. Making a remarkably fine distinction, one Unitarian academic claimed that the government was suppressing the crime of rebellion, not actually fighting a war. Blood flowed nevertheless, and the Quakers especially struggled to find answers consistent with their traditions and interests. Some had seen disunion as a punishment for national sins, most notably slavery, but whether they could remain both pacifists and abolitionists appeared problematic. One editor pleaded with Quakers to set an example for their children by avoiding any expression of warlike spirit, but there were soon reports of young Friends enlisting.[50]

The spring of 1861 seemed hardly the time for cool, rational reflection on the relationship between religion and war, though some believers worried about the effects on the churches. After reading a fiery sermon, Louisianan Sarah Butler regretted that "it embodied the feeling which has made it impossible (to me) to feel enthusiasm on *our* side. I think we should demand and defend our *rights*, but it seems awful to have Brethren arrayed against one another." For most Confederate sympathizers, such feelings passed quickly. Even the gentle Episcopal bishop William Meade noted with sadness but also a certain pride that Virginia would "soon be drenched with blood of the flower of youth, and the strength of her manhood. The piety of all denominations, especially of our Church, will be well represented."[51]

Conservative Presbyterian Charles Wadsworth decided shortly after Sumter that war had become a "necessary evil resulting in good." Great crimes such as the southern rebellion justified Christian governments taking up the sword. Onetime pacifists suddenly decided that nations as opposed to individuals could not be expected to turn the other cheek; when even a Universalist intellectual reverted to the timeless cliché about death being preferable to dishonor, the revolution in religious sentiment appeared unmistakable. Christ had not allowed his followers to fight for him, but he had not forbidden them to fight, claimed one Massachusetts Congregationalist who could obviously split theological hairs with the best of them. The Lord had blessed Israel's fighting men, and Christ had not condemned the Roman centurion's profession. "Nothing from the past worth the having has come to us without blood," the *Independent* added. "Christianity was cemented by the blood of martyrs." Once the churches embraced the necessity for war, there seemed to be no limit. One Methodist bishop declared that he would "fire into them [the Confederates] most benevolently." [52]

Did that wry comment open up the question of how the war itself should be conducted? Few addressed the issue directly, and the clergy often lapsed into platitudes. Rhode Island Congregationalist Leonard Swain offered one list of standards: pray for enemies and avoid hatred; steer clear of profanity, drunkenness, and other vices of the army camps; sustain religion at home. Other pastors warned their flocks against seeking vengeance. The conservative Episcopal bishop of Vermont included a prayer to "restrain the madness of human passion, the army of cruel violence, and the effusion of blood," a sentiment reciprocated by the bishop of Mississippi, who urged his people to pray that their enemies turn from their "evil purposes" rather than lose their lives. At this stage, many northern ministers agreed that the war should be a limited one against the leaders of the rebellion, and not a war on the southern people or a war to emancipate slaves. Even though the devout Eliza Fain in Rogersville, Tennessee, expressed the usual sentiments about loving enemies and overcoming evil with good, she excoriated "holier than thou" northern Christians who ignored the love commandment and indeed most divine ordinances. [53] Both northerners and southerners called for conducting the war in a Christian way but doubted their enemies would do so. Claims to superior morality, just like claims to be fighting for the Lord, only reinforced both sides' deep religious commitment to the war.

The uprising of twenty million people against the rebellion "emanate[s] from the mind of God," a New York Baptist association announced. Conservative ministers might still excoriate Puritan abolitionists and egotistic secessionists for dragging the nation into war, but most believed that government was a divine ordinance and therefore Christians had a duty not only to obey their leaders but also to sustain the Constitution against disloyalty. In many ways the idea of America transcended any narrow nationalism and brought together—at least in Fourth of July sermons—peoples from all nations. The war would obliterate party divisions and make everyone more virtuous because patriotism imposed discipline and encouraged generosity. Misers opened their purses, citizens paid their taxes, and the folks at home boxed up clothing for the sick and wounded. [54] In much of this discussion, the necessary evil of war became transformed into a positive good.

A rural Louisiana woman feared there were many "trials in store for the faithful," but if the southern cause was just, as Confederates believed, God would surely lead them to victory. Even a good Calvinist such as Dabney optimistically assumed that a few battles against superior military talent would bring the Yankees to their senses. Confederates should pray for victory, suggested one Baptist editor, because "frequent prayers are offered in the North for blood to flow in rivers, for slaughter to desolate our homes, for carnage to depopulate our country." Not only would southerners rely on God in this great crisis; they could have the utmost confidence in deliverance because the Lord's blessing counted for more than artillery or gunpowder.[55]

Faith in one's cause became a circular argument for God's favor. Each side saw itself as a chosen people whom the Lord would crown with victory. According to a New York Catholic editor, the Almighty would bring Americans through their fiery ordeal and make them into a true nation with the "pestilent heresy" of state sovereignty "perish[ing] in the flames." Again, it came back to the argument that God would use the wicked rebellion and the resulting convulsions for his own purposes. Even a Unitarian editor affirmed that the nation had entered "Pentecostal days." Themes of religious purification and millennial glory accompanied the waving flags and patriotic airs. To doubt that "Christianity is with us," declared one remarkably enthusiastic Universalist, became nothing but "atheism."[56]

The theological analysis shifted with onrushing events even though affirmations of God's sovereignty and a belief in divine providence remained constants. Ministers might still deny preaching politics, but the war dragged many in that direction; religious editors began to pay much closer attention to events in the secular world. Everyone from Methodists to Mormons, from Catholics to Unitarians, from Baptists to Episcopalians interpreted the conflict in often strikingly similar ways. Although a Philadelphia Catholic wondered whether "the people of both sections are led away more by popular feeling than by a conviction of the justice of their cause," this was true only in part. Publicly and privately, the faithful declared that the Lord would bless their cause. Claiming to hold a "deep christian and inextinguishable hatred toward the demons of the north," an Alabama Methodist preacher advised his brother that "it is doing God service to kill the diabolical wretches on the battlefield." Sitting in a Congregational church in a small Illinois town as he was about to enlist in the army, Will Robinson heard a sermon "running over with patriotism." To him it sounded "quite warlike, and proved that every man who fell sustaining the government, fell in a just cause."[57]

Chapter 4

FIGHTING FOR GOD AND COUNTRY

For the battle is the Lord's, and he will give you into our hands.
— 1 Samuel 17:47

In Littleton, New Hampshire, it was no ordinary, quiet Sabbath, for even the church bells sounded more like a call to arms than a call to worship. The Littleton Brass Band escorted local recruits to the Congregational church; after everyone filed in, the choir sang, "America." The sermon text from Second Samuel sounded the right note: "Be of good courage, and let us play the men for our people." The volunteers reassembled outside after the service, and the band struck up, "Home Sweet Home." In the afternoon, the soldiers attended the Methodist church, again accompanied by the band. Here the text from Matthew concerned Christ's prophecy about "wars and rumors of wars." When the minister mentioned the rebel flag flying over Fort Sumter, many in the congregation wept.[1]

Similar scenes unfolded across the Confederacy. In Germantown, Virginia, Robert Lewis Dabney spoke to raise money for uniforms and blankets for the Prospect Grays, a local rifle company that later became part of the 18th Virginia Infantry. They seemed a "stalwart set of fellows," mostly Presbyterians and Methodists. Dabney noted how the "sun-burned raw-boned and bearded" men "wept like children" during the service but would be fearsome fighters. "Such a people cannot be conquered," he defiantly concluded. In Conecuh County, Alabama, the Reverend George L. Lee urged the Percy Walker Rangers to perform "deeds that will bring glory to God, honor to Christ, happiness to man, confusion to devils, and to all of old Abe's fanatics, and eternal credit and honor to yourselves."[2]

Sending off young volunteers and preparing them to meet the day of battle became an urgent mission for the churches. Here was a chance to present Bibles and Testaments, bless company flags, talk with the young men, and grasp their hands—perhaps for the last time. In Rochester, New York, a beloved Sunday school teacher received a sword, sash, and belt; in Natchez, Mississippi, priests held special masses for Catholic soldiers, making sure they received the sacrament before marching off with a prayer book, crucifix, and medal. The departures were painful. Attending a service in a camp near Abingdon, Virginia, Lizzie Hardin could only describe the scene in the era's sentimental language, whose poignancy, however, remains powerful: "We sat around the immense camp fires which lit with an uncertain light the hills and the distant mountains and fell with ruddy glow into the faces of the wild thoughtless boys, as they looked with thoughtful eyes toward the minister, reading of eternal life to them who must so shortly face death."[3]

On such occasions the messages often became thinly disguised recruiting sermons that relied on time-tested revivalist techniques. Sometimes real recruiters followed the preachers, if not literally into the pulpit, at least into the churchyard to corral young men. In a striking appeal to manhood, Henry Ward Beecher declared that "God hates lukewarm patriotism as much as lukewarm religion and we hate it too. We do not believe in hermaphrodite patriots." Conservatives might disdain Beecher as "a stump speaker who has mistaken his way and stumbled into a church," but there was no question about his effectiveness. Soldiers made a point of attending his Brooklyn church to take in the pulpit oratory, and his optimistic patriotism undoubtedly lifted spirits in the army and on the home front.[4]

But for all the bravado, Christians were still warring against Christians. Ministers routinely called on the soldiers to fight their misguided foes but not hate them, though one candid Virginia Baptist hoped that southern men could summon up the "anger" required to "march on the battlefield and butcher the monsters that have invaded our soil."[5] However that might be, northern and southern clergy reassured recruits that Christians could take up arms in a righteous cause. If the young men felt torn between Jesus's teachings of love and society's demands for military service, few expressed it.[6] Both sides denied being the aggressor and therefore readily cited scriptures justifying self-defense. The Apostle Paul's military metaphors became the basis for sermons extolling the virtues of the Christian soldier, a man who fought both for his country and for the Lord. When a writer in the leading southern Baptist newspaper claimed never to have seen a war that was so compatible with the principles of Christianity, many of his southern and northern brethren would have shouted, "Amen."[7]

For the war to remain a righteous one, it would have to be conducted by righteous men. Ministers warned soldiers to safeguard their moral character through prayer, scripture reading, and especially the avoidance of temptation. Initially the men remained close to home and religious influences as they were mustered in and sent off to training camps. During their first Sunday in uniform, the boys often visited nearby churches—in part because they might not have another opportunity any time soon.[8] Most regiments as yet had no chaplains, so officers and enlisted men conducted prayer meetings or formed Sunday schools; the timid prayed in public for the first time, and the

Henry Ward Beecher (Library of Congress)

frightened found special comfort in a favorite scripture passage while standing guard duty. An Iowa Republican editor was sure that a regiment of praying soldiers with Bibles in hand would prove formidable in battle, far more formidable than traitorous rebels who would "sneer" at such expressions of faith. Yet Confederates were equally proud of the many pious men in their companies; the notion of an army filled with Christian soldiers confirmed the righteousness of their cause. In turn, the Federals countered with assertions that commanders Winfield Scott and Jesus Christ would lead them into battle in sure hope of ultimate victory in this world and the world to come.[9]

The degree to which soldiers absorbed these messages is impossible to determine. Few apparently worried very much about any inconsistency between religious and military obligations. From the outset, a sizable minority at least expressed a clear sense of duty to God and country, and these soldiers assured the home folks that their spiritual health was just fine. One Indiana father rejoiced to hear about "so many good soldiers of the Cross" standing for the "defence of the cause of Truth and Righteousness." Newspapers lovingly quoted patriotic mothers who willingly sent their sons to fight under the banner of their country's God. In life and in death, the Christian soldier belonged to the Lord but of course must never forget why he fought for his country. As a Georgian who had recently lost a wife and daughter informed his parents, the "finger of Providence" had led him to stand for the cause of "truth, of honor, of religion, of property, of national independence."[10]

Bold claims to rectitude and faith in the cause, however, never quite allayed doubts and fears. Even before a major battle had been fought, northerners and southerners had begun to ponder the Almighty's inscrutable ways. Because God was the final arbiter among nations, the more candid admitted, much in war remained uncertain. This might be hard to square with confident assertions of an easy triumph, though tough times demanded a resilient faith that kept everything in perspective. Patriotism had its place but could become a dangerous passion that overshadowed the Gospel teachings. Believers could surely take up arms to fight treason, yet their ultimate allegiance must be to a sovereign God. Therefore, prayers for the nation, suggested one conservative editor, should avoid the "patriotic bombast and moonshine" that became little more than bragging and a "burlesque on prayer."[11]

As the time of battle approached, many people simply affirmed the power of prayer. "Fervent and effectual prayers from the believer's heart . . . will accomplish more than any battery erected by human hands," avowed one Massachusetts volunteer. A Richmond rabbi, whose congregation was ironically called the "House of Love," prayed that the Confederacy's foes would meet the fate described in the 140th Psalm: "Let burning coals fall upon them; let them be cast into the fire; into deep pits, that they rise not up again." Churches held special services for the troops, and ministers visited their families. A northern Presbyterian editor recommended that officers retire to their tents for communion with the Lord as they prepared for battle. Yet, as Dabney warned the men of the 18th Virginia Infantry, "pride and resentment, ambition and animosity" might prevent the Almighty from answering their petitions.[12]

Tearful departures from home became part of this religious drama. Women talked of committing their men to the Lord, but that was so hard. "Buckle on the armour of God, the Helmet of Salvation, and the Sword of the Spirit, which is the Word of God," a South Carolinian advised her brother. "Wherever you go or wherever you may be pray always." In the meantime, the home folks could seek comfort in their own faith. To one Georgia Confederate, knowledge that devout women were praying for the soldiers simply reinforced a belief that southern armies could never be conquered by godless foes. But then that was part of the problem when pious patriots could hardly imagine their enemies thinking along the same lines. "Have Christian mothers North laid their sons with the same loyalty of feeling upon their country['s] altar that we mothers of the South have done," Tennessean Eliza Fain wondered. "I feel it can hardly be possible."[13]

If Confederates were indeed a chosen people fighting in a holy cause, official days of fasting, humiliation, and prayer became public occasions for reaffirming this core conviction. Ministers searched for Old Testament parallels to contemporary events that could somehow propel the Confederate States of America into a larger providential history. Sketching the outline of any divine plan was always difficult, but faith in God's sovereignty remained a bedrock belief. Just as preachers had lent religious meaning to sectional politics, so now they explored the spiritual significance of a new southern nationalism.[14]

On May 14, 1861, Tom Cobb introduced a resolution in the Provisional Congress recognizing the Confederacy's dependence upon an "overruling Providence" and requesting the president appoint a day of fasting and prayer. At this stage of the war, such a proposal reflected more confidence than anything else. Although Jefferson Davis's proclamation called on the people to "humble themselves" before the Lord, it spoke most eloquently about recent signs of divine favor and the evident righteousness of the Confederate cause.[15]

Indeed, the sins most often mentioned on this first Confederate fast day were Yankee sins. Lincoln, like the Egyptian Pharaoh, had hardened his heart against eleven states that sought to leave the house of bondage, Benjamin Morgan Palmer told his New Orleans congregation without apparent irony. The American founders had failed to acknowledge God in their Constitution and therefore had sown seeds of national destruction. Partisanship, corruption, and lawlessness had unleashed a northern majority willing to run rough-shod over the divine right of self-government. In Columbia, South Carolina, the once reluctant secessionist Augustus Baldwin Longstreet preached about how liberty had become licentiousness in the old Union with one inevitable result: despotism. The seceding states had been in grave danger, Episcopal bishop Stephen Elliott informed a fast-day congregation in Savannah, until wise statesmen drafted a conservative Constitution that had corrected many old errors.[16] So, too, the Confederate Constitution's recognition of divine sovereignty made it clearly a work approved by God.

This first Confederate fast day was conscientiously observed in the army, on plantations, in small towns, and in cities. Businesses were closed, and streets seemed Sunday quiet. At one rural meetinghouse, Catherine Hopley noticed a "great deal of unostentatious piety." At this early stage of the war, the secular press both praised and promoted public expressions of unity, patriotism, and piety. Soldiers paused for brief sermons, and Dabney hoped the camps were becoming "places of much prayer . . . shining examples of Christian consistency."[17]

There were no widespread objections to all this civil religion, though a few dissenting voices raised old questions and expressed new doubts. Speaking in language that Thornwell might have used just a few years before, Mississippi Presbyterian James A. Lyon rebuked his colleagues for "prostituting the pulpit to a level with a low and corrupt hustings." Those favoring a strict separation of church and state worried about how quickly that wall was crumbling. Fasting or some other show of "self-denial" to win divine favor, complained one Atlanta editor, amounted to "denying the all-sufficiency of the blood of Jesus Christ." People might well be tempted to make public prayer a substitute for genuine repentance. "Will God hear us?" was the provocative question of a leading Virginia Baptist who thought it far more important for southerners to be "saved from sin than saved from war."[18]

Given assumptions about divine sovereignty and God's role in human history, northerners and southerners anxiously looked for early signs of the Lord's favor. Throughout the war, even small skirmishes acquired religious significance. On June 10, 1861, a badly delayed and poorly managed Federal assault had led to victory for outnumbered Confederates at Big Bethel, Virginia. Colonel D. H. Hill of the 1st North Carolina Infantry lauded his men for their "high moral and religious sentiments," claimed "their conduct has furnished another example of the great truth that he who fears God will ever do his duty to his country," and thanked "the living God for His wonderful interposition in our favor." So did other Confederates as they read about the fight: how else could such a victory against an overwhelming force be explained? And now Confederates could affirm that the Lord had been with them in the day of battle. In the midst of rejoicing, however, a Georgia Baptist editor more somberly noted that providence might still turn against the South and that divine wrath could descend on one side as easily as the other. In fact, one northern Baptist—who obviously had to read the news from Big Bethel much differently—noted how God "may confound our counsels, and smite our strength with weakness."[19] The thinking on both sides of the Mason-Dixon Line reflected deeply imbedded cultural and theological assumptions about how the divine will worked itself out in human affairs, assumptions that would not be easily shaken even by an ever more bloody contest.

Major battles loomed even larger, not only marking the course of the conflict but, for many Americans, serving as religious signposts in an unfolding, and ever mysterious, providential history. The first real test for this thinking came on July 21, 1861, when a bungled Federal flank attack just north of Manassas Junction, Virginia, followed by a fierce Confederate counterattack that drove the Federals back across Bull Run in headlong flight toward Washington, produced a stunning Yankee defeat and a surprising rebel triumph. In the simplest sense, the victory became for many Confederates the answer to prayer. From her temporary refuge in the Shenandoah Valley, Judith McGuire had heard early news of the fight, and the appropriate words quickly came to her lips, "Oh that Providence would now interpose and prevent further bloodshed! Oh, that strength may be given to our men." Several months after the battle a Presbyterian Synod meeting at Staunton, Virginia, picked up the narrative of divine intervention where McGuire's diary entry had left it: "Almost before the weeping worshipers had risen from their knees, the answer came; and gloriously did God at length avenge his own elect." Soon reports circulated about a Georgia infantry company in the thick of the fight that had lost not a man because back home the faithful had been praying for their safety while the battle raged.[20]

Who then could doubt that such a triumph had been providential? The reaction of devout Confederates to First Manassas set a pattern for much of the war: victories became sure signs of the Almighty's blessing. Even in official reports, officers pointed out how the Lord had shown great mercy to Confederate forces. Baptists, Presbyterians, Methodists, Episcopalians, and Catholics all agreed that providence had not only smiled on the Confederacy but had also intervened at Manassas. "It is God alone who has fought our battles," declared one South Carolina minister. Once again the disparities in numbers between the two sides showed that the Lord had miraculously sustained the weaker southern armies against the powerful Yankee host. "Might is not

Right, but Right is Might," William C. Butler told a Richmond congregation as he pointed to the "total paralysis of the gigantic steel-clad foot that was taking its first onward and confident stride toward crushing out our liberties." Now perhaps the entire world would recognize what the Lord had done in this great battle.[21]

"Happy are thou, O Israel: who is like unto thee, O people saved by the Lord, the shield of thy help, and who is the sword of thy excellency! And thine enemies shall be found liars unto thee; and thou shalt tread upon their high places." In preaching on Deuteronomy 33:29 to his rural South Carolina congregation, the Reverend Edward Reed might have been tempted to use the last part of the scripture to prophesy that P. G. T. Beauregard and Joseph Johnston would soon be marching into Washington, D.C., but instead pointed out that "not one of these brave men has fallen, or suffered, without His [God's] permission." No one could discern why one soldier had been hit and another spared, but Reed utterly rejected the idea that any of this could have happened by chance. In an era and among a people where every death and every illness was made to conform to God's will, it is doubtful that this teaching either surprised or offended his listeners—even those who had lost loved ones in Virginia. People could readily believe that God had chosen the field of combat, supplied courage to the soldiers, and had even controlled the timing of troop movements and tactical maneuvers on which the battle's outcome had hinged. In the words of Georgia Baptist editor, the Lord had been the "Commander-in-chief, whose unerring wisdom directed our officers."[22]

Just as God had supposedly strengthened the righteous arm of the southern people so also he had confounded their enemies. Harkening back to Old Testament history, it appeared that the Yankees had scattered as quickly as Assyrians, Midianites, or Philistines before the Lord of Israel. "Were not the Almighty impelling them [the Federals] toward the abyss into which they are destined soon to plunge, they would not invariably make a false move," one anonymous sage suggested. Such a theology threatened to turn human beings into marionettes manipulated by a sovereign but also arbitrary God. Casting aside any reservations on this score, pious Confederates concluded that Manassas signified a great judgment against their enemies. Ignoring Confederate civil religion, Stephen Elliott blasted northern churches and ministers for hauling flags into their sanctuaries, for invoking divine aid against an innocent people, even for encouraging delicate ladies to witness the carnage at Manassas. But in a seemingly apt and familiar biblical reference that must have resonated with everyone from Sunday school children to graybeards, an Alabama minister explained at length how the southern David had slain the northern Goliath.[23] As if to propitiate a fickle deity whose favor could be easily lost, everyone from generals to civilians to preachers to church associations called on southerners to publicly acknowledge the Lord's hand in their deliverance from the Yankee invaders.

Some Christians did not see divine providence as especially mysterious; even wartime deaths were not the decrees of an inscrutable fate. Writing a condolence letter to a friend, one Georgia woman asserted that both God and Jesus Christ must have approved "the sacrifice on the altar of his country, of your glorious firstborn Noble son." Whether such words suggested a steely fanaticism or a sincere piety, after Manassas a Georgia soldier assured everyone back home that should he face the cannon fire and die "like a hero," he could expect a "happy reunion with friends and relatives where there is no war." Noting the deaths of two brothers on the battlefield, Judith McGuire rejoiced that they were Christians, whose "ransomed spirits were wafted from the clash and storm of the battlefield to those peaceful joys" of a heavenly home.[24]

Perhaps this one great victory would end the fighting. "The War Will Be Short" ran the title of a Baptist paper's editorial that argued it would not take long for the Yankees' iniquity to reach the point where the Lord's wrath would be poured out upon them. The southern army would soon advance on Philadelphia and then on Washington and New York, a plan of attack suggesting to the *Richmond Dispatch* passages from the eighteenth chapter of Revelation concerning the fall of Babylon. In the Confederate rejoicing after Manassas, there lurked a danger that people would worship military heroes and ignore a jealous God. Although it was as yet too early in the war for southern preachers to revert to a full-blown jeremiad, there was an occasional pause for reflection. More battles would follow, some ministers conceded, though a firm trust in God should negate both northern fanaticism and numbers. For the time being, as Stephen Elliott remarked, the Almighty had clearly revealed his purposes as he had in the days of the Exodus: "I will sing unto the Lord, for he hath triumphed gloriously: the horse and his rider hath he thrown into the sea."[25]

And thrown into confusion, he might have added. The disastrous retreat from Bull Run had caused a panic in Washington that quickly spread across the country. The shock of having been repulsed by what many considered a much weaker, yea a contemptuous, ragtag enemy raised hard questions. Northerners who had expected an easy triumph now had to figure out where this stunning defeat fit into their theological understanding of the contest. "The judgments of God are upon us," declared one prominent Presbyterian editor who simply could not believe that God willed the republic's destruction. Others were not so sure the nation would be spared, and one New York minister chose an ominous passage on Nineveh from the book of Jonah to warn his listeners about the nation's peril. The somber tone of the leading Methodist journal could be only partially allayed by a typical religious formula: "The unhappy result is doubtless ordered by Providence as part of a severe but wholesome discipline, which in the end will, we hope, cure some desperate evils that have existed among us."[26]

In all the Yankee soul-searching after Bull Run, the idea of God using the debacle to punish the northern people naturally received the most attention. In Indianapolis, a prominent businessman and a Methodist bishop met and "felt it our duty to fall before the Lord" because "great national sins had to be atoned for." The question then became which transgressions had brought down divine wrath, and the answers varied widely. It would be easy to assume that slavery, materialism, or corruption were to blame, but some observers started off with less striking collective and individual offenses. During the antebellum decades, Sabbatarians had fought an increasingly rearguard action against the encroachment of secular and especially commercial activities on Sunday. That Bull Run had been fought on the Sabbath carried great weight for those who had long warned against violations of the Third Commandment. Pointedly referring to the recent battle, the New York Sabbath Committee pressed generals Winfield Scott and George B. McClellan to provide a day of rest for the troops. One leading minister lectured President Lincoln about how Bull Run should have proved the absolute necessity for observing the Sabbath. Others feared that swearing in the ranks might have provoked the Almighty's anger. For evangelical Protestants especially, connections between personal vices and the battle's outcome were readily apparent. "Let the nation read in large characters," one Presbyterian editor admonished his readers, "in the smoke, in the carnage, and humiliation of a lost battle, what vast possibilities of evil are bound up in intemperance."[27]

As the list of sins lengthened, discerning the role of divine providence in the war became more urgent and complex. Echoing biblical language, supporters of the northern war effort feared that discouraged people would cry out for peace when there was no peace. "Religion is at a low ebb, business prostrate, people sad and discouraged," one Methodist minister informed his wife, "This horrible war absorbs everything." Naysayers might claim that the country was hopelessly fractured and that the government could do nothing. In far-off Utah, Brigham Young rejoiced that the Lincoln administration had become so desperate for soldiers that "they have begun to empty the earth, cleanse the land, and prepare the way for the return of the Latter-day Saints to the centre Stake of Zion." Conservative Catholics voiced reservations about the conduct of the war, though Archbishop John Hughes claimed he was not discouraged and believed the government could easily raise more volunteers.

For devout patriots, there could be little doubt that the people's will was being tested and sometimes found wanting.[28]

By far the most penetrating analysis of the Bull Run disaster came in a sermon preached by the prominent Congregationalist Horace Bushnell in Hartford, Connecticut. As a moderate who had sadly watched the country drift into civil war, he understood the despair and anguish that this first great battle had brought to the losing side. Observing how confident prayers had sounded on the Sunday before Bull Run, Bushnell chose an appropriate text (Proverbs 24:10): "If thou faint in the day of adversity, thy strength is small." He quickly slid by the question of fighting on the Sabbath, defensively noting that the enemy had been badly hurt in the battle and that the defeat was not nearly so bad as first reported. Yet he traced present national weakness back to the founding fathers' creation of a government "without moral or religious ideas . . . a merely man-made compact." By grounding the nation in Thomas Jefferson's philosophy and then allowing years of peace and prosperity along with the debilitating effects of slavery to sap the country's character, the United States—like a rudderless ship—had drifted into uncharted and dangerous waters. "We began with a godless theorizing, and we end," Bushnell feared, "just as we should, in discovering that we have not so much as made any nation at all." Consequently there "must be reverses and losses," for "without shedding of blood there is no such grace prepared." Anticipating his later writings on the atonement, Bushnell argued that genuine loyalty grew out of sacrifices.

Turning the conclusions of Confederate preachers on their heads, he seemed to be saying that the defeat at Bull Run was a sign of the Lord's favor. To Bushnell's way of thinking—and there were others who agreed with him—Bull Run marked a divine chastisement that in the end would be a blessing. This argument still assumed that the North stood on the righteous side of the conflict: for Bushnell, "not one doubt is permitted us that we are fighting for the right, and our adversaries for the wrong; we to save the best government of the world, and they to destroy it. Whence it follows that, as God is with all right and for it, by the fixed necessity of his virtue, we may know that we are fighting up to God, and not away from Him."[29] His answer to worried northerners was not only grammatically awkward but coupled a peculiar explanation for defeat with a less than resounding call to arms.

Critics could have pointed out that one problem was Bushnell's failure to deal forthrightly with slavery, but northerners now had to face that question in light of a military disaster. Black ministers debated whether to observe Lincoln's officially declared day of fasting, humiliation, and prayer if the president still refused to move against slavery. Henry McNeal Turner pointedly described the dead at Bull Run as the "bloody victims of slavery's hellish caprice." Antislavery stalwarts pointed to the many compromises Americans had made with slavery, but the cries of the oppressed only grew louder, and now the day of reckoning had come. God would punish the northern people for their entanglement with such an evil institution, a leading Massachusetts Baptist warned, "and may allow us to suffer until our national vanity is mortified." One Iowa preacher could even echo Bushnell, though with rather a different purpose: "Thank God for defeats and disasters, which have shut up the Government more and more to the necessity of doing a grand work of justice. . . . Thank God that the march of the grand army upon Manassas . . . was followed with disgraceful panic and retreat, and resulted in strengthening rather than weakening the rebellion, and, then in strengthening and confirming the conviction that justice to the oppressed is necessary to peace!" [30]

The inscrutability of divine providence suddenly appeared to be much more of a problem. "Exactly what God intends as the future of this nation, no human prescience can divine," the president of Amherst College informed a large congregation on the national fast day. "The cloud is black and impenetrable. Are we to be broken down for our sins, and our free institutions to become a hissing and by-word over all the earth? Are we to be useful only as one more of those terrible examples which are set up along the track of history for the warning of mankind?" There might be a brighter future, but for now northern preachers returned to the old formula of the jeremiad, calling the people to repentance. The confidence of the past spring had given way to a renewed emphasis on divine chastisement. Had not the Lord often destroyed thrones and kingdoms? According to one leading editor, God's way was in the words of the prophet Ezekiel to "overturn, overturn, overturn." In Baltimore, with an equally apt reference to the prophet Habakkuk, moderate Baptist Richard Fuller preached on the theme of "mercy remembered in wrath." [31]

Lincoln and Davis both proclaimed days of fasting or thanksgiving that received considerable public support. In southern Louisiana, William T. Palfrey suspended work on his sugar plantation; patriotic Confederates took time off to attend services. People prayed fervently that the Yankees' wicked designs would be thwarted and thanked the Lord for past mercies. [32] The observance of the early September fast in the northern states seemed equally fervent. In New York, the devout filled the churches, though one editor wryly observed that the less devout preferred afternoon boat or horse races. In Boston, however, virtually all businesses closed, and the newspapers suspended publication for the day. The mood appeared decidedly more grim than in the Confederacy. A rural Indiana couple remarked on the solemnity of worship at home and urged their son in the army to approach "the throne of Grace" on his family's behalf. Sounding like a preacher or a correspondent for a church paper, one Pennsylvania newspaper editor, pointed out how the Lord can "raise up as well as cast down nations." The only recourse was to "cry mightily unto Him, to spare us from His just indignation and from His righteous wrath, which our multitude of National transgressions have so justly merited."[33]

Many of the clergy in both sections repeated shopworn explanations for the crisis. They continued to blame politicians for the war, even as Confederates worried that their own leaders might become just as corrupt and partisan as those in the old Union.[34] Unable to figure out whether any new sins had cropped up during the war, fast-day preachers stuck with old standbys such as covetousness, profanity, intemperance, or worldliness. "Who Stampeded Our Army at Manassas?" an AME editor demanded to know. Citing the nation's embrace of slavery was predictable, but he included all of the offenses just noted while throwing in "thievish contractors" for good measure. Everyone from committed Confederates to ardent abolitionists compiled remarkably similar lists. Laments about the breakdown of order in state, church, and family echoed the jeremiad's standard themes. Yet as one New York Baptist pointed out, the nation's history was "marked by signal deliverances in the day of trouble." Only nations without value were destroyed by God; those that served some divine end—most notably the United States—would only be disciplined.[35]

That idea, of course, could apply equally to Confederates, despite a growing confidence in southern arms. Southern preachers, too, harped on the war as a punishment for sin, and one Georgia Baptist noted how the Lord was using the "wicked" Federals to force wayward southerners back to the narrow paths of righteousness. Yet expositions on southern sins were remarkably general and diffuse, and the clergymen did not seem to have their hearts in it. Condemnations of materialism and mammon worship never quite came up to the mark. Some Confederates predicted that the war could drag on for a long time and admitted that the Lord's exact purposes might be difficult to fathom, though, as Mary Chesnut sardonically remarked, there was "not one doubt . . . in our bosoms that we are not the chosen people of God." After this confusing double negative, she added a peculiar and unsettling observation: "And that he [God] is fighting for us. Why not? We are no worse than Jews, past or present, nor Yankees."[36]

On one point, she was surely correct: the Yankees had exhibited a national conceit worthy of stiff-necked Israel. And after Bull Run, all this self-righteousness suddenly became apparent to anyone looking to explain divine punishment. Too many northerners had become like ancient Pharisees, well aware of others' sins but oblivious to their own, observed one editor who had not entirely avoided that fault himself. Yet even now the self-examination remained narrow and limited. It was easy to admit, for example, that material progress had outstripped spiritual progress, but few shared the pessimism—or, one might have called it, the realism—of the northern Presbyterian who conceded that "history has on record, no example of an insurrection comparable to this, either in extent of territory or apparent unanimity and resoluteness of purpose, that has ever been effectually quelled." [37]

The only answer to that gloomy assessment seemed to be complete trust in the Almighty. Otherwise there would be more Bull Runs until the nation was brought to its knees, forced to confess, in the words of an Ohio Presbyterian, that "God makes History, and men but write and read it." [38] The easy confluence of religion and patriotism that had seemed so orthodox and commonsensical after Fort Sumter suddenly raised disturbing questions. Too many people had confused love for country and with love for God and were now paying a terrible price for that error. Loyalty and self-sacrifice from patriotic businessmen or noble mothers had loomed more important than atoning grace. Somehow the gospel had been perverted to reassure young men—whatever their spiritual state—that, should they fall in battle, their souls would immediately ascend heavenward.[39]

Admonitions to place the war's outcome in God's hands often glossed over these problems. To Confederates, the Lord had smiled on their arms at Manassas. If they would only "walk in his ways," a Baptist minister advised the Georgia legislature, "he would drive the invader from our territories and restore to us the blessings of peace." In other words, final victory lay within the grasp of a people who placed their trust in providence. That the Confederates had to this point held off vastly superior forces surely proved that the Lord intended their ultimate triumph. The God of history had become the God of battles, or, as a young South Carolina woman put it, "The days of the Israelites are returning." [40]

Such statements fostered a dangerous overconfidence. "There has never been an army since the time of Cromwell, in which there was a more pervading sense of the power of God than our own," bragged one Virginia Presbyterian who declared that even irreligious officers had come to believe that the Lord stood with the southern armies on the battlefield. Fighting a righteous war in self-defense placed the South on the right side of history, and Episcopalian stalwart Stephen Elliott airily dismissed any criticism of the government for being too passive. The people needed to understand how the Davis administration's "mature judgment and superior knowledge" had avoided a needlessly aggressive strategy that would have brought about "a waste of human life." If hardly in tune with the wishes of many ordinary Confederates, a defensive policy comported with the belief that the Lord would deliver the Yankees into Confederate hands. Victories would be won "till Old Abe and his cabinet become convinced that a supreme being is sending a just punishment upon them for their wickedness in waging war upon an unoffending country who plead for justice and right," a Louisiana soldier predicted. The Lord had condemned this war of aggression, but the Federals remained hell-bent on self-destruction, and reports of economic distress in northern cities became just another sign of divine judgment.[41]

Whatever the differences over the Almighty's exact intentions, by the fall of 1861 wartime hatreds intensified. In an increasingly rare concession, a New Jersey Episcopalian tried to preach on the sins of both sections, but members of the congregation hissed and stormed out. In St. Joseph, Missouri, one minister's call to "lay aside passion and prejudice" was largely ignored as the state's bitter divisions spilled into the churches, dividing denominations and congregations. Any minister still trying to steer a middle course between sectional extremes seemed oddly if not dangerously out of step. The mere acknowledgment that both Federals and Confederates were praying fervently and sincerely for their cause was about as far as anyone would go.[42] Such opinions seemed exotic even in the war's first year as churches rallied to the powers that be and strove to prove their loyalty.

Southern Baptists appointed committees on the "state of the country" that drafted patriotic resolutions condemning the "religious fanaticism" of hypocritical Yankees and promising "deliverance from the thralldom which an unscrupulous enemy is trying to fasten upon us." In fast-day sermons, prayers, reports, and ceremonies, Presbyterians, Lutherans, Episcopalians, and Catholics who had once shunned entanglement with politics warmly endorsed the Confederate cause.[43]

In the North, too, the churches largely fell into line. Baptists defended the glorious Union and denounced the wicked rebellion; connecting the spiritual with the political was no mere afterthought. Wisconsin Methodists accused Confederates not only of rebelling against the United States but also of committing "treason to the entire race and to Heaven." Anyone who did not rally to his country's cause, claimed the old circuit rider Peter Cartwright, would be "politically damned"–and, he might as well have added, "spiritually damned." Ministers who gave aid or comfort to the rebellion violated the discipline of the Methodist Church, one Indiana conference resolved.[44]

Churches became vital parts of the Union war effort with precious little debate and apparently little thought. The clergy began discussing political and military strategy, and even the Disciples of Christ approved a motion supporting the war, an action shattering precedent in a church that had always avoided political entanglements. A Brooklyn Presbyterian best summed up the gathering consensus among northern churches: "In such a war, religion must be the national reliance."[45]

For a growing number of northerners, however, that great obstacle slavery stood in the way of making the war for the Union into a truly righteous crusade. Besides offering belated justice to the slave, the war should also end northern complicity with this most heinous sin. The *Christian Recorder* bitterly noted how countless presbyteries, synods, conventions, and conferences of several denominations had "engrafted" slavery onto the Gospel.[46] Although cautious churches might simply add slavery to a long catalog of transgressions that included profanity, Sabbath breaking, and intemperance—and not necessarily place it at the top of the list—the trend in religious opinion was unmistakable. No longer were abolitionists' voices crying in the political wilderness. The president had not yet embraced emancipation, though that too would come in time and sooner than expected, given his fundamental conservatism and remarkably persistent support for colonization. Increasingly a war for the Union would become—however slowly and haltingly—a war against slavery. A group of Indiana Methodists warned that the destruction of the government and the perpetuation of slavery would entail far worse evils than war itself. Old School Presbyterians still hesitated to commit their church to any particular position on the issue but admitted that slavery lay at the root of the nation's troubles. Even that arch critic of established religion, William Lloyd Garrison, conceded that the churches were moving in the right direction—albeit much too slowly.[47]

Moral arguments remained at the fore, but even those devout souls with the firmest antislavery convictions were beginning to offer more pragmatic ones as well. Perhaps crushing the rebellion required striking a blow at slavery. The timing remained in God's hands, abolitionist George Cheever conceded, though Cheever seemed to have his own schedule when he disparaged efforts by the cautious Lincoln administration to "please Kentucky." Indeed, the ship of state appeared to be foundering, claimed one Massachusetts Congregationalist, and the only solution was to toss overboard the Jonah of slavery before God's wrath dashed the vessel on the rocks. Yet waiting on the Lord to work his will could just as easily become an argument for moving slowly, and even some antislavery preachers doubted that the time had yet arrived for a proclamation of emancipation. Ironically, once cautious clergy began to believe that slavery must die and die soon.[48]

"The conviction is daily gaining strength in the public mind of the North that the Southern rebellion forms a part of the divine plan for the uprooting of slavery." Even if the Baptist editor who made this claim was correct, much still depended on the course of the war itself and especially on Abraham Lincoln. Some abolitionists already feared the war would end before the administration moved against slavery, and especially after Bull Run, religious impatience grew. Letters, petitions, and denominational resolutions poured into the Executive Mansion. Some insisted that God was using the war to punish the nation or pressed Lincoln to seize the opportunity for eliminating a long-standing evil. To anyone of stern antislavery convictions, the president appeared oblivious to the sufferings of the slaves and far too cautious. When he refused to go along with General John C. Frémont's order emancipating slaves owned by rebels in Missouri, there was a great outcry among antislavery Christians but, as yet, no desire to come down too hard on the administration. Trying to paper over any differences between Lincoln and Frémont, some ministers counseled patience.[49]

In many ways, such a carefully calibrated response made good sense. Despite growing religious support for using the war to rid the country of slavery, this by no means represented majority sentiment in the North even among the devout, and there remained deep reservations if not outright opposition in many churches. "Whenever you preach abolitionism you give me the greatest pain," one Ohio Presbyterian complained to his pastor. Ministers had a right to express their opinions, he conceded, but such sentiments sounded "unpatriotic in the extreme." Old School Presbyterians, Episcopalians, conservative Unitarians, and Catholics might affirm their loyalty to the Union but steered clear of the slavery question.[50]

One Catholic who struck out on a different path was Orestes Brownson. A one-time Presbyterian, Universalist, socialist, freethinker, Unitarian, and transcendentalist, Brownson's peripatetic spiritual pilgrimage ended with his 1844 conversion to Catholicism. Suddenly the radical seeker had become the committed conservative, a lover of order and discipline, a defender of orthodoxy. Yet Brownson remained a reformer within the Catholic tradition and in October 1861 broke ranks with the church's traditionalist leadership. His essay "Slavery and the War" began by suggesting that another disaster such as Bull Run or the more recent Union defeat in Missouri at Wilson's Creek would force citizens of the free states to realize they could not preserve both the Union and slavery. According to Brownson, Christianity encouraged loyalty to government, yet Catholic editors sounded like lukewarm patriots in decided contrast to the church's young men who had flocked to the colors when their country needed them. "The South is more infidel or pagan, and far less Christian than the North, and is and always has been . . . far more anti-Catholic," he asserted.

This provocative article sparked an immediate uproar. In an anonymous response for his newspaper organ, the *Metropolitan Record* of New York, Archbishop Hughes pointed out that the church had condemned the slave trade but had accepted slavery as part of man's fallen nature. Although Hughes acknowledged the evils of slavery and called for gradual emancipation, he would still consign abolitionists to a "lunatic asylum." Yet neither Brownson nor Hughes had much stomach for an angry debate and remained wary of each other. When questioned by Vatican officials, Hughes even defended Brownson's orthodoxy. Some angry subscribers canceled their subscriptions to *Brownson's Quarterly Review*, though perhaps an equal number of good Catholics—including some border state Unionists—praised Brownson's essay despite worries that emancipation might flood the North with free blacks.[51]

Generally speaking, Catholic opinion remained mixed, though by January 1862 Hughes was describing slavery as the "sick man of the United States." He still worried that turning the war into an abolition crusade would demoralize Catholic soldiers and hurt military recruiting, but his rhetoric never became strident. Other Catholics blamed English Protestants for introducing slavery into the country and, in any case, believed that their church could alleviate the slaves' suffering without striking at the institution itself. Whatever their views on slavery, the bottom line for many northern Catholics remained loyalty to the government. Hughes soon traveled to Europe speaking on behalf of the Union cause, and Catholic editors sounded increasingly patriotic.[52]

A notable exception was James A. McMaster, the irascible polemicist and editor of the *New York Freeman's Journal and Catholic Register*. Dismissed from an Episcopal seminary because of involvement in the Tractarian movement, McMaster converted to Catholicism and during the 1840s had become a militant defender of orthodoxy. A longtime Democrat and bitter opponent of abolition, by the summer of 1861 McMaster claimed that many northerners had given up on ever subduing the southern rebellion. He denounced Lincoln for raising armies and suspending habeas corpus without constitutional sanction. Beginning in August 1861 and for nearly eight months, the postmaster general banned the *Freeman's Journal* from the mails. After being arrested on charges of "disloyalty and editing a disloyal newspaper," McMaster was held at Fort Lafayette in New York Harbor for more than a month but never brought to trial. He was released after taking an oath of allegiance under protest. To his fellow prisoners and conservative Catholics, McMaster became a heroic defender of liberty who continued to denounce the Lincoln administration as a cruel despotism.[53] McMaster, however, must have been nearly as frustrated with the leadership of his own church as he was with the government. Hughes and much of the American hierarchy had more than proved their loyalty to the Union cause by the fall of 1861, and a blending of patriotism and pietism had come to define wartime Catholicism. Whatever their differences over slavery and politics, Catholics and all manner of Protestants had become stalwart defenders of the Union.

Many also became eager celebrants of national greatness and divine blessing, although allusions to Union defeats at Ball's Bluff and Bull Run in Thanksgiving sermons emphasizing the Lord's chastisement of a sinful people illustrated the adjustments being made to providential interpretations of the war. Whether many Americans were convinced by clerical admonitions about the benefits of the Lord's discipline—including a sermon from a passage in the book of Hebrews about how Christ became "perfect through sufferings"— remains doubtful. But Presbyterians in particular developed a jeremiad that could seemingly handle defeats more easily than victories. The northern people had learned that they could not rely on superior numbers or resources, that riches could not save them from wrath, and that God had often permitted the weaker side to prevail in battle.[54] No longer could Americans ignore some plain Old Testament truths, claimed one New England Congregationalist, who decided that people needed to appreciate tough scriptures from Jeremiah and Psalms. "We have misinterpreted the gospel of peace and have gone faster than God in bringing on the millennial day when war shall cease," a Massachusetts divine feared. He called up memories of sturdy Puritan ancestors not yet grown soft from the pursuit of wealth and indulgence in luxury.[55]

At certain points, however, such hard-hitting messages seemed to lack conviction. Some of the same ministers who offered stern warnings about divine punishment still maintained that the North had enormous advantages in the war. Everything from good harvests to superior generals to patriotic unity became causes for thanksgiving. Warnings about greed and decadence were all well and good, but northern wealth remained an enormous asset in fighting the rebellion. "King Cotton" has been replaced by "King Corn," Baptist George Ide crowed. Despite defeats during the year, the Lord had safeguarded Washington from attack and helped bring the Federals recent victories at Cape Hatteras and Port Royal. Duly noting how God rebukes man's "practical atheism" with his "majesty and terror," Old School Presbyterian William Sprague nevertheless foresaw a country not only purified but transformed by war: "I see the great work of moral renovation advancing apace, until, by and by, a flood of millennial glory comes pouring in."[56]

A grandiose vision from such an unlikely source surely suggested the stunning ability of Americans to turn their religion into a quite malleable instrument for interpreting the great national crisis. Northerners continued to boast of a superior faith untrammeled by the incubus of slavery, and one Congregationalist predicted that the war would surely "bring great victories of religion pure and undefiled." Such statements illustrated why the twentieth-century theologian Reinhold Niebuhr would later warn how the church always stood "in danger of becoming a community of the righteous who ask God to vindicate them against the unrighteous; or, even worse, who claim to vindicate God by the fruits of their own righteousness."[57] Despite all the talk of a wrathful Jehovah judging the nation's sins, Niebuhr's reservations would probably not have impressed Reverend Sprague or most of his contemporaries. The crosscurrents of civil religion pulled Americans toward repentance and arrogance at the same time, and the line between righteousness and self-righteousness nearly vanished. Recognizing the hand of God in human history fostered neither humility nor even an appreciation for the majesty of inscrutable providence.

Instead, there were visions of a coming millennium that somehow ennobled a terrible war with transcendent purposes. On November 18, 1861, Julia Ward Howe and her husband had witnessed a grand review of General McClellan's troops outside Washington. On their way back to the city, they had joined the soldiers in singing the popular tune, "John Brown's Body." Howe awoke that night, as she later recalled, and the "long lines of the desired poem began to twine themselves in my mind." Springing out of bed, she grabbed "an old stump of a pen" and, without a light, hurriedly scrawled her poem. As a woman steeped in biblical language and utterly convinced that the Union cause was a holy one, Howe turned to images from Isaiah and other prophets as well as from the book of Revelation.[58] In the "Battle Hymn of the Republic," she ironically wrote about the Union cause in words that in a different context could easily have been embraced by Confederates.

Both sides had come to believe that they were about to witness the "coming of the Lord." Both sides could envision the great Jehovah "trampling out the vintage where the grapes of wrath are stored." Both sides believed that God's "truth is marching on," and that the Lord himself was "marching on" with their righteous warriors into battle. Both sides had heard the trumpet sound "that shall never call retreat." And, finally, both sides claimed that they would "die to make men holy" and "live to make men free." Howe's words had come largely from the Bible, but the ideas of the "Battle Hymn" were part and parcel of wartime religion in the Union and the Confederacy.

Here was no warm and sentimental message of salvation. Despite or perhaps because of the often bloodcurdling language, Howe's poem became an inspiring anthem to send so many young men to their deaths. A God of wrath had seemingly supplanted a God of love. Stern judgment loomed larger than saving grace. Meeting a member of a Connecticut artillery battery home on leave, the usually gentle Horace Bushnell bluntly asked, "Killed anybody yet?" The young officer was not sure, but Bushnell offered some unvarnished advice: "Time you had, that's what you went out for."[59]

Chapter 5

TEMPTATIONS OF THE CAMP

Watch and pray, that ye enter not into temptation:
the spirit indeed is willing, but the flesh is weak.
— Matthew 26:41

Bushnell need not have worried about whether soldiers were willing to kill the enemy, but as a minister he might have worried about the war's impact on religious faith. In the spring of 1863, Confederate staff officer Walter Taylor longed for the peace he had experienced after being converted as a young man. "But I am so hardened . . . sad indeed have been the effects of this unhappy war—not the least of which has been the bitter spirit toward our enemies . . . which is entirely at variance with the commands given for our guidance." Despite Robert E. Lee's sterling example, there appeared to be an "utter absence in our army of any external evidence of piety." Marching, fighting, and especially the daily grind of camp life left little time or energy for prayer or worship. Taylor no doubt exaggerated, but many people at home too realized that war had produced what a South Carolina Lutheran synod termed "a callous disposition, and morbid indifference to the demands of humanity and civilization." Soldiers' apparent lack of interest in the Gospel message proved equally disturbing.[1]

During the first two years of the war, soldier attendance at often infrequent religious services remained shockingly low. One surgeon who heard a man saying grace before a meal remarked on the event simply because it was such a rarity, agreeing with many others that there were few genuine Christians in the army. According to an Englishman who had enlisted in a New Jersey artillery battery, any kind of worship in camp "would be literally casting pearls before swine." And by common report, sailors were entirely heathenish.[2]

That faith would not flourish in the military seemed axiomatic to soldier and civilian alike, but explaining that stubborn fact proved more difficult. Evangelical growth and church expansion during the antebellum decades had surely turned Americans into a deeply religious people, though there remained stubborn pockets of resistance. In both the North and the South, many young men held back, perhaps because they associated piety with women and domesticity. If it "becomes fashionable in the army or the navy, to despise religion, confound it with hypocrisy, or with weakness, our strength will be gone,"

Stephen Elliott worried. Northern clergy shared similar fears, as did the more devout soldiers. A Massachusetts volunteer remarked that "keeping religion burning in the heart of the army was like their green wood fires, hard to get into a bright flame." Even for those who had been loyal soldiers of the cross back home, continuing to serve the Lord during the war seemed difficult, if not impossible. "I have gone entirely wild," a Georgia enlisted man confessed to his wife. "If I ever get back I shall have my name taken off the church book for it is a shame and disgrace to the cause of Christ."[3]

The sense of spiritual declension seemed overwhelming. One minister who claimed to have talked with more than two thousand Confederates sadly concluded that the "largest portion of them are irreligious." In three companies of one regiment, he could find no more than seven who professed any kind of faith. "It is sad to contemplate the low ebb to which religion and morality have descended in the army," a Pennsylvania private informed his parents. "And it may be easily accounted for. No one seems to take an interest in the moral and spiritual well-being of the men." Chaplains were of uneven quality, and many regiments did not even have one, but he thought that the root of the problem lay with officers who despised religion and wallowed in vice. At one poorly attended camp service, a New York private noted there was not a single officer present. Despite the pious examples of a Lee or Stonewall Jackson, Confederates too had plenty of general officers who set a poor example. Some insisted on holding reviews and parades on Sunday and bitterly resented anyone who dared criticize them for doing so.[4]

The contrast between companies and regiments led by God-fearing men and ordinary outfits seemed especially striking. One Georgian claimed not to have heard "an obscene word" from any of the company officers in his regiment. A Maine adjutant made a point of praying in sight of the enlisted men, though one joker's "odd expression and actions" set some of the boys to laughing and so the object lesson may have been lost.[5]

Whatever the spiritual state of the officer corps, the biggest concern remained the enlisted men. Even if contemporaries were correct that only a minority of the soldiers was particularly religious, their numbers were significant. Reports of 300,000 Methodists in the Union ranks were no doubt inflated but not by much. Echoing similar sentiments from Confederate ministers, one New Jersey preacher insisted there had not been so many praying men "in the field since Cromwell's days." Optimistic chaplains considered their young charges especially impressionable and therefore amenable to conversion; a Confederate priest assumed that the men who came to confession and communion "do so with a good intention and not just because they are afraid." Whether or not such claims could withstand scrutiny, upright soldiers sought the grace necessary to keep their faith strong in the midst of war and so many ungodly comrades. In calling for domestic missions in the army, a North Carolina presbytery expressed the hope that brave Confederates could return home to "take their places in society—not as reckless and desperate men who cast off fear—who trample upon all law and order, and defy the authorities of the land—but as the independent, yet meek and obedient soldiers of the cross, who would honor and glorify their Lord by a patient, dutiful, and exemplary submission to all which shall uphold virtue, peace, and happiness."[6]

The key appeared to be associating with other godly men in the ranks, a point made by the soldiers themselves and reinforced with advice from home. "I believe as a general thing that a soldier does become demoralized and more sinful in camp, but you must remember that I seldom or never come in contact with them," one Confederate officer assured his wife. "I never associate with them and believe as far I am individually concerned that my morals have been improved."[7] This all may have been true, but worried families must have wondered how long their boys' faith could survive in such an ungodly environment.

"I am very much at a loss to know how to enjoy my self," one Hoosier volunteer admitted to his parents, and that comment summed up what many soldiers saw as a major stumbling block. The monotony of camp life interspersed with grueling marches and horrific combat left a door for mischief far too wide open. The thinking here was clearly contradictory. Some men claimed to have little time for religious devotion but then pointed to the dangers of idle hours spent with convivial comrades. The daily routine, one Confederate recalled, did breed "a restless craving for excitement and recreation." And into this time vacuum, a northern minister noted, came "almost all shapes of vice and all sorts of temptation." A Union chaplain's manual advised telling soldiers not to gamble or play cards on Sunday but warned that going any farther would risk losing influence with men starved for recreation.[8]

Few contemporaries doubted that army camps bred innumerable evils. Military life, as described by one Baptist editor, was a "shore most thickly strewn with the wreck of souls." Reports of demoralization during the war's first year or so were remarkably uniform—often interchangeable between Union and Confederate accounts. Enlistment in a noble cause offered few safeguards against loathsome habits and corrupting influences; the gap between soldier and civilian life seemed to be growing. "My greatest fears arise from the fact that some things are considered right in the army that would be considered greatly out of place at home," a Pennsylvania chaplain informed the readers of one religious paper. "Habit rules to a great degree and may not army habits follow our men after this war closes?"[9]

On an individual basis, the debasing influences of the camp could be subtle but inexorable. "There is so many temptations here that a boy will be almost ruined before he is aware of the fact," an Indiana private remarked to his parents. He added that "the one what were the strictest at home are the first to give way to temptation." From the beginning, chaplains offered stock messages about how men fighting in a righteous war should avoid a host of bad habits, but they seemed to be waging a decidedly uphill battle. "Some are trying to live right," a Pennsylvania volunteer wrote with more hope than confidence from a camp he termed the "roughest and wickedest place i ever saw yet."[10]

What made the camps so morally dangerous seemed simple enough: they were filled with wicked men. A Catholic chaplain described the 73rd New York Infantry as the "scum of . . . society, reeking with vice and spreading a moral malaria around them." And that was precisely the problem: the number of sinful fellows reached a critical mass in the army, and then there was hell to pay. "I am surrounded by the profane," lamented one Confederate who clung to his Primitive Baptist convictions. In such an environment, rough characters only grew worse, and the irreligious gained the upper hand. With unusual candor, a South Carolina chaplain informed an inquiring father that his son was "wild," and in fact "the most profane man in his company, and his influence is evil."[11]

The very concentration of so many immoral men meant that ordinarily good fellows soon turned bad. Like the drunkard so lovingly described in the antebellum temperance literature, their moral descent often came in gradual, almost imperceptible stages. Once-pious young men began by neglecting the Bible and prayer. Soon they were uttering the occasional oath, and before long they were drinking, gambling, and whoring. In a sense there was no necessary inconsistency between denominational claims of sending thousands of good church members off to fight and reports of widespread demoralization in the armies. Young men in camp who ignored the counsels of pious mothers soon enough sank into all kinds of vice, or so many soldier tracts warned. The stereotypical preachers' sons joined the ranks of the publicans and sinners. "Thousands [of men] lose all respect for themselves and those left at home in a short time," claimed one New York sergeant who went on to catalog a range of offenses. Defending such conduct, some men simply stated that they could not be saints in the army or even that a certain amount of moral depravity was necessary to make good soldiers.[12]

On its face, that picture seemed much too dark, as at least a few ministers and soldiers acknowledged. Some men might grow more reckless in the army but others became more pious, especially under the proper influences. As a Hoosier private put it, "we have Swearing, cardplaying, *and* [author's emphasis] Bible reading in abundance." Attempts to assess the soldiers' moral condition became at times strained. One chaplain observed that men of strong character remained so and the vice-ridden pursued their usual pleasures, thus concluding that the army had little moral impact at all. "Camp life is a bad place for religion," a Mississippi volunteer informed his mother but noted "it is not so bad as I expected." Such reports could stir hopes that men might avoid the worst evils, and a Confederate chaplains' meeting declared "that the army is not of necessity a school of vice, but may become of the highest order of virtue."[13]

These sentiments would have seemed utterly utopian to most soldiers (and to many chaplains) at least early in the war. The best that one might hope for was that individuals would persevere in their faith. Having given up swearing and taken up praying, one New York volunteer simply remarked, "I am better in the army than at home." It was perhaps too easy for a man to reassure his family that he was regularly reading the Bible, and some claims about dramatic transformations do invite skepticism. Articles in the religious press assuring anxious mothers that their sons remained models of piety no doubt overstated the case. Yet there were some substantial grains of truth here. A husband and father who decided that he had been leading his family to hell through his own bad example might suddenly urge them to study the scriptures. And, as a Maine chaplain observed, the Federal disaster at Bull Run undoubtedly had a sobering effect on heedless souls who had once scoffed at any mention of religion. But observations of individuals too often turned into broad-brush generalizations that beggared belief. Throughout the war and even beyond, ministers and chaplains on both sides maintained that fighting in a holy cause had weeded out the hypocrites and transformed soldiers into paragons of self-sacrifice.[14]

One could cite examples supporting a range of conclusions, but assessing the moral tenor of armies or even brigades and smaller units was tricky. Certain companies or regiments gained reputations for piety; there was an unaffected pride in claiming that most of the boys in one's outfit were God-fearing men. Union chaplains filed quarterly reports on the moral condition of their regiments, often making comparisons to the rest of a brigade or division. Stories about especially devout regiments appeared in the religious press. On their way by ship to Newport News, Virginia, three hundred members of the 7th New York Infantry sang hymns, interestingly enough on the saloon deck. Commenting on this scene, the *Independent* affirmed that "men who march by prayer will never retreat in the day of battle."[15]

That statement rested on the hope of there being enough pious men in the ranks on the day of battle to merit the Lord's favor. The persistent debate over whether military life hindered, encouraged, or hardly affected the soldiers' spiritual well-being would never be settled during the war or even afterward. Men would promise to keep the faith and sometimes did, families would fret, and frustrated chaplains were often caught between home front expectations and camp realities. The concerns and worries, however, seldom stopped there. Soldiers and civilians saw particular vices as signs of larger trends, as causes of divine disfavor, and indeed as ill omens for the future.

———

War's impact on Sabbath observance was immediately noticeable. As some one hundred men and women gathered in Muscatine, Iowa, to sew for the volunteers who were to depart the next day, a local reporter noted, "There is no Sunday in a time of war." Soldiers soon realized the truth of that statement. The Sabbath often passed unobserved even by men who still considered it a sacred day of worship and rest. Sunday was not only ignored but profaned because soldiers had little opportunity to commune with God amid so much hubbub and confusion. One Confederate officer pointed out how the "bustle" of camp life on Sundays presented "strong evidence of the sin of war."[16]

Contemporary observers blamed the officers. An outraged Pennsylvania chaplain accused one general of making a "profane and deliberate choice" in assigning extra labor on Sunday. Other officers held drills and reviews that interfered with camp services. Men dug rifle pits and erected earthworks, though one scrupulous Tennessee company threw down its picks and shovels at midnight on Saturday. The next day when a solid shot hit an earthwork and killed a man at the bottom of a trench that had been dug that morning, their captain deemed it a "wonderful providence."[17]

Both Braxton Bragg and Robert E. Lee responded to complaints from chaplains who had petitioned Congress to prohibit unnecessary "reviews, inspections, and other parades." Orders confining Sunday activities to only the most necessary duties and scheduling inspections around religious services sounded good, but definitions of necessity in the army could prove quite elastic.[18]

The same pattern held with the Federals. On September 6, 1861, General McClellan noted how the soldiers were fighting in a "holy cause" and "should endeavor to deserve the benign favor of the Creator." He therefore decreed that the men should observe Sunday as a day of rest and "attend divine service after the customary Sunday morning inspection." Work was to be "suspended" and "no unnecessary movements" were to be made except in cases of "extreme military necessity." This order naturally won the approval of soldiers, whose motives were not strictly spiritual. Any distinction between sacred time and leisure time mattered little to exhausted or bored troops. For the moment, McClellan had satisfied those from the clergy, press, and churches who had been agitating the question. Indeed, religious papers waxed eloquent on the fine young men being sent by Christian parents to serve under McClellan's leadership, with the implied promise that honoring the fourth commandment would bring success on the battlefield.[19]

As with the Confederates, however, practical considerations intervened. Sergeant Charles Haydon of the 2nd Michigan Infantry, who resented having to round up men for religious services, scoffed at official efforts to promote piety. One cynic thought McClellan's order had been issued largely for political effect and expected Sunday drill and other work to continue. He was only partially correct, for well into 1862 approving soldiers credited Little Mac with providing a respite for their souls as well as their bodies. An Indiana volunteer summed up the feelings of the devout: "Thank God for the Sabbath the day of rest when you lift our souls from the low groveling earth to the heavens above."[20]

Not satisfied with relying on the religious convictions and goodwill of generals, ministerial organizations petitioned Abraham Lincoln for stricter Sabbath observance in the army, emphasizing the need to respect individual conscience and safeguard young volunteers from moral dangers. Finally, on November 15, 1862, the president acceded to these requests. Citing the importance of a day of rest "for man and beast" and duly noting the "sacred rights of Christian soldiers and sailors," Lincoln requested that "Sunday labor in the Army and Navy be reduced to the measure of strict necessity." He claimed to be acting out of "deference to the best sentiment of a Christian people, and a due regard for the Divine will." Jews or Seventh Day Adventists might ask what accommodations would be made for those who observed the Sabbath on a different day, but Lincoln had undoubtedly gone as far as he deemed prudent in accommodating religious scruples.[21] In any event, military necessity offered a convenient escape hatch.

Despite the best efforts of Lee, McClellan, or Lincoln, Sunday in an army camp or on board a naval vessel just did not feel right. Church bells did not ring; there were no well-dressed people walking to an early morning service. Thoughts naturally ran to the sentimental. Some men hankered for a quiet Sunday worshiping with their family or seeing familiar faces in the congregation and in Sunday school. Even the skeptical Charles Haydon found that the sounds from camp services conjured up memories of Kalamazoo, Michigan, and his mother. As a child, the "solemn mysteries of religion" had inspired in him a "vague terror" that "can never be obliterated," yet he also thought he would like to attend church once again. Corporal Thomas Hart Benton McCain, a much more devout Hoosier volunteer, carefully weighed the religious privileges being given up by the soldiers as he thought about "Hattie, Mattie, and the two Annies" in the Sabbath school class he had taught back home. He longed to again "live as a Christian and a civilized man."[22]

What contemporaries termed "nostalgia" and what a later generation would call "homesickness" flooded over the boys as they hummed familiar hymns or thought about how long it had been since they had heard a good sermon. Given the centrality of singing and preaching to Protestant worship, it is hardly surprising that soldiers would note their absence in the camps. Hearing "none of the Songs of Zion," one Mississippi cavalryman felt literally like "a stranger in a strange land." Many Federals shared these feelings, and attending a nearby church only brought back a host of memories mingled with an ineffable sadness. A Michigan private was locked up in a room with a few of his comrades trying to spend a quiet Sabbath, but he had not attended a real service, and he could not get used to the fact that so many of his comrades showed so little regard for the day.[23]

In fact, even inside the locked room, he might have been able to hear the sounds of revelry and high jinks because blasphemy and profanity echoed through the camps on Sundays as they did on any other day. Vices of all kinds seemed especially annoying on the Sabbath. Yet part of the problem lay with killjoys who objected to innocent recreation such as pitching quoits. After learning that he could not play cards on board a steamer, a Missouri German vented his anger against a pharisaical view of the Sabbath: "What is it if I want to go to hell, it's a free country."[24]

This persistent and almost obsessive struggle over Sabbath observance might seem wildly out of place in the midst of a bloody civil war except for the fact that many Americans connected the issue to the course and outcome of the conflict. Would the Lord pour out his grace upon a nation that ignored his commandments? That question resonated with soldiers and civilians and helps explain why Lee, McClellan, Stonewall Jackson, and a scattering of other generals tried to enforce Sabbath observance in the camps. More than a year after First Bull Run, a young New Yorker still worried that the defeat had been caused by the Federals attacking on the Sabbath. Only defensive fighting on Sunday could be squared with Holy Writ, claimed one southern Methodist.[25] Obeying the Lord's commandments became a solemn duty ultimately connected to the idea of a sovereign God who held the fate of individuals and nations in his mighty hands. Thus, despite the secular pressures that had long threatened strict Sabbath observance, this particular sin loomed large in providential explanations of victory or defeat.

———

The wartime emphasis on Old Testament warnings of judgment on any people who disobeyed divine ordinances made blasphemy an especially egregious offense. Violations of the third commandment would anger a righteous God, who would surely punish anyone who took his name in vain. And few doubted that there were many offenders — especially in the army. "Oaths, blasphemies, imprecations, obscenity, are hourly heard ringing in your ears until your mind is almost filled with them," claimed one Mississippi Confederate. African American chaplains deemed profanity the most common vice in their regiments. That there would be rough-spoken characters in the camps went without saying, but what most worried the more sensitive soldiers was that young men who would never have used such words at home were rapidly becoming prodigious swearers. And cursing in the ranks might easily spill over into civilian life when soldiers returned on furlough; foul language would soon become commonplace in streets and in homes.[26]

War and swearing seemed to go together. When an enlisted man upbraided Harry Smith, a Baptist minister and captain in the 16th Mississippi Infantry, for cussing out a group of men building a bridge across a creek, the good captain declared that "the Lord has given me a furlough until this damn war is over." In a similar incident, a Union colonel lightly dismissed the admonishment of a Methodist chaplain, "We'll make a bargain. I'll do all the swearing for this one [regiment] and you do all the praying." Whether or not such humorous incidents took place in quite the way they were later described, officers, including many with deep religious roots, believed that carrying out their duties required a certain amount of profanity if not blasphemy.[27]

From time to time, there were special camp sermons on the subject but with what effect is impossible to determine. After overhearing a soldier wish that all Yankees were in hell, a Confederate chaplain asked why he did not want them in heaven since "there will be less probability of your meeting them." Several nearby comrades burst into laughter, clearly preferring the wry touch over the usual censorious approach. A bold minister might even dare preach against *officers* swearing at their men. One determined Methodist chaplain drafted a letter to General Winfield Scott Hancock (who had a well-deserved reputation for sulfurous language) reminding him that God commanded men not to swear. Thinking twice, however, about challenging so exalted a figure, the chaplain never sent it. Some officers made fine distinctions in defending their choice of words. After receiving a critical letter from a woman who deplored his reputation as a "profane swearer," General Andrew A. Humphreys replied that he might swear at his fellow men but never at the Almighty.[28] Such give-and-take illustrated how many officers and likely even more enlisted men would dismiss, deflect, or defy efforts to rein in their tongues.

On rare occasions, officers issued orders to curb swearing. At least twice Oliver Otis Howard, who was widely known as a Christian general, admonished the troops under his command. As late as March 1865, Howard still maintained that "every insult to Him [God] is a scourge to ourselves and invites disaster to our noble cause." In one Union company the rule was that any man caught using profanity would have to read a chapter from the Bible aloud. An especially impious fellow in a short time had finished Genesis and Exodus and was well into Leviticus, perhaps not the best example of the policy's deterrent effect.[29]

The clergy struggled to touch the soldiers' consciences or convince them that swearing was—if not a crying evil—at least pointless. Wartime tracts noted that profanity and blasphemy accomplished nothing. Rough language made no one any better or braver; it did not even prod a recalcitrant mule to move any faster. Dabney pointed out that theft, lying, covetousness, lewdness, gluttony, and drunkenness all might be satisfying for a time but that the most horrid oaths did not bring even momentary rewards. Although some might consider cursing and ribaldry signs of manliness, these were hardly habits that would appeal to the ladies. And one day the idle swearer would have to face the day of judgment, and what a penalty there would be to pay for such a pointless sin. For some men the price was exacted in the here and now. Both Federals and Confederates told and retold stories of men who had been killed on the battlefield or even struck dead in their tents with vile blasphemies on their lips.[30]

A few bloodcurdling examples might spark a sudden reformation at least temporarily. Some soldiers admitted their guilt and vowed (one is tempted to say "swore") to do better, especially after a bloody battle. Two Federals on the Virginia Peninsula experienced a change of heart when a comrade counted some fifty-nine oaths that the pair of them had spouted in about ten minutes. Recognizing the problem and giving up the practice, however, were quite different matters. One Mississippi private let slip the admission that he thought about giving up profanity "every day of my life." Chaplains, of course, lovingly recounted how tracts and sermons had convinced such young recruits to abandon the habit.[31]

The benefits would extend beyond individual morality or even personal salvation. Just as with Sabbath breaking, ministers and their most saintly followers held that swearing could call down divine wrath upon nations. In the Old Testament, as one Confederate tract noted, the Lord had smote those who cursed his holy name. Nor would the Almighty protect profane men on the battlefield. Southern Presbyterians even declared the "wicked curse and the rude joke" to be the Confederacy's "crying national sin." According to a Tennessee chaplain, such language should be left to the enemy: "It is not surprising that our invaders should curse and swear. They have drawn the sword in the service of Mammon, of Moloch, of Lucifer, of Beelzebub, and blasphemy beseems them best." [32] The reasoning here was simple if not crude. Whichever side had soldiers who best controlled their tongues would win the war, and men who swore would only help sink their own cause.

―――――

Alcohol presented a different problem for both the soldiers and their spiritual shepherds. The antebellum temperance movement had shifted from condemning drunkenness to promoting abstinence, though defenders of moderate consumption had never entirely abandoned the field. There was not much biblical basis for teetotalism, but the scriptures did include warnings about the effects of strong drink. The temperance crusade had always won more support in the North, and some southerners duly noted that Yankee abolitionists often crusaded against the liquor traffic. Although enlisted men—especially Confederates—had trouble obtaining alcohol, there were widespread reports of drunkenness, especially among the officers. And, indeed, the question of supply proved critical. Union soldiers had more money and were stationed closer to large cities, therefore enjoying greater access to alcohol.[33]

Whatever the differences, tales of heavy drinking in both the Union and Confederate ranks circulated widely. Some contemporaries speculated that the army camps brought together a higher concentration of drunks than the typical town or city, but, however that might be, certain regiments, brigades, and even divisions became notorious. Young recruits wrote home that they had never seen so much inebriation in their life, and religious papers early in the war printed alarming accounts of alcohol abuse in the army. The abstemious often claimed that virtually every fellow in their company drank; even the ostensibly devout joined the tipplers. "I think as much of religion as any man," declared one Confederate sergeant as he took a swig of apple brandy. "But there's such a thing as having too damn much of it."[34]

Little wonder that temperance advocates saw the army as a vitally important but difficult field for any campaign against liquor. In a standard appeal, one Union tract warned soldiers that even moderate drinking was a dangerous first step toward ruin. As with other vices, soldiers removed from the civilizing influences of family and church readily yielded to temptation, making it all the more necessary for people back home to donate money for the distribution of literature and for efforts to suppress liquor sales near the camps. Sutlers who sold alcohol to soldiers seemed little better than traitors, so in a sense reform became part of the war effort.[35]

All these points laid the groundwork for temperance work in the armies, especially among the Federals. Aside from reading tracts, soldiers formed regimental temperance societies and sponsored meetings in which ministers, lecturers, and the men themselves discussed the evils of strong drink. One Irish priest even had a medal struck for the soldiers who would promise to give up the bottle. The temperance pledge that had stood at the very center of antebellum moral reform remained a vital part of wartime efforts to curb alcohol use. In April 1863 Methodist chaplain Louis Beaudry of the 5th New York Cavalry delivered a sermon based on a text in Proverbs warning that the drunkard and the glutton would eventually sink into poverty. By early 1864, he noted how intemperance remained a terrible "scourge" in the army and even gave some credence to a popular notion that the war would have ended by this time had it not been for the influence of whiskey. During the spring, more and more young men began attending meetings, and he greatly rejoiced when one of the hardest drinking officers signed the pledge. What most aided such efforts were the soldiers themselves, who could see the effects of drinking all around them. Scenes of camp debauchery convinced the already sober-minded to promise their home folks that they would never disgrace their families and their country. Temperance—as Lincoln had once pointed out—was not that much of a virtue for those who lacked any taste for alcohol, and there was often an undercurrent of self-righteous pride here.[36]

Candid chaplains readily admitted that condemnations of drinking had little effect on many officers. In one regiment, a besotted major spoke on behalf of temperance but never followed his own advice. Even the indefatigable Beaudry worked for several hours without persuading a single officer to sign a temperance pledge. When his mother suggested forming a temperance society, Fuller Manly dismissed the idea because it was impossible to persuade Confederate soldiers to swear off alcohol. Baptist associations sadly noted growing intemperance in the armies, lamenting how many people at home and in the camps were inclined to embrace worldly vices during a war.[37]

A gathering of Alabama Baptists claimed that alcohol "does more damage to the material, intellectual, and religious interest of mankind, than even the war itself, with all its ravages." A pastoral letter directed to Presbyterians in the Confederate army agreed that intemperance killed more people than war. Northern churches—especially the Methodists—expressed similar views.[38] Such statements reflected a desperate effort to link the cause of temperance to the war's larger purposes, making strong drink as lethal a foe as enemy brigades.

That temperance advocates often fought a losing battle became apparent in their strong criticism of even moderate drinking. In the temperance literature, a single glass of beer or sip of whiskey had long marked an early stage in the slide toward perdition, and during the war Baptist churches in particular tried to hold the line with their members. Part of the difficulty stemmed from the fact that a number of the faithful had decided that the occasional taste of wine did no harm. In 1862 a North Carolina Baptist association cited ten congregations that were "more or less guilty of violation of the constitution" on matters of temperance. Federal chaplains and northern churches too pressed for total abstinence. Worrying that people had come to believe that a moderate use of alcohol was somehow beneficial, Hoosier Methodists deplored the "growing habit of beer-drinking" as the "entering wedge . . . to drunkenness."[39]

Not only were church members imbibing, but they were also directly involved in the liquor traffic. In Indiana, Methodists were reportedly producing and drinking wine, obviously setting a bad example for their children. Baptist associations across the Confederacy admitted that some of their members had been distilling brandy and other "ardent spirits" to profit from wartime inflation. A flurry of reports and resolutions complained of a languishing temperance cause in a church once known for strictly monitoring people's behavior. A group of Alabama Baptists proposed expelling dissipated members—a procedure that once would have been routine—but that now only signified how much the temperance movement was foundering even among once reliable supporters.[40] All this discussion came too late because church discipline had grown lax during the antebellum decades, and the war only made matters worse.

Although one Michigan pastor declared that, "We design the extermination of *King Alcohol* and *King Cotton*," old-fashioned temperance societies, tracts, and meetings could hardly achieve much if the government failed to suppress drinking in the military. After some debate and several amendments, the Confederate Senate passed a bill to "discourage drunkenness" in the army, but the measure died in the House. In proclamations suspending habeas corpus and imposing martial law in various places, Jefferson Davis and local commanders prohibited alcohol sales near the army camps, a policy that pleased some officers and mollified citizens worried about drunken soldiers. States adopted laws against distilling largely because of concerns about grain shortages but also as part of a wartime effort to control drinking. Sobriety supposedly became a hallmark of the true southern patriot. Whatever their effectiveness, some temperance advocates hoped that such measures would win the Lord's approval and perhaps even improve prospects for Confederate arms.[41]

After his regiment spent a surprisingly sober New Year's Eve, one New Jersey chaplain thought about what an effective temperance law might accomplish at home. But aside from abolishing the navy's liquor ration and imposing stiff penalties on anyone in Washington, D.C., caught selling alcohol to soldiers, the Federal government took little action. By 1865, and despite the example set by the teetotaler Lincoln, the *Independent* concluded that the war had weakened the temperance cause and especially support for abstinence.[42]

Unlike swearing or Sabbath breaking, drinking became less of a marker on the war's course. In a broad sense, both Federals and Confederates might point to drunkenness as a sin that could stir the Lord's wrath, though in this case judgment against individuals did not readily translate into punishment for nations. One Confederate tract entitled *Liquor and Lincoln* imaginatively pointed out how God's hard-won favor at First Manassas might be lost if southerners descended into a licentiousness fueled by alcohol. Indeed, whiskey in the hands of southern soldiers could only help their archenemy Abraham Lincoln. Yet the idea that God would chastise the Confederacy for intemperance seemed most prevalent after a series of western theater defeats early in 1862 when people were scrambling to explain these unexpected setbacks. Otherwise, there was little discussion along those lines during the rest of the war.[43]

Providential interpretations of the conflict gave relatively short shrift to alcohol abuse. Because abstinence or signing the temperance pledge had long been signs of conversion and holy living in a strongly evangelical culture, northerners and southerners continued to think about the liquor question largely in terms of personal salvation. Intemperance might harm the armies and even be considered a national sin, but many ministers and other opponents of strong drink worried more about what would happen when so many soldiers who had taken to their cups returned home.

———

A similar pattern occurred in attitudes toward gambling, a vice to be condemned more as a threat to the individual than to the war effort. That soldiers in camp would play cards to pass the time seemed natural enough, and not all played for money. One Mississippian who refused to throw away his deck of cards just before the Battle of Spotsylvania Courthouse recounted how his Episcopalian mother had taught him various games but proudly maintained he had never wagered on them. During the ensuing fight, however, an enemy ball struck his deck of cards and penetrated to the ace of spades, an odd counterpoint to the countless stories about Bibles stopping bullets.[44]

Yet, as with alcohol, an innocent diversion could easily become a serious vice. Like the soldier at Spotsylvania, an Alabama volunteer had learned various card games from his competitive mother and sisters, who had helped hone his skills. In the army he found it easy to beat unwary comrades out of their money. Yet he soon squandered the winnings and, despite finally confessing his guilt to a chaplain, lacked the means to make restitution. No matter, he was soon killed in battle. The young man's story fit into the classic tale of descent from harmless fun to obsessive gambling to steady drinking to thoughtless blasphemy—a straight path to hell in the typical antigambling narrative. Indeed, some soldiers' descriptions of gambling in camp mirrored the familiar drama of the once virtuous lured step by step toward endangering their immortal souls. Soon they would acquire what one tract termed "lewd, base, and wicked companions," and then far more would be lost than the stakes in a card game. They would neglect their duties as soldiers and would forfeit the respect of their comrades, the implication being that they would ultimately weaken their country's cause. Religious tracts graphically described the downfall of naive youth ensnared by temptation doomed to disappoint pious parents and face eternal damnation.[45]

Such graphic warnings, however overdramatic, reflected the pervasiveness of gambling in the armies. Noisy card games disturbed the sleep of upright comrades, who worried as one Virginian did that "our men are becoming lost to all sense of rectitude." Soldiers deprived their poor families of bread by gambling away their earnings; whenever the paymaster arrived, there would be games going on all over camp. A young man who claimed to be an ordained minister won praise as an eloquent preacher in one Pennsylvania brigade toward the end of the war. But he soon acquired a reputation for being a heavy drinker and inveterate card player, and so at the end of one sermon, a fun-loving soldier cried out, "What is trump?"[46]

Even more shocking, gamblers played their games of chance on the Sabbath, cursing their bad luck within earshot of men listening to the word of God. In one Confederate camp, preachers delivered sermons while poker hands were being dealt only a few feet away. Federals too complained of comrades so intent on gambling that they entirely forgot the Lord's day. Pious soldiers could simply not comprehend the attraction, fascination, or addictiveness of faro and other games. One can only imagine the mortification of a Wisconsin chaplain when "chuck-or-luck" drew a larger crowd than his Sunday service. Only the prospect of imminent combat could force men to throw aside their cards or dice right before a battle, and then the reformation proved short-lived.[47]

Resolute chaplains tried to suppress such activities—one Louisiana priest by snapping up the pot from a poker game and donating it to a Richmond orphanage. Clever fellows, however, could easily steer clear of chaplains, and many of these encounters had a humorous quality that suggested efforts to suppress gambling were neither entirely serious nor very successful. One minister serving in a Pennsylvania regiment admitted this particular vice grew out of sheer boredom. Some chaplains did more harm than good when they tried to break up card games among hospital patients; one Confederate chaplain found that his horse's tail had been shaved right after he had preached against gambling. As a Presbyterian chaplain serving in a tough Missouri cavalry regiment concluded, "The devil seems to become more devilish whenever the Lord is correcting souls." He admitted not being able to curb gambling and or prevent officers from holding "another Bacchanalian orgie."[48]

Army commanders enjoyed little more success than the chaplains. In November 1862 Robert E. Lee issued an order to deal with widespread gambling in the army. Such a vice seemed "wholly inconsistent" with the soldier's high character or the Confederacy's righteous cause, but aside from urging officers to police their men, Lee offered no solution to the problem. A few soldiers might read the tracts and throw away their decks of cards, or a mess might agree to avoid any kind of wagering, but in both Union and Confederate camps gambling of all kinds flourished throughout the war.[49] Neither the tracts nor the sermons suggested that poker games would bring down divine wrath on the Union or the Confederacy. Instead, the emphasis remained on the pernicious moral effects and the dangers posed to the individual soldier in this world and the world to come.

In the Civil War era, sexual immorality remained the most hidden, the least discussed, but one of the most popular vices. The combined influence of evangelical religion and Victorian reticence led people to ignore the substantial venereal disease rates in both armies or at least to believe that their boys would never fall prey to the maladies of Venus. There were nearly 200,000 cases of syphilis and gonorrhea in the Union army, and prostitution ran rampant wherever large numbers of troops were stationed.[50]

An Illinois private who deplored the loose morality among officers and enlisted men complained of the "millions of dollars to pay the damage the abandoned women have been to our Government." He clearly exaggerated, but raids on houses of prostitution were widely reported, and newspapers carried large advertisements for venereal disease treatments. The occasional tract delicately warned against a "licentious imagination" leading to "licentious conduct," a habitual sin sure to destroy a young man's moral character. But there was very little open discussion, so for the most part fornication and other sexual misconduct did not enter into larger considerations of sin, national morality, and the war's course. Tract writers and preachers preferred to focus on Sabbath breaking and cursing.[51]

Neither soldiers nor families nor churches cared to dwell on or even to discuss sexual impurity. Aside from veiled references, ribald stories, dirty pictures, and the occasional mention of prostitutes in soldier letters, there remained a vast silence. Clearly the temptations were there, and many a boy succumbed if the venereal disease reports are any indication, but the Civil War generation often conflated rectitude with reticence and euphemism. And in any case, there were plenty of other sins that merited attention. Individual vices of all kinds had become to varying degrees part of the war's unfolding story. From general discussions of the army as a godless place and breeding ground for sin to specific considerations of Sabbath breaking and swearing, soldiers and civilians, Federals and Confederates, weighed in on the relationship between temptation, sin, divine judgment, and the course of the war. In the armies, it would often be left up to the chaplains to deal with camp vices and to reassure worried home folk that their boys were not turning into moral reprobates. Then, too, chaplains would become responsible for the spiritual welfare of the souls placed in their charge.

Chapter 6

THE SHEPHERDS AND THEIR SHEEP

And I will set up shepherds over them which shall feed them: and they shall
fear no more, nor be dismayed, neither shall they be lacking, saith the LORD.
— Jeremiah 23:4

And Jesus, when he came out, saw much people, and was moved with
compassion toward them, because they were as sheep not having a
shepherd: and he began to teach them many things.
— Mark 6:34

In the aftermath of Sumter, as ministers no less than other folks became caught up in the martial frenzy, the first wave of enthusiastic volunteer-
ing inevitably scooped up some of the clergy. But not without controversy. A
ministerial association in Niles, Michigan, condemned "brethren who drop
the sword of the spirit" to take up the "weapons of carnal warfare." A southern religious editor chastised anyone called to preach the gospel of peace who
would "run five hundred or a thousand miles to imbrue their hands in the
blood of their enemies."[1] Such arguments made patriotic duties distinctly secondary to religious ones, but pressures in the opposite direction often proved
overwhelming.

Shortly after Bull Run, sixty Illinois Methodist ministers volunteered, and
their southern brethren were hardly laggards. Preachers did not enlist out of
bloodlust, one Virginia editor defensively remarked, but rather "because they
feel a necessity is laid on them, in the providence of God to uphold a cause that
is interwoven with the progress of Christianity and the salvation of men."[2]

But after several ministers serving in the Army of Tennessee had been killed
or wounded in Georgia during the spring of 1864, the Reverend S. M. Cherry
pointedly reminded men who had ignored their clerical calling about Jesus's
famous warning that those who take up the sword will die by the sword. There
were also doubts whether a minister could maintain his spiritual integrity in
an ungodly military atmosphere.[3] Aside from the obvious problem of joining
in the slaughter, their presence in the army may have weakened the cause of
Christ by contributing to an early shortage of chaplains.

In truth, the chaplaincy never attracted enough healthy and able men willing to endure low pay and other hardships. Acknowledging this fact, various

denominations urged their clergymen to visit the camps for an occasional service or even become army missionaries for a few months. Stonewall Jackson wrote a long letter asking southern churches to send some of the "most prominent ministers who are distinguished for their piety, talents, and zeal" to work with the chaplains. Such men should ignore sectarian differences and help bring "system" to the soldiers' religious lives. Jackson candidly admitted that many chaplains had been delinquent in their duties, making the need all that greater. The General Assembly of the Presbyterian Church commissioned two prominent ministers to organize chaplains and missionaries in the eastern and western armies, though even in the Army of Northern Virginia, as Reverend B. T. Lacy reported, "the harvest is truly great and the laborers are few."[4]

That passage from Luke's Gospel summed up the problem. Beginning in 1862, Baptists took the lead by dispatching twenty-six missionaries to the armies, a number that nearly tripled over the next couple years. The devout expected to get their money's worth, and given Americans' penchant for quantifying everything, including religious faith, it is hardly surprising that Baptists kept tabs on the number of sermons preached and prayer meetings conducted—and, most importantly, souls converted. The costs were considerable. Presbyterians spent $200,000 over a two-year period; congregations often raised substantial sums, and some Baptist associations allocated most of their budgets to army missions.[5] Serving for brief periods, and like chaplains, often pulled in several directions at once, even the most devoted missionaries at times doubted their effectiveness. Besides preaching, they distributed religious literature, visited the hospitals, and helped bury the dead. In the last three years of the war, missionaries led revival meetings, and so there was always more work to do. Presbyterian William J. Hoge, to cite just one example, probably cut his life short with so many visits to the camps, dying of typhoid at the age of thirty-nine as Federal armies closed in on Petersburg.[6]

The Federals faced similar problems. In the summer of 1862, Secretary of War Edwin M. Stanton reported 437 chaplains for 676 Union regiments, a somewhat brighter picture than in the Confederacy perhaps but misleadingly so. Some 29 of these chaplains were on leave or detached service; 13 were absent without leave. Many of these present for duty would be short-termers, and even late in the war several corps and many artillery batteries had no chaplains; in both the Union and Confederate armies, a single chaplain might serve an entire brigade. An Iowa enlisted man reported a situation all too typical: "We have no chaplain now and never one that amounted to much. A good, working Chaplain would be of immense service to this regiment and I do not see why some one does not apply for the place."[7]

To answer this soldier's question and explain why chaplains fell short in both quantity and quality is no simple task, but a good place to start is with the antebellum army. There had been only about eighty, mostly Episcopalian chaplains appointed between 1813 and 1856 and they had largely served as schoolmasters on isolated posts. Neither West Point nor the army itself— despite strict church attendance policies—had been particularly hospitable to religious faith. In 1861 there were only thirty post chaplains. These men did not fit well into the military hierarchy and seemed to be auxiliary if not superfluous; regimental chaplains were virtually unknown.[8]

At the beginning of the war, the government paid little attention to chaplains. According to a War Department plan of organization issued in May 1861, each regiment was to have a chaplain "appointed by the regimental commanders on the vote of the field officers and company commanders." The chaplain would receive pay equal to that of a captain of cavalry ($1,746 annually) and must be a "regularly ordained minister of some Christian denomination." Significantly, the War Department specified no other qualifications and offered would-be chaplains neither rank nor uniforms. Late in the war, a Minnesota chaplain frustratingly noted that he lacked both the "ability" and "authority" to prevent depredations by the troops in his regiment, in part because he "did not wear even the insignia of a soldier or officer."[9] He might have added that no one in Washington showed much interest in his plight.

In August 1861 the War Department instructed chaplains to file quarterly reports on the "moral and religious condition" of their regiments but specified no other duties. Nearly a year later, Congress passed additional legislation, establishing the post of hospital chaplain, requiring that the "fitness, efficiency, and qualifications" of each chaplain be examined by his commanding officer or supervisor, and reducing chaplains' salaries to $1,200 annually.[10] This last provision suggested that some congressmen doubted the worth and perhaps even the necessity for military chaplains, a point not lost on religious editors who complained loudly.[11] Haphazardly drafted legislation, confusion about rank, and the pay reduction all showed stunning indifference to the chaplaincy. Even as ministers declared the cause of Union to be the cause of God, politicians took little interest in supporting religion in the army.

The Confederate Congress appeared equally indifferent. The May 1861 authorizing legislation was even sketchier than the comparable Federal statute but did specify a monthly salary of eighty-five dollars. Even this measure had been adopted only at the urging of Secretary of War Leroy P. Walker, and despite Walker's argument connecting the appointment of chaplains to the Lord's blessing on Confederate arms, neither the Davis administration nor Congress showed any great enthusiasm for chaplains. On May 15, in fact, Congress suddenly slashed chaplain salaries to fifty dollars per month, more than enough, one congressman remarked, for someone who had to preach only once a week. There were immediate howls of protest. Congress had degraded the office of chaplain, complained an outraged Presbyterian, who lectured the lawmakers on their "false economy that starves the soul to feed the body."[12]

Indeed, the debates in the United States and Confederate congresses were richly ironic. The clergy had played an important—albeit often exaggerated— role in the run-up to war. After Fort Sumter, the ministers and churches had rallied to their respective governments with remarkable unanimity and assurances of divine favor. Yet, despite the evangelical growth and church expansion of the antebellum decades, few politicians saw any crying need for a closer alliance between the government and organized religion. They did not share the worries of their pious constituents about the soldiers' spiritual welfare, and however useful civil religion might be, Union and Confederate leaders hardly sought a return to the days of Oliver Cromwell. Neither government appeared anxious to create holy armies, and the state continued to hold the church at arm's length. So military chaplains would be fine in their place, but that place was decidedly humble and secondary.

———

Even the selection of chaplains drove home this point. Although becoming a Confederate chaplain technically required a presidential appointment, it was largely up to the colonels in consultation with company officers and with some consideration for the enlisted men's denominational preferences. There were no educational or other formal qualifications for the job, and the whole process was as haphazard as the chaplain legislation itself.[13] Patchwork procedures also prevailed among the Federals, but the most significant difference revolved around the greater political jockeying in the Union armies. Would-be chaplains gathered clerical support, but rumors persisted that partisan affiliation sometimes mattered more than spiritual qualifications. Moreover, some applicants and their friends readily admitted that poorly paid preachers serving small congregations saw a chaplaincy as a way to improve their worldly status.[14]

Each denomination scrambled for a share of these appointments, though had anyone pointed out how this all smacked of old-fashioned patronage squabbles, the reaction would have been shocked denial. Methodist and Catholic bishops were especially assiduous in looking after their churches' interests; conservative Presbyterians complained about too many appointments going to abolitionists. Faced with one importunate clerical delegation urging him to take more care in appointing chaplains, Lincoln simply said he left such matters with the regiments, adding a droll story about a young boy who complained about not having enough mud to make a clergyman.[15]

The fruits of these irregular procedures were not promising. According to the Union paymaster general Benjamin Larned, many chaplains were "utterly unworthy." Apparently ignoring the requirement that chaplains be ordained clergy, colonels appointed theological students or, more commonly, their friends, some of whom were not particularly religious. Although many regular ministers who did become chaplains early in the war were devoted and capable, as a whole the group was not distinguished. Veteran pastors long past their prime and not likely to endure the rigors of military life or failed preachers foisted off on the army by relieved congregations: critics and cynics could cite many such examples. Men who would never receive a call to preach in "any ordinary church," one Presbyterian editor groused, too often became the spiritual shepherds for an entire regiment.[16]

Men more fitted by training and temperament to become chaplains might have anticipated engaging in fearsome battles with Satan over the souls of their charges but more often faced unanticipated, formidable, and sometimes deadly enemies. Added to the usual strains of military life, disease exacted a fearsome toll. Especially during the first part of the war, resignations for health reasons meant that some regiments ran through several chaplains in a matter of months. Although at first worried that his chaplain might be "lovesick," devout New Jersey colonel Robert McAllister soon had to place the feverish fellow on sick leave, despite the fact that he was "among the best chaplains in the army." An Ohio chaplain died suddenly after holding only two or three camp services, and it was not unusual for an unhealthy chaplain to head home within weeks of enlisting. "As a general thing," a Christian Commission delegate maintained, "ministers have not known much of life, nor of men." They had spent too much time in their studies and too little time in the world, ill prepared to face rough characters and rougher conditions.[17]

Eighteen months was the average term of service, and few chaplains served for the entire war. In the summer of 1862, Massachusetts Congregationalist Alonzo Quint noted the rapid exodus of several chaplains from the fever swamps of the Virginia Peninsula and predicted more would follow. Some ministers had intended to serve for only a few months and return to their congregations, but abrupt resignations reinforced the mounting criticism. In the spring of 1862, the *Independent* reported that two-thirds of the chaplains "are totally inefficient and many disgrace not only religion but humanity by their conduct." A Union soldier agreed that at least three-fourths of them were unfit. Those who sought to defend chaplains from harsh and often unfair newspaper attacks had to admit that there was more than a grain of truth in many of the complaints.[18]

The chaplains themselves knew of colleagues who fell well short of the mark and certainly felt the sting of the broad-brush criticism that came their way. Many ministers volunteered for the most idealistic reasons but immediately faced the daunting challenges of their new position. Reading in a newspaper of his nomination to become chaplain of the 6th South Carolina Infantry, Presbyterian Charles Betts could only pray to God that "no evil may come of this thing." He entered the service with both apprehension and determination. After a couple months on the job, he decided "the camp is not a place favorable to piety, yet I think it is a place where the minister may do good if he is the right sort of man." Betts was the right sort of man, even if he felt diffident about his own abilities, and wondered if God had imposed such duties on him as punishment for sin. At about the same time that Betts was learning about camp life firsthand, Congregationalist Joseph Hopkins Twichell was angling to become chaplain of the 71st New York in the famous Excelsior Brigade. Admitting that the regiment was largely composed of "rough, wicked men," he explained to his father that he nevertheless felt a strong obligation to the soldiers. With the Bible and tracts as his only tools, he would care for the sick and control the unruly. After serving for more than a year and a half, he sadly realized that many men would not even notice if he neglected his duties or merely went through the motions. "So long as I remained benevolent and helpful, I should be called a good Chaplain, even though I forbore almost entirely to preach Christ Crucified."[19]

What helped keep such men going was support from their superiors. Twichell appreciated officers who turned out men for worship and must have been especially pleased (and surprised) when General Daniel Sickles of all people presented him and another chaplain to the brigade as representatives of the "great Commander," adding the firm admonition: "Respect them." To chaplains, however, the best officers did more than offer support. They attended services, occasionally reading a scripture verse or offering a prayer. A few — including generals such as Stonewall Jackson, Braxton Bragg, William S. Rosecrans, or O. O. Howard — showed much more concern for the troops' spiritual welfare.[20]

According to many chaplains and no few soldiers, however, indifference or hostility was far more common. "Fifth wheel," "a nuisance," "time-serving rascals," and "a curse rather than a blessing" were a few of the phrases that came to mind when army officers thought of chaplains. Confederate general D. H. Hill dismissed the lot as "trifling and effeminate," a phrase suggesting persistent masculine resistance to conversion. Lazy and worthless preachers collected their pay but did little else, though the degree of hostility seemed far out of proportion to the chaplains' shortcomings.[21]

Problems began immediately because a chaplain arriving in camp often had little idea what he was supposed to do. In utter exasperation, one Pennsylvanian suggested abolishing the office because a chaplain has "no rights, no assigned sphere, no prescribed duties, no protection from law," and little chance of support from his colonel. Editors of religious newspapers echoed these sentiments. Although the level of frustration for Confederate chaplains seems to have been lower, their duties were equally ill-defined.[22]

In essence, chaplains carved out their own positions in a regiment or brigade. They entered an expansive parish or what Pennsylvanian Andrew Jackson Hartsock termed a "very large and ripe field." There would be much labor required, but the harvest would be uncertain if not meager. Obviously, chaplains were to conduct Sabbath services and prayer meetings, yet that was only the beginning if they were at all conscientious. The energetic organized Christian associations, Sunday schools, and regimental churches. Priests celebrated mass and heard confessions. In the midst of marches, campaigns, and battles, chaplains literally become pastors on the move, and the definition of pastoral duties expanded accordingly. Distributing Bibles and religious literature, caring for the sick and wounded, visiting the hospitals, conducting funerals — the tasks seemed endless.[23]

The work extended far beyond strictly religious activities. A Union army chaplain's manual listed a number of "temporal duties" such as helping hospital patients with their correspondence and securing good reading material. One harried New Jersey chaplain confessed that he could not respond as promptly as he would have liked to all the inquiries from parents and wives. The vital work of maintaining ties between the army and home front required constant attention. Father William Corby received a letter from a Brooklyn woman who was in "complete want" because some twenty-four dollars that her husband had promised to send home had not yet arrived. Although chaplains might shy away from handling such problems, some like Father Corby became virtual bankers for their regiments.[24]

Given the myriad duties and demands, chaplains struggled to address individual needs. The most painstaking compiled lists of soldiers by company with notations about their families, illnesses, and religion. The first step in exerting moral influence was to befriend the lonely and troubled. Patient listening encouraged hesitant young men to share their worries and opened up opportunities for frank talks about the state of their souls. On matters both religious and secular, chaplains became teachers in camp, offering everything from basic literacy instruction to Pennsylvanian James J. Marks's lectures on traveling to the Holy Land.[25]

January 2, 1863, was a typical day for Baptist chaplain William Edward Wiatt of the 26th Virginia. Early in the morning, he stopped by the captains' tents to drop off religious literature. He walked over to see a young soldier who had fallen deathly ill but arrived too late. He talked with several other sick men, urging them to prepare to meet their God. He spent the rest of the day distributing tracts along with his last hymnbook and held a prayer meeting in the evening. Some chaplains kept careful count of sermons, services, and pastoral visits, perhaps to reassure themselves that they were doing some good. But numbers hardly captured the challenges of dealing with so many singular specimens of humanity, ranging from innocent lads who had grown up in Christian homes to wild men who wallowed in depravity. Even for Wiatt and other dedicated chaplains, the demands of the job became overwhelming and left them hardly enough time to reflect on their myriad activities. Some never lost their enthusiastic idealism and simply found satisfaction in helping others. A Brooklyn chaplain frankly hoped for a still higher prize: "I expect to win many stars for my crown of glorification in the kingdom of heaven." More typical were the sentiments of Virginian W. G. H. Jones, who wrote about "striving as best I may to aid our righteous cause."[26]

Because neither Federals nor Confederates officially spelled out a chaplain's qualifications any more than they had defined their duties, the lists of both lengthened. Many chaplains themselves would have argued that piety was the first if not the most important requirement. A popular manual stated that a chaplain should be knowledgeable and doctrinally sound but at the same time lively and kind. Earnestness combined with humility, studious preparation in tandem with a heartfelt faith—the work called for a careful balance of sometimes opposing qualities. At the same time, a chaplain had to be physically and mentally tough enough for military life and the discouragements that inevitably came with the work. J. E. B. Stuart expressed this requirement in negative but clear terms: "I do not want a man who is not both able and willing to endure hardness as a good soldier."[27]

Of almost equal importance was a certain broadness of outlook that allowed a chaplain to deal with all kinds of people in difficult situations. A chaplain had to uphold standards of faith and morality without being either sanctimonious or priggish. Most everyone agreed that theological dogmatism and denominational zeal fatally hampered a minister's effectiveness. With becoming modesty, a young chaplain who thought that "exhortation and counsel are more fitted for maturity and age" noted how he preferred to "work by my life than by my speech," to "rely more on the little kindnesses, attentions, and words of cheer every day than on Sunday preaching, or weekday advice and counsel." This could be carried too far, he acknowledged, but the point was well taken. Cooperation between various denominations became an ideal for both Federals and Confederates, and many chaplains learned that everyone from high churchmen to backwoods Baptists could be good Christians after all.[28]

What the troops most valued was the human touch. A Virginian praised his chaplain as "nice" and "pleasant" but especially enjoyed seeing him play ball or pitch quoits or shoot marbles like one of the boys. Good chaplains were cheerful and hospitable, making the average soldier all that more likely to attend services. Father Peter Paul Cooney thought it useful to crack a joke from time to time. Even more important was the ability to laugh at yourself, a quality played for all it was worth by a footsore Vermont minister who straggled during a long march in Georgia and then preached a sermon on the Genesis text, "See that ye fall not out by the way."[29]

In many respects, it came down to a willingness to live with soldiers and share their hardships. Wise chaplains cared for souls but did not neglect bodies. One Connecticut chaplain could preach well enough, though he no doubt gained more standing in the regiment as a skillful forager who returned to camp loaded down with turkeys, pigs, and sweet potatoes confiscated from godless rebels. A venturesome Wisconsin Methodist even tried to make a plum pudding when the boys seemed downhearted, and his abject failure as a cook greatly amused and likely cheered them up. When such fine fellows left the service, soldiers expressed sincere regrets. As one Confederate summed up his regiment's relationship with an especially beloved chaplain, "We'll *freeze* to him every time."[30]

What truly cemented such bonds was shared suffering on the march and in combat. The great test for many chaplains became whether they could stick with the men as they advanced into line of battle. At this point, one misstep could ruin even the best preacher. One skeptical Federal referred to Methodist Josiah Flower as the "great thunderer"; though at war meetings back home he had promised to join soldiers on the field, "when the shells began to fly and the balls to hiss around, he always concluded that fighting was not in his line of business." Preachers could speak of the glories of heaven but scrambled to remain safely on this earth at the first sign of danger. "Chaplains talk of the good fight," wrote a cynical newspaper correspondent shortly after the Battle of Chancellorsville, "but rarely one is to be seen anywhere near a real fight—a fact that deprives them wholly of influence." Soldiers did not expect the chaplain to grab a gun and start blazing away at the enemy, but they did expect them to stay close by. Certainly they should be cool and calm to steady the nerves of the men who would do the fighting. When a chaplain continued praying as shells fell nearby, the men would likely pay more attention to his preaching in the future.[31]

The emphasis was on courage rather than pugnacity, and praise from ordinary soldiers begged the whole question of a chaplain's appropriate role in combat. In July 1862 a revealing debate erupted in the columns of Richmond's *Religious Herald*, a leading Baptist newspaper. An editorial cited reports of several chaplains wounded in recent battles and then disapprovingly commented that chaplains, like surgeons, belonged safely behind the lines. A letter from "A Wounded Chaplain" noted how being near the lines could inspire the men and aid the injured, tartly suggesting that those comfortably removed from the fighting were in no position to offer advice. The editor responded huffily that chaplains were no more virtuous than ministers at home. In any case, their duties were spiritual, and when they were wounded, their services were lost to the regiment. The controversy dragged on for several weeks until the editor finally allowed that each chaplain should use his own judgment. In point of fact, intrepid chaplains were sometimes ordered to the rear, and while after-action reports often praised their valor, officers never favored placing them in the thick of combat.[32]

Chaplains who risked their own lives to help the fallen won universal respect and admiration. When ordered back to the hospitals by Confederate general Earl Van Dorn, Father John B. Bannon angrily refused: "I am doing God's work, and He has no use for cowards and skulkers." Some chaplains who insisted on riding into battle like ordinary soldiers found themselves becoming hardened to the sights, sounds, and smells of carnage or caught up in the excitement of combat. A Methodist chaplain in a Georgia regiment shouted at retreating Yankees, "Go to hell, you damned sons of bitches."[33]

He apparently did more than shout and was later credited with shooting two Federals and slashing the throat of another. It is hard to say whether it would have been the swearing or the killing that would have most shocked his fellow Methodists. In any case he was hardly alone. Alabama Baptist Isaac Taylor Tichenor turned sharpshooter during the Battle of Shiloh, killing several of the enemy and, more importantly, inspiring his regiment. An equally adept Federal chaplain, Methodist Lorenzo Barber, became known for using his "telescopic-rifle" in battle, and this helped draw good crowds for his services. No doubt some of these accounts are exaggerated, and the press treated reports of fighting chaplains with as much humor as respect.[34]

Facing the danger of battle and the drudgery of camp, chaplains hardly knew what to make of their situation. In many ways they were like so many officers and enlisted men who struggled with fears and frustrations and sought to find their place in this vast and terrifying war. Some prided themselves on having kept to the narrow path of virtue. An Illinois chaplain claimed that he "did not knowingly compromise the truth of the gospel or yield to the solicitations of wrong." He would not even drink toasts with water but, rather like the Pharisees of Jesus's day, he may have mistaken the letter of the law for its spirit. The chaplain's role in promoting moral behavior was an especially delicate task that invited self-righteousness, misinterpretation, and alienation. Many chaplains felt isolated from the common soldiers. A Georgian recalled his struggle "to be a consistent Christian," admitting that "[I was] often sorely tried when I had to kneel in prayer among twenty men not one of whom followed my example."[35]

Looking back over his work in Virginia during the spring of 1862, a conscientious Pennsylvanian thought that his efforts had borne "some fruit" with a "goodly number strengthening in the Christian life." Yet more men appeared to be "hardening in sin," and so he could hardly rejoice over such meager achievements. However much a Federal chaplain's manual extolled the satisfactions, joys, and eternal rewards, it also conceded that a chaplain faced ten times more trials than a regular pastor. Even taking into account the introspection and guilt of a tireless chaplain such as William Edward Wiatt, who could never stop questioning his worth and work, for many the sense of disappointment and disillusionment was real and justified. Relentless criticism in the press and apparent public disdain left chaplains both misunderstood and unappreciated.[36]

Going home sometimes offered the only relief for a pervasive malaise that took a steady toll on the chaplaincy. A soldier in the 11th Louisiana reported that the regiment's chaplain had become so depressed by the men's religious apathy that "he is well nigh crazy, poor fellow." Some felt it necessary to preach a farewell sermon explaining why they were leaving. A Wisconsin chaplain asked the soldiers to forgive his faults but concluded that religious work in the army "seemed like preaching in a bar room." Perhaps that was precisely what chaplains needed to do, but many were not up to the challenge. Vainly trying to sleep in cold weather near a fire without a blanket, a disconsolate Maine chaplain mused that such a life is "totally unfit for me." He could "do these boys no spiritual good" beyond setting a good example, and that was far from enough.[37]

The worst chaplains did considerably less. They preached rarely, never missed a meal, and seldom ventured far from their tents—if they were in camp at all. Some officers tried to prod such lazy fellows into preaching more often but with little success. "Many [regiments] it is to be feared," claimed an 1863 report to the Southern Baptist Convention, "have hirelings who enjoy the revenue, but neglected the duties of their office." Such drones hung onto their posts without showing the least spark of initiative or energy. One chaplain's wife even harbored doubts about her husband's usefulness. Learning that his Wisconsin regiment was on the march, Lucy Fallows sharply commented: "You are not preaching; you are not even holding prayer meetings. I really can't see, dear, what you are accomplishing at all."[38]

Chaplains with a strong but narrow-minded sense of duty became part of the problem. In the summer of 1862, a group of officers in the 8th Connecticut held a meeting to discuss their new chaplain, who had been "nosing round into everybody's business & making himself exceedingly unpopular." He had apparently written waspish letters home and failed to understand that "he is not in New England with all the best part of society around him." That some chaplains never adjusted to such a radically new environment should not have been surprising but remained a problem. After deriding one minister for conducting a "mongrel sort of service," Union general George G. Meade lashed out against chaplains as a group, dividing them about equally between those who "do nothing" and others who "make themselves obnoxious by interfering in matters they have no business with."[39]

To be fair, pleasing officers and enlisted men from various religious traditions (or none) seemed all but impossible. Yet the sorriest chaplains proved worse than failures. In dismissing a chaplain who had "not walked circumspectly before his men," one Hoosier volunteer deemed him more a "renegade than a Teacher of Christ." In what were often termed vice-ridden regiments, a weak chaplain only made matters worse. A Wisconsin private dismissed one chaplain as a Catholic who "plays poker, smokes his cigars, drinks his whiskey," and thereby helped spread "a wrong opinion of Christianity" among already heathenish soldiers. It would be easy chalk up such comments to religious prejudice or temperance fanaticism, but complaints of drunkenness were far from unfounded. Take, for example, the Universalist preacher in a Maine regiment who reportedly could "guzzle more whiskey" than the heaviest drinkers. A New Yorker wryly commented that one Episcopalian chaplain might be of some use if he "only made as many prayers as he drinks glasses of whiskey." Then there was the sad case of Father Paul Gillen, a zealous chaplain much beloved by Catholics and Protestants alike whose drinking problem became so bad he was sent back to Notre Dame on medical leave.[40]

Skeptical and world-weary soldiers never tired of pointing out the chaplains' all-too-human frailties. They reveled in the hypocrisy of ministers who drank, gambled, and swore in part to ward off efforts to tame their own behavior or touch their hearts. A gruff and profane colonel in the 32nd Pennsylvania told Father Peter Tissot: "I know but one text of the Scriptures, 'Cain murdered Abel'; go do likewise." One freethinking Ohio volunteer stationed in western Virginia admitted that his regiment saw little need for spiritual guidance. The boys rather admired their broad-minded chaplain Joseph Fuchshuber, but when he left the regiment, "we had to settle things with heaven in our own way and on our initiative, which posed little trouble for us."[41]

That comment cut to the heart of the chaplains' dilemma. All too many officers and enlisted men doubted that these ministers served much purpose. Outright hostility cropped up from time to time, but polite indifference was much more common. In so often slighting the chaplains, perhaps the Union and Confederate governments reflected broader public attitudes. Churches sent a number of dedicated pastors to the armies, though never enough; the mediocre and poor chaplains in the ranks reinforced both military and civilian assumptions about the limited worth, if not worthlessness, of the entire lot.

―――――

It was hardly fair to evaluate a chaplain solely by camp religious services, but many Federals and Confederates did just that. And in rendering judgments, numbers sometimes counted for a great deal. A dedicated chaplain would preach several times a week or at least hold prayer meetings in between Sabbath services, a pattern often established during the first year of the war, though not always maintained. Less than two weeks after Fort Sumter, a New York Presbyterian editor called for a sermon every Sunday in every regiment so that the soldiers could remember the home they had left and the people gathering there for worship, his hope being that both the sermons and the memories could inoculate them against the evil influences of military life.[42]

Whatever might be said for the wonder-working power of a sermon, that hope often went unfulfilled. The men regularly complained (or perhaps rejoiced) that they had not heard a sermon or attended any kind of service for months. "We have no religious services here, and everything is dead, dead, dead," a staunch Pennsylvania Lutheran informed his parents. "The Lord is still with me," he assured them, but it was sad to note that so many men would be thrown back on their own meager reservoirs of faith. When a chaplain fell ill or resigned, if a regiment had no chaplain, "no services today" became a frequent notation in soldier diaries.[43]

Under the best of circumstances, worship in the army was just not like what men were used to at home. Near Petersburg during the summer of 1864, the location for worship often depended on the likelihood of Yankee shelling, and in any case Confederate adjutant Walter Taylor could not feel as devout in the open air. On the other hand, a beautiful setting might stir religious feeling. Watching soldiers parade in without their arms and then sitting on a clover-blanketed hillside with woods in the background, Charles Brewster of the 10th Massachusetts declared it all a "grand sight" and considered the men's voices raised to sing that favorite New England hymn "Old Hundred" better than any organ music. Once fall came and the air grew crisp, attendance would fall off, and in winter services might be canceled altogether. Yet throughout the 1862–63 lull between campaign seasons, Pennsylvanian Andrew Jackson Hartsock held prayer meetings at night regardless of the cold. Four days before Christmas, he observed how the weather tested men's religious devotion but was pleased by a decent turnout for morning and evening worship. Even in mid-March, his fingers "stiff with cold," Hartsock held his prayer meeting.[44]

From the beginning of the war, shelter became critical for promoting religious life in the army. When McClellan asked the War Department for permission to use boards for erecting places of worship at Camp Denison near Cincinnati, irreverent Secretary of War Simon Cameron wired back, "The Lord's will be done." That ended up being much easier said than done. A Massachusetts chaplain carefully gathered materials and even had carpenters making benches, but before a single service could he held, his surplus hospital tent was hauled away for a court-martial. In some companies and regiments, pious soldiers and chaplains raised money for building chapels; in others, voluntary organizations including the Christian Commission donated tent canvas to cover the wooden chapels.[45]

Catholics often made do with a simple chapel consisting of an altar in a small tent. Peter Tissot described how the "Blessed Sacrament" was kept in a "wooden tabernacle" made by a soldier, and a candle burned there constantly; nearby benches could accommodate a dozen or so men. Protestant chaplains needed somewhat larger structures, usually fashioned from some combination of logs or clapboards and tent canvas. They might decorate the interior with evergreen branches and build a makeshift pulpit with scripture verses carved into pieces of board hanging above. Some chapels were much cruder if not ramshackle; many were drafty and blew down easily in a storm. One Pennsylvanian described a "new church" as "cheap" but the best their small congregation could afford.[46]

Whether the setting was ornate or simple, the singing, praying, and preaching became centerpieces of army religious life. Services typically began with hymns, scripture reading, and prayers, followed by a sermon perhaps delivered from an old hardtack box serving as the pulpit. The men sat on benches or logs or lay on the ground. Most chaplains held Sunday worship after the morning inspection, though some conducted afternoon or, more often, evening services as well. A Union chaplain's manual recommended services last no more than three-quarters of an hour, but it was difficult for long-winded ministers to hold sermons to the suggested twenty minutes.[47]

Priests felt an especially strong obligation to regularly conduct mass—the very soul of Catholic faith and practice. While stationed in Kentucky, Father

*Father Thomas H. Mooney performing mass, 69th New York State Militia
(Library of Congress)*

Peter Paul Cooney heard confessions each morning and held mass on Sunday; others traveled from regiment to regiment administering the sacrament. Even on the march, dedicated priests would quickly set up their altars and tents at the end of the day, offering short sermons urging the men to remember that their first loyalty must be to God. Given the small number of Catholic chaplains, the strain on time and energy could be overwhelming. Serving in the 1st Missouri Brigade (Confederate), Father John B. Bannon once heard thirty confessions in three hours. Near Washington on a July day in 1861, Father Peter Tissot said mass in two different regiments and prepared seventy-five men for communion.[48]

Kneeling in the mud in chapels made of cedar branches, Catholic soldiers partook of their church's ancient rituals, and an altar fashioned from a cracker box would have to suffice. On a snowy Easter Sunday at Guiney Station, Virginia, Louisiana chaplain James B. Sheeran was surprised to find a large crowd gathered early in the morning; despite the cold, men knelt with heads uncovered to receive the sacrament. Such religious devotion became intertwined with patriotism. "First convince the Irish Catholic that the cause is a just one," the editor of the *New York Tablet* advised. Then "assure him" of enjoying the "free exercise of his religion" and "there will be little difficulty in prevailing upon him to take up arms." Catholic soldiers rejoiced at seeing a priest, especially right before a battle, and Father Cooney believed that a priest in the army became a "direct instrument in the hands of God to bring these poor souls from the brink of hell." Men who cared little for religion at home "may die good Catholics in the army" so long as "zealous chaplains" attended to their spiritual needs.[49]

Just as priests administering the sacrament stood at the heart of Catholic worship, a preacher delivering a sermon had long been the centerpiece of a Protestant service. Many chaplains understood they would be judged by a tough audience—in many ways tougher than stiff-necked congregations back home. Soldiers appreciated chaplains who made a sincere effort and willingly listened to those they admired, men who had already befriended them, men willing to hold services under adverse conditions, men who served as earnest ministers of the Lord. To be sure, most soldiers agreed that short sermons were best, and a sense of humor helped a great deal. Seeing that some prankster had placed a pack of cards on top of the Bible right before the service, Chaplain Henry Clay Trumbull of the 10th Connecticut knew he was being tested. Rather than launching into a fiery denunciation of gambling, he quietly put the cards away and said to the regiment's colonel, "Hearts are trumps today, and I have a full hand." Yet Trumbull also recognized that the men needed to take him seriously. Even though at home he had preached from notes, in camp he wrote out his sermons in part to draw a contrast between a minister's formality and a pastor's humanity as he dealt with the troops in different roles and settings.[50]

Preaching to congregations of mixed background and beliefs required fluency and diplomacy, a knack for making short and simple points with good illustrations—imitating methods perfected by Jesus, a Union chaplain's manual suggested. To keep the sermon "interesting," a vague but significant word that cropped up in countless soldier comments about successful preaching, was equally important. And if the chaplain was eloquent as well, so much the better. Hearing a moving sermon with several "allusions to our friends at home, and their prayers for us far away," a Massachusetts volunteer shed "tears which I could not—indeed, which cared not to restrain." On such occasions soldiers felt blessed, comforted, and sometimes seized by the power of the Holy Spirit.[51]

Many would have been satisfied if their chaplain simply preached a little better than usual. That minimal standard often prevailed because mediocre sermons were never in short supply, so the average soldier showed his dissatisfaction by refusing to attend services. One man reported how "it was painful to me to listen" to an especially "poor" preacher; another dismissed the regimental chaplain as the "worst bore we have." Too many chaplains appeared diffident about their pulpit duties. Some spoke so quietly it is little wonder they preached only a few times a year, and the apparent lack of energy always elicited soldier comment. Of course, each man brought to a service expectations about style if not about content, and that became a problem in its own right. A perceptive Union staff officer disdained the "common and often ungrammatical" language of one camp preacher but admitted that his "clear and manly" ideas reached the enlisted men attending the service. Soldiers of simple faith complaining about "intellectual" ministers who failed to preach about salvation or grumbling about stiff Episcopalians and arid Unitarians—all this was to be expected. Words such as "empty," "sonorous," and "dry" readily came to mind and often to tongue and pen. After listening to a Massachusetts chaplain deliver a short but tedious discourse on the relationship of Christianity to government (long a staple in New England churches), the devout young New Yorker John McMahon suspected that such ministers had been unable to find work back home.[52]

But the soldiers themselves were far from agreed on what constituted a weak sermon. Even as some complained about learned discourses, others thought the problems ran in the opposite direction. A Confederate lieutenant was appalled by a chaplain who catered to the "lower class of the regiment." Other ministers seemed utterly ignorant of basic theology. Ranters and shouters offended soldiers used to a more sedate delivery and more sophisticated sermons. Denominational prejudices cropped up in critical comments aimed at Methodists and Baptists who favored a camp meeting style of preaching. Some preachers tried to recycle old sermons, the best example being a Federal chaplain in Louisiana who preached on infant baptism and closed his sermon with an appeal to mothers.[53]

Henry Clay Trumbull adjusted his preaching to the times and to conditions in camp. Rejecting talk about the supposedly demoralizing effects of military life, he maintained that soldiers in the field developed a strong sense of manhood and morality. Like many civilian ministers who became caught up in wartime civil religion, Trumbull thought his men should be grateful for what the Lord had done in preserving their nation and their souls, and he offered a glorious vision of soldiers returning home as triumphant Christians and saviors of the Union. Confederate camp sermons sometimes compared the southern nation to ancient Israel, with suitable references to the prophets. These were not mere experiments in biblical typology but rather efforts to inspire young southerners to become their nation's Joshuas or Davids. On a less lofty and more practical level, chaplains hoped to steel men for the continuing hardships of army life while reinforcing patriotism with healthy doses of religion, though a Michigan colonel worried about his regiment's chaplain putting too much emphasis on facing sickness, death, and a host of other troubles, perhaps with demoralizing effect.[54]

A chaplain with John Hunt Morgan's Confederate cavalry reportedly prayed for the Lord to "strike dead every man, woman, and child in the United States" if that was required to establish southern independence. Though usually handled with less ferocity, a blending of piety with patriotism was predictable and inevitable. Some soldiers—especially those from more conservative churches that shunned political preaching—strongly objected. A Hoosier enlisted man grew tired of bloodthirsty discourses or abolition sermons. "Men of God," a Wisconsin surgeon could almost spit those words out of his mouth shortly after the bloodbath at Fredericksburg, "at their nightly prayers, they in the same breath thank God for the murders we have been permitted to perpetuate—the misery to inflict—and ask for peace on earth, and good will to man." The spiritual hubris sometimes became unbearable. To a Confederate doctor serving on General Sterling Price's staff, an Arkansas chaplain sounded "far too confident of the mind of the almighty and what his designs towards us as a nation are—better not be wise above what is written."[55]

Soldiers expected chaplains to explain (or at least try to explain) God's will and the workings of divine providence—though more in their own lives and than in their nation's history. In point of fact, most camp sermons hewed closely to standard evangelical themes: the men were to love God, follow Christ, and walk in the paths of righteousness. With death all around, the need for salvation became especially urgent. Well might the men ask on the eve of battle how they might be saved, and chaplains pressed that vital question in both sermons and altar calls. Nearly all the sermons of Chaplain J. J. D. Renfroe in the 10th Alabama, for example, covered this familiar ground. Not surprisingly, sermons mentioned the last judgment, anticipated eternal life, and glorified a heavenly home. In the midst of fighting in the Shenandoah Valley during the summer of 1862, a Confederate artillerist found just the right imagery to describe the effects of gospel preaching in his camp: "We are getting in a goodly supply of heavenly ammunition from the arsenal of truth. . . . The ammunition is fixed and ready to fire at all times and under all circumstances, and I hope that we may all pack at least some of it away in the cartridge box of fortitude for immediate and constant use, and not act like the great majority of the world, both saints and sinners, who use it all up in empty ceremonials on Sunday, having not enough left on Monday morning to make a decent skirmish against the inroads of wrong-doing, hypocrisy, and rascality."[56]

The most receptive men variously described services as solemn or impressive with congregations showing considerable feeling; sweet communion with the Lord stirred deep emotion and sometimes moved men to tears. An especially touching service could dredge up fond memories and lead to a bout of homesickness. Private Robert A. Moore of the 17th Mississippi thought of the many soldiers who had no chance to hear the gospel preached in their camps, and he savored every opportunity for Sunday worship.[57]

Indifference or hostility toward religious services is more difficult to interpret or even categorize. Some men felt too righteous in their own eyes to rub elbows with sinful comrades, while others objected to the forms of worship. In the 71st New York one hundred men trooped off to a local Catholic church one Sunday, but another seventy Catholic soldiers chose to drill for an hour in the sun rather than hear Congregational chaplain Joseph Twichell preach. When soldiers did attend a service, many appeared impassive. Early in the war, according to a Confederate chaplain, men would sit with their hats on, chat with each other, smoke, and walk about while he tried to deliver a sermon. In a Pennsylvania regiment, some of the boys played mumblety-peg and largely ignored the service. Despite their dismay over low attendance, the more perceptive chaplains realized that the tepid response may have had little to do with their preaching; a goodly number of men simply had no interest in religious services.[58]

Voluntarism had long been a hallmark of American religious life and now meshed with the idea of the citizen soldier fighting for his country. In the army, however, the price of voluntarism ran high because many officers appeared apathetic and attendance at services lagged. Historian Joseph Glatthaar has estimated that no more than 10 to 20 percent of the men serving with the United States Colored Troops were religiously active, and there is little reason to believe that numbers for the Union or Confederate forces more generally would have been much higher, at least before religious revivals began in the fall of 1862. Some chaplains favored compulsory attendance and occasionally won the support of officers, but such policies caused considerable grumbling from the enlisted men especially on uncomfortably hot or cold days. In the 5th Maine, a corporal's guard patrolled the camp during Sunday worship rounding up stragglers. Watching a chaplain preaching to some prisoners, a cynical Michigan lieutenant sneered that the "only way he can get a congregation is to take those who are under arrest."[59]

At least this chaplain had both a captive and presumably well-behaved congregation. Many services took place in the midst of bustling camps with soldiers pointedly and often noisily going about their duties. Men might be chopping wood, cussing a mule, playing euchre, or wagering their pay (if not their souls) in a game of chuck-a-luck. During one meeting, rowdies danced, whistled, and stamped their feet while the chaplain was praying. One soldier considered such a scene so "ludicrous" that he went back to work on the company accounts. Some men made a point of showing up in a most ragged and unkempt state just to see how the poor chaplain would react. At a camp near Bolivar, Tennessee, a group of impious soldiers held their own service during which "they sang and prayed in blasphemous mockery." In the 154th New York, pranksters squirted mule urine on the men attending a prayer meeting and during another service dropped cartridges down a chimney.[60]

Blaming chaplains for failing to reach or control undisciplined young men away from their families for the first time ignored the deeper roots of such behavior. Before the war, large numbers of Americans had attended church on a regular basis, but their degree of religious commitment varied greatly, and army camps proved to be poor places for nurturing faith, much less piety— especially among men who as civilians had shown little religious interest. In their more candid moments, ministers back home would have acknowledged the formidable and often insuperable obstacles to reaping a bounteous harvest of souls in the army.

A majority of men in any camp found the "worship of God is distasteful," one veteran chaplain candidly observed, and only a minority would likely attend services regularly. A thoughtful enlisted man in the 9th New York tried to explain why chaplains faced so many difficulties. "A minister and a soldier are antipodes in sentiment," Edward King Wightman informed his brother. "The one preaches 'election' and the other fatalism. The minister prides himself upon the clearness and eloquence with which he *elucidates* his principles, and the soldier is equally careful to show by his *actions* that he risks everything on his." Yet even the worldly-wise Wightman believed that the earnest chaplain who preached a "practical" as opposed to a "theoretical" Christianity could touch the hearts of such men.[61] And so the question remained: how many soldiers would become believers? Doubts on that score flowed back and forth from army camps to home front, troubling ministers, churches, and the men themselves. The spiritual stakes of the Civil War mounted with precious souls at risk, especially with so many lost sheep and so few shepherds.

CHRISTIAN SOLDIERS

Put on the whole armour of God, that ye may be
able to stand against the wiles of the devil.
— Ephesians 6:11

Northerners and southerners alike affirmed that Christian soldiers not only would lead their armies to victory but would return as triumphant soldiers of the cross. Many churches came to see the army as one vast home mission field with overtones of millennial glory. Such soaring expectations were doomed to disappointment, and the most candid observers conceded that most soldiers never became Christian soldiers.

The numbers offered by contemporaries and historians are estimates at best. One scholar has recently suggested that the devout made up no more than 10 to 25 percent of the Union armies, a range that certainly appears reasonable. Early in 1862, a Pennsylvania chaplain reported that there were more professing Christians in the Army of the Potomac than in any modern army, but he still suspected their numbers fell "below those who either make no profession, or are among the openly wicked." That the proportions changed later in the war—in the wake of revivalism and thinning of the ranks—is likely, though to what extent is still hard to gauge.[1] Many of the most fervent Christian soldiers came from deeply religious backgrounds in the first place, and weighing the mix of backsliders and converts is impossible. That Christian soldiers remained a minority in the Federal armies is a cautious but useful conclusion.

Some Federals in fact believed that their foes were far more devout and cited evidence of a strong religious spirit expressed in letters found on battlefields. Yet even the most sanguine (and inflated) Confederate estimates claimed that no more than a third of the soldiers in the field (albeit a larger proportion of the officers) were committed Christians. As with the Federals, early in the war the pious appeared to be badly outnumbered by the indifferent or skeptical.[2] The powerful revivals in the Army of Northern Virginia and later in the Army of Tennessee undoubtedly changed this picture, though, as with the Federals, the Christian soldiers were still in a minority.

Perceptions were entirely another matter. Religious editors, speakers on behalf of army missions, and chaplains emphasized how much the soldiers craved the message of salvation. And certainly the idealistic young officers who remained steadfast in their patriotism and their faith exerted a powerful influence out of proportion to their numbers—and were also the most likely to leave behind written evidence testifying to their piety.[3] The idea of the Confederate as Christian soldier proved to be a vital and remarkably enduring part of Confederate identity. Yankees too would have been quick to stake their own claims of armies filled with believers taking up arms against a godless rebellion. But this presents a much too stratospheric view of the matter, because for the Civil War generation the fate of individual souls remained of greatest importance and that was true no less in the armies than at home.

———

Worship and even the process of conversion began with music. In one New Jersey regiment, a group of men gathered up by the chaplain would begin with a hymn, and there would soon be a good-sized congregation. Men in the camps clearly enjoyed singing. Here was their chance to join with comrades whether to express a heartfelt faith or while away time. A Maine volunteer remembered how the boys in his regiment especially loved "The Old Hundred," even when there seemed little occasion for such a song of praise. In the midst of the 1864 Overland campaign, "They would take it up . . . without any apparent occasion for it and without the least suspicion of irony. They didn't bother to think how many voices the war had stopped from praising God. They sang merely because they liked it; the tone was pleasing and the volume of sound was grand." Soldiers especially welcomed the arrival of hymnbooks. "Much of the time formerly spent in card-playing is now spent in singing these sweet hymns," one minister reported to the South Carolina Baptist Convention with perhaps more hope than accuracy.[4]

However that might be, when it came to singing, soldiers had decided preferences. They loved the songs of salvation with words that spoke of the Savior's love and offered hope of redemption. The emphasis was evangelical, though some popular hymns included more martial themes, putting equal emphasis on "Christian" and "soldier." In 1858 Presbyterian minister George Duffield Jr. had written a lively new hymn that began, "Stand up, stand up for Jesus, ye soldiers of the cross" and spoke in decidedly warlike tones. Words such as "victory," "foe," "battles," "trumpet," "armor," "danger," "host," "column," "strife," all evoked images of a holy crusade against sin and the devil. The tune was stirring and easily sung. The promise of victory and the assurance that "death itself is gain" helped steel men not only for spiritual combat but for meeting their temporal enemies on the battlefield.[5]

For the devout, the joy of singing blended with the solace of prayer, as sol-

diers most always enjoyed prayer meetings more than formal worship services. A chaplain might hold sessions during the week, but just as often the
men themselves gathered on their own—if only in groups of two or three. One
stormy night in the middle of the war, a delegate from the United States Christian Commission observed the warmth and enthusiasm of men whose prayers
were "full of penitence and sorrowing for sin, full of love, full of thanks, earnest thanks to God for His benefits and especially for the privileges of the prayer
meeting."[6]

For both believers and seekers, the prayer meeting became a spiritual
haven amid the din of reckless fellows who cared little about the fate of their
souls. Quoting a North Carolina newspaper, one tract claimed that the prayer
meeting "elevates and refines the man, and counteracts that brutish, selfish
disposition, so generally evinced in some portions of the army." In such circumstances, the determination and example of a few soldiers meant keeping
a spark of Christianity alive and even glowing in a regiment or brigade where
piety might have been extinguished altogether. One optimistic Connecticut
volunteer who had just returned from a prayer meeting compared the camp
to the city, "the greater the temptations & activity of life the stronger & brighter
the Christian life." Men spoke from the heart with a kind of rude eloquence
that carried deep conviction. They wanted to get right with God and their comrades in arms, or as one Virginian put it, "My brethren, I'se got notin' agin nobody, and I hope nobody's got nothin' agin me."[7]

Regimental churches and other groups recruited men willing to make more
formal and sustained commitments, foreswearing profanity, alcohol, and
gambling. Camp churches usually required that men subscribe to a general
statement of faith such as the Apostles' Creed without getting down to doctrinal fine points or sacramental details. The emphasis was on being as inclusive
as possible, and in the camp of the 6th Indiana, the chaplain admitted two
Universalists who insisted on crossing out any references to the resurrection
of Christ before adding their names to the church roll.[8]

In a few camps, Sunday schools flourished—yet another evocative reminder
of home. Methodist soldiers organized class meetings, small groups that had
traditionally nurtured faith and monitored behavior. Enlisted men taught
Bible classes, encouraging comrades to memorize passages.[9] For in singing,
praying, and studying the Bible, the men developed a more vibrant faith in the
camp, whether based on a long-standing religious commitment or a recent
conversion. In a nation that been greatly affected by New Measures revivalism,
soldiers learned to seek their own salvation. The belief that ordinary people
could read and expound Holy Writ for themselves seemed readily applicable in

the army where regular services were sometimes scarce. For Protestants especially, the Bible—generally in the form of a pocket New Testament—became essential equipment in camps reportedly filled with unbelievers.

During the antebellum decades, few Bibles had been printed in the South; state and local Bible societies had worked with the American Bible Society. In March 1862 delegates from the major Protestant denominations met in Augusta, Georgia, to form the Bible Society of the Confederate States. A Charleston publisher also produced Bibles, but the supplies were never adequate.[10]

Some Bibles slipped through the blockade, and Virginia Presbyterians approached British groups seeking assistance. Despite fears that "foreigners" might not only try to profit from the war but also promote abolition, Moses Drury Hoge sailed to England representing the Virginia Bible Society. Using a few Confederate bonds and soliciting donations, Hoge secured nearly 300,000 Testaments or shorter selections from the scriptures that were then shipped to the Confederacy in small lots, though many never made it through the blockade. On reading that the Yankees ("creatures who will probably not care a snap for it") had seized a shipment of Bibles, Virginian Nancy Emerson became so enraged she could hardly sleep for thinking about poor Confederate soldiers being deprived of God's word.[11]

But only one of every five or six Confederate soldiers, according to the best estimates, ever received a Bible or Testament, and only a fraction of these had been printed in the South. In striking contrast during the war's first year, at the American Bible Society headquarters in New York, sixteen power presses churned out nearly four hundred thousand Bibles (mostly pocket Testaments), and the yearly distribution of Bibles to northern troops soon reached a million per year. Even at the beginning of the war, twenty-nine New York City regiments left for the camps fully armored with the Holy Scriptures.[12]

Keeping tabs on the supply and demand for Bibles meant far more than maintaining accounts or measuring success through sheer numbers. The New York Bible Society provided German, French, Italian, Spanish, Dutch, Swedish, and Portuguese translations for the many polyglot regiments. Catholic soldiers usually refused the King James Bibles, but copies of the authorized Douay Bible were relatively scarce. In a scathing editorial entitled "Swaddling the Soldiers," one New York Catholic hoped that no member of the church would accept a "spurious and mutilated Bible" and strongly objected to proselytizing by the American Bible Society. He sarcastically asked whether Oliver Cromwell's men had been supplied with King James Bibles when they had slaughtered so many Irishmen. That final remark carried an unintended irony because in fact reprints of Cromwell's brief *Soldier's Bible* appeared in Union and Confederate camps.[13]

Few men turned down a Testament even when they had little use for one. By the middle of the war, importunate delegates from the Christian Commission still assumed that many fellows lacked Bibles and their efforts to thrust a Testament into the hands of any passing soldier bordered on the ludicrous. Battle-hardened veterans noted how they would have preferred better food or extra socks. When a chaplain handed out Bibles in the 5th New York, one young man extracted a sizable wad of tobacco from his mouth, stuck it in the middle of his Testament, and "contemptuously closed it with force, that as much of the book might be destroyed as possible by the saturation of the filthy spittle in the weed." A cavalry officer in Arkansas tore out pages from one Iowan's Bible for use at the camp sinks. Many Testaments were abandoned or lost on battlefields. After the rebels had captured his Bible at Shiloh, one Federal ruefully hoped "the man that took it will make better use of it than I did."[14]

In point of fact, soldiers did read the scriptures, especially in the absence of other reading matter. One Confederate who was not especially religious made it through the New Testament and Psalms twice in one month. Trying to honor the wishes of parents or wives, more pious men studied a few chapters each day and even read aloud to tent mates. An Illinois volunteer found many men making at least some effort to peruse their Testaments, however much "it appears like seed thrown on stony ground." For soldiers who could not always separate religious conviction from army superstitions, the scriptures possessed certain magical qualities. After Confederate general John Bell Hood randomly opened his Bible to Psalms 118:17 ("I shall not die but live . . ."), he somehow knew he would survive the war.[15]

The twice-wounded Hood did survive—barely—but for soldiers trying to buttress their spiritual lives or seeking salvation, religious reading material became virtual lifelines. Chaplains and ministers made this point repeatedly as they begged for money to send Bibles and tracts to the camps. Tireless workers such as Reverend Alfred E. Dickinson, who directed army colportage for southern Baptists, spoke in churches and wrote countless letters to religious papers. "How many leisure hours may be rescued from scenes of vice and turned to good account by having a colporteur in every regiment?" was a question designed to tug at heartstrings and purse strings.[16]

Dickinson proposed that a thousand Baptists donate five dollars each for army colportage—not yet realizing that wartime inflation would soon wipe out the value of even that large a sum. Women's organizations sponsored concerts or went door-to-door soliciting contributions.[17] A congregation could collect a few hundred dollars here and there, but this equivalent of the biblical widow's mite did not come close to meeting the need. Local Baptist associations might raise as much as a thousand dollars, and state conventions proudly reported how many Bibles, hymnbooks, and pages of tracts they had furnished for the camps, yet even then the supply never kept up with demand.[18] The resources of individuals, congregations, and denominations appeared stretched to the limit—especially given the pressing welfare needs of Confederate soldier families and other demands placed on the churches.

The better-organized northerners could rely on the American Bible Society, the American Tract Society, and later the United State Christian Commission along with the greater resources of their churches. If enough Bibles and tracts were not supplied for the camps, one chaplain warned, the poor soldiers might be reduced to reading sensation-seeking newspapers or the vulgar Shakespeare. The thought of men turning to "vile books and pamphlets pandering to the lowest passions," as a secretary for the American Tract Society described the problem, should elicit generous donations from Christians at home. In a special appeal to pious women, a Christian Commission agent claimed that convalescing soldiers quickly threw aside their decks of cards whenever they received religious books and papers.[19]

In the 1840s the American Tract Society had begun using the word "colporteur"—a French term dating back to the Reformation—to describe an agent who distributed religious literature. During the Civil War, northern and southern churches sent colporteurs into the field loaded down with Testaments and tracts. The best ones did more than simply hand out tracts; they talked with the soldiers and encouraged them to keep the faith or to find it.[20]

War itself created a new world for religious publishing. In the Confederacy, inflation and paper shortages forced religious papers to either close up shop or reduce their size, even as editors worked to include more war news, adjust their content to the needs of the soldiers, and more generally support the Confederate administration.[21] Presbyterians, Methodists, and Baptists churned out special soldier papers and often distributed free copies in the camps, where a single issue might be read by a dozen or more men. Reports of soldiers eagerly gathering around a chaplain with his bundle of papers warmed evangelical hearts; one Federal was especially excited about receiving a copy of the Methodist *Northern Christian Advocate* because this was the paper his pious mother always read. With tears reportedly running down his cheeks, he repaired to his tent to devour the entire issue, advertisements and all.[22]

Religious periodicals and tracts presented a consistent evangelical message larded with repeated warnings about the evils of swearing, drinking, and gambling. The nearness of death and the urgency of conversion loomed large for thousands of men preparing to face the enemy in battle. The most popular tracts offered hope of salvation with appeals to home values and especially the influence of pious mothers. *A Mother's Parting Words to Her Soldier* by Virginia Baptist Jeremiah Jeter was a runaway success with 250,000 copies in circulation.[23] As one perceptive northern chaplain observed, the soldiers preferred lively tracts with "narrative and dialogue" to dense columns filled with dry doctrine. Practicality and portability appealed to soldiers seeking simple messages of faith and comfort in the face of danger.[24]

Yet like many camp sermons, most of the tracts were not specifically geared for men in uniform. The theme of salvation was a timeless one, and standard religious fare remained just that, despite the war. Episcopalians issued condensed prayer books with little attention to soldier needs or to civil religion. The American Tract Society and its Confederate counterparts reprinted old tracts for use in the camps with an emphasis on traditional evangelism. A New York chaplain did not hesitate to distribute captured Confederate tracts because they differed little from those found in any northern camp.[25]

Admonitions about the shortness of life belabored the obvious in mid-nineteenth America even without a bloody war, but tracts and sermons urged young people to reckon with their own mortality and to make their decision for Christ today. Because human eyes and hearts could not discern the future or the dangers that lay ahead, Robert Lewis Dabney advised a congregation of Virginia soldiers to avoid "procrastination." A few northern and southern tracts warned about the Day of Judgment, sometimes in graphic detail, but the messages were usually more comforting. All the soldiers needed was a simple, childlike faith, a religion of the heart rather than the head, and salvation was theirs for the asking because, once they received Christ, the priceless gift of eternal life would follow. Here was comfort for the weary enlisted man and officer far from home.[26]

Facing imminent death, whether from disease or bullets, soldiers should be alert and ready. Northern Unitarian John F. W. Ware wrote a special tract for pickets suggesting that young men needed to be as watchful as Christ would be and avoid the sin of being "surprised." By the same token, soldiers must be prepared to meet their Maker because physical and spiritual dangers lurked everywhere. Soldiers fought a two-front battle against their enemies and against Satan, and in either case hesitation and delay could be fatal. The message then for Federals and Confederates was to rally both to the cross and to the flag, and repeated talk of Jesus as the "captain of salvation" drove home the connection between religious faith and patriotic duty. But even then, for all the martial language and occasional references to national deliverance, the primary mission remained the same: each man must enlist in the cause of the King of Kings.[27]

How the soldiers received these messages is a difficult and, in many ways, unanswerable question, but there are some tantalizing hints. A few men preferred having the chaplain hand them a tract privately—safely removed from the mockery of irreverent comrades. One dedicated South Carolina colporteur delighted in men crowding around his tent, hungry for something to read and thirsty for the truths of salvation. Another claimed that soldiers who had never made any profession of faith and even inveterate card players accepted the little tracts politely if not always enthusiastically. Yet few soldiers mentioned religious literature in their letters and diaries, and some who gladly received Testaments had little use for tracts. Denominational reports, the church press, and the colporteurs naturally emphasized successes, but their reams of numbers tended to obscure three important points. Many men were starved for reading material of any kind. Even though some soldiers claimed to crave the tracts, those who did so were often quite pious in the first place. Finally, touching accounts of men reading tracts while shedding tears of repentance and joy contained considerable elements of truth, but they were undoubtedly crafted to help groups such as the United States Christian Commission raise more money for army evangelism.[28]

Even with these qualifications in mind, it appears that a significant number of soldiers genuinely appreciated receiving religious literature. "Give me one of those [tracts]," one rough-spoken Virginian told a minister early in the war, "to keep me out of devilment." Church papers prompted memories of home and promises made to parents and friends. According to one Confederate writer, some soldiers snatched the tracts out of the chaplain's hands while others tossed them aside, and the author could not resist drawing an object lesson about these men's contrasting fates in eternity. On the whole though, the consensus of colporteurs and some soldiers was that uplifting reading material accomplished some good. Men who had once been among the chief sinners in the ranks claimed that a tract had converted them; others reported how religious literature had prevented backsliding in camps filled with vice.[29]

———

Colporteurs typically ignored denominational differences, though Baptists and Presbyterians accused each other of trying to slip sectarian views on baptism into the tracts.[30] And despite much goodwill and cooperation in the army, denominational prejudices hardly disappeared. In a Georgia regiment filled with Methodists and Baptists, one enlisted man asked to be excused from a Presbyterian chaplain's preaching because he could not in good conscience "listen to any but a hardshell [Baptist]." The always censorious Lutheran chaplain John H. Stuckenberg wrote in his diary: "I am surrounded by Methodists who are very clever but lack cultivation."[31]

Such comments, however, were far from typical. In the camps, everyone from northern Unitarians to southern Methodists seemed caught up in an ecumenical spirit that prided itself on suspending sectarian rivalries at least for the war's duration. Patriotism made questions about sprinkling, bishops, and predestination seem less important and certainly not fit subjects for camp sermons. "War liberalizes," one New England Unitarian rejoiced. "The old creeds give way. . . . It is a privilege to live in such an age. The days of the Revolution were less glorious than our own. Christianity was never before such a power in the world." A Mississippi Methodist agreed, claiming that in his camp the "partitions are well-nigh broken down" and that "we know each other here only as Christian brethren traveling to a better world."[32]

The Catholic-Protestant chasm appeared less amenable to wartime good feeling though hardly unbridgeable. Colporteurs, one New York editor complained, "force their pernicious and ranting tracts, bibles, &c upon our Catholic soldiers." In truth, these soldiers received relatively little Catholic reading matter despite efforts by northern and southern parishes to supply prayer books and other devotional works. Complaints about Protestant "trash" did not always prevent Catholic soldiers from reading it when more orthodox materials were unavailable.[33]

Complaints about chaplains were far more serious. According to one Catholic editor, bigoted Protestants had denied Catholic chaplains the "privilege of discharging any of their sacred functions in or around their Puritanical precincts." Protestants and Catholics grumbled about each other's chaplains. Father Peter Tissot in the 37th New York was delighted to overhear a doctor denounce Protestant chaplains as "humbugs" and for his part dismissed them as "worse than useless." In some brigades relations between Catholic and Protestant chaplains were icy at best.[34]

Yet as a practical matter, William R. Eastman recalled, a chaplain simply could not afford to indulge sectarian bigotry. Early in the war, New York Congregationalist Joseph Twichell met Father Joseph B. O'Hagan, also serving in a New York regiment, and the two young chaplains not only concluded a "treaty of amity, peace, and cooperation" but soon became fast friends. Although Twichell still worried about a priest placing himself between a dying man and God, he decided that O'Hagan had reasonable views on matters of faith. For his part, Twichell sounded increasingly less dogmatic about the truths of Protestantism. One cold night shortly after the Battle of Fredericksburg, they lay down to sleep putting their blankets together to stay warm. O'Hagan began laughing, confiding to Twichell how the situation thoroughly amused him, "a

Jesuit priest and a New England Puritan minister—of the worst sort—spooned close together under the same blanket. I wonder what the angels think." He quickly answered his own question, "I think they like it."[35]

Whatever the angels thought, the Catholic chaplains rejoiced (perhaps with a hint of unholy pride) when Protestant soldiers attended their services. Even sermons on blasphemy, mortal sin, and hell drew large, mixed congregations. Dedicated priests won the respect of Protestants in their regiments, and their example undoubtedly reduced religious bigotry. After preaching to many Protestants and baptizing several, Father Peter Paul Cooney claimed that "prejudice to the Church is gone almost entirely." Indeed, such goodwill even became a source of sectional conceit. Hoping to score propaganda points, a Richmond editor pointed to Federal destruction of Catholic Church property while he lauded the Confederacy as a nation that prized religious tolerance and welcomed Catholics in the struggle for liberty against a common enemy—the Puritanical Yankees.[36]

Catholic hostility toward Protestants appeared to wane. Chaplain Twichell found that two-thirds of the men at his services were Irish Catholics, and he thought it best to approach them as a friend rather than as a Protestant clergyman. One gruff colonel pointed out to a skeptical enlisted man that, even though they were both Catholics, it would do them no harm to attend a Protestant service. For sure, this more liberal spirit developed only slowly and then incompletely. An Alabama Baptist chaplain happily prayed with a Catholic soldier but in their discussion kept running up against the "central errors of priestcraft." Sympathy for fallen enemies faced religious roadblocks. A North Carolina Baptist visiting hospitals filled with Federal wounded after the Battle of Malvern Hill was surprised to find "many professing Christians among them" but soon discovered that all too many believed "in the good which can be done departed souls by Popes and Priests." Yet his response was fairly mild: a proposal to establish Sunday schools in the armies.[37]

Rather than becoming model Baptists, perfect Methodists, or exemplary Catholics, the men should simply become Christian soldiers. Both religious and national unity in part rested on this ideal. This was largely a matter of biography, and throughout the war religious newspaper editors and ordinary citizens alike took heart from the saintly lives of everyone from the most exalted commanders to the humblest privates. The spiritual hagiography began at the top with men who acquired reputations as Christian generals. To cite the most famous examples, the well-known piety and powerful example of a Robert E. Lee or a Stonewall Jackson convinced many Confederates that religious devotion permeated their ranks. Faith in Christian generals reinforced a belief that God would surely smile on a cause led by such righteous men.

Robert E. Lee would go down in Confederate history as the ultimate Christian soldier, an outcome that would have surprised the young Lee, who faithfully attended services and prayed but also fretted about his sinfulness and waited until the age of forty-six to join the Episcopal Church. His most frequent expressions of religious sentiments occurred in family letters with brief and quite general references to the role of providence in the war. Even his prayerful agonizing over whether to follow Virginia out of the Union carried with it a kind of stoic sadness rather than any particular biblical or theological content.[38]

During the war, Lee attended camp services and promoted the cause of religion in the army—firmly believing in leadership by example. He quietly encouraged Sabbath observance and was deeply moved by reports of so many soldiers praying for him: "I am a poor sinner, trusting in Christ alone, and . . . I need all the prayers you can offer me." By the spring of 1864, fellow Episcopalian William Nelson Pendleton was convinced that Lee had been growing "more perceptibly in grace and in the knowledge of God during the past year." Yet that knowledge of God contained a heavy dose of fatalism, a kind of resignation that appeared admirable but not always inspiring. To Lee, religious faith meant self-control especially in light of the fact that poor, weak humanity often received (and deserved) as many punishments as blessings. To his officers and men, Lee seemed a model soldier and a model Christian—an image that resonated with a wider public.[39]

As with George Washington, there was a kind of remoteness, almost a statue-like quality to Lee the Christian soldier. The same could be said of Thomas J. Jackson but with Jackson there was also a fervency and indeed a ferocity bordering on fanaticism. As a teenager, Jackson had read the Bible and begun praying nightly, yet did not join a church. After becoming a professor at the Virginia Military Institute, Jackson tried the Episcopal, Methodist, and Baptist churches before joining the Presbyterian Church in Lexington. There he sat bolt upright in his pew, though he often dozed through much of the sermon. Under instruction of his pastor, William S. White, he pored over the *Shorter Presbyterian Catechism*; Jackson and his second wife later read passages together in the evening. Jackson exhibited extraordinary piety: he would not write or mail a letter on Sunday; he avoided small pleasures such as dancing and theater; he eventually gave up whiskey because he enjoyed it too much.[40]

Jackson naturally viewed the Civil War as a providential judgment against a sinful people. A sovereign God literally decreed victories and defeats, and whatever course the war took, it reflected the divine will. One young Virginian noted in the summer of 1862 that "God has Jackson in His special favor," thus explaining the risks that Jackson took and his great success when defeat seemed inevitable. Jackson might appear to be a fatalist, but in fact he poured himself into the war with a relentless sense of duty to his country and his God. Some deemed Jackson a Moses, a Gideon, or a Joshua but the most common comparison was to Oliver Cromwell, surely ironic in light of the widely held notion of a yawning gulf between southern cavaliers and northern Puritans. Yet, if the Episcopalian Robert E. Lee embodied the gentlemanly cavalier, the Presbyterian Jackson seemed to resemble the stern old Puritan Cromwell. Indeed, Ohio congressman James Garfield worried about Confederate troops being "inspired" by "a kind of Cromwell spirit which make their battalions almost invincible."[41]

As a devout general who kept preachers on his staff, Jackson adopted an almost seventeenth-century model of the Christian soldier and once publicly prayed that God would baptize the whole army with his Holy Spirit. General Lafayette McLaws complained in early 1863 that Jackson "panders to the zeal of a puritanical Church, and has numerous scribes writing fancy anecdotes of his peculiarities." Jackson was difficult and rigid—a man reluctant to take into account weaknesses in himself or others. After the Battle of Port Republic, Jackson remarked to Richard Ewell, "General, he who does not see the hand of God in this is blind, Sir, blind!" When it came to divine providence, he remained an unbending Calvinist. After the birth of a daughter in 1862 Jackson solemnly warned his wife, "Do not set your affections upon her, except as a gift from God. If she absorbs too much of our hearts, God may remove her from us." A pious Virginia woman expressed similar fears about Old Jack himself: "I believe that *God* leads Jackson and Jackson his men, just where it is best they should go. My only fear is that people are in danger of worshiping Gen. Jackson instead of God, who rules over all. If we idolize him, he will be taken from us."[42]

However prophetic that statement and however much preachers might warn against relying on an arm of flesh, that is precisely what many people did. Indeed, the religious character of such diverse military men as Jeb Stuart, Joe Johnston, and Braxton Bragg won warm praise. In the battle for historical memory, Confederate generals often emerged as more exemplary Christian heroes, and pious Union generals were largely forgotten. George B. McClellan best illustrates this point. His widely publicized order on Sabbath observance won considerable praise in both the religious and secular press. His restrained approach to war and opposition to emancipation had considerable appeal to conservative Christians.[43]

The problem was that McClellan and most other important northern generals who displayed any kind of religious devotion never could match the military record of a Lee or a Jackson. Oliver Otis Howard was widely known as a Christian general, but his performance—at least in the eastern theater—never came close to matching his piety. In the West, William Starke Rosecrans met with both significant success and bitter disappointment but in the midst of the carnage at Chickamauga turned to the reservoirs of faith. "I prostrated myself in spirit at the feet of Our Crucified Lord and implored His most Sacred Heart to pity us, and repeated to our Holy Lady the prayer of the Church very often," he recalled years later. Nor was this merely the hazy recollections of an old man who had experienced a convenient battlefield conversion. Ardent Catholic that he was, Rosecrans had made arrangements for mass to be said in churches and camps. "What an edifying sight to behold the great leader of the army, humbly kneeling before God's altar among privates," one priest remarked. Even James Garfield, a devout member of the Disciples of Christ, enjoyed listening to Rosecrans recount in late-night conversations how he had changed from skeptic to believer and how he drew a fine line between impermissible blasphemy and necessary profanity.[44]

In the North, the supposed piety of a McClellan, a Howard, or a Roserans received only passing attention and was largely forgotten after the war. Confederate soldiers, civilians, and newspaper editors far more often described their leading generals and even subordinate officers as Christian warriors with suitable biblical comparisons. The reputation of Confederate generals for greater piety was at least partly deserved and, in any case, long survived the war not only in the cult of the Lost Cause but in popular memory.

Whatever the comparisons between the two sides, Christian generals were supposed to inspire officers and enlisted men with their noble examples. Many Federals and Confederates agreed that Christians made the best soldiers period. Yet the relationship between "Christian" and "soldier" was by no means simple. To satisfy the demands and insecurities of male honor, young soldiers needed to reconcile Christianity with manliness and religious obligations with military duties. Rough-and-ready soldiers might well be fine Christians, though one northern Unitarian argued that peaceful, quiet young men who had grown up in the church and Sunday school often proved strongest under fire. This was no mad fearlessness or phony honor but instead a confidence that allowed a soldier to go into battle "calmly, steadily, unfalteringly." The man who had learned to fear God had nothing to fear from man, and his bravery came from the Lord. Whatever the tensions and contradictions, preachers often described the Christian life itself as "heroic," thus combining piety and manliness into a composite portrait of military strength.[45]

Wartime funeral sermons lauded young men whose lives exemplified the highest development of the Christian soldier. Ministers recounted in loving detail the lives of the spiritually precocious who had begun praying at a tender age or who had always been stalwarts in their Sunday schools. Even in their teens, they had performed wondrous deeds of piety. As soldiers, they had shunned degrading vices, read their Bibles, prayed for their comrades, and went about their military duties with a remarkable cheerfulness and efficiency. Simply stated, their loyal service in the army glorified God. In a revealing comment that summed up the melding of domestic, martial, and religious ideals, a prominent Boston divine praised a Massachusetts major killed at the Battle of Fredericksburg as "a good husband . . . a good soldier, a good Christian, a good man."[46]

A powerful sense of duty was often tied to a soldier's religion. Given their commitment to God and country, pious men readily explained to their families why they could not come home. Deserting comrades would mean deserting the Lord, who had blessed both the soldier and his righteous cause. Faithfulness would bring not only earthly victory but eternal life. "I will not come till my time is out," one determined Tennessee Confederate promised his wife. "I left with a character untarnished and by the grace of God I intend to return to you the same way." Praying each night, he could feel God's grace, despite the fact that so many men who professed religion at home seemed to deny their faith in the army. The true Christian, Robert Lewis Dabney added, preferred the peaceful company of loved ones but sacrificed all these comforts for the good of others. And should he die, "the blood of our country's martyrs becomes the seed of our new armies." A Pennsylvania chaplain agreed that this "martyr spirit" constituted "the highest quality of true heroism."[47]

So closely connecting religious faith to military service made it all that easier to justify whatever means were necessary to pursue a holy war to victory. In many ways, Stonewall Jackson embodied contemporary ideals on such questions. That old Presbyterian "knows how to hunt yanks," an Alabama private remarked with admiration. A stern and merciless avenger, or so he seemed to his contemporaries. "There cannot be a Christian soldier," the cynical Mary Chesnut mused. "Stonewall was a fanatic. The exact character we wanted." He knew that to win battles, "men must die." What a contrast to the image of a meek and mild Christian: "The religion of mercy, love your neighbor before yourself . . . why, that eliminates war and the great captains." A German Methodist minister drove home this point during the Confederate defense of Galveston, Texas, saying he would "die a true patriot and a soldier of the cross, a gun in hand and Christ within my heart."[48]

The heart remained the primary concern of pious home folk, who worried about their boys remaining true Christians. Admonitions to read the Bible, pray often, observe the Sabbath, and lead a good life came pouring into the camps, especially from wives, mothers, and sisters. A rural South Carolina woman not only wanted her son to attend services but also inquired about whether he stayed awake during the sermons. "Oh let me entreat you not to forget God my child," a Savannah mother pleaded. "He is the only sure help at all times he will answer if you call upon him in earnest. It does not make a coward of a man to love and serve God. It makes a truly noble and brave man."[49]

For their part, devout soldiers warmly recalled the religious influences of home. "I thank you for making me a Christian man, not a very consistent one I am afraid, but still I owe everything to you and your example," Union general William B. Franklin told his wife early in the war. Other men reported how letters from pious relatives had converted them. Fond memories of examples set by parents and other loved ones seemed especially heartening in times of hardship and danger. A Union captain longed to shout "Hallelujah" over the conversion of sinners in a Methodist meeting back in Michigan and fretted over believers in his camp growing spiritually "cold."[50]

For the poor soldiers, religious conviction remained a pillar of strength. "In God is my trust," declared one well-educated and particularly sensitive Illinois private who hated war, yearned for peace, and nevertheless thought that dying for his country would be "sweet." To rest in the Lord's assurances even in the face of enemy bullets became the real test of faith, and devout soldiers promised their families to stand up for Jesus as well as for their cause. Even if it "should be my lot to be cut down in battle," an enlisted man in the 1st United States Colored Troops wrote, "I do believe from clear experience, that my soul will be forever at rest." Confident Christians rejoiced over sins forgiven, and regardless of lingering doubts and misgivings, knew that the Lord would supply the strength for whatever trials lay ahead. "God is indeed the only refuge for the soldier," claimed a Pennsylvania corporal who believed he was actually becoming a better Christian in the army. The devout rejoiced that their lives had been spared and marveled at God's grace, especially toward the end of the war when veterans had seen and survived the worst. What was there to fear when the cause was just and the Lord's promises certain?[51]

Those who had made their peace with the Almighty claimed to be prepared for anything including their own death. A heartfelt confidence that Jehovah's mighty right arm encircled them even as the lead flew produced a calm determination while comrades fell all around, or at least some soldiers claimed after a big fight. If God looked after every sparrow as the Bible said, the Almighty could turn aside bullets and protect his beloved until the appointed time of their death. Amid the carnage at Fisher's Hill in 1864, observing the cold, stiff bodies still lying on the field, Confederate general Clement Evans could only offer "thanks to the Great Preserver for my safety." Especially for men familiar with Bunyan's *Pilgrim's Progress* and similar works, an unwavering trust in the Lord's tender care helped sustain them. If many soldiers experienced premonitions of their own death right before a battle, others expected to survive the war unharmed.[52]

Such confidence reflected a strong faith in the ways of providence, and perhaps even an ability to discern the Lord's will for individuals as well as for nations. The faithful affirmed, in quite direct and simple ways, the role of providence in human affairs. "All things are in the hands of God. His pleasure be done," Theophilus Perry wrote only a short time before being killed in battle. To accept one's fate suggested a certain melding of stoic resignation with Christian assurance, but all would face death some day, as soldiers and their relatives kept reminding each other. The Lord knew the exact time of each person's passing, and everything would unfold according to plan. Suffering in this world was but a fleeting experience, and so soldiers and their families should simply prepare for that inexorable destiny. In fact, the ordinary traumas of daily life inevitably became entangled in the fate of soldiers and nations. In the midst of war, children died at home while families mourned and asked why. Off with a Mississippi cavalry regiment, Will Nugent tried to comfort his wife about their daughter who had been born with a deformed hand. "If God, my darling in his infinite mercy, see fit to take our babe away from us, we must bow with resignation to his afflicting hand and draw therefrom lessons of fortitude and usefulness. We must recognize the justice of his Providence and bow ourselves in humble supplication at the footstool of grace."[53]

Questions about survival often dominated the thinking of soldiers and their families. The mounting death toll brought an increased interest in heaven, and evangelicals had long talked of a departed soul going to a "better place." As one devout Confederate wrote shortly before his own death in battle, "though life is sweet, Heaven is infinitely sweeter." Soldiers and their families longed for a time and place where there would be no more parting, no more grief, or as one Wisconsin soldier put it, where "pain and death are strangers." Yet this young Badger could not help but wonder if there really were no tears in heaven and if past sorrows were truly forgotten. More commonly, however, soldiers found comfort in the thought of dwelling with their loved ones forever. Indeed, the whole idea of heaven as home became powerfully implanted in the minds of the faithful. Tracts and soldier letters described how earthly homes would pale compared to the eternal home. Even if a man did not survive the war, he would someday be with his parents, wife, and children again. As he lay dying of an inflammation of the bowels in a Baltimore hospital, a young Connecticut volunteer did not appear anxious about his condition but instead spoke about joining his mother and Uncle George in heaven.[54]

"Every one of my boys who fall fighting in this great battle of liberty is going to Heaven," declared a Wisconsin colonel, "I won't allow any other principle to be promulgated to them while I command the regiment." As a practical matter many soldiers (and their families) were universalists who assumed that faithful military service guaranteed redemption; surely dying in a righteous cause sanctified the soul. From the beginning of the war, the orthodox denounced such heresy. The assumption that the southerners killed at Manassas or the unconverted soldiers who died of disease had all gone to heaven was simply, according to one Confederate tract, a "dreadful delusion." To mistake patriotism for religion carried terrible consequences in this world and even worse ones in the world to come. Only the blood of Christ could cleanse from sin, and many a minister and chaplain sought to drive that message home. "Shurely no Catholic is so silly or so ignorant of the teachings of the Catholic church to believe that dying on the battlefield would gain their salvation," a corporal in the Irish Brigade maintained, but he was likely wrong on that score. Even the liberal *Independent* worried that wartime deaths would be misinterpreted: "A profane, licentious, drunken soldier, who dies in battle, though he offers himself freely for a good cause, cannot be called an heir of heaven." Naturally, turning nearly everyone into a holy martyr remained tempting. "Oh my dear child," wrote one worried mother to her son serving in a Texas cavalry regiment, "don't suffer your self for one moment to think the cause however good would save the sole."[55]

There was good reason to worry about any young man serving in a Texas cavalry regiment, but then few assumed that being a Christian soldier during a long and bloody war could be easy. Preachers, churches, and religious editors all pressed the men to be shining lights in the darkness of war, promising that their righteous example could save lost souls and transform the camps from scenes of vice into places of worship. Devout Methodist that he was, seventeen-year-old New Yorker John T. McMahon took Wesleyan teachings to heart and claimed that he was being "perfected" in Christ. Should it be the Lord's will, he would survive the war and enter into his master's service.[56]

At best, however, many of the volunteers could claim only that they were trying to be religious. The parable of the prodigal son surely resonated with the many prodigal sons in uniform because it was still not too late to confess one's sins, beg for mercy, and return to the loving arms of the heavenly father. Despite all the hardship, suffering, and death, men strove to become Christians or to be better Christians; the war could strengthen faith as well as weaken it. "Sarah I am trying to lead a different one [life] here," Michigan private John Pardington told his wife. "I hope the Lord Helping me I shall return a Christian." It was not impossible to lead a Christian life, an Illinois soldier concluded at war's end, but it was terribly difficult.[57]

All in all, many men simply had a hard time finding or keeping their faith. A fellow might neglect religion for a time or grow discouraged but then perhaps discover reservoirs of commitment. "Duty" remained a watchword for soldier and Christian. A young Welsh volunteer wrote to his mother in Ohio about three distinct but connected obligations—to God, to government, and to home. "I feel for one I ought to live a far different life from what I do," a New Hampshire sergeant confessed. "I made resolutions that I will, but how frail I am, how soon do I forget them." Confederate general Dorsey Pender exemplified such difficulties. A man of enormous ego, he "sincerely tried to be a Christian" but could not understand why good works did not earn salvation. He felt the need for conversion yet, at the same time, doubted he was worthy. He read and he prayed, but to what end? Pender wondered if he loved the Savior enough and had trouble concentrating on the scriptures; admittedly, he sometimes confused pleasing a pious wife with pleasing Almighty God. Talks with the chaplain failed to ease his mind, but in the fall of 1861 he was finally baptized. Yet even then he wondered if he were truly saved and worried about how to obey God, often feeling "indolent and weak." By May 1862, he had been confirmed in the Episcopal Church, though months later he still considered himself a "perjured" sinner, having made vows he could not keep. In the spring of 1863, he held out some hope, yet still struggled with doubts about his salvation.[58]

Like Dorsey Pender, other soldiers questioned their faith and wondered why they had not experienced a joyous and dramatic conversion. As one thoughtful Iowan put it, "I do not think I am worse than when I started, pretty much the same old sort."[59] This statement undoubtedly applied to any number of soldiers who remained either hostile or indifferent to religion. Many offered the convenient excuse of there being too many hypocrites and wicked men in the churches, though Alabamian James Williams presented an interesting twist in his criticism of "P-salm-singers" for "making the night hideous with their horrible nasal twang butchering bad music." Such men often made poor soldiers: "Give me a jolly good 'sinner' to stand by me when the hour of danger comes!" But what most troubled Williams was a strong conviction that, had it not been for the preachers, there might not have been a war in the first place. Not surprisingly, he directed most of his ire at abolitionists but then also blasted the ministers who conducted "howling meetings" in camp, men who might be able to face hellfire but would never stand up to enemy fire.[60]

For better-educated soldiers, the criticism of camp religion often contained equal doses of anticlericalism and rationalism. Iowa sergeant Taylor Pierce preferred a philosophical sermon to one based on a "blind faith in the book word of god." Doubting the divine inspiration of the Bible, he had even less use for anything that smacked of sectarianism, preferring instead a religion grounded in nature and morality. Other soldiers enshrined sweet reason and were especially critical of chaplains who railed against sins of the flesh. In one evening campfire discussion, a German serving in a Rhode Island cavalry regiment acknowledged the existence of a "first cause" but denied that prayer could ever change the course of events. Other immigrant soldiers associated Christianity—whether Protestant or Catholic—with political despotism and hoped their new country would avoid bringing together church and state.[61]

The uneasy mix of religion and warfare raised tough questions. "Read all Christs teaching, then tell me whether *one engaged in maiming and butchering men*—made in the express image of God himself—*can* be *saved* under the gospel." This statement from an Indiana soldier was remarkable for both its clarity and its rarity. The far more common concern was that young men would fall prey to vice because army life had hardened their hearts. Old fears of declension appeared: the current generation had lost the faith of their revolutionary fathers and now preferred the sutler and grog shop to the chaplain and the church. In the camps, there were always irreverent fellows who ridiculed the pious and mocked the preachers. In the end, and despite the great army revivals, some men confessed even to their mothers that they could just not become Christians, and the religiously indifferent surely outnumbered the outright scoffers.[62]

They likely outnumbered the devout as well. Despite a widespread assent to standard Christian beliefs, Lieutenant Franklin Butler Crosby, who was later killed at Chancellorsville, wrote about how a Christian could feel isolated in the army, especially on Sunday. The men who consistently practiced and lived their faith remained a righteous remnant. The sprinkling of brief references to the Lord or providence in many soldier diaries and letters seemed perfunctory, and God's word often fell on fallow ground. "There is nothing in camp to satisfy the longings of the soul on the Sabbath, no services," Illinois private Valentine Randolph lamented. "One turns within to enjoy, aside from the frivolities of comrades, the inner life which the world can neither give nor take away." Like many other Christians in the army, he felt "surrounded by wicked and boisterous companions." Yet he still found comfort: "Those who daily strive to do their duty are not left to grovel their way through a dark and sinful world.

They not only have an unerring chart, the Bible, but there is a sure monitor within each one's breast which either approves or reproves accordingly as we do right or wrong."[63] There was more than a hint of self-righteousness (and exaggeration) here, but the way of the faithful, as the Bible said, was a narrow one. This had been true at home, and it would prove even truer during a lengthening and ever bloodier war.

THE GOD OF BATTLES

With him is an arm of flesh; but with us is the Lord
our God to help us, and to fight our battles.
— 2 Chronicles 32:8

After the death of two beloved colonels in a Texas cavalry regiment, Presbyterian chaplain Robert Franklin Bunting drew the orthodox conclusion: "God has come and taken our idols from us in that we may not rely too much upon the arm of flesh, but trust more in Him." At the beginning of 1862, his words reflected the mood of pious soldiers and civilians facing a much tougher war. Each death and, even more so, each defeat reminded the devout of their utter dependence on the Almighty. For Confederates, 1861 had been a good year with a promising string of minor victories and a major one at Manassas. Who could deny that the Lord's hand had been at work?[1]

But would the God receive the glory, or would Confederates still try to rely on the "arm of flesh?" Whether the Almighty would continue to bless southern arms never crossed the minds of the irreligious or the indifferent or the overconfident, but even with few obvious clouds on the horizon, many believers remained uneasy. Ministers naturally discovered the "afflicting hand of God" in any personal or national tribulation. Their admonitions along with an even superficial knowledge of Old Testament history and prophecies provided Confederates (and Federals) both the framework and language required to interpret each twist and turn in the war. Shortly after reading about a sharp engagement and defeat at Mill Springs, Kentucky, with more than five hundred Confederate casualties, a rural North Carolina woman reached for a providential explanation: "Surely God is judging his people, everyone ought to humble themselves in sackcloth and ashes, and fast, and pray to God to spare us, and save us from war and bloodshed."[2]

For the time being, however, the Lord would not spare the Confederates from either. On February 5, Fort Henry on the Tennessee River fell to the Federals; by February 16, the surrender of Fort Donelson on the Cumberland River opened the road to Nashville and all of Middle Tennessee. Confederates mouthed evangelical formulas, adding soon-to-be familiar elements of civil religion. The Lord was rebuking a proud people whose boasting and vanity had brought down well-deserved punishment on their heads. Ultimately, God would deliver his chosen people so long as they humbled themselves. At this point in the war, the idea that the Almighty would allow brave and patriotic southerners to be subjugated by what a Kentucky officer termed "a fanatical mob animated by the most diabolical hate and revenge" remained unthinkable. Defeats would come, a Baptist editor conceded, and he admitted that missionaries, pastors, Sunday school teachers, and godly parents could grow discouraged, but in the end "our great Leader and Commander is infinite in wisdom and power, and he will at last triumph over every enemy."[3]

Nevertheless the gloom that spread over the Confederacy crept into an official proclamation declaring February 28 a day of "fasting, humiliation and prayer." Jefferson Davis, who had recently been inaugurated in Richmond, laid out what became a standard religious response to bad war news. "We are not permitted to furnish an exception to the rule of Divine government, which has prescribed affliction as the discipline of nations as well as of individuals," the president intoned in words that would be echoed in countless southern and northern sermons for the next three years.[4]

Throughout the war, the observance of such occasions became a measure of piety and patriotism, and all across the Confederacy early reports boded well. Businesses were closed and the churches were crowded; even the normally packed barrooms of Charleston were empty. Union services brought together men and women from various denominations to seek the Lord's blessing on the Confederate cause. The thought of the entire nation bowed in prayer warmed the hearts of worshipers, who fervently believed that God would soon turn defeat into victory and mourning into rejoicing.[5]

Echoing Horace Bushnell's sentiments after the Federal debacle at Bull Run, a Georgia minister writing to his son in the army hoped "our reverses are doing us good." The fast day forced Confederates to ponder the providential significance of battlefield losses. Some admitted that the southern people had been overconfident ever since the victory at Manassas. "We need chastisement to rebuke our conceit and vainglory," Methodist bishop George F. Pierce advised his son, but he remained "troubled because the calamities which ought to humble us seem only to harden." Governor Joseph E. Brown of Georgia conceded that the Confederacy's "constant successes" had "caused us to appropriate to ourselves a large portion of the glory that belonged to God alone."[6]

Explanations for the crisis depended on one's historical and theological perspective. Philosophical musings about the failure of popular democracy by Episcopal bishop Stephen Elliott lacked the power of the traditional jeremiad because they ignored immediate problems and said nothing about the future. Clergy and laity alike simply cataloged past transgressions and called for reformation. Just to be on the safe side, a North Carolina preacher offered a list of sins ranging from ingratitude to extortion, from drunkenness to profanity. There were the usual references to wicked Nineveh, the children of Israel, and even the Philistines, but the ministers assumed rather than tried to explain the connection between individual sins and Confederate defeats. So far at least, divine chastisement appeared relatively mild. According to a Presbyterian seminary professor, "We may rejoice, it is the rod of a Father, not the sword of an avenging God."[7]

Affirming that the war remained in the Lord's hands proved comforting despite the many sins that Confederates apparently needed to confess. "Let us look to the Judge of all the earth to judge between us and the foe," a South Carolina Presbyterian editor confidently advised. Reverses and sacrifices were part of any war, and at this stage pious soldiers and their families agreed that God would save the southern nation because he would surely not allow the infidel Yankees to triumph. Recent defeats were nothing but temporary setbacks, for even a Christian people could not escape history's calamities. The justness of the Confederate cause guaranteed its ultimate triumph, but, for all the warnings about bragging and overconfidence, that statement was the most boastful of all.[8]

―――――

True enough perhaps, yet by the spring of 1862, the Confederacy faced a manpower crisis as many of the twelve-month volunteers of 1861 clamored to go home. Jefferson Davis requested and Congress passed a conscription act allowing the president to call into service all white males between eighteen and thirty-five. This law seemingly had little to do with religion in a broad sense or even with the more specific connections between piety and patriotism. In only two respects did the measure present any problem for the churches. Perhaps reflecting earlier debates over whether ministers should join the army, Congress decided to exempt the clergy. By the end of the war, more than two thousand ministers had legally avoided the draft, enough to have more than filled two regiments. A skeptical Texas doctor wondered why the government did not send all the preachers to the army since the most wicked people were there. He sarcastically suggested that a "company of saint catchers [be] . . . organized, armed with the lasso, and sent out with strict orders to haul up every one of the Lord's Shepherds they could find who have no flocks and claim exemption from military service on account of having a license to preach." A Louisiana congressman agreed that ministers might be "much better employed than in preaching to empty meeting houses or to old maids and grannies."[9]

A second issue was not so easily resolved. From the beginning of the war, members of traditional peace churches such as Quakers, Mennonites, German Baptists, and Dunkers had sought exemption from state and Confederate military service. In September 1862 Congress authorized hiring a substitute or paying five hundred dollars. Some religious objectors had already paid an exemption tax to state authorities, and, in any case, to impose a levy on faith raised new issues. In 1864 Congress permitted those with religious scruples to be detailed as agricultural laborers, but, all told, only five hundred or so men were exempted.[10]

Anyone seeking an exemption had to present a tax receipt and a certified affidavit from a church official proving their "regular" membership as of October 11, 1862. Quaker yearly meetings strongly opposed the tax but refused to censure those who paid it. During the spring of 1862, a delegation of Friends had met with members of Congress to explain Quaker teachings on war. The Friends outlined their objections to a draft but, despite receiving a respectful hearing, had failed to win a simple and unencumbered exemption from military service. Jefferson Davis coldly remarked that he was sorry there was a group of people unwilling to fight for their country. Quakers in fact faced a serious dilemma because, as one Virginia meeting put it, "the religion we profess and, as we conceive, the true spirit of Christianity forbid our doing any act in opposition to the laws of the government under which we live." They had customarily refused militia duty and now objected to paying a fine for failing to serve in the army, yet they would continue to pay their taxes. Much of this money went to support the war so sorting out the theological and ethical questions became thorny.[11]

Mennonites in the Shenandoah Valley had traditionally paid a small fee to avoid militia service, but by the summer of 1861 a number had joined the Confederate army. In several cases, congregations excluded from fellowship anyone who went off to fight but avoided holding church trials during the war. Social pressure from neighbors and threats against young men who refused to serve only created more problems for people already suspected of being Unionists and hoarding food. The only recourse for some Mennonite young men and a goodly number of Quakers in others parts of the Upper South was to leave home, flee into the mountains, hide in caves, or perhaps escape to Ohio or Pennsylvania. Others were drafted but quickly deserted. "Don't you know that your first duty is to your country," a Confederate general asked the obstinate young Virginia Quaker Samuel M. Janney. Janney replied, "No, my first duty is to God." He was soon released, but others were not nearly so fortunate. Officers deprived stubborn conscripts of food, water, or sleep; they jabbed them with bayonets and threatened to hang or shoot them, rescinding death sentences only at the last instant.[12]

Harsh treatment perhaps reflected how desperate the manpower situation had grown as Confederate prospects dimmed. The late February praying and fasting could not stem a wave of despondency, especially in the western Confederacy. Not only had southerners been boastful, but they had too readily dismissed the Federals as a cowardly foe. Some had placed their faith in foreign intervention and were now paying the price for turning their backs on God. Comparing peacetime to wartime Sabbaths only added to the gloom. While the congregation sang one of her favorite hymns, "How Firm a Foundation," Virginian Lucy Buck "cried as if my heart would break," remembering old times and contrasting them with present terrors. Stoicism, fatalism, and faith sometimes made for a curious mix even for the most steadfast. "If we fail to trust in God, and to give Him the glory," Stonewall Jackson wrote to his pastor, "Our cause is ruined." A devout Tennessee Confederate feared her beloved southland would become another Ireland, a land brought under the heel of a cruel oppressor.[13]

Well might she succumb to despair. A bold Confederate offensive had achieved remarkable success on the first Sunday in April near Pittsburg Landing, Tennessee, but the following day the Federals reclaimed the bloody Shiloh battlefield. And toward the end of the month yet more shocking news arrived: a Federal fleet had appeared below New Orleans and soon the city was ignominiously surrendered. "Providence seems to be hiding his face from us," one North Carolina woman feared. Did the Confederacy deserve deliverance? Most Confederates would still have answered that question with a resounding yes, and after the initial shock the pious turned to the words of Isaiah: "Behold, the Lord's hand is not shortened, that it cannot save." James Henley Thornwell brought many of these strands of thought together in a widely read pamphlet, *Our Danger and Our Duty*. A "momentary enthusiasm" for the Confederate cause would no longer do, he warned. The crisis required "a steady valor, a self-denying patriotism, protracted patience, a readiness to do, and dare, and suffer through a generation or an age." Such determination could spring only "from a sublime faith in God."[14]

Thornwell had offered nothing new or original, but his thinking mirrored a desperate search for religious meaning in the midst of horrific bloodletting and shocking defeat. Never had the southern people more reason to humble themselves before Almighty God. Catchphrases such as "his chastening hand in our late reverses" continued to pour forth from pulpits and denominational associations, but ordinary believers spoke in much the same language. The Lord sent troubles to test his people's faith; such trials should wean believers away from worldly things. But there was also the temptation to give up on one's fellow Confederates and withdraw into a cocoon of self-righteousness. "The Army is nothing but a bridge for speculators to pack wealth over and a hiding place for Office seekers," one disgruntled Louisiana volunteer raged. "From what I see God will certainly curse us as a people."[15]

Such sentiments could dishearten the home folks as well as the armies, and so the editors of religious papers sought to shore up morale by pointing out that the recent "reverses" had all unfolded according to a providential plan. God still reigned, and defeats on the battlefield proved it. There were no accidents in history, and a belief in divine sovereignty prevailed. Such teachings did not lead to a fatalistic hopelessness. That the Lord responded to penitent hearts and sincere prayers remained a bedrock of faith, especially for soldiers who knew firsthand how desperate the situation had become. Finding comfort in a sermon preached on David and Goliath, a young woman in Front Royal, Virginia, understood a point emphasized by many others: the Lord had often given victory to the weak over the strong. As a Jewish captain serving in a Louisiana regiment tried to reassure his wife, "The cause is a righteous one and God is on our side and will watch over us."[16]

But for Confederates the skies grew ever darker. By May, McClellan's army had laid siege to Yorktown on the Virginia Peninsula, and later, as that old town so rich with memories of the Revolution was being evacuated, Jefferson Davis issued yet another proclamation. "Recent disaster has spread gloom over the land," the president admitted, but the southern people should "unite at their several places of worship . . . in humble supplication to Almighty God." Confederates must petition the Almighty to safeguard their capital from the enemy, and the religious editors in Richmond nervously appealed for people not only to observe the day but to truly bow before a God whose wrath had apparently been unleashed.[17]

If restoration of divine favor, however, depended on how people observed the day of prayer on May 16, Confederate troubles would likely continue. Some churches were again filled, but changes in attitude and behavior since the February fast day were noticeable. Perhaps the ladies for one day, a Memphis editor acidly suggested, could stop purchasing "useless articles" with their Confederate notes. In another sharp reprimand, a Virginia Baptist church noted how few of its members had bothered to observe official days of prayer. Doubts about civil religion itself appeared. There might be less drunkenness for one day, yet little permanent reformation as church members lightly attended religious meetings but packed concert halls. And for the first time there was open criticism of the president for even issuing a proclamation. Surely the country had already had quite enough, editor John M. Daniel of the *Richmond Examiner* groused. "Intelligent men" had come to regard such calls "as either cant or evidence of mental weakness." Nor could this unrelenting critic of the administration resist taking a shot at Jefferson Davis: "When we find our President standing in a corner telling his beads, and relying on a miracle to save the country, instead of mounting his horse, and putting forth every power of the Government to defeat the enemy, the effect is depressing in the extreme."[18]

In a stern rebuke to the Richmond editor, a North Carolina Baptist paper observed that fast days appeared ridiculous only to those who did not believe in prayer and that such petitions "moved God in our favor," whatever infidels might say. But now the jeremiads placed much more emphasis on punishment and suffering than on deliverance and victory. Preachers turned to texts that dealt with the possible destruction of Israel, described the enemy as a "rod of correction," or dwelt on the misery of those who transgressed God's laws. Deserving affliction, people had no choice but to submit to the Almighty's inscrutable will. As one Virginia Baptist bluntly stated, "The Lord's purpose toward his people in this world is not to make them happy but to make them holy." There were many reasons that God might not answer prayers, Dabney suggested in a camp sermon. "We have prayed for revival, and for the redemption of the souls of our heedless comrades," but the "ways of Zion still mourn."[19]

———

In the northern states, prayers ascended toward heaven with many of the same themes but with increasing confidence. Throughout the spring, churches adopted resolutions supporting the government in its war against an unholy rebellion. "Patriotism is a Christian virtue," declared one Methodist conference. Many religious leaders expressed faith in the president, and Lincoln acknowledged this welcome support with gratitude, a mention of divine providence, and vague platitudes.[20] Even once reluctant Old School Presbyterians swung into line. Only a year after passage of the controversial Spring resolutions, the General Assembly met in Columbus, Ohio, under radically altered circumstances. Despite opposition from the border states, the delegates voted 206–20 for a report drafted by Kentuckian Robert J. Breckinridge that condemned the wicked rebellion and warned the churches against disloyalty.[21]

Just as news from Fort Henry and Donelson had dampened Confederate spirits, it had given Union morale a great lift. The newly appointed secretary of war, Edwin M. Stanton, wrote to the *New York Tribune*: "Much has recently been said of military combinations and organizing victory. I hear such phrases with apprehension. They commenced in infidel France with the Italian campaign, and resulted in Waterloo. Who can organize victory? Who can combine the elements of success on the battlefield? We owe our recent victories to the Spirit of the Lord, that moved our soldiers to rush into battle, and filled the hearts of our enemies with dismay." Stanton's sentiments were echoed by many devout northerners. Theologians pointed out how God governed the world with a "general" but also a "particular" providence, and battlefield victories were an example of the latter.[22]

Any simple correlation between Union success and divine will begged any number of questions, but few believers addressed them. In a sermon based on that old standby of civil religion, the thirteenth chapter of Romans, the Reverend William Barrows of Reading, Massachusetts, declared that people should not hesitate to rejoice over recent victories because, after all, the Psalms included "prayers against the enemies of Zion." Both Testaments taught that "we may use physical force and even destructive violence . . . in overcoming evil." Not only did preachers claim an ability to discern the Lord's will, but some even claimed to know the timetable. After hearing of Fort Donelson's surrender, Horace Bushnell decided "the beginning of the end is heaving in sight." A New School Presbyterian editor agreed, "The issue is no longer doubtful, and it cannot be very far off." Prominent Boston Congregationalist A. L. Stone was even more precise, assuring his Park Street Congregation that by July 4 the war would be over.[23]

Only days after the bloody Union victory at Shiloh, Lincoln issued a proclamation calling on the people to "render thanks to our Heavenly Father" who "vouchsafe[d] signal victories to the land and naval forces" and helped the county "avert . . . the dangers of foreign intervention and invasion." For some Union soldiers, the occasion was especially solemn. During the Battle of Shiloh, Iowa sergeant Cyrus F. Boyd had run across a badly wounded Confederate begging for water. Boyd recalled the Lord's command for giving drink to a thirsty enemy but could not pause as his regiment advanced. Thinking later about this incident and the other battlefield horrors, he wrote in his diary, "Oh my God! Can there be anything in the *future* that compensates for this slaughter[?] Only thou knowest." Other soldiers expressed views of providence ranging from the orthodox to the cynical. Attending a camp service, Illinois private Valentine Randolph reflected on the fact that God is "present in the most minute affairs of men." Nothing occurred that failed to reflect the divine will: "On every bullet discharged by a soldier He either smiles or frowns." Ohio cavalry sergeant Albinus Fell would have none of this. "I think the damned old cust of a Preacher lied like *Dixie* for he sayed God has fought our battles and won victorys. now if he has done all that why is it not in the papers and why has he not been promoted."[24]

The officially proclaimed thanksgiving elicited a flood of commentary on God's role in the war with northern ministers reviewing familiar events from Sumter to Shiloh as part of an unfolding and hopeful providential history. Despite mounting casualties, the war could not be wholly evil. The conflict had energized a people in danger of being enervated by prosperity, luxury, and politics, and in the end might prove to be a blessing. A Connecticut Baptist hoped for a "great increase of *physical and manly vigor*" among Americans who had "been degenerating and becoming *effeminate*." Not only had camp life toughened up young soldiers, but, more broadly speaking, the contest with the southern rebels had already revealed the might of a democracy ordained by God. A writer in the *Universalist Quarterly* added that the war must bring some benefits because all evil was compensated by some good, an Emersonian optimism that found expression in more orthodox quarters. To Francis Wayland, the war simply "prepares the way for the reign of Christ."[25]

Though much less prevalent than among the depressed Confederates, a sense that the nation was being punished persisted. For a sinful people humiliated at home and abroad during the past year, there was reason to pause and reflect. The nation had deserved its reverses but could rejoice at finding favor in God's sight once again. "I do not doubt that the ordeal the country's now passing through will . . . give us the nationality we lack, and restore through the alternations of hope and despondence, success and disaster, the virtue, public and private" that had graced the revolutionary fathers, declared General Thomas Williams, who would soon fall mortally wounded in Louisiana. All the evils associated with war had sprung from the American people's own sins, transgressions that in the short term at least would still incite political divisions and fuel the southern rebellion.[26]

Northerners increasingly singled out slavery as a national sin that deeply offended the Almighty. Certainly the Lord had commanded his people to liberate the captive, and the devout had to weigh slavery on the scales of national wrongdoing. "I am rejoiced to see an increasing number of signs of national awakening on the subject of emancipation," the deeply religious James Garfield observed. In communities and families across the North, opinion on the subject appeared to be undergoing a sea change. Revealed religion and divine providence was setting the country on a course toward universal liberty. In the pulpits and press, even staunch conservatives condemned slavery. Leonard Bacon, a once cautious colonizationist, now scorned conciliation with rebels because the war had proved that "God has a purpose in regard to slavery." Old School Presbyterians wondered if the Lord had decreed the death of servitude. A New York Catholic editor noted how the church had long seen slavery as an evil and now endorsed Lincoln's proposals for gradual emancipation. Regardless of continuing hostility to abolitionists, some of the church's leading bishops were inching toward an antislavery position.[27]

This new thinking cut in several directions. Union armies, in fact, might be so successful, some antislavery preachers feared, that the war would end prematurely with slavery intact, and then divine wrath would surely fall on the United States. That the war must lead to emancipation became an article of faith for those who saw God using the conflict for his own righteous purposes. Not only would a new Exodus bring the slaves out of bondage, but one Iowa congressman believed the nation would experience a "Red sea passage" to "that higher civilization and purer Christianity which the Republic is to attain." Little wonder than that so many individuals and churches pressed Lincoln to proclaim liberty throughout the land.[28]

But rather than becoming a Moses, Lincoln had remained a Pharaoh, hardening his heart against the cries of suffering slaves—a biblical reference commonly offered by American and British abolitionists during the spring of 1862, even as Union military prospects brightened. The president had proved to be such a disappointment, AME minister Henry McNeal Turner complained; Turner prophesied that military defeats would soon descend on the land like the plagues of Egypt. An even more venomous comment came from a Methodist women's magazine that excoriated the administration for preserving slavery in the midst of rebellion and then blasted the president and Mary Lincoln for their frivolous parties.[29]

Conservative Christians such as James A. McMaster dismissively referred to Lincoln as a man of "mediocre talent," and so the crosscurrents of opinion were strong, buffeting the politicians and people in various directions. In early April, Congress approved an emancipation bill for the District of Columbia, a small victory for abolition and a hopeful portent. "Let us thank God . . . I believe he will remember us in mercy," Francis Wayland wrote to a Union chaplain. African American meetings celebrated a deliverance marking God's long-delayed answer to prayer. The North Indiana Conference of the Methodist Church even expected the war to bring about a broader "moral purification" of the country. Everyone from Presbyterians to Quakers to Catholics could hope that the nation had more closely aligned itself with the divine will and that the Lord would surely bring an end to rebellion and war.[30]

Yet northern religious opinion remained sharply divided despite ever-louder calls for emancipation. The longer the fighting lasted, the arguments based on military and moral necessity became more hopelessly entwined. Despite emancipation in the nation's capital, a Pennsylvania minister worried that the northern people remained "rebellious" against the Lord's holy ordinances. "The North is not yet worthy of victory—not morally ready for it," he noted scornfully in response to Lincoln's halfway measures on slavery. "And I pray that God may withhold his hand, that disaster on disaster may come upon us, until we are ready, nay anxious, to do the right." Gradualists, however, found their own providential meaning in passing events. Conservative Lutherans, for example, cautiously endorsed "constitutional" measures on slavery because God was surely interposing his will on behalf of human freedom, however slow the process. Henry Ward Beecher could at times sound radical but was essentially a cautious preacher who enjoyed pastoring a large, prosperous congregation, and so his support for Lincoln's approach was hardly surprising. But radical Methodist Gilbert Haven also described the president's push for compensated emancipation as a "divine moment."[31]

The war itself made it extremely difficult to stake out a position without being overtaken by events. Political pressures on the Federal and Confederate administrations mounted as McClellan's forces advanced slowly along the Virginia Peninsula. Toward the end of May, the Army of the Potomac approached the outskirts of Richmond. Throughout that month, James Henley Thornwell like many other patriotic Confederates grasped at any sign that the capital might be saved from the invaders. Believing that the "Lord means to defend the city," he deplored factious opposition to the president. Others equally confident of God's tender care had less faith in Confederate leaders and still worried about godless politicians. Despite good news from Stonewall Jackson in the Shenandoah Valley, pious Confederates remained on tenterhooks with every fresh report of fighting. Near Williamsburg, Confederate belle Harriette Cary noted how church services had been suspended for fear the Yankees would break them up; the people gathered in homes and often in basements to pray for mercy.[32]

By early June she could attend church once again but had also begun to read works on biblical prophecy and wonder if the end times described in the book of Revelation were approaching. A battle of Armageddon loomed, one Tennessee minister declared, and soon the landscape was littered with Yankee corpses. It might seem the Lord had recently neglected to answer the people's prayers, but he was likely teaching stiff-necked southerners a lesson in obedience. Especially as word of heavy fighting on the Peninsula reached southern homes, the faithful had little choice but to trust God that all would work out for the best.[33] They prepared to accept and interpret either victory or defeat, hoping their faith could meet any contingency.

Much however had changed after a year of fighting. The return of hope made some Confederates feel less reliant on the Almighty. Only two weeks after the Seven Days battles ended, a Georgia Baptist editor anticipated the rise of a northern peace party along with possible English and French diplomatic recognition. "King Cotton, with Rice and Tobacco, his ministers, is about to assert his sovereignty," he crowed nearly forgetting to credit God with the recent victories. Editorials in church papers at times had much more to say about military strategy, the political situation, and logistical problems than about divine providence. Sermons had grown both too worldly and too war-like. As for the disheartened Yankees, some of their ministers spent more time excoriating generals and politicians than calling their people to repentance. Even clergymen who would not declare their political opinions from the pulpit privately expressed strong views on men and measures. Conservative Presbyterian Charles Hodge wondered if a military despotism might be necessary. He favored conscription, held Stanton responsible for recent defeats, believed that Henry W. Halleck would make a fine secretary of war, and deplored the influence of Radical Republicans. Other religious leaders blamed the country's troubles on McClellan, and the *Independent* more broadly criticized the lack of energy in the administration, adding "Let all men pray that God would give us a government." [34]

The prudent had steeled themselves for disappointment even when McClellan still seemed to have the Confederates bottled up in the Richmond defenses. A larger army did not always conquer a weaker foe, and the Lord might have other plans for the nation. Just as they had after Bull Run, many northerners now looked for some larger purpose in the repulse of a mighty army. According to a New York chaplain, a victory could well have proved disastrous to a proud people more eager to grab the spoils in the rebel capital than to acknowledge the hand of God. In far-off Utah, Brigham Young rejoiced over how the nation "that has slain the Prophet of God [Joseph Smith] . . . will be broken in pieces like a potter's vessel; yes, worse, they will be ground to powder." [35]

This is not to say the Seven Days destroyed patriotism and or left the devout in utter despair. The large denominations reaffirmed their loyalty, warned against internal divisions, and rallied people to the Union cause. A Pennsylvania Methodist still described the government as "one of Jehovah's right hands of power for the overthrow of despotism, error, ignorance, and every thing which could hinder the coming of His kingdom." Even in the midst of disappointment and doubt, hope revived, pushing aside debates over strategy, men, and responsibility. A New School Presbyterian editor warned that "God does not give victory" to the "weak in heart." The faithful could take stock of national sins but also realize that the stakes involved made this war worth the staggering cost. "How deep a Nation's guilt that must be thus washed out with blood," one minister solemnly told a group of Pennsylvania soldiers on the Virginia Peninsula. Suddenly atonement was no abstract theological concept but rather a powerful image in a world of suffering and sacrifice. [36]

Already prone to see the struggle as a holy war, Confederates now had tangible evidence that the Lord was on their side. The editors of church papers sang the praises of Jackson and Lee, compared the southern armies to the great armies of history, and added thanks to God almost as an afterthought. To recognize the Lord's hand in the great victories that had saved Richmond remained a common theme in sermons and editorials, though a careful listener or reader could not help but wonder if southerners had truly learned much of anything over the past year.[37]

Blessings for the Confederates and judgments against the Yankees—that wish often followed any expression of gratitude. The Lord had not only bestowed victory on the southern people but decreed retribution against their enemies. "God smote the oppressor," one Richmond editor rejoiced. Other Christians acknowledged the hatred that sometimes entered their own hearts, dreaded more bloodshed, and conceded their inability to fathom the principles of divine justice. "War is the province of God and must be meant to scourge nations for national sins," one South Carolina volunteer still believed. Although pride in earthly success could once again prove a stumbling block for Confederates, churches expressed a sometimes bloodcurdling determination to push the struggle through to a triumphant conclusion. A Texas Baptist association well captured this viewpoint: "If need be, we will burn our cotton, spread destruction before the enemy, spend the last dollar, shed the last drop of blood, but be subjugated, never! never!! never!!!"[38]

The soldiers themselves began to think much more seriously about the religious meaning of recent events. "I believe God is with us because our people are more conscientious and religious than our enemies," an idealistic South Carolinian informed his aunt. "He has inflicted this war as an evil upon the wicked ones, and until he has sufficiently punished them, and perhaps us for our sins, the war may be continued to carry out his divine purpose." By early July the sobering effects of intense fighting, heavy losses, and bloody battlefields had become apparent. Combat veterans started reading their Bibles, singing hymns, and attending services; having been delivered from danger, men vowed to lead a better life. "There is something irresistible in the appeal which the Almighty makes when he strikes from your side, in the twinkling of an eye your friend and comrade," one perceptive observer remarked. "Few natures are so utterly depraved as to entirely disregard the whisperings of the 'still small voice' which make themselves so vividly heard at such a moment. Every man unconsciously asked himself, 'Whose turn will come next?'"[39]

Here was the connection between civil religion and soldier faith. The preachers and politicians, the churches and the editors, the Sunday school teachers and the families could all speak of a holy crusade against a heathenish enemy. They could interpret the course of the war to fit widely held notions about providence, they could view the outcome of battles as signs of divine favor or wrath, and they could expound on the war's larger purposes. They might even be able to reach the hardened hearts of men isolated from their families in the camps, but combat itself made such lessons much more vivid and meaningful to the soldiers.

———

A close call on a battlefield brought a man closer to God, as many a soldier recognized and many a chaplain preached. When preparations for combat began, men suddenly stopped joking, threw their playing cards away, and grew serious. "Which of us boys will go up tomorrow?" one stalwart Federal tactlessly asked his comrades shortly before Stones River. Tension, uncertainty, and sheer terror elicited varied reactions from curses to prayers. Some men relied on an assurance of providential protection, while others scoffed at such a naive belief, especially after so many good men had already fallen. "Remember that my life is as safe on the Battle field as it is here," a Confederate soldier tried to reassure his wife early in the war. "God and God alone decrees the death of his children. When he orders me to appear it matters little where I am or under what circumstances." A Massachusetts volunteer reasoned along the same lines. "I am getting to be a believer in pre-destination," Lieutenant Colonel William Franklin Draper informed his wife. "It is the most comfortable belief a soldier can have." Men of quite different religious backgrounds suddenly sounded like Calvinists as they came face to face with the enemy across a field or woods.[40]

Falling into line, some soldiers admitted shaking with trepidation as they searched for reassurance in faith. Those saved by grace could presumably be fearless, as earnest men typically claimed or at least assured their loved ones. Seeking comfort in the arms of the heavenly father might banish doubts and terror at least for a time, and when the moment of truth came, some soldiers found that a surprising sense of peace settled over them. Fear of death had vanished; the prospect of a heavenly home somehow lessened the dangers or at least helped conquer doubt and hesitation. Letters home right before a battle often exuded a heartfelt faith, an unwavering belief in divine protection with references to well-known biblical passages about the Lord numbering the hairs of the head, watching over the sparrows, and wrapping all creation in a caring embrace.[41]

Before going into battle, Christians, Jews, and no doubt a fair number of nonbelievers prayed for strength and the Lord's protection. "I simply breathed faith," an older Hoosier informed his wife, describing his experience lying on the ground at Shiloh awaiting orders to fire on the charging Confederates. "Ever kind Father preserve me" was his supplication. This is not to say that the men thought only of themselves; moving toward the sounds of fighting, they recalled their homes and prayed for their families. Some begged the Lord to give their side the victory as if a last-minute plea could still tip the balance. When all united in prayer, a Confederate tract suggested, southern armies would be invincible. Earnest, conscientious men no doubt mulled over the appropriateness of such pleas, the more sober simply praying that their faith would be strengthened and they would enjoy what a Mississippian called "communion with God" on the eve of battle.[42] Soldiers opened their pocket Bibles to comforting passages from the Psalms, the Gospels, or Paul's Epistles; they sought refuge in the promises of strength in the day of adversity. As the troops moved into formation, a few men would quietly read from the scriptures and perhaps offer one final, silent prayer.[43]

For Catholic soldiers, preparing for combat involved a much more set ritual. Priests typically heard confessions on the eve of battle; shortly before a fight at Munfordville during Braxton Bragg's 1862 Kentucky campaign, one Indiana chaplain listened to soldiers reciting a litany of sins for eight straight hours. The devout and no doubt many others found comfort in having priests around whenever a battle loomed. Confession and communion reportedly made the men fight all that harder, or so some chaplains and soldiers claimed. The most storied scene took place during the afternoon of July 2, 1863, shortly before the Irish Brigade entered the famous wheat field at Gettysburg. Standing on a large rock, Father William Corby summoned the men to make a "sincere act of contrition" and then sternly warned that the church would deny Christian burial to anyone who turned coward. With the soldiers kneeling, heads bowed, Corby stretched out his right hand offering the ancient Latin words of absolution.[44]

Once troops were engaged, men continued to pray. During the Battle of Shiloh, a Tennessean beseeched the Lord so fervently that he became "altogether another person." One West Virginian who tried to maintain a constant attitude of spiritual devotion described how he would "load, fire, and pray at the same time." Men might take advantage of a lull in the fighting to offer an additional appeal for divine mercy. "I prayed as hard as ever any sinner did," a Georgia private reported, and even quite wicked soldiers could not help offering up at least one plea for protection. But the whole process remained mysterious to the men and their families. An African American minister pondered the effects of the prayers uttered by himself, his comrades, and their loved ones back home. Having survived the engagement at Chaffin's Farm, Virginia, in the fall of 1864, he could only conclude that the good Lord had decided it was not yet his time to meet the Savior and that he must still have work to do on earth.[45]

Sometimes it seemed that the devout behaved no differently from the heathen, though believers thought they could discern the hand of God not only in the course and results of particular battles but in the attitude and fate of individual soldiers. During one engagement, a young captain approached a Methodist chaplain as the troops were moving into position and said he wished to join the church, adding "Now if I fall in battle, let my mother know of this transaction. It will afford her great joy." Triumphant Christians rejoiced over reports of lost comrades suddenly converted in the heat of combat. Wounded men remembered calling out to God and feeling a sudden change of heart. "Christ seemed to come and stand by my side all night," one Union soldier told a Washington hospital chaplain. "That was the happiest day of my life!" Soldiers who had survived a horrific battle naturally felt gratitude, decided they needed salvation, and vowed to live better lives. "Nothing but the kind Providence of God would have led me safely through such a fire," a Pennsylvanian confessed, even though he had previously denied God had "anything to do with the government of this world."[46] Undoubtedly the searing experience of combat changed lives in many ways, yet how long these new converts would persist once the danger had passed was by no means clear.

For all too many soldiers, the danger would not pass any time soon. "If a man ever needed God's help it is in time of battle," a Georgian wrote shortly after a close call during a particularly severe engagement. Such men not only believed God *could* safeguard them in combat but fully believed that the Lord *had* done so. Writing to their families after passing unharmed through a battle, soldiers remarked how a merciful God had spared their lives. These comments sounded formulaic and may have been little more than empty clichés, but some soldiers fervently believed that the Almighty had responded to heartfelt prayers from home. A Michigan volunteer assured his wife that on several occasions during the 1864 fighting around Atlanta, the good Lord had caused enemy bullets to miss him. During the Battle of Cedar Mountain, Confederate artillerist Willie Pegram had found himself in a very "hot place." By his reckoning, a Union sharpshooter had drawn a bead on him eight or ten times, and there were four bullet holes in the bottom of his coat. "What have I to fear from Yankee bullets as long as I am under his protection?" he asked his sister. Soldiers used the word "shield" to describe how the Lord had guarded them from danger.[47]

For many men, however, confidence faltered. A battle was a "wonderful place for one who believes he is a Christian to test his faith," one thoughtful Federal informed his father. "I found my hope much weaker than I had thought." Even early in the war, doubts about divine protection came to the fore. One young soldier appreciated the Lord's many blessings but wondered how he could still be shielded from all harm when "in every fight, better men than I go down and fall before my eyes." A war with spiraling casualties and no end in sight raised troubling questions. After the Battle of Chancellorsville, a group of Mississippi enlisted men sat around smoking and discussing the providence of God. One soldier remarked to Private David Holt, "The Lord was mighty good to you to interpose the head of George Pilant between you and that piece of shell." Pilant had been a "sincere Christian" and surely deserved the "protecting care" that Holt had enjoyed. Another soldier took a more fatalistic tack: Pilant's time had come and Holt's had not. Exasperated by such talk, Holt finally said, "Thank the Lord, I don't have to think anything about it. It's none of my business, and I am certain that the Lord can attend to His own affairs. That is my idea of faith." But neither the religious nor the skeptic could help thinking about such matters. Some took refuge in cynicism or sarcasm. After Antietam one soldier suggested that bad rebel marksmanship (rather than Almighty God) had saved the men in his company.[48]

And where was the place for gentleness, kindness, and compassion in such a world? Some Christians remembered to pray for their enemies and might even believe there were religious folks on the other side of the battle lines, but the admonitions found in the tracts and religious papers suggested this was no easy thing and such high-mindedness could easily turn into sinful pride. Jesus had told his followers to pray for their enemies, a Georgia Baptist editor wrote, but that did not mean Confederates could not meet their enemies with "fire and sword" and slay them in a just, defensive war. That reasoning crossed sectional and sectarian lines, causing some Christians to reexamine their view of the scriptures. As one Richmond editor pointed out, the Bible had not been written by "priests and preachers" but by "hard-fisted working and fighting men." Now was the time to read the militant and bloody passages, a Philadelphia Presbyterian maintained. "Men have discovered the Book of the War of the Lord, and congregations are chanting the war psalms now in all their majesty." In sum, "Religion has grown warlike."[49]

With this new attitude, even the most devout began to think the worst of their nation's enemies. Despising and dehumanizing Yankees or rebels seemed natural enough during seasons of horrific and inconclusive combat. To many northerners, the wickedness of the southern rebellion became more apparent each day, and to many Confederates the impiety of the Yankee invaders appeared equally obvious. Each new outrage, each new rumor, and each new exaggeration proved that no "Christian" could possibly be fighting for such a bad cause. Reading northern Baptist resolutions supporting the Union proved to a southern Baptist editor how the vile Yankees "delight in war." A young woman in Murfreesboro, Tennessee, hoped that Lincoln would burn forever in the lake of fire. Women were especially shocked to realize how much they could hate the Yankees, how hardened their own hearts had become in the face of so much suffering and death. What nurse Phoebe Pember termed an especially "pious set" of Christians in Richmond stored various trinkets in a Yankee skull. Writing to her sister and with a strong consciousness of her own Jewish background, she described an evening with these people. "At last I lifted my voice and congratulated myself at being born of a nation, and religion that did not enjoin forgiveness on its enemies, that enjoyed the blessed privilege of praying for an eye for an eye, and a life for a life, and was not one of those for whom Christ died in vain, considering the present state of feeling. I proposed that till the war was over they should all join the Jewish Church, let forgiveness and peace and good will alone and put their trust in the sword of the Lord and Gideon." [50]

Intense loathing readily justified vengeance, all of course rationalized with scriptural proof texts. During the spring of 1862, a leading Virginia Presbyterian wrote to a friend that he wished Confederate armies would invade the North as an act of "retributive justice" so the Yankee "should taste of the cup which he has pressed to our lips." One Tennessee Confederate offered a chilling calculus: "I really believe he who kills the greatest number of abolition thieves and their abettors is the best Christian." The Bible did not sanction personal vengeance, a South Carolina editor conceded, but even the most gentle Christians should rejoice over the slaughter of Yankees in a "religious war," a contest pitting "infidelity against the Bible." Likewise soldiers, whatever their qualms about the carnage, distinguished between combat and murder. Even a Georgia Baptist volunteer who was aghast at the spectacle of the "most enlightened people on the face of the habitable globe . . . daily killing each other by wholesale slaughter" nevertheless concluded that all the butchery had been a "chastisement" to "effect the purpose of the Divine mind." Cyrus Augustus Bartol, a prominent Boston Unitarian, agreed that Christians naturally recoiled at such bloodshed yet also approvingly noted how members of his own congregation had given their lives to redeem the nation. "Our atonement by blood has come," he maintained. "The nation bleeds, and the lives of hundreds of thousands of men—for it is mounting up to that—are the drops." Almost Lincoln-like, he observed that both sections would have to suffer for their sins, though he quickly added that the rebels were much the greater sinners. [51]

Ministers could preach about what Bartol termed the "remission of blood," perhaps all too easily. The mysteries of the atonement had long been central to orthodox Christianity and had generated all manner of learned and often abstruse debate, but now the idea of national atonement helped explain the war itself. So far the battles of 1862 had tested the whole question of providence, and both sides had clung to a belief that the Lord marched with their armies. Devout soldiers meanwhile struggled to sort out God's role in determining their fate. In the hospitals with the sick or wounded, around men's deathbeds, faith might be either precious or despised; the linkage between God's will and the soldier's destiny might seem clear, unfathomable, or meaningless. The search for spiritual comfort, the search for a religious understanding of the war, would continue, but for the soldiers, unlike the preachers, the blood being shed was all too red and all too real.

Chapter 9

CARNAGE

O death, where is thy sting? O grave, where is thy victory?
— 1 Corinthians 15:55

The minié ball struck Private Evan Lawrence's Bible and penetrated to Isaiah 52:7. "How beautiful upon the mountains are the feet of him that bringeth good tidings, that publisheth peace," seemed especially timely and comforting to this young Georgian who later claimed that the text had been on his mind as his regiment moved into action at Kennesaw Mountain. Tales of Bibles stopping bullets cropped up after nearly every major battle, and in point of fact pocket Testaments saved lives just often enough to make such stories believable. In both contemporary telling and later recollection, citing the exact verse where the tip of the projectile stopped somehow lent verisimilitude to accounts that religious skeptics and even some believers might dismiss as wildly improbable.[1]

Whatever the talismanic qualities of the scriptures, soldiers and civilians lovingly described and embroidered such incidents. Reading of a dead soldier found with a Testament inscribed, "Given to the defender of his country by the Bible Society," Mary Chesnut caustically remarked, "How *dare* men mix up the Bible so with their own *bad* passions." But, of course, men (and women) had long done exactly that and would continue to do so. A Virginia artillery officer promised his mother to carry his Testament over his heart but then playfully suggested that it might be just as important to protect "the pit of the stomach." Assuring her that his faith was firm and embraced all "the cardinal points," he could not help asking if she had heard about the man whose life had been saved by a deck of cards in his pocket. Few however assumed such a lighthearted attitude. A Tract Society volunteer sent home a Testament that had failed to save a young soldier's life and reported that the ball had first struck the passage from Revelation, "Surely I come quickly."[2]

However incredible this macabre coincidence—and certainly this tale beggars belief—it did reinforce the point made by countless ministers, chaplains, and soldiers: one must always be prepared for death. A sturdy young man suddenly fell ill, was sent to a camp hospital, and died. Enemy bullets struck down the righteous and unrighteous alike. The ill, the wounded, and the dying could repent of their sins before it was too late, though there were differences of opinion on that score. Chaplains and others tending the sufferers spoke about their immortal souls, being especially careful to observe the men's last moments and record the dying words.[3] Families and friends treasured such information as they struggled with overwhelming grief and kept asking why.

To men and women of the Civil War era, religious faith offered meaning to life and preparation for death. Early on the ravages of camp diseases proved the need for the comforting assurances of a heavenly home, and it was especially sobering when young men died who appeared to lack such assurances. Bloody battles only added to these woes. Having survived one of the first Federal charges toward the famous stone wall at Fredericksburg, a New Jersey volunteer reflected that "there was nothing to protect the union soldiers but the protection that Christ throwed around us when he said it is finished. The plan of redemption is complete and that is the only defences for my protection that I had." Some men figured they would not likely survive the war, tried to control their anxieties, and took comfort in the promises of salvation. For others even the fear of death paled before their fear of hell and doubts about whether they were truly ready to meet their maker; and then there were poignant stories of soldiers who had once had faith but let it slip away.[4]

Serious illness and especially a trip to the hospital became yet another trial of faith or a chance for the wayward. "They [sick soldiers] are most easily influenced," one Union chaplain remarked, but he perceptively added that the "impressions made there [in the hospital] are so apt to be transitory." If the patient recovered, backsliding seemed highly probable—surely an irony for anyone considering the relative importance of saving bodies versus saving souls. As with soldiers facing the prospects of a battle, religious uncertainty haunted the minds of men laid up in hospitals. "I know it must be strange to you to see so many sick, dead & dying," one plainspoken New Hampshire mother wrote to her son. "But be not afraid, when the spirit is gone they are nothing but clay, the same that you and I shall be and everyone else sometime. You know Willie all must die." She hoped that God would protect them both until they met again, but in any case they must trust in the Lord. Family members rushed to the bedsides of young men dying of disease to see whether the fellows could still rely on the promises of eternal life. Deathly ill men reassured loved ones that they had made their peace with God. Suffering from chronic diarrhea, an emaciated Iowan dictated a letter for the chaplain to send home: "So Dear wife prepare for the worst. . . . I have the cold sweat. Do take care of our dear children; and if I never see you more let us try to meet in heaven the home of the good." Two days later he was dead.[5]

The imminence of death had long been a favorite theme for preachers, and there was little need to modify it during the Civil War except to add that soldiers could see tangible proof of that proposition nearly every day. "May we learn from the fickleness of life and the certainty of death," a Hoosier private commented after a comrade accidentally blew his head off when several of the more spirited fellows (in perhaps at least two senses) were randomly firing off their weapons one evening. The contrast between a fixed time on earth and a timeless eternity caused many a man to think about how he planned to face the inevitable, and the promises of heaven seemed especially poignant in funeral sermons offering family and friends hope that a recently deceased soldier was in fact alive and cradled in the arms of a loving God.[6]

"Cut off in the bloom of youth" is a phrase that seems trite and utterly Victorian but one that resonated with the Civil War generation. All the more reason for resignation to God's will when an apparently strapping fellow could so easily succumb to a camp fever. A soldier wasting away from disease did not quite fit the image of the heroic Christian soldier, but this only meant that courage itself must be more broadly defined. "How touching, how manly, how soldier-like, and how replete with religious fervor," one observer described a Kentucky Confederate slowly dying in a camp hospital. Even so death often appeared so random, so sudden, a life of promise ended so abruptly. Above all else soldiers feared dying alone, in the stilted but sincere words of one Indiana volunteer, "with no sympathetic hand of father mother sister brother or wife to soothe their dying pains."[7]

For the deeply or even the nominally religious, however, the ultimate fear was to die without hope of salvation. After receiving news of a soldier's death, the folks back home often wondered whether he had been spiritually prepared, and their own religious convictions sometimes provided little comfort. Preaching a quite conventional funeral sermon for Jacob H. Smith of the 1st Virginia Infantry, Baptist Jeremiah Jeter urged his listeners to "weep not for the pious dead but for the living sinners." Too many men served in the field "without the consolations and hope of the gospel enslaved by sin."[8]

To an Ohio colonel, being a follower of Christ in the midst of so many vexations and temptations "requires higher courage than to stand unmoved before the mouth of a cannon." Feeling insecure about their faith, men refused to seek salvation at the eleventh hour. Another Buckeye dying of a head wound admitted that he had sworn, mocked God, "prayed for sport," and was not a religious man despite occasionally reading the Bible. He was spiritually unprepared for death and did not pretend otherwise. Some men could just not believe that they would soon die and so blocked such questions out of their minds. Between extreme examples lay many soldiers who had tried to prepare

for death, admitted they were not as faithful as they should be, but nevertheless relied on the Lord's promises. These cases presented particular problems
for chaplains caught between offering comfort, inquiring about the state of
a man's soul, and dealing with unanswerable end-of-life questions. Presbyterian James Russell Miller, an earnest Christian Commission delegate, worried about the difficulty of "directing dying men to Christ," especially given the
fearful consequences of failure. All too often a chaplain "smoothes down his
pillow with false hopes, and tried to make him satisfied with his hopes when
in reality the dying man knew nothing whatever of the way of salvation." Typically ministers visiting a hospital found soldiers in various stages of spiritual
anxiety or confidence, and the range of counsel offered was equally broad.
Some continued to preach on the terrors of hellfire, but others came close to
proclaiming that death in battle or even from disease brought sanctification.[9]

Ideally, a believer should be prepared and even welcome the final release
from worldly sorrows. After his brother's death in battle, a Mississippi private
wrote, "It is my earnest wish that we may all be as ready to attend that awful
summons as he was." Those watching men die in hospitals as well as those
struggling with their grief far from the camps found consolation in such statements. The Christian soldier died trusting in Jesus as his savior and, as one
young Virginia woman imagined it, would soon be "quaffing . . . the pure water
from the fountain of Love." With more bluntness than reassurance, Union
general Marsena Patrick urged a group of soldiers gathered for a religious service to "be prepared for what follows death." It was indeed "glorious to die
for one's country," but the men should not neglect their salvation.[10] Speaking
frankly about these matters risked unnerving soldiers on the eve of battle, but
neglecting what could well be a final opportunity to present the message of
salvation seemed far worse.

———

Dealing with the dying and wounded presented a constant challenge, especially for chaplains. And here sectarian differences at times loomed more important than shared beliefs. Priests knelt and prayed with fallen soldiers as
they administered the last rites. Finding the Catholic wounded could be difficult, and these men might not want to speak to a priest when surrounded by
so many nosy and sometimes hostile Protestants. To Father Peter Paul Cooney,
Protestant chaplains who neither baptized the dying nor offered them the
sacrament seemed like spiritual ciphers, "yet they claimed to be *Christian ministers*." Such men were worthless on the battlefield and nearly so in the hospital. On one occasion, Cooney baptized a dying Protestant "conditionally" without hearing a confession and even granted "conditional" absolution, practices

bound to stir up anti-Catholic sentiments. That hardly bothered priests who shared Cooney's belief about serving as a "direct instrument of God to bring those poor souls from the brink of hell."[11]

One Union chaplain's manual offered detailed instructions about how to talk with the sick and the dying, but each minister had to rely on his training, experience, and instincts to build rapport with the men. Specific suggestions on speaking with "inquirers," "desponding patients," and the always difficult "skeptics and infidels" demonstrated how chaplains needed to be both knowledgeable in the faith and ready to deal with all manner of humanity. Conscientious hospital chaplains recorded their patients' spiritual state, noted improvements along that line, and reported conversions.[12]

Aside from holding services, the more ambitious organized small groups of believers into hospital churches whose members promised to lead holy lives and win others to Christ. Here was the place to truly do the Lord's work. "Up at the front," New York chaplain Joseph Twichell discovered, "men are excited— their blood is continually hot, and the gospel of love and peace and charity finds little soil to take root and grow in." There the "savage zeal to smite the enemy" prevailed. "Killing and the Sermon on the Mount do not seem to go together, but where the sick or wounded are laid on beds in still places, the words of our Lord are more fitly spoken and heard." His Pennsylvania colleague Andrew Hartsock agreed that "preaching in the hospital is cheering to the heart" and to the soldiers a "great comfort." After a long day spent with the men, he would "retire to my couch weary but feeling that I have discharged my duty."[13]

Sick or wounded soldiers might be especially receptive to religious conversation, and so for chaplains finding the right words became all important. The tracts distributed in the hospitals often combined comfort with advice. "Do you know Christ?" one asked, and then went on to point out that any disease "is of divine appointment. Its kind, degree and circumstances were all determined by the Lord" for some unknown but holy purpose. Evangelical messages sought to address the inevitable doubts and questions. Convalescence might seem both slow and uncertain, but patients could pray and depend on the promises of Christ; even a long illness was preferable to eternal torment. For those who had neglected their savior, now was the time to set things right. The wounded soldier, one Confederate tract advised, should pause to "think of God's mercy in delivering you" and recognize the need to be born again and so enter the next battle as a soldier of Christ assured of "certain victory over the enemies of your soul."[14]

Sermons, tracts, and chaplains all warned that the sin within a man could do much more harm than enemy bullets, and some soldiers clearly agreed with this spiritual diagnosis. "Oh my God, I offer all my sufferings in atonement for the sins by which I have crucified thee," declared one fellow as he was being lifted onto an operating table. Should he lose an arm or leg, a determined corporal in the Irish Brigade informed his always anxious wife, "i should accept it as the will of God and consider it was for the best for there is not a misfortune in the whole catalogue of human calamitys which if thoroughly investigated will not produce positive evidence that it is for the spiritual benefit of the indevedual to whom it happened." That was hard doctrine especially when death and suffering seemed so random and so purposeless, but the devout at home and in the camps clung to the belief that all worked for good according to God's will. After hearing that her friend Private Francis Stewart of the 49th Ohio had been wounded again, Tillie Foreman—who was herself battling with consumption—reminded him that the Lord chastened those he loved, adding that she felt "more willing to suffer all the afflictions sent upon me if Christ repays us in his love." A surprising number of soldiers agreed that a wound could be a blessing if it drew them closer to God.[15]

The line here between faith and fatalism was never as easy to draw as either the pious or the irreverent believed. Bearing one's pain with Christian fortitude quite often resembled a stoic acceptance of an inevitable fate. Heroes lay in the hospitals as well as on the battlefields when the badly wounded softly repeated the name of "Jesus," or quietly spoke of their salvation, or talked of the savior welcoming them home. Such men could almost stand outside of themselves, viewing their suffering and pain as but a temporary phase during which they might glimpse the glories of heaven. A Confederate badly wounded at Gaines' Mill claimed to feel "rapturous and ecstatic beyond expression." He thought of his redeemer, and "the new Jerusalem seemed to rise up before me in all its beauties."[16] Chaplains and pious volunteers lovingly recorded such statements, and despite many a heartfelt expression, there sometimes appeared to be a set piece quality about them. It was almost as if some evangelical drama were being played out according to a well-established script. The men themselves seemed to know their parts. Yet, at the same time, the words often carried the ring of sincere conviction—a powerful sense of the Lord's presence and the all sufficiency of saving grace.

"I lost an arm, but I have found a savior," one patient in a field hospital informed a Christian Commission delegate. Perhaps even more remarkably, a twenty-four-year-old Maine soldier testified, "It seems to me I can't be grateful enough for losing my arm . . . [because it] ended in my finding Christ. It is better I think to enter into Life halt or maimed, rather than having two hands or two feet to be cast into everlasting fire." Such widely reported statements melded patriotism with piety in ways that defined the ideal of the Christian soldier. A man with both legs amputated talked of his own sacrifice, "My country demands it and my savior demands it." Such affliction reminded patients of how much Jesus had endured to take away their sin. Naturally, not all of the wounded could be such shining examples. In a Richmond hospital, one man whose entire body throbbed cried out, "Lord, what have I done that I suffer so and the pains are sharper than any two edged sword!" He prayed to see his family back in Texas one more time. Although his brother sat by the cot crying and finally managed to read aloud a few passages from Mark's Gospel, this sufferer preferred novels. When a woman visitor tried to offer comforting words, he snapped, "It don't do a damned bit of good to trust in the Lord!"[17]

The pious hope remained that such profane fellows might in their agony see the error of their ways and turn to God. In hospital wards, men had time to think back over their lives—sometimes with guilt and shame—and seek answers to the great mysteries of life and death. Some talked of wanting to be a Christian and perhaps of having long struggled with their faith, but a serious wound had finally led them to take up these questions more urgently. Reading John's Gospel after having a leg amputated gave the words new meaning for one North Carolinian who no longer had much taste for "rude wit and coarse and vulgar ideas." A longing for salvation, however, could not always overcome the reservations of men who felt too wicked to receive the Lord's grace or who preferred putting off such matters until they returned home.[18]

Yet just as often a serious disease or wound laid the groundwork for a change in belief and behavior. The persistence of one plainspoken chaplain who kept asking a wounded New Yorker if he wished to "die for his country and be lost" finally broke down what the soldier termed his "pride and hardened heart." Sometimes a new convert or two helped spark a revival in the wards. Evangelicals had long interpreted tears of repentance as a genuine sign of conversion, and that proved just as true in one western theater hospital where a double amputee found Jesus even though he had no hands left to wipe the tears of joy from his cheeks. When recovery followed on the heels of conversion, the wounded had all the more reason to rejoice, though reports of backsliding sometimes followed. Simply reading a tract in the hospital had brought soldiers to the Lord; the most rudely impious might come around to relishing the scriptures during a prolonged hospital stay.[19]

Though perhaps with less dramatic effects, formal worship yielded some spiritual fruit. In the late fall of 1862 near Fredericksburg, Virginia, the conscientious Pennsylvania chaplain Andrew Jackson Hartsock held services each morning in a camp hospital. He would read a chapter of scripture, talk to the men, pray with them, and sing a hymn or two. Toward the end of the war, meetings in hospitals grew larger, filled with fervent testimonies to God's goodness, conversion narratives, and promises to give up all manner of vice. Soldiers themselves often led meetings in the wards; at White House Landing, Virginia, during the Overland campaign, one group of wounded men enjoyed having evening prayers just like they had at home, ruefully adding, "We are certainly bad boys enough to need them."[20]

Hopeful chaplains often described hospital patients as attentive and grateful, but one wonders how soldiers lying on cots responded to this message from a Virginia Baptist: "Consider then, that you are where you are, and as you are, by the will of God. It was no chance bullet which made that fearful wound." Even fevers, rheumatism, or a cough "came not by accident." All came as an "appointment of God." This was predestination with a vengeance, all part of the Lord's "plan of our life, formed in eternity," and "willed" by him from the time the soldier was a "helpless babe, on your mother's breast." Then there was the Unitarian tract that described "sickness as one of God's best gifts" and listed virtues that could be cultivated in the hospitals—all easily enough said by men who merely visited the wards for a few hours. Although many of the boys welcomed hospital chaplains, some nurses and patients considered them feckless busybodies wandering among the sufferers to no great purpose. One Hoosier chaplain in a division hospital tried to preach a sermon on the theme "prepare to meet thy God," but cursing teamsters drowned out his message. More commonly hospital chaplains like their regimental counterparts were criticized for neglecting their duties and spending too little time with the sick and wounded. An Illinois surgeon derided such "Pharisees who made it a business to pray aloud in public places . . . they were rotten at the core, not caring half as much for their soul's welfare or anybody else's as for the dollars they received." When one of these preachers sat down to talk with patients about being prepared to die, an angry man "threw a plate at him and told him to go the devil."[21]

To be fair, the chaplains had to deal with carnage on an unprecedented scale, and in many cases the horrors of war and suffering in the hospitals must have overwhelmed their physical, psychological, and emotional resources. These men of God were supposed to provide spiritual and perhaps material comfort to men of all sorts, from the confidently religious to the spiritually insecure. And then there were the indifferent, the diffident, and the scoffers. Little in the chaplains' background or training had prepared them for such tasks, and like many of the soldiers and their officers, they had to learn their demanding jobs on the fly and made many mistakes along the way. Above all, like surgeons, nurses, and patients, they had to cope with death all around.

———

What should one say to a man who had just hours or minutes to live? It was often the chaplain who had to tell a badly wounded man that he was dying. Could he convince the lifelong sinner or recent backslider to repent? It would hardly do, as one Massachusetts chaplain pointed out, to urge the man simply to mend his ways or to tell him he would not be punished for his transgressions. Perhaps it was best simply to pray with the dying man and leave the rest to God, though chaplains hardly knew what to say to those without any apparent faith. A Union chaplain's manual recommended avoiding light conversation and getting right to the point but then offered careful advice on dealing sensitively with a variety of patients.[22]

Family members, friends, visitors, and chaplains read scripture to dying soldiers. Young men asked to hear favorite Bible passages, and particular verses sometimes stirred them to one final declaration of faith, an expression of thanks, or even a shout of joy. A bloodstained Bible or well-thumbed Testament with pages turned down to mark certain texts became signs of sanctification—especially to the folks at home. To die with the scriptures near a pillow or lying on one's chest offered a poignant sign of a soldier's faith.[23]

As the chaplains soon learned however, dying soldiers were not all cut from the same cloth, and for every secure believer there were others who expressed doubts or held out no hope at all. Admitting that his wife had given him "good advice at home, but the devil came along and coaxed me off," a Massachusetts cavalryman nevertheless remained fairly certain that his sins were forgiven. Other men confessed to having led reckless lives, but reassuring words from a chaplain or comrade revived their hopes. Even some men who had grown up wild without religious influences trusted all would be well.[24]

Those who had once been faithful church members but had drifted away appeared much more uneasy during their final moments of life. "I have wandered from God," one Confederate acknowledged, "and that troubles me." Perhaps it was not too late for the prodigal to confess his sins and still reach his heavenly home. Using appropriate military language, a young soldier told an Ohio chaplain that he had "left the ranks" and "sinned against God" but now wanted to "reenlist" if "you muster me in." A man ashamed of his past could still pray for mercy. Yet such fellows and even those who led much more dutiful lives could not banish last-minute doubts, and some admitted they were just not ready to die. For their part, chaplains tried to reassure and prepare them, even though many patients were in such excruciating pain with their minds wandering that it was never certain whether those last words of instruction or comfort were even heard.[25]

"I don't want to think," one badly wounded soldier told a Presbyterian chaplain. He wanted more brandy and no more religion. Some men died cursing God, the war, and everything around them. Others could only weakly mutter it was "too late" or "I am lost" when a chaplain tried to speak with them. "I'm dying here without Christ," a Confederate prisoner confessed to a Christian Commission delegate in Chicago. His wife had talked to him about salvation for thirty-five years but he had paid no heed. "I can't die. I can't die," he kept murmuring but soon did. A visiting minister grasped the cold hands of a suffering Hoosier in a hospital at Tullahoma, Tennessee, and kept telling him to come to Jesus. The soldier could only say, "He is not here! He is not here!" and died with those words on his lips.[26]

Chaplains, colporteurs, and the other visitors recounted and no doubt at times embellished or even invented such scenes as object lessons for the living. All that said, the problem of the eleventh-hour conversion troubled many minds. "I cannot come now—I will not," declared one Michigan soldier. "Do you think I'm going to drink the devil's wine all my life up to this last day in hospital and then offer the settlings to Jesus?" Another man in a Virginia hospital was even blunter: "I'll die as I've lived. It's honester." Such men did not want to hear about the thief on the cross and threw back any words of comfort in their visitors' faces. After being wounded at Ball's Bluff, Oliver Wendell Holmes Jr. figured much of the world would consider him "en route for Hell" but decided he would "die like a soldier anyhow" and not give way to fear or "be guilty of a deathbed recantation."[27] For Holmes and those like him, a sense of manliness and principle stood in the way of any surrender to God.

When dying soldiers spoke of being resigned to their fate, their words reflected a phlegmatic stoicism or a deep faith. A providential (if not fatalistic) outlook helped soldiers and their families cope with the war's horrendous and unpredictable losses. Reports of men spiritually ready to die became the most comforting news in many condolence letters. A Virginia artillery officer who had no hope of recovering from his wound described how he had prayed every night for the past three years that God would "prepare me for this day, and save my soul." The words "ready" and "willing" passed the lips of pious soldiers as they spoke of impending death. The philosopher William James later wrote about a state "known to religious men, but to no others, in which the will to assert ourselves and hold our own has been displaced by a willingness to close our mouths and be as nothing in the floods and waterspouts of God." The day of death becomes a "spiritual birthday," and suddenly, the "time for tension in our soul is over, and that of happy relaxation, of calm deep breathing, of an external present, with no discordant future to be anxious about has arrived. Fear is not held in abeyance as it is by mere morality, it is positively expunged and washed away."[28]

A good death anticipating a better life to come had been a Christian ideal for several centuries, and during the Civil War, countless tracts and sermons along with the testimony of dying soldiers all spoke of a believer's peaceful resignation. Ironically, religious sentiments combined with even more ancient traditions that extended beyond the community of faith. A Wisconsin captain visited a badly wounded colonel during the Chickamauga campaign and talked with a surgeon who was "glad to find the Col. so cheerful and resigned, another proof he said, that a freethinker can look death in the face as calmly and unconcerned as the most orthodox minister."[29]

At times the calm acceptance of death blended themes of personal and national salvation. Devout patriots considered themselves ready to die for God and country, as if the atonement of Christ applied to both sinful individuals and sinful nations. "Oh, I am happy," declared a fifty-six-year-old Indiana private who had received a mortal head wound. "For when the Master came, he found me at my appointed work." Indeed, serving in the army meant serving the Lord as men proudly battled for Christ and country. Victory rested both with the cause and with the redeemer; all the pious statements about dying men sanctified their sacrifice and ennobled the war itself.[30]

That was doubly reassuring, but other dying soldiers expressed more ambivalent feelings. Some men appeared more fretful about finding (as opposed to affirming) a consoling faith during their final moments on earth. They seemed anxious to be religious, perhaps even claimed that they had tried to be religious throughout their life, or at least during part of their life. A seventeen-year-old who had run away from his job in Camden, New Jersey, to join the army and was badly wounded at Gettysburg told a chaplain he had no family, had never been to Sunday school, but at least knew "Our father, which art in heaven. . . ." Those even worse off might only be able to whisper back the words of a simple prayer offered by a chaplain. Catholics and Protestants who had never been baptized now received that sacrament as a lifeline; a badly wounded Ohioan told a priest that he had promised his mother to recite a "Hail Mary" some day. Heartfelt pleas often reflected the lingering uncertainty of men who admitted being afraid to die, but then announced they were ready to meet Jesus, and yet finally reverted to a more anxious state, their thoughts and emotions whipsawed by pain and dread. "O Lord, save my body! O Lord, save my soul!," a Confederate prisoner cried out while being treated in a Union field hospital. "And if you do, O Lord, I'll knuckle to You to all eternity." Preachers lovingly recited the dying words of men who at nearly the last instant had surrendered their souls to God.[31]

Chaplains, visiting ministers, Christian Commission delegates, and nurses all recorded soldiers' last words—or at least any religious sentiments expressed. They knew families at home wanted as full an account as possible of their loved one's final moments. The smallest details helped console the grieving. To the chaplains fell the task of carefully composing letters to the deceased's family, and they took heart in what was often described as a "triumphant" death. "He died a Christian," were words that sounded sweet to relatives, friends, and home churches. A man's hope in Christ—duly expressed and recorded—would comfort a pious mother and family members, who could rest assured that their dear soldier boy was with the Lord. Even the grave could claim no victory over a life devoted to God and country, though in almost all accounts of dying soldiers there was far more emphasis on salvation than on patriotism. When a minister tried to talk with Private Edmund Johnson of the 37th United States Colored Troops about the law of the gospel, Johnson replied, "I don't know much about it in de books; but know something about it in my heart. I labored hard to get it into my heart."[32]

Over and over again, the dying simply declared they were thinking about Jesus and praying to Jesus. The personal salvation so heavily stressed by evangelicals in fact embraced a much wider compass and range of religious traditions. To simply trust in God became the touchstone of faith. "Christ is all my hope," declared one New Yorker languishing in a gangrene camp, and his words would have been echoed by many other dying men who saw Jesus as their one true friend guiding them through life's ultimate travail. Chaplains and other hospital visitors looked for signs of patients' acknowledging that Christ had died for their sins. "Tell my wife, that there is not a cloud between me and Jesus," a badly wounded Federal declared shortly after the Battle of Belmont. When men talked of their "precious" savior as they often did, that word resonated with families attuned to a deeply emotional faith in an era that valued both individual conversion and pious homes.[33]

The sentimental and domestic language held great "future" significance for both the soldiers and their loved ones because those who had received God's grace anticipated a reunion in heaven. "I would as soon go to my heavenly home as my native home," a New Yorker announced. Such men recalled how Jesus had promised to prepare a place for them. Reporting on the death of his brother, Ohio soldier David Blair assured his parents that their son "is now in a better mansion than a military hospital." Such words of consolation sounded especially poignant when applied to soldiers who had endured so much in camp, on march, and in battle. Dying men and their families looked forward to a place of rest, of perfect happiness with no pain, sorrow, or parting. People thought of heaven as an idealized Victorian home—in a tangible and material way—but it would also be a nearby place of peace and beauty beyond human imagination. "Meet me in heaven" were among the most common dying words directed to family, friends, and comrades.[34] The thought of an eternal home went beyond powerful metaphor to include a concrete picture of reunited families gathered together basking in the light of their savior.

Given these visions of a glorious future, it is hardly surprising that soldiers wasting away from disease or suffering from wounds affirmed that it was simply better to die. The Christian soldier would soon enter a "better world," long a catchphrase used to describe heaven and console the grieving. "I soon expect to see dear father, grandfather, and above all—Jesus!" wrote one Ohioan who was steadily growing weaker in a Cincinnati military hospital. Agreeing with the Apostle Paul, a West Virginian wounded in one of the last battles around Petersburg insisted that "to die is gain." There was almost a feeling of gladness in some of these statements. Men imagined angels hovering near their cots ready to receive their departing spirit, and a South Carolinian wanted his father to know that he would soon "join the army of Jesus Christ."[35]

Words from dying soldiers reached home and often appeared in religious publications; their simple messages of faith offered comfort and warning to the living. In the army, sermons, tracts, and even the ministers' eulogies sought to tame what could have been an immobilizing fear of death. Some soldiers embraced traditional notions about a "good death" but others—at least according to ministers and other pious souls—had waited too long to receive God's grace. Death came suddenly and often with no warning, and for all the talk of preparing to die, there might not be much time to do so. Whether bodies literally awaited a physical resurrection remained a disputed question in the Western religious tradition,[36] but for the living, that dead body not only required immediate attention but also symbolized the awful mystery of death. One might be tempted to say the "finality" of death, but to believers death appeared only as a prelude to glory. For chaplains and surgeons, for comrades and families, the process of coping with death—whether of a beloved individual or simply the carnage of the war itself—continued.

————

The story of all these deaths and their religious significance extended far beyond the hospitals and even the soldiers themselves. Holding funerals, transporting bodies, and eulogizing Christian soldiers all brought the war home to families, neighbors, and churches.[37] The scale of the suffering and sacrifice in turn raised large and difficult questions about the providential meaning of slaughter on such a massive scale.

On the most basic, practical level, thousands of dead soldiers had to be buried—and, it was hoped, remembered. Among a chaplain's most important and onerous tasks was conducting camp funerals, often right after a battle. Whether simple or elaborate, these services made a deep impression on the living—especially when they marked the first death in a regiment or on board a ship.[38] Soon, however, many a poor soldier was interred without ceremony— his body tossed into a trench. When there was no chaplain available to accompany a funeral procession carrying a cracker-box coffin shortly after the Battle of Fredericksburg, one "rough-looking" but tearful sergeant stretched his arms out toward the sky and simply said, "Great God of battles—we bury poor Tom's mangled body, let his soul enter Heaven—Amen!" The fear and shame of anonymous death made hospital patients think that nobody cared about them; men dug graves for soldiers they never knew, and no words were spoken as the dirt was thrown over a crude box. "Some of the men joke and laugh while they are laying out the dead and seem to think nothing of it," a shocked Iowa volunteer noted during the siege of Corinth. "How inhuman and wicked this thing called War. It brutalizes men and crushes out Christian feeling." A widely circulated tale recounted how a woman had arrived at Hollywood cemetery in Richmond as the body of a Mississippi soldier was being lowered into the ground. He surely deserved a Christian burial so she read the Episcopal service and then chastised some nearby loafers for being utterly indifferent to the poor fellow's death or to their own lost condition.[39]

Even if there was a brief service and a few volleys were fired over the grave, often there were no friends present to remember, no one to mourn. Funeral followed funeral as chaplains and other ministers barely kept track of the numbers and names, much less had anything to say about the dead individually. One cynical Michigan officer described a chaplain's sermon on such an occasion as "about as appropriate and interesting as the driest chpt. of Coke's Commentaries," though he admitted that a military funeral "properly conducted is a very solemn and impressive scene." Chaplains stuck with general and predictable messages: defenses of the noble cause, reminders that life is short, hopes for meeting again on the Resurrection day.[40]

At best, wartime rituals of mourning preserved traditional beliefs and practices haphazardly and incompletely. Nearly all who fell, Yankees and rebels alike, died and were buried far from home and family, leaving all concerned spiritually and emotionally adrift. "At home, when a member of a family is about to go to his last resting place," Confederate nurse Kate Cumming wrote, "loving friends are around the couch of the sufferer, and by kind works and acts rob King Death of half his terrors." But in the military hospital the dying man was usually in a dimly lighted ward with twenty or more soldiers, and there might not even be a nurse nearby when "the death-rattle is heard." Back home, the sound of horses' hooves or a knock on the door seemed to portend the news families dreaded to hear. In Cherokee County, Alabama, Sarah Rodgers Espy felt more fortunate than most. Her son, who had become gravely ill during Braxton Bragg's Kentucky campaign, at least managed to make it home. He soon grew too weak to cough up the mucus filling his lungs but was able to hug each member of the family and weakly tell them he was "going to heaven."[41]

Word of deaths on battlefields or hospitals struck households hard and unexpectedly, bringing sudden anguish and raising hard questions. "I can't believe that dear James is killed," Sarah Palmer wrote to her sister less than a week after their brother's death at Second Manassas. "Poor fellow I know he has passed from a world of sorrow and pain to one of endless happiness." She *thought* he was a Christian but could hardly receive the news without murmuring, as death had for the first time entered the little family circle on their low country South Carolina plantation. Various family members struggled to make sense of it all—one so young taken from them perhaps as a punishment from God. His fiancée Alice Gaillard prayed that God would give them all "strength and resignation." Submitting to the Lord's will became so much harder than they could have imagined, though many commonplace religious sentiments—whatever their formulaic qualities—provided consolation and comfort. The Palmers like so many families had been unable to share their boy's final moments, and they could only hope that Jesus had been at his side. At most a family might receive a lock of hair sent home by a compassionate chaplain, but uncertainty about the state of a loved one's soul caused no end of worry. Families tried to steel themselves for such losses, but mourning often became a numbing experience that involved hardening the heart against an indescribable pain. Pious women especially struggled to accept God's will and could not always do so.[42]

In a hallway or parlor, a wooden coffin became the most tangible sign that the worst had finally happened. Sometimes wives and mothers read from a prayer book and conducted their own services. Neighbors gathered, tears flowed, and the search for spiritual comfort began. Meditations on the ways of providence, a sense of resignation, acknowledgment of divine chastisement, a picture of heaven as a cozy domestic circle—all these conflicting thoughts about the deaths of soldiers (and particularly Christian soldiers) offered consolation to the mourning even as they left many questions unanswered if not unasked. It might be wrong to question the Almighty's role in all the suffering death, but for many people this had become more than an abstract, theological question. Battlefield victories lost their luster for families whose view of the war had largely come down to one particular soldier.[43]

Spiritual resilience sometimes masked a deeper grief or a nagging unease but was nevertheless remarkable. Because the boy had been a Christian, Kate Cumming hoped that a mother who had lost her third son in the war "will weep more in joy than in sorrow." When word reached home that a beloved son or brother or husband had professed his faith and died in sure and certain hope of the resurrection to eternal life, that mattered a great deal. Like the Apostle Paul, family members would "sorrow not, even as others which have no hope." When a grieving wife learned that her dying husband had found Jesus as a Christian Commission delegate softly recited verses of "Just As I Am," she reportedly cried, "Children dry up your tears. Your father is not dead. He is alive in Heaven. Thank God!"[44]

In a time of affliction, the devout affirmed, the Lord would soothe their sorrow. When his son asked, "Well who will be my pa if you don't come back?" a New York soldier hardly knew what to say before experiencing conversion himself. He later wrote to his wife, "I know now how to answer little Henry's question. Tell him the Savior will be his pa, if I don't come back." Women especially talked of leaning on God for strength in present and future trials, a conviction that sustained many during the war's darkest days. Seeking to comfort a friend who had just lost a son at the Battle of Wilson's Creek, the Jewish philanthropist and educator Rebecca Gratz prayed that the Almighty would "open a fountain of consolation" and suggested the grieving mother look to the "hope of reunion in another world." Images of an afterlife complete with loving couples and happy families had become increasingly popular during the first half of the nineteenth century and had obvious appeal during the Civil War when so many families faced both temporary and permanent separation on earth. After the war, books about heaven poured off the presses. Elizabeth Stuart Phelps best-selling novel *The Gates Ajar*, published in 1868, not only described reunited families in their heavenly "home" but even had soldiers meeting Abraham Lincoln on the golden streets.[45]

Meanwhile life in earthly homes continued, and the normal passing of old and young only intensified the wartime anguish for soldiers and their families. In the midst of a military campaign, Robert E. Lee had to write condolence letters to his daughter-in-law when she lost a second child. He rejoiced over the Lord's mercies for both his family and the Confederacy, but a stern belief in providence kept his thoughts and sentiments directed toward God and his work on earth. As they worried about an ill soldier or feared that a breadwinner might soon be forced to enter the army, other families mourned the deaths of children. "I *live* as a great many other people do, carelessly taking great blessings as if they were my just due," Arkansan Virginia Davis Gray confessed. "Just as I receive blessings, I also receive warnings and reproofs, carelessly—too carelessly—may Heaven also forgive me that sin." With her husband in the army, she kept wondering if their child might not in fact be better off for having died at an innocent age. Catchphrases about the shortness of life somehow acquired deeper significance during a war that witnessed so many deaths in the field and the standard complement at home.[46]

What did such a harvest of death signify? Young Emily Dickinson had begun to write poetry but, unlike so many other literary figures of her day, could not see deaths—especially so many deaths in war—as part of any divine plan. Rejecting a theological interpretation of the war, and indeed any theological framework, she could not join Emerson and other intellectuals in believing that good somehow compensated for evil. Others who had seen the carnage firsthand expressed similar doubts. New Hampshire surgeon William Child could not get the dead and wounded of Antietam out of his mind. "I pray God may stop such infernal work, then perhaps he has sent it upon us for our sins," he wrote to his wife shortly after the battle. "Great indeed must have been our sins if such is our punishment." Two weeks later, the "great victory" still troubled him. "The masses rejoice, but if all could see the thousands of poor, suffering dieing men their rejoicing would turn to weeping." Troubling questions kept entering his mind: "Who permits it. To see or feel that a power is in existence that can and will hurl masses of men against each other in deadly conflict—slaying each other by thousands—mangling and deforming their fellow men is almost impossible. But it is so—and why we can not know."[47]

Such thoughts could be dismaying and immobilizing, but just as soldiers often grew hardened to the worst that war might bring, so too did hospital volunteers and civilians. A Union chaplain's manual warned against cold and formal burial services, against carelessly tossing coffins into the ground as if they did not even contain human remains. Were human feelings being utterly destroyed by war? Despite a strong religious faith, a woman living in Natchez, Mississippi, found herself deeply changed by the news of her brother's death: "It seems as though when he died, my pride left us [and] my heart became flint. I am almost afraid to love too dearly any one now." This numbing pain at times produced cries for vengeance. "Subjugate, and if it must be, exterminate every rebel in the land, without delay" was the sentiment expressed at an 1863 funeral for a Michigan cavalry officer. After seeing the graves of twenty Union men executed in North Carolina, a Rhode Island chaplain de-

Dead in front of Dunker Church, Antietam, Maryland (Library of Congress)

clared that God "who said, I will repay, has marked the spot, and the resurrection angel watches their sacred dust; and time will come when Moses and Paul and Luther and Washington from among the glorified martyrs will look these up, and grasp them to sympathetic and honorable embrace." Praising the war dead increasingly meant immortalizing them, wrapping them in the arms of a loving father as heroes who had died for their country and their faith.[48]

The need to be at peace with God became ever more urgent as the toll from disease and battle mounted. An Iowa chaplain sadly asked what had happened to the souls of the dead and how soon the grieving might be comforted during a war that no longer seemed glorious. Although military campaigns absorbed people's attention, one Georgia woman now thought more about Judgment Day. War became the price for sin—a view widely held in the 1860s—but it also offered an opportunity for repentance and redemption. Even all the deaths—thousands of them—might carry a millennial significance only dimly understood by mere mortals. Martyrdom conveyed both purpose and mystery. Recalling a scene at the Battle of Chancellorsville where surgeons were performing an amputation in the woods, Chaplain William Corby of the Irish Brigade concluded that "God wished to punish us for past sins and disregard of His benefits, and that a certain number had to die." [49] That cold and disturbing theology marked the anguish of Americans trying to extract meaning from the war's unprecedented carnage. And in 1862, 1863, and 1864, there appeared no end to the bloodletting. The price of national atonement—if such it was—kept going up, so ministers and churches, the devout and the skeptical and the indifferent alike, the soldiers and even politicians and generals, struggled to make sense of it all.

WAR'S PURPOSE

> He maketh wars to cease unto the end of the earth; he breaketh the bow, and
> cutteth the spear in sunder; he burneth the chariot in the fire. Be still, and
> know that I am God: I will be exalted among the heathen, I will be exalted in
> the earth. The Lord of hosts is with us; the God of Jacob is our refuge.
> — Psalms 46:9–11

By the late summer and early fall of 1862, not only were both sides still proclaiming their own righteousness and praying for their enemies' destruction; they were still searching for some larger meaning in what threatened to become a war without end. After McClellan's defeat on the Virginia Peninsula and the Army of Northern Virginia's sound thrashing of John Pope's ill-starred and short-lived Army of Virginia at the Battle of Second Bull Run, Confederate fortunes had seemingly revived. Soon rebel armies were advancing into Maryland and Kentucky. Had not the northern people, one Presbyterian editor asked, placed too much faith in supposedly great men such as McClellan, Frémont, and Pope?[1]

One northerner who had never joined a church or even declared himself a Christian had begun to look at the whole relationship between divine and human intent with remarkable thoughtfulness, especially for a politician. In many ways, Abraham Lincoln often cut against the grain of his own time and baffled his contemporaries—especially when it came to his religious views. Exposed to a fervid frontier evangelism in Kentucky and Indiana, young Lincoln could imitate the preachers' sermons but never quite embrace their dogmas. Raised in a family of Baptists, Lincoln nevertheless read Thomas Paine and other rationalist works but never exactly espoused their ideas either. He came to believe in what he termed the "doctrine of necessity," a kind of fatalistic philosophy that may have eventually made him receptive to the preaching of Old School Presbyterian ministers but also led to political accusations of being a religious skeptic or worse. At times it seemed as if Lincoln were determined that his contemporaries and even later generations could not categorize or even understand his beliefs.[2]

Early on, Lincoln developed a deep familiarity and apparent affection for the Bible, but he was never a biblical literalist. He once remarked that he would join a church that simply preached the great commandment of love for

Abraham Lincoln (Library of Congress)

God and love for neighbor, but of course the churches insisted on far more. At a time when many Americans embraced particular religious beliefs with an inflexible certitude, Lincoln remained both sympathetic and detached, with an ironic awareness of difficulties and contradictions.[3]

A natural melancholy along with the troubles of life ranging from the disappointment of young love, to a sometimes stormy marriage, to the deaths of children likely made Lincoln more receptive to Christian teachings, but whether he ever came around to believing in the divinity of Christ remains uncertain. As Mary Todd Lincoln put it, her husband was never a "technical

Christian." After their son Edward's death in 1850, Lincoln turned to James Smith, an Old School Presbyterian minister who preached the funeral sermon and had written a massive work on Christian apologetics. Mary Lincoln joined Smith's First Presbyterian Church in Springfield, and the couple attended services there though Lincoln did so irregularly. He would not join this church or any church, then or ever.[4]

Perhaps Lincoln still had too many doubts and questions, but however that may be, he continued to ponder religious matters and even explore the relationship between God's world and public morality. By the 1850s, biblical cadences and scripture references were becoming more frequent in Lincoln's speeches, especially when he discussed slavery. As he increasingly invoked Jefferson's famous phrase about all men being "created equal," he also emphasized that a Creator had made human beings in his own image. And this God hated injustice and slavery, leading Lincoln to express a withering contempt for ministers who would cite scripture to justify enslaving their fellow men.[5]

Lincoln's relations with the clergy were always ambivalent and often carried a bit of an edge. Apparently most of the local ministers in Springfield, Illinois, voted for someone else in 1860, but when Lincoln departed on his circuitous journey to Washington, he pointedly and publicly asked friends and neighbors to pray for him—a gesture that immediately attracted attention and helped build Lincoln's popular reputation as a man of faith. In Washington, the Lincolns attended New York Avenue Presbyterian Church, whose minister, Phineas Gurley, avoided politics in the pulpit and shared Reverend Smith's conservative Calvinism. The president appreciated the northern churches' strong support for the Union war effort but grew impatient with clerical delegations lecturing him about God's will. When one preacher remarked that he hoped "the Lord was on our side," Lincoln reportedly said that he did not know about that. "The Lord is always on the side of the right," the president allowed. "But it is my constant anxiety and prayer that I and this nation should be on the Lord's side."[6]

The distance from a youthful fatalism to a mature contemplation of providence proved to be not that great after all. The president at times saw himself as a humble instrument in God's hands, a man more buffeted by the war and a leader less in control of events than either his friends or enemies imagined. Lincoln could never simply and unequivocally identify the Union cause with God's will as so many preachers did because for him divine providence remained largely mysterious. His faith in the Lord's purposes did not include millennial expectations of an American nation purged of sin or even explicit recognition of Jesus as the savior of mankind. To Lincoln, his fellow citizens remained an "almost chosen" people.[7]

But believers yearning for deliverance from the agonies of war preferred certitude and increasingly came to believe that the president not only shared their faith but was himself an instrument of divine will. The country could be "made peaceful, happy and prosperous under your guidance . . . if you follow the plain teaching of Providence," his old Illinois friend Orville Hickman Browning had advised Lincoln less than a month after First Bull Run. "If you falter God may forsake you." In the fall of 1862, a Michigan Presbyterian synod described the president "as a man of unflinching integrity carefully studying the indications of Divine Providence." And more than a year later a Chicago lawyer remarked, "You may depend upon it, the Lord runs Lincoln."[8]

Confederates expressed similar confidence in their president as a man of faith even though Davis had shown little interest in religion before the war. Baptist parents, early education in a Catholic school, along with Presbyterian and free-thought influences at Transylvania University and West Point Episcopalianism, had made little apparent impression on him. Yet during the war he acquired a reputation as a man of God—largely based on his calls for days of fasting, humiliation, and prayer after Confederate defeats or for thanksgiving after Confederate victories. Such public acknowledgment of divine providence reassured people that the new southern nation was being guided by a Christian president.[9]

Davis and his wife Varina attended St. Paul's Episcopal Church in Richmond where the Reverend Charles Minnigerode became a family friend and spiritual counselor. In the spring of 1862 there was talk of Davis formally joining the church, and on May 6 he was baptized in a private service at the Executive Mansion. This event was highly significant for the president but less so in the larger scheme of things because his contributions to southern civil religion remained largely pro forma. Davis had little doubt that the Confederacy merited the Lord's favor and never appeared to struggle with the difficult questions about God's purposes that so troubled Lincoln.[10]

And with the war going well for the Confederates during the late summer and early fall of 1862, there was naturally danger of overconfidence turning into self-righteousness. "Our arm is nerved with almost super-human strength," Episcopal Bishop Stephen Elliott declared. "We are moving forward, as I firmly believe, as truly under his [God's] direction, as did the people of Israel when he led them with a pillar of cloud by day and of fire by night." Recognizing the hand of God in recent victories, preachers and churches spoke of deliverance from a wicked foe with apparent assurance, but there remained nagging doubts about whether the southern people deserved such blessings. Even after Democratic gains in the fall northern elections, Georgia Methodist bishop George F. Pierce sounded a Lincolnesque note of foreboding: "We are in the Lord's hands, and I know not what he means to do with us. In many re-spects the prospects before us are dark. We have wrought wonders, but seem to have gained nothing. The war is without a parallel in the past, as to its ori-gins, its battles, its progress, and its results so far. I hope for the best, but I am looking to God alone—vain is the help of man."[11]

———

Northern religious thinking moved along similar lines, though in even gloomier tones given the latest military setbacks. "The war does not seem to improve public morals in the slightest degree," remarked one Iowan as if he had somehow expected it might. With two sons in the army, he feared self-ish speculators were prolonging the war so they could continue to line their pockets with ill-gotten gain. Everyone from abolition preachers to conserva-tive Catholics could see the hand of God chastising the people as evidenced by recent defeats. Everyone from Congregationalist preachers to AME editors tried to discover which transgressions had provoked the Lord's wrath. Even Quakers and Unitarians echoed the standard themes of the Jeremiad—a time-less and flexible form of preaching that explained everything and nothing at the same time.[12]

Intellectual and theological confusion reigned as preachers denounced every imaginable sin. Perhaps simple partisanship had become one of the na-tion's besetting vices, or maybe poorly attended prayer meetings had angered the Almighty. Yet the assumption remained that divine sovereignty worked perfectly, irresistibly, and efficiently. "There is no waste of patriotism or sac-rifice in this great plan," wrote one Connecticut soldier to a newspaper back home. "The mismanagement of his human agents is all provided for, it is part of the allowance for friction in the running of His machinery. There is no such thing or word as mistake with Him. And all this blundering, wasteful, extrava-gant war is an economical, well-ordered part of His system, and shall promote the great general progress of virtue and liberty in the world and the glory of His own great name." This attempt to discern a beneficent order amid the war's bloody chaos was remarkable. Even that voice of liberal reform, the *Indepen-dent*, at the end of a long article blasting the generals and the Lincoln admin-istration, agreed that northerners had no choice but to "wait God's time of Vic-tory." Perhaps the nation would have to pay a still-higher price in blood for the remission of its sin or, as one Presbyterian minister observed, for its failure to reckon with the power of evil.[13]

Confederates might well have agreed but would obviously have defined "evil" much differently. After all, Yankee claims to being a people of faith were all a sham. "The element of religion, of course, is used only as a foul hypoc-risy," the *Charleston Mercury* declared. "That a just or holy God can regard with favor their invasions—their robberies—their murders—their sacrilege—the Abolitionists know is impossible. To get rid of Him as an obstacle, they deny His existence. They have openly declared that they are actuated by a higher law than the Bible." Denunciations of northerners as atheists and idolaters resonated with Confederates who defined their own faithfulness by condemning their enemies' faithlessness. According to another South Carolina editor, all present difficulties stemmed from the spread of "French skepticism and German rationalism" in the northern states, where even Baptist ministers had abandoned "sermons warm from the heart" in favor of "written essays and stilted compositions." [14]

On the heels of denouncing the enemy came new claims about the Confederacy fulfilling millennial hopes, hopes that remained firmly anchored in slavery. "Ours seemed to be the place where God has chosen above all others for the pure unalloyed propagation of the Gospel Truth," the wife of a small East Tennessee slaveholder avowed. As would often be the case throughout the war, Stephen Elliott became a bellwether for Confederate civil religion. In an important sermon preached in Christ Church, Savannah, on September 18, 1862—an official day of thanksgiving—he proclaimed that the Lord had "caused the African race to be planted here under our political protection and under christian nurture," thereby preserving the institution "until the fullness of his own times." Black Republicans and northern abolitionists had examined slavery in the most superficial, human light, forgetting that God had once placed his chosen people in bondage to the Egyptians. After this odd twist on the Exodus story that had more typically served as a lesson in liberation rather than bondage, Elliott went on to show how God had permitted slavery to grow and prosper in the southern states. The Almighty had in turn led southern armies to victory, but the war would continue until England and the North acknowledged that slavery "is a divinely guarded system, planted by God, protected by God, and arranged for his own wise purposes." [15]

The persistent religious defense of slavery that linked the institution to recent Confederate victories paralleled the equally abstract northern defense of democracy as a divinely sanctioned system of government. No northern minister expressed more faith in democracy than Henry Ward Beecher, the most famous preacher of his day and, to Confederates, the very symbol of Yankee apostasy. Beecher took a much rosier view of the war and humanity in general than many clergymen who were quick to see the suffering and bloodshed as simple punishment for sin. "God is the great democrat of the universe," Beecher cheerily informed his Brooklyn congregation, despite the apparent lack of progress in the war and recent Democratic victories at the polls. Pointing to European advances toward republican government, he optimistically predicted that hierarchies have "had their day" and that democracy would spread inevitably not only into politics but into virtually every field of human endeavor. The association of religious faith with human progress—an idea that was often brutally satirized by Confederates—promised that the work of God and his church would surely triumph. Although many northerners still worried about the prevalence of national sins, others talked of providence in wildly optimistic ways. Only weeks after the disaster at Second Bull Run, a prominent Philadelphia Presbyterian minister with a long-standing interest in missions proclaimed once again that America can "become a mountain of holiness for the dissemination of light and purity into all nations, a dwelling-place of righteousness and liberty for the oppressed and poor of all lands, a name and a praise for all the earth." [16]

If northerners at times vacillated between formulaic jeremiads and millennial optimism, Confederates expressed a simpler, unalloyed thanksgiving to God for his many blessings to the southern cause. Ministers offered thanks for the deliverance of Confederate armies from "boastful" Yankees but appeared to be going through the motions or sounded wildly overconfident themselves. Gloating over the despair of their enemies, secular and religious editors not only detected the hand of God in recent victories but even predicted a speedy end to the war. In Raleigh, North Carolina, Joseph Atkinson told his congregation how the "wonder-working providence" had grown more evident in the Confederate "revolution" than in the American Revolution. Anticipating later arguments by Lost Cause advocates, a Virginia Baptist interpreted recent victories as nothing short of miraculous because Federal armies supposedly outnumbered Confederates by at least four to one. [17]

Certainly during the war's first year, the churches had largely fallen into line behind their respective "nations." On the Confederate side, there were the usual diatribes against the Yankees for waging a war of aggression against the South, indeed a war against women and children. Not only had the new nation's "sacred soil been polluted by the monster's tail," claimed one especially fervid preacher, but her "noble daughters have been threatened with dishonor." The Methodist Annual Conference in Georgia deemed northern armies "enemies to the human race." Yet variations in content and tone struck slightly discordant notes. The war itself, warned one South Carolina Baptist association, had kept too many people from their religious duties at home and in camp. An influential North Carolina Presbyterian tactlessly praised the unselfishness of pious soldiers from the best families who had been willing to serve under the command of their social inferiors. [18]

The often irresistible force of the war itself would push virtually all northern churches into declaring their loyalty to the Union. Maverick Orestes Brownson's endorsement of emancipation in early 1862 had failed to turn northern Catholics into abolitionists, but the church—despite persistent and serious divisions—became highly patriotic. In Cincinnati, Archbishop John Purcell issued a September pastoral letter detailing the evils of slavery and denouncing a secessionist conspiracy going back at least three decades. At the other extreme, James A. McMaster still blamed a "false and prostitute [Protestant] clergy" for the "ruin of the country," but he hardly spoke for more than a noisy minority in the church, and by this time many good Catholics were serving in the Federal armies. Returning from a European speaking tour on behalf of the Union cause, Archbishop Hughes preached a regular war sermon at St. Patrick's calling for more volunteers and urging one great effort to crush the rebellion. Bristling over criticism from conservative Catholic editors, he declared himself "a patriot rather than a politician."[19]

What had become unacceptable was neutrality. One could be a good citizen without being a Christian, an Indiana Baptist association conceded, but one could not be a Christian without being a good citizen. Loyalty to the nation could not be separated from loyalty to God, and at times the former loomed more important than the latter. Even though many denominations offered little more than general support for the government and for the president, others exuded both a soaring idealism and a fiery resolve. Methodists, Baptists, and Presbyterians still hoped that the war could purify American life as they discerned the workings of divine judgment against national sins. Like Lincoln, a group of Indiana Methodists warmly declared that "our Union shall never be separated, and that only in the execution of our own principles of liberty and equality, as laid down in the declaration of independence, can she expect to perform her high mission." Many resolutions expressed growing bitterness toward Confederates and spurned talk of compromise.[20]

The widely publicized denominational support for the Union war effort elicited howls of protest from Confederates who accused their northern brethren of political meddling and outdoing the politicians in their rancor toward beleaguered southerners.[21] All these statements (along with remarkably similar ones made on the northern side) breathed a fair amount of hypocrisy. But then bloody defeats and victories along with the war's mounting costs hardly encouraged a thoughtful, dispassionate, or charitable attitude toward one's enemies.

———

One especially devout Confederate soldier blamed Lincoln for the country's woes and, for good measure, looked forward to the Yankee president standing before the judgment seat of God. By the summer of 1862, northerners might not have gone that far but were rendering harsh judgments of their own. This was especially true of those who had run out of patience on the slavery question. Leading northern Methodists pressed the administration to pursue a more vigorous military strategy and proclaim emancipation. As one Chicago preacher pointedly observed, "policy" and "expediency" had too long ruled the White House, and in calling for "moral heroism," he implied that Lincoln had yet to display that essential quality.[22]

Even though many churches and religious editors still hung back, New School Presbyterians, various Methodist conferences, and Baptist associations grew more and more outspoken. Some applauded the progress of the antislavery cause and expressed a hope that liberty could soon be proclaimed throughout the land; others warned Lincoln that the nation was being punished for the sin of slavery; a few went further urging the president to enlist African American troops to suppress the rebellion. Even though their petitions occasionally recognized the delicacy of the question in the border states, they reflected the growing influence of antislavery views across a wide denominational spectrum.[23]

That the president had moved slowly on the slavery question should not have been surprising. Lincoln had reached political maturity as a Whig with a conservative reverence for both the Union and the Constitution, and he did not share the moral certitudes of the abolitionists or other reformers. His evolving ideas on the inscrutability of divine providence separated him from the more zealous and self-righteous members of his own party—and certainly from many clergy and churches. He had proposed gradual, compensated emancipation in the border states but without success. "Suppose God is against us in our view on the subject of slavery in this country, and our method of dealing with it?" he had once asked Browning. This most unsentimental of politicians had long favored colonization—one of the least practical and most unjust approaches to the country's racial dilemma. As president, he would continue to promote the idea though haltingly and inconsistently; during the war, not only conservative Catholics but antislavery Methodists and others clung to that chimera.[24]

Nevertheless, Lincoln had come to believe that somehow God willed the death of slavery and perhaps willed that Abraham Lincoln would help bring it about. In June 1862 meeting with a group of "progressive" Quakers, he agreed that slavery was wrong but doubted that simply decreeing emancipation could unloose the slaves' shackles. Recognizing the need for "divine assistance," he sometimes thought he might become an "instrument in God's hands of accomplishing a great work" but could not be entirely sure of the Lord's will or purpose.

Even as he had privately decided that the government must move toward emancipation, he continued to spar with visiting preachers, perhaps testing some of his own ideas in often pointed, at times tense, and occasionally humorous exchanges. At a September meeting with two ministers who had come to present a memorial on emancipation adopted by a large interdenominational meeting in Chicago, a bemused Lincoln noted how he was bombarded with a range of opinions from "religious men" all "equally certain that they represent the Divine will." After this gentle rebuke, there followed a playful observation, "I hope it will not be irreverent for me to say that if it is probable that God would reveal his will to others, on a point so connected with my duty, it might be supposed he would reveal it directly to me; for, unless I am more deceived in myself than I often am, it is my earnest desire to know the will of Providence in this matter. *And if I can learn what it is I will do it!* These are not, however, the days of miracles, and I suppose it will be granted that I am not to expect a direct revelation." After canvassing the practical, constitutional, and military difficulties in the matter, and after listening to the ministers for nearly an hour, Lincoln cautioned them against expecting too much from an emancipation policy, referring again to the delicate matter of the border states and assuring them "the subject is on my mind, by day and night, more than any other." Then he added enigmatically and prophetically, "Whatever shall appear to be God's will I will do."[25]

The right and wrong of the question seemed clear enough—Lincoln would later claim to not remember a time in his life when he had not considered slavery a great moral wrong—but political and military considerations muddied the waters. On July 22, he had read a draft of an emancipation proclamation to the cabinet but on Seward's advice decided not to issue it until after some striking success of Union arms. Two months later shortly after news of McClellan's costly victory at Antietam reached Washington, Lincoln again met with his advisers. According to Secretary of the Treasury Salmon P. Chase and Secretary of the Navy Gideon Welles, the president claimed to have made a promise to himself and to the Almighty that if Lee's army was driven out of Maryland he would issue a proclamation of emancipation. That statement must have stunned those in the room as Lincoln no doubt anticipated, and it was a most extraordinary statement to make to the cabinet. Welles recorded the substance of what followed: "It might be thought strange, he said, that he had in this way submitted the disposal of matters—when the way was not clear to his mind what he should do. God had decided this question in favor of the slaves." Ever since his son Willie's death early in the year, Lincoln had spoken more often and more feelingly about the ways of providence, and now he had finally reached the conclusion that the ministerial delegations, editors, and antislavery reformers had been pressing for so long.[26]

The president must have wondered, however, about how the men doing the fighting would react to this dramatic change in policy. Soldiers had long seen slavery as the war's root cause, but only a minority had been strongly antislavery. Increasingly, however, more of them decided that striking a blow against slavery was a military if not a moral necessity. At the same time, many would also have insisted they were fighting solely for the Union, for their homes, for their families, and for their comrades. "Sunday I attended divine service," a Rhode Island artillery sergeant wrote from Hilton Head, South Carolina. "The services were conducted by some abolitionists who came from the state of Massachusetts and there was so much talk about the confounded niggers that I came out disgusted." He complained about contrabands being treated much better than the boys in blue, adding "there is not a soldier who does not hate the sight of a nigger. . . . I despise them more than dirt." In truth, military opinion ran the gamut from deep-dyed conservatism to abolitionism. Vermont Private Justus Gale wanted to see slavery "wiped from our land," and the blacks colonized because he had "seen as much of the dirty nasty creatures as I care about." On the other hand, perhaps the nation was being punished for the sin of slavery, and the rebellion could only be crushed by crushing slavery. Lincoln's preliminary Emancipation Proclamation gave some men confidence that the "God of battles" had joined them in the fight for Union and liberty.[27]

The Lord's hand at work was a claim repeatedly heard after the president's dramatic announcement. To antislavery churches, clergy, and editors, emancipation reflected the fundamental reality of God's sovereignty in the world—a point made by Quakers and conservative Presbyterians alike. The war had come as a divinely ordained punishment for the sin of slavery, but now Christians could renounce evil and hail with joy the president's welcome—albeit tardy—conversion to the cause of righteousness. "The progress of the war clearly indicates the purpose of God to be the summary extinction of slavery," an Ohio Baptist convention declared, and Antietam became proof of that proposition.[28]

God had inspired the president to act, in the stern words of some Ohio Methodists, as an agent of "retributive justice." Frederick Douglass and other African American leaders increasingly interpreted the course of the war and destiny of their race in providential terms regardless of doubts about how much of a Moses Lincoln would turn out to be. "O Lord command the sun & moon to stand still while your Joshua Abraham Lincoln fights the battle of freedom," one black minister prayed. Christians would have preferred that the president had grounded emancipation upon principles rather than expediency, the *Independent* sniffed. Abolitionist Lydia Maria Child was even more dismissive: "Providence sometimes uses men [Lincoln] as instruments whom I would not touch with a ten-foot pole."[29]

Even that sour remark could not overshadow millennial hopes, which soared over news of the president's proclamation. Words such as "light" and "glory" appeared in religious commentary on emancipation, and that old stalwart of the benevolent empire, the American Broad of Commissioners for Foreign Missions, even predicted that "peace, prosperity, and righteousness will be permanently established in our land." A war lasting two to three years with losses of a hundred thousand or so lives would be well worth the cost, a leading New School Presbyterian editor calculated, so long as slavery was destroyed, and then the nation might well enjoy a hundred years of peace. The "cause of human liberty and the cause of pure religion," Pennsylvania Baptists avowed, would surely triumph.[30]

Sketching out the implications for this grand fulfillment of divine prophecy and national destiny summoned forth great imaginative and descriptive powers. "A new dispensation of things is now upon us," declared the African American minister Henry McNeal Turner. Talk of an epochal historical transformation became contagious. Spurning otherworldly religion, a Unitarian editor pointed out that Christ had been very much interested in this world and especially its poor and enslaved. "There are those who, in the commotions of the time, hail the second advent of Christ, and the coming of his kingdom," he observed. "So do we. But not in any personal appearance of Christ. He comes a second time in his principles, in his truths. . . . He comes in new thoughts, higher disclosures of duty, fresh manifestations of the glory and safety of his Gospel. He comes, blessed be God, in the captive freed; in manacles broken; in systems of cruelty and wrong shattered; in the new kingdom of righteousness, freedom, justice, humanity." Here was the vision of a reborn country, a beacon of civil and religious liberty to oppressed people. Ending slavery and crushing the rebellion, one Presbyterian editor maintained, would prepare the nation to lead the way "for the conversion of the world."[31]

No one wanted to consider the limits of human achievements or ambition, or what theologian Reinhold Niebuhr would later term the "provisional meanings in history," much less the "provisional judgments upon evil in history." The contemporary voices of moderation were not that thoughtful, they were merely cautious. Following Lincoln's lead and defending emancipation on the basis of military necessity suited the temper of some Methodists and Old School Presbyterians who refused to be caught up in the excitement of the antislavery moment, kept seeing the practical difficulties, remained concerned about state's rights, and worried about the futures of the freed slaves and southern whites. Yet even Presbyterian George Duffield, who not long ago had condemned John C. Calhoun and William Lloyd Garrison as equally wrongheaded, welcomed the preliminary Emancipation Proclamation as a providential gift.[32]

This is not to say that northern churches stood foursquare behind emancipation. Conservatism—especially among Episcopalians and Catholics—remained a powerful force, and however hard it might be to measure, a fair amount of indifference among preachers and their congregations prevailed in many parts of the North. Official denominational statements and the sermons of the more outspoken ministers undoubtedly ran ahead of lay opinion, though by how much is difficult to say. Worries about insurrections, race war, and former slaves migrating to the free states all stoked fears and made some clergy hesitant to embrace emancipation. The splintered views of Catholics were symptomatic of broader doubts and divisions across the northern states. James McMaster and other Catholic editors accused the president of selling out to radicals and succumbing to political pressure from Protestant preachers, but they also had to counter claims by Orestes Brownson that the Catholic Church had stood against slavery by pointing to traditional defenses of order, authority, and property rights. Caught in the middle, Archbishop Hughes had agreed to join other conservative clergy in New York to write public letters disapproving Lincoln's emancipation policy, but the Protestants backed out and so nothing came of this effort.[33] Perhaps Hughes also thought better of it. After all, he had been a firm friend of the Union and of great assistance to the government in rallying Catholic opinion at home and abroad; in the end, his public silence on this issue may well have represented a large swath of church opinion that wanted nothing to do with the extremes of McMaster or Brownson. Religious northerners were moving toward emancipation on both pragmatic and moral grounds, but many believers still had little to say about the issue and there remained strong pockets of resistance.

––––––

In the Border South, the battles over loyalty and slavery raged with much more intensity even among Catholics. Louisville bishop Martin J. Spalding continued to blame any agitation for emancipation on bigoted Protestant abolitionists. In Maryland, western Virginia, Kentucky, or Missouri, it often seemed best to hold one's tongue, though Unionist charges of Catholic disloyalty could hardly be ignored, and not surprisingly priests who passed through Union lines ministering to the Confederate sick and wounded aroused suspicion. Discussion about whether bishops and other clergymen should swear a loyalty oath revealed the pressures faced by Catholics in the border areas.

Yet keeping the church together proved much easier for Catholics than for many Protestants, ironically vindicating arguments made by McMaster and Spalding.[34]

Strong personalities compounded church troubles, especially for Old School Presbyterians. Kentuckian Robert J. Breckinridge had long condemned both slavery and abolitionists in strident fashion, and his *Danville Quarterly Review* published many articles on the war, all aligning Unionism with the scriptures and Presbyterianism. Admitting there were many disloyal pastors in Kentucky churches, and despite initial opposition to Lincoln's emancipation policy, Breckinridge could never conciliate the church's more conservative elements and preached a fiery Unionism bound to alienate southern sympathizers and their clerical allies.[35]

Intellectually and temperamentally, if not politically, Breckinridge met his match in the Irish-born editor of the *Louisville True Presbyterian*, Stuart Robinson. For someone who remained ostensibly silent on political questions, Robinson was a born controversialist. His sarcastic editorials condemned political preaching with the fervor of a Thornwell. Sharply attacking Breckinridge in the spring of 1862, he lauded a "free church" devoid of secular and political influences. Distinguishing between his duties as pastor and citizen, Robinson felt no obligation to endorse any particular form of civil government. His opposition to emancipation supposedly sprang from the atheistic character of abolitionism, but his strong opinions and self-proclaimed neutrality naturally led to charges of disloyalty, and his paper was suspended by Union authorities. He spent much of the war in Canada.[36]

Border state Presbyterians largely fought their battles in the columns of church papers and in synod meetings, but long-standing competition between northern and southern Methodists proved more serious. Ever since the church had divided along sectional lines in 1844, there had been tension in the border conferences, but secession and war brought matters to a head. Northern Methodists had a clear advantage in western Virginia, but the southern church claimed the lion's share of members in Kentucky and Missouri.[37]

Despite the state's official neutrality, Union and Confederate armies would eventually do battle in Kentucky, and consequently church quarrels heated up. Unionism remained strong, and in 1862 thirty-six southern Methodist preachers threatened to join the northern church if the state seceded. One Federal chaplain claimed that half the members of the Annual Conference of the Methodist Episcopal Church, South, were traitors, and soldiers threatened to arrest clerics who refused to swear an oath of allegiance. Some ministers steered clear of politics and concentrated on revival preaching, but suspicions of disloyalty lingered long after the war.[38]

This all paled beside the much deeper conflicts in Missouri where sectional bitterness (including the enduring effects of the 1850s Kansas border clashes) and guerrilla warfare spilled over into the churches with threats of violence and occasional assaults against ministers. Citing the familiar "render unto Caesar" text, determined Unionists rejected the southern rebellion as an illegitimate revolution against lawful authority without embracing emancipation much less radical Republicanism.[39] Old School Presbyterians had long struggled to avoid political questions and maintain theological orthodoxy; in November 1861 the Synod of Missouri unanimously rejected the General Conference's controversial Spring resolutions. This supposed neutrality, however, failed to prevent both Confederate guerrillas and Union troops from burning churches. "It was no use to try to do good, or do right, the Lord left Missouri . . . and religion was off on furlough," remarked one disheartened Presbyterian. Baptist Galusha Anderson recalled how discreet pastors refused to preach on subjects that might further alienate already divided congregations, but after seeing a secession banner flying from a church in St. Louis, he pointedly prayed for the president of the United States and closed the service with the singing of "America." The next Sunday a brickbat came flying through a church window.[40]

Badly outnumbered, northern Methodists in Missouri often felt besieged, and most of their ministers fled at the beginning of the war. Reports of suspended services and vandalized churches along with complaints about mobs — invariably described as "drunken" — filled the pages of the *St. Louis Central Christian Advocate*. A minister in Shelbyville received a note threatening him with a coat of tar and feathers should he dare preach again. The predictable epithet "abolitionist incendiary" offered a convenient excuse for secessionists to surround a minister's home and threaten to burn the place or worse. Federal troops provided some protection but whenever they left an area, guerrillas and other ruffians grew bolder, intimidating clergymen and their congregations. Throughout 1861, tensions mounted when reports spread that the Methodist Episcopal Church intended to plant more churches in the state to undo influence of the southern branch.[41]

As Federal troops occupied portions of Missouri, complaints about the arrest and abuse of ministers associated with the Methodist Episcopal Church, South, multiplied. Accusations of disloyalty and outright intimidation often drove these men of the cloth into exile. They claimed to preach Christ crucified and nothing more — never flying flags on their churches — but refused to profess loyalty to the Union, and some clearly had strong Confederate sympathies. They naturally denied persecuting northern Methodists, yet what appears most striking amid all the charges and countercharges is that cries of political persecution and proscription by one side largely mirrored—in often the same words—the charges made by the other side. And in most cases, threats against ministers were never carried out, though the war's disruptive effects on the churches were striking. Many preachers tried to avoid the political and social turmoil, but war inevitably crept into the churches. Reports of sick and elderly preachers dying in Federal custody further inflamed Confederate sympathizers.[42]

Lincoln had been right to tread warily in the border states but perhaps overestimated the importance of the slavery question there. Although many Presbyterians and Methodists—not to mention Episcopalians or Catholics— opposed emancipation, it was the war itself that most deeply divided denominations, neighborhoods, and congregations. Missouri became the most extreme example with the atrocities committed by guerrillas and Federal troops making religious tensions appear mild by comparison, but deeper and deeper wedges were being driven between believers. The antebellum division of the major denominations had born especially bitter fruit in the border states.

So 1862 had been a year of decidedly mixed blessings and seemingly mixed purposes for the American Union. Federal armies had largely triumphed in the western theater, but Robert E. Lee and the Army of Northern Virginia had won a series of dramatic victories. Even though Confederate offensives had been thrown back at Perryville, Kentucky, and Antietam, Maryland, and Lincoln had issued a preliminary Emancipation Proclamation, doubt and division—not only in the border states but across the North—still caused great unease. That fall Republicans faced resurgent Democrats in state and national elections. In September a group of Jewish congregations petitioned the president to declare a national fast day near the end of October as a suitable prelude to Thanksgiving. Lincoln did not do so nor would he issue a Thanksgiving proclamation until the following year, perhaps thinking that this especially gloomy November hardly seemed the time. Thanksgiving became a painful reminder of family losses yet also a marker for the war, a time to think about the meaning of the year's tumultuous history.[43]

Surely the Lord had blessed the nation, even though the rebels had been allowed to triumph for a time. The plain truth, according to one Pittsburgh Presbyterian of a strongly Calvinist bent, was that "God can do without this Republic!" He hoped the Almighty would still save the nation but could hardly be sure.[44] As a remarkably candid preacher in Scranton, Pennsylvania, admitted, "the household of faith is divided against itself." Anticipating Lincoln's elegiac mediation in the second inaugural address, Reverend J. H. Hickok added four telling sentences that exposed the perils of civil religion: "In this suicidal strife, both sides have made special appeal to Heaven. The combatants are Christian brethren—Christian ministers of the same communion. They are not only fighting against each other, they are praying against each other. Prayer meeting is pitted against prayer meeting; fast days counteract fast days; generals and soldiers on both sides are supplicating the same God, for success in the same engagements."[45]

After running through the usual litany of individual and collective sins, however, ministers more often assured their congregations that the Lord would not possibly allow the wicked rebellion to prevail. Pointing to the progress of Union arms, they still affirmed that all the sorrow and suffering served a holy purpose, and, however much God afflicted his people, he would still deliver the nation from its enemies. A government founded on righteous principles could not fall. Even Reverend Hickok seemed to forget his somber meditation on a religiously divided country and wrapped up his Thanksgiving sermon with an inspiring vision of the Union "sweeping steadily onward toward the eternal morning and summer of millennial glory."[46]

Despite the dominant strains of an untempered civil religion, more cautious voices could occasionally be heard. Northerners had by no means abandoned Calvinism, and indeed some of its sterner tenets still held sway. In suitably Presbyterian fashion, several divines urged people to be grateful because no greater disaster than war had yet befallen their sinful nation. And, as always, one could be thankful for calamities that betokened the chastening hand of the Almighty. Perhaps the people had expected too much of their generals and had been too impatient, declared one Philadelphian who favored restoring McClellan to command the Army of the Potomac. Political conservatism naturally made some clergy and congregations skeptical of the millennial rhetoric that filled so many Thanksgiving sermons. Some believers desperately clung to traditional ideas about the narrowly spiritual character of the church, hoping to ride such a solid raft safely through the swirling currents of war and revolution. Doubts that the Lincoln administration could prudently free the slaves often ran up against a growing sense, even among cautious Old School Presbyterians such as George Duffield, that failure to rid the nation of slavery had brought on the war. Despite his own traditional preaching, Duffield at times mistook divine purpose for the Union cause. Little wonder an outraged Catholic editor in Baltimore blasted Protestant Thanksgiving sermons for exhibiting the "most repulsive partisan rancor and abound[ing] in shocking blasphemies of God's providence."[47] Even for stout defenders of the strictest and narrowest theology, the ground kept shifting in unexpected and dangerous ways.

Ministers who denounced abolitionists and other "ultraists" acknowledged that the country had moved toward emancipation because Confederates had rebelled against a constitutional government. Others more readily embraced emancipation as a crowning moment of divine history. It seemed most fitting to give thanks for the impending triumph of human freedom under the rule of divine providence. Deliverance of the nation from such a heinous sin presented a glorious prospect, as Henry Ward Beecher and other ministers rejoiced over how the Lord had inspired the president to free the slaves.[48]

Would that matters were that simple. For those of a strict antislavery faith, such lofty sentiments seemed out of place, the joyous celebrations premature. Abolitionists wondered if the cautious Lincoln—who had yet to publicly link his change in policy to the divine will—could be trusted to issue a final Emancipation Proclamation. In any case, the Lord's work of reform would remain incomplete so long as northerners failed to confront racial prejudice in their midst, an evil that had already produced disastrous consequences and divine disfavor. Quaker editors criticized military abuse of the contrabands and deplored widespread alarms over freed slaves flooding the northern states. In a broader sense, Americans had ignored the downtrodden—whether slaves, Indians, or the poor. Social caste, declared a Connecticut Congregationalist, had created a "chattelism" that extended far beyond race and defined many a category of "nigger."[49]

Few ministers addressed such sensitive questions, but viewing the war as punishment for sin remained a standard theme in sermons and editorials, not to mention private mediation. For many northerners, the end of 1862 dramatically reinforced this belief. The stunning defeat and horrific casualties suffered by the Army of the Potomac at the Battle of Fredericksburg raised anew hard questions about God's will. Everyone from newly elected Ohio congressman James Garfield to Unionist Julia Chase living in Winchester, Virginia, interpreted this disaster as but the latest sign of divine chastisement. "I am every day asking myself what this nation has done which is so much more wicked than the deeds of all others that the scourge of God should fall so heavily and not be lifted," Garfield wailed. Chase wondered if "our Country's cause must be a very unholy thing" but still hoped that "Providence [might] raise up a leader like Joshua of old . . . to crush the enemies of our beloved country." This calamitous defeat even produced a temporarily humbler approach to divine providence. A recently delivered Thanksgiving sermon had offered a prescient warning: "Let us stop then, our infidel questioning, our heavy tongued murmuring, our vain guesses, our ambitious attempts to interpret the ways of God, our arrogant dictation and still more arrogant prophecies."[50]

Shortly before the battle, one Georgia volunteer had marveled over how the Federals fought in an "unholy cause . . . blinded by their folly, and maddened by their own wickedness," and now another Confederate victory marked the Lord's verdict against northern wickedness. Pious southerners immediately declared Fredericksburg a righteous judgment against the Yankees and additional evidence—if any were needed—that God would strike down abolitionist fanaticism. Confidence threatened to become hubris, even though the southern people were urged to seek the mercy of God. The usual talk of a just cause and imminent deliverance, especially among the devout at home, led to bragging about divine favor, literally "Lording" it over the enemy. Calls for humility either rang false or seemed pro forma and could hardly compete with soaring hopes, yea expectations, that the war would end in a matter of months.[51] Morale, and to some degree religious faith itself, followed a predictable course with periods of confidence often followed by defeat and gloom, with times of repentance giving way to hope and optimism. A strictly providential view of history offered little comfort, and human beings had trouble accepting the inscrutability and unpredictability of God's ways.

Even cheerful Confederates had to acknowledge that the victories of 1862 had come at a staggering cost, but for the Federals it would be an especially dismal Christmas season. "Every paragraph we read now-a-days, seems to be a disaster to our cause and arms," General John White Geary lamented. Yet he refused to be disheartened, and still believed God would protect him and his command. An equally somber Maine volunteer longed to see the war end but realized that the Lord would bring peace only "in His own good time and way."[52] It all came back to that thorny relationship between national purpose and divine will, between human plans and providential designs.

Chapter 11

THE LORD'S WORK

Seek ye the Lord while he may be found, call ye upon him while he is near.
— Isaiah 55:6

And the King shall answer and say unto them, Verily I say unto you,
Inasmuch as ye have done it unto one of the least of these my brethren,
ye have done it unto me.
— Matthew 25:40

There had been signs of religious stirring in the armies for several months, not exactly a surprising development during a season of intense combat. Seeing the dead at Antietam, one Union chaplain asked the question that must have weighed on many minds: "Oh God! how coust thou permit thy own creatures to butcher each other so cruelly?" Soldiers naturally struggled with such matters in the midst of so much ordinary and extraordinary suffering. Earlier attempts to organize army prayer meetings had met with indifferent responses, and even once devout fellows had lost their spiritual bearings in camp. There were always deeply religious men scattered through the regiments, brigades, and divisions, but whether this righteous remnant could leaven the often inert mass remained in doubt.[1]

By the fall of 1862, however, the prospects appeared much more promising. Lengthening lists of dead and wounded followed by any sustained period without active campaigning often laid the groundwork for bringing men to the Lord. At Winchester in a camp of the reserve artillery, evening meetings complete with singing, prayers, and the occasional sermon marked the first signs of religious revival. By late November in one Virginia regiment, a terrible backslider suddenly began praying with the men in his mess, and the chaplain hoped that this might be the beginning of a "great and good work in the camp."[2] Such small affairs portended a more sustained evangelism, which would gain momentum that winter and continue intermittently for the rest of the war. Some men found the courage to profess a renewed faith among comrades who continued to drink, curse, and indulge all manner of vices; as soldiers of the cross, they gathered around the campfires to sing hymns of salvation and comfort.[3]

Cold weather hindered outdoor services, but hastily built log chapels helped accommodate the swelling number of worshipers. The sermons were earnestly evangelical with much less attention paid to turning the men into better soldiers. Reports of growing religious enthusiasm as evidenced by wholehearted singing, fervent praying, and even occasional shouting spread, especially in Robert E. Lee's army. Chaplains, visiting missionaries, and local preachers showed new energy. Some men praised the services, while others noted a dearth of good preaching, yet references to fallen comrades often helped drive the main points home and brought tears to the eyes of hardened veterans.[4]

Well-attended, sometimes nightly services offered hope that the army would enjoy a season of religious awakening. Pious soldiers duly noted how men packed the meetings or when interest slackened. A sergeant in General William Barksdale's Mississippi brigade—where the fires of revival seemingly burned brightest—commented in the spring that services had been going on for a month, often three times a day, with more than a hundred joining the church, and fifty currently on the mourner's bench. Rejoicing that on the "crest" of war "rides a pure Christianity" and that the "grace of God shines through the smoke of battle," Virginia Baptists joyfully declared that the "camp becomes a school of Christ."[5]

Eventually northern churches made the same claim, but the early stirrings of religious interest in the Federal armies never matched the intensity or scope of the first Confederate revivals. By the beginning of 1863, with the aid of chaplains and delegates from the recently organized United States Christian Commission, the first signs of a spiritual stirring appeared. "There is a great many very good men here in the army as well as some very bad ones," one hopeful Pennsylvania private concluded. The soldiers were getting religion, he thought, but only a week later sadly noted "a grand army horse race and ending up in a drunken debauch and niger show, a disgrace to our army." Chaplains, who carefully recorded the names of officers and enlisted men who had joined the worshipers for the first time, often had to be satisfied with a dozen in attendance at evening prayer meetings rather than the much larger numbers reported among the Confederates.[6] Chaplains held more evening services, soldiers erected chapels, but attendance remained spotty and the lure of more worldly diversions strong. By April 1863 a Wisconsin volunteer claimed that even "rough and hard hearted soldiers" had become receptive to the Gospel message. Yet news of religious excitement in the Confederate camps alarmed a Maine chaplain, who marveled over how "God is reviving His work wonderfully at the South and in the army also."[7]

He was right: there were unmistakable signs of religious fervor among Lee's troops. Reports of fifteen thousand or more conversions in the Army of Northern Virginia were likely exaggerated, but the excitement that spread from brigade to brigade was real. Regiments without chaplains or with apathetic officers did not share this experience, and some resistance came from Episcopalians, Lutherans, and Old School Presbyterians who had never warmed to revivalism. Even so, these Confederate army meetings loomed far larger than any on the home front or those among the Federals on the other side of the Rappahannock River.[8] The past year had shown that the war would not end any time soon, triumphs and defeats had whipsawed emotions, and easily made claims about divine favor were beginning to ring hollow. Then, too, the deprivations of camp life and the horrific casualties, along with a lull in campaigning, made soldiers more receptive and in some cases eager to experience and promote the work of the Holy Spirit.

By early 1863, in camps around Fredericksburg, chaplains and visiting preachers were holding "protracted meetings." Private Robert Moore of the 17th Mississippi began attending in mid-February and came under the powerful influence of veteran Presbyterian evangelist Joseph Clay Stiles. Moore was "seeking the salvation of my soul" and seemed "weighed down with sin." But soon he had "found Christ in the pardon of my sins" and felt enormous "relief." He attended several services a week, rejoicing over all the "mourners" seeking the throne of grace. For the entire winter and into spring, there were prayer meetings in the mornings and afternoons and preaching at night. Stiles estimated that forty or fifty souls were being saved each week.[9]

Remarking on the "season of refreshment from the presence of the Lord" in the Army of Northern Virginia, Chaplain Robert Franklin Bunting of the famous Terry's Texas Rangers could only hope that such an outpouring would soon occur in the western armies. Perhaps these troops moved about too much or inclement weather prevented meetings in often widely scattered outfits, though one Louisianan stationed at Vicksburg concluded that "hardness of heart seemed the more to prevail among the soldiers here." Feeling especially alienated from many comrades and doubting that the Lord could look kindly on such a wicked lot, he decided that "sin has undoubtedly brought the dreadful calamity upon us." Such sentiments were far too gloomy. As in the eastern theater, there were signs of religious interest in the hospitals, and in some camps groups of soldiers gathered for prayer, and soon others followed their example. By spring there were small meetings in various regiments, but nothing yet to compare with the eastern revivals.[10]

The evangelical fervor ran up against indifference if not determined opposition; some officers remained uncooperative and occasionally hostile. One Alabamian doubted that all the religious excitement had much affected his regiment because the chaplain was "one of those cold men who never shows life in preaching." On the other hand, would the emotional excitement of revivals have a lasting effect on the soldiers? The men might show "some interest in the things of the Gospel," one frustrated Baptist preacher noted, but few appeared to be "decidedly awakened." Even among the supposedly upright Mississippians, irreverent fellows spread an oilcloth and began gambling and cursing within earshot of a Sunday service. One normally enthusiastic religious editor admitted that vices ranging from robbery to Sabbath breaking to "irreligion" remained widespread. To many believers, it still seemed that the irreverent and heedless far outnumbered the faithful.[11]

———

During the war and ever since, the question of numbers has proved quite difficult. Estimates of between 100,000 and 200,000 Union converts—something less than 10 percent of the total enlistments—are little more than educated guesses. How many of these had already joined a church at home is impossible to determine, and many church members would not be included in these totals. Even if the numbers had a more solid basis, though, they reveal nothing about the intensity or persistence of faith.[12]

Estimates on the number of Confederate conversions present similar problems. At the high end, 150,000 conversions would mean that roughly one in five men experienced some kind of spiritual rebirth. But given the social nature of evangelical religion, including revival meetings, it is impossible to tell how many "new" converts were won. And the deeply pious J. Williams Jones placed the total number of converts in Lee's army at under 15,000 (though he deemed this "conservative" and also threw out a possible figure of 50,000), so the extent and success of revivalism remains in doubt. How many Confederate soldiers were "praying men"? Perhaps one in three, as one historian has claimed, but when, for how long, and under what circumstances is hard to say.[13]

By Jones's own admission, the seemingly large numbers may have been misleading because they do not take into account how much of this renewed interest in religion actually amounted to a "genuine and permanent work of grace." Even if there was little falling away, historian Bell Wiley has concluded that a "majority of Confederates made no profession of faith and had no church affiliation." More recently, Joseph Glatthaar has made two important points about the Army of Northern Virginia that obviously have broader application: young males were not the most promising candidates for conversion; and, despite the importance of the services, prayer meetings, and revivals, the level of religious activity remained relatively low.[14]

Many soldiers would have agreed with these more cautious assessments, but then that was all the more reason for the preachers to see the armies as a vast if difficult field for evangelism. After all, Christians had to win over souls one at a time, so from the war's beginning, the emphasis had been on individual witness. Believers posed a simple but vital question for their fellow soldiers: are you saved? Chaplains labored at converting a man here and there in hopes of sparking a larger revival of religion.[15]

The religious press, denominational committees, Christian Commission reports, and compilations of testimonies, not to mention soldiers' letters and diaries, all described conversions and their significance for the individuals and the armies. These often moving stories form a crucial part of the war's religious history and, to many believers, the most important chapter in the narrative.

The themes were predictable and familiar. For instance, more than the certainty of death, the imminence of death drove home the evangelical message. When chaplains asked men to contemplate the vastness of eternity, they stirred deep fears. As soldiers struggled to repent, sound theology or even consistent behavior took a backseat to raw emotion. A Massachusetts corporal overstated the problem but nevertheless recaptured the sometimes mixed results of camp religion: "I see so much bad Christianity, I am discouraged."[16]

But erstwhile believers had other ways to win over wavering hearts. As one Federal chaplain remarked, "There are three words by which the soldier is readily influenced—Mother, home, Jesus," and the mere mention of the first two laid the groundwork for discussing the third. Thoughts of home along with the camp services often sowed the seeds of conversion. A religion of the heart remained at the center of evangelical faith, and appeals to spiritual affections deeply touched men removed from their families and beset by wartime trials.[17]

Recounting their conversions, soldiers often gave credit to their loved ones. Remembering the Sunday school back home and his pious mother, one uneasy Federal admitted being a "wanderer," full of anxiety and unable to find comfort. A camp sermon spoke directly to his anguish, and he concluded that "God has heard my mother's prayers." Likewise the desire to meet one's family in heaven made a man more receptive to the revivalist message. "The voice of a Mother and Sister, the early death of a brother, [and] two bloody battlefields all warn me of the shortness and uncertainty of life," an earnest volunteer in the famous Stonewall Brigade admitted. "And still I remain a hardened sinner. . . . the world lures me on and again I am in the same old state." He wished to believe but excused his laggard ways by pointing to men "profess[ing] to be Christians who really are not." Yet a couple weeks later, he talked with a sympathetic comrade and finally decided he had received salvation. "I trust that I have not deceived myself and pray that I may not fall back," but he found great delight in religious meetings and anxiously awaited his certificate of church membership to reach home.[18]

Converts spoke of joy and peace washing over them. "I have God in my heart, Christ in my soul, and heaven for my home," declared Private Peter Jones of the 36th United States Colored Troops. That conversions improved camp morals became an article of faith, but not everyone was convinced that wartime religious fervor was real or even desirable. A skeptical Unitarian chaplain admitted there might be less profanity heard in the camps but offered a sharp critique of revivalism: "I do not believe in any adequate gage of moral influence like that which is flaunted before our eyes by evangelical sectarians in statistics of conversions and degrees of conversion."[19]

Chaplains, missionaries, and Christian Commission delegates probably paid too much attention to the numbers but also found the baptisms quite moving. Somehow washing away sin — especially on the eve of battle — seemed both fitting and essential. According to a Catholic chaplain from Louisiana, some twenty-five "simple, country boys" who were baptized and later died in a Virginia hospital had found peace, and their families consolation.[20]

The type of baptism was not important, a Union chaplain's manual instructed, but that was hardly true for everyone. A perhaps apocryphal anecdote recounted one clash over immersion versus sprinkling. After hearing a Baptist chaplain tell about baptizing two soldiers in the chilly waters of the Potomac River, a Maine colonel ordered sergeants to take a man from each company and baptize them in the Methodist fashion, adding "I can't allow any damned Baptist to supplant my authority either spiritual or temporal." For the most part, converts could choose the method, and diplomatic chaplains with contrary beliefs went along. Even the rigid and censorious Lutheran John Stuckenberg agreed to immerse one soldier, recognizing the need to meet the "spiritual wants of men of all denominations." This was especially true for dying soldiers, though remarkably a Baptist chaplain who poured a healthy quantity of water on one poor fellow was censured by a group of ministers and later apologized to his home congregation for not following his church's practice of immersion.[21]

A final measure for successful evangelism was the admission of converts into a church. Especially during camp revivals, a fair number of the newly saved had to decide which one. Even soldiers who might have lingering doubts on this score thought it best to settle the matter immediately. There were some nondenominational camp churches, but usually a chaplain or preacher sent the information on a "saved" man to a congregation back home. Letters from chaplains certifying baptism qualified a soldier for admission to a local Baptist church.[22] Such news from the army, especially given worries about the effects of military life on the boys' morals, must have been heartening to congregations and families. Conversions, baptisms, and church membership all proved how the Lord's work was prospering despite the war or perhaps because of the war. Indeed, hope that the suffering and bloodshed might yield some good made reports of religious revivals all the more welcome.

———

The voluntary associations of the antebellum decades that Tocqueville had seen as so quintessentially American laid the groundwork for wartime benevolence. Churches often provided the setting, especially for women who had long served as the foot soldiers of charity. Only days after the firing on Fort Sumter, the women of Grace Baptist Church in Richmond joined a sewing circle to make clothing for the soldiers. By summer volunteers were carrying food to military hospitals and serving as nurses. In New York, a Presbyterian editor advised women to visit destitute working-class families in their neighborhoods. These new philanthropic opportunities reinforced the idea that the war would bring great and untold social benefits. In early 1863 the editorial voice of northern Methodism spoke of countless opportunities to help "cripples and widows, and orphans," along with "multitudes of freedmen."[23] To carry the Lord's work from the churches into the world had become both a practical and moral necessity.

Nowhere was this more apparent than in the military hospitals. As more and more women became nurses, their work brought physical and spiritual comfort to the suffering soldiers. Offering patients not only the soft bread that so many craved but also the "bread of heaven" seemed a noble calling, though one fraught with difficulty. Working at a Confederate hospital in Chattanooga, Kate Cumming, realized that many mothers could not abandon their work at home but still thought that many who could have volunteered had not done so. "How can we be expected to succeed when there is such a gross disregard of our Savior's own words?" she asked pointedly. In Columbia, South Carolina, young Grace Elmore felt the sting of such remarks. Having to care for her mother (or at least that was her excuse), she could not volunteer in a hospital and had instead donated money, but this was not the same as joining in the good work. She fretted about "disregarding the voice of God in my heart" and felt guilty about a "life of ceaseless ease that had been my lot for twenty two years."[24]

Those women who did enter the hospitals treasured opportunities for staying with soldiers during their final moments of life, reading the Bible, praying, or even bringing about a deathbed conversion. Those assigned to watching sick and wounded patients at night might have one last priceless opportunity to converse with a man about his immortal soul. And if there was one thing that many Federals and Confederates agreed upon, it was that the Catholic Sisters of Charity—along with nuns from eleven other orders—performed these tasks as well as anyone. In many ways, they embodied the highest ideals of pious womanhood in selfless service, and from Charleston to Baltimore to New York to Vicksburg, Catholic sisters tirelessly cared for grateful patients.[25]

Most of the trained nurses were in fact nuns, and even if their medical knowledge was limited, devotion to the work made them invaluable. When the number of wounded overwhelmed army medical resources, the sisters became ever more important and, given a shortage of priests, they helped ease the spiritual anxieties of Catholic soldiers.[26] In a gray serge dress, blue apron from neck to toe, and white bonnet with wide, starched flaps, their appearance was distinctive and, to some men, slightly comical. The neatness bespoke a determined efficiency and deep piety that could not help but impress even skeptical surgeons and hard-bitten soldiers. Above all, the sisters were no respecter of persons and cared for enemy prisoners like any other patients. "Dey Sisters day ain't for de Noff nud Souf," remarked one slave woman working in a Kentucky hospital. "Dey's for God." Their tender mercies, including care for men suffering from combat fatigue, impressed even the more cynical doctors.[27]

The war enhanced the reputation of various Catholic orders while reducing religious prejudice, as the sisters believed, and countless soldiers would have agreed. Initially unsure what to make of these women in the odd headgear and hardly knowing what to say to them, patients soon learned to appreciate their dedication. "We have for nurses the Sisters of Charity," one Union private wrote from a Washington hospital. "I assure you it looks queer to see them around without hoops." When a bell rang, they retired to pray, but despite their unusual appearance and behavior, he decided "it seems like home to have their soft hands to smooth one's pillow, to feel and wet our heated brows." For their part, the sisters liked men who expressed a "childlike" gratitude or made sure that none of their comrades spoke rudely to these angels of mercy.[28]

Catholic soldiers especially viewed the nuns as both nurses and comforters. Observing that some sisters had been tending more than a thousand sick and wounded soldiers at Monroe, Louisiana, Bishop William Henry Elder was pleased that "nearly all who die are reconciled to the Church, chiefly by baptism." Sisters sat by the beds of hopeless cases and, when necessary, administered the last rites. Despite difficult and often disgusting conditions, one nun rejoiced over "conversions, repentances, and the removal to a great extent of certain prejudices to our Holy Faith."[29]

That last point illustrated how successfully the sisters worked with all sorts of patients. Their compassionate deeds and hard work often meant more than the preaching of hospital chaplains. But when necessary these women too could deliver a sermon of sorts. After asking permission to obtain ice and beef for Confederate prisoners and being rebuffed by a Union general, one Sister of Charity held her ground: "Rebel or Federal, I do not know; Protestant or Catholic, I do not ask. They are not soldiers when they come to us; they are simply suffering fellow creatures. Rich or poor, of gentle or lowly blood, it is not our province to inquire. Ununiformed, unarmed, sick and helpless, we ask not on which side they fought. Our work begins after yours is done. Yours the carnage, ours the binding up of wounds. Yours the battle, ours the duty of caring for the mangled left behind on the field." When sneers or insults did not seem to faze them, that only enhanced the nuns' reputation and melted away distrust. In wards where not one in twenty soldiers was a Catholic, a Louisiana priest observed, the Sisters of Charity worked wonders in reducing bigotry against the church. Men who at first expected these "emissaries of the Pope" to poison their food, or worse, expressed deep regret when the sisters left. One Maine volunteer in a Confederate prison had nothing but praise for the sisters "with their black bonnets and white bonnets" who paid so much attention to suffering soldiers. "I am far from being a Roman Catholic," he wrote in his journal. "But from what I have seen during this war, I am convinced that the Roman Catholics have done more for sick and wounded soldiers North and South than any other religious sect."[30]

Sterling examples of Christian service changed minds and hearts. Shortly after the battle of Gettysburg, Sister Camilla O'Keefe reported, sixty Confederate prisoners converted to Catholicism. Some Protestants were deeply impressed by their nurses' example, but sisters also talked about faith with men (including the occasional deserter condemned to death) who had little religious knowledge of any kind. "Sister, I'm ready for you now," declared one soldier in a Baltimore hospital. "It's just as if the Almighty threw something at me, and when it struck me, I felt that your religion was the true one." Without much knowledge or interest in theology, men in the wards who had grown close to the nuns suddenly wished to embrace their faith. "I want to belong to the religion to which the Sisters belong," one wounded Confederate at St. Louis told Father Patrick J. Ryan, who had been attempting to explain the basic tenets of Catholicism. He kept asking a Sister of Charity if she believed these things, and when told that she did, he said he believed them too and agreed to be baptized.[31]

The Catholic sisters, just like the chaplains and visiting preachers, felt a deep responsibility to share the message of salvation whenever the opportunity offered. For the soldiers, hard service, deadly disease, and bloody campaigns meant that dangers lurked everywhere. Immortal souls were at risk, and there were never enough shepherds to mind all the sheep, never enough dedicated chaplains, army missionaries, or pious nurses to attend the men's physical and spiritual needs.

———

Although a tradition of organized benevolence in the northern states had established important precedents for wartime service, the sheer size of the armies required a more systematic and organized effort to care for the soldiers' bodies as well as their souls. So along with a fervent patriotism (and often strong Republican ties), both revivalism and perfectionism became driving forces behind the formation of the United States Christian Commission. The leadership had deep roots in Sunday schools, temperance, and any number of religious and reform organizations.[32]

Early in the war, branches of the Young Men's Christian Association handed out Testaments to troops, arranged for publishing devotional books, and gathered hospital supplies. By the summer of 1861, these haphazard measures had proved inadequate, and, perhaps more significantly, the regimental chaplains—then as always in short supply—needed help. The demand for pious men and women with practical skills and a desire to succor the soldiers and share the gospel was obvious, but the problem became how to harness the idealism and enthusiasm. In November representatives from across the northern states met in New York to create the United States Christian Commission, whose purpose was to seek "the spiritual good of the soldiers in the army, and incidentally their intellectual improvement and social and physical comfort." Twelve commissioners were appointed from evangelical churches in the Northeast and Midwest.[33]

During the summer of 1862, the Christian Commission moved its headquarters from New York to Philadelphia, where, under the leadership of the wealthy merchant and Presbyterian layman George H. Stuart, it began collecting money, gathering supplies, and sending volunteers to the armies. The work slowly gathered momentum with only fifty-five delegates in the field by the end of the year. These volunteers traveled to camps, hospitals, and battlefields, ideally spending six weeks without pay helping the sick and wounded, distributing devotional literature, and conducting religious services. By the end of the war nearly five thousand delegates had joined the work. Just as evangelicals had long counted the souls saved, the Christian Commission proudly reported the numbers of sermons preached, prayer meetings conducted, letters written for soldiers, books and pamphlets distributed, and the value of donated supplies.[34] "There is a good deal of religion in a warm shirt and a good beefsteak," George Stuart once remarked. Meeting the soldiers' spiritual and temporal needs in the tradition of John Wesley and Florence Nightin-

*Headquarters of the United States Christian Commission, Germantown, Virginia
(Library of Congress)*

gale became the overarching purpose. Viewing the men as "absent members
of Christian homes and communities," the Christian Commission aspired to
take the place ("imperfectly at best") of "father, mother, brother, sister, wife,
and friend, minister and church, to cheer and sustain them in their hardships
toils and perils, temptations and privations."[35]

Only evangelicals who could present a letter of recommendation from a
clergyman need apply to serve as delegates, so there was never any doubt that
the commission's religious work was all important. Many delegates were ministers, though according to one Christian Commission report, too many of
the clergy "pray for the country, make donations, and hope that the war would
be vigorously prosecuted—and do nothing more." Those who did volunteer
might be older men in delicate health, and camp conditions forced many to
return home. "The Christian Commission, so called, I am sorry to say I regard
as an unmitigated humbug," a Vermont preacher's son informed his father.
"Its agents are mostly Methodist ministers who can't be trusted with congregations North, and are a pretty slim set." Any money donated would only go to
support a "worthless set of imbeciles."[36]

Not surprisingly the Copperhead (and rabidly anti-Lincoln) *Chicago Times*,
dismissed Christian Commission delegates as "sanctimonious gentlemen
[who] are afraid of bullets" and visited the troops only when no battle loomed
so they could spend their time "among the skulkers in the rear of the army."

Soldiers sometimes echoed such criticisms. A Massachusetts volunteer who had seen more than his share of fighting suspected that a young teacher he had known back home who cheerily spoke of "see[ing] the thing out" with the Christian Commission was simply dodging the draft. Most likely, this soldier's comrades concluded. Just as with the chaplains, soldiers noticed and commented about Christian Commission delegates who slept late and rode about camp doing little or nothing. In Rosecrans's army, however, Catholic priests worried about the commission being all too active. They sounded the alarm over this "new-fangled and self-proclaimed band of protestant ministers," even though Father Peter Paul Cooney claimed that soldiers would pay little attention to men who embodied "the impotency of Protestantism which has no power over the heart and therefore can work no change." [37]

Such pointed criticisms, however, ignored the larger picture. During the Petersburg campaign, a Maine chaplain pointed out that, with but few exceptions, the Christian Commission delegates tirelessly sought out the sick, wounded, and dying. Persistent chaplain shortages—particularly in the western armies—made these visits all the more welcome, but everywhere, despite lingering suspicion and hostility, soldiers welcomed the supplies, religious publications, and most of all the attention. As a surgeon in the Army of the Potomac observed, there was little need for "good readers of sermons" but there could never be too many "steady, hard-working Christian men [possessing] . . . cheerful conversational qualities." [38]

The delegates' memorandum books recorded countless meetings held, literature distributed, hospitals visited—at times with a mathematical precision that suggested as much faith in organization as in the Lord. Given their myriad activities, including the distribution of badly needed food and supplies, delegates must have often found it burdensome to keep tabs on the spiritual condition of hospital patients and soldiers in camp. One field agent began a typical day by sending a half-dozen delegates to the front in a two-horse wagon. These men tried to cover two brigades during the morning, to hand out something to every man, and to speak with each one briefly. After a noon meal and well-earned rest, they visited a hospital, a single delegate handling four or five wards. After a break for tea, they held a brief service in each ward. Soldiers obviously relished any special food or supplies, but many sufferers also asked for reading material, longed for sympathy, or sought out spiritual comfort. [39]

"Soup first, then Testaments," could well have been the motto of one Hoosier delegate who understood the proper order of business; hot coffee, stationery, and kind words opened a path to men's souls. Such routine activities were one thing, but a major battle was quite another matter. Gettysburg overwhelmed everyone involved and certainly tested the Christian Commission's logistical abilities. Besides problems with loading and transportation, agents and delegates often had trouble finding the field hospitals, and many of the wounded were still lying on the ground or had been carried to farmhouses and buildings in town. Chaos and confusion led to criticism and second-guessing. Surgeons and nurses preferred strictly controlling the distribution of food, but in an emergency any help was welcome especially by hungry patients.[40]

Right after Gettysburg, Reverend P. A. Strobel entered a barn filled with wounded from the 11th Corps. He quickly found a thick comforter to replace a coarse woolen blanket that was causing untold agony to one fellow whose back was nearly raw. He scrounged a circular cushion to comfort one soldier with a fractured hip who had developed a nasty bedsore. For other men, he wrote letters or simply listened to stories about home and family or whatever they wanted to get off their chests. One captain who had just undergone a third amputation of a leg—this time above the knee—seemed inconsolable as he held pictures of his wife and daughter, tears running down his cheeks, but Strobel at least tried to calm the poor man until he fell asleep. He conversed and prayed just as easily with two hundred wounded rebel prisoners. Here was a man living out the teachings of Jesus, a thought that certainly crossed other delegates' minds as they offered a cooling drink or washed a feverish face. The soft bread, the coffee, and marmalade in one regimental hospital all signified a deep love and commitment to the soldiers.[41]

Christian Commission delegates watched patients at night to relieve the nurses or met the wounded arriving at Washington and Philadelphia hospitals. A Maine chaplain greeting the sufferers with food and warm drinks added "words of sympathy and direction to Christ." Assisting the wounded off steamboats and loading them into ambulances served both God and men. In the broadest sense, the delegates proclaimed that Jesus was the "Great Physician," who might heal patients physically and would surely heal them spiritually, and he offered the only source of real and lasting comfort. Working with chaplains, Christian Commission delegates assisted with burials, conveyed a man's dying words to a wife or mother, and shipped his precious effects home. In short, the delegates acted as brothers in Christ.[42]

With hospital chaplains in short supply, the Christian Commission often took charge of worship in the wards. Busy transporting supplies and handing out tracts, they kept services short, singing a hymn, reading a scripture, making a few remarks. One nurse, however, deplored a delegate's gloomy preaching and apparent obliviousness to more down-to-earth matters; a Massachusetts volunteer thought that one minister and his wife sang so horribly that they could be drowned out only by the "groans of a fellow who had just suffered amputation at the shoulder."[43]

Such criticisms likely stretched the truth but resembled those leveled against regimental chaplains. After all, worship in the hospitals was a delicate matter, especially given the Spartan conditions and suffering patients, and so a certain amount of grumbling was unavoidable. More often services seemed especially welcome where, in the words of a Vermont private, there had been "very meager religious privileges of any kind." In an artillery brigade in the Army of the Potomac, one minister thought there had not been more than ten men in five hundred trying to lead a Christian life, but he believed more regular religious services were bringing about a marvelous change. The evening prayer meeting anchored the Christian Commission's work. "It was sweet to be able to tell them of Jesus and of home," a Massachusetts delegate reported. "We miss them at home, at the prayer-meeting and in the social gathering. It was sweet to tell them so, and pleasant for them to know that we loved them, thought of, and prayed for them. But a home in heaven is better, and the love of Jesus is sweeter."[44]

In March 1864 at Brandy Station, Virginia, some two hundred worshipers filled a large Christian Commission chapel tent. Each evening at half past six, a delegate preached a short sermon, and then for the next hour and a half anyone who wished to speak, sing, or pray did so. The men relished the spontaneous singing and soldier testimonies. Official instructions warned visiting ministers to keep their sermons "brief, kind, tender, breathing of home, earnest, and fervent for Christ" because the men "cannot be impressed or moved by abstractions, or dry and dull discussions." Soldiers likewise appreciated how the Christian Commission tamped down denominational differences. Even in the navy where the more fiery Protestant ministers would make little headway with the sailors, Christian Commission services were considered an improvement over those conducted by ship captains. By evangelical standards, the meetings led by Christian Commission volunteers were successful because they encouraged revivals that would not otherwise have taken place, and delegates joyfully publicized the conversions.[45]

One visiting minister described his mission as "a personal agency to individuals for their conversion" with the emphasis on "personal." What was required, explained an official report, were "kind words to the soldier as a man, not a machine; as a man beloved for his heroic devotion to the Union, not despised as merely hireling food for powder and shot." After seeing the gospel personified in acts of kindness and compassion, a man would then exclaim, "Well, this is religion! . . . Tell me about it, and how I can become a real Christian?" An experienced delegate recommended walking about camp distributing tracts and saying little to the men; then return half an hour later, sit on a bunk, and strike up a conversation. Rebuffed no more than three or four times, he found many opportunities to quietly press home a biblical truth with some practical illustration. Such discussions could then lead to requests for private prayer during which both parties poured out their souls to each other and to the Lord. A few final words with a dying man might be one last opportunity to direct him to Christ. Addressing the common fear that soldiers would come home full of wild habits and worse morals, one delegate anticipated a more glorious possibility. He envisioned "pure, temperate, reverent, manly Christians" returning to "towns and villages to become the heroes and educators of admiring youths, and to be elected by a grateful people to every public office from constable to president." All that was necessary to make this happen was to bring the "power of religion to bear on the consciences of the soldiers."[46]

Success depended entirely on how receptive the soldiers were to the message. In early January 1864, a devout Pennsylvania private concluded that meetings held each evening by the Christian Commission were doing much good—a verdict confirmed by a couple Michigan volunteers and with even greater emphasis by hopeful and idealistic delegates. Although soldiers were hard to impress and their criticisms stung, the Christian Commission received high marks for a combination of needed food, timely assistance, sympathetic care, and spiritual comfort. After one delegate in perhaps a conscious imitation of Christ washed a Confederate prisoner's feet, tears ran down the man's cheeks, and he kept saying, "I can't stand it." Gratitude for warm blankets, soft bread, and kind words could transform soldiers used to hard campaigning and foul-mouthed officers. Compared to the chaplains who shirked their duties but were around to collect their pay, Vermont Private Wilbur Fisk considered Christian Commission volunteers to be selfless servants of God doing great good in a vast mission field—the Union army.[47]

In all their labors, delegates were supposed to supplement, not supplant, the chaplains, a point emphasized in their instructions. But that left a great deal of work to be done and created a few friction points. Christian Commission officials no doubt exaggerated the defects of the whole chaplaincy system to justify sending at least one delegate to each brigade. The best chaplains recognized the pitfalls of this makeshift system but welcomed the help so long as the Christian Commission men understood their place. A few chaplains resented would-be interlopers and perhaps feared the soldiers might be more receptive to fresh faces newly arrived from home.[48]

Christian Commission delegates greatly assisted in the commissary, medical, and religious work of officers, surgeons, and chaplains. Just as the government struggled to muster enough manpower to fill the armies, so the

Christian Commission eventually sent women delegates into the hospitals, perhaps hoping that a gentler touch would have a softening effect on rough soldiers and lead them to Christ. In their own way, female volunteers became disciples of Jesus not just in comforting hospital patients but in working with their churches to raise money. Some women, by donating jewelry and reportedly even their own wedding rings, became models of loyalty, piety, and sacrifice. Lists of suggested activities filled the pages of evangelical publications, and even little girls in Sunday school could put together a "housewife"—a bag with buttons, needles, thread, some tea, with perhaps a tract or enclosed letter—that would carry the message of pious devotion to the soldiers. Biblical references to Mary and Martha or the widow's mite justified women's unprecedented involvement in charity work—albeit in prudent and conventional ways.[49]

To mobilize the churches became the fondest desire of Stuart and other leaders who aspired to see a home front on fire for the Lord. Indeed, estimated contributions to war-related charities in the northern states ran to more than $200 million. Aside from general fundraising appeals, the Christian Commission took up special collections right after bloody engagements when volunteers and supplies were most needed. Even foreign missionaries sent in donations, as did some soldiers. A delegate from Chicago loved recounting the tale of a six-year-old girl and her widowed mother who scraped together two dollars for soldier Testaments—an inspiring example sure to bring tearful penitents to the mourners' bench.[50]

The commission even tried to enlist Lincoln. In February 1863 an invitation for the president to chair a meeting in Washington led to a brief cabinet discussion, but only the pious Chase spoke in favor, and Lincoln did not attend. Nevertheless, he commended the commission for "turn[ing] our thoughts from the unreasoning, and uncharitable passions, prejudices, and jealousies incident to a great national trouble" and instead "strengthen[ing] our reliance on the Supreme Being, for the final triumph of the right." From the beginning, Lincoln had given rather perfunctory approval to this work; perhaps Christian Commission officials seemed too much like the pesky clerical delegations that kept showing up at his door. In any case, during a trip to Philadelphia, Lincoln offered warmer praise for the rival Sanitary Commission.[51]

Organized by prominent business, civic, and medical leaders, the United States Sanitary Commission collected millions of dollars and sent out hundreds of paid agents to distribute medicine, food, clothing, and incidentals to the soldiers. Prominent Unitarian minister Henry W. Bellows served as president, and in some ways the liberal Christianity of the Sanitary Commission presented a striking contrast to the stoutly evangelical Christian Commission. Organization and efficiency became hallmarks of the Sanitary Commission along with a socially conservative, patrician approach to philanthropy. There seemed little religious fervor or cloying sentimentalism here, but women who ran the Sanitary Fairs often embodied warmer ideals of Christian self-sacrifice.[52]

In the minds of many Americans, the Sanitary and Christian commissions seemed interchangeable as soldiers, volunteers, and ministers often praised both groups in the same breath. In the field, the two organizations normally cooperated, but among the leadership there was tension. Bellows for one worried that the Christian Commission "without accomplishing its own object, will weaken and defeat ours." And there was more at work here than simple rivalry. Early meetings with representatives of the Christian Commission convinced George Templeton Strong of their "shallowness, fussiness, and humbug." At the end of the war, he was still railing against George Stuart as an "evangelical mountebank" and dismissed a Christian Commission delegation he met in Stanton's office as an "ugly-looking set." Accusations that the Christian Commission was hostile to Catholics and Jews or that its work in the hospitals failed to reach enough soldiers rounded out the list of criticisms. One Sanitary Commission partisan derided the rival organization for wasting money on "tracts and broken down preachers."[53]

Such disparagement only fed a self-righteousness that cropped up in defenses of the Christian Commission. Simply labeling the Sanitary Commission "Unitarian" was the equivalent to calling it atheistic in some evangelical circles. Christian Commission supporters kept a sharp eye out for any deviations from religious orthodoxy by the Sanitary Commission. A raffle and dance at the Great Western Sanitary Fair in Cincinnati outraged Methodists who deemed such activities a "direct insult to the Christian Community and Christian Churches."[54]

Perhaps the problem was that there was no nationwide Christian "community," and churches themselves were hardly united on the proper approaches toward charity and certainly not on the war's larger questions. Both the fervent support and, at times, sharp criticism received by the Christian Commission reflected not only sectarian differences but a persistent gap between believers and nonbelievers. Just as the success of the Second Great Awakening had been partial and incomplete, so too the camp revivals and work of the Christian Commission could not meet the lofty goals for evangelizing the army and the larger society set by ministers, their lay supporters, and the churches. Meanwhile the war ground on, and at the beginning of 1863, both sides would have to contend with internal divisions as they struggled to discern the ways of providence. Civil religion remained strong in both the Union and the Confederacy, but emancipation, conscription, calls for peace, and persistent debate about the war's religious meaning and purpose would place new strains on the connections between patriotism and faith.

Chapter 12

TESTING FAITH

When they fast, I will not hear their cry; and when they offer burnt
offering and an oblation, I will not accept them: but I will consume
them by the sword, and by the famine, and by the pestilence.
— Jeremiah 14:12

It just did not seem like Christmas—a common enough lament among older folks—but true enough for most everyone in 1862. The absence of familiar treats and familiar faces marked but another sign of how the war ruined everything, especially in the Confederacy. "With the shadow of God's judgment and displeasure still over our beloved country, and no ray of absolute light breaking from any quarter," the planter (and Presbyterian minister) Charles Colcock Jones wrote to his son in the army. "I do not know that we can greet each other with a 'Merry Christmas.'" Despite the recent Confederate victory at Fredericksburg, a young South Carolina volunteer in Virginia offered an even more somber assessment: "If all the dead (those killed since the war began) could be heaped in one pile and all the wounded be gathered together in one group, the pale faces of the dead and the groans of the wounded would send such a thrill of horror through the hearts of the originators of this war that their very souls would rack with such pain that they would prefer being dead and in torment than to stand before God with such terrible crimes blackening their characters."[1]

Like Reverend Jones, northern Methodist Heman Bangs worried about "God pouring out His vials of wrath upon us." And, to his way of thinking, deservedly so for the hoary idea of war as divine chastisement seemed as applicable as ever. "We are having a baptism of blood," one leading editor remarked, adding with some hope, "but it is a baptism not unto death but to resurrection." The promise of light and salvation, however, appeared quite dim—perhaps too distant to glimpse. A New School Presbyterian editor who welcomed the government's move toward emancipation nevertheless warned that an army where three-fourths of the volunteers were "profane" had become in itself a "sufficient cause for disaster and defeat." A dedicated Vermont sergeant was determined to see the war through to victory but was convinced that the Lord was giving the nation a well deserved "scurging."[2]

Whether Americans had yet been humbled or even much chastened seemed doubtful. Deriding the boastful northern press crowing over "superior physical power," the *Charleston Mercury* ridiculed the Yankees for failing to put the Almighty into the equation. For his part, the editor was just as boastful, asserting that a "God of justice and holiness" could not possibly sustain such a band of "robbers and murderers" and calling on righteous southerners to "scourge them from our land, and make them the hissing scorn and detestation of the world." Editors and preachers and soldiers continued to assert—often without qualification or reservation—that God most decidedly favored southern arms. Confederates were blind to their own sinful pride, but they were right about their enemies. That God would subjugate the rebels remained the unwavering conviction of many devout northerners, whether Unitarians or Baptists. The Almighty will yet vindicate the nation's "free institutions," a Michigan lieutenant explained in a long letter to his wife. To such true believers, there was no mistaking the divine will regardless the cost in dollars and blood.[3] This persistent linking of the war to God's purpose made people more willing to bear that cost and continue the fighting.

A providential framework still explained the war's course. According to conservative Presbyterian Charles Hodge, God carefully calibrated the "distribution of good and evil in this world," all governed "by mysterious wisdom for the accomplishment of higher ends than mere punishment or reward." Unlike expositors of a simpler civil religion, Hodge not only explicitly acknowledged the inscrutability of the Lord's will but implicitly suggested the possibility that divine purposes might not mesh with northern war aims or methods. Hodge questioned the whole idea of wartime suffering as a punishment for individual and collective sins and instead saw the affliction of individuals and nations as more redemptive than punitive. Yet more often ministers as well as soldiers reaffirmed that, whatever the mysteries of providence, all would work out for the Union cause, indeed that God would directly assist in restoring national unity. Many northern Christians still equated providence with progress and cast American destiny as part of an unfolding and beneficent plan for mankind. "Jesus is revolutionizing the globe," a Pennsylvania chaplain declared even after the carnage at Fredericksburg. "Each successive annual not only brings nearer, but with accelerated speed, His reign of peace and love."[4]

"Thus saith the Lord," might well have been added to these public pronouncements and private affirmations. But that was the problem: theologically questionable and logically slipshod interpretations of the war produced dogmatic assertions of providential intent. In doing so, the chief defenders of such a position, Union or Confederate, ironically left open the door for other and, to their minds, less congenial understandings of divine purpose. Perhaps the Prince of Peace did not sanction war at all, as the Quakers and others would have argued. The so-called Peace Democrats in the North might have agreed, though a Baptist editor in Columbia, South Carolina, was eager to show that there could never be peace societies in the Confederacy because Christ had offered his highest praise to a Roman centurion and slaveholder—a tortured reading of scripture, but that hardly seemed to matter. And for good measure, border state Catholic bishop Martin John Spalding held that "Puritanism, with its preaching and Common Schools has at length ruined the Country." Such a result had been quite predictable, but Americans would have to realize that "their only salvation is to be found in conservative Catholicity."[5]

Many of these arguments were hard to follow or seemed illogical, but they illustrate how at the beginning of 1863 religious voices still sounded remarkably dissonant. Nor would they converge any time soon because the war itself along with rancorous debates and internal dissent would place enormous strains on the governments and the people, making any kind of consensus on the meaning and direction of the conflict elusive if not impossible.

———

Slavery remained the most divisive and most explosive question as Lincoln prepared to issue the final Emancipation Proclamation. Proslavery clergymen had done their work all too well, so the response fell into a familiar pattern. An *Address to Christians throughout the World* signed by a who's who of southern divines denounced this supposedly desperate measure for inciting a slaughter of women and children while unsettling the natural affections between masters and slaves. In their view, the triumph of abolition could only produce "bitterness and sorrow and pain and infidelity and moral degeneracy." Such sentiments were echoed by many southern Christians who foresaw a satanic triumph in the North. Virginian Nancy Emerson repeated the commonplace charge that Yankees had thrown away their Bibles to embrace fanaticism and therefore would suffer the consequences.[6]

In point of fact, celebrations of emancipation by African Americans beginning on January 1, 1863, assumed a nightmarish quality for Confederates. In speeches, sermons, and especially song, the celebrations of deliverance reached a crescendo. For a time ignoring the government's halting and still incomplete commitment to emancipation, a black minister in Washington led a group of former slaves in singing "Go Down Moses." The line "Let my people go," was delivered in a "perfect shout." Elsewhere worshipers joined in the old Methodist hymn, "Blow Ye the Trumpet, Blow," whose chorus now suddenly took on new meaning:

The year of jubilee is come!
The year of jubilee is come!
Return, ye ransomed sinners, home.[7]

References to Exodus and the year of jubilee touched important themes in African American religion, but a long editorial in the AME *Christian Recorder* reinterpreted the standard jeremiad, making emancipation both inevitable and providential. "God has a controversy with this nation": that variation on a warning from the prophet Hosea explained the anguish of war. The chastening hand of God was striking down slavery, as Lincoln and millions of Americans had concluded. The realization of this fundamental truth had taken time, but the president's proclamation proved how the Lord hated oppression and was determined to free those in bondage.[8]

The Almighty had at last redeemed the innocent, but the question then became, Would the southern pharaoh continue to harden his heart and ignore the northern Moses? Whether either president exactly fit those roles seemed beside the point. Northern black leaders began adding Lincoln to the honor roll of politicians, even though abolitionist Henry Highland Garnet warned the congregation at New York's Abyssinian Baptist Church, "My friends, we must remember that it is God who has brought about this great event." Even Frederick Douglass adopted apocalyptic and millennial language in exulting over how the American crusade promised to bring about worldwide freedom. Praise for the Lord reached ecstatic heights but also led black ministers and editors along a treacherous path toward a civil religion that confidently discerned a providential meaning for each new twist and turn in history. A day after Lincoln had issued his famous document, the Union army had won a great victory at Stones River. But should the next defeat then be interpreted as a repudiation of an antislavery war?[9]

Ironically, the final Emancipation Proclamation itself made no mention of providence, although the pious treasury secretary Salmon P. Chase had persuaded Lincoln at the last minute to invoke the "gracious favor of Almighty God." The document's legalistic and uninspiring language, however, did not prevent Unitarians from praising its "moral magnitude and grandeur" or calling it a second Declaration of Independence. Could one dare think, as Lincoln never did, that emancipation would make the United States a Christian nation? To antislavery preachers, there could be little doubt on that score. To Henry Ward Beecher, the Emancipation Proclamation proved that the Almighty had a plan for liberty and the northern people should go forth with the cry of "God and justice." To the *Independent*, the glorious document had become a "pillar of fire" marking the "steady progress of a Higher Plan in the history of this land." To the leading organ of northern Methodism, emancipation brought "bright omens of success" and God's "grace will be vouchsafed to help us, and his wisdom to guide to a perfect result."[10]

The spirit of antebellum perfectionism lived. "To withdraw ourselves from every brother, from every church, from every association, that it in any way justify or uphold American slavery, intemperance, secret societies, or any other sin, is not to divide the church of Christ, but to separate ourselves from all that is anti-Christian," an Indiana Baptist association announced. Emancipation itself became an act of repentance to atone for the country's manifold sins. The war's darkest hours reminded Christians of the Crucifixion, but here too darkness was but a prelude to light, the glorious resurrection of a nation at last doing its moral duty. Upright churchgoers overwhelmingly supported the government's new emancipation policy, the resolutely antislavery *Zion's Herald and Wesleyan Journal* editorialized, and "the vast preponderance of sin and moral infidelity is on the other side."[11] The war became more righteous than ever with little doubt expressed about where the Lord stood.

There were naturally exceptions. Quakers rejoiced over emancipation while somehow trying to deny it was a military measure; Catholics remained divided and ambivalent.[12] In a broader sense, clerical conservatives may have spoken for a sizable though often silent segment of religious opinion, but the grounds of the discussion were shifting. In spurning both northern and southern extremists and holding up George Washington as a symbol of constitutional and national unity, Presbyterian John C. Lord sounded like a voice crying in the political wilderness. His cautious embrace of emancipation might once have seemed bold but now sounded tepid. That doctrinaire opponent of abolitionism, Vermont Episcopal bishop John Henry Hopkins, persisted in a biblical defense of slavery that appeared ever more tendentious, if not bizarre. Even though Democratic clubs in Pennsylvania issued a reprint of his pamphlet, *Bible View of Slavery*, as a campaign document in 1863, Republicans enlisted Pennsylvania Episcopal bishop Alonzo Potter to blast the piece as "unworthy of any servant of Jesus Christ."[13]

However unpopular Hopkins's views were, a fair proportion of churchgoers remained indifferent to the plight of slaves. Like Lincoln himself, many soldiers who supported emancipation placed much greater emphasis on the evils of slavery than on the evils of racism. A Michigan surgeon who concluded that free labor must come to the southern states still saw blacks as "inferior by nature" and greatly in need of guidance from paternalistic, Christian whites. "Any country that allows the curse of Slavery and Amalgamation . . . should be cursed," a junior officer from Illinois believed, and it was difficult to separate his aversion to slavery from his aversion to race mixing. In far-off Utah, Brigham Young maintained that "if the white man who belongs to the chosen seed mixes his blood with the seed of Cain, the penalty, under the law of God is death on the spot." Radical preachers such as Methodist Gilbert Haven realized that deep-seated racism would be difficult to eradicate but pressed northern churches to live up to the American ideals of democracy and equality. Massachusetts minister Edmund Willson pointedly reminded his congregation that "under every dusky skin is a soul as much in the care of God, as is he who issues proclamations."[14]

To those of an unwavering antislavery faith, the best way to fight bigotry was to enroll blacks in the Union armies. The hope for a change if not a revolution in white opinion rested on this military experiment. A Baptist missionary in Burma wrote to her brother supporting the use of black troops as part of the Almighty's emancipation plan. AME leaders urged African Americans to serve the country's cause in a grand fight for liberty—even in the face of mistreatment and pay discrimination. The Emancipation Proclamation, claimed the pious Indianapolis businessman Calvin Fletcher, "proposes to recruit all able bodied men as soldiers." His hope remained that God "may yet raise up a Moses whom we shall fear and respect and that he will give his countrymen character and standing among the whites."[15]

Whatever the importance of "character and standing," the Union cause badly needed able-bodied men. In 1863 the United States government finally resorted to conscription but, unlike the Confederates, provided no exemption for ministers. Massachusetts senator Henry Wilson opposed protecting a "favored few," and John B. Henderson, representing the bitterly divided state of Missouri, took an even harsher view. He sarcastically recommended putting all the clergy in service and "trust to God in the future they would not bring on another war."[16]

Congregations might pay the perfectly legal three-hundred-dollar commutation fee to keep their pastor at home but that hardly settled matters. Patriotic ministers considered such gestures insulting, while others complained when their strapped parishioners refused to come up with the money. Democrats kept a sharp eye out for any "abolition preacher" who failed to enlist. But the practical question remained whether ministers should serve in the military and whether they made good soldiers. Complaints about anticlerical prejudice in Congress likely reflected worries that the draft would hurt the northern churches, but each congregation and its minister were largely on their own.[17]

The federal conscription law posed a much larger problem for the peace churches. Quakers had little sympathy with a slaveholders' rebellion, regularly proclaimed their patriotism, and despite their pacifist principles were hardly neutral in the conflict. Yet, like many conservatives, Quakers claimed to shun the partisan strife and political hatred that had led to war. Their periodicals offered few comments on the conflict and often seemed mired in the church's eighteenth-century history. Despite such precautions, young people could not help but get caught up in the war fever, while traditionalist Quakers criticized any church publication that printed military news.[18]

Maintaining the church's peace principles proved difficult in a nation consumed by a bloody and relentless civil war. "When the sound of armies is heard," the Western Yearly Meeting in Indiana advised, "Let us betake ourselves to prayer that our everlasting Father, the Prince of peace may hasten the day when nation shall not lift up sword against nation neither shall they learn war any more." Officially, Quaker meetings condemned the southern rebellion but could not support its forcible suppression. All wars were incompatible with the Christian faith, and this one was no exception, though some pacifists made a distinction between suppressing a rebellion and fighting a war. And even if the conflict destroyed slavery, it remained difficult to rationalize the violent means involved. Not all Quakers lived up to such exacting standards, and there was a natural tendency to rejoice over Union victories and forget that the dead on both sides had immortal souls. After all, war "deprave[d] the morals of the people," one editor warned, and so "there seems little room for Friends to do more than meekly and unyieldingly maintain their peaceable principles in conversation and example."[19]

In reality, the peace witness had already been weakened, and Quakers had not been active in antebellum peace societies. Only weeks after Fort Sumter, reports circulated of Quaker companies enlisting, and many Amish and Mennonite young men followed suit. They volunteered for largely the same reasons as other soldiers—patriotism, adventure, employment—though some also saw themselves as crusaders against slavery, but their decision to take up arms saddened families and raised questions about church discipline. One further irony: the lyrics to a popular recruiting song, "We Are Coming Father, Abraham," were written by a Quaker abolitionist.[20]

During the summer of 1862, a militia draft had tested Quaker convictions. "We are encouraged by tidings . . . that there are yet among our young men those who are prepared to stand firm in adherence to the peaceable principles of Christianity," the *Friends' Intelligencer* commented. The more sobering implication seemed to be that a number of Quakers had already volunteered. Various meetings instructed members not to serve in the military, and in a strict sense, even substitution and commutation violated religious principles.

What Quakers preferred was a blanket exemption that recognized pacifist scruples, and they reassured government officials that only small numbers of men would seek such protection.[21]

As a practical matter, Quakers (or their families) often paid commutation fees especially during the final year of the war, and the Friends were seldom harassed by the government. Members of Congress and state governors were often sympathetic. Lincoln acted with kindness and understanding; even the imperious Stanton took a surprisingly tolerant attitude toward conscientious objectors. Under a revised law, a drafted man could work in a military hospital but that hardly satisfied strict pacifists who objected to helping a soldier recover so he could resume fighting. However one interpreted such provisions, some Quakers still complained about being punished for conscience sake, though yearly meetings expressed deep gratitude to Lincoln and Stanton.[22]

A few Quakers were hauled into army camps and made to wear uniforms, but they refused to bear arms. Persuasion and even force failed to change their minds. Officers and enlisted men often sympathized with anyone willing to suffer for their convictions, but resisters were not always treated gently. In July 1863 Cyrus Pringle was drafted at Burlington, Vermont. He refused to serve or pay a commutation fee and so was confined at Brattleboro with very little food. Later held on Long Island, Pringle and another Quaker faced constant bullying from a major determined to break them. At a camp in Virginia, they were issued guns but would not carry them; junior officers threatened them with severe punishment or death. When Pringle refused to perform hospital duties, he was staked to the wet ground and left out in the sun for nearly two hours. Eventually sent to Washington, Pringle won release from Lincoln himself.[23]

Making such men fight would have been either impossible or far more trouble than it was worth, and in any case a few conscientious objectors hardly endangered the Union war effort. For the Quakers, how to avoid providing any support for the war posed a greater difficulty. Some thought they should pay no taxes that directly financed military operations but did not object to taxes in general; the New England Yearly Meeting recommended that Quakers pay all taxes. When Ohioan Joshua Maule urged other Quakers to withhold any "war tax," some Friends advised him not to disturb the monthly meeting with such talk. Despite Lincoln's sympathetic attitude toward Quakers, there was some debate over whether Friends should vote in the 1864 presidential election.[24]

A quarter or more of the military-age Quaker men from Indiana served in the army, and the peace witness seemed weaker in the western states. Any church proceedings against those who enlisted were usually postponed until after the war when it was easier to excuse such behavior as a youthful indiscretion. Boys with a still developing religious faith would not always make the most principled choices during times of high excitement and embittered passions. Any who later confessed their error were readmitted to fellowship, but the substantial number of enlistments by Friends and other members of peace churches certainly proved how war disrupted even tightly knit religious communities.[25] The Lincoln administration could have hardly tolerated draft resistance from any of the larger denominations, and the Quakers along with other peace churches wisely avoided aligning themselves with the so-called Peace Democrats, who shared neither their pacifist nor antislavery principles.

In September 1863 a group of New York Quakers complained about the "embarrassment" caused by "unscrupulous men, assuming the name of peace makers, [who] are doing all they can to further the objects of those who seek to destroy our general Government, and to rivet the chains of slavery in this land." Such a statement echoed Republican condemnations of Democratic "Copperheads," who during the late winter and spring of 1863 were flexing their political muscle. Exalting McClellan as a Christian general, some Democrats described themselves as disciples of peace who deplored abolition preachers' bloodcurdling sermons. At the most extreme, one Copperhead editor even claimed that the early Christians had all been pacifists and denounced those "fighting parsons" who now "shouted for the slaughter of God's family." Anyone preaching politics rather than Jesus mistook loyalty to the Lincoln administration for loyalty to God and more often than not dodged the draft himself or sought a safe position as chaplain or Christian Commission delegate. Outraged religious conservatives objected to denominations adopting "political" resolutions on the war and, like many Confederate preachers, detected the spirit of Puritan intolerance in national fast and thanksgiving sermons. The venomous C. Chauncey Burr claimed that Cheever, Beecher, and other radical ministers had made Negroes their idol and then sarcastically asked, "What must be the priest, where the monkey is a god?"[26]

Inflamed by such rhetoric, Copperheads not only walked out of services but occasionally disrupted them. During a revival meeting in Johnstown, Pennsylvania, a half dozen "ruffians" brandished pistols, cursing both abolitionists and the war; at a later service, another group of hecklers denounced Union chaplain Andrew Jackson Hartsock as a "damned abolition son of a bitch." Yet, as one Presbyterian minister perceptively noted, "Few men have objections to the preaching of politics, so long as it is their own politics which are preached."[27]

The point is well taken because conservative ministers at times preached their own brand of politics. In Fairfield County, Ohio, Methodist James F. Given felt threatened by "political rowdies," in this case Republicans who angrily withdrew support from his church after he had endorsed the notorious Copperhead Clement L. Vallandigham for governor. In condemning emancipation and Republican clergy, some conservatives delivered what amounted to Democratic stump speeches, and so attacks on political preaching rang hollow.[28]

If Democrats used "abolition minister" as a handy epithet, Republicans just as vigorously denounced "proslavery preachers." In December 1862 Illinois Methodist Rumsey Smithson reportedly called it a sin for any person of color not to have a master. Forced to resign the following April, Smithson spoke at a Democratic rally in May and was expelled from the Central Illinois Conference in September. A Republican editor sarcastically remarked that Copperhead ministers might not preach politics on Sunday but freely spoke at public rallies during the week. All told some thirty "disloyal" ministers had their licenses revoked by Methodist conferences in Ohio, Indiana, and Illinois. An article in a women's church paper called on readers to "detect and expose the covert traitors in your neighborhood . . . Hunt them out. Make the place, the society, the neighborhood too hot for them."[29]

In response, an independent church movement in several midwestern states sought to divorce religion from Republican politics; Democrats declared themselves Christian martyrs, being driven from the pews by infidels and partisans. But attracting only a few dissident clergymen, these new congregations remained small and struggling. Democratic newspapers touted them, and Republicans ridiculed them, as well they might because these breakaway groups hardly helped the Democrats or Vallandigham in the fall 1863 elections. The complaint of one Democratic editor likely reflected more political pique than religious conviction: "Democrats have as good a right to pray and share the blessings of grace as any beings on this green earth."[30]

Perhaps so, but for many northerners the word "loyalty" struck the keynote as United State flags were prominently displayed at denominational meetings. "It is this holy spirit of devotion on the part of the whole, this jealous patriotism, this unconditional loyalty that can alone save the land," Unitarian Henry Bellows avowed. In this manner, every church and home and business could help "Christianity and civilization to triumph over Barbarism and Slavery." The establishment of the New York Loyal Publication Society in early 1863 reflected the commitment of men such as Bellows and Horace Bushnell to a stronger clerical voice in politics. Catholic supporters of the government's war policies, despite any misgivings about religious bigotry in the Republican Party, made a point of proclaiming their loyalty to the Union.[31]

The politics of loyalty deeply affected the leading Protestant denominations, especially the Methodist Church. At a meeting of the Illinois Conference, Governor Richard Yates showed up to administer an oath of allegiance, even though more conservative clergy—including famed circuit rider and ardent Democrat Peter Cartwright—vigorously objected to resolutions supporting emancipation, conscription, and the suspension of habeas corpus. Simply avoiding political discussions could be interpreted as a sign of disloyalty. According to the Wisconsin Annual Conference, "Neutrality is treason, silence crime, and inaction unpardonable." The Reverend Granville Moody reportedly specialized in "skinning Copperheads, crushing butternuts, and flaying peace men."[32]

Because Copperheads were enemies of both God and country, strong words, including "traitor," came out of the churches. Worse still, denominational bodies saddled opponents of the war with bloodguilt, charging them with responsibility for the slaughter of their countrymen on southern battlefields.[33] The only answer—at least for the more extreme partisans—was to outlaw Peace Democrats. "While those at the front kill rattle-snakes, we at home must kill copperheads," a leading Methodist editor suggested. Political and religious proscription against rebel sympathizers extended to children, with one little boy reportedly praying, "O Lord, if there are any little 'butternuts' in this house, I'll kick them out."[34]

All quite amusing, except for what many church leaders considered a real danger—that Copperheads would convince northerners to compromise with rebels for the sake of a peace that sacrificed the sacred principles of Union and emancipation. "We can make no peace with the Confederacy but by submitting to its despotic will," the North's most influential Methodist editor feared. After nearly two years of stalemate and mounting bloodshed, even gentle Unitarians held that waging war was the Lord's work. Democrats who cried for peace when there was no peace, Baptist Francis Wayland maintained, had been rebel sympathizers all along. As for peace itself, had not Jesus told his disciples that he brought not peace but a sword? Therefore an unjust peace negotiated with traitors would be a far greater calamity than civil war itself.[35]

———

Confederates would have largely agreed with that assessment because they showed little interest in any settlement short of recognizing southern independence. People should not be seduced by that sweet word "peace," Episcopal bishop Stephen Elliott warned; otherwise they might be tempted to "yield up either right or truth or justice for its attainment." In March 1863 Jefferson Davis's call for yet another day of fasting, humiliation, and prayer expressed great faith in deliverance by force of arms—always, of course, under the providential guidance of the Lord of Hosts who was teaching the Yankees that the battle was not to the strong. Confederates should pray that the Almighty "will continue his merciful protection over our cause, that he will scatter our enemies, set at naught their evil designs, and that he will graciously restore to our beloved country the blessings of peace and security."[36]

Elliott was not so sure. Confederates had placed too much hope in foreign intervention and their own efforts, while "God had thought it best for us that this cruel war should endure yet longer and should be waged with an increased ferocity." The lesson seemed perfectly clear and by now perfectly familiar—that "we must take Divine will into reasoning" about the war and "must school ourselves into an acquiescence with his divine arrangements." Yet the fast-day sermons and services more often conveyed a shopworn sort of repentance, as if Confederates were confident that God would soon deliver them, but they should at least go through the motions of appearing humble. The clergy expressed few if any doubts that God stood with the Confederacy, whatever its weaknesses in resources and men. Even though ministers might still caution against boasting, their sermons often conveyed a different message.[37]

Talk of sackcloth and ashes on the official fast day sounded ritualistic and empty. Ministers and congregations repented of the usual sins: drinking, swearing, Sabbath breaking, and, with increasingly greater emphasis, extortion. A Baptist minister deplored the opening of a new theater in Richmond where "lewd dances" and "burlesque negro songs" along with vulgarity and blasphemy had created a "school of immorality and vice." Upbraiding people for worshiping mammon remained as popular as ever and calls for repentance sounded fervent but were overshadowed by denunciations of Yankees as arrant hypocrites and worse sinners. Confederates would be punished for their transgressions, but Cornelia McDonald seemed most worried that this would occur *after* Confederate independence had been established. An Alabama enlisted man was "all moste purswaded to believe that solgers are not accountable for there deeds hereafter" because of all they had endured in war.[38] With God on your side, all manner of sin could presumably be forgiven, and recent Confederate victories hardly elicited much soul searching.

In the Army of Northern Virginia, Lee and Jackson ordered observance of the fast day and instructed chaplains to hold special services, though with mixed results. Despite the recent revivals, many regiments even in Jackson's Corps still had no chaplains, and there were not nearly enough visiting preachers and missionaries. In some hospitals and camps, no particular attention was paid to the day. One chaplain in Tennessee delivered a lengthy blast against modern infidels (mostly Yankees) who no longer believed in hell; he later remarked, however, that "little [religious] good seems accomplished in the army."[39]

Despite a suitable amount of solemnity and fasting along with the usual acknowledgment of dependence upon divine protection, private and public reflections breathed a spirit of self-righteousness. God has "wrecked his heavier vengeance upon the northerners for the mutilation of his world and their sins," one Tennessee preacher declared. In sermons delivered to the Georgia General Assembly, two eminent southern divines, George F. Pierce and Benjamin Morgan Palmer, agreed that the Yankees were far and away the chief transgressors against the Almighty's sacred commands. Holding southerners "blameless" for the war, Palmer unequivocally declared where the Lord stood in the matter: "Our cause is preeminently the cause of God himself, and every blow struck by us in defense of his supremacy." Unlike the infidel northerners, the Confederates had not "corrupted the gospel of Christ."[40]

Such statements went too far even for loyal Confederates. "Blood-thirsty ferocity" gave one Baptist editor pause: "If Christians are not careful while striking for their country, to maintain the spirit of their Master, how shall they hope for that Master's help?" Young Amanda McDowell—ironically echoing long-standing criticism against northern clerics—complained that ever since the war began, her minister had more to say about politics than about Jesus. With unusual candor, a Georgia Baptist editor questioned the all too common "God is on our side" theology that seemed "irreverent and flippant, sometimes self-complacent, boastful and patronizing." Suggesting that the doctrine of divine providence had more application in times of adversity, he admonished his fellow citizens for indulging in "a transient, shallow piety" when things were going well.[41]

Even with Confederate fortunes on the rise, a few of the devout and the doubtful alike expressed reservations about cheap talk of divine favor. "We are a wicked people," not yet humbled by the Lord's chastisement, the pious General Frank Paxton told his wife. Soldiers wallowed in "blasphemy and wickedness," while the home folks indulged in "avarice and extortion." He drew a withering conclusion: "Fasting and prayer by such a people is blasphemy, and if answered at all, will be by an affliction of God's wrath, not in a dispensation of his mercy." A disaffected Mississippian bluntly informed his church, "I don't intend to fast and pray just because Jeff Davis tells me to do so. When they were instigating this war, they didn't call on the churches to pray them into it; and now they needn't call on them to pray 'em out of it. I don't owe allegiance to Jeff Davis nor Abe Lincoln."[42]

Less than a week after the Confederate fast, Lincoln called on northerners to observe their own day of "prayer and humiliation." Given recent defeats, political turmoil, and the low state of northern morale, the president's proclamation naturally dwelt on sin and punishment, an acknowledgment of divine judgment on nations as well as individuals. The American people had forgotten the Lord, had tried to rely on human strength, and must mend their ways; all in all, the proclamation covered the jeremiad's standard points but did not presume to understand the ways of God.[43]

For northerners, religious expressions of loyalty often remained little more than glittering generalities or empty piety, the preaching lofty and vague. In an otherwise ordinary and excruciatingly long sermon with predictable and chauvinistic references to the Puritan fathers and sweeping generalizations about a religious people, one Massachusetts Congregationalist briefly noted a contrast between a chosen people (the ancient Israelites) and those having a special relationship with God (the Americans) but left the point hanging. Hazy references to a patriotic revival unintentionally highlighted the pressing need to maintain (or, indeed, restore) national unity in the face of a tenacious rebellion, a faltering administration, peace rumors, and Copperhead machinations. Little wonder that throughout the late winter and early spring cautious voices stuck with emphasizing the legitimacy of a war to save the Union.[44]

In harking back to the American Revolution, preachers could not help but mention the Tories and apply their sad example to contemporary dissenters. Copperheads appeared more dangerous than Confederates to those who believed that only a divided North could open the path to a rebel victory. More than two months before that summer's New York draft riots, a Massachusetts Congregationalist warned of demagogues such as New York politico Fernando Wood who might encourage resistance to conscription, which could easily lead to bloodshed. Ministers increasingly emphasized a loyalty that equated unquestioning patriotism (and support for government measures such as emancipation) with true Christianity. To sustain the nation (and the Lincoln administration) meant fulfilling biblical injunctions about obedience to civil authorities. The greatest sin in the present crisis of American affairs was to murmur against the Union's political and military leaders, and familiar passages about Moses, Aaron, and the children of Israel drove home that crucial point.[45]

The churches' had grown more entangled with a civil religion that made little distinction between sacred and secular loyalty. Ever since First Bull Run, northern ministers had pointed to Sabbath breaking, swearing, and drinking as offenses sure to provoke the Lord's wrath. In an era when Americans claimed—or at least aspired—to take all ten commandments seriously and literally, what might seem for example a tenuous connection between blasphemy and war was both self-evident and vital. So flaying faithless chaplains, indifferent soldiers, and godless politicians while tossing out conventional condemnations of mammon worship made perfect sense to ministers and congregants, who sniffed out sin in all manner of thought and deed. "Nominally a christian nation, but now practically atheistic have we been in the development of wealth," an Episcopalian chaplain thundered. Deeply engrained habits such as pride, boasting, and apathy all proved how countless Americans had ignored God through two years of war and were now paying the price. More damning still—especially in an era of soaring millennial hope—the American nation had failed to fulfill its exalted mission. A people who had received so many blessings had yet to realize that God had a higher purpose in mind than slaying rebels.[46]

Nor were the churches spared a few stinging rebukes. "Time-serving clergy, and a membership satisfied with 'smooth things,' who appear reluctant to submit to a faithful application of the gospel," distressed a small-town New York minister, who complained that too many of his fellow Presbyterian pastors had become mere pleasure seekers ready to abandon their calling for trivial or monetary reasons. Even the normally cheerful Unitarian Henry Bellows worried that despite vast material and technological progress, Americans had advanced little in piety or morality. Religion had become a tame and timid affair with "no enemies" but "few devoted friends." For the more conservative clergy, materialism and greed still eclipsed slavery and racism as besetting national sins. As contractors cheated the government and the soldiers to line their pockets, patriotism waned, and more ominously the spirit of sacrifice appeared to be much stronger in the Confederacy.[47]

The ardently antislavery Baptist pastor George Ide chastised northerners for worshiping "Business, Enterprise, Industrial Development, Material Prosperity" and southerners for bending their knees to the "Moloch" slavery but also choked on his fellow pastors' still-equivocating approach to the slavery question. Northern complicity with southern sin had long been a theme of abolition ministers, and even in the wake of the Emancipation Proclamation, such preaching continued. Confederate sympathizers and administration critics did not want to touch slavery, and so all talk of peace was premature; indeed, the length of the war itself proved that the process of moral purification must run its course. A Union still constituted as an unholy mix of free and slave states must surely displease the Lord, and the fact that the Emancipation Proclamation did not touch slavery in the border states meant the bloodshed must continue. One antislavery Methodist had only "kind words" for Lincoln but doubted he was a leader of "profound ability or a great statesman." The president had proclaimed emancipation but had not achieved victory on the battlefield, a still more outspoken Iowa preacher remarked at a union prayer service: "Our fasts will never avert the judgments of the Almighty, or receive his blessing, until it be the result of a deep and abiding conviction of national guilt." The nation should do its duty by destroying slavery completely. Otherwise, the Lord's wrath would still be poured out, and for radicals even the obliteration of slavery would not assuage God's anger. The sin of racism meant that proclamations of freedom left much of the work incomplete, and the mistreatment of blacks even in the northern churches cried out for redress. Calling for an end to segregation and all other racial distinctions, Gilbert Haven presented a millennial vision of the great human family worshiping together and speaking a common language.[48]

In the meantime, however, Americans with less elevated views must suffer for their sins. Fast-day preachers interpreted divine chastisement in tones ranging from wildly apocalyptic to almost soothing. In the past, nations grown too wicked and corrupt had been overthrown—a stock warning of the jeremiad that seemed appropriate enough at this low point in Union fortunes. Border state Baptist Richard Fuller saw divine wrath descending upon the nation and, with a suitably stern text from Jeremiah, called on his listeners to turn away from their sins and acknowledge that God is God. Offering a much milder explanation for recent defeats, Thomas Brainerd, a member of a prominent Presbyterian family long active in mission work, maintained that the nation had made considerable religious progress but that recent battlefield losses reflected "the moral discipline through which God purifies us from remaining corruptions." Soldiers adopted similar reasoning, believing that once the nation had been sufficiently humbled the fighting would end.[49]

The war's entire course appeared consistent with the workings of a heavenly plan that always unfolded slowly and never without suffering for the Lord's chosen ones. The Almighty hated the hypocrisy and pretenses of a supposedly religious people who would not even observe a national fast in any great numbers. According to Baptist William Lamson, the bloodshed would continue until God's as yet undisclosed ends had been achieved. To this point, both sides had been frustrated, as Lincoln himself would readily have admitted, and the nation had now entered what a Maine preacher called the "furnace of purification." To insist that the Lord's purposes remained shrouded in mystery offered little comfort to family and friends mourning the loss of so many men and was all too often overshadowed by more bombastic pulpit oratory North and South.[50]

In this hour of despair, devout northerners clung to the long-held assumption that the Lord could not possibly will the destruction of the glorious Union. "It is my fixed faith," Secretary of the Treasury Chase maintained, "that God does not mean that this American republic shall perish." Given their glorious and sacred heritage, Americans should not falter. A chaplains' council in the Army of the Cumberland expressed an unwavering belief that "the heaven-inspired principles of American liberty shall not only be more firmly established in our own country, but shall become the settled political faith of the world."[51]

Whether soldiers absorbed such a hopeful message remained uncertain. Reports of fast-day observance in the camps were spotty, and a Massachusetts minister's claim to having discovered a "power of religion [in our army], never known to the same extent in any army of the world," would have amazed even the most pious and dutiful volunteers. A faltering Union war effort along with the carnage at Fredericksburg and Stones River forced many men to think more about war's relationship to divine will. An Illinois private doubted that rebels who stripped the dead after a battle could ever "find favor in sight of Heaven." Eternal torment would be their lot, so "let us leave them in their guilt." But looking over the same battlefield at Murfreesboro, Tennessee, a less self-righteous Hoosier cavalryman took a broader view, wondering "why is man the only portion of God's creation that does not live in harmony and peace." Instead people scrambled to take advantage of each other, and "is it not a wonderful mercy that the Blessed God does not blot man out of remembrance?" The warnings of Old Testament prophets sounded ever more appropriate and ominous. Although firmly believing that a "fearful load of guilt" must fall on southern traitors, Vermont private Wilber Fisk conceded that the "whole Nation is involved, and deep grief and poignant sorrow must be borne by the North, to expiate the crimes of the South." He knew that God hated slavery and rebellion but that no one escaped divine judgment.[52]

That was hard teaching in such a dark hour. All across the North, mayors and even New York Democratic governor Horatio Seymour had issued proclamations calling for the observance of the national day of fasting, humiliation, and prayer. Businesses and places of amusement were to be closed as people confessed their country's sins and prayed for deliverance. One Brooklyn newspaper, which had often slyly derided Beecher's political preaching, nevertheless published substantial excerpts from ten fast-day sermons—including one by Beecher. According to a Presbyterian editor, the day had been solemnly observed, and the northern people had acknowledged their many transgressions, thus paving the way for the Lord of Hosts to save the American Union. But a southern editor sharply observed that several Confederate victories had followed instead, smugly adding (a little over a month before Gettysburg), "A retributive providence is often seen among men in the present life." That of course was precisely what bothered so many loyal northerners during this spring of despondency. One Philadelphia preacher concluded that "little effect . . . has been already produced by the calamities of this nation." A people refusing to humble themselves needed to recognize that God could easily set brother against brother in the northern states.[53]

The chaplain of the Senate wondered if Americans still trusted the Lord to deliver them from the ravages of war. How many people would instead make the day of prayer a "mockery in the sight of God?" With portentous references to Jonah and Nineveh, he saw the nation "descending every hour and at every step in the path of inevitable destruction."[54] And in many cases Christians were either leading the way or following in the wake. A spirit of selfishness had too often overwhelmed a spirit of sacrifice—a point made with equal fervor and frequency by rebel preachers. The Emancipation Proclamation had heartened some northern religious leaders but had produced neither mass revival nor moral reformation. Among Confederates, battlefield victories had not inspired a feeling of greater dependence on God but instead had produced a dangerous overconfidence. Considering what many deemed the sorry state of religious life on the home front, neither side could find much comfort or hope as the war continued to destroy lives, shatter families, and depress communities, for what purpose God only knew.

DECLENSION

> But my people would not hearken to my voice; and Israel would none of me.
> So I gave them up unto their own hearts' lust: and they walked in their own
> counsels. Oh that my people had hearkened unto me, and Israel had walked
> in my ways! I should soon have subdued their enemies, and turned my hand
> against their adversaries.
>
> — Psalms 81:11–14

Civil religion created an alliance between church and state in the United States and the Confederate States, but paradoxically the war weakened church attendance and ministries in the short if not in the long term. "Patriotism is a Christian virtue," an Illinois Presbytery declared during the fall of 1863, yet it duly noted that the churches would languish so long as people's minds were preoccupied with war. Once the Union had finally been restored, those who had survived the crisis "will arise with new strength to do the work of the master."[1]

As a practical matter, excitement and tumult would deeply affect the churches, and alarms about the war's moral impact soon spread from the army camps to the home front. Conservatives still hoped that pious folk would not wish to hear anything preached but the Gospel. The reality proved quite different because the war encroached on religious life throughout the week and especially on Sunday, when worship services and family devotions brought sad reminders of absent loved ones or those who had already died as martyrs in their country's battles. That piety must take priority over patriotism was a truism easily expounded but not easily lived, especially when ministers touted religious devotion as a way to secure divine favor and save the Union.[2] Millennial optimism proved surprisingly hardy, and as the months of gloomy news, bloody battles, and deep anguish continued, people naturally looked for any sign of religious health.

Aside from the revival meetings in the army, there were few such signs. Was the falling away of the faithful unavoidable? People going about their daily lives still faced timeless questions about death and eternity, commented one Presbyterian editor, who believed a "just war . . . may be the most powerful means of exalting national character." On the other hand, during a visit home, a plainspoken Pennsylvania chaplain decided that "this war is crippling our churches and injuring every department of society." In a narrow sense, it was a matter of simple arithmetic: the vast wealth expended on the war would not pour into church coffers. In a broader sense, the national crisis was bound to disturb conventional beliefs and practices. Ralph Waldo Emerson gleefully informed a visiting Catholic priest that during such exciting times people had no interest in hearing him discuss theological questions. Emerson likewise noted with apparent satisfaction the decline of family religious observance and Sabbath keeping. For the more orthodox, the fear arose that the war not only encouraged all manner of vice but even raised doubts about biblical authority.[3]

Contradictory speculations might appear fanciful or overblown, but for churches in the Confederacy the problems were both real and tangible. With a large proportion of the military-age population away from home, even public worship took on a much different cast. Most of the major and minor battles were fought in the Confederacy or the Border South, and the churches there faced much greater challenges and disruptions. Southern preachers naturally feared that religious duties might be entirely neglected, and denominational associations sometimes had little to report. Even in isolated western North Carolina, Reverend William Graves complained that "excitement and confusion have carried the mind of the major part of this community too much from the great subject of religion."[4]

As the war continued, words such as "lukewarmness" appeared more frequently in denominational minutes. In September 1861 a Georgia Baptist association admitted that "coldness" appeared "universal" among its churches and candidly blamed ministers for preaching the "war spirit" rather than the "spirit of the Gospel." The rapidly spreading army revivals made the condition of the home folks appear all that much worse; toward the end of the war, a Louisiana private heard that "religion is dying in Claiborne Parish."[5] From the very beginning there had had been alarming reports of a growing worldliness. People neglected worship, Sunday schools languished, Sabbath observance declined. Even prayer meetings were becoming rarities in some neighborhoods, and Texas Baptists were reportedly neglecting the Bible in favor of secular reading.[6]

Confessions of sin appearing in denominational reports were standard fare, and the idea of churches being scourged for their transgressions certainly fit into the wartime jeremiad. That good old Puritan word "declension" popped up in discussions of religious affairs, and indeed citing the war as an excuse for any falling off in devotion seemed itself a sin. "Impatience and irreconciliation to the providential dealings of God," declared a Georgia Baptist association, "often cause murmurings, despondings, coldness of affection, neglect of duty." Nor had the churches' well-deserved suffering led to repentance. The war had begun with the church praying for the army, one Baptist editor sharply noted in the early fall of 1863, but "many in the church have lost the spirit of prayer and the army is now praying for the church."[7]

The implications were frightening. "If we are defeated, whose fault will it be?" asked the *Christian Index* of Macon, Georgia. But then the jeremiad had always concluded with a final conditional warning, and a Mississippi Baptist association understood the logic perfectly, "If the cause of religion goes down, so must the cause of our country go down." By neglecting the churches, the people would surely call forth the Lord's wrath and face the unspeakable horrors of subjugation.[8]

This is not to say that all was doom and gloom. In the fall of 1861, an optimistic North Carolina Presbyterian predicted that the war would not impede the cause of Christ, and two years later some churches were denying the crisis had done much harm. Was not the gospel still being preached? Congregations were "passing through the fiery furnace, heated by the blasts of war," a South Carolina presbytery concluded, but "it is a pleasing thought that the Master has not forsaken her, in the time of her trying ordeal." A quiet Sabbath spent singing old hymns, a familiar liturgy, or the customary worship service became quite a comfort for civilians in a time of alarming news and ceaseless tumult. Some associations, synods, and presbyteries even reported a healthy spiritual state, and the word "progress" occasionally cropped up in descriptions of their work. Sunday schools and Bible classes still met, despite the fact that many of the teachers were off fighting. Churches rejoiced over adding members and performing baptisms, even if those joining were mostly women and slaves.[9]

On the surface at least, the condition of northern churches seemed largely unchanged and much healthier, though here too believers had to contend with wartime distractions and internal divisions. The editor of the *American Standard* in Jersey City worried about "coldness and apathy" enveloping the churches. Ironically, local church records barely mention the war because normal congregational life could be more easily maintained than in the Confederacy. In the fall of 1863, a Pennsylvania Presbyterian minister concluded that the northern churches had suffered little from the conflict in part because many of the young men leaving home to serve their country would become missionaries in the army.[10]

This glossed over one of the more noticeable effects of these departures. An editorial headline in a New School Presbyterian paper, "The Blood of the Church Poured Out for the Salvation of the Country," summed up the problem for both churches and nation. According to many pastors, the best young men, the future leaders of congregations, had enlisted. Minutes of monthly church meetings often carried the notation that the clerk was in the army. In September 1862 a Michigan Sunday school superintendent read off the names of young men who had been active in the church and were now in uniform. A quarterly report on Sabbath schools in Greencastle, Indiana, described what must have been all too common: with so many young men in the army, the remaining members were "endeavoring to hold on as best we can under the circumstances."[11]

The same might be said for other northern churches, despite scattered reports of strong attendance. "The troubles of the times seem to have led men to the house of God," a Cleveland presbytery hoped, though now the pews and benches were largely filled by older people, women, and children. Patriotic sermons included reminders that the church's main work remained saving souls and that people still had a duty to attend worship and support the good work in all the usual ways. There were reports of home front revivals, new congregations, and other promising signs, but the northern churches were not exactly flourishing. Presbyterians held their own and even gained members toward the end of the war; northern Baptists saw declines in some states. Claiming that no Christian denomination had supplied more soldiers to the Union army, one Methodist editor reported "greatly diminished numbers" in churches and Sunday schools, along with lagging financial support. By the end of the war, northern Methodists had lost more than sixty thousand members.[12]

Confederate losses dwarfed these numbers. In four years, southern Methodist membership had fallen by a third; Presbyterian congregations had shrunk; Baptist associations had disappeared. Was this all inevitable during a long war? From the beginning, gloomy reports of declining membership, no baptisms, and fears of worse to come had appeared in the religious press and denominational reports. In some churches, the only new members were soldiers converted in the army revivals. At best, struggling congregations gained a few communicants, but more suffered declines. Ecclesiastical bodies either canceled meetings or gathered in what amounted to rump sessions with many churches unrepresented.[13]

In Virginia, political excitement had reportedly already reduced church attendance in the spring of 1861, and the outbreak of war only made the problem worse. A countrywoman in North Carolina described an all-too-common scene: "I felt very sad to look around at the vacant seats of many, who had gone, perhaps never to return." By the end of the year, many churches had fallen into a nearly comatose state, and members of one congregation even appeared reluctant to come out in the rain. War-related excuses multiplied. Long rides in the hot sun from widely scattered plantations were even less appealing with rumors of Union cavalry in the neighborhood. Because candles were soon in short supply, there were fewer night services, and in any case it no longer seemed safe for "ladies" to be out after dark.[14]

By 1862 in Virginia and Tennessee, the advance of Federal forces was already causing the suspension of worship services. Threats to coastal areas forced denominational meetings to move inland, and eventually churches were left vacant as many of the faithful became refugees. By 1863 church records noted the mounting casualties among members, and services in many places became even more irregular. By 1864 a Tennessee Baptist simply remarked on low attendance and the prevalence of sin in the land—the two presumably connected.[15]

———

When denominational bodies reported coldness and indifference in the churches, that often meant preaching no more than once a month. Calls for more frequent services sounded futile with so many ministers in the army and so many pulpits vacant.[16] Even more disheartening in the wake of shrinking congregations and absent ministers were churches fallen into disrepair or abandoned. This was especially true in coastal and border areas where Federal armies sent people flying to safer places or where sanctuaries were converted into hospitals. Landscapes dotted with largely empty and ramshackle churches only added to a sense of ineffable sadness.[17]

Dwindling congregations became largely female. Ministers and ordinary worshipers often commented when a few more men were present or if the male contingent was especially small. After seeing only one man at a crowded service in Columbia, South Carolina, Mary Chesnut sardonically remarked, "It is plain why there is no marrying nor giving in marriage to heaven. The church is the gate to heaven, and the church is apparently filled with women only going up there." These numbers, however, did not translate into temporal power. Late in the war, the Silver Creek Baptist Church inquired about the rights and responsibilities of female members, and the Pearl River (Mississippi) Baptist Association replied that the women are "entitled to all the privileges of male members" but then quickly contradicted that statement by adding that, on ecclesiastical policy and secular issues, "the business [should be] . . . transacted by male members."[18]

Yet, with a goodly number of Sunday school teachers serving in the army and despite some reluctance, calls soon went out for women to take up the slack. Working with children fit safely into domestic and nurturing roles, but wartime change was hard to contain. One South Carolina Baptist association approved "pious females" taking charge of the Sunday school program, and denominational reports suggest that is exactly what happened. Toward the end of the war, some churches were even ready for women to serve as Sunday school superintendents.[19] Such opportunities, however, came during the worst of times.

Small congregations and struggling denominations became righteous remnants facing an uncertain and frightening future. If that future rested with young people, the irregular worship services made Sunday schools even more vital for spiritual growth. Optimists at first expected these mainstays of evangelical faith to prosper during the war. Despite an immediate shortage of teachers and materials, the state Baptist convention in South Carolina hoped that regular classes would still make "good soldiers of Jesus Christ." Even in 1863 and 1864 Baptist leaders such as Basil Manly Jr. and John A. Broadus worked to revive a Sunday school movement that had fallen on hard times. At best, however, the reports sounded iffy. Classes were small and teachers were few in churches that still had any Sunday school at all. Words such as "neglect" and phrases such as "a sad record" summed up conditions from Virginia to Texas. A North Carolina Baptist gloomily reported that "vice and ignorance are increasing at a fearful rate among the boys and girls who are at once the hope of the country and the church."[20]

"In these times of war and confusion," an 1864 report of the Edgefield, South Carolina, Baptist Association maintained, "the weeds of business, trouble, and anxiety have grown so rank in adult minds as to render them almost impervious to religious impressions; while the untroubled mind of childhood is a rich garden, ready for the seed." How untroubled children's minds could remain after three years of war seems doubtful, and for all the dogged persistence, hard work, and a few promising signs, the future grew ever darker. "The fault lies at home," a Virginia Episcopalian committee bluntly declared. Parents had come to depend too much on the now languishing Sunday schools and had failed to provide instruction for their children. The war had only made matters worse by fostering what a Georgia Baptist association termed a spirit of "restlessness and insubordination." Therefore, pious Christians must "disinfect the children of our country" by surrounding them with the safeguards of revealed religion.[21]

Religious education more generally suffered serious blows as soon as the war began. Many academies, colleges, and seminaries closed their doors as students and no small number of teachers rushed off to fight. Buildings occasionally became hospitals, and money ran short. Even as Confederate nationalists boldly declared intellectual independence from Yankeedom, they lacked the means to accomplish such an ambitious goal. Southerners might vow to pour money into their own schools rather than into northern coffers or brag they would no longer hire northern ministers, but such brave words yielded few tangible results. Like so much wartime propaganda, this all rang hollow as schools shut down or barely survived.[22]

Such failures all reflected a simple fact of Confederate religious life: church coffers were nearly empty. In the fall of 1861 a committee of the Bethel Baptist Association in Georgia urged congregations to contribute one dollar for each white member and ten cents for each colored member into a colportage fund, but a year later only five of thirty-five churches had met this goal. Typically people fell behind in their pledges, and giving to both congregations and denominations dropped off. With skyrocketing inflation, the relative contributions sometimes increased but that was misleading. "Money abounds more than anything else, and not being worth much, people would as soon give it to the Lord as not," Methodist pastor Enoch Mather Marvin remarked. By 1864 some churches had grown reluctant to accept Confederate money. Excoriating tight-fisted southerners, Episcopal bishop Richard Wilmer turned to sarcasm: "I rejoice to think that a people who made scorn of paying tithes to establish the Kingdom of Peace are compelled to disgorge them for the purposes of making war."[23]

Few northern churches experienced any remotely comparable problems, though if anything the status and perhaps influence of the northern clergy further deteriorated. On the eve of the war, the average minister made no more than three hundred or four hundred dollars a year with considerable variation in salaries by denomination and region. Inflation was far less a problem in the wartime North, but ministers' families felt the pinch. Early on, there was fear that hard-pressed pastors would have to supplement their income. A devout doctor serving in the army advised his wife back in Michigan to give up some luxury or comfort so she could set aside money to help support the minister, but not many followed this example. Few congregations apparently raised salaries, and some actually reduced them, leading clergymen to complain about expenses exceeding incomes, forcing them to rely on special offerings or what amounted to alms from their congregations.[24]

These largely manageable difficulties in the North became major problems in the Confederacy. So many ministers had volunteered as either soldiers or chaplains that from the start of the war pulpits stood vacant. In 1863 the Alabama Methodist conference reported a substantial increase in members but eighty fewer clergymen. Some churches limped along without a preacher for two or three years. Those ministers who remained often worked a second job to make ends meet as inflation ate up already modest salaries, and few young men were ordained. At the beginning of 1864, one Baptist editor worried that three-fourths of the churches would soon have no pastor.[25]

Even churches with a preacher hardly flourished. By 1862, as both membership and giving fell off, churches reduced ministers' salaries or simply did not raise them in the face of rapidly increasing prices. Then too congregations fell into arrears. Parishioners acted as if faith and prayer could feed a family, one pastor's wife bitterly complained to a Presbyterian paper. In other cases, ministers went into debt simply to keep food on the table; they or their wives often had to teach school to make ends meet. Louisiana Methodists complained that their best ministers had been driven from the pulpit by miserly congregations whose members thought nothing of spending lavishly on themselves and even on their slaves.[26] Customary complaints about low salaries took on a harder, more desperate edge.

Ministers and their parishioners might have turned to the familiar biblical passage about making bricks without straw. Baptist churches struggled to raise salaries by a hundred or two hundred dollars, but even clergy in larger churches could never stay ahead of inflation. Some congregations tried to retain a good preacher by doubling his pay, but spiraling prices soon ate up this seemingly generous sum; by 1864 what would have been astronomical salaries a few years earlier now seemed woefully inadequate. Church officials encouraged congregations to supplement their preachers' income with special offerings or even donations in kind, and perhaps some produce or a few chickens were more appreciated than worthless Confederate notes. Yet as one disgruntled minister's wife pointed out, such support was sporadic and often of doubtful value. What minister, for example, needed three pair of slippers? Nor were elders or other church leaders above taking advantage of a man's devotion to a particular congregation by not even paying the agreed upon salary.[27]

The ministers' struggles mirrored the churches' struggles, and indeed the war made formal religious life less important. In many ways, spiritual commitment now appeared most noticeably in prayer meetings or family devotions as individual and collective piety became part of Confederate civil religion. In November 1862 from Chapel Hill, North Carolina, came a call for women at noon on December 1 (along with their "female domestics") to pray for an "honorable peace." Churches filled with worshipers, and even women who had been unwell or had not been to a service in weeks made a special effort to attend. Devout civilians and soldiers alike hoped their earnest petitions might bring peace, but there were always skeptics. When asked how some military problem might be solved, Texas senator Louis T. Wigfall sarcastically suggested that Jefferson Davis might encourage women and children to pray about it.[28]

During a long war, many others must have doubted the efficacy of prayer, yet it remained the most powerful witness to faith. In the spring and summer of 1861, both Baptists and Presbyterians had worried about the vitality of family worship, but now women had to take charge of what once had been a father's or husband's domain. This marked a decided shift from public liturgy to private devotion, though one made with some reluctance. At the end of the war, ardent Confederate Eliza Fain finally "was enabled to bow at the family altar myself for the first time in my life" and decided that "I shall from this time forward be enabled to do my duty." For many women, only faith could hold their lives together. "Nothing but the influence of Religion can keep down the bitter sorrow and sad repining," a North Carolinian wrote, even though others in her family had trouble submitting to the Lord's will or had increasingly little to say about religion.[29]

In the more prosperous and less hard-pressed North, home front religion at times languished, though for different reasons. The war disrupted family routines even as it opened up opportunities for some women to work publicly for the Union and emancipation. Here too women were cast as stalwarts of both domestic and civil religion, patriots equally devoted to home and country. Women "have reason to prize the great institutions of civil and religious freedom, which furnish them with the richest means of culture and advance, which open to them the most varied paths to happiness and usefulness," one religious paper maintained. Not only through their charitable and public activities but in letters to their loved one in the armies, many women breathed a spirit of pious sacrifice. And in reality they relied heavily on religious faith, including a strong belief in divine sovereignty to sustain their own morale. Indeed, their orthodoxy and devotional practices were often remarkable.[30] Many women believed that the northern people should trust in the Lord to lead them through a dark period in their nation's (and their own) history, but they too could help defeat the rebels by sewing for the soldiers and raising money for charitable and religious causes.

———

The war therefore presented both opportunities and dangers. Philadelphian Rebecca Gratz, who had long been active in Jewish philanthropies, discerned the "wickedness of man in this unholy strife" and ironically feared that women would "step out of the sphere God designed them to fill in such times of trouble." However that might be, the more immediate question became how the North's diverse religious communities would respond to the sudden demands on their generosity. Would charitable contributions dry up? What would happen to the poor, the insane, and the disabled? Large donations to the Christian and Sanitary commissions were a promising sign, claimed one Christian Commission delegate who still worried about the war's effect on northern churches. Most denominations not only proclaimed their loyalty to the Union but took pride in what an Illinois presbytery termed "liberal contributions for the spiritual and temporal welfare of the Soldiers both in camp and hospital."[31]

Catholic organizations raised money for soldier families and attempted to succor the growing number of orphans. In Philadelphia, the Ladies Hebrew Association for the Relief of Sick and Wounded Soldiers cooperated with the Sanitary Commission to gather supplies; elsewhere various aid societies (with support from the Jewish press) sent volunteers to hospitals and raised money. According to one Methodist editor, all this charity work revealed how large cities "proverbial for their wickedness" had become "abodes of active piety and unostentatious philanthropy."[32]

In the Confederacy, soaring prices and vast needs meant that increased giving accomplished much less. Even early in the war, church leaders feared a retrenchment as families felt the pinch of hard times, but ministers and women's societies actively promoted benevolence. According to one Methodist bishop, "Lazy girls are at work, and everybody is alive to the great interests involved." That may have been true in the summer of 1861, but by 1865 only five women in one prosperous Richmond congregation volunteered to knit socks for the soldiers, and attendance at sewing societies elsewhere had fallen off.[33]

With charitable contributions lagging behind inflation, ingenuity in fundraising stirred controversy. The strait-laced shunned lotteries, balls, and even tableaux vivants, especially if held in churches, as sure signs of a creeping worldliness. Such objections raised broader questions about how directly churches should become involved in the war. For example, should congregations donate their bells for use by the Confederate Ordnance Department? Some agreed to do so, but Catholic bishop William Henry Elder wondered if bells consecrated to God's service should be cast into artillery, certainly a reversal of the familiar prophecy about turning swords into plowshares.[34]

In a more traditional vein, churches had long followed biblical teachings about caring for widows and orphans, but now this required more than the occasional act of charity. By 1862 churches faced a daunting task. Surely, appeals to educate the children of men who had given their lives for the Confederacy would stir hearts and loosen purse strings. When women donated rings and other jewelry, however, their contributions bespoke desperation as much as patriotism. Church members visiting the homes of soldier families found that some had enough food but needed salt while others appeared completely destitute.[35]

The vast needs of the poor along with other wartime demands forced churches to cut back on traditional evangelizing. Baptist William R. Williams, who had long been active in the American Tract Society and the American Bible Society, saw the war opening up a wide field for missions, but in fact missionary societies often withered. A Virginia Baptist association report on the subject clearly revealed how war consumed people's thoughts and energies: "Who now feels the love of Jesus? It is too often displaced by hostility to our enemies." Overseas the situation was especially dire as donations to missionaries dried up. "I fear God will not bless his people if they leave the Missionaries to starve and the Heathen to perish," Deborah B. Lapham Wade wrote from Burma. As long as the war lasted, many missionaries would have to fend for themselves, and only peace promised to reinvigorate evangelism around the world.[36]

Domestic missions (including work with Indian tribes) suffered badly. By 1862 churches admitted doing little or nothing for families that lacked any kind of religious reading matter or instruction. By 1864, given the Confederate inflation rate, paltry collections seemed especially pitiful. Early in the war a North Carolina Baptist association had sought a colporteur to counter the "rapid spread of error" among the people, but if doctrinal soundness depended on sending ministers and laity out into the countryside with Bibles and tracts, heresy must have flourished.[37]

Reports from churches and ministers along with political speeches and newspaper editorials confirmed what many upright souls suspected: sin was rampant not only in the camps but at home. Young men had long been warned against the temptations of the saloon, the gambling den, and the brothel, and the war made that message even more urgent. Newspapers reported alarming (though seldom specified) rates of debauchery and crime; ministers worried about growing Sabbath desecration, profanity, and drunkenness as the war loosened moral standards.[38]

Even in Eufaula, Alabama, a committee of the First Baptist Church uncovered apparently widespread Sabbath breaking, profanity, horse racing, card playing, dancing, and drinking among church members. If sin could ruin armies as chaplains often claimed, the Confederacy itself was turning into a modern-day Sodom or Babylon, at least according to the alarmists. A satirical "proclamation of Satan" published in a Baptist newspaper mockingly praised stay-at-home secessionists (including church members) whose distilleries had turned corn into a scarce commodity. And then there were more subtle "sins." Writing letters on the Sabbath would once have seemed quite wicked, but South Carolinian Mary Leverett thought the "exigencies of the times demands a relaxation of these rules," and now correspondence with a family member became an "act of piety." The problem became where to draw the line. According to a Georgia newspaper, young men *and* women were smoking pipes in church, chewing tobacco, and even spitting on carpets and steps; a Baptist congregation in North Carolina had to discipline male and female members alike for using profanity.[39]

Perhaps these problems were isolated or reflected a long-term decline in church discipline, yet the uncertainty and upheaval of the 1860s surely heightened a sense of moral decay if not moral crisis. The question of dancing, for example, had long been a contentious issue. Attending a picnic in the spring of 1863 with some "country ladies and none of them pretty or entertaining," a Confederate captain (and Episcopalian) stationed in North Carolina found the whole affair "boring" because the Methodist and Baptist women refused to dance. However, many of their sisters elsewhere were now more than willing to indulge in such worldly recreation. An Alabama woman believed that dancing was wrong, claimed she did not enjoy dancing, but nevertheless spent most of an evening dancing. The remorse she expressed the following day hardly seemed genuine.[40]

"Southerners! This is not a time to dance!" declared a leading Baptist editor late in the war. Ministers condemned social dancing during a time of widespread suffering and want. "Is there not something heartless in the music of the ball-rooms and theaters?" Methodist Bishop James O. Andrew asked plaintively. The scandal of frivolous entertainment in the midst of so much bloodshed and heartache outraged the pious but hardly plumbed the depths of worries about moral decadence. The real danger, as a Mennonite preacher in the Shenandoah Valley told his congregation, was that parties and dances would "provoke the God of heaven to anger."[41]

All this promised disaster for the Confederate cause, so when churches disciplined their members for dancing, they acted as righteous patriots. But by 1864 this monitoring did little good especially in places that had yet to hear the tramp of enemy armies. Not only were brothers and sisters being led astray by others, but some were holding parties in their own homes. Yet what could be done? Even during the Confederacy's final months, churches accepted the repentant revelers back into the fold and expelled stiff-necked sinners with little apparent effect.[42] At times, it seemed as if thoughtless men and women were determined to dance on their nation's grave.

The sheer extravagance of parties and balls in a time of severe shortages and threatened starvation struck a discordant note. Quaffing wine and liquor while engaging in meaningless chatter revealed a shocking selfishness and dangerous indifference to the Confederacy's desperate struggle. Such disgusting scenes devalued the blood sacrifice of noble soldiers who would have been shocked to witness such civilian decadence. So ran the religious critique of social excess, and not only in the Confederacy. Unitarian Cyrus Bartol condemned elaborate displays of dress and food as "irreligious" in addition to being "unpatriotic" and "unjust." An Iowa woman whose husband was marching with Sherman to the sea received a "big taking down" at church one Sunday when she donned a hat that had been refashioned for winter. Those suffering deprivations resented seeing the still prosperous enjoying the good things of life. "There is a great wrong somewhere," Alabamian Sara Rodgers Espy remarked in her diary. "If our confederacy should fall, it will be no wonder to me for the brunt is thrown upon the working classes while the rich live at home in ease and pleasure."[43]

Reminders that the soldiers were fighting, bleeding, and dying for the home folks reinforced the point, but calculating the proper amount of civilian sacrifice proved tricky. Rather than strictly adhering to rigid economic laws such as supply and demand, Virginia Baptists suggested, people should follow the dictates of "Christian philanthropy and patriotism." A Presbyterian editor had grown tired of people whining about hard times and murmuring against the stern but just decrees of providence. Patience if not stoicism remained a Christian virtue, yet the war inevitably strained social and religious unity. After the infamous Richmond bread riot in April 1863, when a mob consisting largely of women and boys sacked some twenty businesses, a priest serving as a chaplain in a Louisiana regiment railed against Protestants for blaming the troubles on Irish and German Catholics but then claimed the whole affair had been planned in Baptist and Methodist churches. More commonly, complaints arose about indifference to the plight of the poor. According to a woman living in Spotsylvania County, Virginia, with three small children and very little to eat, rich people had "hearts of steel" and would rather toss food "to their dogs than give it to a starving child." She wondered how God could grant the Confederates victory so long as widows and children cried in vain.[44]

When it came to condemning extortion and speculation, Confederate ministers soon warmed to the task. "The foulest, blackest spot that will stain the page of the historian, will be the record of the heartless villainies of extortioners," a Presbyterian hospital chaplain thundered. His congregation of convalescing soldiers was no doubt receptive to this message, having already received word from home about the crimes of such bloodsuckers. In the still evolving Confederate jeremiad, extortion became a major cause of divine displeasure, but it also revealed cracks in the new nation's vaunted social and religious unity. Prominent Christians thought nothing of hiking up prices for soldier families. "What shall we say of the religion of the man who can, in these times, hoard up in his barns and storerooms, more than he needs himself?" a Presbyterian editor asked sharply. One reason to pray for revival at home was to soften the hearts of extortioners, but citing scriptural condemnations of this sin had seemingly little effect even on church members. The

Georgia Baptist Association issued a solemn but likely futile warning: "Extortioners and the covetous, no more than adulterers and fornicators, idolaters, thieves and drunkards shall inherit the kingdom of God."[45]

The nature of the problem, however, seemed more obvious than the solution. By suggesting that repentance could accomplish more than coercion, a Presbyterian editor clearly preferred voluntary measures. Sellers might not be able to control the market, Reverend J. W. Tucker observed, but they could control their own appetites and donate excess profits to the poor. Or perhaps the producers of corn and wheat should stop selling to speculators and market their crops directly to soldier families at a fair price. Such proposals were as unworkable as they were idealistic in a society where individualism and self-interest increasingly trumped communal and even patriotic values. Indeed, the more conservative clergy did not question the market system. Arguments for the harmony of interests made it seem dangerous to interfere with property rights, so religious leaders drew back from legislative remedies.[46] Churches condemned extortion in resolutions filled with moral indignation but went no further, perhaps reluctant to offend influential members of their congregations.

Instead of examining their own consciences and actions, some Confederates preferred finding a scapegoat, in this case a familiar one. Confederate war clerk John B. Jones claimed that Jews had been "scouring the countryside in all directions" buying up goods to hoard in anticipation of rising prices. In August 1862 a citizens' meeting in Thomasville, Georgia, denounced Jewish peddlers for price gouging and ordered them to leave town. These angry Georgians were not alone. Congressmen and newspaper editors spouted anti-Semitic slurs, many directed at Secretary of State Judah Benjamin, who was blamed for any unpopular administration policies. More broadly, Jews were condemned as Shylocks demanding their proverbial pound of flesh from soldier families. Even the normally mild-mannered Baptist editor of the *Religious Herald* in Richmond alleged that many "extortioners" were Jews who were violating the principles of their own faith. When newspapers appealed for women to stop wasting money on fancy clothes, editors threw in references to Jewish sharpers.[47]

Such charges certainly fueled public anger, and Jewish leaders responded quickly to defuse a potentially dangerous situation. In a sermon delivered on a Confederate fast day in Richmond, Rabbi Maxmillian Michelbacher denied that Jewish merchants were selling out (or even buying up) the Confederacy and cited their many philanthropic contributions. Michelbacher himself had composed a long prayer for distribution to Jewish soldiers and exuded a bloodthirsty patriotism leaving little doubt about whose side the Lord favored. As a religious minority in a Protestant society, Jews went out of their way to prove their fidelity to the fledgling southern nation. In Savannah, Georgia, a committee of five German Jews drafted resolutions defending constitutional liberties, criticizing newspapers for repeating anti-Semitic slanders, and pointing to their brethren serving in the Confederate army.[48]

Tarring Jews with a broad brush went too far for some Confederates. A citizen of Petersburg wrote a long letter to the *Richmond Examiner* (whose editor had bitterly complained about Benjamin and other "Israelite" representatives of the "synagogue") arguing that many Christians had joined in the carnival of speculation and extortion. He denounced the "cruel injustice" of blaming a "separate class of scapegoats" for financial or military disasters yet presented a stereotypical picture of the Jews as a people of great achievements in many fields who worked hard, accumulated wealth, and seldom became a burden on society. In point of fact, southern Jews posed no threat to the social order. Although few became planters or owned slaves, they had seldom criticized the institution; indeed, the northern rabbi Morris Raphall's defense of slavery had won applause from the fire-eaters during the secession crisis.[49]

By far, the most infamous case of wartime anti-Semitism involved General Ulysses S. Grant's December 1862 order expelling Jewish merchants from his department. Earlier the general had attempted to prevent such men from traveling south and had denounced them as a "privileged class" of cotton speculators. Claiming that Jews had persistently violated Treasury Department regulations, Grant demanded they leave the Department of the Tennessee within twenty-four hours and forbade anyone from visiting his headquarters to apply for trade permits (or presumably to protest the order). With his troops immobilized in northern Mississippi, Grant had grown frustrated, and his father Jesse's entanglement with three Jewish merchants in Cincinnati made him furious.[50] The degree of the general's own anti-Semitism remains impossible to determine with all the charges and countercharges that swirled around, especially in 1868 when Grant was running for president. Two things are clear: Grant expressed the common prejudices of his day; he disingenuously tried to explain away the order.

How many Jews were actually expelled is equally uncertain, but protests erupted immediately. After a Jewish merchant from Paducah, Kentucky, accompanied by an Ohio congressman met with Lincoln, General-in-Chief Henry W. Halleck revoked Grant's order. Jewish leaders warmly praised this decision while reminding the president that Grant's order had been an "unjust and tyrannical mandate" proscribing an entire of class of citizens in clear violation of the Constitution.[51]

The Jewish press tried to counter religious prejudice by publishing lists of

Jewish soldiers fighting for the Union and challenging anti-Semitic newspaper comments. Politically, Jews in the United States had kept a low profile, and this probably prevented wartime hostility from getting any worse. Editors and rabbis had steered clear of partisan politics during the secession crisis and followed that same course during the war. Like Episcopalians and Catholics, many Jews deplored sectional divisions and refused to engage in anti- southern invective; a few blamed Protestant ministers for exacerbating sectional tensions. Once the war had begun and despite lingering conservatism in some quarters, Jewish leaders rallied to the Union cause. They honored national fast days and flew flags over synagogues, but then southern Jews joined in similar Confederate observances.[52]

Such displays of "loyalty" became an important feature of civil religion and a way to solidify support for the war but exacted a considerable cost. For Confederates, early divisions over secession and wartime disruption of congregational life created much deeper and more complicated problems of national allegiance and social cohesion. During the 1850s, some northern-born ministers had gone out of their way to embrace slavery and other southern values, though suspicions about their true convictions lingered during the war. Worries about the influence of a so-called Yankee element persisted. In some areas, Unionists stopped attending services rather than join in warlike prayers, and churches expelled members suspected of disloyalty. Over a three-year period, the Holston conference of the southern Methodist church in East Tennessee charged some thirty-five ministers with disloyalty to the Confederacy and expelled nine of them. With strong encouragement from the notorious editor William G. "Parson" Brownlow, who could excoriate religious opponents, political enemies, and Tennessee rebels with equal venom, pro-Union Methodists organized a separate conference.[53] In a sense, secession begat secession.

The appearance of the enemy further tore the social fabric. Federal armies captured coastal areas and eventually penetrated deeply into the Confederacy, putting further strain on ministers and their congregants, who suddenly became refugees—displaced from their homes, uncertain where to go, and sometimes less than welcome elsewhere. Often the first to sound the alarm, pastors became leaders of the exodus, though they hardly brought their people to any kind of promised land. If pastors faced a seemingly rootless life in unfamiliar surroundings, their refugee parishioners felt even more adrift. At least some churches welcomed the newcomers in part because they helped make up for wartime losses in membership. Given the chaotic circumstances, Baptists decided they had little choice but to admit refugee members without the usual letters of "dismission" from home churches. In the spring of 1864, two

South Carolina Episcopal churches described how the influx of "many excellent people" from the low country offered a wonderful opportunity to practice Christian charity.[54]

That may have been wishful thinking. Other congregations were apparently not so hospitable because ministers and the religious press kept urging church members to greet the newcomers as brothers and sisters in Christ. A South Carolina Lutheran synod even praised refugees for their patience and cheerfulness despite a sometimes cool reception from local churches. In Lynchburg, Virginia, one minister ordered refugees to sit in the gallery—a place traditionally reserved for slaves. Such powerful symbolism spoke volumes about refugees' tenuous status in a society feeling all the strains of a long war. According to a Kentucky congressman, a woman attending a revival (he would not say where) had heard a preacher announce there would be no refugees in heaven, leading an older woman to cry out, "Thank God! . . . I want to go there!"[55] Yet the refugees themselves could be equally standoffish. In Texas, young Kate Stone—the privileged daughter of a Louisiana planter family forced to flee from the Yankees and their own slaves—wrote condescendingly about the poorly dressed country people who shouted far too many "hallelujahs."[56]

So churches could just as easily keep people apart as bring them together. Congregations no longer had the wherewithal to support themselves, much less help others. The war kept disrupting religious life in countless and unpredictable ways. For many people, larger questions of loyalty and disaffection, of victory and defeat often paled beside the travail of families and the suffering of individuals, but the two could not always be so neatly separated and at times placed well-meaning people at cross purposes.

When churchgoers prayed or adopted resolutions supporting the troops, they could not help but focus on the men they knew best. The assumption was that these soldiers would bravely face the enemy, yet that would not always be the case. By 1863, congregations increasingly had to deal with deserters who had once sat among them. Some sought advice from other churches and held out hope that the wayward might yet confess and mend their ways.[57] Churches hesitated to act and often postponed decisions as long as possible. One Virginia Baptist congregation patiently waited for nearly a year and a half until finally deciding that one deserter would not heed General Lee's plea to return. Brother Lafayette Whitman, according to the note in a North Carolina Baptist record book, "was expelled from the church for deserting his country's flag and going to the enemy."[58] No doubt, congregations delayed taking such a drastic step in part because they did not want to acknowledge that any of their members could be so disloyal.

All the losses, whether from desertion or death, placed other problems faced by denominations and congregations in a broader perspective. That war had seriously shaken the foundation of religious life was undeniable. Northern churches could better weather the storm because the battles were not fought in their backyards, but they too faced vacant pews and lengthening casualty lists. In the Confederacy, the effects were more immediate and more dramatic. Services were still being held, sermons were still being preached, and members tried to maintain the normal rhythms of church life, but hard times overwhelmed many pious and charitable impulses. And all the while more battles were being fought, and at times the Lord seemed so far away.

Chapter 14

WRATH

> Therefore wait ye upon me, saith the Lord, until the day that I rise up to
> the prey: for my determination is to gather the nations, that I may assemble
> the kingdoms, to pour upon them mine indignation, even all my fierce
> anger: for all the earth shall be devoured with the fire of my jealousy. For
> then will I turn to the people a pure language, that they may all call upon
> the name of the Lord, to serve him with one consent.
> — Zephaniah 3:8–9

The air felt warmer, the trees were budding, and the roads were starting to dry out—all sure signs of another campaign season in the offing. And in
the spring of 1863, there appeared still another sign of approaching combat.
Soldiers about to begin slaughtering each other seized one last opportunity to
make their peace with God. The Confederate revivals along the Rappahannock
River continued as men figured they would be on the march any day now. In
the Federal camps near Falmouth, Virginia, prayer meetings had grown larger
and more enthusiastic.[1]

Now was the time to write home, thumb through a Testament, or perhaps
take more seriously the message in that tract the chaplain had just distributed. The soldiers could not know that this would be the year of Gettysburg,
Vicksburg, and Chattanooga, turning points all in what had seemingly become a war without end. But first there was Chancellorsville, a masterstroke
for Robert E. Lee, another disaster for the Army of the Potomac, a horrific
bloodletting, and the final curtain for that fierce Presbyterian Stonewall Jackson. General Joseph E. Hooker thought he had a surefire plan to outflank the
Army of Northern Virginia and force the rebels to fight for their supply lines.
By April 30 the Federals had crossed the Rappahannock, but the following day
Hooker seemed to lose his nerve, and Lee approved the audacious flank attack
that would win a battle he should have lost.

Sunday, May 10, was a day to celebrate this Confederate victory by order
of General Lee himself. Louisiana Sergeant Reuben Allen Pierson acknowledged the battle's terrible bloodshed but repeated a familiar formula: "If we
are only true to ourselves and God be for us the time will surely soon come
when we shall be redeemed from the miseries of this horrid war and restored
to our homes in peace." Other soldiers would not have made final victory so

conditional, and one costly result of Chancellorsville was a dangerous over-confidence in part resting on assumptions about divine purpose. Some of Lee's soldiers even sounded optimistic about the increasingly dire situation at Vicksburg because after all, as one South Carolina corporal informed his aunt, "God is certainly on our side, and we should trust in Him to deliver us from the hands of our enemies." Such sentiments echoed thinking back home, where assumptions about Confederate victories and God's will were just as simplistic and perilous.[2]

Ironically, many northerners reeling from news of Hooker's retreat back across the Rappahannock expressed almost equal confidence in the Lord's favor—at least in the long term. "God will protect the right and punish sin-ners," one Methodist editor affirmed. "But God works by laws that require a long time for the development of his purposes, and history abounds in many apparent eclipses of the right, and triumphs of evil." Such reverses were only temporary, however, because the war would ultimately destroy slavery and save the Union. At this point, such reasoning was predictable and much too pat—a ritualistic response to another humiliating defeat. Yet even pious sol-diers who had seen the worst believed that the horrors of Chancellorsville simply meant the country had not been punished enough. Too much reliance on human strength and fallible generals, too little reliance on the Lord of Hosts had again proved fatal, and now loyal northerners once again cataloged their country's transgressions. Archbishop Hughes added infidelity, heresy, and schism to the usual list of sins but also believed that had the nation built more churches, orphan asylums, and hospitals, "the thunders of the battle-field" would have ceased.[3]

In this scattershot theology, surprisingly few people bothered to rethink their assumptions about the relationship between God's will and military de-structiveness. A war for "union and freedom," Boston Unitarian Cyrus Augus-tus Bartol still claimed, "is as Christian and holy as it is patriotic and neces-sary." Premature cries for peace were not merely pointless but sinful because it was God who would decide when and under what conditions the guns would fall silent.[4]

There was little chance that even the more conservative churches would offer much comfort to Copperheads or other opponents of the war. Meeting in Peoria, Illinois, Old School Presbyterians adopted some confusing and equivo-cating resolutions on the state of the country and on slavery—their customary caution still quite evident. Yet after some debate, the United States flag flew over their meetings, and the delegates reaffirmed their loyalty to the govern-ment—this time with virtually no opposition. Accompanied by oblique but critical references to their Old School rivals, the New School General Assembly in Philadelphia heartily endorsed the Lincoln administration and the Emancipation Proclamation. Some sixty-five delegates then hastened to Washington eager to present their resolutions to the president. Lincoln cryptically replied that some denominations were perhaps more loyal to the Union cause than others but that all claimed to be loyal. He found their support most "gratifying because from the beginning I saw that the issues of our great struggle depended on Divine interposition and favor." Lincoln did not say whether the cause of the Union had actually secured the Lord's favor, simply noting, "The end is not yet."[5]

Just two days after Lincoln met with the Presbyterian delegation, Virginia Baptists adopted a long address blasting northerners, "who claim to be the followers of the meek and lowly Jesus," for ferociously attacking slavery and treating southerners as "felons" in the Lord's house. As a warning against the dangers of fanaticism, future generations would surely point to "this atrocious war, waged in the name of Christ, by descendents of the Puritans, by high-priests of philanthropy, the once meek advocates of peace, who would scarce admit the lawfulness of defensive war." Although these Virginians also acknowledged the sins of the southern people, they did so only in passing and with not nearly the zeal they used to excoriate northern Christians.[6]

Rather than considering their own faults (such as waning religious enthusiasm at home) or heeding scriptural warnings about judging others, Confederates asked how long the Lord would allow this horrible war to continue. Even in the wake of Chancellorsville, an Alabama lieutenant wrote of a "dark time" in the Confederacy's short history, and "no man" could know when it would end. "God constituted this war for some good and wise purpose and when his purpose is accomplished then comes the end of the war." Yet, like many other Confederates, he believed that northern armies represented the "scum of their population," but now Lincoln would have to raise regiments and brigades that "will draw members from all of the families in his Government." Such a thought made him more hopeful: "Let them [the Federals] tremble for their day of retribution is not far distant."[7]

———

By the same token, news of prayer meetings and continued revivals in the armies (again despite worries about declension at home) further convinced southern churches that the Confederate cause remained God's cause. "The Church of the South can with a clear conscience, take her stand by the side of her battling children," a North Carolina minister told an Episcopalian council. The church "can send her soldiers to the field" in a "religious war" against "northern religious fanaticism." It became more imperative than ever for

Christians to obey the conscription laws and support the war. Although "God in scourging us has used the hand of a wicked nation as His avenging instrument," Virginia Baptists admitted, "We are daily more convinced of the righteousness of our cause, and have abiding faith, through His favor, of ultimate, and we trust not distant deliverance from our ruthless enemy."[8]

The death of Stonewall Jackson would seemingly shake their faith in a benign providence, but Confederates' theology and their reading of scripture remained tied to a cycle of victory and defeat, sin and repentance, punishment and redemption—all pointing to the achievement of southern independence. One aspiring poet described Jackson as the Confederate Moses who would not enter the promised land, but few doubted that others, including Robert E. Lee, would get there. To the devout, Jackson had been the general sent from God, and Old Jack himself had always detected the Lord's hand in wartime events large and small.[9]

As news of Jackson's wounding after the successful flank attack at Chancellorsville had spread through the army, the ways of providence became for a time at least more mysterious and certainly not as beneficent. Taken to the small plantation office at Guinea Station, Jackson himself appeared ready to die. "You find me severely wounded, not unhappy or depressed," he told one minister. "I believe it has been done according to the will of God, and I acquiesce entirely in His holy will." Drifting in and out consciousness, when told it was Sunday, the general rallied enough to reply, "It is the Lord's day. My wish is fulfilled. I have always desired to die on Sunday."[10] And so he did on May 10, 1863.

At the funeral service in Stonewall's home church in Lexington, Virginia, his pastor William S. White read from First Corinthians, with special emphasis on the verse, "The last enemy that shall be destroyed is death." And here began the apotheosis of Jackson as martyr to the Confederate cause. Although to countless Confederates the news at first seemed overwhelming, the loss unbelievable and unexplainable, the orthodox knew how to respond. By October 1863 Virginia Presbyterians concluded that Jackson's "untimely" death marked a "further chastisement for sins, especially for our ingratitude, pride, and dependence on an arm of flesh." In an even more Calvinist vein—though one often forgotten when Confederate confidence soared—Kate Cumming mused about the Lord's "dark and mysterious" ways.[11]

Jackson's military reputation and accomplishments had long appalled, frightened, and impressed his foes. Jackson seemed to be one of those "men of narrow minds, but strong passions and tremendous will," Washington journalist John W. Forney remarked. "Religious enthusiasts of all religions and

Lieutenant General Thomas Jonathan ("Stonewall") Jackson (National Archives)

creeds have often devoted themselves with conscientious and determined energy to a wicked cause." Yet many northerners could not help but admire their enemy's zeal. Abolitionists fumed when Henry Ward Beecher called Jackson a "rare and eminent Christian," but the Reverend Beecher was not alone. Northern editorial comments on Jackson's passing were often restrained, respectful, and even reverent. "No man rejoices at his [Jackson's] death," a Massachusetts chaplain wrote to a church newspaper. He considered Jackson "a man of prayer and Christian experience, a brave, gallant and chivalric soldier." The good chaplain added: "May God pardon his one fault! I wish *we* had more generals like him."[12]

Emphasizing Jackson the devoted Christian over Jackson the relentless fighter turned the general's life into an evangelical object lesson. No longer would the mighty Stonewall accomplish great deeds on the battlefield, but his example of pious patriotism could still point the way to others seeking salvation for themselves and their country. Young men beset by temptations need look no further than Jackson for inspiration. The general had driven his men hard, eulogists conceded even as they tried to soften the image of the relentless warrior indifferent to human needs and weaknesses. Yet, in the end, Jackson's greatest virtue was his utter reliance upon God rather than man—a belief the general himself would have used to comfort Lee and other Confederates who could not imagine the Army of Northern Virginia without him.[13]

Struggling to understand why the Lord had taken away their great hero, pious Confederates settled on a thoroughly orthodox answer: the southern people had relied too much on the arm of flesh. "They made an idol of him, and God has rebuked them," the general's sister-in-law Margaret Junkin Preston wrote only days after his death. Many other Confederate Christians made nearly identical statements, though some thought the southern people had been guilty of idolizing other generals, which might have raised a troubling question about excessive veneration for Lee. The Lord was a "jealous god" as the Old Testament said repeatedly. "God will be honored," Tennessean Eliza Fain warned, "and if we in any way rob him of the honor and glory due to him alone he will bring us to see the evil of our ways." Many men in Jackson's own command, according to the deeply religious artillery officer Willie Pegram, had "lost sight of God's mercies."[14]

Devout Confederates made subtle but, in their minds, important points on this score. Many people had not realized how closely Jackson's deep piety connected to his military successes, and they would have to learn anew the lesson that Jackson himself so well understood: the need to rely upon God absolutely and unconditionally. Now all the people could do, one Virginia woman suggested, was to "bow in meek submission to the great Ruler of events." But this was no fatalistic message. If politicians, generals, and the southern people only embodied the "spirit of Jackson," one minister suggested, the war might have already ended in a Confederate triumph.[15]

Nor was Jackson's death the end of the story. The same God who had raised up one Jackson could raise up another, a fond hope even as Confederates mourned their loss. "He will provide another whose arm he will strengthen to drive the invaders from our soil," a Kentucky staff officer predicted. The

Lord had given, the Lord had taken away, and the Lord would give again—that seemed the most reassuring if not the most logical way to assess the meaning and consequences of Jackson's death.[16] Such confidence in the workings of providence greatly simplified the understanding of everything from bloody battles to individual deaths. It offered comfort and reassurance but also laid the groundwork for disappointment, disillusionment, and even the loss of faith. A belief in God's sovereignty did not prevent humans from claiming to understand the unfolding of the providential design, an understanding deeply imbued with their own hopes. A common assumption was that Stonewall's example would inspire Confederates to enter future battles with greater spirit, élan, and even ferocity. As a chaplain in the Army of Tennessee remarked as he searched for spiritual and military meaning in Jackson's death, "God can remove the chief of workmen, and still carry on the cause of liberty."[17]

———

The campaign season would in any event proceed, and the Army of Northern Virginia soon moved north into Pennsylvania buoyed by the victory at Chancellorsville and inspired by memories of the fallen Jackson. Confederate confidence contained an admixture of arrogance, a quality in seemingly plentiful supply on all sides during the summer and fall of 1863. Even hope that Lee's men in Pennsylvania would refrain from pillaging carried as much self-righteousness as sincere conviction. And hatred now threatened to overwhelm gentler virtues even among the deeply religious. Because "extermination is the watchword of our enemies," one Georgia Baptist editor rationalized, "Mercy ceases to be a virtue in a contest with devils." Instead, the government should adopt "those extreme measures of retaliation which shall put fear into the hearts of the Yankee soldiery and demoralize the invading armies."[18]

Fear and demoralization had already spread across the northern states, with Hooker's recent defeat only deepening the gloom. "Truly God has a controversy with this people," Maria Lydig Daly wrote as the Confederates entered Pennsylvania. Worse still, she thought, the Lord "raises for us no deliverer." Methodist ministers in Philadelphia tried to rally volunteers to defend the city, even wielding picks and shovels to throw up makeshift fortifications. This all reflected panic for sure but also an abiding confidence in divine favor. The deeply religious Salmon Chase had lost faith in his friend Hooker but not in God or the Union: "If our cause is just and right will He not bless it? Will He suffer the cause to fail because of the unworthiness of those who sustain it?"[19]

Just as Pennsylvanians and other northerners nervously followed the advance of Lee's army, for an even longer time anxious Confederates had awaited news about the halting, slow, but apparently inexorable progress of General Grant's campaign against Vicksburg, a vital outpost on the Mississippi River.

"God being on our side we will assuredly gain the victory," a Tennessee major had written back in March. Yet, as the Yankee grip gradually tightened, people in Vicksburg asked if the Lord would somehow miraculously feed them. At the end of May, Emma Balfour along with thirty other hardy souls worshiped in a church filled with rubble from the Federal shelling, disheartening for even the sturdiest patriot. Increasingly Confederates both inside and outside the city no longer expected a miraculous deliverance, began thinking about what sins had brought on such a disaster, and prepared to live with the Lord's inscrutable decrees. One chaplain reported more soldiers turning to God as the situation grew more hopeless.[20] These diverse reactions, however, all fit into an overarching set of religious convictions. In Vicksburg as elsewhere, faith offered consolation but also provided set explanations for victory or defeat, ways for both understanding and coping with the vicissitudes of war.

Military high and lows (along with their political and social fallout) led people to either exult too much or despair too easily. The early days of July were a case in point. After three days of hard fighting, the Army of the Potomac emerged victorious from the bloodbath at Gettysburg, and on July 4 Grant's army accepted the surrender of Vicksburg. The psalmists and prophets provided the hosannas to the Almighty after these stunning triumphs over the wicked rebels. But only a little more than a week later a mob in New York City attempted to stop the draft, and a full-scale riot erupted. Conscription and long casualty lists had enflamed political, ethnic, and religious tensions. Ever since the slaughters at Antietam and Fredericksburg, if not before, Irish Catholic support for the war had wavered. Emancipation had won few friends among working-class immigrant families, the Catholic press highlighted evidence of Protestant nativism, and a draft call only fueled a common belief about the poor bearing the brunt of the war's burdens. Cries for peace from the city's leading Democrats helped stir a seething cauldron of resentment until it boiled over into the worst violence in the city's history.[21]

A mob stormed the draft office and began ransacking businesses and homes. Screaming for the blood of abolitionists and Republicans, rioters swarmed around newspaper offices, and attacked any well-dressed man suspected of having paid the three-hundred-dollar commutation fee to avoid military service. The more vicious targeted African Americans, lynching several and burning the Colored Orphan Asylum. The Catholic hierarchy was caught in the political and religious crossfire. Archbishop Hughes had been a stalwart Unionist and even endorsed conscription. He had little use for Copperhead Democrats and, while the riot was still raging, had issued a public letter appealing for the Irish and other Catholics to peaceably return to their homes. But Hughes discreetly suggested to his friend Seward that the draft be suspended for a couple weeks or more.[22] As usual planting himself between the antislavery Brownson and the reactionary McMaster, the ailing archbishop had made one final effort to align his church with a firm but moderate loyalty to the government.

Not surprisingly, church leaders claimed that few of the rioters in New York (or in the smaller disturbances elsewhere) had been good Catholics, but religious divisions assumed even greater importance once order had been restored. Protestant leaders of various stripes piously condemned the rioting and worried that it might hearten Confederates. Beecher and the more moderate clergy conceded that the Irish had played a large role in the disturbances but claimed they had been misled by demagogues—an undoubted reference to New York Copperheads. The draft had been only a pretext for men who reveled in anarchy and were mostly interested in plunder, the leading New School Presbyterian organ charged.[23]

Other Protestants adopted a harsher tone. The hostility to Republicans and reformers of various stripes and especially the attacks on inoffensive blacks recalled the mob spirit that had crucified Jesus. Modern-day Pharisees had incited brutal attacks against the weakest members of society. "Such a course of persecution will most assuredly cause the Irishman to sink and the colored man to rise," a New Jersey minister predicted. Editors ranted about foreigners attacking Americans and doubted any priests had tried to stop the violence.[24]

It would be going too far to say there was a resurgent Know-Nothingism at work here, but Catholics had reason to fear that old prejudices had been rekindled. And in this case, religious questions became once again entangled in the politics of loyalty and the politics of slavery. Differences among Catholics along with broad-brush attacks on the church made matters worse. The *New York Irish-American* praised the Catholic clergy for refusing "to preach the nigger from their pulpits," while William Lloyd Garrison accused Irish Catholics of being "the very bitterest enemies of the antislavery cause." Crosscurrents of religion, ethnicity, and politics created a flurry of comment but offered far more rationalization than enlightenment.[25] Yet it would be misleading to take all the rhetoric on both sides too seriously because the New York draft riots were no more than a short-term problem for northern Catholics.

After all, the recent victories at Gettysburg and Vicksburg loomed much larger than the draft riots in most people's minds. Even while the rioters were still rampaging through the New York streets, Lincoln issued a proclamation calling for a national day of thanksgiving. The president carefully balanced references to "wonderful things he [God] has done in the nation's behalf" with sympathy toward the many families in mourning. Whether Lincoln or Seward drafted this document is not known, but it was certainly less circumspect than other presidential statements in claiming God's favor. The proclamation described "repentance and submission to the Divine Will" as a sure path to "the perfect enjoyment of Union and fraternal peace."[26]

Repentance and submission, however, proved to be in even shorter supply than usual. Stunning victories instead sent hopes soaring to greater heights; the spiritual naiveté and arrogance that had characterized Confederate civil religion in the spring of 1863 now appeared all across the North. The devout turned the victor of Gettysburg into a Christian hero. Major General George Gordon Meade's order offering "thanks to the Almighty Disposer of events, that in the good of his providence He has thought fit to give victory to the cause of the just" touched the major themes of wartime civil religion. One Presbyterian editor contrasted Meade's words to the drunken Hooker's "profane boast that he should capture or destroy the rebel army in spite of providence." God would not be mocked, and so the disaster of Chancellorsville had been followed by the victory of Gettysburg.[27]

Triumphalism encouraged neither humility nor thoughtfulness, especially on the official day of national thanksgiving. After delivering a standard defense of the clergy's right to speak on political questions, a New Jersey Presbyterian threw all modesty to the proverbial wind: "It has been conceded on all hands that the world has never seen a better class of men than the Protestant ministers of the present age—pious, honest, self-denying, laborious, and devoted especially to their great work of advancing civilization and saving the souls of men."[28] Was there a hint of anti-Catholicism here? Perhaps so, but more importantly, these words reflected a millennial expectation that kept cropping up during the war, notably after any great success on the battlefield. Despite acknowledgment that the Lord continued to work in mysterious ways, clouds of doubt appeared to be lifting.

The temptation to anticipate still greater victories if not a final, crushing blow against the rebellion became overwhelming. On the day of national thanksgiving, an Illinois schoolboy asked a classmate, "Aint you glad God is going to the stop the war?" Preachers contrasted recent despair with present jubilation as they reminded congregations how Almighty God had rendered a harsh but righteous judgment against the rebels. All the anguish caused by the military disasters of the past two years had been only a prelude to the American republic's glorious and final vindication. The Lord had determined there would be no breakup of the Union, and some ministers even anticipated "permanent" peace and prosperity. For those with a strong antislavery faith, Gettysburg and Vicksburg proved how once the eyes of the president and the generals had been opened to the necessity for striking a blow at slavery, national deliverance was assured. According to a Pennsylvania Methodist, "God hastens its [the war's] termination in the triumph of the democratic principle, in the elevation of all men to the freedom and equality for which He created them."[29]

All the lofty sermons, a New York Times editorial predicted, would strengthen the government, inspire the army, and make the people more patriotic. Repeating the catchphrase "God reigns" was obviously more comforting after victories than after defeats, but those words came far too easily. Affirming divine sovereignty further aligned the Almighty with northern war aims and turned Confederates into rebels against the Lord and his holy word. God loved the United States and had yet greater work for this blessed nation in the future. On August 6 Lincoln and his secretary John Hay heard Reverend Phineas Gurley refer to the Lord as "the Guardian-God of the Republic" who, "though we have offended him, we can not believe He will have us to perish." The president observed that Gurley had never preached with such confidence about the Union cause before.[30]

God stood above all governments, all armies, and indeed above any human means. Politicians and generals could hesitate and delay, the people could lose heart, yet the almighty hand steadily guided the course of history, in this case toward the promised land of reunion and peace. At a joint service in Chicago, Methodist bishop Matthew Simpson described how the Lord worked through "secondary agencies" and "subordinate influences" to "direct the armies of the earth." With reasoning similar to that of Confederate Christians after First Manassas, northern believers credited God with providing the Army of the Potomac a strong defensive position along Cemetery Ridge and even arranging the tactical deployments.[31]

Aside from some extended consideration of slavery's role in the continuation of the war, northern sermons paid only passing attention to the nation's transgressions or ignored them altogether. Somehow, talk of divine judgment carried an expectation of divine deliverance, as the Union's enemies appeared to be in full retreat. Preaching about God pouring out his wrath on the nations and even attempts to tie the course of the sectional conflict and Civil War to prophecies in Daniel and Revelation became less a cause for lamentation than thanksgiving. If Gettysburg had in fact been Armageddon, as one student of the Bible concluded, then perhaps the final victory of the Lord (and the federal Union) was at hand. By the same token, the whole idea of blood sacrifice and even martyrdom gave all the deaths and wounds a transcendent meaning boding far more good than ill.[32]

Seeing Gettysburg and Vicksburg as sure signs of divine favor opened up the prospect for making republican government universal, a project growing out of the era's drive for worldwide evangelization. There was no need to "crusade against foreign despotisms," a Philadelphia Unitarian maintained; "the darkness of oppression, here and everywhere, shall vanish even as the morning mists disappear at the rising of the sun." These great victories marked the nation's purification, again showing how God viewed the events of history far differently than fallible humanity. A German Reformed editor even chastised Lee's invading Confederates for boasting that God was on their side, as if he were not committing the same deadly sin.[33]

Northern church support for the war remained strong, and by the fall of 1863, several denominations reaffirmed their commitment, often with an unseemly pride. With perhaps a sly reference to Judas and the disciples, the Pennsylvania Baptist Convention claimed that eleven out of twelve Christian ministers and an equally large proportion of the laity were unswervingly loyal to the government. "True patriotism," a New York Methodist preached, "is a high grade of New Testament piety." Did all this overstate the case? Although the Methodist Church took great pride in its clergy's patriotism and all the members who served in Union regiments, a conference in southern Indiana felt it necessary to advise every minister to "be as clear on the subject of loyalty as on the subject of honesty."[34]

Churches of various stripes came close to abandoning all pretense of political neutrality. Baptist associations, Methodist annual conferences, and other bodies were no longer satisfied with simply sustaining the government against an unholy rebellion. Many resolutions explicitly supported Lincoln and the Emancipation Proclamation. Some adopted detailed statements approving a whole range of war policies, including the suspension of habeas corpus, and even exulted over Republican victories in the fall elections.[35]

Denominational groups lauded the president as a humble man with a profound faith in providence, and the politically astute Lincoln surely appreciated the timely endorsements. In brief remarks to delegations from two Presbyterian synods, the president noted how with the Lord's help he simply had done his duty. "If God be with us, we will succeed; if not, we will fail." Many preachers had been making this point for more than two years, and Lincoln claimed that from the beginning he had realized that human strength alone would never suffice. When he admitted wishing he had been a more "devout man" or stated with disarming frankness, "When I could not see any other resort, I would place my whole reliance in God," such statements resonated with churchgoers used to confessing their own weaknesses and doubts.[36]

The slow but steady public transformation of the president into a Christian statesman made the battle against the southern rebellion into a still holier crusade. Patriotic resolutions from various religious bodies poured into Lincoln's office. After the Republicans made important gains in the fall elections, one

Methodist editor detected the "voice of God."[37] Whether this was some new revelation remained to be seen, but loyalty to the Union, the success of northern arms, and the equation of patriotism with piety left little room for objections. An ever stronger belief that the Lord's guiding hand was leading Federal armies to victory, a faith often coupled with millennial hope, transformed the great Jehovah into a much more benign and less mysterious force in human history. Abstract confidence could not always calm the fearful, much less comfort the grieving, but it helped make a terrible war at least superficially more comprehensible. Devout Christians hardly need question their own motives, beliefs, or actions when their political and religious allegiances appeared so closely aligned.

For Confederates, the times, the war, the Lord's will, and their own lives seemed badly out of joint. Not only had the suffering and bloodshed mounted, but so many Christian soldiers, including the sainted Jackson, were gone. Yet, as a timely tract pointed out, a triumph as followers of Christ would be far greater than any victory of southern arms. The latter had suddenly become problematic in any case, and so now was the time to seek the Lord. Salvation did not depend on human circumstances or earthly hopes; bad news from the battlefield could not overshadow the good news of the gospel. Indeed, a divine "amnesty" for sinners offered far more than any presidential amnesty for deserters. Only Christ could bring true peace if not in this world at least in the world to come. Soldiers still hoped the war would end soon and with southern independence established, but the Lord's promises of salvation were of infinitely greater value. All of this marked a turning inward. Depressing reports from Vicksburg and Gettysburg led families to focus more than ever, and sometimes almost exclusively, on the safety and survival of *their* soldiers. Yet, with a husband in the army and a baby recently dead, one Arkansas woman wondered if heaven was gained only through the blood of others. Devout soldiers praised the Lord for having safeguarded them thus far, prepared to meet their own death, and increasingly expected to die in the next battle.[38]

The theological reasoning here remained simple but to many folks still powerful. Defeat forced conscientious Confederates to consider their own transgressions, a matter that had been more easily avoided during the winter and spring of soaring hopes. "God is angry with us for our sins," a Georgia editor stated, offering the readiest explanation for the depressing battlefield news. To be cast out by the Lord would surely be an even worse fate than subjugation by Yankees. "Sins of the people have rose like a dark cloud between us and God, yes between us and the mercy seat," William Stillwell of the 53rd Georgia feared. As any student of the scriptures knew, the Lord punished nations as well as individuals for their sins—a point often made before and one that sounded more ominous than ever in the wake of Gettysburg and Vicksburg.[39]

Never had there been a greater need for confession and prayer, indeed for a heartfelt acknowledgment that Confederates had brought these troubles on themselves by violating God's most holy ordinances. Recalling the dangerous self-confidence that had been so widespread in the Army of Northern Virginia and on the home front, the *Central Presbyterian* observed how Confederates had chosen to ignore God with all too predictable and disastrous consequences. Chaplains, ministers, and denominational associations cited any number of offenses that had stirred up divine wrath. Army officers had not lived up to their high calling as Christian gentlemen and had set a poor example for the enlisted men. At home, the people had been guilty of murmuring against their rulers and coveting their neighbor's possessions, if not engaging in outright extortion—the one sin that had recently become a staple of the Confederate jeremiad. Patriotism itself had waned, and desertion had grown.[40]

Jefferson Davis too felt God's "chastening hand" and so declared yet another day of fasting, humiliation, and prayer. "Trials and reverses" should lead to "self-examination," and the president admitted that unwarranted confidence and rampant greed had led people to forget the Lord's mercies. Unlike the standard jeremiad however, his proclamation dealt almost exclusively with the "anguish and sufferings of defeat," making no apparent reference to hope for redemption. People desperately searching for comfort at this low point in Confederate fortunes paid little heed to such subtleties. Instead, Davis still won praise for being a man raised up by God to lead the southern nation, a Christian fit to stand with General Lee.[41]

On August 21 the preaching and praying in camp left a strong impression. A member of the Richmond Howitzers imagined "our bleeding nation bowed . . . at the Throne of Grace" in prayers that would surely be answered. In letters and diaries, righteous soldiers recapped the day's sermons and sought to elevate commonplace religious expressions into transcendent ones, marking a turning point in Confederate history. In Chattanooga, however, Federal artillery fire ominously interrupted services, including one conducted by that famous Presbyterian divine and ardent secessionist, Benjamin Morgan Palmer.[42]

Chaplain Robert Franklin Bunting outlined how each fast day had been followed by a Confederate victory, which unfortunately had been followed by a period of vainglory with all too many southerners placing too much faith in generals, armies, and their own virtue. Yet under God's chastening discipline, those same generals and armies must fight on. Chaplain J. J. D. Renfroe of the 10th Alabama denied that much had been lost at Gettysburg or Vicksburg; he fully believed that affirming the "battle is God's" would ultimately bring victory and southern independence. That message too had been heard before and still the war continued.[43]

In Richmond and elsewhere, businesses closed and the churches held special services. The anti-Davis *Richmond Examiner* continued to rail against the fast days as Puritan-Yankee contrivances, but that was to be expected. Signs of civilians' losing heart seemed far more ominous because in some places few people observed the day. "We fast, certainly," War Department clerk John B. Jones commented sardonically, "feel greatly humiliated at the loss of New Orleans and Vicksburg—and we pray, daily."[44]

Such statements expressed the raw emotions of people struggling to square the realities of war with assumptions about the righteousness of the Confederate cause and the overweening role of divine providence. "Everything seems dark and threatening," eighteen-year-old Lucy Buck lamented. "Yet I will not despair but commit our cause to His hand who 'out of chaos' brings forth order." Realizing the Yankees had a "foot hold in *every* state" made Alabamian Joshua Callaway in a camp near Chattanooga "tremble with apprehension," but even then he expressed faith in God and the justness of the Confederate cause. The Lord would care for his people; though many intoned that comforting thought, how and when remained the unanswerable question.[45]

Then, too, the people must show far more humility, at least according to pious soldiers and civilians. Confederates should stop criticizing generals or even excoriating Yankees and instead examine their own sins—a familiar enough message but now especially apropos. Even the *Southern Churchman* in Richmond, the leading Episcopalian newspaper in the Confederacy, quoted a woman in Pennsylvania who had remarked that the rebel army would soon be leaving the state because it had placed more trust in that fine Episcopalian general Lee than in the Lord. Lee himself might well have agreed that Confederates had become too confident and had forgotten the mercies of God. The logic was simple, and the syllogism seemingly ironclad. The southern people had grown arrogant; the Lord had visited them with condign punishment; they must now humble themselves before the throne of grace. Or, alternately, the southern people had been brought low; this required a true spirit of repentance; the Lord's wrath would then abate. As in every previous morale crisis, unswerving patriots believed that God would never desert the Confederacy, and this was about as comforting a message as could have been delivered in the summer and fall of 1863. Even in the midst of self-abasement and calls for unconditional submission to the Almighty's ever more mysterious will, there remained the promise that true repentance might still open a path to victory.[46]

This meant viewing recent defeats as part of God's sovereign will, but that required answering some hard questions. Perhaps all this suffering would impose what one editor termed a "salutary discipline." The Lord governed the world and nothing could be done without his help, so the issue became restoring divine favor. In a sermon later reprinted by the Soldiers' Tract Association, a Virginia Methodist counseled obedience and patience, two qualities increasingly in short supply. But what if the southern people were not truly a chosen people? The idea that God would work out the question of war and peace in his own way and own good time might offer some reassurance but could arouse new fears. Having largely given up on the war, North Carolina editor William W. Holden offered his own take on the ways of God: "If it should please Him to build up and perpetuate this new nation of Confederate States, He will do it; if not He will not do it—that is all we know about it."[47]

From a much different perspective, General William Nelson Pendleton plaintively asserted that "God has not vacated His throne nor will He except for wise purposes, permit iniquity to triumph ultimately." That word "ultimately" had been used after every Confederate defeat but now offered much less consolation. Pendleton's advice to his family was thoroughly orthodox yet hardly cheering: "And if, for such purposes, although impenetrable to us, He sees fit to allow our enemies to triumph, we can, I hope, submit to Him . . . as did our Saviour under the hands of his enemies,—'Not my will, but thine, be done.'" Reminders that peace would come only on the Lord's terms stuck a disturbingly fatalistic note. Perhaps Confederates had misinterpreted the divine will all along, and one Methodist editor even doubted "that God had always been on our side, or that he operates *actively* in this controversy at all."[48]

Was the Lord not only chastising the southern people but also entering a final judgment on their iniquity? Hearing of Vicksburg's surrender, young Sarah Lois Wadley sank into despair. "All is dark, I cannot look ahead. I shudder to think of the future." For the first time she actually considered the possibility that the Confederacy could fall. Talk of the Almighty's "chastening hand" was no longer a pro forma response of people who still expected deliverance. "We have deserved all we have suffered," one Tennessee infantryman admitted, and he could only hope God would "spare the rod of Thy anger before we are utterly destroyed." But the day of the Lord had become not a day of triumph but a day of reckoning. A providential interpretation of events (small and large) made this low point in Confederate fortunes portend an apocalypse, especially for those weak-kneed hypocrites who had claimed to trust the Lord but in fact had placed their confidence in man. Once unthinkable thoughts caused people to scramble, seeking ways to soften the judgment. God most severely punished those he most loved; in the end, the "judge of all the earth will do right"; the Lord's fiery anger would purify the southern people.[49]

Under great emotional strain, people began lashing out at neighbors, especially those suspected of disloyalty or, even worse, collaboration with the heathen Yankees. Never having made any secret of his doubts about secession, Presbyterian minister James A. Lyon faced mounting hostility in Columbus, Mississippi, where a raucous meeting tried to drive him from the pulpit. Still ardent Confederates considered murmuring and faultfinding against the president and other officials to be a great sin. Charges of "submissionism" divided communities, spreading rumors and suspicion. Ministers and soldiers alike blasted Holden and other peace advocates for demoralizing the people and even usurping the role of the Almighty, who alone would determine when the war would cease.[50]

Especially for civilians at home, the war sorely tested long-held religious beliefs. Novelist Augusta Evans criticized women for not wielding their customary moral influence to stem demoralization, but perhaps others had decided that both their menfolk and the Lord had failed them. If not exactly a full-blown spiritual crisis, the war at the very least produced rebellious thoughts and at worst led some to conclude that God had forsaken the Confederacy. Even Basil Manly wondered about trusting the Lord should Charleston or Mobile fall: "Righteous causes long before now have been subdued by violence and cruelty and God has looked on." He still could not quite believe that the great Jehovah willed a Yankee victory, but he came perilously close. And perhaps God was judging both the southern nation and the southern church. To advance the Kingdom of Christ was it necessary that vain hopes in southern independence be dashed? Raising such a disturbing question struck at the very marrow of civil religion and individual faith.[51]

Yet a test of faith could produce a reaffirmation of faith, and it was sometimes amazing to see how talk of despair, declension, and judgment could so quickly turn to words of determination, revival, and vindication. From the pulpits and religious press came pleas for Confederates to gird themselves for the worst, to take heart in the promises of revealed religion. Seasons of defeat and disaster had come before and would come again, but then the Lord would deliver those who remained steadfast. "Cowardice is sin," declared one Presbyterian editor, and another claimed there was no reason to despair even after Vicksburg and Gettysburg. In the deepening gloom, with many of the devout falling silent, churches still called for resistance to the invaders.[52]

Some stalwart patriots denied that the news from the battlefields was all that discouraging; after all the Yankees had yet to prevail in their war of conquest. The southern people remained willing to make sacrifices, revivals were taking place in the armies, and Confederate forces still appeared formidable. In short, there were no genuine grounds for despair. Deep faith, wishful thinking, and outright delusion all combined to paint a positive picture of a united people fighting for their rights.[53]

On the Confederate fast day, Stephen Elliott delivered a most conventional jeremiad. The Lord's righteous judgments had cast a deep gloom over the Confederacy, but that would surely be lifted in his own good time. For a while the infidel Yankees might be allowed to prevail, yet in the end God would defend the right. Why then did Confederates have to suffer so? Because the Almighty would discipline his chosen people, especially when they murmured against their leaders and against providence itself, came the orthodox reply. Shopworn arguments poured forth from pulpits and press. According to one Mississippian, the southern people "will rally around the sacred tombs of our honored dead" and "come out of the furnace [of affliction] doubly purified for the good work and fight that God has given us to do."[54]

"If God be for us, who can be against us?"—that familiar passage from Romans should have comforted soldiers and civilian alike, but people had been intoning it for more than two years, and it now sounded more fatalistic than hopeful. An Alabama lieutenant serving in Virginia wrote home that the Lord "*has* smiled on our cause, and will never forsake us, tho we lose our whole army."[55]

That last clause was not quite so ominous as it sounded because individual faith, not to mention the staples of civil religion, proved remarkably resilient. As a Virginia cavalry officer affirmed, "God will give us victory even when we are driven to the wall, which certainly is not yet." And presumably, as the old saying went, the Lord would help those who helped themselves. "It will not do to fold our hands, and wait for the Lord to help us," the editor of the *Southern Churchman* counseled his readers. "We must strain every nerve and make use of every means God has given us. And what are the means? Guns, powder, men, horses, food, brains, and bayonets." This message contradicted the usual warnings about placing too much faith in human means, but even the clergy urged the southern people to muster all their strength and prove themselves worthy of liberty.[56] This new covenant of works would supposedly bring victory, though theological confusion reigned on that point.

After all, even the self-righteous could confess their sins or at least go through the motions. That patriotism had often been supplanted by covetousness certainly became a commonplace observation for pious southerners railing against everything from merciless extortion to light entertainment. Citing the warnings of Jonah against Nineveh and with a passing mention of the "wicked Shylocks" at home, a Georgia infantryman complained about men who "would sell their interest in Heaven for a few dollars." Worrying not only about people who heedlessly ignored divine commandments, he also feared that "our young Confederacy" might become a "vessel of wrath fitted out for destruction." Yet all too often the focus was on someone else's sins, and when earnest Confederates admitted that the southern people had not yet become humble enough, they seldom referred to themselves. How much conviction calls for fasting, humiliation, and prayer still carried remained anyone's guess. Preachers could point out that Confederates had failed to acknowledge the workings of providence or had neglected the task of evangelism, but such confessions sounded too pat. "This is no time for honied words," one Episcopalian editor warned. "We are being punished for our sins, and these sins should be pointed out plainly and people should be told plainly they must forsake their sins or they will be ruined in this world and the next too." But warnings that God might deliver the southern nation into the hands of the Yankees had been heard before.[57] The orthodox might complain that Confederates remained too stiff-necked, though in fact they appeared to fluctuate between repentance and self-righteousness. The search for reassurance or even a glimmer of good news kept too many people on tenterhooks, caught between despair and faith, fearing judgment but clinging to hope. And one final irony would become apparent at least in hindsight: the Yankees themselves had experienced remarkably similar cycles of confidence and despair, of pride and humiliation.

Indeed, the Confederates might have been well advised to have paid some attention to the words of their archenemy Lincoln in that famous fall 1863 address at the new Gettysburg cemetery. Here was the scene of a great Yankee victory and a stunning rebel defeat, though ironically at times the president spoke in tones that his enemies might at least have understood if not embraced. The language of the Gettysburg Address—a speech more memorized than analyzed—sounded much more secular than sacred, yet in its brief compass there were distinctive biblical phrases and cadences. "Four score and seven" along with words such as "consecrate" and "hallow" echoed scriptural language. At the same time they evoked memories of the American founding to which Confederates had laid their own claims. Indeed, Confederates still thought their claims were superior. Even Lincoln's call for a "new birth of freedom" would fit into Confederate rhetoric about purifying republican government.

How and why Lincoln added the phrase "under God" to his original text when he referred to the nation's "new birth freedom" remains a matter of dispute.[58] After all, he strongly maintained that it was the soldiers fighting at Gettysburg who had consecrated that ground. In this speech, Lincoln the youthful fatalist had disappeared; equally absent was the Lincoln who would later invoke themes of providence with such eloquence and insight. He was moving in that direction but had not gotten there yet. The Confederates even before the first shots were fired had called forth divine favor, most dramatically in their constitution. And Jefferson Davis had been much more willing than his northern counterpart to assert that God was on his "nation's" side. Now both men and their two "countries" stood at a great crossroads, not only on military and political matters but on religious questions. Divine purpose, national deliverance, personal salvation, and even millennial hope had all become entangled in a war that had become more destructive than even sinful human beings could ever have imagined.

Chapter 15

JUBILO

Ethiopia shall soon stretch out her hands unto God.
— Psalms 68:31

"If the negro should be set free by this war, which I believe he will be, whether we gain or not, it will be the Lord's doing. The time has come when his mission has ended as a slave, and while he has been benefited by slavery, the white race has suffered from its influence." Thus, nurse Kate Cumming looked to the future, combining traditional complaints about the effects of slavery on her race with a typically providential view of history. She blamed northern abolitionists for most of the trouble, and her analysis remained confused, but as Confederate hopes sagged, she had at least begun thinking about possibilities that few white southerners had been willing to face. Here and there, other devout Confederates weighed the prospects of everything from a gradual emancipation policy to the enlistment of black soldiers.[1]

The long festering slavery question was reaching a glorious, complicated, spectacular, disappointing, and still unpredictable climax. Slaves, soldiers, and civilians were playing large roles in this drama, and much of the discussion remained explicitly or implicitly religious. People continued to debate slavery and freedom in providential if not millennial language, all shaped by battles and alarms. Remarkable, and in some ways revolutionary, change was afoot often refracted through the lens of faith.

Writing after the war, Robert Lewis Dabney predicted that future historians would marvel at how the "the Christianity and philanthropy of our day have given so disproportionate an attention to the evils of African slavery" when so "many other gigantic evils were rampant in this age." He may have been mystified, but many of his fellow Confederates had thought a good deal about slavery during the war. Hearing the distressed cries of a slave being whipped, a young Louisiana woman wrote in her diary that "surely God will not wink at such cruelty." But many white southerners did wink at, or simply ignored, such cries.[2] A few claimed to have always hated the institution and no doubt did; others expressed varying degrees of remorse and guilt, but there is little evidence that such feelings were either deep or widespread. There are far more examples of callous indifference, paternalistic indulgence, or fervid support, and with Dabney as a case in point, the proslavery argument remained alive and well throughout the Civil War and far beyond.

That slavery had been sanctioned by God, as had the war itself, remained a bedrock position of the churches, the preachers, and the laity. As the chairman of a Texas Baptist association stated, the Lord ordained slavery just as he had ordained marriage. Should slaveholders lose their slaves, they risked losing their religion, so closely had the two become entwined. When Thornton Stringfellow's Virginia plantation was overrun by Federal troops, the seventy-five-year-old rheumatic minister presented one soldier with copies of his proslavery pamphlets, fully confident that he remained on the right side of Christianity and history. Indeed, a southern commitment to slavery—an institution that some still believed would endure throughout the course of human history—guaranteed Confederate victory in a war against godless abolitionists. "Success on our part will be the complete vindication of Slavery as a divine institution," one Baptist editor predicted. "The certain eventuation of that destiny which the Lord has allotted to the South."[3] Millennial dreams refused to die even as Confederate fortunes crumbled.

But whether slavery buttressed or undermined a conservative social order grew more doubtful. By the summer of 1863, cries for peace brought simmering class resentments bubbling up, and the Richmond bread riots remained a disturbing memory. Even ministers saw the need to shore up doubts about slavery's broad social benefits. "I have never owned a slave in my life, and yet I contend that I have more interest in slavery than the man who owns five hundred," Alabamian J. J. D. Renfroe preached to a brigade in Lee's army. "Abolish the institution of slavery, and your children and my children must take the place of that institution. . . . In our country, color is the distinction of classes— the only real distinction. Here the rich man and poor man and their families are equals in every important respect." He asked the assembled troops to think for a moment about what the Confederacy's subjugation would mean. Their "worthy offspring" would end up "grinding in a factory, scouring a tavern, tilling the soil of the wealthy, and blacking the boots of the dandy." How these appeals to class distinctions were supposed to reinforce Confederate unity, the good reverend did not explain. But now the clergy more often appealed to fears rather than to hopes. Even when ministers and churches proudly and publicly pointed to the absence of slave insurrections in the aftermath of Lincoln's incendiary Emancipation Proclamation, years of alarms raised about the plots of abolitionist firebrands added to private panic. Perhaps a violent and bloody future loomed after all.[4]

Yet religious slaveholders had trouble seeing themselves as part of the problem or acknowledging the implications of their own beliefs. Some spoke of "precious souls," of "high missionary ground," and "friendship" between masters and slaves. When it came to the lofty sentiments of paternalism, no one hesitated to lay it on thickly. A Kentucky preacher congratulated himself on his Christian forbearance in yielding to the pleas of a slave who begged not to be whipped and claimed to be deeply sorry for his misdeeds. Familiar descriptions of slavery as both burden and duty often preceded self-righteous statements about offering weak and easily deluded Africans protection from the pseudo-philanthropy of northern abolitionists. Such reasoning made masters and ministers and churches all responsible for the immortal souls in their charge, and calls for meeting these obligations became a regular part of the wartime jeremiad.[5]

In December 1861 at a Presbyterian assembly in Augusta, Georgia, Charles Colcock Jones, who had labored for some thirty years on slave missions, spoke for more than an hour urging southern Christians to take such duties far more seriously. Pointedly remarking that slaves were not cattle but "men created in the image of God," Jones extolled a reciprocal dependence between the races. If southern slaveholders claimed to be "patriarchs," a word that echoed from the Old Testament, they must act in the best interests of their black and white families because the "eyes of the civilized world are upon us."[6]

If anything, wartime worries about security and possible slave insurrections made religious instruction ever more urgent. South Carolina Methodists deemed slave missions useful for "securing the quiet and peaceful subordination of these people." At the 1863 Alabama Baptist state convention, delegates discussed the need for expanded religious instruction as a show of gratitude toward slaves who had remained faithful to their masters. Talk of "political dangers" obliquely tied to slave behavior barely concealed mounting anxieties.[7]

For fears arose that slaves would be neither grateful nor faithful. Even as they fretted about their human property running off to the Federals, slaveholders claimed to be deeply concerned about the poor blacks falling into the hands of northern hypocrites. Proper religious instruction should immunize them against the siren calls of freedom. According to Virginia Episcopalians, only the church stood between the African race and "extermination." The rhetoric was paternalistic, but the sense of panic among slaveholders and church leaders was palpable. Eliza Fain wildly claimed that the heartless Yankees might talk about the Exodus in glowing terms but would "fasten upon them [the blacks] a bondage more cruel, more exacting than the Egyptian."[8]

Slaveholders themselves became the first line of defense in safeguarding slaves from both the Yankees and Satan. Taking their religious obligations quite seriously, some masters read scripture, sang hymns, and even preached sermons. Eliza Fain took great interest in the spiritual lives of a dozen or so slaves. The Bible spoke plainly about the mutual obligations of masters and servants, and she expressed a deep concern for their salvation. Reading aloud to several slaves about the crucifixion of Christ, she prayed the Lord would work his will "for the moral good of Ham's abject sons." As Fain listened to them sing, she imagined a heaven where family and "servants" alike would be reunited. "Christ will make them all free," she wrote in her diary with no apparent irony.[9] Yet even Fain lacerated herself at times for neglecting these Christian duties, and contemporary descriptions suggest that such paragons were very much the exception.

In the end, the churches could hardly rely on the slaveholders and so tried to reach the slaves more directly. Episcopalians and Baptists proudly counted wartime baptisms; Methodists duly reported expenditures for slave missions; congregations tallied the ups and downs of black membership. Churches held meetings for slaves complete with scripture readings and prayers; Sabbath afternoon preaching or colored Sunday schools received warm endorsements from various denominations.[10]

At the First Baptist Church in Aberdeen, Mississippi, part of the main auditorium had been set aside for black members, but eventually separate services were held. White ministers took the lead, though there were occasional sermons by black preachers. Other congregations allotted one afternoon a month for special services but, in any case, reinforced the slaves' lowly status even among God's people. In Vicksburg at the beginning of the war, young Sarah Wadley had watched with great fascination as the white members and then the black members received communion. Even in this most important sacrament, the established order had to be maintained, yet Wadley noticed something interesting about the slaves and their relationship to the faith. "Their position in society makes their deportment so much more humble," she thought. "It is peculiarly interesting to see them receive the spiritual body and blood of Christ."[11]

Thanks to their churches' educational efforts, Virginia Baptists proudly declared in 1863, black members now held much sounder views on such doctrines as divine grace. One could observe the principles of Christ dramatically at work in their lives, yet such promising signs were hardly unambiguous. Watching a group of slaves "perfectly happy, some of the older ones fairly dancing with joy" after a Methodist service on Easter, Kate Cumming considered the response "in keeping with the excitable character of the Negro." At a communion service, Eliza Andrews noticed that slaves "looked very much edified while the singing was going on, but most of them slept through the sermon."[12] The chances for misinterpretation and misunderstanding were high, especially as war put great strains on slavery itself. Whites became keener but not necessarily more perceptive observers of black behavior, and slaves themselves responded to the readings, songs, and preaching in ways that at once fulfilled and baffled expectations. They too had to wrestle with questions of faith during a time of great hope, uncertainty, and fear.

Just as with the soldiers, by 1862 there were reports of slave revivals and a goodly number of conversions—the ultimate measure of evangelical success. In some congregations, blacks made up as much two-thirds of the wartime membership, though given the disruptive effects of the fighting and prospects for emancipation, many churches and denominations also lost African American members.[13] The black converts' shouts of joy at once pleased, amused, and exasperated white worshipers, but both celebrating and critiquing slave piety raised important questions. Toward the end of the war, Eliza Andrews, despite her strong preference for Episcopalianism, decided "there ought [not] to be any distinction of classes or races in religion." She then added, with how much sincerity is impossible to say, "I only wish I stood as well in the recording Angel's book as many a poor negro that I know." More commonly, signs of success in slave missions fostered a self-righteousness that reinforced conventional views. Even in 1863, Methodist bishop George F. Pierce still maintained that "slavery has shown itself to be a great missionary institution." That same year the General Assembly of the Presbyterian Church in the Confederate States of America could hardly praise the slaveholders too much: "The best vindication of our system of domestic servitude is the generous provision of masters for the temporal and spiritual well-being of their servants, and the faithful, affectionate, and grateful service of those who enjoy their protection and care."[14]

It logically followed that Christianity strengthened the "natural" bonds between slaveholders and slaves. In Charleston, South Carolina, an Episcopal minister used this argument to protest efforts to curb black religious meetings if martial law was declared. The pious, faithful slave praying for the safe return of old and young masters from the army became a staple of Confederate propaganda. Such slaves risked ostracism in the quarters, but as one slave preacher slyly told his deacons after being chastised for beseeching God to kill more Yankees, "Don't worry children; the Lord knew what I was talking about." Descriptions of devoted slaves searching for their master's body on a bloody battlefield warmed paternalistic hearts and fostered paternalistic delusions. When news of a master's death reached home, some slaves no doubt expressed genuine sorrow, but others' groans, screams, and sobbing rather overdid it and were likely gotten up for white consumption.[15]

Skepticism about such effusive displays of piety and loyalty offered a convenient rationale for reining in religious activities. At a prayer service in Savannah held just as Georgia was leaving the Union, black worshipers sang the lines from a hymn, "Yes, we shall all be free / When the Lord shall appear" so enthusiastically that police broke up the meeting. Three years later with Federal cavalry riding freely through Alabama, one master asked young W. B. Allen "to pray to God to hold the Yankees back." Whatever his own reservations about the Yankees, Allen spoke his mind: "[I] told my white folks straight-from-the-shoulder that I could not pray along those lines. . . . I could not pray against my conscience: that I not only wanted to be free, but that I wanted to see all the Negroes freed! I then told them that God was using the Yankees to scourge the slave-holders just as He had, centuries before, used heathens and outcasts to chastise His chosen people—the Children of Israel." No wonder that some slave owners had long since decided to take better care to monitor any slave gatherings. Widespread fears led some churches to abandon religious instruction for slaves or at least discontinue separate services. It was easy to criticize what a group of Virginia Baptists labeled "extremely cautious people" or blame northern abolitionists for any disturbances, but many whites clearly dreaded the volatile effects of the war and the Gospel on the social order.[16] As more slaves fled into Union lines, this became another pretext for opposing or at least curtailing mission work. Even where slaves remained with their masters, churches might excuse their own dereliction by pointing to the prejudices and superstitions of the slaves, including those who were ostensibly Christians.[17]

Quite often, however, the churches candidly admitted their shortcomings. The word "neglect" appeared frequently in official statements about their work with the slaves and free blacks as home front conditions grew more unsettled. The usual committee reports on the "religious instruction of the colored people" became revealingly brief.[18] By 1863, one leading Baptist editor considered the whole a matter a huge scandal. "Beyond all controversy the overwhelming majority of our slave population is but a grade above heathenism," declared one blistering editorial. A few months later in decrying this "great national sin," he noted how God sanctioned slavery but no longer approved the conduct of slaveholders. The failure to fulfill religious obligations had become the great "curse" connected with slavery, a Mississippi Episcopal bishop concluded. Surely the Lord's wrath had been stirred, a fearful accounting would have to be rendered, and the war with all its attendant evils would continue until this great wrong had been righted.[19]

In an August 1863 fast-day sermon, Baptist minister Isaac Taylor Tichenor spoke with unusual candor: "We have failed to discharge our duties to our slaves. I entertain no doubt that slavery is right, morally, socially, politically, religiously right. But there are abuses of it which ought to be corrected." Other ministers joined in the sometimes pointed criticism, including an acknowledgment that southern whites had spent much time defending slavery from a biblical standpoint yet had neglected scriptural teachings about the mutual obligations of masters and slaves. Those pushing for reform may have included some who would have ultimately favored emancipation, but most were interested not only in squaring slavery with their religious convictions but in strengthening the institution.[20] A few leading Episcopalians, Presbyterians, Methodists, and Baptists all supported proposals that would once have been dismissed as little short of aid and comfort to abolitionists. Tichenor and others argued for correcting various evils and abuses in no uncertain terms, but reformers worried most about the religious stakes in the debate. Perhaps carried away by his own idealism, Methodist George F. Pierce pulled no punches in preaching to the Georgia legislature: "If the institution of slavery cannot be maintained except at the expense of the black man's immortal interests, in the name of Heaven I say—*let it perish*."[21]

Whether the good bishop actually meant that last statement or was merely indulging in a bit of pulpit hyperbole, reformers did hit the slaveholders in sensitive and vulnerable spots. Richmond's Catholic bishop John McGill warned that the Lord would surely punish southern whites for their "neglect or refusal to respect in slaves, the holiness, the unity and indissolubility in marriage." Given restrictive southern divorce laws and church condemnations of adultery, the absence of any legal protection for slave marriages amounted to a moral double standard and a major sin of omission. The wrong seemed especially striking given the long-standing defense of slavery as a civilizing influence—but then to defend an institution treating human beings as both property and persons had always posed a great challenge. All in all, however, the reformers' blunt honesty about the evil effects of slavery on black men and women was at times striking. A Baptist editor complained that "marriage" hardly existed for slaves if the bonds could be dissolved at the slaveholders' "whim and caprice"; worse still, failing to legitimate black unions made all their family relations sinful.[22]

A closely related question revolved around the breakup of marriages and families through sale. With unwarranted optimism, a group of Episcopal bishops expected state legislatures to remedy this evil. As McGill scathingly observed, this failure of "civil government" allowed slaveholders to "treat the matrimonial union among them [slaves], as if they were really little more than the chance association of unreasoning animals." That posed an enormous challenge to devout Christians who placed family relations at the center of religious and social life. By October 1864 Georgia Baptists had gone on record favoring a law protecting slave marriages.[23] But this late in the war, such a proposal seemed like nothing so much as a final, desperate effort to win back divine favor. Even then the language seemed oddly formal and dispassionate as if they were simply going through the motions with little expectation of tangible results.

No doubt speaking for many slaveholders, an article in the *Southern Presbyterian Review* outlined some powerful objections. Slavery was a biblically sanctioned "domestic" institution, the slave being the "subject of family government." Once slave marriages received legal sanction, the author warned, emancipation would inevitably follow. Even were that not so, slave owners would be stuck with incorrigible bondsmen whom they could not sell, and in any case the morals of the Africans, including their "deplorable sensuality," would not improve. Remarkably enough, the article concluded with a suggestion for lifting the legal restrictions on slave literacy.[24]

Especially for Protestants who viewed reading the Bible as central to their faith, telling pious masters they could not teach their slaves to read the scriptures seemed outrageous. According to one Baptist editor, studying the Bible was a "God-given right of humanity." Only Catholics had attempted to keep the holy book from the common people, one correspondent added with a touch of sectarian relish. Much depended on how one viewed the relationship between slavery, religion, and authority. In a broad sense, some ministers and editors argued, restrictions on literacy violated the rights of masters as well as slaves.[25]

Despite wide if not particularly powerful support for reform from the main Protestant denominations, nothing much came of these efforts. Georgia lifted a ban on licensing black preachers; Alabama and Texas expanded slaves' rights to legal defense and trial by jury. Bills on marriage and literacy, however, never emerged from committee, and there was no significant discussion of these matters in any legislature.[26] Slavery reform died aborning.

Instead, the disintegration of slavery itself weakened the churches. Expectations about slaves' loyalty to their congregations and to their masters, if not to the Confederacy, were often dashed. Congregational minute books recorded the admission of new slave members even as others ran off to the Yankees, and by the fall of 1862, a genuine exodus had begun. Clerks and pastors noted how slaves had deserted their owners, joined the "abolitionists," and enticed others to do likewise. Some congregations investigated how many members had been lost, suggesting that the numbers may have been considerable.[27]

By their lights, white church leaders had treated slave members as brothers and sisters in Christ, but the blacks had apparently deceived them. As with slaveholders more generally, it was easy to lament such betrayals and draw broad conclusions about the ingratitude of the entire race. But then slavery had always fostered such delusions. The further assumption that the naive and ignorant slaves had been tricked by evil men or that the churches had simply failed in their religious teachings helped whites avoid more painful questions about slavery and about themselves. So instead congregations and denominational associations adopted resolutions and began expelling scores of slaves who had gone over to the "public enemy."[28]

Had the Lord indeed rendered a final judgment on the slaveholders if not on slavery itself? That conclusion had to be avoided at all costs, and sermons had carefully distinguished between the abuses of slaveholders and the justness of slavery. Calls for renewed evangelism in the quarters became part of the wartime jeremiad, and as more and more slaves left the churches and their owners, the warnings from the pulpit sounded more prescient. But neither the churches nor the slaveholders could muster the will or political support to reform slavery. In any case, it was too late to save an institution that was steadily crumbling before the invading northern armies and through the actions of slaves themselves. In many ways, the southern churches had simply reaped the whirlwind.

Black churches and black preachers had occupied anomalous and often insecure places on the antebellum southern religious landscape, but the war brought new troubles and opportunities. It no doubt astonished northern missionaries and teachers, not to mention the Union troops, to find a flourishing African American religious life in a slaveholding society, to discover African American churches and preachers, most notably in the cities, conducting their own services and blacks already leaving the biracial churches.[29]

White Union soldiers found all this especially exotic. Slave worship services seemed far too emotional, indeed far too freewheeling, filled with what a Massachusetts corporal termed "funny logic and quaint grammar." Yet the raw eloquence of the slave preachers won at least grudging respect, and even northerners from Brahmin backgrounds decided that some sermons merited close attention. Here were black men speaking of the Lord Jesus with a moving simplicity. Despite vast differences in worship style, New Englanders expressed amazement over ministers who had endured slavery yet remained men of faith and power, men who could pray and preach as well as anyone.[30]

On the South Carolina Sea Islands, a Gullah preacher explained how the whites grasped the logic of religion but not its feel. There did not seem to be much "spirit" in their worship especially compared to a people whose joyous songs expressed a poignant longing for spiritual freedom, and perhaps other

First African Church, Richmond, Virginia (Library of Congress)

kinds as well. At Beaufort, a Baptist missionary heard a black preacher named Harry talk about Christ and salvation with unusual authority. "I was ashamed of myself," the missionary later recalled. "Here was an unlearned man, who could not read, telling of the love of Christ, of Christian faith and duty in a way which I have not learned." Even the shrieks and shouts brought the spirit of the gospel alive and deeply stirred the religious imagination. As one Sea Island missionary put it, the black preachers have "God in their soul."[31]

Perhaps the appearance of Yankee liberators was a prelude to the Second Coming, and so freedom not surprisingly assumed a millennial significance. It was that kind of theology that most worried Confederates. "Preachers are rising up among them [the slaves] who are blind leaders of the blind," an 1864 report on slave missions in Mississippi noted with alarm. "They are generally found to be the worst men among them, with a few exceptions." How subversive such preachers were had always been a matter of debate among southern whites (and likely too among slaves), but many simply preached the Gospel as they always had. At New Bern, North Carolina, a Connecticut chaplain listened to an old traveling evangelist read with great difficulty. Yet the man had no trouble capturing the spirit of the Scriptures: "De Lord Jesus come to de poor de lowly. Dat's a comfort." In his view the grace of God was all-sufficient. A standard and simple message for sure, and perhaps even a "safe" one, but also one that offered hope for the oppressed.[32]

With the coming of the war and especially the arrival of northern armies, black preachers found their prophetic voice. Ministers in both sections had tried to figure out how the eleventh chapter of Daniel describing a war between a "king of the north" and a "king of the south" had foretold the American struggle. Thomas Lewis Johnson recalled how literate slaves would puzzle over this confusing and complex passage searching for verses that would portend northern victory and black freedom. More often, it had been the Exodus story that spoke most directly to their current state and future hope but now the war brought the promised deliverance, so white and black preachers alike compared African American slaves to the children of Israel. An otherworldly Jesus would for a time give way to a this-worldly Moses. During one such sermon, a white missionary noted how members of the black congregation would nod their heads in approval at each such reference. A strong belief in divine intervention, a confidence that the newly free would meet their once enslaved but now departed friends and relatives in a wondrous heaven impressed even skeptical and condescending observers.[33]

How glorious it was to pray openly for Confederate defeat, to believe that the day of the Lord had come, to witness the great promise of freedom fulfilled. The masters had long feared the power of such prayers, claimed one northern missionary who heard former slaves recount how they had prayed for northern victories and for the northern president. At the end of the war, one slave recalled how his people had been emancipated from sin and from slavery "through the sacrifice of Abraham Lincoln and Jesus Christ." To many African Americans, the president literally became their Moses or even their redeemer. Reverend James Lynch, a dedicated AME minister, had found his own heart fired by contact with southern slaves. "Ignorant though they be, on account of long years of oppression," they exhibited a great thirst for knowledge and the Spirit. "Every word you say while preaching, they drink down and respond to, with an earnestness that sets your heart all on fire, and you feel that it is indeed God's work to minister to them."[34]

Their voices expressed a remarkable richness of experience and emotion. The music of African American worship deeply impressed white missionaries and soldiers as powerful voices sang about the year of Jubilee and the coming of God's kingdom. The preacher might "line" a hymn from the pulpit—a practice going back nearly two centuries—and, as described by a New England minister, "the song rolled on like a flood, winding, twisting, quaint, and weird, and trembled in the air." There would always be a rising enthusiasm, especially on favorites such as "Roll, Jordan, Roll." Some worshipers would beat time with their feet, while others might move in a circle, jerking, shouting ever louder. These sounds and movements elicited white skepticism, but one sympathetic Vermont private even considered the most uncontrolled parts "original, and full of power, whether of pathos, of warning or exultation."[35]

Evangelical religion flourished amid the ebb and flow of armies, with the arrival of northern ministers, and even in many areas still held by the Confederates. Testimonies about dreams and visions struck one Baptist missionary as "artless" and "stereotyped," but he decided there was great religious potential among the former slaves. Their spiritual lives in turn became part of the war's religious landscape. Even as they were baptized, African Americans prayed for northern victories and saw freedom coming with the arrival of Union troops. With little on earth to call their own, a sympathetic Wisconsin chaplain noted, blacks sought the "durable riches" of heaven where they would no longer be a "despised and oppressed class." Indeed, their devotion and endurance moved others. An old woman working as a laundress in a Union camp near Vicksburg kept asking an ailing and depressed Christian Commission delegate, "Massa, does ye see de bright side dis morning?" That question did not cheer him up, but she persisted. Hearing her tell how even after seeing her children sold away, she could still find the "Lord Jesus" and "den it's all bright an' cl'ar," he felt abashed and humbled. Such faith shamed the proud and the educated. Although few slaves could read and oral instruction was hit or miss, a Methodist minister decided that "God himself teaches them even as he taught the bondmen in Egypt." He refused to disparage what many whites considered their ignorance and superstition.[36]

Like many white ministers and soldiers, some officers (whether deeply caring or coldly indifferent) tried to control what they deemed barbaric excess. More often a kind of religious accommodation was reached, and the best chaplains adjusted their ideas about proper worship to the desires and practices of the newly recruited black soldiers. And, indeed, the unaffected devotion displayed in religious services could be contagious, especially when men prayed so fervently for Lincoln. According to the abolitionist reformer and commander of the all-slave 1st South Carolina Infantry, Thomas Wentworth Higginson, the former bondsmen knew phrases from scripture by heart, but their knowledge was "chaotic" and "most of the great events of the past they straightly credit to Moses." Yet many black soldiers yearned to read and greatly treasured Bibles, so the Christian Commission along with missionary teachers used old primers and spelling books for camp instruction.[37]

As with many white regiments, there were never enough chaplains to go around. Even though the American Missionary Association and other groups provided volunteers who ministered to African American regiments, Quartermaster Sergeant James H. Payne wrote a long letter to the *Christian Recorder* chiding the AME church for not sending more preachers. He pointedly criticized the "babyish local ministers . . . [who] want to see God work a miracle before they start." However that might be, many chaplains believed their mission was to root out the influences of slavery by conducting orderly services, insisting on regular Sabbath observance, and stamping out vice. Some strongly discouraged shouting and dancing, but the wisest chaplains refused to stifle their men's earnest response to the Gospel.[38]

Like the white soldiers who experienced conversion, many of the black troops enjoyed what evangelicals would have termed a season of "spiritual refreshment." Noisy meetings appalled the more fastidious officers and chaplains; Higginson commented on prayer services led by the "greatest saints and scamps of the regiment" that had continued past the "usual bedtime" for the "children." Such racial condescension failed to acknowledge how black soldiers were caught between two religious worlds. Chaplains conducted regular services that presumably solidified African American identity with the Union army and inculcated white Protestant values. But the black soldiers often held their own meetings, sometimes conducted by slave preachers, where they could worship more freely. "Every black face was sober and reverent. The leader 'lined off' the words of the hymn and all sang the line together," Freeman Bowley recalled. "The voices rose sweet and mellow. Then came prayers and exhortations. The words were those of ignorant men, but there was in them a pathos which I have never heard equaled." Just as with the white troops, fervent and emotional prayers helped men prepare to face death.[39]

"The moral state of our men will compare quite favorably with any other regiment in the service," one captain bragged. After all, these troops had recently been living as slaves "raised in ignorance, and denied every facility for acquiring information pertaining to the ways and works of God." And many had become "strongly attached to worship," so he anticipated a bright future for them and indeed for the entire race. Reports from Christian Commission delegates and northern missionaries were equally optimistic, describing black soldiers as faithful to both God and country. A group of "colored teamsters," one observer remarked, are "among the most earnest Christians that I have seen in a long time." Men who had been held in bondage expressed surprisingly little bitterness or hatred. As one soldier confessed during a prayer meeting, "I love my Savior, I love the Church of Christ, I love the world, I love everybody, and I love them that don't love me."[40]

Such men warmly embraced the gospel without qualification. "I doubt if there is a colored infidel or free thinker in the South," one northern missionary rejoiced after five soldier converts had come forward at the end of a service. Many of these troops reportedly thirsted for God's word. The chaplain of a black regiment in Louisiana, despite many of his comrades' complaints about noisy services, described the men in his outfit as "so tractable, with such unlimited confidence in their liberators, as to yield up set forms of expression, religious customs and manners, familiar from infancy for those of *another* race." Ignoring the fact that many of these soldiers conducted their own religious exercises away from prying white eyes and ears, he thought them "easily molded and shaped by the stronger minds which press upon theirs, and which command them." Such racially charged comments showed a naive confidence in military authority, but these remarks also reflected a kind of admiration for men of simple yet stalwart faith. As one observer stated, black soldiers "seem to believe more and doubt less." Then too a desire for literacy would lead them to the Holy Scriptures and elevate their position in society.[41]

At least that was the hope of white ministers and many of the soldiers themselves. A member of the 56th United States Colored Troops later thanked a missionary for having led him from "darkness into light" by teaching him to read, write, and love God. A sergeant from the same regiment agreed, adding a wish that his race would "behold the glorious full light of liberty wich have bin hidden behind the cloud of slavery." Just as in Old Testament times, the Lord was liberating an enslaved people. God's judgment against slavery gave African American troops something worth fighting for and hope for the future. Higginson overheard one of his men pray about going forward with a musket in one hand and the Bible in the other, facing the future without fear because he had Jesus in his heart. The liberation of the slaves and the enrollment of black troops all promised a glorious fulfillment of the nation's destiny and prophetic witness. As people from nearby plantations assembled for a Thanksgiving service in a small South Carolina Baptist church, Charlotte Forten Grimké, a northern African American teacher raised in privileged circumstances, observed a "crowd of eager, happy black faces from which the shadow of slavery had forever passed." She could not help saying to herself, "Forever free! Forever free!"[42]

This all marked a fulfillment of America's promise of freedom for all, and some northerners even expected the country's racial troubles to miraculously disappear. Whether it was faith in free labor, a belief in an approaching millennium, or hope that the degraded South could be regenerated, many religious groups greeted the death of slavery as an opportunity for evangelism. Besides planting northern churches on southern soil, many Christians turned their attention to the people General Benjamin F. Butler had called "contrabands" of war.

Here was a providential opportunity to save many more souls, to bring the light of the gospel to a benighted land and people. Such rhetoric made the southern states appear to be a strange and exotic land, the sort of place where some intrepid foreign missionary might go to convert the heathen. Groups established to provide relief and education multiplied, all seeking support from the churches, and the larger denominations sent their own missionaries. Congregationalists had established the American Missionary Association, but there was little cooperation with the Presbyterians or other Protestant churches.[43] All too many bright hopes and promises of evangelical success remained just that: hopes and promises.

Old School Presbyterians had only reluctantly endorsed emancipation but by 1864 had established a Committee for the Education of the Freedmen to send teacher missionaries into the South. For all the brave talk about promoting moral behavior and limiting Catholic influence with the former slaves, these badly financed efforts won few black converts. The more antislavery New School fared little better. In point of fact, Presbyterians showed little confidence or enthusiasm, attributing the inevitable failures to the lingering effects of slavery and African American character flaws. "Indeed from the peculiar emotional nature of the Negro, together with his extreme ignorance," one missionary in Beaufort, South Carolina, concluded, "very special care is needed to have the right instruction in the right manner."[44]

Few appeared ready for such a demanding task. Northern Methodists approached the whole matter from a more narrowly denominational standpoint, seeing themselves as the saviors of black Methodists suffering under the oppressive rule of the Methodist Episcopal Church, South. Like the Presbyterians, they drew connections between Catholicism, slavery, and rebellion, promising to rescue the former slaves from all three. Blacks coming into Union lines, an Indiana conference reported, were the "poorest of the poor," the very sort of people that John Wesley himself had most effectively reached back in England.[45] For a time that idealistic vision overshadowed a host of practical difficulties, yet like the Presbyterians, northern Methodists vastly overestimated their appeal and potential strength in the southern states.

In an address to the American Baptist Home Missionary Society, George Ide sketched out a glorious prospect: "In place of a Gospel so corrupted by false views of human rights, so distorted by the selfish greed of the oppressor, as to stand forth an abomination to heaven and earth, we must plant the Gospel which He taught who came to save the poor and lift up the fallen—a Gospel which proclaims liberty to the captives, and the opening of the prison doors to them that are bound." Meeting in Philadelphia, Baptists from the "loyal states" rejoiced over the Lord's decree of a "brighter, grander future for our country and the world." Inspired by a vision of teaching former slaves to read the Bible and seeing the southern states as one vast mission field, northern Baptists eventually dispatched some 120 missionaries, teachers, and assistants into Dixie.[46]

Stirred by news of emancipation, appalled by reports of conditions in the contraband camps, or moved by fundraising sermons, idealistic men and women believed that God had sent them on a noble mission. Reverend Marvin Richardson Vincent, a Methodist minister recently turned Presbyterian, spoke passionately about what he considered the greatest obstacle to missionary success: "Slavery has stood beneath the very shadow of the cross, and called its bleeding Victim to witness that its atrocities were all for Christ's sake, and, as a commentary on its christian intentions, had compelled the slave to incorporate into his christianity the toleration of the foulest lusts; the denial of the marriage rite, the necessity of ignorance, the abrogation of all his rights as a father, or brother, or husband." Then too many a former slave remained tied to what George Ide termed the "wild Fetishism of his ancestral African" religion that placed a premium on emotion and excitement rather than holy living. Given the prevalence of both racial and cultural prejudices, appeals for donations oddly played on both compassion and fear. Unitarian John F. W. Ware, author of soldier tracts and a strong opponent of slavery, nevertheless decided that the freed slave was dangerous because "he is without the wonted restraint." Failing to support the mission work in the former Confederate states, Ware warned a Baltimore audience, would lead to thousands of blacks showing up on their doorsteps. "Your city will be the charnel house of vagabondism and vice and crime."[47]

But here was both a problem and an opportunity. As missionaries fervently believed, slavery rested on a foundation of ignorance, and slaveholders had greatly feared the spread of knowledge among the common people. From those two premises came the conclusion reached by George Ide and many others that northern Christians must "pour the light of education and a pure Gospel" into the former slaves. The school of bondage had left African Americans unprepared for freedom, but Yankee teachers could shine a light into the darkness. After observing a large class of former slaves who were learning the alphabet, a Vermont private wrote in his diary, "In the education of the black is centered my hope for the redemption of the race, and the salvation of my country." This project could redeem the nation, though few northerners were yet ready to face questions about suffrage and citizenship. Indeed, all the talk of education and progress carried a good degree of racial condescension, strikingly illustrated by this Unitarian assessment of the problem: "The Freedmen are like the Irish, poor, degraded, and animal; and it is now the prime work of our nation to reorganize their industry, free them, educate them, and make men of them."[48]

Many former slaves longed for the bread of life, though they preferred to receive it from their own people. To the extent that slavery and racism had helped forge a sense of African American identity, white missionary efforts often faltered. The AME and AME Zion churches seized the opportunity by sending their own ministers and teachers into the southern states. The energetic James Lynch arranged for a local pastor in Savannah to lead black worshipers out of the Methodist Episcopal Church, South, and soon an AME congregation had been organized. "The African Methodists are going to sweep the field," a Christian Commission delegate predicted shortly after the war ended. "Even the Methodist brethren north cannot hold the churches they have organized, against the tide toward the African."[49]

In many ways, the AME missionaries preached a standard Protestant message of uplift, discipline, and education, but in calling for more black teachers, they also emphasized racial pride and independence. Arriving in Virginia even before the Emancipation Proclamation had been issued, George A. Rue claimed to have "no fear in preaching the whole gospel" to the "contrabands" at Harrison's Landing and enrolled more than two thousand adults and children in a Sabbath school. Like the northern Methodists, the AME ministers had a denominational agenda but one closely tied to rising hopes about their race's destiny. Ethiopia was indeed reaching out her hands to God, and it would be the African American preachers who would clasp those hands. New AME congregations were springing up, mostly in cities, and there were requests to set up conferences. Rivalries with northern Methodists and the AME Zion church might slow progress, and the countryside remained largely under the control of slaveholder churches, though not for long. As the Congregationalists and Presbyterians faltered, the Methodists and Baptists held out greater hopes for success, but the AME church was laying the groundwork for a postwar explosion in membership.[50]

—————

Was this too evidence of the Lord's work? In August 1863, only a little more than a week after Lincoln's official day of thanksgiving, an editorial in the AME *Christian Recorder* described in some detail how the hand of God had shaped the course of the war and emancipation. First, the incubus of slavery had been removed from the nation's capital, and then western Virginia had become free soil. Slavery was dying in Missouri and Maryland, and the president's Emancipation Proclamation had promised to set free the "captives" in all the rebel states. Many slaves in Kentucky and Tennessee were virtually free, and the unholy institution was rapidly dying there. Black men were slowing gaining their rights and now wore blue uniforms. "Every one of these things seemed impossible," the editor commented. "God has accomplished them in spite of the opposition of man." The proslavery conservatives and temporizing moderates in the North had been routed. The divine intent had become clear: "to establish on this Continent one undivided, free, Christian, American Nation."[51]

Fighting for freedom as opposed to merely fighting for the Union—admittedly a sacred cause in itself for many devout northerners—gave the war a more transcendent purpose. A report for the Philadelphia Baptist Association captured these soaring expectations: "That the universal prevalence of Freedom in this country will be the climax of that series of events which indicate that God has appointed this nation to be the harbinger and model of the world's civilization."[52]

The moral necessity for emancipation readily translated into a political necessity for supporting Republicans in the fall 1863 elections. As active laymen, especially in the Methodist, Presbyterian, Congregational, and Unitarian churches, many party leaders had no trouble wrapping political ambition in divine authority. Whatever the lingering objections to "political preaching," churches had become increasingly part of a partisan political culture. Resolutions forwarded to Lincoln from the Ohio United Brethren in Christ claimed that anyone supporting Vallandigham for governor lacked not only "patriotism" but also "Christianity" and even "manhood." That covered all the bases and reflected a political sea change with powerful religious overtones. Pennsylvania private and devout Lutheran George Washington Beidelman wrote back to his local newspaper asking how Episcopal bishop John Henry Hopkins could still defend slavery when it clearly violated the golden rule. Instead, the bishop should rejoice that the Lord had changed men's hearts on slavery, and indeed the change was so dramatic that lifelong-Democrat Beidelman had switched parties.[53]

Church support for emancipation emphasized moral arguments but hardly ignored political ones, and this disturbed conservative Catholics along with no small number of Protestants who remained highly critical of abolitionism and partisanship. War, race, politics, and religion made for a volatile mix, and one not to everyone's liking. At a Pennsylvania church, an angry parishioner claimed the minister had said "It was no sin to marry a negro," and all hell had apparently broken loose. Watching the turmoil, a chaplain home on furlough tartly remarked, "The negroes may get to Heaven and some whites shut out." Yet he deplored political excitement because it meant that "no religious sentiment can reach the mind," and there was "no hope for a revival this side of the Election."[54] For pious folk of a more conservative bent, that was exactly the point: civil religion remained an obstacle to revealed religion. Sermons and denominational resolutions endorsing emancipation therefore told only part of the story. Flights of rhetoric about the dawning of freedom could not cover up persistent divisions in both church and state.

Nor would emancipation usher in the promised millennium because even though racial attitudes had changed or were at least evolving, the future looked uncertain and war's legacy doubtful. Many northerners clung to the chimera of colonization because they still could not believe whites and blacks could live together in peace. With slavery dying, a few voices called for the churches to more honestly address racial issues. In August 1863 a Methodist preacher delivered a powerful sermon against what he termed "that unchristian prejudice against color, which so often has its violent demonstration in the cities and villages of our land." It was easy enough for ministers and churches to maintain that people should love everyone just as God did, but only the most radical got down to specifics, such as having blacks and whites mix freely on street cars or in public schools. Then, too, segregated Sabbaths had become the rule even in evangelical churches that had once been much more biracial. Escaping the clutches of prejudice more generally proved equally difficult. Even James Thome, an old Lane Seminary antislavery firebrand who rejoiced over the wondrous prospects for the freed slaves in America, held that the Indians essentially had no future in the country. And one more irony: a long letter in the nation's leading AME paper suggested that it was time to strike the word "African" from the church's name, though the author admitted that some congregations had refused to admit white members or allow them to become Sunday school superintendents.[55]

Inconsistencies, contradictions, and divisions all stemmed from the nature of the peculiar institution itself. Antislavery ministers and politicians, and even abolitionists, had underestimated how slavery and race had woven themselves into the very fabric of American society. So despite the recent success of northern arms and of emancipation, it might well be doubted that the Lord's wrath had been spent. "The day of God's vengeance has come," a Buffalo pastor warned in a sermon delivered for the Christian Commission. "The streams have been turned into pitch, and the dust into brimstone. God is treading the wine-press alone. . . . He is treading us in his anger. He is trampling us in his fury. Our blood is sprinkling his garments. . . . For the day of vengeance is in his heart, and the year of his redeemed is come." The echoes of Revelation (and Julia Ward Howe) were unmistakable. Slavery represented a kind of national apostasy foretold in the book of Daniel, George C. Phillips argued in a lengthy and turgid work entitled *The American Republic and Human Liberty Foreshadowed in Scripture*. Phillips compared the current conflict to the biblical clash between Michael and the angels on one side and Satan and the Dragon on the other. For all the references to fire and judgment, however, Phillips foresaw a glorious future in which "God, through the instrumentality of the Church is preparing the world for the universal dominion of republican government." So if the Lord was purging the land with blood, he was also readying the nation for a prophetic fulfillment. At last, humanity would acknowledge duties to God and neighbor, and the liberation of the slaves would be a harbinger of lasting peace.[56]

While constructing earthworks along the North Anna River in Virginia, Private John Haley of the 17th Maine noticed a house once occupied by a minister who had "not been slow in securing a share of the *world's* goods." Seizing a piece of china plate, Haley began reflecting on how part of his mission was to root out a false religion: "A theology that sanctions slavery savors too strongly of Satan to be tolerated. The religion of Jesus Christ has nothing in common with the auction block or the lash." Haley was no great friend of blacks and in part deplored slavery because it had encouraged race mixing, but he was nevertheless a foot soldier in the army of emancipation. Attending a celebration at a black church in New Bern, North Carolina, on the first anniversary of the Emancipation Proclamation, a northern Methodist minister noted how the children carried freedom banners and sang throughout the service, while the "deepest feeling was manifested from time to time."[57] Here was joy in unleashing the shackles of slavery and of sin, rejoicing in emancipation and grace. These children and their parents in one way or another saw the hand of the living God in the war, a God who would liberate their people and save their souls.

Singing about the "year of jubilo" sounded glorious but also premature. A substantial number of northerners had yet to embrace either the justice or necessity for emancipation, and the politics of race remained a popular ploy for scheming politicians and reactionary clergy. Loyal Confederates still linked the preservation of slavery to both Christianity and republicanism, sometimes with millennial overtones. Even their talk of sin, punishment, and reform largely focused on ways to preserve and strengthen the institution. Yet in a broader sense, Federals and Confederates also anticipated a similar redemption. The year 1863 had brought not only the Emancipation Proclamation but more religious revivals, mostly in the armies but at times spreading to the home front. As Americans of various faiths thought about all they had witnessed and suffered, hopes for national and personal salvation endured and at times still soared.

Chapter 16

ARMIES OF THE LORD

It was meet that we should make merry, and be glad: for this thy brother
was dead, and is alive again; and was lost, and is found.
— Luke 15:32

And David spake to the men that stood by him, saying, What shall be done
to the man that killeth this Philistine, and taketh away the reproach from
Israel? for who is this uncircumcised Philistine, that he should defy the
armies of the living God?
— 1 Samuel 17:26

"Every day my conviction becomes firmer that the hand of *God* is in
this and that in spite of victories and advantages he will deny us Peace unless
we grant to others the liberties we ask for ourselves—'break every yoke and let
the oppressed go free,'" Lieutenant John Quincy Adams Campbell wrote on
November 12, 1863, as the 5th Iowa marched toward Chattanooga to reinforce
Grant's beleaguered forces. Adams expected a "great victory for our army" but
wondered to what effect. "The difficulties of this war have proved knotty questions to our Belshazzars and our 'wise men' but in a generation from this time,
every child will be a Daniel—able to interpret the handwriting of God, telling
us that we have not been faithful to the charge he committed to our trust. My
earnest prayer to God is that we may have mercy and not judgment. I believe
that our Nation will yet emerge from the conflict, entire and triumphant but it
will only be after she has been purged with fire."[1]

Two months earlier, Confederate war clerk John B. Jones had more briefly
ruminated about similar questions but along different lines. Expecting battles
in Virginia and northern Georgia, he scrawled in his diary a commonplace
phrase, "May God defend the right!" But for many Confederates by the fall
of 1863, confidence in divine favor had waned, and so Jones added a couple
more somber and thoughtful sentences: "If we deserve independence, I think
we shall achieve it. If God be not for us, we must submit to His will." There
soon followed the dramatic victory at Chickamauga where Braxton Bragg and
the Army of the Tennessee reinforced by James Longstreet's corps from the
Army of Northern Virginia routed William S. Rosecrans and the Army of the

Cumberland. "May a merciful God deliver the enemy entirely into our hands!" an Atlanta minister prayed. He was convinced that the Lord had decreed Rosecrans's "crushing defeat," offering a "signal answer to a nation's prayers." Such sentiments had been expressed many times before, but a Georgia sergeant who had actually been in the battle refused to exult over a field strewn with the dead from both sides: "Will nations never prosper by a knowledge of the past! Eighteen hundred years of Christ, and five thousand of historical experience and today we are slaying each other with no better instincts than prehistoric brutes with improved machines to accomplish it."[2]

If moral progress was uncertain, so too was military progress. Only a little more than two months after their great triumph at Chickamauga (September 20, 1863), Bragg's army besieging Chattanooga suffered stunning defeats at Lookout Mountain and Missionary Ridge (November 24–25, 1863). The Army of Tennessee retreated all the way to Dalton, Georgia, and Bragg soon resigned the command. The battered Confederates prepared to settle into winter quarters; soldiers licked their wounds, and some contemplated God's inscrutable ways. There was no disguising the fact that matters had reached a fearful pass. The usual talk of sin, chastisement, and repentance sounded much more ominous, no longer a ritualistic hedge against bragging or overconfidence. "There is not a state in the Confederacy that will not be scourged by the invader," Kate Cumming predicted. Confidence that God stood with the southern nation suddenly gave way to doubts, including a realization that Yankee and rebel alike turned to the Lord in their hour of need. Lincoln, Seward, and the abolitionists prayed for peace, a North Carolina Baptist editor conceded, but for them peace meant the destruction of the South. He then sounded a note that would ironically be echoed in Lincoln's second inaugural address: "May it not be, that the war will go on until the people on both sides are willing to give up their own preferences and selfish ends and submit entirely to the will of God?"[3]

For the Federals, too, 1863 had been a year of mounting casualties and unimaginable heartbreak. Border state Episcopalian Noah Schenck preached a Thanksgiving sermon with the usual expressions of gratitude and celebrations of progress, but he refused to ignore the war's staggering loss of life or that his fellow citizens had turned into a "warlike people." Toward the close, he let out a cry of anguish that was seldom heard from northern or southern pulpits: "When victories mean but wholesale slaughter and no great permanent advantage secured, the victory mainly ascertained by measurement of blood and calculation of corpses, I fail to see in it the occasion of thanksgiving to God." At best other preachers made only passing mention of the great sorrow that had descended on their communities or referred obliquely to what one Presbyterian called the "occasional excesses and outrages" that are "inseparable from a state of war," quickly adding that these were the crimes of a few depraved individuals.[4]

Even Lincoln's call for the first national Thanksgiving Day—evidently drafted by Seward—offered a conventional list of items for which people should express their gratitude and coldly noted that the country's population had steadily increased "notwithstanding the waste" of warfare. An allusion to national sins and divine punishment was brief, perfunctory, and easily missed.[5] Many preachers held forth on the occasion whether they had much to say or not. The *Brooklyn Eagle* gave extensive coverage to the sermons delivered, but the editor tartly noted that the "pastors seldom venture to run contrary in politics to those who pay their salaries." The usual talk of abundant harvests, business prosperity, and general health competed with war-related matters. Rabbis joined in discussing themes of national iniquity and divine punishment, and even spoke of the coming triumph of human liberty in almost millennial terms.[6]

The American Civil War had become part of a worldwide struggle in which Christ would deliver all men from the shackles of slavery and sin. The great upheaval had scrambled traditional political categories and had at last brought northern conservatives and radicals together as lovers of both the Union and liberty. Talk of trumpets summoning forth the friends of freedom to a final victory sounded a note of great hope with little hint of an apocalypse. Even Episcopalians became caught up in the promises that revealed religion held not only for the emancipated slaves but for the entire African continent. Playing on universal themes of redemption, one Old School Presbyterian spoke of a crusade against "superstition and oppression" with God confronting and defeating "false religions, false principles, false institutions." The Emancipation Proclamation itself marked a divine triumph over ignorance and prejudice. Indeed, the northern armies were winning a great victory over the rebellion, an Ohio Presbyterian declared, because the morals of the camp were so much better than the morals of the plantation.[7]

That gave each battlefield conquest a transcendent meaning, and certainly Thanksgiving Day 1863 became an occasion for offering thanks to the God of battles. "The battle is the Lord's." How many times had these words of young David already been invoked by both sides in the conflict, but how much easier to affirm them after signal victories at Gettysburg, Vicksburg, and Chattanooga? A New York Congregationalist predicted that "pilgrims" would one day visit "Fort Donelson and Shiloh, Vicksburg and Port Hudson, Murfreesboro, Antietam, and Gettysburg, as we have gone to examine those of Thermopylae and Marathon, of Cannae and Pharsalia, of Brannockburn, Agincourt, and Waterloo." He omitted Fredericksburg, Chancellorsville, and Chickamauga from that list, but a Pittsburgh Presbyterian pointed out how such defeats had all worked for the good of the northern people, leading them away from a vain trust in frail humanity and toward a deeper faith in the living God. And whenever the nation had humbled itself, victory had followed; pointing to this cycle of defeat, repentance, and triumph had by this time become a staple of pulpit oratory. Yet that lesson could quickly be lost even on those clergymen who announced that the rebellion had proved itself a great failure and that the end of the war was in sight.[8]

For Confederates the outlook appeared much darker politically, militarily, and theologically. William Bingham, a devout North Carolinian, even wondered whether the southern people deserved freedom. The growing strength of a peace faction in the Tar Heel State, not to mention the prevalence of sins ranging from extortion to Sabbath breaking, led him to fall back on an orthodoxy where no human government, indeed no endeavor of depraved humanity, could be anything but a stopgap before the second coming of Christ. "We certainly are not fit for peace yet," he wrote to a cousin. "I don't believe we ever will be; but God does not deal with us according to our deserts, and I believe he will deliver us whenever we realize that our only hope is in him." The equally pious East Tennessean Eliza Fain sounded even more pessimistic as she surveyed the war's wreckage: schools were suspended, the Sabbath was ignored, crime was rampant, and "woman [was] losing sight of all that has ever given her any position in social life." Worst of all, the country appeared to be ruled largely by "demoralized men forgetting there is a God." A good thing she had not overheard a recent conversation in Richmond. "The parsons tell us every Sunday that the Lord is on our side," Virginia senator Robert M. T. Hunter cynically remarked. "I wish, however, he would show his preference for us a little more plainly than he has been doing lately."[9]

Too many battles had been lost, too much territory occupied, and too many lives sacrificed. The Confederacy had been cut in two as the Federals at last held the Mississippi River line. Benjamin Morgan Palmer admitted the desperate military situation and at least uttered the word "defeat," if only to rally the disheartened by reciting a litany of horrors that would inevitably follow a Yankee triumph. His call for people to enlist under the banner of God even as their sons became martyrs, however, struck an oddly fatalistic note for one who avowed that the Almighty would strike down the "haughty and the proud." Presumably he was referring to the Yankees, though that was not entirely clear. Confederates might once have proclaimed that they could never be conquered, but as the devout Mary Jones pointed out, now such statements only sounded foolish.[10]

This all signified a turning inward, with a greater emphasis on individual than national salvation though for the past year the two had become ever more closely entwined. The continued religious awakening in the armies presented the most heartening evidence that the Lord had not yet abandoned his people. Discouraging war news led many people at home and in camp to focus more and more on their own redemption. If, as Lincoln would later say, both sides prayed to the same God and read the same Bible, both sides in this increasingly bloody war also placed a great deal of faith in evangelism to save souls if not nations.

———

Revivals in the Army of Northern Virginia during the winter of 1862–63 had set the tone, but the western theater had lagged behind. Despite scattered reports of well-attended services and prayer meetings in the Army of Tennessee, it had not been until the spring of 1863 after Bragg had withdrawn from Murfreesboro to Tullahoma, Tennessee, that there appeared the first major signs of a spiritual stirring. Meetings were held in several brigades, and there were reports of nearly five hundred converts. Chaplains and local ministers conducted services, and by fall the revival had spread to even a few hard-bitten cavalry regiments. As Bragg's forces moved toward Chattanooga and into northern Georgia during the summer and early fall, revivals had grown larger and more enthusiastic. Three chaplains in one brigade held "brush arbor" meetings for five weeks with impressive results. Elsewhere, army missionaries gathered the troops in local churches for evening services. There were promising signs even among the Trans-Mississippi forces, though the more widely scattered brigades there made the work more difficult.[11]

After Lee's army returned to Virginia following the retreat from Gettysburg, chaplains began organizing sunrise prayer meetings followed by conversations with "inquirers" at ten and preaching at eleven. Interdenominational Christian associations conducted nighttime prayer services. Visiting ministers and lay leaders helped make the winter of 1863–64 a high point in army evangelism. Camp revivals reportedly reached the indifferent and prodded the faithful, but then discouraged Confederates had every reason to welcome the gospel message, and the end of the campaign season as usual proved an opportune time.[12]

This harvest of souls often grew from small seeds. A few men began gathering informally; one soldier would read a passage of scripture, offer a prayer, and sing a hymn; anyone who wished could then give his testimony. In this manner, some two-thirds of the men in one artillery battery confessed their faith. Others found the Lord in much larger settings. A Mississippian recalled a communion service where fifteen chaplains administered the sacrament from a great platform, distributing cracker crumbs on plates and wine in cups.

Near Orange Courthouse, the preaching continued for several weeks with outdoor crowds of more than a thousand and several hundred coming forward each evening for prayer. Finding a place to meet was a challenge, but a good hillside with log benches formed a rude amphitheater that made an excellent backdrop for the drama of conversion, scenes that veterans remembered years later.[13]

When the armies settled into winter quarters and there was a chill in the air, worshipers needed warmer accommodations. Some forty log chapels, typically seating around three hundred, were erected along the Rapidan River; in the Army of Tennessee, one makeshift structure could hold nearly a thousand worshipers. A Baptist chaplain described an idealized scene: "The sea of upturned, earnest faces, and the songs swelling from hundreds of manly voices making the forests resound."[14] Tent flies supplied by the Christian Commission covered log huts, and more than sixty of these chapels were built for the Army of the Potomac. In one camp along the Rapidan, a thirty feet by eighteen feet structure with log benches sat 150 worshipers; no Solomon's temple, a Connecticut soldier remarked, but a "temple of riven pine overlaid with Virginia mud." The more skilled volunteers erected garlanded archways and even chandeliers fashioned from tin cans as ingenuity often compensated for a shortage of conventional building materials and interior furnishings. After all, the men could worship as well in hastily erected "shebangs" as in the most picturesque New England chapel, a Maine chaplain informed his wife.[15]

Just as with western Confederates, the revival spirit touched the Federals in winter quarters around Chattanooga. When the weather began warming up during the new year, "large congregations" gathered for evening services. Perhaps the anguish of Chickamauga and the miraculous victories at Lookout Mountain and Missionary Ridge led men to seek solace in the Lord and to sing his praises. Yet, as more conscripts and substitutes entered the Union ranks, it became more difficult for the preachers to touch the hearts of such tough cases. Racial tensions occasionally flared as well. When an Indiana chaplain preached at a service for both whites and blacks, one outraged soldier refused to attend and denounced him as a "nigger lover."[16]

Most men remained outside the fold of religious faith, and the small groups of believers revealed much about the armies' religious character. As with the Confederates, a couple Union soldiers would start meeting for evening prayers, and soon others would join them. Pious fellows praying alone in the woods to avoid scoffing comrades discovered they were not alone. Regular churchgoers formed the heart of such groups, and this was certainly true of the small bodies of men gathered in the winter huts for evening devotions. To be sure, there was evidence of spiritual growth, especially when attendance improved at prayer meetings and revival services. Between early September and mid-November, 30 hardy souls grew into 150 worshipers in one Rhode Island regiment. Yet, in most brigades, a core of professing Christians became the mainstay of camp religion, and at best only a few officers participated.[17]

Much still depended on the chaplains, and so a persistent shortage even in the Army of Northern Virginia no doubt hindered the work. The quality of chaplains had reportedly improved, and certainly missionaries along with laymen took up some of the preaching slack. Once the revivals were well underway, however, the quality of sermons seemed to matter much less, or at least that's what Methodist Morgan Callaway told his wife: "I have never seen a time when men hear the Word with such gladness. Anybody's preaching is acceptable—even mine." A South Carolinian agreed that "the most ordinary preachers drew large congregations." For the first two years of the war, the soldiers might have been fortunate to hear a sermon every couple of weeks, though now in some brigades there were services nearly every day. The very success of revivals boosted Confederate morale but at the same time fostered either a spiritual complacency or a striking hubris. "The world has perhaps never seen a mighty army under the influence of one general revival," a Georgia Baptist association crowed. "The camps, designed to train men to butcher their fellows are the places where souls are prepared for heaven."[18]

Would these preachers and laymen concede the possibility of similar holiness in their enemy's ranks? Although the revivals appeared less widespread among the Federals, they too enjoyed a season of spiritual renewal. An optimistic (and perhaps myopic) Maine chaplain even thought the temperance cause was "gaining ground," though one abolitionist preacher was convinced that the armies on both sides were still composed of "profane men" charging into battle like "incarnate fiends." The reality was much more complex than either of these statements suggests. Men were being converted, and demoralization in the camps had no doubt been exaggerated, but when a Michigan doctor talked about a "spirit of prayer and earnestness among religious men in the army," he was choosing his words carefully.[19] The implication was that a good number were not "religious men," and so there remained much work to do.

Families back home (just as they closely followed the war against the rebels) longed to know how the battle against Satan was going, but neither the Christian Commission, the chaplains, nor visiting ministers gathered information very systematically, and so the reported numbers of converts and other statistics are both scattered and suspect. The Union revivals seldom extended beyond the regimental or brigade level and generally proceeded soul by soul. After a meeting, a chaplain might receive only two or three converts but still feel the Lord's presence among them; likewise a handful of baptisms was certainly noteworthy. On the other hand, a mass baptism or the occasional hundred or more soldiers won over during a weeklong protracted meeting—one of the more traditional means of evangelism—seemed to prove how the Holy Spirit was moving through the ranks.[20]

Confederates made even more expansive claims of success. One soldier simply reported revivals *throughout* the Army of Tennessee, and vaguely worded statements about hundreds of penitents cropped up in letters home and the religious press; indeed, an Alabama private later concluded that "thousands of Confederate soldiers owe their salvation to the influences brought to bear upon them during service in the army." Good evangelicals that they were, chaplains along with sympathetic officers and enlisted men sometimes reported more exact figures: 94 men in one regiment "returned" to the faith or 146 men who had "found peace in Christ." Some accounts defied belief: had there really been 200 men converted during a single meeting? Some figures—1,000 professors of faith, 2,000 inquirers, 2,000 converts—seemed suspiciously round, raising more doubts about reports from army missionaries.[21]

Lee tried to encourage the chaplains, and soldiers were always impressed when Marse Robert unobtrusively showed up for worship. And by this time many Confederates had virtually deified him into a national savior. During the spring of 1864, General Pendleton concluded that Lee himself "has grown more perceptibly in grace and in the knowledge of God during the past year. . . . He expresses full assurance that the Judge of all the earth will do right, and entire submission to His holy will." When fourteen generals dutifully marched into church one Sunday, however, Mary Chesnut sardonically commented that "less piety and more drilling of commands would suit the times better." This bit of sarcasm ignored the connection between faith and morale. In both Union and Confederate armies, officers had important roles to play, sometimes leading prayers, reading scripture, or even delivering a sermon. The conversion of officers who had once been wicked men became a special cause for rejoicing, and perhaps yet another sign of growing righteousness.[22]

From mass conversions to pious officers, all of this added to the standard narrative of Confederates as Christian soldiers. But despite voluminous evidence of piety, questions lingered. "All our boys were not good boys," a Confederate artillerist confessed, stating the obvious. Even when there was preaching in a nearby church, another Virginian wryly commented that "the boys are slow about going to the altar" because there "are too many vegetables here for them to steal." In the midst of revivals, a substantial number of men remained coldly indifferent, and even those who were baptized might quickly fall back into their old ways—a fact noticed by the devout and skeptical alike.[23]

Then there was the practical question of whether religion made men better soldiers. In a season of defeat and despair, hope that faith could sustain Confederate morale survived, though the preaching remained heavily evangelistic in the traditional style. The emphasis as always was on conviction and conversion, on baptism and the church. Soldiers longed for guidance and comfort as they faced hardship, suffering, and death. Whether the Confederacy remained a sacred cause was another matter, but there was far more talk of personal than national salvation. When an Alabama chaplain spoke about enlisting under the banner of Christ, he was seeking to nurture and encourage young converts rather than to prepare men for the battlefield. Religious editors and even former Episcopal bishop and Confederate general Leonidas Polk simply hoped that army revivals would prevent the men from returning home wild and uncontrollable heathens. This is not to say, however, that the religious awakening in the camps had supplanted civil religion. Methodist bishop James O. Andrew viewed the revivals as a sure sign that God stood by the Confederacy. Repeating an argument that had appeared in one form or another since the beginning of the war, a Presbyterian editor avowed, "It would be extraordinary and unaccountable for God to pour out his blessing upon an army which was engaged in a lost cause."[24]

Jefferson Davis would have agreed, and as camp revivals continued into spring he issued yet another call for a day of fasting, humiliation, and prayer. Even the relentlessly anti-Davis *Charleston Mercury* welcomed the fast day and warned of a "future the most awful that the imagination can contemplate" should the Confederacy fail. But the usual affirmation that all rested in God's hands sounded more fatalistic than hopeful, and there was increasing uncertainty about how to connect divine providence to the war's course. An emphasis on confessing individual faults and saying daily prayers resonated from the camp revivals, but whether a people facing another grim year of war would flock to the churches, observe the fast (as if food supplies were not already tight), ignore the president, or even spend the day in dissipation was anyone's guess. A South Carolina Baptist editor complained that on previous occasions there had been an "obtrusive display of ungodliness" and citizens had preferred "idle sports" to sacred worship. It was a welcome day off from business but no occasion for sincere contrition or true humility. "Our people at home," he lamented, "have become more selfish, extortionate, oppressive, gay, and frivolous."[25]

Perhaps Mammon worship did flourish, but it was difficult to tell from widely scattered reports about how well the day was observed. In the Confederate capital, several thousand gathered in the New Richmond Theater to hear a sermon by the Reverend J. L. Burrows, though his chosen text told how the Lord had repeatedly punished people for sin—hardly a message to bolster sagging morale on the eve of a campaign season. General Lee issued an order instructing officers and men to "beseech the aid of the God of our forefathers in the defense of our homes and our liberties." Indeed, the camps in Virginia and Georgia were unusually quiet with little drilling or other activities, and many officers attended services. Soldiers sat through preaching and prayer meetings and reportedly fasted, though there were naturally some wry comments on the latter, given the often short rations in the Confederate armies. The turnout for camp worship was unusually large according to most accounts, but one North Carolinian thought only the religiously disposed paid much attention.[26]

When it came to flailing sinners, the fast-day preachers did not disappoint. Impiety of all sorts along with drunkenness and greed came in for the usual condemnations, and a close connection was drawn between individual vices and national suffering. A Baptist editor made the link between sin and defeat perfectly clear: "Let all who are conscious of unrepented sins read in these reverses a Divine rebuke in themselves. . . . Let us cease to fight against Him, that he may fight no longer against our country and ourselves." Yet, as usual, the ministers excoriated Yankee wrongdoing with considerably more enthusiasm. Not only would Federal troops—the very dregs of a society that promoted all sorts of heresies—free every slave, but they would soon close down every church.[27]

Why this was all happening or about to happen could be only partly explained by the people's wicked disregard for God's holy ordinances. In a rural Virginia church, a Baptist preacher spoke of "calamities and scourges" that fall on nations, "ordered by . . . [an] Allwise, though mysterious Providence." There was presumably a design in all this, but one that lay beyond human comprehension. The only way to end the war was for the people to humble themselves, and then God would heed their prayers and heal the land. His listeners had heard all that before, but then he added that the Lord sometimes "may withhold success from his most faithful servants even in his own cause." Yet for how long? Even Episcopal bishop Richard H. Wilmer, who was certainly an ardent Confederate, talked of "present reverses" being designed for "future good" and rejected the idea of praying for the southern cause with the expectation that God could be bought off like some "mercenary." Too many people sought "temporal prosperity" and failed to realize they might have to wander in the wilderness before being delivered from their enemies. Because fast-day sermons so often painted the immediate future in such dark hues, themes of suffering and destruction overshadowed any hope that might be offered in their conclusions. Even camp revivals—a cause for rejoicing mentioned by many preachers—presented a striking and depressing contrast to the apparent declension at home. Stephen Elliott tried to minimize Confederate military losses in passages that would have done any politician proud but sadly conceded how often civilians murmured against their rulers.[28]

On that score, Union and Confederate soldiers expressed quite similar sentiments. Having warned his mother against complaining about troubles and brooding over the poor soldiers, a Federal staff officer observed how "Christ has suffered for us all, both mental and physical pain." Given their own hardships, perhaps the soldiers could better understand the theology of the atonement as they already had witnessed plenty of blood sacrifice. Camp religion would presumably strengthen home front religion, and by the same token a family's love and piety helped sustain men in battle against enemies both temporal and spiritual. One northern Presbyterian reassured a group of volunteers assembled at a camp near Boston that "not only your godly fathers and mothers, wives and sisters, pastors and friends are praying for you continually; the whole northern church is bowed on her face before the Eternal God on your behalf."[29]

Camp revivals heartened both Federals and Confederates but had made pious soldiers even more anxious about the religious state of their families, churches, and communities. Unfortunately the home front often proved rocky soil for the seeds of evangelism. An October 1863 report from an Ohio presbytery was typical in noting "no general tokens of spiritual blessing," despite all the families that had lost loved ones and undoubtedly needed to think on "eternal things." On the surface at least, northern church life often seemed far removed from the war. But pious Confederates too detected spiritual coldness on the home front in the absence of revivals such as had graced the armies. With news of invasion and the alarms of battle, church meetings seemingly held little interest for families struggling to survive the economic, social, and emotional hardships. "War and its rumors sap the life of the church," one Kentucky Confederate perceptively observed, and the Lutheran Synod of North Carolina was equally terse: "Our Zion now seems to languish."[30]

In many southern communities, revivals were rare, and war's distractions overshadowed everything. Yet this all seemed a weak excuse for neglecting religious duties, and a Presbyterian editor warned about impending humiliation if soldiers who had experienced a "work of grace in the army" returned to find "religious deadness at home." Perhaps the camp services would somehow inspire what some Richmond Baptists termed the "slumbering churches." Indeed, civilians should not simply await a spiritual awakening but, in the mode favored ever since the days of Finney and the Second Great Awakening, must pray and labor for an outpouring of the Holy Spirit.[31]

Whether a burst of home front revivalism that began in 1863 rallied much support for the war was hard to tell. The message often remained narrowly evangelistic even when visiting soldiers helped fill the empty pews. By this point, War Department clerk John B. Jones thought there was no need to remind anyone about the horrors of death. Indeed, allusions to the war were infrequent; as always, the emphasis was on winning souls—especially young souls—to the Lord. The primary hope remained that God's work of conversion could spread to men and women across the Confederate states. Yet the war itself at times stifled piety, not to mention charity, forgiveness, and other virtues. On her North Carolina plantation, Kate Edmondston dreaded losing "the little Christianity I have got!" Her hatred of the Yankees knew few bounds. "I rejoice when I hear of their slaughter by thousands."[32]

The picture was equally spotty in the northern states. Experienced preachers might still conduct fall meetings in the old Finneyite way, and indeed, by 1863 reports of a religious awakening spread from New England into the Midwest. A growing ethnic and religious diversity, however, further hamstrung efforts to create any kind of evangelical unity, and civil religion remained largely a matter for official fast and thanksgiving days. In Catholic enclaves across the North, priests conducted missions that served to spread the church's influence among both the native and immigrant populations.[33]

Few ministers dared point to any of this as a sign of God's returning favor. Indifference and distraction, demoralization and decadence all worked against broad-based revivals; the converts and the devout, just as in the armies, made up a distinct minority.

————

A Mississippi lieutenant stationed in Virginia was dismayed to learn of the "deplorable state of religion at home" but happily reported that "the opposite was the case in the army." On the eve of the spring campaign season, attendance at services swelled and in some camps, worship services of one kind or another took place almost daily. Soldiers conducting prayer meetings and Bible classes turned to religion with a desperate intensity.[34] In March 1864 an army evangelist urged other ministers to visit the brigades in Virginia and organize meetings, because they could work without hindrance for several weeks before the troops took the field again. Large interdenominational services had become the order of the day with Holy Communion being an especially solemn occasion as the inevitable rumors of impending troop movements spread.[35]

More ominous still near Dalton, Georgia, where the Army of Tennessee was in winter quarters, a smoldering tree fell into a crowd of worshipers one evening and killed ten soldiers from the 4th Tennessee. There followed an impressive mass burial and no doubt much sober reflection. Ironically, this macabre accident occurred during a season of unprecedented revivalism among western theater Confederates. Visiting preachers delivered sermons that broke up the monotony of regular camp worship, and in some brigades there were nightly meetings. Chapels overflowed and walls had to be knocked out.[36]

Reports of large crowds over a period of several weeks sounded like the sweetest of hymns to those hoping for an abundant harvest of souls in what had often seemed a God-forsaken army. Beginning shortly after the Chickamauga campaign, revivals extended to at least eleven of the army's twenty-eight brigades, though again there was much less attention paid to the course of the war than to the state of men's souls. More soldiers began to carry Bibles. Mass baptisms dramatized evangelical success, with soldiers preferring immersion because it symbolized complete submission to the crucified Christ and a dramatic change in their lives.[37]

Even the highest-ranking Confederates bowed in prayer, confessed their sins, and received baptism. In the summer of 1863, Episcopal chaplain Charles Todd Quintard had talked to Braxton Bragg about the state of his soul, bringing the crusty and often sour general to tears. Bragg's baptism by Bishop Stephen Elliott failed to improve his generalship, something that seemingly lay beyond divine power, but that hardly stopped the preachers from working on the Army of Tennessee's high command. In May 1864 Leonidas Polk baptized Joe Johnston, John Bell Hood, and several other generals, though that too failed to prevent the fall of Atlanta. Nevertheless, with prominent officers very much a part of the revivals, the devout took heart if not in the Confederate cause at least in God's care. "I have never seen such a spirit as there is now in the army," one Georgian rejoiced.[38]

There was equally good news in the Army of Northern Virginia where the revivals reached a new intensity. "Many are turning to the Lord," a pious Georgia private wrote home, but exactly how many remained uncertain. He reported eleven joining "the church" one evening, and the most reliable information showed that the conversions generally came in dribs and drabs. Five here, six there, occasionally more; the cumulative effect was no doubt impressive, but talk of many men awakening from their spiritual lethargy was often imprecise and in some cases clearly exaggerated. Individual brigades claimed a remarkable number of longtime believers and recent converts, but then chaplains and religious papers had every reason to cite impressive figures without worrying too much about their accuracy. One Episcopalian editor, however, questioned the depth of sincerity in camp conversions and expressed a general skepticism about the whole system of religious revivals.[39] Men who had been quite pious before the revivals offered the most enthusiastic assessments, but many soldiers said little or nothing on the subject, raising questions about how much camp services had touched the mass of men and with what lasting effects.

As spring approached, the Federal armies experienced their own spiritual stirrings. Christian Commission delegates reported enthusiastic meetings but tended to paint a bright picture with very broad brush strokes. Vague comments about "a good feeling" in a regiment or the "earnest labors" of a visiting Baptist minister along with accounts of deeply moving services suggested both a growing religious feeling and perhaps the limited reach of camp revivals. Private Wilbur Fisk, a Vermont schoolteacher and perceptive observer of army life, believed that the novelty of the meetings attracted men seeking an hour of diversion. Weekly services, nightly prayer meetings, and regular Bible classes all served social as well as spiritual needs. Packed chapel tents warmed the hearts of Christian Commission delegates; whether many thousands were converted as was sometimes claimed is anyone's guess. Many regiments still had no chaplains, and in some outfits even prayer meetings were rarities. "There is so much evil going around," a Michigan doctor working at an army hospital in Tennessee admitted. "It is almost impossible to keep God in the thoughts."[40]

That statement summed up the problem, especially for soldiers struggling to find faith. In Crab Orchard, Kentucky, a Massachusetts sergeant sounded disheartened as he noted how the local people ignored the Sabbath, but the state of his own heart was little better. "Feel I have not that thirsting of soul for the spiritual good of my comrades, which ought to be in the heart of the disciple." A New York private found it hard to pray, and despite feeling a certain conviction of sin, he had not yet experienced the work of redemption in his life. The revival meetings—however extensive and lively—left residues of doubt, and resistance to the gospel undoubtedly remained strong with many men.[41] In other words, the usual rhythms of spiritual life, struggling, questioning, losing faith, finding faith persisted during the war, and though the revivals surely touched hearts and changed lives, they hardly molded battle-hardened veterans, the conscripts, and new recruits into Christian armies.

What all the religious meetings in the army added up to may have been less than met the eye. A crusty Wisconsin sergeant saw little value in prayer meetings and had "no confidence in the spasmodic and transient results of so-called revivals." Even in Virginia, where the fires of religious enthusiasm had burned brightest, a young sergeant described Sunday as like any other day in his camp. The more skeptical soldiers denied there had been any moral progress in the army, all claims to the contrary notwithstanding. A New York volunteer who believed there were more "bold witnesses for Christ" nevertheless admitted that most officers and men "are reprobate concerning the faith and care nothing of these things." Many a young man went straight from the afternoon service back to the card game. An Ohio German serving in the Army of the Cumberland saw little point in having Baptist preachers in camp and thought his comrades "rather inclined to the opinion that a little more sensual gratification would not be amiss here in Ringgold, [Georgia]." [42]

Among Confederates, too, religious indifference remained a problem even though devout soldiers still connected a spiritual awakening to southern independence. The more sanguine even held that the revivals had strengthened the armies' moral tone and augured well for the future. Yet, in writing home, many men had little to say about religion, and one North Carolinian—no doubt exaggerating the case—told his parents that despite regular preaching in camp, "there is so much wickedness going on it appears that the men don't care what they due." [43]

For the past three years, some ministers had argued that soldiering would make men better Christians—indeed, "Christian soldiers" in the fullest meaning of both words. Regiments with large numbers of converts had reportedly stood their ground in battle while more heathenish outfits had broken ranks. One Tennessean even connected the revivals to declining rates of desertion. Devout soldiers embodied the highest ideals of the early Christians without regard for sect, uncomplaining patriots who loved God and served their country without reservation. [44]

Plenty of these fellows would be needed because in the spring of 1864 the slaughter was about to begin anew. As another campaign season approached, the uncertainty of life and the certainty of death once again weighed heavily on the soldiers' minds and hearts. Some 200,000 lives had already been lost repelling the Yankee invaders, one Confederate tract claimed, and this proved how angry God had grown with southern sinners. A promise of eternal peace with the Lord was nearly lost in the appeal to raw fear, and hard questions simply would not go away. Sergeant William Pitt Chambers of the 46th Mississippi spoke for many others in asking "what induced thirty millions of the human race living under the same government all speaking the same language to engage in such an unholy strife?" Would the Lord continue to punish the southern people ever more severely for their transgressions? In Virginia, with the contending armies camped so near each other, Father James Sheeran deeply wished to be spared "the approaching scenes of blood and carnage." [45]

Sheeran still expressed confidence in the troops and in the Confederacy, so his brooding remarks hardly reflected an irreversible despair. Simply look to the Lord in this latest hour of crisis, the pious would advise the generals, officers, and enlisted men. The price of independence would continue to rise as many Confederates had finally come to realize. The war's course remained in the hands of an inscrutable God who controlled the destiny of nations and would bring peace strictly according to his purposes and timetable. William Nelson Pendleton conceded that the Lord might choose not to deliver the southern nation from its enemies and instead "cause the wrath of man to praise Him," though he quickly added, all would "work for good." In the midst of such confusing assessments and efforts to shore up morale, the only recourse was to repent and leave the rest in God's hands. This did not yet signify an immobilizing fatalism or mean that soldiers and civilians had stopped praying for victory. The Almighty was still testing his people, and they must not question either their faith or their cause.[46] Whether such a theology would reassure enough people and renew their commitment to the fight must have been a troubling question especially for the preachers and their friends in the government and in the army.

The righteousness of the Confederate crusade remained vital for many believers. Identifying the Confederacy as a Christian nation sanctified the war itself, especially for the idealistic and upright young officers who formed the heart and soul of the southern armies. Yankee victories and depredations had been demoralizing, but they could also rekindle a determination to keep fighting in a holy contest for both individual and national redemption. Therefore, despite setbacks and gloom in many quarters, a religious confidence in ultimate victory survived and helped prolong the fighting. The Lord "will never suffer a determined and Christian people to be overcome by a cruel tyrant," a Louisiana sergeant informed his father. God would deliver the southern people from the Yankees just as he had delivered the Israelites from the Egyptians. Many a devout soldier expected success in the spring campaigns, a hope strengthened by religious faith. The ancient idea of covenant resurfaced: if Confederates would renew their commitment to God's cause, the Almighty would preserve their nation. Commenting on recent news of army revivals, a Virginia woman drew the predictable conclusion: "With such an army may we not look for his [the Lord's] blessing?" That point was not lost on their enemies. Struck with both awe and fear, a Maine private remarked about the rebels: "Their army is sure that God is on their side."[47]

Camp conversions became tokens of divine blessing not only for the soldiers but also for the Confederacy. On the eve of the spring campaign season, a Baptist editor reassuringly claimed that rebel armies were much more Christian than Yankee armies. To others, the sheer volume of prayers ascending from the ranks ensured a Confederate victory in the next big fight. In the most desperate circumstances, soldiers could still rely on the Lord who would never abandon them to a godless enemy—or so they thought and hoped. Why this was so or exactly how it all would come about was far from clear, and the most confident assertions of faith in the righteousness and ultimate triumph of southern arms hardly plumbed any great theological depths. On the recent Confederate fast day, a Methodist chaplain had simply observed that perhaps the Lord could be "propitiated and will manifest His favor towards us in the coming campaign." More simply yet, an Alabama preacher had told a group of soldiers that, if they kept doing their duty, their enemies would flee. Faith became coupled with notions of invincibility that ensnared many Confederates blinded by patriotic devotion and religious fervor.[48]

Surely such naive ideas were, as many soldiers would have said, "all played out" by this time, and the platitudes of Confederate civil religion must have rung hollow to many men facing another season of war. The fear of death had undoubtedly spurred conversions, and now men began to recalculate their chances of dying, and perhaps even more sadly of having their unidentified bodies tossed into a burial trench. For his part, Father Sheeran found great consolation in helping Catholic soldiers (and Protestants for that matter) "make peace with their God before meeting the enemy again." Being a Christian provided comfort when the bullets flew. But faith and orthodox beliefs also forced men to take a hard look at what might lie ahead. The spring campaign promised another "great tournament of Death," a Mississippi cavalryman advised his wife. Echoing the Old Testament Job far more than any New Testament assurance of salvation, his words struck a fatalistic chord: "If the all seeing eye of that Jehovah, who rules the whirlwind and directs the storm, be favorably inclined towards [us], we have nothing to fear."[49]

A very big "if," and the problem became overcoming fear for the body if not for the soul. Both stood in mortal danger, pious Confederates and Federals would have readily acknowledged. As the Army of the Potomac prepared to leave the winter camps, a Presbyterian kept preaching "the great Bible doctrine of instantaneous regeneration—of God's immediate claim on the heart, and his precious promise to pardon and accept at once every returning prodigal." Time was shorter than ever, and many men would soon die on battlefields or in hospitals, and so sinners must "hasten" to Jesus. Some soldiers appeared more receptive to the gospel than ever, or as a Christian Commission delegate put it, "listening as if they were anticipating the baptism of blood which awaits them." A goodly number even signed a temperance pledge just to be on the safe side.[50]

In the rush of new orders and frantic preparations to take the field, observing the Sabbath, reading the Bible, or even meditating on matters of faith might be easily neglected. Agreeing for once with their enemies, many Federals hoped that camp conversions had strengthened the armies. To believers, it appeared self-evident that the better a man was prepared to meet his maker, the better soldier he became. More fearless perhaps, and certainly more devoted to duty, but in any case even veterans who felt they had already done more than their share must still answer the call of duty—a summons from their officers, their comrades, their country, and ultimately from their God. Perhaps the fast-day preachers and chaplains were right; they all truly fought in the armies of the Lord. Meanwhile families prayed hard for their boys in the army, and one Iowa woman remained confident that "the Lord *will* surely take care of the soldiers and soon give us victory and peace."[51]

WAR COMES TO THE CHURCHES

I exhort therefore, that, first of all, supplications, prayers, intercessions,
and giving of thanks, be made for all men; For kings, and for all that are
in authority; that we may lead a quiet and peaceable life in all godliness
and honesty.

— 1 Timothy 2:1–2

Wherefore I will bring the worst of the heathen, and they shall possess
their houses: I will also make the pomp of the strong to cease; and their
holy places shall be defiled.

— Ezekiel 7:24

On May 9, 1864, Abraham Lincoln released a brief statement to the
press stating that "enough is known of Army operations within the last five
days to claim our especial gratitude to God" and urging "all patriots at their
homes, in their places of public worship, and wherever they be, unite in common thanksgiving and prayer to Almighty God."[1] Five days earlier the Army
of the Potomac had crossed the Rapidan River. On May 5 the Army of Northern Virginia had attempted to stop and indeed wreck the advancing Federals
in what became known as the Battle of the Wilderness, and the two armies
would slug it out in a confusing series of attacks and counterattacks in dense
thickets and second-growth forest all that day and the next.

Lincoln thought he had at last found a general in Ulysses S. Grant who
could defeat Robert E. Lee, and so his invocation of thanks to the Almighty
after a rare victory over the Army of Northern Virginia sounded a suddenly
more hopeful if not exactly confident note. Reverend Gilbert Haven, an ardent
Methodist and firm supporter of the administration and emancipation, admitted to his Boston congregation that "telegrams, not texts are our spiritual
food. The battle, not the Bible, draws our attention." Now that Federal armies
(including African American regiments) stood on the right side of the slavery
question, "how must the trembling sinners of Richmond look aghast as they
see the dark face of their slaves riding insolently up to their walls." The religious press became so caught up in the news from Virginia (and of William T.
Sherman's halting advance on Atlanta) that editors were paying more attention to General Grant than to the Lord of Hosts. Grant would not likely waltz

into Richmond after a few days of fighting, as they readily conceded, and James McMaster was soon blasting the new general-in-chief for "the great feast of blood" in Virginia, but many Christians of various stripes looked for the current campaign to prove decisive.[2]

Even for this war, victories in the Overland campaign (such as they were) took an unimaginable toll. At the first major engagement in the Wilderness, the two armies suffered nearly thirty thousand casualties, and worse was yet to come. Federal assaults on hastily built Confederate entrenchments around Spotsylvania Courthouse from May 10 through May 12 produced some of the most prolonged and brutal fighting of the entire war.

Ignoring Lee's aggressiveness, a Richmond Presbyterian editor excoriated Grant as a butcher, indifferent to human suffering, who plied his troops with whiskey to drive them into battle. Fortunately, an "avenging Providence" had thwarted his plans. Farther south, Confederate success in Georgia, according to one Lutheran synod, proved that southerners were the "innocent and injured party" in the contest. Northern soldiers had not died martyrs to the cause of Christ, as Yankee preachers claimed, but instead had received the just reward for what Macon's *Christian Index* termed "robbers and blood-thirsty murderers" who foolishly equated the Union and abolition with religion and the gospel. As always, pious Confederates fell back on the assumption that such devilish armies could never prevail and that the infidel northerners would soon pay for their crimes.[3]

Despite all the deaths that weighed so heavily on families, northern preachers still talked about the sacrifices needed to preserve the Union, the government, and liberty itself. Harriet Foote Hawley, a Union general's delicate wife who went to South Carolina to teach the freed slaves and work in the hospitals, expected a "baptism of blood" to "purify this county and cleanse it of greed and selfish ambition, as well as of Heresy." War was by nature destructive, as a pastor in a rural New York Presbyterian church pointed out to his congregation with more truth than profundity. The prophets of the Old Testament had warned people about the consequences of sin and disobedience. Even the most peaceful Christians at home could hardly be immune from the suffering that touched nearly all aspects of life.[4]

That now included the Lord's own sanctuaries. On the morning of May 21, 1864, Grant, Meade, and their staff, on the way from Spotsylvania Courthouse toward Guinea Station in yet another attempt to steal a march on Lee, reached the Massaponax Baptist Church. Orderlies dragged out pews, and the Federal high command held a council of war outdoors. Grant with the usual cigar in his mouth pored over maps, worrying about the whereabouts of Winfield Scott Hancock's corps. This incongruous scene—of the generals and staffs sit-

Council of War, Grant and Meade, Massaponax Church, Virginia (Library of Congress)

ting on the pews in the churchyard—was captured by photographer Timothy O'Sullivan. The great war had reached deeply into the southern countryside and had even touched peaceful little churches; later three enlisted men from the 114th Pennsylvania scrawled their names on a wall inside the sanctuary.[5] The pews in the churchyard and those names on the wall were small details that loomed large. Slavery and sectionalism had already divided three major denominations, and almost as soon as the first shots were fired, new fissures opened as the war arrived literally on church doorsteps.

———

Factious border state congregations faced invasion, occupation, and military rule. In May 1861 Samuel B. McPheeters, a native Virginian, graduate of Princeton Seminary, and minister of Pine Street Presbyterian Church in St.

Louis, wrote a long pastoral letter explaining his political neutrality. When the Old School Presbyterians adopted the famous Spring resolutions affirming the denomination's loyalty to the Union, many border state ministers felt alienated from their own church. Their political conservatism could easily be mistaken for rebel sympathies, and sometimes their strident defense of the church's strictly spiritual nature barely masked clear political preferences. In this case, the good pastor's own indiscretions—including the baptizing of a baby named after Confederate general Sterling Price—aroused the suspicions of Unionist members.[6]

Clashing with Robert J. Breckinridge at the 1862 Old School General Assembly, McPheeters denied the church owed any allegiance to civil government. In June, George P. Strong and some twenty-nine other members of the Pine Street congregation signed a letter inquiring about McPheeters's loyalty. They denied any wish for him to "preach politics" but considered a forthright condemnation of the rebellion as "good morals" because Confederates warred against both the government and the Almighty. Their conclusion was all too typical of contemporary attitudes: "There are only two sides to this controversy. There can be no neutral ground." McPheeters drew a clear line between his duties as a minister and his duties as a citizen, denying the right of anyone in the congregation to catechize his political opinions and further commenting that he preferred to pray for all those in civil authority rather than singling out President Lincoln. This tone of wounded innocence was bound to displease Strong and the others; it hardly allayed their misgivings whether real or imagined.

An October meeting at the Pine Street Church for those "who are in favor of sustaining the Government of the United States" declared McPheeters's response "not satisfactory." This vocal minority refused to "countenance, by our attendance, a Church whose moral influence encourages the rebellion and where treason is unrebuked." McPheeters should either pray for the success of Union arms or leave the church. The minister again explained why he would not deliver "political sermons," quoting one parishioner as saying, "I have the war all the week, and want the gospel on Sunday." Each exchange widened the breach. Strong and two others members excoriated McPheeters for allowing charges of disloyalty to taint his ministry, adding that "moral traitors, men who secretly take the side of the enemies of our Government, but who have not the manliness or courage openly to espouse their cause or join their armed bands, have been encouraged in their sinful course."

Accusations of disloyalty led General Samuel R. Curtis to bar McPheeters from preaching and to order him to "take up residence" somewhere "north of Indianapolis and west of Pennsylvania." Curtis handed over control of the

Pine Street Church to "three loyal members" who were to see that "its pulpit be filled by a loyal minister of the Gospel, who can invoke the blessing of the head of the church upon the efforts of the Government to re-establish its authority."[7] McPheeters immediately complained to Attorney General Edward Bates, a Missourian, active Old School layman, and friend of the family, who arranged for him to meet with Lincoln. By this time, conservative editors had taken up the cause, raising the predictable cries of military despotism; Curtis, McPheeters, and the feuding Presbyterians had all placed the president in a tough spot. As Lincoln told McPheeters and others, he could not have ministers preaching treason but would not allow generals to take over churches. Lincoln was convinced of McPheeters's rebel leanings yet doubted he had done anything to justify banishment. The president instructed Curtis to suspend that portion of the order, but the general intemperately protested by pointing out how loyal men in St. Louis were now complaining that rebel sympathizers wielded undue influence with the administration. Other Missourians including members of the powerful Blair family raised similar objections.[8]

Missouri affairs had turned into a constant headache for the beleaguered president, and this helps explain why he devoted so much attention to the Pine Street squabbles. In meetings with various Missourians and even official correspondence, Lincoln's irritation clearly showed. In early January, he sent a carefully worded dispatch to Curtis. Describing the charges against McPheeters as vague and insubstantial, Lincoln left it up to the general to decide whether the minister should be allowed to resume his duties. The president made it clear, however, that he did not think the government should "undertake to run the churches," a none too subtle swipe at Curtis's order. "When an individual, in a church or out of it, becomes dangerous to the public interest, he must be checked," Lincoln allowed. "But let the churches, as such take care of themselves."[9]

Despite Lincoln's suspension of the expulsion order, McPheeters could still not preach in Missouri and so attempted to resign his pastorate. But the Presbytery would not accept the resignation, and a large majority of members in the Pine Street congregation asked McPheeters to reconsider. By late fall, more letters reached Washington complaining that McPheeters was still being kept out of the pulpit. Lincoln bristled over the "monstrous" suggestion that he was somehow responsible and complained that those petitioning on the minister's behalf presented contradictory accounts of his status. By January 1864 McPheeters was preaching again, but an outspoken minority in the congregation remained determined to drive him out and won support from the St. Louis Presbytery. Eventually the Old School General Assembly voted to sustain the presbytery's decision to remove this "disloyal" minister. As the war was ending, McPheeters moved to Kentucky where he died in 1870 at the age of fifty-one.[10]

The cantankerous McPheeters had been far from an ideal defender of religious liberty, but many Old School Presbyterians bitterly resented his rough handling by both the military authorities and the General Assembly. Aside from the doubtful constitutionality of such actions, as Lincoln no doubt understood, military intervention in religious affairs hardly made anyone more loyal. How the hapless McPheeters threatened the Union war effort, no one could say, but his case proved how the politics of loyalty could directly touch the lives of ministers, their congregations, and the denominations.

———

At the height of the McPheeters controversy, Confederate authorities in Arkansas arrested several Baptists accused of "preaching disloyalty and distributing Lincoln proclamations and otherwise attempting to excite the people to disloyalty." Some ministers pointedly refused to pray for Jefferson Davis or insisted on praying for the Union government and thus incurred the wrath of Confederate officers. Reports of clergymen being hounded from the pulpit—sometimes by armed men—for a supposed lack of patriotism perhaps helped reinforce community solidarity but also provided grist for Union propaganda mills. And heaven help the poor preacher attempting to steer a course between Confederate officials, Union occupiers, and their own consciences.[11]

Once Federal forces arrived, Confederate persecution of Unionist ministers became a convenient excuse for weeding out "disloyal" preachers. Often blaming southern clergy for inciting the war, northern soldiers talked of vestments splattered with the blood of thousands slain in battle. Such beliefs reinforced the idea of the Federals as the Lord's avenging angels against rebel churches that blasphemously called on the Almighty to support an unholy cause. One Unionist in Columbia, Tennessee, reported the treasonous talk of a local Presbyterian pastor to newly appointed military governor Andrew Johnson. Similar complaints regularly reached Union commanders. To these officials, the solution to the problem was clear: suppress these rebel preachers and place loyal men in the pulpits.[12]

Insistence on a demonstrable proof of allegiance caused no end of trouble. In areas under Federal control, swearing an oath of loyalty to the Union became necessary for conducting all kinds of business, including church services. Whether the clergy could make such affirmations in good faith naturally became the most difficult question. Confederate patriots cried, "Never!" and condemned anyone—and especially any man of the cloth—who would betray his country by swearing a false or meaningless oath. Such an offense against God, Benjamin Morgan Palmer declared, would undermine civil government and corrupt the people. Had not devout Christians always been willing to suffer for conscience sake? In Kentucky, Methodist farmer and part-time preacher George Richard Browder was appalled that Federal officials would arrest ministers for refusing to take an oath. He took some comfort in the fact that the Lord had allowed Job to be persecuted, Jeremiah to be imprisoned, and the various apostles to suffer. He wrestled with the question of whether to "swear against his conscience" but also recalled the Apostle Paul's admonition about submitting to the powers that be and so finally traveled to Russellville and signed the hated piece of paper.[13]

In the Department of Missouri, General William S. Rosecrans required those attending official religious meetings such as synods and annual conferences to give "satisfactory evidence of their loyalty to the Government of the United States." Such assemblies might easily "concoct treason," and the nation's enemies should not be allowed to plot behind the cloak of a spurious religious freedom. As for those objecting to his order, Old Rosy simply dismissed them as rebels in disguise. Prodded by Attorney General Bates, Lincoln quickly suggested that Rosecrans reconsider but did not insist that the order be suspended. The general regaled a group of Methodist ministers with rumors of a vast rebel conspiracy to bring in disloyal preachers from surrounding states but eventually allowed them to meet. When Presbyterians gathered in St. Louis, they reportedly used the "Rosecrans oath" to expel ministers.[14]

War, invasion, and occupation posed equally stern tests for churches that had managed to remain united during the sectional crisis. Catholic claims to being the church universal—and, indeed, charges that Protestant principles had inevitably led to ecclesiastical and finally political schism—perhaps led some priests and bishops to believe they could escape the troubles roiling other denominations. Yet, like the Episcopalians and Presbyterians, Catholics ritualistically prayed for those in civil authority. As Mississippi left the Union, Bishop William Henry Elder in Federal-occupied Natchez amended the standard prayers to recognize the new order. By the spring of 1862, as Grant's forces were threatening to enter Mississippi, the bishop took what he considered a principled approach to the enemy. He would make the rounds of Federal camps and hospitals and would even minister to thousands of runaway slaves barely surviving and often dying from epidemic diseases in Federal contraband camps but would not dine with the officers. A native southerner who claimed to treat sufferers on both sides with kindness, Elder hesitated to visit his archbishop in occupied New Orleans for fear of being forced to take an oath of allegiance. At first Elder gave his priests and their congregations much latitude but later decided that subscribing to such an oath (a solemn vow before God) and not intending to keep it would be a "mortal sin."[15]

In the spring of 1864, General James Tuttle asked Elder whether a prayer for the president and Federal authorities was being used in the Catholic churches; the bishop replied this was up to each priest's discretion. Elder naturally bristled at the idea of a military officer meddling with worship services and warned this would outrage Catholics across the country. In June, Colonel Joseph F. Farrar demanded that a prayer for the president and other civil officials be read at every service. By the time an irate Elder had composed a nineteen-page protest, Farrar had been replaced by General Mason Brayman, who insisted that all military orders be obeyed. There followed an exchange of ill-tempered notes. Brayman determined to test the bishop's loyalty, and Elder dramatically declared that "liberty of conscience" for the entire church and country was at stake. He decided on a course of "passive resistance" and would "leave the consequences to God." Claiming to fear that military authorities would seize St. Mary's Cathedral for use as a hospital, "defacing and desecrating everything beautiful and holy," Elder carefully explained his position to a stream of sympathetic Catholic and Protestant visitors. On July 22, 1864, a special order from General Brayman declared Elder a rebel and ordered his expulsion from Natchez; military authorities seized control of St. Mary's.[16]

When Elder prepared to cross the Mississippi River to Vidalia, Louisiana, Catholic sisters and their orphan charges cried as a group of men gathered to accompany the bishop; those in the crowd fell to their knees—seemingly on cue—and Elder melodramatically declared, "God forgive me for not doing much more for such people." In Vidalia, Elder lived in a small room for seventeen days until released and allowed back into Natchez. Several federal commanders had accomplished nothing in their ham-handed orders other than to turn the bishop into a living martyr. In the end, Brayman petulantly conceded that "all Persons conducting Divine Worship [were] at liberty to manifest such measure of hostility, as they feel against the Government and Union of these States." Elder returned to a hero's welcome and ringing bells; his first sermon pointedly referred to friends and enemies praying before the same altar.[17]

The bishop's triumph was complete. A Natchez resident had fed information about the contretemps to the fiery James A. McMaster, so the whole matter soon became a cause célèbre in the Catholic press. Even editors sympathetic to the Lincoln administration refused to defend the military's treatment of the prickly Elder.[18] Prescribing or prohibiting certain forms of prayer was bound to stir up trouble, but the politics of loyalty often trumped good sense. Military commanders and local Unionists, not to mention northern politicians and their patriotic constituents, all demanded submissive behavior if not submissive hearts.

Worship services inevitably became a battleground. Whatever one thought of Mr. Lincoln, a Unionist editor in Memphis wryly remarked, should not good Christians pray for everyone, no matter how great a sinner? Despite the playful tone, this was a deadly serious matter to people on all sides. Generals such as Benjamin Butler banned prayers that showed any support for the Confederacy or its leaders but also insisted that standard prayers for the president of the United States (such as in the Episcopal liturgy) must be used. Grant took a more pragmatic approach, advising one general in West Tennessee that he could "compel all clergymen within your lines to omit from their church services any portion you may deem treasonable, but you will not compel the insertion or substitution of anything." Whether in fact leaving out the customary prayer for those in civil authority was acceptable very much depended on the local commanders.[19]

With their ears attuned for sins of omission as well as commission, Union officers and enlisted men often attended southern churches. They noted with approval a "loyal" minister praying for the president and reacted with outrage if a preacher failed to do so. In Pine Bluff, Arkansas, after an Episcopal minister had deviated from the liturgy, a Federal colonel cried out "Stop sir!" and marched toward the altar to read the prayer. At other times, irate soldiers brandished weapons and arrested the offending clergyman or closed the church.[20]

Talk of noble patriots being dragged from their pulpits became staples of Confederate propaganda, often followed by the usual rant against Beecherism, free-loveism, Mormonism, and other peculiarly Yankee heresies. The reputedly mild-mannered Episcopalians seemed especially defiant; a few insisted on praying for Jefferson Davis, and others simply refused to pray for Lincoln. In true mock heroic style, a minister in Alexandria, Virginia, whose service had been disturbed by Federal troops, declared, "I summon you to answer at the judgment seat of the King of Kings" for interrupting the people's prayers.[21]

Some members of the clergy adopted a cleverer strategy, much to the frustration of both staunch Confederates and anxious Federals who wanted to know where everybody stood. When a minister prayed for the president and Congress, a Michigan surgeon remarked, the men wondered which ones. "For some reason," he added, "preachers south nearly all preach and pray in this ambiguous manner." Such trimmers had perhaps been equally evasive when Confederates were in charge and clearly honed their survival skills. But trying to steer a neutral course aroused suspicions all round.[22] Satisfying Confederate parishioners and Union occupiers was a delicate task, and those who preached a message devoid of political references could presumably escape the scrutiny of Federal authorities. Their congregations might miss the prayers for the Confederacy and dismiss such clergymen as weak-kneed at best, but discreet pastors considered staying out of trouble an important service to people who badly needed them as times grew harder, casualty lists lengthened, and churches suffered accordingly.[23]

In Winchester, Virginia, after the third battle fought near that unfortunate town, a Presbyterian minister opened up his church and then preached a sermon about how northern "fanatics" and southern "demagogues" had tried to subvert the Constitution. He prayed earnestly for peace though, as a visiting Union soldier noted, he said nothing about restoring the Union. Appearing to pray with equal fervor for the soldiers on both sides, one Tennessee pastor left an Illinois surgeon wondering where his true sympathies lay. Praying for the soldiers in general or for all Christian rulers appeared safe enough, but with loyal Confederates and Yankee soldiers in the pews, there was always the danger of going too far in one direction or another. About the same time Bishop Elder was running afoul of the military authorities, Methodist preacher William H. Watkins in Natchez started off innocently praying for peace, for comfort, and for various other blessings. But he then asked the Lord to bless "our enemies" and "give them the spirit of justice, humanity, and the fear of God!" This last bit crossed the line, and he was soon arrested.[24]

Typically such ministers were soon released. Captured on horseback near Warrenton, Virginia, during a sweep against suspected guerrillas, a Methodist preacher could not explain why he was carrying a revolver but was freed the next morning. Especially in Missouri or areas freshly occupied by Union troops, officers might detain clergymen for several days without bringing any charges; perhaps the poor pastors had refused to take a loyalty oath or had incurred the wrath of Unionist neighbors.[25] In Tennessee, Andrew Johnson, with no small amount of plain spite imprisoned "secession preachers" and even contacted several midwestern governors about shipping them north under threat of being treated as spies should they dare return to Nashville. "Who are these reverend traitors that they should go unpunished for their crimes?" Johnson thundered. "They have pursued and corrupted boys and silly women, inculcated rebellion, and now let them suffer the penalty." Johnson himself had never shown much religious interest, and one of the ministers remarked—with no apparent irony-that in addressing them, the governor sounded most like an angry overseer speaking to slaves.[26]

Once a rebel preacher had been driven from his pulpit, the question became what to do with his church. Declaring an entire congregation disloyal,

Union officers might seize the building and grounds, a decision that solved one problem but created several more. As a practical matter, the church was often quickly restored to the trustees. Lincoln himself made the sensible point that if the army had need of a church building, "let them keep it," but otherwise "leave it and its owners alone." This was politically astute because Democrats in Congress had begun introducing resolutions about the seizure of churches, and the behavior of Federals troops did not help matters. When a group of soldiers played poker in an Alabama Baptist church, they treated the rebel house of worship with sly contempt. Churches sometimes became horse stables or even ammunition dumps but more commonly served as temporary field hospitals. This often involved removing pews and other items from the sanctuary; believing that "secesh" preachers had helped cause the war, some soldiers demolished pulpits for good measure.[27]

From the beginning of the war, the movements of armies, rumors, alarms, and of course battles had led churches to cancel services and even close for several weeks or longer. In Charleston, for instance, worship schedules largely depended on whether the Federals were shelling the city. To ardent Confederates, the silent sanctuaries where brave clerics had defied godless Yankees symbolized the despotism of their would-be conquerors and showed why the fight must continue. Doubting that the Federals would allow observance of a Confederate fast day, young Kate Carney in Murfreesboro, Tennessee, defiantly wrote in her diary, "They can't deprive us of our thoughts though I have no doubt they would, if they could." Even a children's magazine, after describing how the enemy arrested ministers, desecrated churches, and disrupted prayers, observed that such men were surely "blinded by fanaticism and infidelity."[28]

The damaged churches showed how in war there were literally no sanctuaries. Near Fairfax, Virginia, a church that had been used as a field hospital stood with a door open, windows torn out, stripped of furnishings. Many Baptist meeting houses in the state suffered extensive vandalism or complete destruction; in some counties, few churches survived the war unscathed, and eight colonial-era churches had reportedly been used as stables. After Sherman captured Savannah, Federal troops began constructing a new defensive line in a Catholic cemetery outside the city, and that provoked a heated exchange of letters between Bishop Augustin Verot and Edwin Stanton. At one point, the bishop even warned about excommunication, though it is doubtful that the fervently Protestant Secretary of War quailed at that threat. "Brutal force or infidel ideas may make light of such an ecclesiastical penalty, but there is a Power above which sides with the weak and defenseless and will act

Ruins of Circular Church, Charleston, South Carolina (Library of Congress)

in due time, slow or obscure its operation may be," the adamant Verot lectured the equally irascible Stanton. In the end, the bishop won the argument and the cemetery was restored.[29]

For churches, such as those in Vicksburg, caught between the contending armies, bursting shells ignited fires, or cannonballs left gaping holes in roofs and walls. What a later generation would term "collateral damage" caused no little sadness and outrage. Reports of churches burned or otherwise destroyed only reaffirmed commonly held Confederate assumptions that the Yankees waged war against the Almighty himself.[30]

The intentional destruction and desecration of sanctuaries proved even more shocking. Some church buildings were torn down for the lumber, which was then used for everything from soldier huts, to breastworks, to pontoons.

In one South Carolina town, Illinois troops ripped out the pews and pulpit from a large and beautiful church; siding and blinds suffered a similar fate; finally through the use of axes and poles, the entire building came crashing down. "There goes your damned old gospel shop," one derisive fellow yelled. Playing lewd songs on organs or scrawling obscenities on walls showed contempt for both Confederates and their religion. Conservative northerners deplored pointless mischief and destruction, even as Confederates wondered if their enemies were trying to destroy the consolations of faith. After visiting a badly damaged church, where Yankees had scribbled their names along with "blasphemous oaths" and "horrid pictures," Virginian Anne Frobel thought of a passage from Paul's first letter to the Corinthians: "If any man defile the temple of God, him shall God destroy."[31]

A Michigan lieutenant compared soldiers splitting wood and knocking out bricks to French revolutionary mobs. Nothing appeared sacred, at least if it was somehow associated with the hated southern rebellion. Smashing everything from pews to pianos, some men stole whatever they could get their hands on, including communion cups. If the local minister had been a notorious rebel, so much the better. Worse yet, whether intentionally or not, churches were sometimes burned to the ground as fire—one of the age's great terrors—became a weapon. After the sack of Darien, Georgia, and the burning of an Episcopal church by a South Carolina regiment made up of former slaves, their commander bluntly declared that southerners "were to be swept away by the hand of God, like the Jews of old."[32]

Despite considerable damage and sporadic destruction, churches remained places of worship for both members and visitors. Any northern soldier marching into a southern church on a Sunday morning attracted attention, curiosity, and plenty of stares. Congregations could be polite, sometimes even welcoming, but more often there was tension and discomfort on all sides. After the service, conversations tended to be awkward, stilted, or worse. At an Episcopal church near Baton Rouge, Louisiana, a dozen or so Union officers knew how to use the prayer books, and knelt at the proper times, but Sarah Morgan could not help being self-conscious, feeling so distracted she missed half the sermon. Members of such congregations simply kept their distance. "I cannot bear to be nearer than three or four pews," one Mississippi woman noted with precision. In a Kentucky church, worshipers had good reason to avoid contact because the Federals had been camping in the sanctuary and the place was crawling with lice. When soldiers crowded into churches and perhaps even occupied some of the choicest seats, they were bound to be met with hostile looks.[33]

Indeed, staring daggers at the Federals became one of the safest and in many ways a preferred form of resistance by ardently Confederate women. After attending a Methodist church in Jackson, Tennessee, an Illinois sergeant summed up the situation well: "The ladies no more come near us than they would a snake." This was especially insulting because the boys in his regiment had cleaned up to look respectable. A communion service in Winchester, Virginia, brought "the oppressors and the oppressed at the table of the Lord together," much to the dismay of diarist Cornelia McDonald. Some women simply refused to attend any service likely to be crowded with bluecoats, though it became a matter of some debate whether one was honor bound to beard the foe in the Lord's house. Wearing a thick veil conveyed the proper note of mourning and helped maintain a certain distance from the hated Yankees. It could be risky to push hostilities much further. In Vicksburg, General James B. McPherson banished five women who had stormed out of an Episcopal church when a minister dared pray for Lincoln.[34]

Such incidents raised fine points of etiquette involving worship and politics, but any soldiers entering a church in occupied territory were likely to run into what one Iowan termed "irreconcilables." He and several comrades joined a Sunday school near Carrollton, Louisiana, but were soon asked by the superintendent to stop attending. This was not an uncommon occurrence, and even men eager to teach children were ignored or turned away.[35] The local people might well consider such visitors a distraction, or at least that was the commonly offered excuse. At the same time, receiving the cold shoulder or worse on the Sabbath convinced many northern soldiers that any reconciliation with their erstwhile foes might take many more years.

———

Rebel fears that the Yankees intended to take over the southern churches were far from groundless. Chaplains preached in sanctuaries that stood empty or soldiers simply told the local minister that they would hold meetings in his church. All might appear harmonious when soldiers and members of the congregation sang in a joint choir, yet conflict and resentment were inevitable. For the Federals to gather in a church that held precious memories for its members (many of them rabid Confederates) brought a deep sadness as well as a mounting anger. According to one Alabama minister's wife, a Wisconsin chaplain apparently considered all the local people "quite heathenish" and even shoved a children's religious paper "highly perfumed with the extract of abolitionism" under her front door.[36]

Repeated denunciations of rebel preachers soon led to more serious efforts at spiritually transforming the southland. From the beginning of the war, northern Christians proposed sending missionaries south to advance the cause of the sacred Union and true religion. By early 1863 the Methodists were searching for the means to bring wayward southern brethren back into the fold. Bishops conferred about the need to "explore" Confederate territory and perhaps even lay claim to property owned by the Methodist Episcopal Church, South. Why not plant loyal, antislavery churches in Dixie? "It seems to me that Methodism must play a great part in the re-organization of Society in the South and South West," General Clinton B. Fisk advised Bishop Matthew Simpson. "We must 're-possess hold and occupy' the 'citadels of truth' that were captured from us twenty years ago." The devout and strongly antislavery Fisk hoped to excise the word "south" from the church and proposed starting in Missouri. Any delay in launching an aggressive missionary program in the southern states, a Methodist women's magazine warned, might allow the "treason-polluted and blood-stained" southern church to reoccupy its customary haunts.[37]

Talk of the Methodist Church as a body appointed by God to redeem the South blended hostility, self-righteousness, and arrogance in a mix that gave the whole endeavor a blinkered, crusading zeal. Annual conferences discussed sending ministers into conquered territory to redeem a benighted people from the twin thralldoms of rebellion and slavery.[38]

On November 30, 1863, Stanton issued the first of a series of orders granting Bishop Edward R. Ames authority to take over any church that did not have a "loyal" minister—meaning most churches under the jurisdiction of the Methodist Episcopal Church, South. The secretary of war believed that "Christian ministers should, by example and precept, support and foster the loyal sentiment of the people." The fifty-seven-year-old Ames had been a Methodist minister for more than three decades, had traveled widely in the South and West, and had acquired a reputation as a staunch antislavery man. Less than a month after receiving authorization from Stanton, he moved to take over churches in Arkansas, Tennessee, Mississippi, and Louisiana. In some cases, ministers suspected of rebel sympathies were turned out and consequently attendance remained spotty. In New Orleans, one northern Methodist warned that "if the Caucasian should reject the Gospel and refuse to fill the churches . . . we turn to the sons of Africa."[39]

Leading northern Methodists made little distinction between spreading the truth of the gospel and bringing the light of Unionism to the rebel states. They dismissed the inevitable criticism of political interference in the churches, but in fact Stanton's order and Ames's zeal became another embarrassment for the Lincoln administration. The bishop's supporters rightly worried that the president might well modify or rescind Stanton's order, and the protests from Missouri were especially strong. Not surprisingly, Attorney General Bates believed there was "not a shadow of law for what was done" and even accused northern Methodists of "coveting their neighbors' land." Once again church controversies exasperated Lincoln, who quoted earlier instructions to General Curtis and others while complaining of all the "embarrassment" caused by Stanton's order. The secretary finally had to exempt Missouri because it was not a Confederate state and claimed he had simply hoped to "rally the Methodist people in favor of the Union." Lincoln would have preferred the whole question disappear but patiently explained to one border state Methodist that, though the order was "liable to some abuses" even in the rebel states, "it is not quite easy to withdraw it entirely, and at once."[40]

Talk of moral regeneration exposed a kind of reckless chauvinism that hardly promised to win many southern converts—at least among the white population. The ambitious plans to crush the spirit of rebellion, plant northern churches, and at the same time promote reconciliation not only suffered from contradictory goals but also ran into considerable resistance. A complex and rancorous conflict over control of McKendree Chapel in Nashville, Tennessee, illustrated the volatile mix of local religion and national politics. Only a few months after the city fell to the Federals, that future giant of evangelism Dwight L. Moody held prayer meetings in the church; at the same time, however, military officials coveted the building for use as a barracks. Soon McKendree Chapel turned into a Methodist battleground. Bishop Matthew Simpson wanted one M. J. Cramer installed as pastor, but southern Methodist Samuel Baldwin pressed his claim, having courted conservative generals, and appealed directly to military governor Andrew Johnson. After telling anyone who would listen that Baldwin was a dangerous rebel, Cramer abruptly resigned to become an army chaplain. Johnson decided the church's former trustees were loyal enough to regain possession. Bishop Simpson soon learned that the keys to the building had not been handed over, so there was still a slim chance for the northern faction to retain control. Like the hopes of Ames and other northern church leaders, however, this one too was quickly dashed. When Johnson became president after Lincoln's assassination, he no longer breathed fire against "secesh preachers" but did get into a heated discussion with Simpson about McKendree Chapel. The church eventually reverted to the Methodist Episcopal Church, South, whose bishops still fumed over the entire affair.[41]

Fearing that Methodists and Baptists might gain the upper hand, Presbyterian leaders apparently asked the War Department to issue an order for military cooperation with their mission efforts. Exactly what that meant was far from clear, and in any case this was a more circumscribed document than the one Stanton had given to Bishop Ames. The Old School officially described the South as a "mission field" but hesitated to do much more during the war. The

New School commissioned a few missionaries, yet despite an occasional burst of crusading rhetoric was not much more energetic or successful.[42]

With political backing from Senator Ira Harris of New York, the American Baptist Home Mission Society received authority to take charge of abandoned Baptist meetinghouses or those without a "loyal" preacher. They seized control of some thirty buildings (though not for very long) and appointed pastors in several churches.[43] But the Baptists were little more successful than the Presbyterians and, along with the Methodists, faced stiff competition from the two main African American denominations.

After all, much of the mission work was directed toward southern blacks as well as southern whites. In 1863 AME bishop Daniel Payne arrived in Nashville where he was received by Andrew Johnson and soon took over a sanctuary formerly affiliated with the Methodist Episcopal Church, South. Payne preached a conservative message of sobriety, thrift, and piety, and his work prospered. Local black preachers were at times hostile or intimidated by the better-educated AME missionaries, and there were battles over worship styles and ordination requirements. AME ministers considered themselves agents of racial uplift and suggested that other northern churches limit their proselytizing to southern whites. Denominational rivalries and racial tensions flared up from the time to time, though AME bishops seldom visited the southern states and had little money to spend on mission work. Yet energy and optimism sometimes made up for the lack of resources. "The colored preachers North and South are truly loyal, heartily opposed to the rebellion and favorable to the government," one leading Methodist editor declared, but this cheerful statement could not mask the growing competition, or the fact that the AME (and to a lesser extent the AME Zion) churches were slowly winning the battle for black converts.[44]

"We must have a free Gospel, free labor, free press, and free education, and we must have ministers, and teachers and publishers to secure these blessings to us," was the way a leading Presbyterian organ summed up the views of Virginia Unionists about the church's mission in the South. In many ways, the missionaries of both races were the vanguard of efforts to reconstruct southern society and not coincidentally southern churches, all the while denouncing treason and slavery and proclaiming a gospel of freedom.[45]

In the view of many northern religious leaders, southern churches had been irredeemably tainted by slavery and rebellion. This meant that Yankees must head south to plant northern churches and deliver the souls of benighted whites and oppressed blacks. The missionary emphasis on racial progress applied equally to white southerners whom one Pennsylvania chaplain described as "very little less ignorant and degraded" than slaves. Grateful southerners would presumably welcome their northern benefactors and flock to their worship services. Unionists, refugees, or what one New York Congregationalist candidly termed "poor white trash" all offered an unprecedented opportunity for philanthropy.[46]

Here was a chance to redeem a desolated land and downtrodden people. The Lord had hardened rebel hearts just as he had Pharaoh's, but there remained a righteous remnant of Unionists. Northern civilization—and the more specific reference was of course to New England civilization—could yet save the churches. A millennial optimism suffused much of this thinking because there lay before the nation a vast and glorious prospect for true reform. The *Independent* predicted that southerners would turn against those religious leaders who had misled them into a disastrous war. Liberty would flourish in a land freed from oppressive hierarchies, cruel injustice, and perhaps even denominational squabbles. This new birth of the republic, an exultant Unitarian avowed, would foster "the noblest growths of civilization and Christianity" because the nation had arrived at a period of "glorious transfiguration." The dawning of righteousness in the southern churches and among the southern people would mark another triumph for the Kingdom of Christ.[47]

Chapter 18

CITIZENS, SAINTS, AND SOLDIERS

Render therefore unto Caesar the things which are Caesar's; and unto God the things that are God's.
— Matthew 22:21

And fear not them which kill the body, but are not able to kill the soul: but rather fear him which is able to destroy both soul and body in hell.
— Matthew 10:28

"Paul, in death, was not more loyal to his Lord than I . . . am to the cause of the Union," an Illinois Methodist minister proclaimed in 1864, and he spoke for a growing number of people in both sections of the divided land who had long since stopped drawing much of a distinction between patriotism and religion. The impetus for sending missionaries south and perhaps even for vandalizing rebel churches stemmed from a belief that the flag and the cross marched together, that national allegiance and religious faith could not be separated. For many northern Methodists, loyalty to the government also meant loyalty to the Lincoln administration and support for its policies. Ministers and lay leaders came to sound like Republican politicians when they accused Democratic critics of prolonging the war. This left little room for dissenting views, and editor Thomas Eddy called for the "social outlawry of every man and woman whose position is doubtful."[1]

In May 1864 the General Conference meeting in Philadelphia did not go quite this far but did call for prosecuting the war until the "wicked rebellion is subdued." And, at last, northern Methodists took a bold and unequivocal stand on slavery. Asserting that the nation's "calamities" had stemmed from "our forgetfulness of God and from slavery," the delegates endorsed permanent abolition by constitutional amendment. "Providence has at length mysteriously led us through the struggles of ages to the highest unity in the assertion and vindication of the highest right," the pastoral address concluded. The delegates voted overwhelmingly (207–9) to amend the church discipline to prohibit church members from holding slaves.[2]

The Methodists were proud of their work, so proud in fact they sent five delegates from the General Conference to present an address to Lincoln trumpeting their patriotism and commitment to emancipation. The president no doubt appreciated their warm support and welcomed even more the thousands of Methodists in uniform. He noted how all the churches had sustained the government and did not want to "appear invidious against any" but added, "it may be fairly said that the Methodist Episcopal Church . . . [is] by its greatest numbers, the most important of all." It "sends more soldiers to the field, more nurses to the hospital, and more prayers to Heaven than any." Such generous remarks only made the Methodists more confident about following God's will—indeed far more confident than the president. Nor were they much concerned about the relationship between means and ends. One Illinois Methodist who favored "confiscation, subjugation, and extermination" suggested using "Negroes, mules, brickbats. . . . small arms, large arms and bayonets to kill rebels and crush rebellion."[3]

He might have added "emancipation" to the list because by 1864, several denominations—including conservative ones—were moving in that direction. In May 1864 Old School Presbyterians decided that "the time has at length come, in the providence of God, when it is His will that every vestige of human slavery among us should be effaced" and that "every Christian" should take "his appropriate part in the performance of this great duty." Some church leaders admitted they had been wrong (or at least laggard) on this question, and now the Old School finally and forthrightly endorsed the government's emancipation policies. Lutherans and Episcopalians with some hesitation and equivocation fell into line. Objections to "political preaching" suddenly seemed quaint and antiquated (though not exactly dead); those who did not want to proclaim freedom from the pulpit nevertheless privately acknowledged that the hand of God had turned against slavery.[4]

Heavily pro-Democratic Catholics remained divided and as with other northern Christians, racial considerations shaped both political and religious thinking. Claims that emancipation would spawn miscegenation or that enfranchised blacks would outvote the Irish or that abolitionists planned to revive Know Nothingism all struck a responsive chord, and one persistently played by Democrats. Fear that partisan considerations might enter into church business or worse contaminate church life often served as a convenient excuse for sidestepping questions surrounding both the war and slavery. Indeed, leading Catholics still had to fend off old canards about their faith being hostile to democracy itself, and some Protestants, such as the editors of the *Independent*, cited the church's official calls for peace as evidence that the papacy was somehow in league with the rebels. Worries about Catholic power persisted, thus making church leaders especially sensitive to Protestant attacks on their loyalty.[5]

American emphasis on religious voluntarism left the relations between faith and politics to be continually worked out because for all the conventional talk about separation between church and state, that word "separation" seemed clearer in theory than it ever proved to be in practice. Some religious leaders believed the problem went back to the nation's founding documents and their silence on religion. Ever since Horace Bushnell in the summer of 1861 had questioned the idea of resting government on Jeffersonian theorizing, orthodox voices had complained about a "godless Constitution" that made no reference to a higher power. The "absence of any recognition of the sovereignty of God," Presbyterian Henry A. Boardman lamented, gave the lie to the whole idea of the United States being a "Christian nation." What another minister termed the "almost entire separation of the principles of the gospel from our political life" had left public affairs in the hands of "ungodly men" and an "ungodly press." As a pious New York soldier put it, "our head men and rulers was ones that was so wicked" they "did not care for any thing, only for their own good, and not for the good of the Nation."[6]

In early 1864 representatives from eleven Protestant denominations established the National Reform Association. They proposed amending the Constitution's preamble by adding the words, "humbly acknowledging Almighty God as the source of all authority, the Lord Jesus Christ as the Ruler among nations, his revealed will as the supreme law of the land, in order to constitute a Christian government." Methodists, Presbyterians, and several smaller denominations offered their support, and petitions were presented to Congress and the president. When a group of ministers visited the White House, Lincoln was on his guard. "The general aspect of your movement I cordially approve," he responded warily. It would, however, take time to deliberate on the details because "amending the Constitution should not be done hastily."[7]

The president never referred to the United States as a Christian nation, but Byron Sunderland, Presbyterian and chaplain of the Senate, readily declared that the "mighty elements of pure Christianity" gave the country its character and shaped its destiny. In an early 1864 sermon preached in the House of Representatives, he denied that the constitutional protection against established religion meant that the founding fathers "intend[ed] to make us an infidel nation, nor our Government an impious and God-forsaken iniquity." And increasingly there were calls for explicit recognition of Christ in official proclamations and in the Constitution. In asking, "Shall we be a Christian nation?" one Presbyterian dismissed any "senseless clamor about church and state." An angry Methodist considered it an outrage that "our Presidents dare not speak the name of Jesus in their messages."[8]

Confederates had proudly invoked the name of God in their Constitution. Even late in the war, a South Carolina editor pointed to what he saw as a revealing fact: the Federal Constitution—with no reference to the Almighty—"could have been passed and adopted by Atheists or Hindoes or Mahometans." Yet the Confederate founders had not gone nearly far enough for the more devout. Their acknowledgment of the Lord, Methodist bishop George Foster Pierce advised the Georgia legislature, "uses the language of deism, or natural religion, rather than of Christianity." The Jews had remained isolated and scattered because they had refused to recognize the son of God, and perhaps a similar fate now awaited the Confederacy.[9]

Portentous signs always appeared to those obsessed with looking for them. As each side debated whether it was a Christian nation, the war itself kept intruding into the discussions. By September 1864 Grant was starting to encircle Petersburg, and Sherman had advanced to the outskirts of Atlanta, so both Federals and Confederates sought to read the signs of the times and place them within a providential framework.

———

"May God hasten the day when this cruel war will be brought to a close," one Iowan wrote in his diary in the midst of the Atlanta campaign. He hoped the Lord would "hasten the day when the rebels will lay down their arms and return again to their homes" but recognized that many good men might yet fall. "May God be with us and help us as we stand in need, for he is a God of battles." The belief that the Lord threw his loving arms around faithful soldiers still comforted some men even as they longed for the fighting to cease. Would God forgive their bloody work, one Michigan soldier wondered, but decided the only thing he could do was "utter my own prayers for the safety of my poor soul and my country."[10]

After three years of hard fighting, however, religious thinking on the war—especially among the soldiers—had fractured. Even the Federal capture of Atlanta, which guaranteed Lincoln's reelection, produced reactions that ran the gamut from simple gratitude to deep cynicism. "I believe the Lord is on our side," a New York private stationed at Hilton Head, South Carolina, wrote on hearing the news. "It cant be other wise . . . we shall as a nation shine forth in the world as free people and nation whoes God is the Lord and him will I serve." This conventional statement might have been made at any time over the past three years, but the faithful also began to sound more sober-minded. In Atlanta, General John W. Geary naturally rejoiced over the "glories of victory which God has vouchsafed to give us" but also felt sad for the poor sufferers in the city, who "mope around the corners as if some unearthly catastrophe had occurred." Geary could only conclude, "Babylon is fallen." For other soldiers, seeking any heavenly purpose in all the misery and destruction seemed absurd or obscene. After observing firsthand the "ruin and desolation in Atlanta," Captain John Henry Otto from Wisconsin sounded almost like Sherman himself: "War is cruelty and barbarism on a large scale." He could hardly believe that people "argued and upheld stubbornly that a mercifull, All-wise, Allmighty God ordains and conducts wars to obtain his ends." Adding a note of skepticism typical of many German volunteers, he asked, "Is there not a considerable sprinkling of pure, genuine blasphemy hidden in such arguments?"[11]

A few Confederates might have agreed with that last assessment because despite revivals in the Army of Tennessee, it had become hard to find signs of divine favor. Throughout the summer, the meetings had continued even as the armies maneuvered and occasionally fought. "There will be more Christians under the leadership of General Johnston in the next great battle than ever faced the foe in this army," claimed one report. "Some of the happiest men I have ever seen were in the battle of Resaca." Such a combination of fervor, expectation, exaggeration, and nonsense showed how reports of revivalism still fueled Confederate optimism. As Johnston's army fell back into the Atlanta defenses, the prayer meetings continued, and soldiers attended local services, where they appeared far more intent on worship than the well-dressed civilians. There was preaching within sight of the enemy lines, and the Federals reported hearing songs and even shouts late into the night, though occasionally skirmishers mischievously broke up the proceedings.[12]

The Confederate withdrawal toward Atlanta stunned patriotic civilians. During what one farmer's wife living near Marietta, Georgia, termed the "dark, dark days," affirming the Lord's promises would "never fail" buttressed civilian courage but added to the emotional and spiritual jolt when Atlanta finally fell to the Federals. Hope gave way to despondency and fear that perhaps God had at last abandoned the Confederacy. A Mississippi Baptist association pledged to "bow with submission to our lot," words that bespoke more convention than conviction. The usual warnings about divine chastisement and even laments about southerners ready to prostrate themselves before the northern Baal sounded at once formulaic and ominous.[13]

Familiar religious comforts survived, a bit shopworn by this time but still serviceable. As a soldier's term of enlistment was about to end, he might marvel over all he had endured and survived, but sitting beside a mortally wounded friend made an Ohio volunteer recall that "God's ways are not our ways." However clichéd, such expressions suggested a higher purpose and sense of order that during the summer and fall of 1864 must have seemed quite hard to fathom. After several men had been killed near Petersburg, Alabama chaplain J. J. D. Renfroe preached a sermon, "The Resurrection of the Confederate Soldier," pointing out how the price of liberty had to be paid in blood. Had not Jesus said without the shedding of blood, there is no remission of sin? On the other side of the lines, with the ultimate sacrifice paid, Chaplain Garland H. White of the 28th United States Colored Troops rejoiced, "some of our troops fell in the harness of faith and hope in Christ, and to-day I believe they are far away from a land of battle, carnage and blood, where prejudice and scorn are not known."[14] For soldier and civilian alike, the continuation of a religious awakening in the armies and occasional sparks of revival at home rekindled hopes of personal if not necessarily national salvation.

———

Confederates still relied on army missionaries to assist the chaplains in promoting revivalism, though one artillerist complained that fewer evangelists appeared to be visiting the camps. A skeptical Alabama soldier decided it would be better if the "whole set of Chaplains had guns put in their hands." A real and immediate "fear of death" would no doubt improve their sermons, he thought.[15] However that might be, revivals in the Confederate camps had been going on for more than two years and had become a regular feature of army life. At the same time, more continuous fighting and 1864's long casualty lists may have simultaneously thwarted evangelism and made the need for saving souls seem ever more urgent. By September and especially in the Petersburg entrenchments, there were renewed signs of religious interest. Despite the North's ostensible organizational superiority, when it came to camp religion, Confederates appeared to have the advantage. Even in the trans-Mississippi theater, worship services attracted good crowds.[16]

For the Federals, the hard fighting of the spring, summer, and early fall had also made it harder to keep the spiritual fires glowing. A devout New Jersey colonel had reported "pretty good attendance" at evening prayer services even during the summer but sadly added that "many of those that formerly met with us are now killed, wounded and missing." With the beginning of the Petersburg campaign as the armies became more stationary, interest and attendance picked up. By November there were some seventy meetings a week in the 5th and 9th corps. As the weather grew cooler, soldiers erected the usual wood and canvass chapels, and at Poplar Grove near Petersburg, the 50th New York Engineers constructed an elaborate structure of hewn logs complete with an impressive Gothic spire.[17] After the fall of Atlanta in September, more regular services resumed in Sherman's army as well. Chaplains preached to fair-sized congregations and Christian Associations added members. By late September a group of believers in an Illinois regiment was planning a series of protracted meetings; camp Sunday schools and even choirs flourished.[18]

The most conventionally evangelical messages could not avoid touching on the soldiers' anguish during this year of horrific bloodshed. In late Octo-

Log Church built by 50th New York Engineers, Poplar Grove, Virginia
(Library of Congress)

ber a New York chaplain preached on the text from the prophet Amos, "Prepare to meet thy God," reminding the men how their lives had thus far been
spared while many of their comrades had been wounded or killed. A Christian Commission delegate preferred Paul's exhortation, "present your bodies
a living sacrifice unto God." Such passages naturally led men to think about
their families and reflect on their own mortality. Yet rather than focusing on

national troubles, chaplains simply called on the men to repent of their sins, and some soldiers turned their thoughts from earthly troubles toward heavenly mansions. There was no doubt that the Overland campaign and Grant's relentless pressure against Lee's army had stirred new doubts and fears. The tireless Alabama chaplain J. J. D. Renfroe noted how the children of Israel had often faced bitter disappointment and had murmured against Moses and the Lord. Indeed, in the current situation, God appeared at times to "crush out hopes," but Christ would lead men to the tree of life.[19]

That was precisely the point: individual salvation loomed much larger and certainly more achievable than southern independence. Wartime events almost seemed beside the point. Repentance and especially the conversions in the army raised the usual hopes that better men might make better soldiers, or at least more virtuous ones. Camp revivals, according to one New York pastor, had led to sharp declines in "drunkenness, gambling, and licentiousness" and therefore the returning veterans would not "deluge our cities and villages with vice and blasphemy." In turn, these righteous believers waged a holy war against just the kind of traitors King David and the Old Testament prophets had so condemned and detested. Among men who had seen the worst of the fighting, however, civil religion could wear thin. "There is no God in war," an Illinois surgeon wrote in disgust as Sherman's men neared Savannah, Georgia. "It is merciless cruel, vindictive, unchristian, savage, relentless. It is all devils could wish for."[20]

For most Confederates, the war had become all these things and more, yet piety and specifically prayer still offered comfort for the individual soul if not for the nation. Pleas for deliverance grew especially intense on the eve of battle during this year of unimaginable carnage. In the Petersburg trenches during the fall and winter, the praying, singing, and preaching all proceeded despite general misery and occasional shelling. Small groups gathered to hear the scriptures expounded, but unfortunately enthusiastic services could draw enemy fire. One chaplain distributed tracts as mortar rounds arced across the lines, and even baptisms could be interrupted by calls to battle. Worshipers were occasionally wounded, and one hapless Georgian was reportedly killed by a Parrott shell while still clasping his Bible.[21]

Heart-rending accounts of such incidents soon reached the home folks, yet at the same time any news of civilian revivals heartened Christian soldiers. Reports of meetings, conversions, and baptisms circulating between camp and home encouraged the pious by reaffirming that the Lord still stood with the Confederates. Whether success in the camps had bred success at home, accounts of large meetings, intense interest, and more Christian soldiers again made the fall and winter a time of spiritual renewal. "I never saw men pay better attention to preaching," a Methodist chaplain serving with Lee's army rejoiced. It was moving to see "hardy sunburnt" warriors eagerly listening to a sermon as they prepared for battle. Even in bad weather and in the absence of pulpit spellbinders, the turnout for services remained impressive. Reports of two dozen converts here or a hundred men baptized there all signified the continuance of what many Confederates considered a great religious awakening. From the army of Northern Virginia to the widely scattered forces in the trans-Mississippi came enthusiastic and optimistic accounts of a bounteous spiritual harvest.[22]

Some of these claims were no doubt overblown, but even toward the end of the war, church leaders were still trying to figure how best to organize army missions. When there was little good news for the Confederate cause, descriptions of army revivals in both the religious and secular press showed the staying power of evangelical religion in the beleaguered southern nation. Yet how powerful this great work of the Holy Spirit had been remained a matter of dispute; some soldiers doubted the revivals had yet touched most of their comrades. "The papers state that there is a very perceptible improvement in the religious feelings of this [Lee's] army," General Bryan Grimes told his wife. "If so I have been unable to discover it, for I fear we are all an ungodly lot." In the West, a Georgia soldier agreed that "it is awful to think of the wickedness and corruption attending an army," and he doubted there was "enough goodness" in the ranks to save them from destruction.[23]

Many pious folk clung to the belief that the conversion of so many soldiers would surely cause the Lord to smile on Confederate arms once more. In some cases, camp revivals literally revived confidence in both the Lord and the cause, with optimists still anticipating victories against the forces of darkness, whether spiritual or temporal. Indeed, there was an important cultural contrast here between revivals in the Federal and rebel armies. Confederate revivals were news and not only in the religious press. Reports of meetings and conversions reinforced widespread claims to superior virtue and ultimately laid the groundwork for the persistence of such beliefs even in defeat. Lee himself hoped that a religiously regenerated southern nation would eventually receive its just reward. If not, the comforts of heaven would have to suffice. For the most devout and the most patriotic, as one Confederate recalled, "disaster seemed only to strengthen the faith," though increasingly this faith would have to rely on some miraculous deliverance that defied human comprehension. Even so, all these outpourings of God's spirit must eventually be followed by Confederate independence; such was the theological and political reasoning.[24] The Confederate revivals had in fact been more widespread and certainly more publicized than those in the Union camps; so too Confederates were more likely to link the army meetings to military success.

———

"Stand by the flag and the cross," advised one young Federal soldier on his deathbed as he affirmed both the Union's civil religion and the preachers' evangelical message. More than any signs of spiritual renewal among the soldiers, many northerners looked to the war itself for evidence of divine favor. Even if the Confederates managed to "whip Grant and drive Sherman to the Ohio and burn the cities of Pa.," remarked one private, "I will still believe that they must be finally destroyed. I cannot believe that Providence intends to destroy this Nation." These words expressed a bedrock faith that could not be easily shaken, even by the butcher's bill of 1864. The nation appeared to be passing through what chaplain Henry McNeal Turner of the 1st United States Colored Troops termed a "terrible revolution" to "purge her from the dross of base corruption." Then, echoing Horace Bushnell's famous sermon delivered after the Federal disaster at First Bull Run, Turner concluded, "Reverses, political and moral, may sometimes be commuted for glorious ends." Religious thinking could focus on the immediate or even the distant future, though there was much more of the millennium than the apocalypse here. Even bitter laments often carried with them a conviction that all things would work for the glory of the Lord and of the Union. Peace seemed far away and reports of discord at home certainly disheartened one Hoosier volunteer, who nevertheless expected the Almighty would "put to naught the designs of wicked men."[25]

This all assumed that the Union still merited divine favor. Just to be on the safe side, and with the war once again in an apparent stalemate, Congress had passed a joint resolution in early July calling on the president to appoint a "day for humiliation and prayer," but this time Lincoln's proclamation did not elaborate on the lawmakers' pious platitudes. In their customary way, the religious press prodded public officials and private citizens to be truly repentant, but calls for people to humble themselves before God had already been overused. Were the ministers and their congregations merely going through the motions, reciting the usual litany of sins? Northerners seemed deeply depressed if not demoralized—as well they might be from scanning the long casualty lists in the newspapers.[26]

Perhaps the people themselves, including many good Christians, had grown cold and indifferent, not only to their country but to their redeemer's cause. Too many citizens were quick to criticize while seeming to stand aloof from the bloody contest, one Catholic editor lamented. A Pennsylvania minister complained about "professed Christians" ignoring the Sabbath by taking a "pleasure trip on an excursion train." Maintaining both patriotic commitment and religious faith became much harder after more than three years of war even if much pious nationalism survived. Conflicting beliefs and emotions tossed people this way and that, especially during a summer of intense fighting. Only God could carry the Union cause to victory, claimed one Hoosier who deplored the political divisiveness back home; at the same time, he could not help but express soaring hopes for his country: "May America yet carry liberty and religion to all the nations of the earth."[27]

Christian patriotism sometimes consisted of little more than glittering generalities. Talk of a righteous nation included partisan blasts against dissenters that in turn provoked Democrats to make their usual denunciations of politics in the pulpit. Like the preachers, soldiers speculated that the nation had not yet suffered enough for its transgressions or that the bloodshed was being used to achieve some end known only to God. The war itself had become the ultimate punishment for sin and, according to one Quaker editor, could produce only an "insidious moral poison" that would destroy countless lives and encourage vices such as intemperance. In the face of such evils, human beings appeared powerless to stop the young men not only from being corrupted but also from being slaughtered.[28]

Providential interpretations of the conflict still found adherents. For some people, invoking divine providence remained a least common denominator of civil religion; for others, it was the best way to express both patriotic and spiritual fervor. Expectations of easy victory had long since vanished, and certainly repeating the ancient wisdom that the ways of God were not the ways of man carried a new ring of truth. At least the nation had finally realized the sinfulness of slavery, one Michigan Presbyterian minister declared, so the war had proved once again that the Lord's justice must ultimately triumph. Faith in providence also meant affirming—as had been done ever since the summer of 1861—that God was instrumental in conducting the war, directing the campaigns, and fighting the battles. "I firmly believe the Lord is laying out a work for me to do," one midwesterner explained to his wife, and that was why he had to be away from home so long. Serving the Union cause still meant serving the Lord. As one African American private put it, "The blessing of Almighty God is better than the army of Butler, surer than the rifle of Burnside, and sharper than the sword of Grant." Battles would be fought and men would fall, but the Lord's kingdom could not be shaken by even the bloodiest war.[29]

Religious orthodoxy proved to be remarkably flexible, and the Christian patriot had little trouble explaining disappointments and defeats. Did not the scriptures warn against crying for peace when there was no peace? Thus, even copperheadism had a biblical precedent. Preachers, editors, and countless ordinary believers readily found a providential, if not exactly a heartening, explanation for all the anguish and bloodletting. References to the darkest days of the American Revolution accompanied calls for remaining faithful to the Lord and to the Union.[30]

For their part, Confederates had always claimed to be the legitimate heirs of the American founding fathers and by the fall of 1864 must have believed their suffering more than equaled that of those great patriots. Worse still, the war had unleashed the most destructive passions. In late July 1864, when rebel cavalry torched Chambersburg, Pennsylvania, even a few devoted Confederates were frightened and appalled when they recalled that vengeance belonged to the Lord. How could they ask God's blessing on such work? Eliza Fain suggested southerners use the official day set apart by Lincoln to pray for (though perhaps not forgive) their enemies. Confederates might ask the Lord to show the Yankees the error of their ways so they would end the foraging, raiding, and killing. One Methodist missionary advised displaying "Christian kindness" toward the "vandals of the North who have come to desolate our homes and destroy our country."[31]

Increasingly, Confederates placed themselves in a great narrative of suffering. In this hour of woes, some thought the privations and bloodshed had prepared them to read, study, and embrace the word of God like never before. Newly converted soldiers could serve their country devotedly, go into battle calmly, and if necessary die confidently. At the same time, even the orthodox wondered if God had forsaken the Confederacy but could always fall back on the proposition that the people were simply being punished for their manifold sins. In the midst of darkness and gloom, hope survived that the Lord would still vindicate the Confederate cause. After General (and former Episcopal bishop) Leonidas Polk had been killed by a stray Union artillery round at Pine Mountain, Georgia, in June 1864, Stephen Elliott warned that northern Christians faced a terrible reckoning at the "judgment-seat of Christ" for "fanning . . . the fury of this unjust and cruel war" and predicted that the lives destroyed by northern armies "will be returned upon you [the Federals] in blood a thousand-fold." Elliott would leave such vengeance to God (so he said), but he eagerly invoked divine judgment and wrath. A South Carolina woman living on a farm near Columbia believed that the Almighty would severely judge Yankee women, "a cold, hard, unfeeling set who will sell their very souls for fine clothes and fine furniture."[32]

The Confederacy had become caught up in a military, political, emotional, and theological whirlwind. Each new battle, each bit of news, and each rumor raised painful questions and summoned up a welter of contradictory thoughts and feelings. "It seems like the Lord has turned his face from us and left us to work out our own destruction," a Georgia soldier worried. Growing anxiety about the southern nation's fate could not always be separated from increasing worry about individual salvation. "My mind has been so full of doubts of God's goodness and mercy today," young Virginian Lucy Breckinridge wrote in her diary. "I have been so sinful. I read my Bible and prayed, but the light of God's countenance was withdrawn from me." A typical lament, but she quickly connected her own dark thoughts to the "gloomy state of the country." Perhaps the Lord had, according to a circular letter sent to several Georgia Baptist churches, "forsaken us and left us to wail, to weep, and to mourn."[33]

No longer did public statements avoid raising the most troublesome questions, including the possibility that the Almighty willed the scattering and destruction of southern churches. Talk of divine chastisement or the rod of correction had taken on a much deeper meaning in the lives of denominations, congregations, and believers. When preachers ran through the familiar list of sins, there was more emphasis on a looming judgment than there had been in the past, as the whole tenor of Confederate civil religion took on an almost funereal tone. Preachers trotted out Jeremiah and other gloomy prophets as appropriate sources of wisdom on both individual and national declension. Men especially, one South Carolina woman pointedly suggested, needed to place less value on personal honor and more value on their country's welfare and on Christ's kingdom.[34]

Human endurance, not to mention human power, had seemingly reached its limits. On a fast day proclaimed by Georgia governor Joe Brown in September 1864, Stephen Elliott chose to preach on the Psalmist's cry, "Vain is the help of man." That Confederates had been dependent on God from the beginning of the war but had too often tried to rely on the "arm of flesh" seemed by now obvious. Every six months or so, Elliott observed, the people had humbled themselves and prayed for deliverance, and their prayers had always been answered, a pattern noted many times before. Elliott detailed the devastation of the southern landscape, including the burning of churches, but then sounded an even more ominous, grave, and confessional note. Many men of property, including politicians, had failed to make the necessary sacrifices or even support the cause; worse yet selfish extortioners had taken full advantage of the people's suffering. Like the children of Israel murmuring against Moses, Confederates had been quick to lose heart and complain.

Though proceeding entirely according to a divine plan, war had brought nothing but what Elliott termed a "harvest of death." He still held that God could not possibly intend the South's "subjugation," yet the sermon also touched on some vulnerable and sensitive points before retreating into denial. Leading southerners had long dismissed northern abolitionists as "false" philanthropists, but Elliott maintained in the face of substantial evidence to the contrary that southern slaves had remained quietly contented. Yet, without worrying about the inconsistency, he then pointed to the horrible suffering of those black men and women who had run off to the Yankees, claiming that at least half of them had perished. In an even bolder leap of illogic, Elliott expected recent Union victories and the anticipated reelection of Lincoln to strengthen the southern cause by sparking a patriotic revival. The northern people, Elliott predicted, would turn against each other in a reenactment of the French Revolution.[35]

It was hardly surprising that Elliott warned his listeners against expecting the European powers or northern Democrats to save the situation, but this surreal combination of combativeness and delusion did not mesh well with calls for the southern people to cast their cares on the Lord. The rhythms of Confederate civil religion proved to be remarkably persistent in the face of military disasters. The sight of women and children fleeing their homes around Petersburg, Virginia, led a South Carolina enlisted man to wonder if his country remained under divine protection. Yet his only advice was for all people to humble themselves and acknowledge their dependence on the Almighty. "May we live," one pious Alabama farmer intoned in October 1864, "as to draw off gods frowns from us in this terrible war." Talk of sackcloth and ashes strongly suggested that Elliott was right: Confederate armies could accomplish nothing unless the Lord of Hosts once again smiled on the southern cause.[36]

Raising the point to a still more abstract level, an editorial in the *Charleston Mercury* appearing on an officially proclaimed day of worship in November 1864 seemed to echo from seventeenth-century New England: "Human reason is incompetent to [explain] the ways of God to man, and therefore humility, submission, and trust are the height of wisdom." Jefferson Davis's own pastor, Charles Minnigerode, preached about the power of God being beyond the comprehension of human beings, whose only recourse was to redouble their faith. Members of the congregation must have surely noticed the contrast between divine omnipotence and the all-too-human power that was steadily slipping away from both the Confederate government and their most prominent parishioner, Jefferson Davis. Even while emphasizing the fiendishness of the enemy, the president's call for a day of prayer had used the word "chastisement" in one form or another three times.[37]

Suitably enough for such a despondent period, when the day of prayer brought rain across the Confederacy, many civilians stayed home or there was no preaching. In Columbus, Mississippi, Episcopal chaplain Charles Todd

Quintard turned to that most difficult text from Matthew: "Think not that I am come to send peace on earth: I came not to send peace, but a sword." Whether that sword would slay the Yankee invaders or the southern people remained an open question, despite the many pious voices affirming that Confederates were still the chosen ones. "God does not forget his elect amidst wars and desolation," a Presbyterian editor bravely maintained. After reviewing how denominational strife had led to war and while admitting the guilt of many Confederates, a Baptist preacher concluded that "faith once delivered to the Saints has been maintained in its integrity and purity throughout the States of the South." Despite the North's now overwhelming advantages in numbers and strength, God's favor would yet bring Confederates to the promised land of independence.[38]

The weaker side could emerge victorious so long as the southern people passed the test of faith. To recognize that God ruled, that his will prevailed over all human plans and expectations meant standing firm and not having one's convictions buffeted by every alarm or defeat. Did not the Bible include many accounts of miraculous deliverance? Trying to shore up courage at home, a Methodist chaplain wrote to his wife of "unchanged hope in ultimate success." The prayers of the righteous remained mightier than mere carnal weapons, and the preachers repeatedly pointed out how victories had often followed seasons of repentance and prayer, a providential interpretation of the war's course that refused to die. The staunchly patriotic Episcopal bishop Richard Wilmer believed the cloud of despair and rod of punishment would be lifted once the erring children had truly repented. Yet Wilmer and others had been preaching the same message for three years now, and still the war dragged on with Confederate prospects growing ever dimmer. A soldier stationed at Fort Sumter tried to split theological hairs by saying he did not believe in a "general dispensation of an Almighty Providence" but held out hope for a "particular dispensation of a special Providence." Other pious men looked for signs of divine blessing and an early peace, straining to catch the faintest glimpse of any portent that was in the least promising.[39]

But would the Lord offer this generation any sign at all? "God's hand alone can draw curtains aside and reveal what He has so wisely hidden from our view," a young Georgia woman mused. The future would be "drawn by a Master's hand . . . directed by a hand of love and mercy." That the Almighty would "overrule all" for the good of his children became a catchphrase for Confederates who had no other basis for expecting much good news. Sufferers had long declared that God would never lay more burdens upon them than they could bear. That proposition must have seemed increasingly doubtful, though civilians and soldiers alike had little choice but to embrace it.[40]

Citing a famous passage from Jeremiah about how the Lord shapes nations like a potter molds clay, the Reverend J. L. Burrows believed this image presented a "striking illustration of the passive helplessness of the nations in the hands of God!" The great Jehovah could "build them up, or He can dash them to pieces," he observed, echoing the psalmist. Whether the Confederacy survived was up to the Almighty; General Lee himself remained only an instrument of divine will. "God has not altogether forsaken us," the president of a North Carolina Lutheran Synod declared, though his choice of adverb was not very reassuring. Providence had made the ancient Hebrews an independent and separate people and could do the same for the Confederacy, but that analogy perhaps raised more fears than hopes because the Lord had ultimately destroyed ancient Israel, sending the Jews into exile, and eventually scattering them across the face of the earth. Even believers who held that the Almighty would ultimately give the southern people peace were no longer sure he would also grant them victory.[41]

The emphasis shifted from military or political triumphs to spiritual ones; saving souls had become more important than even saving a nation. In the trenches around Petersburg, Virginia, captain Richard Joseph Manson prayed that the Lord would "spare the lives of our soldiers and give them of Thy holy spirit." He yearned for peace but again there was no mention of military success. Admittedly, Manson was more devout than even many of his pious comrades, but others too found comfort in the fact that the enemy might destroy their bodies but could not touch their souls. While seeking to rally support for the war, religious editors put increasing emphasis on spiritual assurance. If sinful Confederates had indeed lost God's favor, they must turn their minds and hearts to securing a heavenly home.[42]

Their earthly homes and, indeed, most of their earthly dreams had seemingly been like the biblical house built on sand, and no Union general did more to prove that point, especially in Georgia during the autumn of 1864 and the Carolinas during the winter of 1865, than William Tecumseh Sherman. Sherman believed that war unfolded according to natural, in some ways mathematical, laws and doubted that God played any role at all. War took on a life of its own, beyond human understanding and control, hardly amenable to even the Lord's will. Sherman had a deep, almost spiritual commitment to the Union and certainly viewed the southern rebellion as satanic in origin. As a young army officer, however, he had denied professing any "particular creed" while accepting "the main doctrines of the Christian religion." Sherman refused to embrace his wife's Catholicism, once remarking that Ellen was "pious enough for half a dozen ordinary families." "Providence," he admitted, appeared entirely "inscrutable to me."[43]

As Sherman's army left burned-out Atlanta and began the famous March to the Sea, soldiers had to adjust to a new (though hardly unprecedented) type of war characterized by relentless foraging and, at times, mindless destruction. Confederates then and later would exaggerate their suffering, but the blue-coats themselves remained often painfully ambivalent about what they saw— if not necessarily about what they did. Religious and moral scruples hardly disappeared. With considerable overstatement, one Union general and staunch Presbyterian compared the devastation in Georgia to the Israelites ravaging the land of Canaan.[44]

White Georgians could easily believe that Lucifer himself had taken on the shape of General Sherman or that the Beast mentioned in Revelation had suddenly conferred superhuman power on the Yankees. Many civilians bravely tried to keep up their spirits or even defiantly face the onslaught. But patience and simple prayers for deliverance became the more common responses among those who still believed that the Lord might spare them the worst. A resilient faith, familiar scriptures, and spiritual reassurance both steeled them for the arrival of Sherman's men and helped them survive the ordeal. "Helpless, oh, how utterly helpless!" one plantation mistress cried out on a day when her house was searched by Federal troops. "And yet blessed be God! We feel that we are in the hollow of His almighty hand. It is a precious, precious feeling that the omnipotent, omnipresent Jehovah is with us, and that Jesus, our Divine Redeemer and Advocate, will be touched with our sorrows."[45]

Believers who escaped the worst or fared better than other families attributed it all to God's mercy and goodness. If the Yankees decided not to burn a house, it was the Lord's doing. Like many soldiers, civilians bravely declared they need not fear those who could harm the body but not the soul. In the midst of so much suffering, some prayed that the Almighty's avenging hand would strike Sherman and his minions. That God would leave such deeds unpunished seemed unthinkable, but then that assertion had been made almost since the war's beginning.[46]

By the time Sherman's men reached Savannah, the Confederacy was physically, emotionally, and spiritually exhausted. On Christmas Day, some of the Federal troops took up a collection for orphans in the city because Confederate money was now worthless. Despite reports that Sherman's men were a godless lot, many crowded into local churches or regimental meetings. Civilians appeared disheartened and subdued though at times rebellious.[47]

Yet the heart of Confederate resistance, including religious defiance, had been seriously weakened. Although many soldiers would stay with their regiments until the end, and some civilians still hoped for a *deus ex machina* to bring about a miraculous deliverance, little of this mattered in the greater scheme of things. Despairing Confederates looked to their inner resources and to their God, but the war's horrific toll became evident. By early September 1864, young Grace Elmore in Columbia, South Carolina, felt the anomaly of living a quiet life in the midst of so much suffering. "We know not what a day may bring forth, nor at what hour this peaceful town may be spread in ruins, and another instance of barbarous spite added to the long list of outrages committed by the Yankees," she wrote prophetically. "Yet our life flows evenly on, we hear of battles, we see friend after friend brought home coffined and ready for the churchyard, the mourning garb is no longer uncommon, and the cork leg and one armed men have ceased to attract attention, we have gotten used to it all, war does not interrupt a quiet breakfast nor does it disturb our night's rest."[48]

Chapter 19

THANKSGIVING AND DESPERATION

Blessed be the Lord my strength which teacheth my hands to war, and my fingers to fight.

— Psalms 144:1

In September 1864, James F. Wood, the Catholic bishop of Philadelphia, called for observing a day of thanksgiving and prayer for recent Union victories. The reach of civil religion in light of growing optimism about the war had spread into the more conservative churches. The combined operations of the army and navy in Mobile Bay but especially Sherman's capture of Atlanta had induced Lincoln to issue an official call to thank the Lord for his many mercies.[1] Absent, however, were the usual references to sin or chastisement. The "finger of God" had been "put forth for our help," a New School Presbyterian rejoiced, just "when men at the North were beginning to repine and be discouraged, and to talk of the impossibility of subduing the South." From Atlanta to the Shenandoah Valley, northern arms had triumphed under the Almighty's guiding hand.[2] Pride and self-righteousness (never in short supply) had replaced repentance and humility; northern religious leaders stood more than ready to pronounce a final judgment against the southern rebellion.

"The hand of God is to me so conspicuous in this struggle, that I should almost as soon expect the Almighty to turn slaveholder, as to see this war end without the extinction of its guilty cause," Presbyterian theology professor Roswell Hitchcock wrote privately. As for grieving families, Professor Hitchcock preached a sermon minimizing their pain. "The loss is not so great as may at first appear," he declared in a remarkably cold-blooded (and cold-hearted) way. "Death will come sooner or later to us all. The man who falls in battle only dies a little sooner than he expected." Rejoicing over northern victories with little consideration for the cost accompanied renewed condemnations of anyone who cried out for peace or compromise.[3]

Maintaining a clear distinction between God's ways and man's became increasingly difficult in the face of religious, political, and military triumphalism echoing from the pulpits. Fewer and fewer people could avoid falling into this theological trap. Quakers for instance welcomed emancipation as they struggled to maintain a peace witness. They respected Lincoln as a man sympathetic to their religious scruples, and in August 1864 Eliza Gurney, who

353

had exchanged letters with the president for the past two years, told how she prayed that the Lord might strengthen him to accomplish the great purpose of liberating a people. She added that many Quakers fully believed that Lincoln should be reelected. Although debate continued over whether Quakers should vote and how best to avoid becoming involved in the war, most remained silent or cast their ballots for the president.[4]

Northern churches drew an ever-sharper line between "loyalty" and "disloyalty," often freely mixing the religious with the political and church with state in their discussions and resolutions. Any who failed to "heartily sustain the government," an Indiana Baptist association declared, "are in league with the Southern Confederacy" and had become "enemies to their Country, and to their God." The churches themselves had contributed to the divisiveness by taking increasingly aggressive stands on the war, positions that inevitably bled over into partisan politics. "It is no little thing," Boston Unitarian George H. Hepworth informed Lincoln, "that every pulpit in the North sent up its most fervent prayers" each Sunday for our "hard working, careworn, but much loved Leader." And now the clergy was ready to "pray at an election."[5]

Lincoln's more pious allies pointed to the religious language often sprinkled through official statements and proclamations as signs that the president had been chosen by the Almighty to crush the rebellion and uphold the nation's most sacred principles. For his part, Lincoln increasingly courted the churches and their leading ministers. The occasional complaint that he remained at heart a deist, or worse, were largely drowned out by a chorus of clerical support. Throughout the presidential campaign, the Union League reprinted patriotic sermons from various parts of the country, and even if the preachers did not directly endorse Lincoln's reelection, few could mistake their implicit and often explicit political message.[6]

Many churches pledged to stand by the president as both the clergy and the religious press sounded like mouthpieces for the Republican Party. Even denominational bodies that called on members to set aside partisan considerations to support the government and the president were sounding a partisan note. "An army of Christ with the banners of the cross" and at least a million strong should "march to the ballot-box," the *Independent* editorialized. In doing so they would be "true to Christ and his cause . . . until the glad cry resounds throughout the land, throughout the world, Abraham Lincoln is re-elected President of an entire and undivided country!"[7] Some churches merely expressed support for the government though others—especially Methodist conferences and Baptist associations—endorsed the administration. According to one Unitarian editor, 1864 would be the most momentous political contest in American history: "He who acts and votes aright in this approaching election will most effectively serve the Lord and his Christ." Talk of a negotiated peace at this critical time could only hearten traitors and help preserve slavery because in a still broader sense the children of light were battling the children of darkness. "While nearly every pulpit gives its utterance in favor of war," the nation's most prominent Methodist editor declared, "the cries from the dram-shops and all the purlieus of vice is peace! peace!"[8]

As religious minorities, Jews and Catholics remained more wary of entering into partisan politics but often expressed strongly Unionist sentiments. Conservative Catholic editors favored the Democratic nominee, General George B. McClellan, without necessarily endorsing the party's peace platform and tried to avoid Republican and Protestant charges of disloyalty. Indeed, clerical support for McClellan was neither vocal nor visible. Republican sympathizers, including ministers and religious editors, naturally saw an opening here and took full advantage, hurling invective at both their religious and political foes.[9]

Strong partisan statements naturally outraged conservatives, who charged that the politicized denominations were neglecting eternal truths. Preaching the gospel had given way to preaching politics. Ohioan Jonathan Palmer Finley after graduating from Princeton Seminary had become a Presbyterian minister in Fulton, Missouri. Though believing that the "spirit of secession" had "blinded and perverted men," he decided not to vote in the 1864 elections. His neighbors would be watching closely, and he feared casting a ballot might "have injured the cause of Christ more than would have been compensated by any good my vote might have done." Others argued that partisanship could harm both church and state by undermining national unity. Even an anti-slavery Unitarian regretted seeing a "war" and "peace" party "claim to speak in the name of conscience and Christianity." Whatever their congregations might desire or demand, some ministers proudly declared they would never deliver a political sermon. One New York Episcopalian even conceded that the prayers of the church were "fallible," expressing at times more human wish than divine will.[10]

Condemning partisanship was easy for those who clearly had a partisan agenda, just as the most conniving politicians loved to pose as disinterested statesmen. Then too, as one New Jersey editor pointed out, those who accused the northern clergymen of preaching politics when they spoke out for the Union and emancipation never seemed to criticize ministers who sympathized with the rebels and defended slavery. If anything, Horace Bushnell argued, there needed to be a much closer connection between divine and human government, and he welcomed the recent placement of "In God We Trust" on United States coins.[11] By the same token, believers had a duty as citizens to elect loyal men, to "reinforce our bullets by our ballots," as one Presbyterian put it. Despite claiming to eschew political preaching of any kind, Baptist George Dana Boardman maintained that during the presidential election, God "visibly makes bare his arm" and ministers must speak.[12]

And speak they did in what often sounded like little more than Republican stump speeches. If McClellan wins, the republic dies, claimed one Boston Presbyterian who deemed it "a Christian duty to prosecute this war to the point of victory complete." In several sermons during the campaign's final weeks, Henry Ward Beecher held forth on the war, emancipation, and the election. He made no bones about preaching politics, though one disgusted listener reportedly stood up and gave three cheers for McClellan. In the early fall, Methodist bishop Matthew Simpson began delivering a stirring war speech that boldly proclaimed: "God cannot afford to do without America." Requests poured in from Republican committees, and Simpson kept up a busy speaking schedule, commanding honorariums as high as four hundred dollars.[13]

Praising Republicans naturally meant condemning Democrats and especially their peace platform. No true patriot can accept the nomination on such a basis, *Zion's Herald and Wesleyan Journal* sneered. "We believe it is rank treason to ask for an armistice under these circumstances." That pretty well summed up the thinking of the religious leaders most actively engaged in the campaign. Ironically, like some desperate Confederates, northern ministers observed how Jesus himself had promised to bring not peace but a sword. Even if the Democrats were honestly calling for peace, the terms of that settlement remained unclear, and that made their motives all the more suspect. Even a Methodist women's magazine accused Lincoln's opponents of favoring peace at any price and truckling with the rebels.[14]

"I fear much Indiana Democracy is idolatry and witchcraft," a prominent Indianapolis businessman and attorney wrote in his diary on the eve of that state's election. Copperheads, "nursed and promoted by ignorance and catholicism," would "destroy the union and oppose all religion and mores and pull down ev[e]ry institution." The more enthusiastic religious leaders claimed that all educated and upright people stood on one side with all the corrupt and Jesuitical (the anti-Catholic reference was no accident) rebel sympathizers on the other side.[15]

Devout soldiers echoed many of these sentiments and voted Republican in overwhelming numbers. Believing that the Lord had plainly shown his displeasure with slavery, one company officer in an Indiana regiment favored Lincoln in the election because the president was reportedly a believer, and the Bible taught the necessity for choosing upright rulers. By this time, the dramatic but spurious tale about Lincoln becoming a Christian at Gettysburg was already in circulation. More importantly, many soldiers had come to despise

Copperheads and knew that the Almighty could not possibly favor the Democrats' cowardly peace platform.[16]

The election and its aftermath became a time for political but also religious celebration. Pious partisans could rejoice and thank the Lord for delivering the nation from disloyal Democrats. McClellan and his allies, one AME minister declared, "were buried in the political sea of oblivion, never to rise any more." Picking up on the Exodus theme, he noted how the Lord had sounded the trumpet of freedom across the land. At the same time voters had, in the words of an enthusiastic Baptist, sustained the "noble, honest, patient, patriotic and Christian Chief Magistrate."[17] More and more, the devout linked the president to the Almighty. During a torchlight parade shortly after the election, a minister in Middletown, Connecticut, displayed a lighted transparency with a cleverly selected passage from Genesis: "And the angel of the Lord called unto Abraham out of heaven the second time." Not surprisingly, Lincoln's most enthusiastic religious supporters saw the hand of providence in his reelection.[18]

"There probably never was an election in all our history in which the religious elements entered so largely, and so nearly all on the one side," the editor of the Methodist *Christian Advocate and Journal* crowed. Heathenish Copperheads had suffered a crushing defeat. Republicans were pleased that the "disloyal" vote had been small and tried to explain away much of McClellan's quite respectable showing. Reckoning that many young men had voted Democratic because their fathers had or had supported McClellan because they believed he would suppress the rebellion, Vermont Baptist William Aspey added that a fair number were "too illiterate to cast an intelligent, independent ballot." So too, his argument ran, Catholics voted Democratic in mindless lockstep. Once all these factors were taken into account, Aspey believed, "you reduce the positively disloyal to an insignificant minority." Beyond revealing class and sectarian prejudice, such an analysis flew in the face of preelection rhetoric that had defined the contest as one simply between loyalty and rebellion, between good and evil. Other Protestants railed against the influence of immigrant Catholics and urban corruption, crediting both the churches and the Sunday schools with fending off these dangerous elements. In truth, Democrats did show considerable strength among Catholics, Episcopalians, and some Old School Presbyterians, while Republicans did well with Methodists, Baptists, New School Presbyterians, and smaller Protestant denominations.[19]

Coming on the heels of Lincoln's electoral triumph, Thanksgiving acquired a stronger political-religious cast. Here would be another opportunity, one conservative Democrat charged, for "Abolition preachers" to "relieve themselves of an excess of gall and bitterness." The *Chicago Times* denounced the

President's Thanksgiving proclamation for suggesting that the "Almighty has indorsed the political principles of the administration." Lincoln had done no such thing but rather had spoken in vague terms about the year's blessings with only the slightest allusions to the war and none to politics. Despite complaints that the president and most governors had failed to acknowledge Jesus Christ in their proclamations, a national day of Thanksgiving that simply recognized divine providence won widespread approval. On the appointed day, Lincoln attended the New York Avenue Presbyterian Church where he made a pledge to the Christian Commission and listened to Reverend Phineas Gurley preach for an hour.[20]

A rising sense of national self-confidence burst forth, especially from the pulpits. Recent Union victories capped by Lincoln's reelection meant that few preachers would deliver somber messages. Were not heartfelt thanks for Union victories, emancipation, and the president's reelection in order? And with the coming of emancipation, the Kingdom of Christ itself appeared imminent. In the words of one Pennsylvanian, "God is going around the earth shaking the nations, and preparing the way for the bright millennial dispensation." Equally cheering, Americans had joined wholeheartedly in the benevolence of the Christian and Sanitary Commissions, a further sign of sectarianism breaking down. All told, the Redeemer's cause was advancing rapidly in America as a war apparently nearing its end promised a glorious fulfillment of national destiny.[21]

The nation's victories were in reality God's victories. Providence had repeatedly confounded the traitors in Richmond and those closer to home. Reviewing more than three years of war and especially recalling the dark days of 1862, a New York Presbyterian explained how people had learned to place their faith in the Lord rather than in generals: "God told us awful truths in the swamps of the Chickahominy, in the trenches of Yorktown."[22] The staggering costs of war acquired new meaning as if a great light had suddenly revealed how the nation's suffering fit into the divine plan. A Connecticut Congregationalist spoke of witnessing "the vials of Jehovah's wrath pouring their dread contents upon the guilty land, filling it with these gory battle fields, these groaning hospitals, these shrouded homes and crushed hearts." The terrible price to be paid for upholding a civil government ordained by God was clear, but so were the incalculable benefits. "Every gory body which is planted in her [the nation's] bloody soil is the seed of a future and perennial harvest of national honor, permanence and power," a Buffalo Presbyterian exulted.[23]

For several years, families had worried a great deal about the war's effects on the soldiers, many fearing they would come home ungovernable heathens to wreck both church and society. No more. Because the troops had been so thoroughly evangelized, Reverend Charles Wadsworth predicted they would return as "armies of self-denying, God-fearing, law-abiding men, making the earth fairer with their peaceful ministries and heaven's air pure and sweet with the breath of praise in these old songs of Zion." Reiterating a by now common theme, other ministers described how Americans would go forth with a purer Christianity to convert the world. But millennial hopes soared even higher and, indeed, well beyond those expressed only a few months earlier. There was little danger of the republic sinking into vice, Horace Bushnell rejoiced, but instead a "great sublime progress in character" would make government itself less and less necessary—a kind of Christian withering away of the state. Nor would history any longer proceed through inevitable cycles; nor would future historians ever have to write about the rise and decay of American civilization. In St. Louis, Congregationalist Truman Post preached on the theme "social regeneration." Pointing to the familiar story of decline in ancient Greece and Rome, he announced what amounted to a new historical dispensation: "I believe in no necessary mortality of states or civilizations, at least in the present or future." His faith in moral and social progress was unshakable because now Christianity had become the great force of liberation. A reborn American nation "shall defy the corrosions of time."[24] National immortality must have seemed an alluring prospect to a people struggling to comprehend a war of such carnage and destruction. The ministers offered the usual comfort to the grieving and consolation to sinners, but they also spread out before their congregations the temptations of spiritual (and political) hubris.

———

The suffering and shrinking Confederate nation appeared all too mortal. Imprisoned on Johnson's Island in Lake Erie, Colonel Daniel R. Hundley scorned the Yankee Thanksgiving and wondered "how long the Almighty Father will endure such blasphemy." To his way of thinking, southerners understood and accepted divine chastisement, but northern preachers "eat their fat turkeys and other good things with a pious unction worthy of the most self-complacent Pharisees."[25] Such scathing remarks, however, barely concealed deep anxieties.

On Christmas Day in Petersburg, a North Carolina captain attended two crowded services at St. Paul's Episcopal Church. The Gothic sanctuary was festooned with evergreen boughs; officers and ladies were finely dressed; presiding clerics wore luxurious vestments. Yet all these attempts at keeping up holiday spirits could not shut out the war, especially after the demoralizing defeats in Tennessee at Franklin and Nashville along with the unrelievedly bad news from Georgia. Even after hearing a quite good camp sermon from his chaplain, an artillery officer in Lee's army did not mince words: "The future looks dark, gloomy, bloody, and hopeless." Across the Confederacy, devout patriots noted how sad the Christmas season had been, and feelings of depression could not be easily dispelled. In Newton County, Georgia, the slave children's traditional cry of "Christmas gift, mistress! Christmas gift, mistress!" only caused Dolly Lunt Burge to pull the covers over her head and cry. With Sherman about to enter Savannah, Grace Brown Elmore was sure the Yankees would soon reach her home in Columbia, South Carolina. "Our hope in man has failed," she wrote in her diary. "We can look alone to God."[26]

Even then, people turned to the Lord for spiritual comfort rather than national deliverance. Hearing the picket firing at night and noting how several men had frozen to death, William Nelson Pendleton wished his family a "happy New Year . . . in a spiritual sense." We could not "expect to retain our earthly blessings," he explained, and would instead "find our chief happiness in those which are spiritual and unfailing." Such thoughts rang especially true as the Confederacy's military prospects faded. It was perhaps some consolation to realize that temporal comforts, which in any case had grown rare of late, were fleeting at best. Unlike the northern divines who increasingly talked of a glorious national fulfillment, an Augusta, Georgia, minister reminded his congregation how nations and empires rose and fell, yet the kingdom of Christ was indestructible and not subject to the ravages of disease or time. To think of eternal things and a future heaven helped make life in the Petersburg trenches endurable and helped steel believers for another campaign season.[27] During the revival services and prayer meetings throughout the winter and spring, the men prayed for their own safety, their own souls, and their own families.

Yet somehow the link between spiritual fervor and patriotic devotion survived. A brigade serving in the Shenandoah Valley adopted resolutions promising to resist "crafty, cruel, and merciless" Yankees who "come with the Bible in one hand" and "the dagger in the other." They spurned talk of a negotiated peace and expressed unlimited confidence in General Lee, "the Christian gentleman and chivalrous soldier." At the same time, however, sagging morale remained a problem, and chaplains increasingly decried the sin of desertion. The ranks had grown thinner, though a devout core of men affirmed that God stood by the Confederacy, and the religious meetings would continue until the armies were disbanded.[28]

Equally heartening were any signs of resilient faith and occasional reports of revivals at home. Soldiers especially noticed when local churches held protracted meetings or other special services, and the work of evangelism proceeded. "Every thing looks so dark that our only comfort is in looking to God for His blessing," a Virginia refugee commented. "The Union Prayer-Meetings are great comforts to us." In turn, families sent words of encouragement to their boys. "Never be ashamed to own your faith in God," one father advised his son. Without the Lord, he would be only "a moldering piece of clay good for worms." By this time, many young men's bodies had literally returned to the earth, so such words became more a reminder of death's great harvest than a counsel of hope. Better to rely on personal witness as in Petersburg, where a Georgia Baptist was impressed that local women still flocked to a Methodist church that seemed dangerously exposed to enemy fire.[29]

South Carolinians grew frantic as Sherman's men neared their borders, rightly expecting the Yankees would wreak special havoc on the birthplace of secession. In Columbia, young Grace Elmore candidly expressed her fear of rape and even considered suicide as she contemplated how the invading troops had "taught us how impotent is the weakness and helplessness of women." She wondered whether the Lord would approve such a desperate act but found no answer. By February, Elmore could only write, "We must bear up, God is our friend." A few days after the burning of Columbia, she marveled at the feelings of vengeance unleashed in herself: "My whole nature is changed, I feel so hard so pitless, gladly would I witness the death of each of those wretches, God hear the curses poured upon their heads, God grant they may suffer in their homes, their wives their children as they made us suffer." Knowing that "God is greater than Sherman," she would still cling to her faith even as the Almighty was "leading us by crooked paths, but though he slay me yet will I trust in him." She had seen "the wicked flourish" yet would "bide the Lord's time."[30]

Hearing of Columbia's fate from her refugee home in Eatonton, Georgia, Tennessean Ellen Renshaw House reeled from shock: "Surely this state [of affairs] cannot last much longer. God will not permit it." But he apparently would. The Lord meted out justice—that was readily affirmed—but more and more Confederates meditated on the mysteries of that justice. "The magnificent movements of the divine mind are revealed only by the lapse of time; and we must wait the developments of Providence, before we presume to decide concerning the righteousness of God's judgments," a Georgia Baptist wrote plaintively. The resort to theological abstractions, however, reflected how more tangible signs of divine favor had nearly vanished. Even words of assurance and hope became increasingly conditional. Despite the sins of the people and the incapacity of their leaders, the Lord's strong right arm could still save, but that all depended on a rebirth of public virtue. Weighing the chances for South Carolinians resisting Sherman, Episcopalian James Warley Miles offered little comfort: "If they rise to the emergency, we will be independent. If not, we deserve subjugation." Miles no longer expected a miraculous deliverance, and even reading scripture no longer calmed fears. "We talk of the prophecies of the Bible," one Arkansas woman noted, "and became almost scared at the thought of the world coming to an end."[31]

Few Confederates talked of an apocalypse, but they struggled to read the "signs of the times" and glimpse what looked to be a horrifying future. God had been steadily withdrawing his favor, and just like Moses's generation, the Confederates would be kept out of the promised land. Interpreting wartime events as punishment for sin had long been standard, but by the spring of 1865 the focus had narrowed. More than ever, covetousness now seemed the besetting evil as devout Confederates pondered individual and collective guilt. Emma Holmes explicitly connected Yankee raids in South Carolina to the fact that "the love of money had swallowed love of country." The distillers of whiskey who had kept precious grain from reaching hungry widows and orphans, to cite just one example, would one day have to approach the judgment seat of God. This was not simply a matter of people committing sins, which after all was part of the human condition; the real problem was that the southern people had failed to repent of those sins. They had gone through the motions on days of fasting, humiliation, and prayer, but they had not truly humbled themselves before God and therefore were reaping the fruits of hypocrisy. If God decreed that the Confederacy must be overthrown and the enemy should triumph, who could claim that his erring children did not deserve such a righteous judgment?[32]

During the spring of 1865, soldier meetings adopted resolutions confessing sins and promising to live new lives. Not only would sins be forgiven but divine favor would return; southern independence, peace, and prosperity would surely follow. All hope had not been lost, and there was still talk of purifying the people, but now the soldiers as well as the preachers pondered the Lord's unfathomable will. The devout Willie Pegram took comfort in the phrase "God reigneth," but the more cynical General Edward C. Walthall remarked to a fellow officer, "From the way that things are going now, I am afraid the Lord is a Union man." Resignation to divine chastisement was easy enough to describe, but to quell a questioning and rebellious spirit was much more difficult. A search for answers might well be in vain.[33]

"Job is my comforter now," Mary Chesnut commented while declining a friend's gift of religious books, and ironically many preachers turned to texts from that less than orthodox source. Other comparisons quickly came to mind: the darkest days of the American Revolution or the suffering of the Israelites in Egypt. All expressed a similar anguish, but the soldiers simply prayed for the strength and courage needed in the next battle. Gratitude for whatever mercies God chose to bestow on the Confederates became a mantra for a chastened and deeply distressed people. To pray without ceasing, to seek anew the throne of grace, the preachers and religious editors offered familiar counsel. Yet after witnessing the destruction of Columbia, Grace Elmore kept asking why wicked men were allowed to rampage through the land and why the horrible war continued; many other Confederates must have echoed her final question, "How long oh Lord, how long?"[34]

The pat answer was that all of human history remained in God's hands, but a belief in providence could tug the heart and mind in several different directions. The Lord might somehow lead the Confederates to victory; he might abandon them to the Yankees' tender mercies; the war might simply drag on. A despairing cry or quiet confidence seemed equally appropriate. To express trust in God was to repeat a central tenet of the faith that offered at least some comfort in the Confederacy's darkest hours. Or perhaps repeat the now tattered assertion—made by Virginia senator Robert M. T. Hunter among others—that a righteous God would not allow the wicked Yankees to ultimately prevail. Or would he? Increasingly, it seemed that only what a North Carolina farmer's wife termed "a miraculous intervention of the God of battles" could save the southern nation. Others talked of "faint hope" or "almost" losing hope. One desperate chaplain's prayer even offered the Lord some advice—to "get thyself a great name" through "a deliverance from our enemies."[35]

Such a pathetic plea echoed those of Moses trying to intercede for the children of Israel. Yet for every disheartened soul, there was another Confederate clinging to hope or even expecting a miraculous deliverance. Any promising development, no matter how small, became a sign that the Lord might yet save the Confederacy. All the people need do was humble themselves before God, keep the faith, and the final victory would be theirs, one Mississippi preacher advised. A pastor in Charleston offered far more bloodcurdling counsel: "Fight! fight, my friends till the streets run blood!" Lee's perceptive artillerist Edward Porter Alexander later recalled that the "generally religious character of the people" and belief "in a God who overruled all human affairs" had led some Confederates to anticipate success even after Lincoln's reelection. This in turn prevented any strong demand for peace negotiations.[36] In sum, Confederates often remained convinced that the Lord was on their side. The devout spoke of an unshaken faith in God, and the phrase "ultimate triumph" kept cropping up in both public and private remarks.[37]

How long would that "ultimate" victory be in coming? Did religious faith needlessly prolong a bloody war? Civil religion had been from the start a vital component of a nascent Confederate nationalism, and by the end of the war it remained critical for buttressing sagging morale in the army and at home. As he often had done before, Jefferson Davis at the urging of Congress summoned his fellow citizens to "acknowledge our dependence on his [God's] mercy." The official proclamation for a day of fasting and prayer on March 10, 1865, included words such as "humble submission," "contritely," "chastening hand," and "sufferings" that, besides whatever theological truth they expressed, showed how dramatically the military and political situation had deteriorated. Like Mary Chesnut, the *Richmond Dispatch* suggested that preachers find their texts in Job. In the Confederate capital, despite rain and cold, many people gathered in churches that remained open for much of the day.[38] The weather no doubt reduced attendance at camp services, but for many of the men in uniform as well as the folks at home, special days of fasting, humiliation, and prayer had run their course. Even the reputedly more pious female population now seemed lax if not indifferent. "The prayers and fastings of one or two will avail nothing," an Arkansas woman sadly remarked.[39]

But if the faithful lost heart and even expressed some cynicism, then all indeed was lost. "The final issue of this war," a Virginia Episcopalian warned, "may probably depend on the manner and the spirit, in which our people discharge the duties of this day." The dark clouds might still lift, and devout patriots could no more give up their faith in the Confederacy than they could give up their faith in God. Nor could they relinquish the idea that divine wrath would surely descend on the Yankee invaders. After all, the Confederates had already won many victories against long odds and could do so once again. To an Arkansas artillery officer, the pattern of providential history had already been set: in his eyes, "all most every national day of humiliation and prayer has been followed with some marked triumph on some bloody battlefield."[40]

For the remaining weeks of the Confederacy's national life, some believers maintained that trusting in God rather than men must bring success, and that link in Confederate civil religion was never entirely broken. At the same time, however, more ominous signs appeared. If not necessarily outright despair, an ineffable sadness and quiet resignation descended on people who still viewed the war through the lens of faith. Whatever fate might await the Confederacy, a Baptist editor wrote shortly before news of Lee's surrender reached Georgia, Christians knew they would eventually be "heirs" to a "better country" in the afterlife. When a black Union officer in Sumter District, South Carolina, brandished a pistol, veteran schoolteacher Mary Hort dared him to kill her, "I shall go straight to heaven. I am a Christian."[41] Even as the war entered its final weeks and days, in camps across the Confederacy some men read their Testaments, attended services, or built a chapel. But now the language of catastrophe and even apocalypse appeared more often. "I take it there will now be war in this country fully as long as you or I will live," wrote one South Carolina

Baptist to a fellow minister in Alabama.[42] War without end, and with seemingly no escape for Confederates short of defeat and destruction.

———

These dour assessments would have resonated with prisoners held on both sides, especially once the exchange cartel was suspended at the end of 1862. There were special and informal exchanges from time to time, but in the spring of 1864 these largely stopped.[43] More prisoners held for longer periods meant worsening conditions and more deaths. Where was God for these soldiers, who increasingly lost hope of ever surviving the ordeal? If anything, the fear of anonymous death—unknown to family or friends—must have reached its greatest intensity in the prison camps. As spirits sank in the midst of increasingly horrific treatment, the consolations of faith must have seemed ever more valued but at the same time more elusive.

What the whole prisoner question could produce was impassioned words. Northern church publications highlighted the abuse of Union prisoners and other rebel cruelties, and there was plenty of self-righteous posturing all round. In a funeral sermon for a soldier who had died in prison at Salisbury, North Carolina, on Christmas Day, 1864, a Massachusetts minister emphasized both the man's spiritual character and the brutality of the Confederates, who would not even grant the poor fellow a Christian burial. Nurse Kate Cumming expressed the same kind of outrage over the harsh treatment of a southern chaplain in a northern prison camp, but like many who entered into the debates over whose prisons were the worst, she maintained that her side was largely innocent of abuses and had indeed followed the Savior's commands about how to treat enemies.[44] Such a preposterous claim was unfortunately all too typical.

The whole prisoner question generated white-hot rhetoric that would not cool for several decades. An anonymous pamphlet written by a northern conservative blasted efforts to inflame popular passions by displaying photographs of half-starved Union soldiers released from Richmond prisons. Not surprisingly, he saved his moral indignation for marauding Federals in the South, the shelling of southern cities, and the use of black troops. On this question, as on so many others, there appeared to be little if any neutral ground. Reading about the condition of Confederate prisoners at Point Lookout, Maryland, Grace Elmore envisioned a tenfold vengeance against "this race of liars and murderers." A rare exception to this pattern was African American chaplain Henry McNeal Turner, who deplored calls for killing rebel prisoners in retaliation for atrocities against black troops.[45]

The charges and countercharges largely focused on food, shelter, and medicine, paying little attention to the moral and spiritual aspects of prison life. Just as in the army camps, however, the more upright men complained of having to live with the depraved and irreligious. "Surrounded by none but the wicked," was how one Hoosier described, and no doubt exaggerated, his situation. Blasphemous and profane language was a common problem, and some irreverent fellows would create disturbances whenever worship services were held. A Confederate chaplain arrested in Winchester, Virginia, and sent to Baltimore found the southern prisoners there a hard lot of inveterate gamblers and dedicated hell-raisers. In a more balanced assessment, a Rhode Island Methodist observed how "prison life makes men hard, selfish and rough," though occasionally a "prodigal son" or "backslider" would inquire after the way of salvation.[46]

Yet as the hours and days stretched out endlessly, the boredom and ennui no doubt encouraged men to haul out their Testaments. When a Massachusetts sergeant confined in Libby Prison and later at Andersonville felt especially sad or homesick, he would "read from God's words, of its precious promises, and our Saviour's teachings, felt I had in them much to cheer, and had no right to be despondent." Given the mortality rate in such places, he had every right to feel despondent at least about his earthly prospects. In testimonies cherished by the Christian Commission and other evangelical groups, feeble and emaciated men later recounted how their well-worn Testaments had helped them survive the worst. Prisoners had to keep their own Sabbath, but memories of Sundays back home or thoughts about a wife praying with the family kept flooding over them.[47]

To throw men into crowded places and keep them there certainly promoted long, rambling conversations. Once prisoners had recounted their personal histories, once all the old stories, amusing anecdotes, and smutty jokes had been exchanged, the talk might eventually turn to spiritual matters. In one Virginia prison, a Union major got into a long discussion with a fellow officer about the finer points of Calvinism, including predestination (he remained unconvinced). Elsewhere, Universalists debated those who believed in a literal hellfire. As had always been true in Civil War armies, the nightly prayer meetings along with Sunday schools and Bible studies became the real centers of religious devotion.[48]

In Libby Prison, Ohio chaplain Charles McCabe became known for his enthusiastic singing and cheerful disposition, both surely welcome in such a gloomy place. After an especially effective sermon, men offered moving testimonies and entered into lively discussions, seeming to relish the preaching whether for spiritual sustenance or momentary diversion. According to one German soldier, even the freethinkers and skeptics "could stand an occasional sermon," though he thought, in too many cases, "the windiest of windbags babbled and blustered." Generally, however, ministers preached from texts that helped men endure suffering or promised deliverance, and in any event, the hope was that somehow the light of God's countenance would shine in this darkest of worlds.[49]

For many Christians, what counted were the conversions or, more to the point, counting the conversions. After an Ohio minister at Andersonville had preached a sermon just past sunset, four men asked for prayer—"one back-slider, one new convert, and two who were just beginning to feel the infinite importance of eternal things." An agent of the Christian Commission reported more than a thousand men had found the Lord in Andersonville. Potential converts joined "mourners" as the first step in the process. "If I am not a chris-tian I am determined to become one," Edmund Dewitt Patterson at John-son's Island allowed. He had at first resisted the preachers' appeals, could not "understand my feelings entirely," but finally stood ready to join the church.[50]

This new convert and his comrades did not pray exclusively for their own souls. In early May 1864 there were almost daily prayer meetings "for the spe-cial purpose of invoking God's blessing on our arms during the coming cam-paign." At one point, according to Patterson, a soldier stood up and prayed that the life of General Lee be spared. To the Alabamian, the prayer meetings were "one good sign for the country," and he believed "almost every man in the prison, whether saint or sinner," had sought the Lord's blessing for the Army of Northern Virginia as it prepared once again to defend Richmond. Yet even here Confederate prayers for national salvation sounded increasingly condi-tional: "Help us to pray aright for our country," an Alabama officer on John-son's Island wrote in his diary. "If it is consistent with Thy will, give us Inde-pendence and Peace."[51]

Prison authorities hardly appreciated such petitions to the Almighty, and Confederates especially hated to hear Union soldiers praying for Lincoln. But some captured Federals were even bolder. An Iowan loudly called on "God to crush this rebellion and cut off all traitors from the face of the earth." After being reprimanded for calling down "damnation and disaster on the rebels," one Union chaplain reminded a Confederate officer that the Apostle Paul had prayed in prison. "When they found that they could not frighten him [the chap-lain]," one admiring observer remarked. "They let him pray unmolested."[52]

Any visiting local pastors faced skepticism if not hostility. At Libby Prison, officers debated (but failed to adopt) a series of resolutions against having "Rebel ministers" conduct services. The discussion was lively, and one Penn-sylvania captain remarked, "They [the local pastors] had better teach humanity to their own people before they attempt to preach Christianity." Given the shortage of Catholic chaplains in the Union army, however, priests were more warmly received. Soldiers welcomed the opportunity to make their confessions and receive the sacrament, though one embittered Wisconsin skeptic was sure the bishop in Richmond arranged for Catholic soldiers to be more quickly exchanged than other prisoners. More often, Protestant soldiers were happy enough to see the priests and praised their work. At Andersonville, Father Peter Whelan remained with the men for several months, sharing their rations and even winning the confidence of the crusty commandant Henry Wirz. According to one prisoner, Whelan and other priests would crawl into the dugouts on their hands and knees to hear confessions or administer Extreme Unction.[53]

Then again religious activities of any kind were better than none at all, so even a sermon from a Confederate minister could draw a crowd. As several soldiers noted, whether grudgingly or not, some of these preachers were devoted servants of God. A visiting Methodist preached on charity, illustrating his message by giving each man a plug of tobacco wrapped in a tract. Further cementing himself in the men's affections, he brought some precious eggs for the sick. The wisest and most discreet ministers avoided political allusions in their messages and simply presented the gospel to any who would listen. In Libby Prison, a great crowd gathered around a North Carolina chaplain who urged them to tell the folks back home how southern preachers had offered them "comfort and cheer."[54]

The same could be said for northern clergy ministering to Confederate prisoners, who also preferred religion free of politics. Hearing too much "abolition" in one sermon, an officer sniffed that "the clerical world in Puritandom has not changed altogether from the happy days of Quaker whipping and Papist hanging." More often, however, local preachers gathered large and more or less receptive groups of prisoners in the barracks and yards. At Elmira, New York, the inmates chose the ministers, Thomas K. Beecher, the eccentric and conservative brother of Henry Ward Beecher, being a special favorite. Everyone from Catholic priests to Dwight L. Moody preached to these literally captive congregations.[55]

Religious life in Union and Confederate prisons could hardly remain untouched by the bloody battles that raged beyond the walls, nor could spiritual concerns always take priority. Worship itself remained fraught with political meaning. Attending a service conducted by a local minister, Edmund DeWitt Patterson could not help raging against the indignity of it all: "After dragging our own ministers from the pulpit and thrusting them in prison, simply because they would not pray God's blessing on old Abe, I think they could offer us no more gross or great insult than to offer to preach their Yankee religion to us."[56]

But the northern ministers would soon be doing much more, lording it over the downtrodden Confederates as the war entered its final phase. The November Thanksgiving sermons had offered a taste of a greater triumphalism still to come. All that was needed was for Richmond to fall and the rebel armies to surrender. Would the worst nightmares of devout Confederates come to pass? Would northern victory mark a final chapter in the providential history of this war? Would millennial hopes at last be fulfilled? Those northerners who had most loudly proclaimed a civil religion tying Union and emancipation to the divine will prepared to celebrate what they considered a complete vindication of a righteous cause. This was hardly the time to think very deeply about the Almighty's purposes, so the Yankees would simply revel in a victory that reaffirmed their political and religious virtue.

THE FINAL DECREES OF PROVIDENCE

The judgments of the Lord are true and righteous altogether.
— Psalms 19:9

Know ye not that there is a prince and a great man fallen this day in Israel?
— 2 Samuel 3:38

Sometime in 1864 Lincoln offered a far more thoughtful reflection on God's purposes than did the most learned clergy on either side of the conflict. He privately outlined his conclusions in a document that came to be known as the "Meditation on the Divine Will." Distilling in only ten sentences his thinking on the war's ultimate meaning, Lincoln began with a simple premise: "The will of God prevails." Although both sides claimed to be fighting on God's side, "in the present civil war it is quite possible that God's purpose is something different from the purpose of either party." The Lord worked through "human instrumentalities" but for whatever reason the war continued. "I am almost ready to say this is probably true—that God wills this contest, and wills that it shall not end yet." Such a statement reflected either persistent fatalism or deep faith—or perhaps a mixture of both. The Lord could have "saved or destroyed the Union" without a war but had not done so. Even now "he could give the final victory to either side any day. Yet the contest proceeds."[1] As Lincoln said, the course of events reflected God's will, but unlike countless fellow citizens, he would not even pretend to discern God's will.

Shortly before another bloody campaign season began in the spring of 1864, Lincoln was still crafting and testing ideas about the war's course and its relationship to God's purpose. He told a delegation of Kentuckians, "I am naturally anti-slavery. If slavery is not wrong, nothing is wrong. I cannot remember when I did not so think, and feel." Later putting down these thoughts on paper, Lincoln explained to Albert G. Hodges, a Kentucky newspaper editor, how, despite his own constitutional scruples and natural conservatism, his hand had been forced on the emancipation question. He then added a paragraph that injected a new set of themes. Here was some of the old fatalism ("I claim not to have controlled events, but confess plainly that events have controlled me")—presumably a revealing passage for biographers. Yet Lincoln did not stop there. "Now, at the end of three years struggle the nation's condition is not what either party, or any man devised, or expected. God alone can claim it. Whither it is tending seems plain. If God now wills the removal of a great wrong, and wills also that we of the North as well as you of the South, shall pay fairly for our complicity in that wrong, impartial history will find therein new cause to attest and revere the justice and goodness of God."[2] These points meshed well with the views of many northern clergy but also carried a deeper sense of awe and humility all too often missing from their sermons.

More than ever, Lincoln was struggling with large questions about the war's purpose, and he deliberately chose to share his thoughts with an increasingly wide audience. In response to a petition from "persons under eighteen" in Concord, Massachusetts, calling on the president to free all the slave children, Lincoln summed up a still evolving view of divine providence: "Please tell these little people I am very glad their young hearts are so full of just and generous sympathy, and that, while I have not the power to grant all they ask, I trust they will remember that God has, and that, as it seems, He wills to do it." Lincoln almost claimed the ability to fathom the Lord's will but not quite, because he included the all-important word "seems." Upon being presented a Bible by the "Loyal Colored people of Baltimore," he returned to the relationship between divine will, human agency, and black freedom. "I can only now say . . . it has always been a sentiment with me that all mankind should be free" was how he expressed the moral nub of the issue. At the same time, however, he had to reckon with constitutional and pragmatic considerations; he therefore hesitated to claim too much credit for his own virtue or judgment. "So far as able, within my sphere, I have always acted as I believed to be right and just; and I have done all I could for the good of mankind generally." Responding to a petition of support from the American Baptist Home Mission Society, Lincoln used some uncharacteristically harsh language to condemn those who would cite scripture to justify human bondage and added that, when southern ministers appealed to the "Christian world" to aid a slaveholders' rebellion, they "contemned and insulted God and His church, far more than did Satan when he tempted the Saviour with the Kingdoms of the earth. The devil's attempt was no more false, and far less hypocritical." Yet, perhaps thinking he had gone too far, Lincoln quickly added, "But let me forbear, remembering it is also written 'Judge not, lest ye be judged.'"[3]

An exultant (and at times gloating) victor's theology proved most satisfying to countless northern soldiers and civilians, including many of the president's most ardent supporters. But not to Lincoln himself. Even with the war going well by the fall of 1864, the president was still working out his own sense of the war's meaning, a meaning by no means tethered to the ebb and flow of military news. In a letter to Quaker Eliza Gurney, Lincoln crafted an interpretation of divine providence that confronted the classic problems in dealing with a sovereign and inscrutable God head-on: "The purposes of the Almighty are perfect, and must prevail, though we erring mortals may fail to accurately perceive them in advance." That one sentence in many ways summed up Lincoln's views of God's role in the war, and he candidly confessed that human beings found this to be hard doctrine. "We hoped for a happy termination of this terrible war long before this; but God knows best, and has ruled otherwise." Again, a most unpleasant truth, especially in light of all the blood already shed, but a truth that had to be recognized. Yet this was no immobilizing fatalism: "We shall yet acknowledge His wisdom and our own error therein. Meanwhile we must work earnestly in the best light He gives us, trusting that so working still conduces to the great ends He ordains. Surely He intends some great good to follow this mighty convulsion, which no mortal could make, and no mortal could stay."[4]

Lincoln had arrived at a position that would have been more or less acceptable to many orthodox Christians and Jews, but both the humility and uncertainty of these statements could not fully satisfy people seeking assurance that the nation's agony had served some understandable and unalloyed purpose. Lincoln had often been out of step with the religious thinking of many believers, and in the hour of Union victory, he remained so. By the time of the second inauguration on March 4, 1865, recent military successes and Lincoln's own reelection brought the war's end in sight. The large crowd gathered to hear, and the many more who would later read the second inaugural address likely expected a speech celebrating recent successes and northern virtue. If so, they would be sorely disappointed because once again Lincoln cut against the grain of public expectations and popular theology.[5]

Lincoln barely mentioned "the progress of our arms, upon which all else depends," noting that the news must be "reasonably satisfactory and encouraging to all." No review of recent victories, no defense of his administration's policies. He closed the first paragraph of his speech on a surprising and equivocal note: "With hope for the future, no prediction in regard to it is ventured."[6]

Surely the coming Union victory represented a triumph of righteousness to many northerners. Lincoln, however, described a conflict, which though "somehow" caused by slavery, was really no one's responsibility. Rather than excoriating the secessionists as traitors like so many orators had done for the past four years, Lincoln merely claimed that "both parties deprecated war" and then added that brilliantly mystifying sentence: "And the war came."

Who had in fact brought about all the subsequent carnage, Lincoln did not say. Who could end the war and how it could end, he did not say. Many northerners believed that a wrathful God was at last striking down the wicked rebellion, but Lincoln would offer his fellow citizens a much more complex and disturbing message—a sobering variation on the wartime jeremiad. The tone and even the cadence of the speech suddenly changed.[7] "Both [parties] read the same Bible, and pray to the same God; and each invokes His aid against the other." Had Lincoln's wartime calls for prayer and thanksgiving ever crossed that line? Perhaps, but he was surely referring here to the foolishness and sinfulness of human beings petitioning the Lord to advance their own purposes by such bloody means. The Confederates had called for the Almighty to sustain their slaveholding republic, as Lincoln clearly acknowledged, and he pointed out the moral perversity of such a prayer. Yet—and here his thinking surely ran contrary to many northerners—Lincoln still warned those assembled, "let us judge not that we be not judged."[8]

Human beings had ignored that admonition for nearly two millennia, but the president let no one off the hook. "The prayers of both [parties] could not be answered; that of neither has been answered fully." He conceded precious little ground to those who would simply declare the approaching Union victory a righteous triumph. Throughout the war many preachers and countless others might have agreed with Lincoln's next statement, "The Almighty has His own purpose," but they had seldom dwelt upon or thought deeply about what to most people is both a difficult and unpalatable idea.[9] "Woe unto the world because of offenses; for it must needs be that offenses come, but woe to that man by whom the offense cometh." Lincoln quoted this passage from Matthew, and his listeners might reasonably have assumed that he was referring to the rebels. And, indeed, he quickly pointed to "American slavery" as one such offense that God would deal with in his own good time. Significantly, Lincoln termed slavery an "American" and not simply a southern sin.

That in turn led to the speech's most somber passage. Lincoln raised the possibility that the "mighty scourge of war" might continue "until all the wealth piled by the bond-man's two hundred and fifty years of unrequited toil shall be sunk, and until every drop of blood drawn with the lash, shall be paid by another drawn with the sword." Even with such a butcher's bill, he would still affirm in the words of Psalm 19, "the judgments of the Lord, are true and righteous altogether."[10] This was a most difficult teaching indeed. Had all the dead and wounded met their fate according to some horrific decree? The Almighty might have his own purposes, but did those purposes require slaughter and suffering on this scale? Here Lincoln had dodged some troubling questions. If people simply affirmed, "thy will be done," that hardly left human beings as helpless victims in a great metaphysical drama, at least as far as Lincoln was concerned. He urged the northern people to show mercy toward a defeated enemy and at the same time finish the work. Lincoln called on his fellow Americans to "bind up the nation's wounds" without specifying how that was to be done. For nearly two years, the president and Congress had sometimes disagreed over the goals and methods of reconstruction, and even now he laid down no blueprint for the future.

Rejecting the moral certitudes not only of the proslavery preachers but also of their northern critics, Lincoln stood witness to a remarkable belief in providence shorn of pride, overconfidence, and hubris. The heart of his address had presented another brief meditation on the connections between slavery, war, and divine purpose, though Lincoln had not exactly unraveled that mysterious relationship. He left much unsaid, and that is not surprising for a political leader who had developed a civil religion that was both timely and timeless.

He was speaking to a people with little appetite for the paradoxes or ironies that he would never escape. Less than two weeks later, in replying to a letter praising the speech from veteran New York politico, Thurlow Weed, Lincoln himself offered the best assessment: "I expect . . . [it] to wear as well as— perhaps better than—any thing I have produced; but I believe it is not immediately popular. Men are not flattered by being shown that there has been a difference of purpose between the Almighty and them. To deny it, however, in this case, is to deny that there is a God governing the world."[11] In both the short and long term, Lincoln was right.

Any immediate praise for the address came from both expected and unexpected quarters but was oddly muted. Democratic editors blindly misread the address as showing Lincoln's spiritual arrogance. A Maine chaplain lauded the president's "moral tone" without carefully considering what Lincoln had actually said. The usually critical *Independent* concluded that the president's "moral vision" had greatly improved, though again without a very thoughtful analysis of the speech itself.[12] It seemed as if Lincoln's carefully selected words had fallen if not on deaf then perhaps on largely unperceptive ears. Frederick Douglass considered Lincoln's speech a "sacred effort," but one can imagine Lincoln responding that it had been a "half sacred" effort directed at an "almost chosen" people.[13] Only a few weeks later the president would be dead from an assassin's bullet, and his clerical eulogists would demonstrate how little they had learned from the Second Inaugural. Even in his own death, Lincoln might have detected the inscrutable ways of divine providence.

But that all lay in the unknowable future; for the time being the northern people could anticipate and then celebrate the triumph of the Union cause. After news of Richmond's capture reached Washington, the Capitol was brightly illuminated. A gas-lit transparency emblazoned a biblical message that appeared to cut through both the physical and spiritual darkness: "This is the Lord's doing; it is marvelous in our eyes." This was especially suitable because hastily prepared sermons celebrated not only the "justice" but the "government" of God whose light had at last shone fully on the American republic. To the devout, the long-delayed entrance of Union troops into the rebel capital marked the Almighty's direct intervention in human history. From camp prayer services to formal presbytery sessions came thanks to God for such a dramatic triumph over treason.[14]

There soon followed news of Lee's surrender (suitably enough on Palm Sunday), and so from pulpits, congregations, and homes, the hallelujahs rose ever higher. "Glory to God in the highest!" Indianapolis businessman Calvin Fletcher scrawled in his diary. The Lord could save nations as well as souls, and now was the time for an even greater outpouring of divine love. After what a Pennsylvania presbytery termed a "baptism of blood," there should come a "baptism of the Holy Ghost."[15]

Even in the hour of victory, this was too much for some northern conservatives. A Boston priest deplored the "processions of truckmen and ministers of the abolition and puritan type, making addresses to the mob on the fall of Richmond." But war's end opened the floodgates for "political preaching." Henry Ward Beecher pointed out how the northern people had been forced to wander in the wilderness like the children of Israel before entering a promised land of peace, reunion, and emancipation. Here he hit on what became a popular analogy, and preachers often turned to Exodus for sermon texts. Methodist Gilbert Haven cast Jefferson Davis in the role of a latter-day Pharaoh thrown into the sea by the Union's Moses and Aaron: Lincoln and Grant. On the day Lee sent word that he could no longer defend Richmond, the Confederate president had "received his death-blow in the church of his idolatry, at the altars of a false god whom he had set up in the place of the true God and our Savior Jesus Christ." In doing so, Davis, like the biblical Pharaoh, had played out the role he had been destined to follow. Changing biblical analogies, the *Independent* called the late Confederate capital "Babylon the Great, Mother of Harlots and Abominations of the Earth."[16]

Already Lincoln's recommendation of "malice toward none" and "charity for all" was being forgotten or ignored. Some ministers and religious editors pushed for the arrest of prominent Confederates including Robert E. Lee for the mistreatment of Union prisoners, among other crimes. Even after pointedly remarking how both sides had sinned, abolitionist and Unitarian James Freeman Clark insisted that Georgia and South Carolina deserved to be ravaged and leading rebels exiled.[17]

Once again, soaring hopes competed with lingering fears. The battles of reconstruction had already been joined, and that was part of the problem because the meaning of emancipation and freedom remained very much in dispute. Presbyterian Henry A. Boardman no doubt spoke for a broad swath of northern religious opinion in welcoming the providential death of slavery while worrying about the racial consequences. With some trepidation, he noted "the abrupt and violent enfranchisement of four millions of ignorant slaves" but again saw a wonderful parallel in the Exodus. Such statements reflected uncertainty and confusion. Boardman urged northerners to be "peacemakers," but how to square that advice with the demands of justice, much less to tackle the difficult and intractable problems peace would bring, he did not say. Others pointed out how the prayers of pious slaves had hastened the day of liberation, even though supposedly wise statesmen had failed to recognize the power of such humble petitions. Indeed, as one Methodist editor pointed out, the Lord had prevented an earlier triumph for Union arms "in mercy to ourselves and the colored race."[18]

Such statements pushed against the limits of northern opinion and prejudice, no doubt exaggerating the potential for revolutionary change. Despite the Emancipation Proclamation, the enrollment of black troops, and even congressional passage of the Thirteenth Amendment, neither the northern clerics nor their congregations had moved so far as the more radical ministers hoped or expected. In sermons hastily prepared right after the capture of Richmond and the surrender at Appomattox, it seemed more appropriate to emphasize national deliverance and celebrate the Lord's blessing on popular government and free institutions. One Baptist preacher rejoiced over how "God Almighty created Abraham Lincoln, and hid him away just as he did Moses, till he wanted him, and then he brought him forth to lead his people out of Egypt."[19]

But Lincoln, like Moses, would not lead his people into the promised land. Instead, he would be almost literally crucified on a cross of bitter hatred and smoldering rebellion as the biblical typology shifted to the New Testament. Exodus gave way to Easter: Good Friday, Ford's Theater, John Wilkes Booth, and beatification. Even as the Union armies were winding up their work and religious meetings continued with enemy guns now silent, news arrived in the camps that Abraham Lincoln had been assassinated. For the soldiers, stunned disbelief mingled with raging anger. All around the country, clergymen searched for some suitable text for a message far different from the joyous Easter morning sermon they had planned to deliver. Although by this time scores of war sermons had already been printed, on this unique occasion an unprecedented number would eventually appear as pamphlets or in published collections.[20]

Almost all the preachers began by noting how Easter joy had turned to Easter sorrow. Contrasting the recent news from Richmond and Appomattox with this unexpected, unbelievable calamity made it all that more painful.[21] Cries of anguish from the pulpit—and they often seemed palpable even in the published sermons—must have echoed those from the congregations. Lincoln's death seemingly mocked the meaning of Easter Sunday. The message "He is risen," a Boston Unitarian observed, had been overwhelmed by the message, "He is dead." Normally long-winded preachers suddenly found themselves almost speechless, hardly prepared to address the meaning of such a tragedy or soothe people's jangled nerves. Some pastors forged ahead with an Easter sermon dealing with the assassination, but many of these said much more about Easter than about Lincoln. Other ministers admitted having little to say of any consequence and promised to derive deeper lessons at some future date.[22]

"I do not know the meaning of this awful transaction," Reverend Charles Robinson conceded with a modesty all too rare in the clerical fraternity. "Let silence speak," a Wisconsin chaplain advised his sorrowful troops, urging them to wait for the Lord to make his ways plain to mortal men. Talk of a sovereign God who presided over human history at its worst offered little reassurance on this Easter morning.[23] The applicable passages from Psalms and other scriptures readily came to mind, and they surely brought some peace, but they could not shut out the hard, nagging questions that demanded answers.

The assassination upset spiritual equanimity by casting doubt on the more pat and rosy affirmations of civil religion. "Why did a just and merciful God permit this thing to happen?" one Vermont soldier wrote in anguish, and his question no doubt resonated with many believers. The lack of a ready answer hardly prevented ministers and laity alike from probing the issue more extensively if not more deeply. Naturally enough, many began by asserting the will of God moves along unknown paths or, as a Michigan surgeon serving with Sherman's army in North Carolina expressed it, "leads us in a way we know not." And just because even the subtlest theologians could add little here, that was hardly a reason to lose faith. An article in the Methodist *Ladies' Repository* simply described Lincoln's assassination as "one of the inexplicable mysteries of Providence."[24] These words echoed those of Lincoln himself, who ironically might well have offered a similar interpretation. "Be still and know that I am God," that sound advice of the Psalmist, became a favorite text.

A providential view of the assassination, however, left little room for silence, much less chance, in effect refuting the fatalism of the young (and, at times, older) Lincoln. Either Satan's plot or Booth's plans—whatever your preference—had all proceeded according to some as yet unrevealed design. The randomness of nature or of life had little place in contemporary reactions to the president's murder; luck or even accident (including the series of remarkable decisions, actions, and mistakes that made the deed itself possible) failed to explain much of anything, at least to those who affirmed the sovereignty of God in all of life. When ministers repeated that "God reigns," they duly noted how Lincoln himself had pondered the inscrutable ways of providence in his Second Inaugural, yet he remained a humble servant of the Almighty who never tried to usurp divine prerogatives.[25]

Because so many patriotic citizens had failed to learn that lesson, placed too much faith in their leaders, and often failed to acknowledge the nation's dependence on God, the Almighty had allowed and perhaps decreed Lincoln's death. Connecting political assassination to the divine will was not that different from preachers' persistent warnings against relying on an "arm of flesh." The Lord had demonstrated anew that no man was indispensable either to the nation or to Christ's kingdom; as a Boston Congregationalist observed, a "prince" would easily be removed by a "bullet." Even Lincoln's own pastor, Phineas Gurley, preaching at the funeral in Washington, once more hauled out that favorite biblical image: "the rod of correction," to explain why the president had been taken from the people. A Cincinnati Unitarian sounded especially dogmatic on the general relationship between the Lord's will and untimely death: "All shedding of blood is by God's permission. Not one act of violence, not one destruction of life, not one drop of human blood shed, without his knowledge and consent." It was then but a short step to affirming that the assassination had been "foreordained."[26]

Divine omniscience meant divine control; the initial reaction of the devout was often a simple reaffirmation of God's providence. The Lord's will was reflected not only in the president's death, a Lutheran pastor maintained, but in all the "calamities that have befallen us for the past four years." A Pennsylvania minister agreed that "God's way was to soak our soil with gore and redden our rivers with blood, and thicken the very air with groans for four long years."[27] In several ways, this kind of reasoning gave the war and human suffering in general too much meaning and therefore raised a host of thorny questions about heavenly benevolence and free will. Yet many ministers kept declaring that history unfolded according to a divine plan with events rigidly ordered by the Almighty. Such a theology might and did appear callous to the human mind but reflected a fairly pervasive orthodoxy that extended beyond the clergy. That

"GOD'S WAYS UNSEARCHABLE."

A DISCOURSE,

ON THE DEATH OF PRESIDENT LINCOLN,

PREACHED BEFORE THE

𝕿𝖍𝖎𝖗𝖉 𝕻𝖗𝖊𝖘𝖇𝖞𝖙𝖊𝖗𝖎𝖆𝖓 𝕮𝖔𝖓𝖌𝖗𝖊𝖌𝖆𝖙𝖎𝖔𝖓,

IN MOZART HALL, PITTSBURGH, PA.

SUNDAY, APRIL 23d, 1865.

BY

Rev. HERRICK JOHNSON, Pastor.

PUBLISHED BY REQUEST.

W. G. Johnston & Co., Printers, Stationers and Blank Book Makers, 57 Wood Street, Pittsburgh.

Herrick Johnson, sermon title page, God's Ways Unsearchable the assassination fulfilled some as yet undisclosed but holy purpose echoed from many pulpits but also mirrored the private views of people struggling to fit this latest horror into their understanding of the war.[28]

Study the designs of God, that was the only advice forthcoming from several pulpits. At least since First Bull Run, many believers had been doing exactly that; they later tried to fathom the significance of Antietam, discern the meaning of Gettysburg, or find some message in the slaughter of the Overland campaign. Lincoln's assassination would send them back to their Bibles, forced to relearn ancient lessons. God might hide himself for a time, especially in the gloom of the assassination, claimed New York Baptist William R. Williams, but the good minister's own attempt to wrestle with the implications of recent events led to intellectual confusion and a rather weak and Emersonian assertion that in human affairs God created a kind of "epic symmetry."[29]

Williams who had over many years accumulated a vast private library of learned tomes made the question far too intellectual and abstract. Ministers coming face to face with the great problem of providence in Lincoln's assassination fell back on the conventional but still powerful conviction that some future good would emerge from the present evil. All through the war, both northerners and southerners had repeated and relied on Paul's promise that "all things work together for good to them that love God." After all, the president's death did come in the hour of victory, a last gasp of treason, and there was still much cause if not for rejoicing at least for hope. "God has made no mistake," Brooklyn Presbyterian Samuel T. Spear forcefully declared, but "has permitted apparent calamity for some wise reason." Even taking into account the inscrutable and irresistible decrees of providence, familiar assertions about God being on the Union's side still echoed from Yankee pulpits. To a Dutch Reformed minister from New Jersey, one aspect of the divine will remained quite clear: "God means the perpetuity of our free institutions."[30]

If that was true, it also became necessary to extract from Lincoln's life some deeper meaning. Everyone from ordinary citizens to the most famous pulpit orators recounted the president's humble origins and his improbable path to the nation's highest office. Even those simple points, however, created complications because it was hard to describe Lincoln as both a self-made man and an instrument of divine will. In any case, this unlikely leader had emerged from what one preacher called "the American Nazareth," though whether that was located in Kentucky, Indiana, or Illinois, he did not say.[31] Yet many ministers displayed at least some understanding of Lincoln's virtues. Several pointed out that Lincoln had a great mind, at once strong and benevolent; others praised his judgment and sense of duty. There was even some recognition that Lincoln was not only an extraordinary but a complex person. Sharp humor, common sense, and basic honesty complemented a political shrewdness anchored in a steady moral purpose.[32]

At times, Lincoln's contemporaries reduced his character to caricature, and certain blinders inevitably narrowed their perspective on the man. A prime example would be the shocked reaction in some quarters on learning that the president had been shot in a theater by an actor. The assassin Booth, an Ohio minister sniffed, "is a legitimate product of the theatre, the drinking saloon, and the gambling hall." Ministers who greatly valued holiness saw the theater as a natural breeding ground for such criminals. Perhaps God intended this terrible deed to "awaken anew our fears and suspicions of the dangerous influence of the stage on the moral sentiments and habits of the people," an earnest Presbyterian warned.[33] This was a new twist on the whole theme of providence, but few ministers traveled far along this path.

For the president to be murdered in a theater seemed disgraceful in its own right, and one preacher uttered some sanctimonious claptrap about how no man should enter a place where he was not willing to die. Had Lincoln actually sanctioned sin by attending the play? That was the verdict of an Episcopalian rector, and remarkably Reverend Gurley expressed similar sentiments. Yet even the most strait-laced ministers had a convenient way to absolve most of Lincoln's guilt. Ignoring his love for everything from Shakespeare's plays to Artemus Ward's humor, they claimed that the president had only reluctantly agreed to attend the performance. A careworn Lincoln had simply made his appearance so as not to disappoint the public. The direct evidence for this assertion was thin, though that hardly mattered to these ministers; the great man had perhaps erred, but his motives were pure and the sin was readily forgiven.[34]

The whole question of place and timing fit into a much larger theological framework. However regrettable the location may have been, clerics had much less trouble explaining why the president had been snatched away in the very hour of victory. Putting aside general considerations of national sin and providential design, they pointed out that Lincoln's work was finished. With the surrender of Lee's army (and despite the fact there were still Confederate forces in the field and Jefferson Davis remained at large), the Union had been preserved and the slaves emancipated; as countless sermons noted, God had therefore released his faithful servant from all earthly cares. The president's death literally marked the end not only of the war but of his assigned part in human history. This almost made the president into just another "soldier" fallen at the end of a successful war. The Lord had appointed the time and place of Lincoln's birth and death just as he had for all persons, and a thoroughly orthodox Vermont Congregationalist used the phrase "determined his days." And he might have added, that was all for the best. Had Lincoln lived he would have faced a future fraught with difficulties that could well have tarnished his historical reputation. After the assassination, stories immediately circulated of the president's own dreams and premonitions, so it could easily be argued that Lincoln himself understood the designs of providence at work here.[35]

The preachers' assertions about timing meshed perfectly with the idea widely bruited about at the time that Lincoln had above all else been an instrument of the Almighty. Several ministers talked about how the God had "raised up Lincoln" as a "man of providence." How marvelous of the Lord to select a man born to a hardscrabble family in a slave state to deliver the nation from traitors and lead the people toward the promised land of freedom. And to complete the picture of Lincoln as the Lord's servant, there were the president's own statements about the role of providence in the war. When future generations considered the ways of God in history, a New Jersey Episcopalian believed, they would always think of Abraham Lincoln.[36]

The president had completed his work and would lead the people no farther. America as a New Israel had long been a popular idea, especially in New England, and therefore the Exodus story brought new meaning to Lincoln's story. Some Jews compared Lincoln to their patriarch Abraham or to David, but Moses was far and away the most popular analogue among both preachers and editorial writers. Like Moses, Lincoln had been born in humble circumstances and had to contend with a mighty slave power. Like Moses, Lincoln had been a great and good man with a special mission from the Lord. Like Moses, Lincoln had become the unlikely leader of a chosen people. Like Moses, Lincoln had come to the end of his journey, and God had called him home. Like Moses, Lincoln had died at a most dramatic moment in his people's history.[37]

Yet it was emancipation that capped the comparison between Moses and Lincoln. They had each delivered a people from the house of bondage, and despite a good deal of wandering in the wilderness and a still uncertain future, the day of jubilee had arrived. "The black people of America will never forget the name of Abraham Lincoln," a New Jersey Presbyterian predicted. Unlike some historians, former slaves appeared to have little doubt about Lincoln being the great emancipator. At an African American school in Charleston, the children cried over news of the assassination, and some of the older students complained about a local teacher "speaking with disrespect" about the late president. Among former slaves, there was much talk of the Red Sea and even of Lincoln as a redeemer messiah.[38]

The events of Good Friday followed by the sermons on Easter Sunday undoubtedly strengthened that last connection, but transforming Lincoln into a conventional (or some would say any kind of) Christian had several pitfalls. Some ministers said little about the president's religious views other than simply observing that he must have been a believer. More often, they mustered as much evidence as they could find—or invent. One chaplain discovered spiritual devotion even in the very young Lincoln: "Born of a pious mother, and brought up to [sic] the Bible, Abraham Lincoln was taught to pray before he could pronounce his Maker's name." And had not a much older Lincoln asked the good citizens of Springfield to pray for him as he left for Washington? Lincoln had enjoined observance of the Sabbath in the army; he had reportedly devoted an hour to prayer and the Bible each day. Any little scrap of information made for good sermon material.[39]

Whatever their complexities and ambiguities, the president's many references to providence were proof enough. "That he was a sincere Christian we have every reason to believe from the frequent declarations of his lips and the acts of his life," a Dutch Reformed minister assured his congregation. Lincoln's great decisions and especially the Emancipation Proclamation had grown out of a powerful moral sense that surely partook of the sacred. His famously tender heart along with familiar anecdotes and public statements had revealed what a Pennsylvania Presbyterian termed a "Christ-like quality of forbearance toward his enemies." Yet Lincoln had been largely "shut-mouthed"—to use his law partner William Herndon's famous phrase—about many things and especially about his religion, so when clergymen tried to marshal thin evidence and contradictory reports, they invariably created more confusion. One New York minister, for instance, claimed that somehow Lincoln had "enlisted the fellowship of all Christians." A belief in the sovereignty of God made him "Calvinistic," yet he also leaned toward rationalism; he appeared "at once orthodox and liberal, devout and humanitarian."[40]

For all the speculation and downright wishful thinking, the fact remained that Lincoln had never formally professed faith in Christ or joined a church. Yet surely he must have been a Christian, many Americans thought or at least hoped. Ministers (and undoubtedly many in their congregations) put great stock in stories about Lincoln's "conversion," which supposedly had occurred either right after the death of his son Willie or—in the more widely circulated version—during his trip to Gettysburg. The visit to the battlefield and cemetery there reportedly had been a heart-changing experience. When asked later if he loved Jesus, he supposedly replied, "I do love Jesus," though the exact wording varied from account to account (none of them very direct or believable) and even then subject to widely varying interpretations.[41]

Had the president in truth died for the nation's sins, as so many ministers declared or at least implied? The assassination on Good Friday obviously stirred many believers to wonder if Lincoln had been an American Christ. A freedman in Charleston expressed it this way: "Lincoln died for we, Christ died for we, and me believe him de same mans." Both had been the liberating saviors of humanity, and each had ascended to heaven with their work on earth complete. In comparing the assassination to the crucifixion, preachers of various stripes searched for parallels between the two events. The American people felt as depressed as the apostles had on Good Friday, yet surely Lincoln would have forgiven his enemies just as Jesus had done from the cross. All this went too far for conservative Democrat Maria Lydig Daly, who scoffed at all the saccharine Easter sermons on Lincoln. "It seemed to me that they gave Our Lord only the second place in his own house," when in fact God alone had brought Union victory. To elevate a mere man—and a deeply flawed one at that—to the status of national savior seemed utterly blasphemous.[42]

And, indeed, comparisons of Lincoln to Christ made the search for meaning in the assassination all that more theologically significant (and troublesome). Americans would now associate Good Friday with Lincoln, that seemed clear enough. Then, too, the preachers insisted that this terrible tragedy had to serve some larger, divine purpose. Reducing the matter to a single proposition, a Connecticut Baptist declared: "Jesus Christ died for the world; Abraham Lincoln died for his country." Easily enough said, but the whole idea of progress brought about by the shedding of blood—though certainly repeated often enough during the war—remained a difficult teaching. To interpret the president's death as a blood sacrifice meant that he had died for the remission of national sins. This went along with current thinking about the atonement, especially the idea of "vicarious sacrifice" hinted at in several assassination sermons but later developed more fully by Horace Bushnell. Bushnell argued that not only Lincoln but also the patriotic soldiers had made a "vicarious sacrifice" for their country.[43]

Atonement for sin in turn suggested forgiveness of sin, though that issue became much trickier when applied not only to Booth and his fellow conspirators but also to rebel leaders or Confederates more generally. Lincoln would surely have advised northerners to curb their anger and help heal the broken nation, a Philadelphia rabbi told his congregation. Warnings against vengeance or blanket condemnations of southerners came from the more conservative clergymen, who still held out hope that the president's generous spirit would survive. Catholic editors praised Lincoln for accepting the liberal terms of surrender that Grant had offered to Lee and thereby throwing off the vindictive spirit of New England radicalism.[44]

Such an emphasis on a cautious or merciful Lincoln hardly fit the tenor of the times. "Ministers who have preached peaceful conciliation when they meant aid and comfort to the foe," one influential Baptist maintained, must share blame for the assassination. Such false servants of God had received their inspiration from Richmond and used the Bible to defend slavery. Notorious Copperheads became favorite targets. After all, they had most harshly criticized their own government and had seldom found much fault with the rebels; "loyal" ministers excoriated them as hardly better than traitors serving the interests of the rebellion, little more than tools of the notorious slave power.[45]

Just as the slave power in 1856 had assaulted Charles Sumner on the Senate floor, so it had struck down Abraham Lincoln. For anyone caught up in the joyous celebrations over Lee's surrender, this latest atrocity served as an important reminder of the connections between slavery, rebellion, and violence. As for John Wilkes Booth, he was but a pawn of a brutal aristocracy that had often lashed out against any friend of freedom. And here again northern sympathizers with the rebellion—and that label was bandied about loosely—must share responsibility for the crime. A conservative Presbyterian who had been "repelled by the Infidelity" of the abolitionists now decided that Lincoln himself had been guilty of not coming down hard enough on slavery.[46]

The president's well-known tenderness and mercy became a central theme in providential interpretations of the assassination. One fear, a prominent New York Methodist observed, had been that Lincoln would be "too forgiving" and "too Christ-like." Perhaps the key to understanding the role of God's will in the assassination was to explain how kindhearted Lincoln would have been unable to deal with treacherous southerners on difficult matters of reunion and reconstruction. Even the conservative Presbyterian George Duffield observed how the Lord had once punished the children of Israel with a plague for treating the sin of rebellion too lightly.[47]

To many northerners, the assassination taught one unmistakable lesson: there should be no more concessions to rebels because treason still stalked the land. This murder had occurred, according to Reverend Villeroy Reed, a New Jersey Presbyterian, because "God saw it necessary to check the spirit of unholy fraternizing with the abettors of the worst forms of social and political crimes." The president's death, a New York minister added, put a halt to any kind of "charity" that "ignores the guilt of sin." Surely even the most naive would now understand the rebels' true nature. Southern chivalry stood unmasked, the assassination conspirators its legitimate representatives. The most vengeful Old Testament texts now spoke to the needs of the hour as preachers thundered against weak-kneed moderation. Lincoln's death marked the culmination of rebel atrocities, ranging from the abuse of Union prisoners to the notorious massacre of African American troops at Fort Pillow to the foiled plot to burn New York. And had not Confederates now become party to premeditated assassination, a plot that revealed much about their darker purposes? As New Jersey Presbyterian William Hornblower explained, Confederates operated at "the suggestions of the Devil"; and "as long as Jefferson Davis lives, this nation will feel that the death of Abraham Lincoln is unavenged."[48]

While a Pennsylvania chaplain was wrapping up a camp sermon for soldiers who had participated in the final assault on the Petersburg lines, word had arrived of Lincoln's assassination. Some men cried out for revenge, but the chaplain wondered if God had allowed Lincoln to die because a more radical leader was needed to take charge of reconstructing the southern states. He reminded the troops, "This is God's war." If many religious people compared Lincoln to Moses, then Andrew Johnson must play the role of Joshua, whom the Lord had appointed to bring the chosen people into the promised land, a comparison echoed by the *New York Herald*. Some ministers even predicted that the Tennessean would prove superior to Lincoln, agreeing with Republican Senator Zachariah Chandler of Michigan that "the Almighty continued Mr. Lincoln in office so long as he was useful and then substituted a better man to finish the work." Strong talk about crushing out the spirit of rebellion once and for all continued because, in the words of a Boston Methodist, the traitors at last faced "eternal damnation"[49]

"Just at this juncture I do rejoice that he [Lincoln] did not survive the fall of the Confederacy," but this comment by a Georgia Baptist who had served in the Army of Northern Virginia carried a far different message than similar sounding statements by northern ministers or the late president's Republican critics. To many southern whites, Lincoln's death appeared both heartening and frightening. Some Confederates simply rejoiced, and women in Charleston reportedly fell on their knees to praise the Lord. "God grant so may all our foes perish," wrote refugee Eleanor S. Cohen in burned-out Columbia, South Carolina. It was easy to find a few such outspoken rebels, and certainly the northern press played up such comments and incidents, but Confederates in general reacted with deep shock and no little ambivalence to the news. One Richmond woman was ashamed of exulting over Lincoln's death but could not feel too sorry and so finally concluded the whole affair signified the "vengeance of the Lord."[50]

Yet few southern whites probably believed the assassination had accomplished anything. In fact, there was a fairly widespread belief that Lincoln's death would bring only more trouble. Like their northern brethren, Confederates might affirm that God reigned and everything would work out for the best, but in a strange way it seemed that providence had dealt them another hard blow. Some ministers strongly advised their congregations to condemn the crime or face worse consequences. Signs of defiance and talk about southern independence being secured by the next generation could do little good and much harm. "God has taken the matter in his own hand," young Grace Brown Elmore wrote in her diary, and "is commanding us, with a mighty voice to be patient and be still." [51]

Such patience was difficult under the best of circumstances, and now it proved nearly impossible. Lincoln and many devout northerners had offered widely varying providential interpretations of the war's course and outcome. His assassination provoked a new round of soul-searching, though not always of the deepest kind. It would be easy to stress signs of disillusionment, loss of faith, and even the demise of civil religion, but that is only part of the story and not the most important part. Many Americans would continue to view their own and their nation's wartime experience through a religious lens. Northerners and southerners alike would cling to the old verities, repeat familiar words of comfort, and carry them into a tumultuous postwar world. They would seek to rebuild their lives and their churches, often reaffirming their most cherished beliefs even as they struggled in coming to grips with the events of the past four years. The devout would turn to their families, their churches, and their God for direction, comfort, and meaning in a time of dramatic changes, deep fears, and unrealized hopes.

EPILOGUE

"I saw strong war worn smoke begrimed, powder burnt men . . . lying upon the ground with tears streaming from their eyes and crying like children," a corporal in Parker's Virginia Battery recalled. The news of Lee's surrender had unnerved them and many were "praying God for help in this their hour of great distress." The word "anguish" well captured the reaction of countless Confederates who felt as if the heavens had collapsed upon them, and all was indeed lost. Some were so disheartened they could no longer write in their diaries and so fell silent. Others poured out their sorrow about shattered hopes and dreams in words that evoked an overwhelming despair. So many hard questions preyed on people's minds. Had all the blood been shed in vain? Had costly sacrifices and ardent prayers all gone for naught? Had God at long last utterly forsaken them? Imprisoned at Fort Warren in Boston Harbor, Alexander H. Stephens, the former Confederate vice president, who was melancholic enough under normal circumstances, took to reading the book of Job before breakfast.[1]

Perhaps the Confederates had depended too much on General Lee and not enough on God; that was one predictable explanation for the Confederate collapse. Having returned home from the Army of Northern Virginia, a pious Georgian concluded that by making an idol of Lee just as they had with Jackson, southerners had greatly displeased the Lord. Theological thinking on the war and especially its outcome inevitably fragmented. The poor Confederates had no longer been able to resist the Yankees' overwhelming numbers, the Episcopal bishop of North Carolina observed, anticipating a central tenet of the Lost Cause, but "we must as Christians see the finger of God in it." Others maintained that understanding divine providence remained vital for explaining and accepting the reality of defeat. Few would express any doubts about the righteousness of secession or the war itself; after all, religious faith had helped sustain the southern armies and people for four long and bloody years;

this powerful blend of piety and nationalism had stood at the heart of the southern nation. The downfall of the Confederacy simply reflected the Lord's will, however mysterious it might appear to soldiers who had given so much to the doomed cause. And then there was always the longer and more personal perspective: because final victory would not come on this earth anyway, Appomattox did not necessarily shatter religious faith.[2]

How many people continued to embrace these various and at times contradictory ideas is impossible to say. And though many white southerners continued to speak of providence in quite conventional ways when wrestling with Confederate defeat, there certainly were exceptions. When his brother referred to God's "inscrutable workings" or pointed to examples of "divine mercy," South Carolinian Louis Blanding dismissed such ideas as "vague scholastic playthings, fit for the keen edge of discussion and of no earthly account." Perhaps civil religion itself, at least for many Confederates, was as the soldiers would have said "all played out." Cynical War Department clerk John B. Jones found a perverse consolation in the apparent demise of civil religion: "We shall now have no more interference in Caesar's affairs by the clergy—may they attend to God hereafter."[3]

At the same time, catchphrases about it always being darkest before the dawn reflected a belief that the Lord might completely abase his chosen people before saving them. Wartime theological assumptions survived. The notion of God's "appointed time" proved especially important for Confederates still trying to fit their experience into a providential framework. Lingering talk of "ultimate triumph" placed the vindication of the Confederate cause in some vague and indefinite future and avoided raising more painful questions about present suffering and the divine will. Only two weeks after Appomattox, young North Carolinian Elizabeth Collier expressed what would soon become an empty maxim: "We are bound to rise again."[4]

Confederates had repeatedly avowed that God could not possibly intend their subjugation, but in April 1865 the truth slowly dawned on them that perhaps God did so intend after all. Although this seemed beyond comprehension, a sudden shift in thinking—especially among civilians—revealed how flexible providential theology could be. To believe that "what is" reflected the Lord's will actually smoothed the transition to peace though it hardly soothed the pain for the more ardent Confederates. Talk of laboring under a heavy yoke or bowing to the Lord's mandate marked a reluctant acceptance of a once unimaginable reality.[5]

"We deem it our duty as patriots and Christians to accept the order of Providence" and "yield to unreserved and faithful obedience to the powers that be," a Virginia Baptist association resolved. But despite urging their members to "prove themselves loyal citizens of the United States," exactly what that signified was never spelled out. Accepting the verdict of history or even submitting to God's will seemed standard enough counsel, but Methodist bishop James O. Andrew—whose wife's inherited slaves had sparked his church's sectional schism more than twenty years ago—was much more specific. In a July 1865 pastoral letter, he insisted that bushwhacking and guerrilla warfare cease. "To sum up in a few words," he advised, "God seems to have ordained that we should live together in civil compact with the North as formerly, and the sooner we can bring about a state of kind feeling between the two sections, the better for all concerned."[6]

Providence had decreed that the Confederacy fall, the Union survive, and the slaves be free. Many Americans regardless of section or race might well have affirmed that statement, though with varying emphases and tones. Victorious northerners could more readily embrace God's will in all these things, yet the Almighty had accomplished his purposes in a most costly way. Working out a new interpretation of the atonement, Horace Bushnell viewed the Union dead as the price that had to be paid for national salvation. "Without the shedding of blood there is almost nothing great in the world," he told a group of Yale alumni gathered to honor former students who had died in the war.[7]

Implicit in all this was the idea that Americans remained a chosen people. In the summer of 1865, Henry Clay Fish reviewed the entire course of the conflict for his New Jersey Baptist congregation. He began by quoting Secretary of War Stanton, who attributed Union victories to the "Spirit of the Lord." In fact, the Almighty had been at work all along even in the early reverses and defeats, slowly forcing the northern people to place their trust in him rather than in man. God had decreed that Richmond not be captured in the summer of 1862 before the slaves could be emancipated. And the much-needed victory at Stones River had been the Lord's way of making sure that Lincoln—himself an instrument of the divine will—issued the final Emancipation Proclamation. As for the future, Fish predicted that veterans would acknowledge how God had preserved their lives and so would lead the entire nation to repentance. In a series of lectures given in Europe, Swiss-born theologian Philip Schaff explained how the Almighty had used the conflict to reunite the American nation and how Lincoln's death had consolidated the triumph of the divine will.[8] At least in the short run, memories of the war's religious history remained very much alive, and long-held beliefs about providence, sin, and judgment still held sway, though for northerners there was now an equal emphasis on the blessings of victory and peace.

Where emancipation fit in remained a much-clouded issue. Slavery in one way or another had been central to civil religion in the Union and the Confederacy, and with the coming of peace, the theological questions remained just as knotty. Even though the Lord had chosen not to perpetuate the institution, Tennessean Eliza Fain remained convinced that slavery was biblically justified. Why God had acted so, "we cannot know now, but he does and this is all we deserve to know." Meeting in Macon, Georgia, in December 1865, the southern Presbyterian General Assembly resolved that condemning slavery as a sin would be "unscriptural and fanatical," and thus there had been no shame for southerners who had simply walked in the footsteps of Abraham, Isaac, and Jacob—slaveholders all. Despite claims of accepting the Lord's will in this matter, these church leaders hardly welcomed emancipation: "This relation is now overthrown, suddenly, violently—whether justly or unjustly, in wrath or in mercy, for weal or for woe—let history and the Judge of all the earth decide."[9]

Racial bigotry remained cloaked in the garb of humanitarian paternalism. The war's effect on the "minds of our poor Negroes" disturbed Eliza Fain, who feared there was much "calculated to excite pride, haughtiness of spirit and every feeling contrary to the word of God and that it tended only to lead them to hell."[10] As if replying directly to Fain, an editorial in the leading paper of the AME Church pointed out how "new ideas have possessed the masses of the people" as the nation was being "regenerated and born anew." Ironically, the southern rebellion had vindicated the "universal brotherhood of the human race." The contrast in assessing African American character appeared striking: "Before the war little was known of him, except as a 'nigger,' to be degraded, out-lawed, and spit upon; chattels, to be bought and sold and traded as beasts of burden. But his very condition before, being the cause of the war, has brought him before the nation and the world in a new light: 'He is a man and a brother,' brave in battle, humane in victory, and he has shown, that in his ignorance he possesses all the attributes of enlightenment."[11]

This new status included the cherished right of free people to worship as they pleased. Dramatic preaching, ecstatic dancing, and heartfelt shouting—however criticized and caricatured by white (and some black) observers—celebrated emancipation both from slavery and from the white churches. The black exodus from the white churches marked a sea change in southern religious history, one that shocked and alarmed not only former Confederates but northerners as well.[12] "The ebony preacher who promises perfect independence from white control and direction carried the cold heart at once," one northern missionary observed condescendingly and perceptively. But, in fact, on the heels of emancipation African Americans were celebrating what amounted to a second, spiritual liberation.[13] One black woman explained with a raw eloquence why so many of her sisters and brothers had left the white churches: "I goes ter some churches, an' I sees all de folks settin' quiet an' still, like dey dunno what de Holy Sperit am." Did the scriptures not speak of the very stones crying out? She simply could not understand such staid worship: "Not make a noise! Why we makes a noise 'bout ebery ting else; but dey tells us we mustn't make no noise ter praise de Lord." She had endured slavery, and for former slaves that agony had continued during the often fruitless search for lost family members once freedom came, but surely emancipation was worth celebrating in the most joyous way. A new day had dawned with the promise of God's grace shinning brighter than ever. Echoing both Union and Confederate statements on the role of providence, a letter to the *Christian Recorder* celebrating the entrance of black troops into Richmond remarked how "the hand of God has been made visible to all who have not sunk entirely out of the reach of his mercies."[14]

Devout Confederates might certainly have wondered if that last clause described their situation. Talk of useless sacrifices appeared to reflect a deepening crisis of faith. Even Grace Brown Elmore, who had long shown patriotic devotion and stoic patience, gave way to bitterness about the injustice of it all. "I find no consolation in religion," she finally confessed, having lost confidence in virtually everyone. "I cannot be resigned," she raged. "Hard thoughts against my God will arise, questions of His justice and mercy refuse to be silenced." She struggled to "find truth at the bottom of this impenetrable darkness." But she discerned no light, no relief, no comfort, no hope. "Sometimes I feel so wicked, so rebellious against God, so doubtful of his mercy." Present suffering perhaps counted for little in the Lord's sense of time, but she had trouble embracing such a long view of things.[15]

God had seemingly abandoned both the Confederacy and its people. Perhaps the whole experiment had gone wrong from the beginning, and there was even the occasional reassessment of Confederate civil religion. Presbyterian Moses Drury Hoge wrote of "the idolized expectation of a separate nationality, of a social life and literature and civilization of our own, together with a gospel guarded against the contamination of New England infidelity" but quickly noted how that dream had "perished." He fell back on an orthodox Calvinism: "God's dark providence enwraps me like a pall. I cannot comprehend, but I will not charge him foolishly; I cannot explain, but I will not murmur."[16]

There had been plenty of murmuring during the war against politicians and against generals and against God, and as Confederate fortunes had declined, thoughts had turned both inward and upward. "I am trying to live for heaven," the introspective Abbie Brooks wrote from Nashville, and many other southerners shifted their attention from the earthly to the eternal. In the wake of military disaster, it is hardly surprising that pious Confederates often remarked on the fleeting nature of all human concerns. To fix one's mind on holy things was to escape from the mundane and depressing aspects of daily life in a conquered land. In a chaotic time, faith in God, claimed Episcopal bishop Stephen Elliott, brought a sense of order and hope even if people could not exactly discern the order or always find much hope. "The Christian cannot be defeated," the Texas Baptist Convention bravely maintained. "In the midst of the turmoil, agitation, and strife incident to human affairs the mind of God is serene, the virtue of the atonement is unimpaired, human instrumentality preserves its place in the divine economy, and the will of God concerning the redemption and salvation of man is being accomplished." Believers stood outside human history and rose above the temporal and unimportant, setting their minds on higher and more transcendent matters.[17]

Southern churches would simply have to rebuild congregational life in a most difficult time. In the wake of defeat, some preachers swore off politics altogether. "War . . . made the Confederacy our idol," a North Carolina Presbyterian sadly observed, and God has "left us neither name, nor country nor inheritance among men." No longer would southerners worship the state but in the words of the prophet Micah would instead rest under their own "vine" and "fig tree." The "spirituality of the church"—a doctrine long favored by Thornwell and other conservatives—now loomed larger than ever along with revivals as a predominant form of religious expression, with Confederate veterans often in attendance. As Stonewall Jackson's own minister remarked at the end of the war, "True religion has prospered under all forms of civil government. Our blessed Lord can surely do more to make his people permanently happy than men and devils can to make them miserable."[18]

In many ways, religious life in the North was moving in similar directions. According to one postwar estimate, at least one in six or seven northerners was a church member, though more attended services regularly. Any faithful reader of the religious press, or secular newspapers for that matter, would assume these numbers might be much higher given the extensive coverage of church affairs.[19] A triumphalist civil religion and evangelical strength seemed to promise an even brighter future. "This nation will be an example for the whole world," a Connecticut artillery lieutenant wrote a little less than a month after Appomattox.[20]

For most churchgoers, however, civil religion was often overshadowed by a renewed emphasis on individual salvation, and peace would allow Americans to turn their attention back to spiritual matters. Historian David Bebbington has written of the "dominant force" of evangelicalism in the "English-speaking world in the last half of the nineteenth century," and that simple generalization speaks volumes about what mattered most to millions of Americans. If anything the war itself, along with its horrific death toll, made the standard messages of salvation all that more appealing. Christ's mysterious sacrifice on the cross remained at the center of faith, and heaven became the chief consolation for those who had suffered grievous losses. A flood of books, tracts, and articles pictured heaven as home, a place where families would be reunited, and consolation became a major function of the postwar churches.[21] But the kind of orthodoxy that Horace Bushnell and others yearned for would not necessarily prevail.

Disturbed by a series of lectures on the theory of evolution, a New Yorker feared the country tolerated "every form of belief and unbelief." In the United States, "the Atheist, the Deist, the Jew, the Romanist, the German Sunday pleasure seeker, and the Mormon have thrown their respective banners to the breeze." Yet these same groups often sought to banish Christianity from "our civil and organic life." The rough ecumenicism of the army camp had perhaps loosened denominational loyalties across the entire nation, and complaints in both the North and South about declining discipline in the churches may also have reflected a weakening commitment to particular historic creeds and practices. After the war, liberal theology, the emergence of the Social Gospel, and a growing faith in science competed with a rising fundamentalism.[22]

At the same time, however, the faith of ordinary people often appeared little shaken by such competing forces, and the winds of theological and intellectual change in biblical criticism, evolution, or psychology would hardly touch most Civil War veterans or their families.[23] How much the war experience affected their faith remains a matter of conjecture and perhaps some dispute. "After the Civil War, the world never seemed quite right again," Oliver Wendell Holmes Jr. once remarked, but even after being seriously wounded at Antietam, Holmes had pridefully refused to seek religious consolation.[24] Disillusioned intellectuals often had interesting things to say but hardly spoke for countless fellow citizens who still embraced quite conventional and orthodox religious views.

The faithful clung to idealistic images of the war and its participants. Aside from the usual talk of divine favor, both sides had claimed to have armies with a core of deeply religious soldiers. In the aftermath of camp revivals, Confederates had been especially adamant on this point but during a reinterment ceremony in 1871, a former Confederate chaplain (perhaps unintentionally) interrupted the postwar mythmaking when he admitted that "the vast majority of our soldiers were its [Christianity's] nominal adherents." He cast this statement in a positive light, though he added that only a minority had been consistently devout, and he clearly preferred dwelling on Stonewall Jackson and other paragons.[25]

That word "nominal" likely revealed much, and the same adjective could have easily been applied to the Federals. Yet, on claims to being Christian soldiers, northerners refused to yield any ground. Like the most fervent Lost Cause preachers, Yankee ministers eulogized their warriors' physical and spiritual perseverance. The soldiers had fought the good fight in a righteous cause, a New York Presbyterian declared in a sermon welcoming the returning troops. They had served both God and country. Their example and that of Christ, the prolific Congregationalist scholar Joseph Parrish Thompson explained during a memorial service for the Union dead, should teach people to have "faith in the great principles of justice and humanity by which God orders the world."[26]

In some ways such, claims and counterclaims simply continued long-standing rhetorical battles over comparative spiritual virtue. But there is one final irony. Historians seeking to explain the outcome of the Civil War are not likely to refer to divine providence; after all, in dealing with questions of causation historians do not usually turn to teleology or metaphysics.[27] "Those who complain of the aridity of technical history . . . evading the majestic issues that relate to a man's larger destiny," Herbert Butterfield once remarked, "are crying out precisely for the thing which the Biblical writers were doing with the human drama, and to the dignity of which the academic historian could not pretend to reach."[28] True enough perhaps, and the absence of virtually any reference to religious forces in the standard Civil War narratives is remarkable. That in itself would have struck those in the Civil War generation as very odd because many of them believed that the origin, course, and outcome of the war all reflected God's will.

Stephen Alexander Hodgman, a northerner who had lived in the South for thirty-two years before the war, observed that God had not just sealed the doom of slavery but that all wars helped prepare the way for the reign of Christ. In his view, the advance of both science and religion led to one inescapable conclusion: "There may be some now living, who, though not very young, may be permitted to see the last bloody conflict, which is to precede the dawning of the millennial day, when the olive branch of peace shall be seen throughout the world."[29]

Had the American Civil War been that "last bloody conflict?" That would be revealed in due time, but many Americans remained firmly wedded to the idea of providence shaping their lives. The war had in many ways highlighted the role of God in history for believers who had searched for meaning in events large and small. Naturally the coming of peace shifted the emphasis from the extraordinary to the ordinary but many people still interpreted the trials and vicissitudes of daily life in providential terms. Nor was a providential interpretation of their nation's recent history quickly forgotten. Religious certitudes had sustained morale and had likely prolonged the bloodshed. The Civil War had in fact been the "holiest" war in American history. Never before and likely never again would so many ministers, churches, and ordinary people turn not only to their Bibles but to their own faith to explain everything from the meanings of individual deaths, to the results of battles, to the outcome of the war itself.

In an oft-cited and likely apocryphal story, George Pickett was asked after the war to what he attributed the Confederate failure at Gettysburg. Perhaps his questioner hoped to elicit some sharp comments about Longstreet, Stuart, or even Lee, but the former general instead simply remarked, "I think principally to the Yankees."[30] This is usually rendered as "I've always thought the Yankees had something to do with it," but in either version the statement remains clever and perhaps unintentionally illuminating. And with a slight variation, it also offers a suitable conclusion to a religious history of the American Civil War. Because if asked to explain the causes, course, and consequences of the conflict, many Americans—northerners and southerners, African Americans and whites, Protestants and Catholics and Jews alike—might well have replied, "I've always thought God had something to do with it."

NOTES

Abbreviations

AAS	American Antiquarian Society, Worcester, Massachusetts
ABHS	American Baptist Historical Society, Rochester, New York
ADAH	Alabama Department of Archives and History, Montgomery
DePauw	Archives of DePauw University and Indiana United Methodism, DePauw University, Greencastle, Indiana
Drew	Methodist Collection, Drew University, Madison, New Jersey
LC	Manuscripts Division, Library of Congress, Washington, D.C.
Notre Dame	University of Notre Dame Archives, University of Notre Dame, Notre Dame, Indiana
OR	*War of the Rebellion: A Compilation of the Official Records of the Union and Confederate Armies.* 128 vols. Washington, D.C.: Government Printing Office, 1880–1901.
PHS-M	Presbyterian Historical Society, Montreat, North Carolina
PHS-P	Presbyterian Historical Society, Philadelphia
SBHLA	Southern Baptist Historical Library and Archives, Nashville, Tennessee
SHC	Southern Historical Collection, University of North Carolina, Chapel Hill
UVa	Alderman Library, University of Virginia, Charlottesville
VBHS	Virginia Baptist Historical Society, University of Richmond
VHS	Virginia Historical Society, Richmond

Prologue

1. *Christian Observer* (Richmond), August 11, 1864.

2. Doggett, *A Nation's Ebenezer*, 14.

3. Hall, *Worlds of Wonder, Days of Judgment*, 77–78, 91–94; Saum, *Popular Mood of America, 1860–1890*, 13–17.

4. Dabney, *True Courage*, 10.

5. Niebuhr, *Kingdom of God in America*, xi–xvii, 17–44; *Evangelist* (New York), December 6, 1860; Rees, *Sermon on Divine Providence*, 3–7; Miles, *God in History*, 5–31.

6. For a useful summary of the various strands of American civil religion, see Angrosino, "Civil Religion Redux," 239–67. For a very useful recent study on the role of providentialism in America, see Guyatt, *Providence and the Invention of the United States*.

7. The best discussion of these ideas remain Niebuhr, *Kingdom of God in America*, 45–163; Tuveson, *Redeemer Nation*, 1–90.

8. Aamodt, *Righteous Armies, Holy Cause*, 2–15. See especially the excellent and indispensable analysis in Mark A. Noll, "The Image of the United States as a Biblical Nation, 1776–1865," in Hatch and Noll, *Bible in America*, 39–51. For the continuation of millennial expectations during the war, see the excellent treatment in Moorhead, *American Apocalypse*. Moorhead's work deals with northern Protestants, but Confederates also talked of millennial hopes and expectations for their new republic. On the Confederates, see the narrower but still occasion-

ally useful study by Silver, *Confederate Morale and Church Propaganda*. For a penetrating and provocative analysis of the connections between Confederates' religious faith and slavery reform, see Genovese, *A Consuming Fire*.

9. Dabney, *True Courage*, 3–4; Niebuhr, *Faith and History*, 15, 22–29, 38; Frederickson, *Inner Civil War*, 3; Walker, *Sermon Delivered before the Executive and Legislative Departments of Massachusetts*, 7–8; *Independent* (New York), December 19, 1861. For a brilliant and moving reflection on how modern minds (and historians) have trouble understanding people who viewed God as the "Great Narrator" of history, see Faust, "Civil War Soldier and Art of Dying," 37–38.

10. This was duly noted directly and indirectly in a fine collection of essays that suggested both the potential benefits and difficulties of integrating religious themes into broader examinations of the Civil War era. Miller et al., *Religion and the American Civil War*. For a comprehensive overview that assembles a good deal of factual information on the general subject of religion and the Civil War, see Miller, *Both Sides Prayed to the Same God*.

11. The question of representative evidence is always difficult and tricky, and especially so here. This explains why I chose to dig deeply into the sermon literature as well as the periodical literature and denominational proceedings. Seldom is it possible, for example, to estimate how influential any particular sermon proved to be, but when a number of preachers from different denominations and parts of the country emphasized similar themes, that in itself was revealing. Unfortunately, however, there is also a significant denominational imbalance. The Presbyterians and to a lesser extent the Baptists were much more likely to publish sermons. Methodists are definitely underrepresented, and there are relatively few published Catholic or Jewish sermons. Again, however, common themes that cut across denominations along with the existence of some dissenting voices make all of this evidence quite valuable for exploring religious approaches to any number of issues.

12. On this type of material, Baptist association proceedings must take pride of place. The same is true for the minute books of Baptist congregations.

13. There is a great need to examine the attitudes of Catholic soldiers as well Catholics at home to supplement two valuable recent studies that focus on northern Protestants, Rolfs, *No Peace for the Wicked*; and Scott, "'A Visitation of God.'"

14. For an unfailingly stimulating and indeed international examination of the relationship between theology and the war, see Noll, *Civil War as a Theological Crisis*. Unfortunately, the latest and most comprehensive survey of theology in America does not extend into the war years. Holifield, *Theology in America*.

15. Stout, *Upon the Altar of the Nation*.

16. For the relationship between religion and southern identity with an emphasis on the central role of the clergy and churches in the sectional conflict, see Snay, *Gospel of Disunion*. Although I have placed more emphasis on persistent doubts and clerical divisions during the secession crisis, I have found Snay's study extremely illuminating. For the broader question of the relationship between religion and sectional politics, a description of vast cultural differences between north and south, and an emphasis on the vital role of religion in the sectional crisis, see the comprehensive and indispensable Carwardine, *Evangelicals and Politics in Antebellum America*.

17. There is extensive treatment of the wartime jeremiad in Stout, *Upon the Altar of the Nation*. Civil War preachers from many denominational backgrounds adopted this old Puritan rhetorical style in their sermons. It could be either a blunt instrument lambasting sinful

humanity in general or a scalpel cutting to the heart of some wartime dilemma. It was probably more often the former than the latter, but in the chapters that follow this prologue, there will be many examples of both.

18. The chaplains themselves were of decidedly mixed character. For a useful though a bit too positive assessment of Union chaplains, see Armstrong, *For Courageous Fighting and Confident Dying*.

19. On the all-important but until recently neglected subject of death and the Civil War, see two excellent works: Faust, *Republic of Suffering*; Schantz, *Awaiting the Heavenly Country*.

20. Alexander, *Fighting for the Confederacy*, 58–59. Such faith was much more likely to strengthen than weaken the will to fight. For a contrasting view, see Beringer et al., *Why the South Lost the Civil War*.

21. Jones, *Christ in the Camp*; Bennett, *Narrative of the Great Revival*. Historians have paid surprisingly little attention to comparable compilations of northern piety. Billingsley, *From the Flag to the Cross*; Hackett, *Christian Memorials of the War*. For contrasts in the postwar assessment of religious faith among both northerners and southerners, see the useful discussion in Shattuck, *A Shield and Hiding Place*, 127–36.

22. Steven Woodworth's excellent treatment of religion in Civil War armies, *While God Is Marching On*, supports this generalization while presenting voluminous evidence about the most deeply religious soldiers. For recent works that offer equally conservative estimates on the proportion of pious men in the ranks, see Rolfs, *No Peace for the Wicked*, xviii; Glatthaar, *General Lee's Army*, 236–37, 240–41.

23. On this point see McPherson, *For Cause and Comrades*, 62–76. For the important role of idealistic and devout officers, see Carmichael, *Last Generation*. Gerald Linderman has pointed out but also exaggerated the amount of religious disillusionment during the war; see Linderman, *Embattled Courage*, 158–59. For biographical treatments of especially pious Confederates, see Dollar, *Soldiers of the Cross*.

24. These themes all carry over into postwar America. I have chosen to conclude this book with the end of the war itself and do not take up the very large subject of the war's long-range impact on the churches, including the rebuilding of congregational life, growing racial segregation, religious themes in Reconstruction, and religion in the Lost Cause. On these topics, see Stowell, *Rebuilding Zion*; Blum, *Reforging the White Republic*; Wilson, *Baptized in Blood*; Moorhead, *American Apocalypse*; Blum and Poole, *Vale of Tears*.

Chapter 1

1. Schaff, *America*, 91, 118. Schaff did allow that Scotland might be just as religious as the United States.

2. For a fascinating study of "numeracy" in early American history, see Cohen, *A Calculating People*.

3. For high estimates of church adherence, see Smith, *Revivalism and Social Reform*, 17–21; Johnson, *Redeeming America*, 4–5; Cannon, "United States Christian Commission," 61. For lower estimates, see Butler, *Awash in a Sea of Faith*, 283–88; Carwardine, *Evangelicals and Politics in Antebellum America*, 4–5.

4. Finke and Starke, *Churching of America*, 54–108; Korn, *American Jewry and the Civil War*, 1–14.

5. Thornbrough, *Indiana in the Civil War Era*, 597–619; Smith, *Revivalism and Social Re-*

form, 18; Crowther, *Southern Evangelicals and Coming of the Civil War*, 40–45; Dicey, *Spectator of America*, 254.

6. McLoughlin, *Revivals, Awakenings, and Reform*, 112–40; Bruce, *And They All Sang Hallelujah*, 3–35, 70–95; Saum, *Popular Mood of Pre–Civil War America*, 62–77.

7. Miller, *Life of the Mind in America*, 78–84; Griffin, *Their Brothers' Keepers*, 3–22; Smith, *Revivalism and Social Reform*, 148–75.

8. On this point, see Niebuhr, *Kingdom of God in America*, xi–xvii.

9. Loveland, "Evangelicalism and 'Immediate Emancipation' in American Antislavery Thought," 172–88; Stewart, *Holy Warriors*, 13–49; Guyatt, *Providence and the Invention of the United States*, 232–35; Strong, *Perfectionist Politics*, 26–43; Walters, *Antislavery Appeal*, 37–42.

10. Dunham, *Attitude of Northern Clergy toward the South*, 81–104.

11. Chesebrough, *God Ordained This War*, 177–78.

12. Freehling, "James Henley Thornwell's Mysterious Antislavery Moment," 383–87; Palmer, *Discourse Commemorative of J. H. Thornwell*, 3–57; Holifield, *Gentlemen Theologians*, 110–11; Farmer, *Metaphysical Confederacy*, 170–74, 201–20.

13. In examining the relationship between scripture and the debates over slavery, I have relied heavily on Mark Noll's penetrating and brilliant analysis in "The Bible and Slavery," in Miller et al., *Religion and the American Civil War*, 43–73. See also Noll, *America's God*, 386–421, and additional comments on the weaknesses of the biblical argument against slavery and how European Protestant thinkers echoed some of these debates in Noll, *Civil War as a Theological Crisis*, 31–50, 95–111.

14. Johnson, *Life and Letters of Robert Lewis Dabney*, 128–29; Rosen, *Jewish Confederates*, 37–44. Larry Tise has pointed out that many of the antebellum proslavery writers were clergymen and that a fair number were northern born. Tise, *Proslavery*, 124–79.

15. Smith, *In His Image But*, 129–52; "Christianity and Caucasian Theory," *American Quarterly Church Review, and Ecclesiastical Register* 11 (July 1858): 249–58; Haynes, *Noah's Curse*, 3–40; Long, *Saints and the Union*, 11–12; Mitchell, *A Bible Defense of Slavery, and the Unity of Mankind*, 3–31. European religious commentators critiqued the racial suppositions of American attitudes toward slavery. Noll, *Civil War as a Theological Crisis*, 118–19. References to Ham actually reinforced the idea that all people had descended from a common ancestor—Adam—and set the stage for a potential clash with newer "scientific" studies of race. By the 1850s some theologians—North and South—grew more uneasy about the direction of scientific research that might reduce life to a series of chemical reactions or, worse, adopt ideas of polygenesis that contradicted biblical accounts of creation. It is equally important to note that readings of the Genesis text were also closely tied to notions of honor, hierarchy, and order. Bozeman, *Protestants in the Age of Science*, 3–159; Haynes, *Noah's Curse*, 65–104.

16. Heathcote, *Lutheran Church in the Civil War*, 40–65; Fortenbaugh, "American Lutheran Synods and Slavery, 1830–1860," 72–92.

17. Howe, *Unitarian Conscience*, 270–300; Robinson, *Unitarians and Universalists*, 83–85; Gannett, *Ezra Stiles Gannett*, 285–302.

18. Edwards, *Of Singular Genius, Of Singular Grace*, 49–54; Barnes, "The Idea That Caused a War," 73–83; Cole, "Horace Bushnell and the Slavery Question," 19–30; Luker, "Bushnell in Black and White," 408–16.

19. Ahlstrom, *Religious History of the American People*, 455–68; Marsden, *Evangelical Mind and New School Presbyterian Experience*, 59–87; Noll, *America's God*, 308–11.

20. Hodge, *Life of Charles Hodge*, 333–36, 359; Murray, *Presbyterians and the Negro*, 116–12; Noll, *America's God*, 413–17; Sandlund, "Robert Breckinridge, Presbyterian Conservative," 145–52.

21. Furman, *Rev. Dr. Furman's Exposition of the Baptists Relative to the Colored Population*, 10–11; Fuller, *Chaplain to the Confederacy*, 11–42,.212–27.

22. Johnson, *Life and Letters of Robert Lewis Dabney*, 129.

23. Milburn, *Ten Years of Preacher-Life*, 350–51; Genovese, *A Consuming Fire*, 18–22; Cornelius, *Slave Missions and the Black Church*, 40–46; Perkins, "Religion for Slaves," 237–39; *Southern Churchman* (Alexandria, Va.), September 2, 1860.

24. Mathews, "Charles Colcock Jones and the Southern Evangelical Crusade to Form a Biracial Community," 310–20; Stacy, *History of the Midway Congregational Church, Liberty County, Georgia*, 212–44; Smith, *History of the Washington Baptist Association of Georgia*, 38–40; Carroll, *A History of Texas Baptists*, 253–55.

25. Strout, *New Heavens and New Earth*, 143–44; Carroll, *History of Texas Baptists*, 255–57.

26. Jones, *Religious Instruction of Negroes*, 206–19; Clarke, "An Experiment in Paternalism," 223–30. Most recently, Robert Bonner has shown the close connection between evangelizing the slaves and evangelizing the slaveholders in both southern thought and practice. Bonner in turn connects these projects with claims for separate southern national identity. Bonner, *Mastering America*, 114–27.

27. Alexander Glennie Parish Diary, 1832–69, South Carolina Historical Society; Vander Velde, *Presbyterian Churches and the Federal Union*, 104; Wills, *Democratic Religion*, 67.

28. Williams, "Plantation Experiences of a New York Woman," 390, 394–95; April 15, 1860, Centre Ridge Presbyterian Church (Dallas County, Alabama) Minute Book, ADAH; Baptist Church, Virginia, Rappahannock Baptist Association, *Minutes of the Seventeenth Annual Session*, 14–16.

29. West, *Methodism in Alabama*, 606–8; Daniel, *Southern Protestantism in the Confederacy*, 126–28; Margrett Nickerson (Florida), Charlie Van Dyke (Alabama), Alice Sewell (Missouri), William Sherman (Florida), Della Bess Hillyard (Florida), *Slave Narratives* (CD-ROM).

30. Nack Mullen (Florida), Maria Calloway (Georgia), Annie Davis (Alabama), *Slave Narratives* (CD-ROM); Thomas, *Secret Eye*, 194; Adams, *South-Side View of Slavery*, 54–56.

31. Boles, *Black Southerners*, 163–67; Raboteau, *Slave Religion*, 243–66; W. L. Bost (North Carolina), Adeline Hodge (Alabama), William Henry Towns (Alabama), Ellen Payne (Texas), Levi Ashley (Mississippi), *Slave Narratives* (CD-ROM).

32. Daniel, *Southern Protestantism in the Confederacy*, 123–24; Clarke, *Our Southern Zion*, 189–99; Blackburn, *Life Work of John L. Girardeau*, 31–51.

33. Sernett, *Black Religion and American Evangelicalism*, 114–16; Carroll, *History of Texas Baptists*, 257–60; Cornelius, *Slave Missions and the Black Church*, 103–23; Mathews, *Religion in the Old South*, 197–202; Bacon, *Letters of a Family during the War for the Union*, 1:14–15.

34. Heyrman, *Southern Cross*, 46–52; Genovese, *Roll, Jordan, Roll*, 255–79; Raboteau, *Slave Religion*, 212–43, 288–301.

35. Litwack, *North of Slavery*, 187–213; Walker, *A Rock in a Weary Land*, 4–29; Carol V. R. George, "Widening the Circle: The Black Church and the Abolitionist Crusade, 1830–1860," in Perry and Fellman, *Antislavery Reconsidered*, 75–95; Fordham, *Major Themes in Northern Black Religious Thought*, 33–53, 85–107, 139–50.

36. Smith, "Righteousness and Hope," 21–45; Sandeen, *Roots of Fundamentalism*, 42–58; Moorhead, "Between Progress and Apocalypse," 524–42.

37. Maddex, "Proslavery Millennialism," 46–57; Calhoon, *Evangelicals and Conservatives in the Early South*, 185–91; *North Carolina Presbyterian* (Fayetteville), June 30, 1860.

38. Lincoln, *Collected Works*, 2:255–56. For the context see, Lehrman, *Lincoln at Peoria*.

39. Mathews, *Slavery and Methodism*, 212–45; Matlack, *Antislavery Struggle and Triumph in Methodist Episcopal Church*, 146–54.

40. Pearne, *Sixty-one Years of Itinerant Christian Life*, 44–45; Bucke et al., *History of American Methodism*, 2:47–59; Smith, *Life and Letters of James Osgood Andrew*, 336–75; Buckley, *History of Methodism in United States*, 2:70–105.

41. Swaney, *Episcopal Methodism and Slavery*, 192–99; Barclay, *History of Methodist Missions*, 3:51–54.

42. Bucke et al., *History of American Methodism*, 2:157–67; Buckley, *History of Methodism in the United States*, 2:137–42.

43. Deborah Bingham Van Broekhoven, "Suffering with Slaveholders: The Limits of Francis Wayland's Antislavery Witness," in McKivigan and Snay, *Religion and the Debate over Slavery*, 196–220; *Domestic Slavery Considered as a Scriptural Institution*, 13–125.

44. Eighmy, *Churches in Cultural Captivity*, 10–20; Goen, *Broken Churches, Broken Nation*, 90–98; McCardell, *Idea of a Southern Nation*, 188–93.

45. Snay, *Gospel of Disunion*, 113, 138–43; Chesebrough, *Clergy Dissent in the Old South*, 4–5. For a recent effort to draw some important distinctions between the Methodist and Baptist schisms and a discussion of what is termed "evangelical nationalism," see Bonner, *Mastering America*, 127–40.

46. Noll, *America's God*, 228; Sutherland, *Expansion of Everyday Life*, 79; Saum, *Popular Mood of Pre–Civil War America*, 3–26.

47. Carwardine, *Evangelicals and Politics in Antebellum America*, xv–xix, 17–49. In analyzing the role of religion in antebellum politics, I have relied heavily on Carwardine's superb book.

48. Hatch, *Democratization of American Christianity*, 3–46; Tocqueville, *Democracy in America*, 1:357; 2:30–31. This last point is especially emphasized in Noll, *America's God*, 187–208.

49. Noll, *America's God*, 9–18, 53–92, 210–24; Tocqueville, *Democracy in America*, 1:355, 361–62; Moorhead, *American Apocalypse*, 5–22.

50. Cole, *Social Ideas of Northern Evangelists*, 133–58; Hanley, *Beyond a Christian Commonwealth*, 13–41.

51. Scott, *From Office to Profession*, 18–35; Carwardine, *Evangelicals and Politics in Antebellum America*, 7–17.

52. Weiss, *Life and Correspondence of Theodore Parker*, 2:100–102, 114; York, *George B. Cheever*, 135–36; Bolster, *James Freeman Clarke*, 236–37; Bacon, *Leonard Bacon: A Statesman in the Church*, 341–48; Sernett, *Black Religion and American Evangelicalism*, 157–61.

53. Carwardine, *Evangelicals and Politics in Antebellum America*, 180–86; Boardman, *American Union*, 5–56; Lord, "'The Higher Law' in Its Application to the Fugitive Slave Bill," 3–16.

54. Smith, *In His Image*, 167–69; Hoge, *Moses Drury Hoge*, 138; Jacobs, *Committing of Our Cause to God*, 3–24; Palmer, *Life and Letters of James Henley Thornwell*, 477–78; Carwardine, *Evangelicals and Politics in Antebellum America*, 186–91.

55. Matlack, *Antislavery Struggle and Triumph in the Methodist Episcopal Church*, 209–26;

Clark, *Matthew Simpson*, 193–95; Thompson, *Presbyterians in the South*, 1:540–50; Goen, *Broken Churches, Broken Nation*, 134–39; McKivigan, *War against Proslavery Religion*, 161–82.

56. Thompson, *No Slavery in Nebraska*, 3–30; Bacon, *History of American Christianity*, 284–85; Carwardine, *Evangelicals and Politics in Antebellum America*, 235–44; Foster, *Rights of the Pulpit*, 5–36.

57. Wayland, *Dr. Wayland on the Moral and Religious Aspects of the Nebraska Bill*, 1–8; Mullin, *Puritan as Yankee*, 210–19; Gannett, *Relation of the North to Slavery*, 3–12.

58. Foster, *Rights of the Pulpit*, 37–72. See also, March, *The Crisis of Freedom*, 5–6.

59. Dolan, *Immigrant Church*, 121–27, 141–48; McGreevy, *Catholicism and American Freedom*, 13–14, 43–60; Murphy, "Catholic Church in United States during the Civil War Period," 274–305; Shaw, *Dagger John*, 334–36; Blied, *Catholics and the Civil War*, 20–28. Southern Catholics were not ardently proslavery but, as a relatively powerless religious minority, they posed no threat to the institution. Nor did their ineffective mission work among slaves challenge Protestant dominance in that field. Miller and Wakelyn, *Catholics in the Old South*, 11–12, 86–92, 211–39; Randall M. Miller, "Slaves and Southern Catholicism," in Boles, *Masters and Slaves in the House of the Lord*, 127–41.

60. Dunham, *Attitude of Northern Clergy toward the South*, 14–18; Allen, "Slavery Question in Catholic Newspapers," 120, 136–37; McGreevy, *Catholicism and American Freedom*, 60–67.

61. Carwardine, *Evangelicals and Politics in Antebellum America*, 80–89, 199–234; Shaw, *Dagger John*, 291–92.

62. Fish, *Voice of Our Brother's Blood*, 5–22; Sears, *Rebellion or Reform*, 3–10; Haven, *National Sermons*, 57–86.

63. Gannett, *State of the Country*, 3–20; Gannett, *Ezra Stiles Gannett*, 302–3; *Boston Pilot*, June 7, 1856; *Presbyterian of the West* (Cincinnati), September 6, 1855.

64. Howard, *Conscience and Slavery*, 143–55; Carwardine, *Evangelicals and Politics in Antebellum America*, 248–55; McGreevy, *Catholicism and American Freedom*, 75–81; Black, *Essays and Speeches of Jeremiah S. Black*, 51–67.

65. Carwardine, *Evangelical and Politics in Antebellum America*, 285–92.

66. York, *George B. Cheever*, 169–71; *Independent* (New York), October 20, November 10, December 8, 1859.

67. Beecher, *Freedom and War*, 1–27.

68. Strong, *Diary of George Templeton Strong*, 3:12; *Pittsburgh Catholic*, October 20, 1859; *New York Freeman's Journal and Catholic Register*, October 22, 29, 1859.

69. Fox-Genovese and Genovese, *Mind of the Master Class*, 636–46; Lee, *Memoirs of William Nelson Pendleton*, 123–24; *Central Presbyterian* (Richmond), February 25, 1860.

70. On his inaugural journey, Lincoln used this evocative phrase in a speech before the New Jersey senate. He invoked memories of the revolutionary generation, noted as a young man how he had been greatly taken with Mason Weems's didactic biography of George Washington, and then described how anxious he was that the Union and Constitution be preserved. As for himself, he only hoped to be a "humble instrument" of God and of an "almost chosen people." Lincoln, *Collected Works*, 4:235–36.

Chapter 2

1. Phelan, *History of Early Methodism in Texas*, 442–58; Chesebrough, *Clergy Dissent in the Old South*, 33–41; *Southern Christian Advocate* (Charleston), July 21, 1859; Norton, "Method-

ist Episcopal Church and Civil Disturbances in North Texas," 317–41; Reynolds, *Texas Terror*, 148–67.

2. Ridgaway, *Life of Rev. Alfred Cookman*, 218–21; *Zion's Herald and Wesleyan Journal* (Boston), January 4, March 21, 1860; Robert D. Clark, "Methodist Debates and Union Sentiment on the Border, 1860–1861," in Auer, *Antislavery and Disunion*, 152–70.

3. Carwardine, "Lincoln, Evangelical Religion, and American Political Culture," 35–42; *New York Freeman's Journal and Catholic Register*, May 5, 12, 26, June 30, July 14, September 1, November 3, 1860; *New York Tablet*, September 8, 1860; Carwardine, *Evangelicals and Politics in Antebellum America*, 300.

4. Riforgiato, "Bishop Timon, Buffalo, and the Civil War," 70; *Independent* (New York), July 5, 1860; Gladden, *Recollections*, 92–93. For a somewhat different analysis of the campaign that emphasizes the Republican achievement in mobilizing evangelical support, see Carwardine, *Evangelicals and Politics in Antebellum America*, 296–307.

5. Brevard, *Plantation Mistress on the Eve of the Civil War*, 41, 43, 45, 47; *Southern Presbyterian* (Columbia, S.C.), November 9, 1860.

6. Bangs, *Autobiography and Journal*, 316.

7. Holifield, "Penurious Preacher?," 17–36; Schweiger, *Gospel Working Up*, 78–79; Wyatt-Brown, *Shaping of Southern Culture*, 136–53.

8. Maddex, "Proslavery Millennialism," 57–62; Wakelyn, *Southern Pamphlets on Secession*, 63–77; Wayne C. Eubank, "Benjamin Morgan Palmer's Thanksgiving Sermon, 1860," in Auer, *Antislavery and Disunion*, 291–309; Johnson, *Life and Letters of Benjamin Morgan Palmer*, 219–23; Monroe, "Bishop Palmer's Thanksgiving Day Address," 105–18. For a complex reading of Palmer's sermon, see Bonner, *Mastering America*, xi–xv.

9. *Fast Day Sermons*, 9–56; Johnson, *Life and Letters of Robert Lewis Dabney*, 223–24.

10. Duffield, *A Thanksgiving Discourse*, 11–31; Brantly, *Our National Troubles*, 7–32; Vinton, *Thanksgiving Sermon*, 3–23; *German Reformed Messenger* (Chambersburg, Pa.), November 28, 1860; McIlwaine, *Necessity of Religion to the Prosperity of the Nation*, 3–21.

11. McPherson, *Political History of the United States*, 513; Evans, *Intrepid Warrior*, 45–47; Presbyterian Church, Synod of South Carolina, *Minutes, 1860*, 28–29.

12. Van Dyke, *Giving Thanks for All Things*, 3–24; Gannett, *Ezra Stiles Gannett*, 303; *New York Tablet*, November 17, 24, 1860.

13. "Politics at Home," *Brownson's Quarterly Review* 23 (July 1860): 360–91; *New York Freeman's Journal and Catholic Register*, November 17, 1860.

14. *Christian Observer* (Philadelphia), November 15, 1860; Smith, *Two Discourses on the State of the Country*, 3–26; Dunning, *The Godly Heritage and Its Heirs*, 5–16.

15. Daniel, *Southern Protestantism in the Confederacy*, 6–7; Overy, "Robert Lewis Dabney," 96–97; Robertson, *Life and Letters of John Albert Broadus*, 177–78.

16. *Christian Advocate* (Nashville), November 29, 1860; *North Carolina Presbyterian* (Fayetteville), December 15, 1860; *Religious Herald* (Richmond), November 29, 1860; Fleet and Fuller, *Green Mount*, 42; Kollock, "Letters of Kollock and Allied Families," 155; Clark, *Papers of Walter Clark*, 1:42; Ramsey, *True Eminence Founded on Holiness*, 16. On various approaches to the role of providence at the beginning of the war, see Guyatt, *Providence and the Invention of the United States*, 259–64.

17. Flynt, *Alabama Baptists*, 110; Crowther, *Southern Evangelicals and the Coming of the Civil War*, 199–201; Eighmy, *Churches in Cultural Captivity*, 21–24.

18. Crowther, *Southern Evangelicals and the Coming of the Civil War*, 201–4; George W. Farmer, "Seven Sides of the Itinerancy," pp. 53–54, Farmer Papers, Drew; Silver, *Confederate Morale and Church Propaganda*, 18.

19. McCash, *Thomas R. R. Cobb*, 88–91. For an excellent analysis that places more emphasis on clerical unity, see Snay, *Gospel of Disunion*, 151–56.

20. Bonner, *Colors and Blood*, 24–25, 60; Bettersworth, *Confederate Mississippi*, 285–86; Wooster, *Secession Conventions*, 258.

21. Bertram Wyatt-Brown, "Church, Honor, and Secession," in Miller et al., *Religion and the American Civil War*, 98; *Religious Herald* (Richmond), December 6, 1860, February 21, 1861; *Christian Advocate* (Nashville), January 17, 1861.

22. "The State of the County," *Princeton Review* 33 (January 1861): 1–36; Post, *Our National Union*, 5–20; Wilson, *The Cause of the United States*, 3–13; Perkins, *Northern Editorials on Secession*, 1:505.

23. *Presbyter* (Cincinnati), January 17, 1861; Moorhead, *American Apocalypse*, 27–35; *Christian Inquirer* (New York), December 15, 1860; Hodge, *Life of Charles Hodge*, 464–66; Robert J. Breckinridge to Charles Hodge, April 3, 1861, Hodge Papers, Princeton University Library.

24. *Christian Inquirer* (New York), December 22, 1860; Ellis, "The Preservation of the States United," 3–29; Myers, *Children of Pride*, 637; Chesire, *Church in the Confederate States*, 10–11, 13; Henry C. Lay, Pastoral Letter to the Clergy and Congregations of the Church in Arkansas, December 6, 1860, Lay Papers, SHC.

25. *Christian Watchman and Reflector* (Boston), December 13, 1860; Wilson, *Causes and Remedies of Impending National Calamities*, 15–16; Williams, *Freedom of Speech and Union*, 1–12; Bangs, *Autobiography and Journal*, 324–25.

26. Moore, *Rebellion Record* 1 (Documents):17; Scott, "'A Visitation of God,'" 12–13; *Independent* (New York), December 20, 27, 1860, February 14, 1861.

27. December 1860, Yeopim Baptist Church (Chowan Co., N.C.) Record Book, SBHLA; *Religious Herald* (Richmond), December 6, 1860, January 10, 1861; Taylor, *Life and Times of James B. Taylor*, 260; Simpson, *Echoes of Mercy—Whispers of Love*, 2–3; January 4, 1861, Sarah Lois Wadley Diary, SHC.

28. Atkinson, "*On the Causes of Our National Troubles*," 3–15; Verot, *A Tract for the Times*, 2–14; Stanton, *Church and the Rebellion*, 212–18.

29. Hovey, *The National Fast*, 2–5; Thompson, *President's Fast*, 5–26.

30. Niles, *Our Country's Peril and Hope*, 9–30; Moorhead, *American Apocalypse*, 34.

31. Fiske, *Sermon on Present National Troubles*, 18–19; Perkins, *Northern Editorials on Secession*, 1:491–94; *Fast Day Sermons*, 227–46; Allen, *Constitution and the Union*, 3–34; Wadsworth, *Our Own Sins*, 10.

32. *Fast Day Sermons*, 255–64; Anderson, *Dangers and Duties of the Present Crisis*, 5–18; Duffield, *Our National Sins to Be Repented Of*, 3–40. Mark Noll emphasized a diversity of clerical opinion on slavery during the secession crisis that turned into an "interpretative standoff." Noll, *Civil War as a Theological Crisis*, 1–4.

33. Humphrey, *Our Nation*, 3–13; Roset, *A Sermon on the Preservation of the Union*; *New York Herald*, January 7, 1861; Hall, *Our Sins and Duties*, 3–10.

34. Glover, *National Sin and Retribution*, 3–19; Seiss, *The Threatening Ruin*, 17–38; Lord, *Causes and Remedies of the Present Convulsions*, 3–7.

35. Salter, *Our National Sins and Impending Calamities*, 3–8; Duffield, *God of Our Fathers*, 5–29; McGill, *Sinful But Not Forsaken*, 3–11; Beecher, *Freedom and War*, 57–83.

36. Vinton, *God in Government*, 3–24; Chew, *God's Judgments Teaching Righteousness*, 3–13; Adams, *Prayer for Rulers*, 7–26; Smith, *Two Discourses on the State of the Country*, 27–28; Grimes, *The National Crisis*, 5–16.

37. Bangs, *Autobiography and Journal*, 324; *German Reformed Messenger* (Chambersburg, Pa.), January 2, 1861; *Fast Day Sermons*, 295.

38. Baum, *Shattering of Texas Unionism*, 53–57; Spain, *At Ease in Zion*, 13–15; Cain, *Methodism in the Mississippi Conference*, 295; Purifoy, "Southern Methodist Church and the Proslavery Argument," 337–41; Moore, "Religion in Mississippi in 1860," 234–37; Evans, *History of First Baptist Church, Aberdeen, Mississippi*, 25.

39. Thornwell, *State of the Country*, 4–32; Brevard, *Plantation Mistress on the Eve of the Civil War*, 68, 85; Betts, *Civil War Diary of Rev. Charles Bowen Betts*, 14; Palmer, *Life and Letters of James Henley Thornwell*, 486.

40. *Fast Day Sermons*, 127–226; *Presbyter* (Cincinnati), January 17, 1861; *Christian Inquirer* (New York), February 16, 1861; Sloane, *Review of Rev. Henry J. Van Dyke's Discourse*, 3–40; *Evangelist* (New York), January 3, 1861; January 7, 1861, Sarah Lois Wadley Diary, SHC.

41. Prentiss, *A Sermon Preached At. St. Peter's Church, Charleston*, 3–20; *Christian Index* (Macon, Ga.), January 16, 1861; February 12, 1861, Susan Cornwall Book, SHC. Stephen Douglas's newspaper organ in Washington noted the large number of slaves who had joined the various churches in the slaveholding states. Perkins, *Northern Editorials on Secession*, 1:498.

42. Wight, "Some Wartime Letters of Bishop Lynch," 24–25; Pillar, *Catholic Church in Mississippi*, 156–60; Randall M. Miller, "A Church in Cultural Captivity: Some Speculations on Catholic Identity in the Old South," in Miller and Wakelyn, *Catholics in the Old South*, 16; David Summerville to Archbishop John Baptist Purcell, February 12, 1861, Catholic Church, Archdiocese of Cincinnati Papers, Notre Dame.

43. Blied, *Catholics and the Civil War*, 37–38; Wimmer, "American Catholic Interpretations of the Civil War," 99–101; Pittsburgh *Catholic*, January 5, 1861; *New York Freeman's Journal and Catholic Register*, December 8, 1860, February 2, 16, 1861.

44. *New York Freeman's Journal and Catholic Register*, November 24, 1860, March 2, 30, 1861; Blied, *Catholics and the Civil War*, 73–74; Wimmer, "American Catholic Interpretations of the Civil War," 117.

45. Wimmer, "American Catholic Interpretations of the Civil War," 96–99; November 3, 1860, First Baptist Church (Darlington, S.C.) Minute Book, SBHLA; Butler, *Republican Loyalty*, 3–23; Stanton, *Civil Government of God*, 7–26.

46. Lincoln, *Collected Works*, 4:268–71.

47. *Christian Watchman and Reflector* (Boston), March 14, 1861; Perkins, *Northern Editorials on Secession*, 1:496. Samuel Dennison to Abraham Lincoln, January 31, 1861, Lincoln Papers, LC; Talmage, *Admonitions for the Times*, 5–22.

48. *New York Tablet*, March 16, 1861; *Evangelist* (New York), March 7, 1861; March 11, 1861, Mary Jeffrey Bethell Diary, SHC; Crowther, *Southern Evangelicals and the Coming of the Civil War*, 205–6.

49. *Central Presbyterian* (Richmond), December 8, 1860; *Southern Churchman* (Alexandria,

Va.), December 14, 1860; Robertson, *Life and Letters of John Albert Broadus*, 178–80; *Christian Advocate* (Nashville), February 14, 1861; *Christian Advocate and Journal* (New York), February 21, 1861.

50. Johnson, *Life and Letters of Robert Lewis Dabney*, 214–20; Robert Lewis Dabney to Elizabeth Randolph Dabney, January 12, 1861, Dabney Family Papers, VHS.

51. Green, *Memoir of James Hervey Otey*, 91; Johns, *Memoir of William Meade*, 491–92.

52. Breckinridge, *Our Country, Its Peril and Its Deliverance*, 1–43; *Southern Presbyterian* (Columbia, S.C.), April 6, 1861; Johnson, *Life and Letters of Benjamin Morgan Palmer*, 196–205.

53. *Independent* (New York), March 28, 1861; *Christian Watchman and Reflector* (Boston), April 11, 1861; *Southern Churchman* (Alexandria, Va.), April 12, 1861; Eddy, *Secession:—Shall It Be Peace or War?*, 17–21.

54. In some ways the secession crisis reflected the confusion of voices on the relationship between religious faith and modern civilization described in the opening passages of H. Richard Niebuhr's classic, *Christ and Culture*, 1–5. In this case, however, it might be fair to say that culture posed more of a challenge to Christianity than Christianity did to culture.

Chapter 3

1. Trumbull, *War Memories of a Chaplain*, 65–66.

2. Holmes, *Diary of Emma Holmes*, 10; Towles, *A World Turned Upside Down*, 296; April n.d., 1861, Mary Hort Diary, South Caroliniana Library; Elliott, *The Bloodless Victory*, 8. For a lengthier providential analysis of Sumter, see Smyth, *Battle of Fort Sumter*, 8–37.

3. *Christian Recorder* (Philadelphia), January 19, 1861; Hackett, *Christian Memorials of the War*, 190–92; Morris, *Christian Life and Character*, 674.

4. Eddy, *A Discourse on the War*, 3–9; *Christian Recorder* (Philadelphia), April 27, 1861; Taylor, *Israel against Benjamin*, 3–18; George W. Woodruff to Abraham Lincoln, April 18, 1861, T. B. Gary to Lincoln, April 18, 1861, Lincoln Papers, LC; *New York Times*, April 22, 1861; *New York Tablet*, April 27, 1861; *New York Freeman's Journal and Catholic Register*, April 27, 1861; *Christian Watchman and Reflector* (Boston), April 18, 1861. For a perceptive discussion of the transition in northern opinion, see Moorhead, *American Apocalypse*, 35–41.

5. Walmsley, "Change of Secession Sentiment in Virginia in 1861," 100; *Central Presbyterian* (Richmond), April 20, 1861; Reynolds, *Editors Make War*, 208–9.

6. Heathcote, *Lutheran Church in the Civil War*, 72; Wyatt-Brown, *Shaping of Southern Culture*, 166–74; *Christian Index* (Macon, Ga.), April 17, 1861; *History of the Baptist Denomination in Georgia*, 228–29.

7. Duryea, *Loyalty to the Government*, 5–28; Watts, *The Scriptural Doctrine of Civil Government*, 3–24; Hornblower, *Sermon on the War*, 3–7; Morris, *Christian Life and Character*, 678–79; Moore, *Rebellion Record*, 1 (Diary of Events):28.

8. By the same token works on just war theory have either ignored or made only passing mention of the American Civil War. For example, see Walzer, *Just and Unjust War*. For a partial exception (because the author pays considerable attention to the thinking of Henry W. Halleck and Francis Lieber about the legitimate conduct of war), see Johnson, *Just War Tradition and the Restraint of War*.

9. Abijah Martin, "Sentiments Appropriate to the Present Crisis," unpublished sermon, April 21, 1861, AAS; Jackson, *Sentiments and Conduct Proper to the Present Crisis*, 3–13; Nason,

Our Obligations to Defend the Government of Our Country, 1–6; Elias Nason to Abraham Lincoln, April 16, 1861, Lincoln Papers, LC.

10. Long, *Saints and the Union*, 14–16, 19–20, 24–26, 28–30.

11. Jenkins, *Thoughts for the Crisis*, 5–24; Goodrich, *A Sermon on the Christian Necessity of War*, 14–15; *Christian Advocate and Journal* (New York), April 25, 1861.

12. Taylor, "Diary of Mary Taylor," 921; Luker, *A Southern Tradition in Theology and Social Criticism*, 110–11; *Biblical Recorder* (Raleigh, N.C.), May 8, 1861; McMillan, *Alabama Confederate Reader*, 96.

13. Swain, *Our Banners Set Up*, 3–14; Swain, *God in the Strife*, 3–13; Perkins, *Northern Editorials on Secession*, 2:1072; James R. Doolittle to Abraham Lincoln, April 18, 1861, Lincoln Papers, LC. Not everyone became caught up in the martial excitement. For thousands of armed men to invade states filled with Christian brethren appalled a conservative Presbyterian who doubted that even ending slavery could justify the cost in blood and treasure. Hornblower, *Sermon on the War*, 1–3.

14. Stout, *Upon the Altar of the Nation*, 39–40; Daniel, *Southern Protestantism in the Confederacy*, 10–11; *Christian Advocate* (Nashville), May 9, 1861.

15. Bryan, "Churches in Georgia during the Civil War," 287; Chittenden, *Invisible Siege*, 7; Scott, "'A Visitation of God,'" 23; Howard, *Life Story of Henry Clay Trumbull*, 176–77; New York City Welsh Congregational Church to Abraham Lincoln, April 16, 1861, Lincoln Papers. LC; Moore, *Rebellion Record*, 1 (Diary of Events):38, 40, 57, 62; Conway, *Autobiography*, 1:324–26; Blied, *Catholics and the Civil War*, 40–44; Strong, *Diary of George Templeton Strong*, 3:125–26; *New York Herald*, April 22, 1861; Perkins, *Northern Editorials on Secession*, 2:1065. At the same time, the secular press employed the language of providence in editorials extolling the Union and supporting the war. Scott, "'A Visitation of God,'" 24–26.

16. A phrase that repeatedly cropped up during the first months of the war in Richmond's largest circulation newspaper, the *Dispatch*.

17. Bellows, *The State and the Nation*, 3–16; Bartol, *The Duty of the Time*, 5–16. For a broader discussion of how American intellectuals believed that war would strengthen the nation, see Frederickson, *Inner Civil War*, 65–72. In some ways, an early belief in a connection between the war and progress marked the birth of a standard Civil War narrative that still exerts such a dominant influence. See the pointed critique in Edward L. Ayers, "Worrying about the Civil War," in Ayers, *What Caused the Civil War*, 103–30.

18. Vander Velde, *Presbyterian Churches and the Federal Union*, 21, 31–33.

19. [Charles Hodge], "The State of the Country," *Princeton Review* 33 (January 1861): 1–36.

20. Vander Velde, *Presbyterian Churches and Federal Union*, 35–36; Thomas, *Correspondence of Thomas Ebenezer Thomas*, 113; *Presbyter* (Cincinnati), February 14, 1861; John H. Rice, "The Princeton Review on the State of the Country," *Southern Presbyterian Review* 14 (April 1861): 1–44.

21. Vander Velde, *Presbyterian Churches and Federal Union*, 43–44; Jones and Mills, *Presbyterian Church in South Carolina since 1850*, 77–79; Myers, *Children of Pride*, 669–70; *North Carolina Presbyterian* (Fayetteville), May 11, 1861.

22. Vander Velde, *Presbyterian Churches and Federal Union*, 46–64; Spring, *Personal Reminiscences of the Life and Times of Gardiner Spring*, 2:178–94.

23. Vander Velde, *Presbyterian Churches and Federal Union*, 65–70; "The Church and the

Country," *Princeton Review* 33 (April 1861): 322–40; "The General Assembly," ibid. (July 1861): 511–68.

24. *Evangelist* (New York), June 20, 1861; *Presbyter* (Cincinnati), May 2, June 13, 1861; Vander Velde, *Presbyterian Churches and Federal Union*, 83–91, 160–64.

25. Vander Velde, *Presbyterian Churches and Federal Union*, 105–7, 141–43; Graham, *A Kingdom Not of This World*, 135–50, 219–45.

26. John B. Adger, "The General Assembly of 1861," *Southern Presbyterian Review* 14 (July 1861): 296–347; Presbyterian Church, Synod of North Carolina, Orange Presbytery, *Minutes of One Hundred and Eighty-third Session*, 12; Johnson, *Life and Letters of Benjamin Morgan Palmer*, 240–46; Red, *History of Presbyterian Church in Texas*, 108.

27. Thompson, *Presbyterians in the South*, 2:13–35.

28. Protestant Episcopal Church, Diocese of Louisiana, *Extracts from the Journal of the Twenty-third Annual Convention*, 3–24; Chesire, *Church in the Confederate States*, 14–35; Elliott, *Address of the Rt. Rev. Stephen Elliott*, 3–10.

29. April 27, 1861, Episcopal Convocation of Edenton Records, Diocese of Eastern North Carolina, SHC; Quintard, *Doctor Quintard, Chaplain, C.S.A.*, 164–66.

30. [Hopkins], *Life of Right Reverend John Henry Hopkins*, 322, 324–25; Moore, *Rebellion Record*, 2:528–29; Butler, *Standing against the Whirlwind*, 146–58, 163; Smythe, *History of Diocese of Ohio*, 313; Hawthorne, *Episcopal Church in Michigan*, 4–7.

31. Atkinson, *Extract from the Annual Address*, 1–8; April 9, 1862, James Hervey Otey Diary, Otey Papers, SHC; Protestant Episcopal Church, *Journal of Proceedings of an Adjourned Convention of Bishops, Clergymen and Laymen*, 3–47.

32. *New York Tablet*, July 27, 1861; *New York Freeman's Journal and Catholic Register*, June 1, August 3, 1861; S. C. Hayes to James A. McMaster, July 6, 1861, McMaster Papers, Notre Dame; Wimmer, "American Catholic Interpretations of the Civil War," 123–26, 281; Allen, "The Slavery Question in Catholic Newspapers," 163.

33. Allen, "The Slavery Question in Catholic Newspapers," 99; Welsh, *Irish Green and Union Blue*, 65, 70; *New York Freeman's Journal and Catholic Register*, May 4, June 22, July 13, 1861.

34. McCann, "Archbishop Purcell and the Archdiocese of Cincinnati," 77–78; Freidel, *Union Pamphlets on the Civil War*, 1:118–27.

35. Connor, "Northern Catholic Position on Slavery and the Civil War," 39–40; William Henry Elder to John Mary Odin, June 15, 1861, Catholic Church, Archdiocese of New Orleans Papers, Notre Dame; Pillar, *Catholic Church in Mississippi*, 160–65; Wight, "War Letters of Bishop of Richmond," 262; *New York Tablet*, September 14, 1861.

36. *Charleston Mercury*, May 3, 1861; Faust, *Creation of Confederate Nationalism*, 22–23; Holmes, *Diary of Emma Holmes*, 47–48. In discussing the common religious language of North and South, I have relied on the excellent analysis in Snay, *Gospel of Disunion*, 181–98.

37. Rosen, *Jewish Confederates*, 256–57; Aamodt, *Righteous Armies, Holy Cause*, 60–73; Genovese, "King Solomon's Dilemma—and the Confederacy's," 55–75; Guyatt, *Providence and the Invention of the United States*, 264–66.

38. *Journal of the Confederate Congress*, 1:32–33, 858–59; Myers, *Children of Pride*, 725–26; [Barten], *A Sermon Preached in St. James' Church*, 5–8.

39. Stiles, *National Rectitude the Only True Basis of National Prosperity*, 3–15; Pierce, *Sermons of Bishop Pierce and Rev. B. M. Palmer*, 10–15, 27.

40. James A. Lyon, "Religion and Politics," *Southern Presbyterian Review* 15 (April 1863): 569–610; "The Rev. Dr. Thornwell's Memorial on the Recognition of Christianity in the Constitution," ibid. 16 (July 1863): 77–87; Thomas Peck, "Church and State," ibid. (October 1863): 121–44; Gregg, *Primary Charge, to the Clergy of the Protestant Episcopal Church, in Diocese of Texas*, 25–39; Palmer, *Life and Letters of James Henley Thornwell*, 507; *Religious Herald* (Richmond), January 14, February 11, March 10, 1864.

41. Stout, *Upon the Altar of the Nation*, 44–46; Jones, *Christ in the Camp*, 25, 32; J. B. Jeter Notes and Sermons, Matt. 22:21, Fall 1861[?], VBHS; Miles, *God in History*, 24.

42. Slaughter, *Coercion and Conciliation*, 1–8; Pierce, *The Word of God a Nation's Life*, 5–14; *Christian Advocate* (Nashville), July 4, 1861. For examples of continuity in wartime sermons, see April 1861–March 1863, Mary Hort Diary, South Caroliniana Library; J. B. Jeter Notes and Sermons, VBHS.

43. Pierce, *The Word of God a Nation's Life*, 14; Smith, *Smite Them Hip and Thigh!*, 31.

44. *Southern Presbyterian* (Columbia, S.C.), April 20, 1861; Hoge, "The Christian Statesman," 5–23; Stiles, *National Rectitude*, 17–32; *Anecdotes for Our Soldiers, No. 1*, 2–3, 17–18.

45. Pierce, *The Word of God a Nation's Life*, 14–19; Stiles, *National Rectitude*, 26–27, 32–34; James Z. Branscom to his brother, February 11, 1862, Branscom Papers, ADAH. For clashes between hopes and reality with similar themes from more secular sources, see Rable, *Confederate Republic*, 56–87, 111–31.

46. Sweet, *Methodist Episcopal Church and Civil War*, 111–32; *Presbyter* (Cincinnati), May 19, 1861; Marlay, *Life of Rev. Thomas A. Morris*, 316–17; *German Reformed Messenger* (Chambersburg, Pa.), May 22, 1861; Perrin, *The Claims of Caesar*, 3–20; Ide, *Battle Echoes*, 9–23; Duffield, *Courage in a Good Cause*, 5–37.

47. Webb, *The Christian Religion the Only True Foundation of National Perpetuity*, 3–13; Harris, *Our Country's Claim*, 3–13; Hackett, *Christian Memorials of the War*, 17–18.

48. Moore, *Rebellion Record*, 1 (Documents):175; Paludan, *People's Contest*, 345–46; *German Reformed Messenger* (Chambersburg, Pa.), May 1, 1861.

49. Ide, *Battle Echoes*, 24–34; Harris, *Our Country's Claim*, 13–16; *Friends' Intelligencer* (Philadelphia), May 4, 1861.

50. Brock, *Pacifism in the United States*, 689–96, 713–15, 725–26, 843–49; *Friend* (Philadelphia), December 15, 29, 1860; *Friend's Intelligencer* (Philadelphia), May 11, August 10, 1861.

51. Sarah E. Butler to Margaret Butler, April 16, 1861, Anna and Sarah Butler Correspondence, Louisiana State University; Johns, *A Memoir of the Life of the Right Rev. William Meade*, 494–95.

52. Wadsworth, *American Patriotism*, 5–7; Goodrich, *A Sermon on the Christian Necessity of War*, 3–11; G.H.E., "Christianity and the War," *Universalist Quarterly* 18 (October 1861): 373–95; Quint, *Christian Patriot's Present Duty*, 3–23; *Independent* (New York), April 25, 1861; Peter J. Parish, "From Necessary Evil to National Blessing: The Northern Protestant Clergy Interpret the Civil War," in Cimbala and Miller, *An Uncommon Time*, 61.

53. Swain, *Our Banners Set Up*, 14–16; Demund, *Subordination to Government*, 5–15; Form of Prayer by Bishop of Vermont, April 25, 1861, *Services of the Protestant Episcopal Church in the United States*; Protestant Episcopal Church, Diocese of Mississippi, *Journal of the Thirty-fifth Annual Convention*, 65; Fain, *Sanctified Trial*, 8–9.

54. Morris, *Christian Life and Character*, 685–87; G. B. Wilcox to Abraham Lincoln, June 30,

1861, Lincoln Papers, LC; Vinton, *Christian Idea of Civil Government*, 3–12; Moorhead, *American Apocalypse*, 129–30; Baptist Church, Ohio, Cleveland Baptist Association, *Minutes of the Thirtieth Anniversary*, 7; Ayers, *In the Presence of Mine Enemies*, 160; S. W. S. Dutton, "The Duties to their Country in the Present Crisis," *New Englander* 19 (July 1861): 674–84.

55. Nancy Willard to Mary and Micajah Wilkinson, May 28, 1861, Micajah Wilkinson Papers, Louisiana State University; Robert Lewis Dabney to Elizabeth Randolph Dabney, April 25, 1861, Dabney Papers, VHS; *Religious Herald* (Richmond), June 13, 20, 1861; *Southern Churchman* (Alexandria, Va.), April 26, 1861.

56. *New York Tablet*, May 4, 1861; Breed, *The National Nest-Stirring*, 14; "The War," *Christian Examiner* 75 (July 1861): 95–115; *Presbyter* (Cincinnati), May 9, 1861; *Christian Advocate and Journal* (New York), May 2, 1861; *Christian Watchman and Reflector* (Boston), April 25, 1861; E.G.B., "Our Civil War," *Universalist Quarterly* 18 (July 1861): 276.

57. William A. Nolan to James A. McMaster, June 7, 1861, McMaster Papers, Notre Dame; Frear, "'You My Brother Will be Glad with Me,'" 121; Hess, *Union Soldier in Battle*, 103. A conservative New York editor excoriated the church in both sections for being as guilty as the politicians in causing the "present disasters" and feared the effects of turning the conflict into a "holy war." Perkins, *Northern Editorials on Secession*, 2:1090–93.

Chapter 4

1. Abbott, *First Regiment New Hampshire Volunteers*, 87–91.

2. Johnson, *Life and Letters of Robert Lewis Dabney*, 232; Flynt, *Alabama Baptists*, 114.

3. Lyle, *Light and Shadows of Army Life*, 14–16; Bonner, *Colors and Blood*, 81; Davis, *Civil War Journal of Billy Davis*, 4; Washburn, *108th New York*, 8; Pillar, *Catholic Church in Mississippi*, 190–91; Hardin, *Private War of Lizzie Hardin*, 18.

4. Sullins, *Recollections of an Old Man*, 197; Paludan, *People's Contest*, 344, 348; Kinsley, *Diary of a Christian Soldier*, 88; Beaudry, *War Journal*, 105.

5. Quimby, "Recurrent Themes and Purposes in the Sermons of the Union Army," 428; Moe, *Last Full Measure*, 29; *Religious Herald* (Richmond), June 6, 1861.

6. On the classic question of the relationship between Christ and culture, many believers in the Civil War generation saw no essential conflict between their religious and cultural values. They would have readily identified Christ with culture. In their view, Christianity should, could, and eventually would bring their war-torn society into a glorious, millennial future. See the still invaluable analysis of the general question in Niebuhr, *Christ and Culture*, especially 83–115.

7. West, *Sermon Delivered at the Military Encampment, Near Hestonville, West Philadelphia*, 5–13; Henry Champlin Lay, "The Devout Soldier," March 6, 1864, Lay Papers, SHC; Wadsworth, *The Christian Soldier*, 3–24; *Religious Herald* (Richmond), May 9, 1861.

8. Henry Augustus Boardman, "Address to Col. Gray's Regiment, the Scott Legion in My Church," May 21, 1861, Boardman Papers, PHS-P; Holcomb, *Southern Sons, Northern Soldiers*, 5–6; R. Henry Campbell to his sister, May 29, 1861, Campbell-Varner Family Papers, Virginia Military Institute.

9. Garfield, *Wild Life of the Army*, 10–11; Chester, *Recollections of the War*, 14; Perkins, *Northern Editorials on Secession*, 2:1084–85; Wilkinson and Woodworth, *A Scythe of Fire*, 36–38; *Biblical Recorder* (Raleigh, N.C.), July 10, 1861; Stewart, *Camp, March and Battlefield*, 2–4.

10. Campbell, *Union Must Stand*, 2; Skidmore, *Alford Brothers*, 59, 75; Moore, *Rebellion Record*, 1 (Rumors and Incidents):43; White, *Sketches of the Life of Captain Hugh A. White*, 44-45, 47-48, 55; Myers, *Children of Pride*, 725.

11. "The National Crisis," *Christian Review* 26 (July 1861): 517-21; Bellows, *How We Are to Fulfill Our Lord's Commandment*, 3; *German Reformed Messenger* (Chambersburg, Pa.), July 17, 1861.

12. James Bates to William Corthell, May 24, 1861, Civil War Papers, AAS; Michelbacher, *Prayer of the C.S. Soldiers*; Jones, *Christ in the Camp*, 31; June 17, 1861, Jonathan Palmer Finley Diary, PHS-P; *Evangelist* (New York), July 4, 1861; Robert Lewis Dabney "Encouragement to Prayer, A Sermon," June 1861, Dabney Papers, Union Theological Seminary.

13. April 29, May 13, July 12, 1861, Mary Jeffreys Bethell Diary, SHC; Towles, *A World Turned Upside Down*, 297; *Religious Herald* (Richmond), July 4, 1861; Wetherington, *Plain Folk's Fight*, 75; Fain, *Sanctified Trial*, 11.

14. In this and the following paragraphs, I have especially benefited from the analysis in Silver, *Confederate Morale and Church Propaganda*, 25-30; Faust, *Creation of Confederate Nationalism*, 26-29; Snay, *Gospel of Disunion*, 164-75; Stout, *Upon the Altar of the Nation*, 48-52; Bonner, *Mastering America*, 241-51.

15. *Journal of the Confederate Congress*, 1:218; Davis, *Messages and Papers of Davis*, 1:103-4.

16. Chesebrough, *God Ordained This War*, 201-20; Longstreet, *A Fast-Day Sermon*, 3-14; Elliott, *God's Presence with the Confederate States*, 11-20.

17. Myers, *Children of Pride*, 697; Hopley, *Life in the South*, 1:354-56; Bennett, *Narrative of the Great Revival*, 97; Stone, *Brokenburn*, 24-25; *Charleston Mercury*, June 13, 1861; Johnson, *Life and Letters of Robert Lewis Dabney*, 236-37. For an excellent discussion of the changing attitudes of secular editors toward Confederate fast days, see Harry S. Stout and Christopher Grasso, "Civil Religion, and Communications: The Case of Richmond," in Miller et al., *Religion and the American Civil War*, 330-32.

18. Bettersworth, "Mississippi Unionism," 39-40; Bryan, "Churches in Georgia during the Civil War," 293-94; *Religious Herald* (Richmond), June 13, 1861.

19. *OR*, ser. 1, vol. 2, p. 97; McGuire, *Diary of a Southern Refugee*, 31; *Christian Index* (Macon, Ga.), July 17, 1861; "The National Crisis," *Christian Review* 26 (July 1861): 517-21.

20. *Southern Churchman* (Richmond), November 22, 1861; McGuire, *Diary of a Southern Refugee*, 41; Presbyterian Church, Synod of Virginia. *Minutes, 1862*, 314; Bennett, *Narrative of the Great Revival*, 110.

21. Woodworth, *While God Is Marching On*, 132-33; Baptist Church, North Carolina, State Convention, *Proceedings of the Thirty-Second Annual Session*, 19; Blied, *Catholics and the Civil War*, 61; Vedder, "*Offer unto God Thanksgiving*," 13-15; Armstrong, "*The Hand of God upon Us*, 5-7; Butler, *Sermon: Preached in St. John's Church, Richmond*, 5-9.

22. Reed, *A People Saved by the Lord*, 3-6; Armstrong, "*The Hand of God upon Us*," 3-5, 7-9, 12-15; *Southern Presbyterian* (Columbia, S.C.), August 10, 1861; *Christian Index* (Macon, Ga.), July 31, 1861.

23. Thomas Smyth, "The Victory at Manassas Plains," *Southern Presbyterian Review* 14 (January 1862): 593-617; *Providential Aspect and Salutary Tendency of the Existing Crisis*, 26-27; Blied, *Catholics and the Civil War*, 65; Elliott, *God's Presence with Our Army at Manassas!*, 9-18; Winn, *The Great Victory at Manassas Junction*, 1-8.

24. Joslyn, *Charlotte's Boys: Civil War Letters of the Branch Family*, 72–73; Owen, *The Sacred Flame of Love*, 97; McGuire, *Diary of a Southern Refugee*, 42–43.

25. *Christian Index* (Macon, Ga.), August 7, 1861; *Richmond Daily Dispatch*, August 10, 1861; *Christian Advocate* (Nashville), August 1, 22, 1861; Elliott, *God's Presence with Our Army at Manassas!*, 5–9. The text quoted is Exodus 15:1.

26. *Evangelist* (New York), August 1, 1861; Fowler, *National Destruction Threatens Us*, 3–16; *Christian Advocate and Journal* (New York) August 1, 1861.

27. Fletcher, *Diary of Calvin Fletcher*, 7:158; *Evangelist* (New York), August 1, 8, 22, 1861; New York Sabbath Committee, *Plea for the Sabbath in War*, 1–8; *Independent* (New York), August 1, 1861; *Christian Recorder* (Philadelphia), July 27, September 7, 1861; *Christian Advocate and Journal* (New York), August 1, 15, and 29, 1861. Confederates self-righteously chided the Federals for attacking on the Sabbath, fully satisfied that the devils had received their just desserts. *Christian Index* (Macon, Ga.), August 14, 1861; White, *Sketches of the Life of Captain Hugh A. White*, 58–59.

28. *Evangelist* (New York), August 8, 1861; Ware, *Our Duty under Reverse*, 3–15; Bangs, *Autobiography and Journal*, 327; Long, *Saints and the Union*, 36; Edward C. Donnely to James A. McMaster, August 31, 1861, McMaster Papers, Notre Dame; *Christian Advocate and Journal* (New York), August 8, 1861.

29. Bushnell, *Reverses Needed*, 5–27; Fletcher, *Diary of Calvin Fletcher*, 7:181; *Christian Watchman and Reflector* (Boston), August 15, 1861.

30. Angell, *Bishop Henry McNeal Turner*, 42; Eddy, *Liberty and Union*, 23; *Evangelist* (New York), July 25, 1861; Carey, *The War an Occasion for Thanksgiving*, 20–21.

31. Stearns, *Necessities of the War and the Conditions of Success*, 16–23; *German Reformed Messenger* (Chambersburg, Pa.), August 21, 1861; *Independent* (New York), October 10, 17, 1861; Fuller, *Mercy Remembered in Wrath*, 3–9. For a scathing and stimulating indictment of the wartime jeremiad (Union and Confederate) that condemns it for justifying both a longer and more brutal war, see Stout, *Upon the Alter of the Nation*, 92–93. I have preferred to emphasize subtle but significant shifts in sermon themes and language as responses to the events and carnage of the war.

32. Roland, *Louisiana Sugar Plantations during the Civil War*, 37–38; Fleet and Fuller, *Green Mount*, 85; McGuire, *Diary of a Southern Refugee*, 72; *Christian Advocate* (Nashville), November 28, 1861; November 15, 1861, Sarah Lois Wadley Diary, SHC.

33. *New York Tribune*, September 26, 1861; *New York Herald*, September 27, 1861; Skidmore, *Alford Brothers*, 117; Ayers, *In the Presence of Mine Enemies*, 225. Despite some observance of official fast days in the army, the soldier response was often tepid. Few Confederates appeared eager to turn out for extra preaching in the evening if their officers had not given them a day off. Federals admitted that recent defeats cast gloom over their meetings as they prepared for what promised to be a long war. Hieronymus, "Chaplains of the Confederate States," 291; Daniel, *Soldiering in the Army of Tennessee*, 115–16; Hackett, *Christian Memorials of the War*, 188–89; Downing, *Downing's Civil War Diary*, 10; Quint, *Potomac and the Rapidan*, 26–28.

34. For typical sermons (one Union and one Confederate) cataloging the usual political sins, see Leeds, *"Thy Kingdom Come: Thy Will Be Done,"* 3–16; Tucker, *God in the War*, 20.

35. *Christian Advocate* (Nashville), December 19, 1861; *Independent* (New York), September 12, 1861; Skinner, *Comfort in Tribulation*, 5–28; *Christian Recorder* (Philadelphia), September 7, 28, 1861; Weston, *Incentives to Prayer and Hope*, 41, 49–50.

36. Tucker, *God in the War*, 5–11; Moore, *God Our Refuge and Strength*, 5–18; Couture, "Bolling-Cabell Letters," 25; September 15, 1861, Sarah Wadley Diary, SHC; Chesnut, *Mary Chesnut's Civil War*, 233.

37. Hedge, *The National Weakness*, 3–10; *Presbyter* (Cincinnati), October 24, 1861; Hitchcock, *Our National Sin*, 5–21; "The Moral Aspects of the Present Struggle," *American Theological Review* 12 (October 1861): 710.

38. Leeds, *"Thy Kingdom Come: Thy Will Be Done,"* 16–25; Larimore, *A Discourse on Our National Dependence on God*, 5–15.

39. *Christian Recorder* (Philadelphia), August 10, 1861; *Religious Herald* (Richmond), October 10, 1861.

40. *Charleston Mercury*, November 15, 1861; Tucker, *God in the War*, 11–17; Baptist Church, Alabama, Coosa River Baptist Association, *Minutes of the Twenty-eighth Annual Session*, 8–9; Amelia S. Montgomery to Joseph A. Montgomery, October 16, 1861, Montgomery Papers, Louisiana State University; Elmore, *Heritage of Woe*, 11–12, 28–29.

41. Moore, *God Our Refuge and Strength*, 13–14; Elliott, *How to Renew Our National Strength*, 7–8; *Southern Churchman* (Richmond), November 29, 1861; Cutrer and Parrish, *Brothers in Gray*, 66; *Christian Observer* (Richmond), November 19, 1861.

42. Stearns, *The Sword of the Lord*, 3–15; Stout, *Upon the Alter of the Nation*, 78; "The Moral Aspects of the Present Struggle," *American Theological Review* 3 (October 1861): 733; Mahon, *Winchester Divided*, 13.

43. Baptist Church, Virginia, Goshen Baptist Association, *Minutes, 1861*, 3; Presbyterian Church, General Assembly, *Minutes Presbyterian Church in the Confederate States, 1862*, 21–22; Lutheran Church, Virginia Synod, *Minutes of the Thirty-second Convention*, 10; Protestant Episcopal Church, Diocese of Georgia, *To the Clergy of the Diocese of Georgia*; Bettersworth, *Confederate Mississippi*, 287.

44. Baptist Church, Illinois, Baptist General Association, *Minutes, 1861*, 31–32; October 18–20, 1861, Huntington (Ind.) Baptist Association Minute Book, ABHS; Bennett and Lawson, *Methodism in Wisconsin*, 192–93; Chrisman, "For God and Country," 80; Methodist Church, Indiana, Southeastern Indiana Conference, *Minutes, 1860–61*, 37–38.

45. E. R. Ames to R. L. Sewall, May 12, 1861, Ames Papers, Drew; Harrell, *Social History of Disciples of Christ*, 1:156–59; Carpenter, *Relations of Religion to War*, 4.

46. *Christian Watchman and Reflector* (Boston), October 24, 1861; McPherson, *Political History of the United States*, 475–76; William Patton to Abraham Lincoln, October 12, 1861, Lincoln Papers, LC; *Christian Recorder* (Philadelphia), November 23, 1861.

47. Cole, *Impact of the Civil War on Presbyterian Church in Michigan*, 1–5; September 18, 1861, Methodist Church, Indiana, Indiana Conference, Evangelical Association Minutes (translated from the German), DePauw; Guyatt, *Providence and the Invention of the United States*, 277–82; Stokes, *Church and State in the United States*, 2:204; *Liberator* (Boston), January 3, 1862.

48. Cheever, *God's Way of Crushing the Rebellion*, 3–20; Moorhead, *American Apocalypse*, 99; Walker, *The Offered National Regeneration*, 13–24; Simmons, *Our Duty in the Crisis*, 15–24; Thompson, *The Sword; A Divine Judgment for Sin*, 21–25.

49. *Christian Watchman and Reflector* (Boston), August 1, 1861; John L. Scripps to Lincoln, September 23, 1861, E. G. Cook to Lincoln, September 21, 1861, Simeon Jocelyn to Lincoln, September 26, 1861, Lincoln Papers, LC; Stewart, *Camp, March and Battlefield*, 44–47; Methodist Church, Illinois, Illinois Annual Conference, *Minutes of the Thirty-eighth Session*, 15;

Howard, *Religion and Radical Republican Movement*, 12–18; Stone, *Divineness of Human Government*, 37–55; Bellows, *Valley of Decision*, 17–25.

50. Thomas, *Correspondence of Thomas Ebenezer Thomas*, 119–20; [Hopkins], *Life of Right Reverend John Henry Hopkins*, 323; "A Word about the War," *Monthly Religious Magazine* 26 (November 1861): 324–30.

51. "Slavery and the War," *Brownson's Quarterly Review*, 23 (October 1861): 510–46; Andrews, "Slavery Views of a Northern Prelate," 60–71; Hassard, *Life of the Most Reverend John Hughes*, 435–36; John Hughes to Cardinal Alessandro Barnabo, September 30, 1861, Hughes to Orestes Brownson, October 3, 1861, M. L. Linton to Brownson, October 16, 1861, R. J. Howard et al., to Brownson, November 10, 1861, Richard Vincent Whelan to Brownson, December 14, 1861, Basil T. Elder to Brownson, January 4, 1862, Brownson Papers, Notre Dame. One of Brownson's harshest critics was the soon-to-be-infamous Dr. Samuel A. Mudd, who had equally little use for Archbishop Hughes. Mudd to Brownson, January 20, 1862, Brownson Papers, Notre Dame.

52. Sharrow, "John Hughes and a Catholic Response to Slavery," 254–69; Shaw, *Dagger John*, 344; Spalding, "Martin John Spalding's 'Dissertation on the American Civil War,'" 75–82; *New York Herald*, September 4, 1861; Rice, *American Catholic Opinion in the Slavery Controversy*, 118–23.

53. *New York Freeman's Journal and Catholic Register*, June 8, August 10, 17, 31, September 7, 14, 1861, April 19, June 15, 1862; Charles J. Faulkner to James A. McMaster, October 26, November 16, 25, December 1, 1861, George William Brown to McMaster, November 7, 1861, John A. Kasson to William B. Taylor, February 21, 1862, Kasson to E. A. Richardson, March 7, 1862, Kasson to McMaster, April 8, 1862, McMaster Papers, Notre Dame, *OR*, ser. 2, vol. 2, pp. 801–4.

54. Mears, *Life of Edward Norris Kirk*, 282–94; *Evangelist* (New York), November 28, 1861; Miller, *"Perfect through Suffering,"* 1–8; Demerest, *Thanksgiving Sermon*, 3–16; Spring, *State Thanksgiving during the Rebellion*, 5–20.

55. Mead, *Occasions for Gratitude in the Present National Crisis*, 19–20; Eggleston, *Reasons for Thanksgiving*, 3–21.

56. Mead, *Occasions for Gratitude in the Present National Crisis*, 7–19; Thompson, *Thankful for Everything*, 3–22; Ide, *Battle Echoes*, 35–59; Duffield, *Great Rebellion Thus Far a Failure*, 3–19; Foss, *"Songs in the Night,"* 3–42; Sprague, *Glorifying God in the Fires*, 35–58.

57. Gage, *From Vicksburg to Raleigh*, 47–48; Leonard Bacon, "The Wars of the Lord," *New Englander* 21 (January 1862): 115–34; Niebuhr, *Faith and History*, 238.

58. Howe, *Reminiscences*, 271–76. For useful analysis of Howe's words, see Wilson, *Patriotic Gore*, 91–98; Tuveson, *Redeemer Nation*, 197–202; Aamodt, *Righteous Armies, Holy Cause*, 81–87; Snyder, "Biblical Background of the Battle Hymn of the Republic," 231–38.

59. Niven, *Connecticut for the Union*, 276–77.

Chapter 5

1. Taylor, *Lee's Adjutant*, 51; Lutheran Church, South Carolina Synod, *Minutes, 1862*, 6; Robertson, *Life and Letters of John Albert Broadus*, 188–89. For a good discussion of those soldiers (a minority to be sure) who continued to struggle with the necessary compromises between military duties and religious faith, see David W. Rolfs, "'No Nearer Heaven Now But Rather Farther Off': The Religious Compromises and Conflicts of Northern Soldiers," in Sheehan-Dean, *View from the Ground*, 120–44.

2. Wiley, *Life of Johnny Reb*, 174–75; Holt, *Surgeon's Civil War*, 168–69; Horrocks, *My Dear Parents*, 120–21; Bennett, *Union Jacks*, 126–30.

3. Elliott, *How to Renew Our National Strength*, 14–15; United States Christian Commission, *First Annual Report*, 58; Fitzpatrick, *Letters to Amanda*, 39.

4. Bennett, *Narrative of the Great Revival*, 101; Beidelman, *Letters of George Washington Beidelman*, 149–50; Seth Gilbert Evans to his sister, December 5, 1861, Evans Letters, Pearce Civil War Collection, Navarro College, Corsicana, Texas; *Religious Herald* (Richmond), February 17, 1862; *A Kind Word to the Officers of Our Army*, 2; Gould, *Civil War Journals*, 442; Clinton B. Fisk to Matthew Simpson, February 9, 1863, Simpson Collection, Drew.

5. Evans, *Intrepid Warrior*, 79; Gould, *Civil War Journals*, 290.

6. Sweet, *Methodist Episcopal Church and Civil War*, 93–94; Twichell, *Civil War Letters*, 24–25; Jones, *Give God the Glory*, 103; Tuttle, *Civil War Journal*, 21; Gache, *A Frenchmen, a Chaplain, a Rebel*, 28; Presbyterian Church, Synod of North Carolina, Fayetteville Presbytery, *Minutes of the One Hundred and First Sessions*, 7–8.

7. Dollar, *Soldiers of the Cross*, 65–72; Upson, *With Sherman to the Sea*, 23; J. Maxwell Couper to Dora Harper Couper, December 15, 1861, Couper Family Papers, SHC.

8. Skidmore, *Alford Brothers*, 163; Duke, *Reminiscences of General Basil W. Duke*, 416; Griffin, *Their Brother's Keepers*, 245; Hammond, *Army Chaplain's Manual*, 87–102.

9. *Religious Herald* (Richmond), May 23, 1861; Bennett, *Narrative of the Great Revival*, 31–34; Van Wyck, *A War to Petrify the Heart*, 27; *Christian Advocate and Journal* (New York), August 15, 1861; Hartsock, *Soldier of the Cross*, 166.

10. Clark, "'Please Send Stamps,'" 103, 221; Adams, *Memorials and Letters of Rev. John R. Adams*, 31; McJunkin, *The Bloody 85th*, 15; Miller, *Bound to Be a Soldier*, 7.

11. "Father Joseph O'Hagan," 178; Jones, *Christ in the Camp*, 271–72; *Primitive Baptist* (Milburnie, N.C.), December 3, 1864; Post, *Soldiers' Letters, from Camp Battle-field and Prison*, 220; Betts, *Civil War Diary*, 202.

12. Charles Rockwell, "The Evils of War, and Our Duty to Those Engaged In It," *National Preacher and Village Pulpit* 38 (February 1864): 34–42; [Weld], *Pitching the Tent toward Sodom*; [Royal], *Advice to Soldiers*; *Christian Recorder* (Philadelphia), August 31, 1861; Haines, "In the Country of the Enemy," 34; Hartwell, *To My Beloved Wife and Boy at Home*, 217; Pettit, *Infantryman Pettit*, 8; Ayers, *Diary of James T. Ayers*, 15.

13. Clark, "'Please Send Stamps,'" 89; Urwin, "'The Lord Has Not Forsaken Me and I Won't Forsake Him,'" 324–25; Armstrong, *For Courageous Fighting and Confident Dying*, 49–51; Evans, *Sixteenth Mississippi*, 9; Jones, *Christ in the Camp*, 575.

14. Billingsley, *From the Flag to the Cross*, 234; Huckaby and Simpson, *Tulip Evermore*, 26; *Religious Herald* (Richmond), October 3, 1861; Jones, *Christ in the Camp*, 34; Adams, *Memorials and Letters of Rev. John R. Adams*, 33; Foster, *The Constitution Our Ark in the Storm*, 36; Henry Champlin Lay, sermon, "The Devout Soldier," March 6, 1864, Lay Papers, SHC; Hight, *Fifty-eighth Indiana*, 538.

15. Martha White Read to Thomas Griffin Read, August 7–12, 1861, Read Family Correspondence, Notre Dame; Callaway, *Civil War Letters*, 17; McAllister, *Letters of Robert McAllister*, 210; Eddy, *Sixtieth New York*, 87–89; *Independent* (New York), May 9, 1861.

16. Piston and Hatcher, *Wilson's Creek*, 52; Charles H. Eager to his wife, January 4, 1863, Eager Letters, Lewis Leigh Collection, U.S. Army Military History Institute; Ayling, *A Yankee at*

Arms, 102; Boyd, *Civil War Diary*, 24–25; Hartsock, *Soldier of the Cross*, 32; Evans, *Intrepid Warrior*, 332.

17. Twichell, *Civil War Letters*, 181; Gavin, *Campaigning with the Roundheads*, 229; Garey, *A Keystone Rebel*, 42; Romero, *Religion in the Ranks*, 71–72.

18. Cross, *Camp and Field*, 1:73; Jones, *Christ in the Camp*, 49–50, 599; *OR*, ser. 1, vol. 32, p. 1150.

19. *OR*, ser. 1, vol. 51, pt. 1, pp. 472–73; Dexter, *Seymour Dexter, Union Army*, 46; Baptist Church, Ohio, Grand River Baptist Association, *Minutes of the Forty-ninth Annual Meeting*, 4; *Christian Recorder* (Philadelphia), August 24, 31, September 21, October 19, 1861; *Evangelist* (New York), September 12, 1861.

20. Haydon, *For Country, Cause and Leader*, 7, 15; Brewster, *When This Cruel War Is Over*, 39; Stewart, *Camp, March and Battlefield*, 165–66; January 4, 1863, Henry C. Marsh Diary, Marsh Papers, Indiana State Library.

21. United Presbyterian Synod to Abraham Lincoln, October 28, 1861, Lincoln Papers, LC; Morris, *Christian Life and Character*, 784–87; Lincoln, *Collected Works*, 5:497–98; B. Behrend to Lincoln, December 4, 1862, ⟨http://www.geocities.com/Athens/Forum/1867/shabbat .htm⟩.

22. Daniel, *Soldiering in the Army of Tennessee*, 116; Meade, *Life and Letters of Meade*, 1:328; Sturtevant, *Josiah Volunteered*, 58–59; Bates, *A Texas Cavalry Officer's Civil War*, 94–95; Haydon, *For Country, Cause and Leader*, 190; McCain, *In Song and Sorrow*, 3–4, 27, 31.

23. Nugent, *My Dear Nellie*, 113; McCain, *In Song and Sorrow*, 3–4, 10, 14, 68; Rhodes, *All for the Union*, 20; Macmillan, *Methodist Episcopal Church in Michigan*, 26.

24. Price, *One Year in the Civil War*, 29; Hubbs, *Voices from Company D*, 39–40; Washburn, *108th New York*, 114; Kircher, *A German in the Yankee Fatherland*, 119.

25. Siegel, *For the Glory of the Union*, 94; Molyneux, *Quill of the Wild Goose*, 208; McMahon, *John T. McMahon's Diary*, 29; *Southern Christian Advocate* (Charleston), February 20, 1862. This reasoning applied equally to naval warfare. A Presbyterian editor claimed that in the famous fight between the *Alabama* and the *Kearsarge*, the Confederates lost the engagement because Captain Raphael Semmes had opened fire on a Sunday. *Evangelist* (New York), August 4, 1864.

26. Wiley, *Life of Johnny Reb*, 48; Redkey, "Black Chaplains in the Union Army," 340; Squier, *This Wilderness of War*, 29; *German Reformed Messenger* (Philadelphia), January 18, 1865.

27. Holt, *A Mississippi Rebel in the Army of Northern Virginia*, 159; Fallows, *Everybody's Bishop*, 187; Upson, *With Sherman to the Sea*, 103–4.

28. Washburn, *108th New York*, 122; Hoge, *Moses Drury Hoge*, 148; Fellman, *Inside War*, 150–51; Stuckenberg, *I'm Surrounded by Methodists*, 30–31; J. D. Mather to Andrew A. Humphreys, November 19, 1862, Humphreys to Mather, January 1, 1863, Humphreys Papers, Historical Society of Pennsylvania.

29. Gates, *Civil War Diaries*, 70; *Christian Recorder* (Philadelphia), November 22, 1862; *OR*, ser. 1, vol. 38, pt. 3, p. 417, vol. 47, pt. 2, p. 686; Shannon, *Organization and Administration of Union Army*, 1:228.

30. Andrews, *Why Do You Swear?*, 1–8; Dabney, *Swear Not*; Jeter, *Don't Swear*; *The Bold Blasphemer*, 1–7; Rogers, *War Pictures*, 228–33; Fain, *Sanctified Trial*, 235.

31. Norton, *Army Letters*, 111; Wiley, *Life of Johnny Reb*, 48.

32. [Curry], *Swearing*; Stewart, *Camp, March and Battlefield*, 255–58; Newell, *10th Regiment*

Massachusetts Volunteers, 181–86; Presbyterian Church, General Assembly, *Pastoral Letter of the General Assembly*, 5–6; Cross, *Camp and Field*, 1:137.

33. For a useful comparison of alcohol consumption in the Union and Confederate armies, see Wiley, *Life of Billy Yank*, 253.

34. James Bates to "Brothers and Sisters of Old Social," September 22, 1863, Civil War Papers, AAS; Dexter, *Seymour Dexter, Union Army*, 11–12; Brewster, *When This Cruel War Is Over*, 52–53; *Evangelist* (New York), March 26, 1863; Haydon, *For Country, Cause and Leader*, 64–65; Nisbet, *Four Years on the Firing Line*, 43–44.

35. Dulles, *Soldier's Friend*, 11–12; Collins, *The Prospect*, 12–15; *Evangelist* (New York), December 26, 1861.

36. Tobie, *First Maine Cavalry*, 20–21; Corby, *Memoirs of Chaplain Life*, 286–98; Beaudry, *War Journal*, 26, 90–91, 97, 100, 106; John M. Jackson to his father, January 12, 1863, Jackson Letters, Notre Dame; Evans, *Intrepid Warrior*, 506.

37. Twichell, *Civil War Letters*, 69; White, *Civil War Diary*, 136; Beaudry, *War Journal*, 93; Fuller, *Chaplain to the Confederacy*, 298–99; Baptist Church, North Carolina, Western Baptist Convention, *Proceedings of the Seventh Annual Session*, 16.

38. Baptist Church, Alabama, Coosa River Baptist Association, *Minutes of the Twenty-Eighth Annual Session*, 9–10; Presbyterian Church, General Assembly, *Pastoral Letter of the General Assembly*, 7–8; Methodist Church, Indiana, Southeastern Indiana Conference, *Minutes 1863*, 27.

39. Baptist Church, Texas, Union Baptist Association, *Minutes of the Twenty-Second Annual Meeting*, 4–5; Baptist Church, North Carolina, United Baptist Association, *Minutes 1862*, 8; Trumbull, *The Knightly Soldier*, 117–19; Methodist Church, Indiana, Indiana Conference, *Minutes . . . 1861*, 17.

40. Methodist Church, Indiana, Indiana Conference, *Minutes . . . 1861–62*, 17; Baptist Church, Alabama, Shelby Association, *Minutes of the Eleventh and Twelfth Annual Sessions*, 7; Baptist Church, North Carolina, Chowan Baptist Association, *Minutes of the Fifty-Eighth Annual Session*, 5–6; Baptist Church, Virginia, Rappahannock Baptist Association, *Minutes of the Twenty-Second Annual Session*, 11–13; Baptist Church, Alabama, Cahaba Baptist Association, *Minutes of the Forty-Fourth Anniversary*, 12.

41. Griffin, *Their Brothers' Keepers*, 244; *Journal of the Confederate Congress*, 2:127, 161–64, 7:293, 758; Neely, *Southern Rights*, 29–42; *Southern Churchman* (Richmond), January 24, 1862; Baptist Church, Mississippi, Choctaw Baptist Association, *Minutes of the Twenty-Third Anniversary*, 12–13.

42. *Newark (N.J.) Daily Advertiser*, January 13, 1863; Moore, *Rebellion Record*, 2 (Documents):479; *ORN*, ser. 1, vol. 7, p. 584; *Independent* (New York), January 12, 1865.

43. *Liquor and Lincoln*, pp. 1–4; January 25, March 21, 1862, James Hervey Otey Diary, Otey Papers, SHC; *Southern Christian Advocate* (Charleston, S.C.), February 13, 1862.

44. Stephenson, *Civil War Memoir*, 39–41; Holt, *A Mississippi Rebel in the Army of Northern Virginia*, 263–64.

45. J. J. D. Renfroe, "The Great Revival," 1863, Renfroe manuscript sermons, SBHLA; *Don't Play Cards, Boys*; Smith, *Here's Your Mule*, 22; *The Gambler's Balance Sheet*, 1–4; Jeter, *Evils of Gaming*, 1–6; Finley, *The Broken Vow*, 1–4.

46. Wiley, *Life of Johnny Reb*, 36–40; Apperson, *Repairing the "March of Mars,"* 188; *Christian Index* (Macon, Ga.), March 16, 1863; Wiley, *Life of Billy Yank*, 249–52; Newton, *A Wisconsin Boy in Dixie*, 77; Gavin, *Campaigning with the Roundheads*, 592.

47. Richard and Richard, *Defense of Vicksburg*, 83; Wiley, *Life of Johnny Reb*, 39; McCain, *In Song and Sorrow*, 143; Curtis, *Twenty-Fourth Michigan*, 138.

48. Sheeran, *Confederate Chaplain*, 34–35; Hartsock, *Soldier of the Cross*, 27–28; Stuckenberg, *I'm Surrounded by Methodists*, 106; Jones, *Christ in the Camp*, 207–8; Daniel, *Protestantism in the Confederacy*, 69; February 13, 1864, Robert Wharton Landis Diary, Landis Papers, PHS-P.

49. *OR*, ser. 1, vol. 19, pt. 2, p. 722; Bennett, *Narrative of the Great Revival*, 22–23; Comey, *A Legacy of Valor*, 24; Stewart, *Camp, March and Battlefield*, 60.

50. For very fragmentary data on venereal disease rates in the Confederate army early in the war, see Wiley, *Life of Johnny Reb*, 55–56.

51. Barnes, *Medical and Surgical History*, 6:891–96; Wiley, *Life of Billy Yank*, 257–62; Wiley, *Life of Johnny Reb*, 50–57; Barber, *Civil War Letters*, 169–70; Dwight, *The Seventh Commandment*; Sheeran, *Confederate Chaplain*, 52–53.

Chapter 6

1. Macmillan, *Methodist Episcopal Church in Michigan during Civil War*, 32; *Religious Herald* (Richmond), October 3, 1861.

2. Shaw, *Twelve Years in America*, 310; *Biblical Recorder* (Raleigh, N.C.), March 19, 1862; Mitchell, "Southern Methodist Newspapers during the Civil War," 29.

3. Bennett, *Narrative of the Great Revival*, 381; Smith, *Life and Letters of James Osgood Andrew*, 439–40; Methodist Church, Indiana Conference, *Minutes, 1861–62*, 13.

4. Yearns and Barrett, *North Carolina Civil War Documentary*, 228; Bennett, *Narrative of the Great Revival*, 51–53; Presbyterian Church, General Assembly, *Minutes, 1863*, 138–40; Lacy, "Address of the Chaplains of the Second Corps," 353–56.

5. Daniel, *Southern Protestantism in the Confederacy*, 82–86; Baptist Church, North Carolina, Union Baptist Association, *Minutes of the Twentieth Annual Session*, 14–17; Baptist Church, Mississippi, Choctaw Baptist Association, *Minutes of the Seventy-sixth Annual Session*, 12; Baptist Church, Georgia, Columbus Baptist Association, *Minutes of the Thirty-sixth Annual Session*, 11.

6. Robertson, *Life and Letters of John Albert Broadus*, 196–208; *The Victory Won: William J. Hoge*.

7. "Regimental Chaplains," *House Executive Document* No. 136, 37th Cong., 2nd sess., 1862, p. 1; Holcomb, *Southern Sons, Northern Soldiers*, 105.

8. Quimby, "Congress and Civil War Chaplaincy," 246–50; Coffman, *Old Army*, 78–81, 178–80; Trumbull, *War Memories of a Chaplain*, 1–2.

9. *OR*, ser. 3, vol. 1, p. 154; Hammond, *Army Chaplain's Manual*, 23–25; Armstrong, *For Courageous Fighting and Confident Dying*, 12–14; July 5, 1864, Elijah Evan Edwards Diary, DePauw.

10. Hammond, *Army Chaplain's Manual*, 16–17; *OR*, ser. 3, vol. 1, p. 382.

11. Armstrong, *For Courageous Fighting and Confident Dying*, 7–10; *OR*, ser. 2, vol. 3, p. 278; *Evangelist* (New York), January 23, 1862; *Christian Advocate and Journal* (New York), April 7, 1864. Even after the Federals began enlisting black troops, there were only a few African American chaplains. Wilson, *Campfires of Freedom*, 109–26. Congress had thoughtlessly required that chaplains belong to some Christian denomination, but eventually amended the law to simply require that any applicant be "a regularly ordained minister of some religious denomination." Only one Jew served as a regimental chaplain, but several were appointed hospital chaplains by Lincoln. There were apparently no Jewish chaplains in the Confederate army. Korn,

American Jewry and the Civil War, 56–97; Rosen, *Jewish Confederates*, 209. During the Civil War, there were only forty Catholic chaplains in the Federal armies but approximately 200,000 Catholic soldiers. And there were a mere twenty-eight Catholic chaplains serving Confederate troops. Throughout the war, the Catholic hierarchy lobbied for more Catholic chaplains and scrambled for priests to fill the positions. Randall Miller, "Catholic Religion, Irish Ethnicity, and the Civil War," in Miller et al., *Religion and American Civil War*, 263–68; Blied, *Catholics and the Civil War*, 108–11.

12. Matthews, *Statutes at Large of the Provisional Government*, 99, 116; *OR*, ser. 4, vol. 1, p. 252; *Christian Observer* (Richmond), May 13, 1864; *Southern Churchman* (Richmond), December 13, 1861; Moore, *God Our Refuge and Strength*, 12–13.

13. Brinsfield et al., *Faith in the Fight*, 59–62; Romero, *Religion in Rebel Ranks*, 9–10.

14. *Christian Advocate and Journal* (New York), September 12, 1861; Samuel V. Leech to Matthew Simpson, September 19, 1864, P. Coombe to Simpson, December 18, 1861, Simpson Collection, Drew; Hight, *Fifty-eighth Indiana*, 42–43.

15. J. K. Moorehead to Matthew Simpson, November 30, 1861, Simpson Collection, Drew; Vander Velde, *Presbyterian Churches and Federal Union*, 429–32; Lincoln, *Collected Works*, 4:559; 5:8–9, 53–54; Carpenter, *Inner Life of Abraham Lincoln*, 277.

16. *OR*, ser. 3, vol. 1, p. 728; Eastman, "Army Chaplain of 1863," 340–41; Hieronymus, "Chaplains of the Confederate States Army," 274–79; *German Reformed Messenger* (Chambersburg, Pa.), March 30, 1864; *Christian Advocate and Journal* (New York), July 11, 1861; *Evangelist* (New York), December 5, 1861.

17. McAllister, *Letters of Robert McAllister*, 493; Tourgée, *105th Ohio*, 170; Miller, "Two Civil War Notebooks," 77; *Christian Observer* (Richmond), December 24, 1863.

18. Shattuck, *Shield and Hiding Place*, 63; Quint, *Potomac and the Rapidan*, 182–83; Fletcher, *Diary of Calvin Fletcher*, 7:537–38; *Independent* (New York), April 3, 1862; Wiley, "'Holy Joes' of the Sixties," 290–92; Stewart, *Camp, March and Battlefield*, 53–54, 301–5.

19. Betts, *Civil War Diary*, 18, 28, 69, 131–41; Twichell, *Civil War Letters*, 16–18, 210.

20. Eastman, "Army Chaplain of 1863," 338; Smith, *Seventy-sixth New York*, 88; *Christian Recorder* (Philadelphia), June 15, 1861; Daniel, *Southern Protestantism in the Confederacy*, 65–66; Camp Notes by Chaplain, *Religious Herald*, July 17, 1862, Una Roberts Lawrence Papers, SBHLA. For a balanced assessment of the relations between officers and chaplains, see Armstrong, *For Courageous Fighting and Confident Dying*, 43–48.

21. Rogers, *War Pictures*, 14; Norton, *Army Letters*, 111; Sabine, "The Fifth Wheel," 20; Hays, *Life and Letters of Alexander Hays*, 165; Lord, *They Fought for the Union*, 253; Stuckenberg, *I'm Surrounded by Methodists*, 103; Daniel, "An Aspect of Church and State Relations in the Confederacy," 52.

22. Marks, *Peninsula Campaign in Virginia*, 47–52; *Evangelist* (New York), March 17, 1864; *Independent* (New York), February 2, 1865; Hieronymus, "Chaplains of the Confederate States Army," 111–25.

23. Trumbull, *War Memories of a Chaplain*, 106–9; Hartsock, *Soldier of the Cross*, 164; Armstrong, *For Courageous Fighting and Confident Dying*, 18–24; Corby, *Memoirs of Chaplain Life*, 27–28; Hieronymus, "Chaplains of the Confederate States Army," 166–76.

24. Hammond, *Army Chaplain's Manual*, 71–86; Siegel, *For the Glory of the Union*, 99; Betts, *Experience of a Confederate Chaplain*, 9; Mrs. Thomas Moleny to William Corby, August 23,

1862, Receipts, Emigrant Industrial Savings Bank, New York, 1863–65, Corby Papers, Notre Dame.

25. Bennett, *Narrative of the Great Revival*, 54–55; Armstrong, *For Courageous Fighting and Confident Dying*, 120–25; Twichell, *Civil War Letters*, 29; Hammond, *Army Chaplain's Manual*, 130–32; Lord, *They Fought for the Union*, 254; Hieronymus, "Chaplains of the Confederate States Army," 180–90.

26. Wiatt, *Confederate Chaplain William Edward Wiatt*, 22; Eagleton, *Memorial Sketch of Rev. George Eagleton*, 41; *Christian Recorder* (Philadelphia), April 26, 1862; McDonald and Searles, *Life of John S. Inskip*, 136; W. G. H. Jones to ?, July 21, 1862, Barbour Family Papers, VHS. Although historians have often been critical of chaplains, for two substantive (though rather one-sided) defenses of their performance, see Armstrong, *For Courageous Fighting and Confident Dying*, 55–58; Hieronymus, "Chaplains of the Confederate States Army," 299–314.

27. Brown, *Army Chaplain*, 13–20; Hammond, *Army Chaplain's Manual*, 43–70; Van Wyck, *A War to Petrify the Heart*, 74; Quint, *Potomac and Rapidan*, 11–12; Jones, *Christ in the Camp*, 102–3.

28. Bradford, "Chaplains in the Volunteer Army," 157–67; Humphreys, *Field, Camp, Hospital, and Prison*, 16; Watford, *Civil War in North Carolina*, 153.

29. Barclay, *Ted Barclay, Liberty Hall Volunteers*, 142; Beidelman, *Civil War Letters*, 54; Cooney, "War Letters," 68; Bishop, *Second Minnesota*, 163.

30. Sprague, *13th Connecticut*, 17–18; Fallows, *Everybody's Bishop*, 189–90; Hieronymus, "Chaplains of the Confederate States Army," 297.

31. Wiley, *Life of Johnny Reb*, 189–91; Norton, *Army Letters*, 100; Lusk, *War Letters*, 88–89; Small, *Road to Richmond*, 85; *New York Herald*, May 16, 1863; Magee, *72d Indiana*, 221–23.

32. *Religious Herald* (Richmond), July 10, 17, 24, 1862; Jones, *Christ in the Camp*, 36, 522.

33. Tucker, *Confederacy's Fighting Chaplain*, 46–47; Upson, *With Sherman to the Sea*, 87; Quimby, "Chaplains' Predicament," 34–37; Tucker, *Confederacy's Fighting Chaplain*, 39–59; Wiley, *Life of Johnny Reb*, 188.

34. Hieronymus, "Chaplains of Confederate States Army," 153–64; *OR*, ser. 1, vol. 25, pt. 1, p. 863; Isaac Taylor Tichenor, "Reminiscences of the Battle of Shiloh," Tichenor Papers, SBHLA; Stevens, *Berdan's United States Sharpshooters*, 275–76; Moore, *Rebellion Record*, 2 (Rumors and Incidents): 74; *Independent* (New York), March 30, 1862.

35. *Story of the Fifty-fifth Illinois*, 442–43; Smith, *Smite Them Hip and Thigh!*, 47.

36. Stewart, *Camp, March and Battlefield*, 86–87, 151, 198–99; Hammond, *Army Chaplain's Manual*, 28–42; Wiatt, *Confederate Chaplain William Edward Wiatt*, 21.

37. Daniel, *Soldiering in the Army of Tennessee*, 116; Reid, *Uncommon Soldiers*, 85; Mills, *Chronicles of the Twenty-first New York*, 282.

38. Wheeler, *Letters of William Wheeler*, 368; Bennitt, *"I Hope to Do My Country Service,"* 143–44; McAllister, *Letters of Robert McAllister*, 252–86; Baptist Church, Southern Baptist Convention, *Proceedings of the Ninth Biennial Session*, 39–40; Fallows, *Everybody's Bishop*, 187–88.

39. Charles M. Coit to "Dear All," June 4, 1862, Coit Papers, Sterling Library, Yale University; Meade, *Life and Letters of George Gordon Meade*, 2:144–45.

40. Rolfs, *No Peace for the Wicked*, 170–71; Amandus Silsby to his father, April 1, 1863, Silsby Correspondence, Archives Division, Stones River National Military Park, Murfreesboro, Tenn.; Haley, *Rebel Yell and Yankee Hurrah*, 250–51; Brandegee, *Charlie's Civil War*, 76; James Dillon

to "Very Dear Brother," July 20, 1863, Civil War Soldiers' and Chaplains' Letters, Miscellaneous Manuscripts, Notre Dame; J. H. Walters to William Corby, March 2, 1864, Corby Papers, Notre Dame.

41. Hight, *Fifty-eighth Indiana*, 564–65; Tissot, "A Year with the Army of the Potomac," 52; Grebner, *Ninth Ohio*, 67.

42. Barclay, *Ted Barclay, Liberty Hall Volunteers*, 20; Betts, *Civil War Diary*, 145–48; Durkin, *Stephen R. Mallory*, 142; *Evangelist* (New York), April 25, 1861.

43. Halsey, *Brother against Brother*, 122; Callaway, *Civil War Letters*, 33; Beidelman, *Civil War Letters*, 96; Downing, *Downing's Civil War Diary*, 54, 107.

44. Taylor, *Lee's Adjutant*, 173–74; Brewster, *When This Cruel War Is Over*, 30–31; Hartsock, *Soldier of the Cross*, 19, 46, 76.

45. *OR*, ser. 1, vol. 51, pt. 1, p. 338; Humphreys, *Field, Camp, Hospital, and Prison*, 12–13; Wiatt, *Confederate Chaplain William Edward Wiatt*, 31; Carter, *Four Brothers in Blue*, 380.

46. Tissot, "A Year with the Army of the Potomac," 55; Smith, *Anson Guards*, 174; Small, *Road to Richmond*, 125; Twichell, *Civil War Letters*, 235; McJunkin, *Bloody 85th*, 75; Trumbull, *War Memories of a Chaplain*, 19, 34–37.

47. Romero, *Religion in Rebel Ranks*, 165; Beaudry, *War Journal*, 10, 22, 36–37, 40–41; Humphreys, *Field, Camp, Hospital, and Prison*, 13; *Christian Recorder* (Philadelphia), April 26, 1862; Hammond, *Army Chaplain's Manual*, 106–10.

48. Cooney, "War Letters," 56–57, 62, 230. Corby, *Memoirs of Chaplain Life*, 51–52, 307–11; Tucker, *Confederacy's Fighting Chaplain*, 24–27; Tissot, "A Year with the Army of the Potomac," 44, 47, 62. Jewish Confederates tried to observe holy days and even keep kosher in camp but appreciated opportunities to attend services in Richmond and other cities. Rabbis visited the Federal camps on occasion, and Jewish soldiers practiced their faith despite the absence of Jewish chaplains. Rosen, *Jewish Confederates*, 97–98, 210–13; Korn, *American Jewry and the Civil War*, 56–98.

49. Welsh, *Irish Green and Union Blue*, 41; Corby, *Memoirs of Chaplain Life*, 42–43; Sheeran, *Confederate Chaplain*, 39–40; *New York Tablet*, October 5, 1861; Cooney, "War Letters," 52–53.

50. July 24, 1864, Elijah Evan Edwards Diary, DePauw; Cutrer and Parrish, *Brothers in Gray*, 186; Beidelman, *Civil War Letters*, 143; Wiley, *Life of Billy Yank*, 270; Trumbull, *War Memories of a Chaplain*, 15–16, 98–99.

51. Hammond, *Army Chaplain's Manual*, 110–14; Post, *Soldiers' Letters from Camp, Battlefield and Prison*, 34; Wiley, *Life of Billy Yank*, 270.

52. Boots, "Civil War Letters," 208, 214; George T. Chapin to John E. Chapin, February 17, 1863, Chapin Family Papers, Indiana Historical Society; Bahnson, *Bright and Gloomy Days*, 53; Richard Henry Watkins to Mary Watkins, January 4, 1863, Richard Henry Watkins Papers, VHS; Strother, *Virginia Yankee in the Civil War*, 28; Haydon, *For Country, Cause and Leader*, 321; McMahon, *John T. McMahon's Diary*, 60.

53. Romero, *Religion in Rebel Ranks*, 31; English Combatant, *Battle-Fields of the South*, 195; Guerrant, *Bluegrass Confederate*, 185, 209; Dougan, *Confederate Arkansas*, 113; Wiley, *Life of Billy Yank*, 270.

54. Trumbull, *War Memories of a Chaplain*, 100–104; Trumbull, *Good News!*, 3–18; Fiske, *Mr. Dunn Browne's Experiences in the Army*, 160–61; Hieronymus, "Chaplains of the Confederate States," 220–29; Wiley, *Life of Billy Yank*, 270.

55. Moore, *Rebellion Record*, 8 (Poetry and Incidents):11; Clark, "'Please Send Stamps,'" 93, 95, 203; Castleman, *Army of the Potomac*, 65–66; McPheeters, *"I acted from principle,"* 69.

56. March 9, 1862, William Scandlin Diary, AAS; Quimby, "Recurrent Themes and Purposes in the Sermons of Union Army Chaplains," 431–33; J. J. D. Renfroe, manuscript sermons, SBHLA; Adams, *Memorial and Letters of Rev. John R. Adams*, 40–41; Tissot, "A Year with the Army of the Potomac," 44; Neese, *Three Years in the Confederate Horse Artillery*, 78.

57. McPheeters, *"I acted from principle,"* 77; Beaudry, *War Journal*, 19; Barclay, *Ted Barclay, Liberty Hall Volunteers*, 30; Moore, *A Life for the Confederacy*, 146–47, 157.

58. Twichell, *Civil War Letters*, 35–36; Rhodes, *All for the Union*, 74; Jones, *Christ in the Camp*, 187; Chisholm, *Civil War Notebook*, 12, 31; Humphreys, *Field, Camp, Hospital, and Prison*, 17; Hight, *Fifty-eighth Indiana*, 130–31. Even a Georgia planter noted the general indifference of Union soldiers attending nearby camp services. August 7, 14, 1864, William King Diary, SHC.

59. Glatthaar, *Forged in Battle*, 225–26; Miller, *Fighting for Liberty and Right*, 115; Gavin, *Campaigning with the Roundheads*, 23; Wiley, *Life of Billy Yank*, 270; Bicknell, *Fifth Maine*, 71; Haydon, *For Country, Cause and Leader*, 160.

60. Siegel, *For the Glory of the Union*, 99–100; Robertson, *Soldiers Blue and Gray*, 183–84; Taylor, *Mission Ridge and Lookout Mountain*, 123–25; Regan, *Lost Civil War Diaries*, 176; Peirce and Peirce, *Dear Catharine, Dear Taylor*, 36; *History of Thirty-fifth Massachusetts*, 201; Boyd, *Civil War Diary*, 67; Dunkelman, *Brothers One and All*, 176.

61. Hammond, *Army Chaplain's Manual*, 109–10; Wightman, *From Antietam to Fort Fisher*, 56.

Chapter 7

1. Rolfs, *No Peace for the Wicked*, xviii; Stewart, *Camp, March and Battlefield*, 96–100. Reid Mitchell has pointed out that estimates of religiosity in northern ranks have often failed to consider the large of numbers of African American and Catholic soldiers. Reid Mitchell, "Christian Soldiers? Perfecting the Confederacy?," in Miller et al., *Religion and the American Civil War*, 297–305.

2. Lusk, *War Letters of William Thompson Lusk*, 100; Bennett, *Narrative of the Great Revival*, 413; *Religious Herald* (Richmond), June 20, 1861; Jones, *Christ in the Camp*, 496, 501, 564. Bell Wiley concluded that Confederate soldiers were more religious than were Union soldiers. But even then, most southern soldiers neither made a profession of faith nor joined a church. Wiley, *Life of Billy Yank*, 358–59; Wiley, *Life of Johnny Reb*, 191. From a more theological perspective, Steven Woodworth has argued that a majority of Americans generally and Civil War soldiers in particular held more or less orthodox views but that a "far smaller number" had met what evangelicals considered the requirements for salvation. Woodworth, *While God Is Marching On*, 52–56.

3. Elmore, *Heritage of Woe*, 71–72; Carmichael, *The Last Generation*, 149–51.

4. McAllister, *Letters of Robert McAllister*, 329; Small, *Road to Richmond*, 145; Huckaby and Simpson, *Tulip Evermore*, 26; Baptist Church, South Carolina, State Convention, *Minutes of the Forty-second Anniversary*, 155.

5. Abbott, *First New Hampshire*, 125–26; Wiley, *Life of Johnny Reb*, 186; Wiley, *Life of Billy Yank*, 269.

6. Romero, *Religion in Rebel Ranks*, 72–77; Price, *One Year in the Civil War*, 32; *Evangelist* (New York), October 1, 1863; Miller, "Two Civil War Notebooks," 69–72.

7. Bragg, *Letters of a Confederate Surgeon*, 16; *Anecdotes for Our Soldiers, No. 1*, 18; Henry Grimes Marshall to "Dear Hattie," January 25, 1863, Marshall Letters, Schoff Civil War Collection, Clements Library, University of Michigan; Robertson, *Soldiers Blue and Gray*, 172.

8. Hackett, *Christian Memorials of the War*, 122–24, 128–30; Howard, *124th Illinois*, 402–13; Parker, *Twenty-second Massachusetts*, 56–57; Daniel, "Southern Protestantism and Army Missions in the Confederacy," 187; Skidmore, *Alford Brothers*, 121.

9. Culver, *"Your Affectionate Husband,"* 268; Pettit, *Infantryman Pettit*, 29; McKinley, "Civil War Diary," 277; Jones, *Christ in the Camp*, 602.

10. Daniel, "Bible Publication and Procurement in the Confederacy," 191–97; Bible Convention of the Confederate States, *Proceedings, 1862*, 3–24; State Bible Convention of South Carolina, *Proceedings, 1862*, 8–9.

11. Daniel, "Bible Publication and Procurement in the Confederacy," 197–201; Robert Lewis Dabney to William Thomas Hoge, December 21, 1862, Dabney Family Papers, VHS; Hoge, *Moses Drury Hoge*, 168–97; August 9, 1864, Nancy Emerson Diary, UVa.

12. Bennett, *Narrative of the Great Revival*, 46–49; White, *Lincoln's Greatest Speech*, 102–6; Griffin, *Their Brothers' Keepers*, 246; Moore, *Rebellion Record*, 1 (Documents):262–63, 3 (Diary of Events):107.

13. Smith and Judah, *Life in the North during the Civil War*, 254–57; Moss, *Annals of the United States Christian Commission*, 698; Fuller, *Chaplain Fuller*, 191–92; *New York Tablet*, April 26, 1862; Stewart, *Camp, March and Battlefield*, 58–60; *Soldier's Pocket Bible*.

14. Jones, *Christ in the Camp*, 536; Adams, *Reminiscences of the Nineteenth Massachusetts*, 5; Davis, *Three Years in the Army*, 2; Beaudry, *War Journal*, 14; Urwin, "'The Lord Has Not Forsaken Me,'" 336; William R. Stimson to his wife and children, April 10, 1862, Stimson Letters, LC.

15. Wiley, *Life of Johnny Reb*, 180; Cate, *Two Soldiers*, 10–11; Kauffman, *Civil War Letters*, 29; Smith, *Incidents of the Christian Commission*, 353; Randolph, *Civil War Soldier's Diary*, 19; McMurry, *John Bell Hood*, 32–33.

16. *Religious Herald* (Richmond), May 16, 1861; Baptist Church, North Carolina, Beulah Baptist Association, *Minutes of the Twenty-ninth Annual Session*, 8–9.

17. *Religious Herald* (Richmond), June 13, 1861; December 1863, Fork Baptist Church (Fluvanna County) Minute Book, VBHS; July 1864, Bybees Road Church (Fluvanna County) Minute Book, VBHS.

18. August 1862, Red Oak Church (Appomattox County), Minute Book, VBHS; Baptist Church, Georgia, Bethel Baptist Association, *Minutes, 1862*, 2; ibid., *1863*, 12; Baptist Church, North Carolina, State Convention, *Proceedings of the Thirty-forth Annual Session*, 22–24; Jones, *Christ in the Camp*, 160–61.

19. *Christian Recorder* (Philadelphia), February 27, 1864; *Independent* (New York), January 2, 1862; Griffin, *Their Brothers' Keepers*, 251; *German Reformed Messenger* (Chambersburg, Pa.), May 13, 1863.

20. Romero, *Religion in Rebel Ranks*, 98–99; *A Tract for the Soldier*, 1–8; Baptist Church, Virginia, Appomattox Baptist Association, *Minutes, 1862 and 1863*, 12–13.

21. Stowell, *Rebuilding Zion*, 18–19; Silver, *Confederate Morale and Church Propaganda*, 58–63; A. L. Alexander to Abner Addison Porter, August 5, 1861, Porter Papers, PHS-M.

22. Romero, *Religion in Rebel Ranks*, 102–3; Thompson, *Presbyterians in the South*, 2:45;

United States Christian Commission, *First Annual Report*, 58–59; "The Heart of the Soldier," *Ladies' Repository* 24 (February 1864): 127.

23. Jones, *Christ in the Camp*, 171, 182–83; *Religious Herald* (Richmond), July 10, 1862.

24. Hammond, *Army Chaplain's Manual*, 114–17; Quint, *Potomac and the Rapidan*, 244–45; *Christian Inquirer* (New York), February 14, 1863.

25. Protestant Episcopal Church, Diocese of Virginia, Diocesan Missionary Society, *Prayer Book for the Camp*; Griffin, *Their Brothers' Keepers*, 247; Beaudry, *War Journal*, 63, 120.

26. Robert Lewis Dabney, "God's Eminent Mercy," "Spurious and Genuine Repentance Contrasted," "The Immediate Decision," "Procrastination," "Faith," Dabney Papers, Union Theological Seminary; *How Do You Bear Your Trials?* 1–6; Deems, *Christ in You*, 1–2; [Alexander], *Christ's Gracious Invitation*, 1–8; McGready, *An Appeal to the Young*, 1–4; *Are You Prepared?* 1–4; *Blood upon the Door Posts*; *Prepare to Meet Thy God*, 1–4; Dulles, *The Soldier's Friend*, 3–7, 13, 16–20, 21–22, 24–30, 32–33; *The Day of the Trial*.

27. *Delay; or, The Accepted Time*, 1–5; *Now!*; Ware, *On Picket*, 3–9; *The Sentinel*; Quintard, *Balm for the Weary and the Wounded*; Teasdale, *Season of Divine Mercy*; *Soldier's Great Want*; *The Muster*; *Prepare for Battle*; Ware, *To the Color*, 3–9; Penick, *The Captain of Salvation*; Jones, *The Christian Regiment Encamped in Every Soul*.

28. Armstrong, *For Courageous Fighting and Confident Dying*, 24–26; Baptist Church, South Carolina, State Convention, *Minutes of the Forty-second Anniversary*, 154; Bennett, *Narrative of the Great Revival*, 79, 117–18, 121; Wiley, *Life of Billy Yank*, 273–74; Walker, *Quite Ready to Be Sent Somewhere*, 164; *Southern Churchman* (Richmond), November 22, 1861; Baptist Church, North Carolina, United Baptist Association, *Minutes, 1862*, 10; United States Christian Commission, *First Annual Report*, 36–37.

29. Moore, *A Life for the Confederacy*, 164; Jones, *Christ in the Camp*, 191; Bennett, *Narrative of the Great Revival*, 82–83, 101, 141–42, 151; "The General Assembly," *Princeton Review* 34 (July 1862): 467–68; Madison, *The Contrast*; *Biblical Recorder* (Raleigh, N.C.), September 17, 1862; Hackett, *Christian Memorials of the War*, 86–87.

30. Bennett, *Narrative of the Great Revival*, 279; *Religious Herald* (Richmond), July 16, 1863, April 28, 1864.

31. William Flinn to Abner Addison Porter, August 22, 1861, Porter Papers, PHS-M; Springer, *The Preacher's Tale*, 45–46; Stuckenberg, *I'm Surrounded by Methodists*, 56.

32. Quint, *Potomac and the Rapidan*, 13; E. J. Y., "A Glimpse at the Army, the Hospitals, and the Freedmen," *Monthly Religious Magazine* 31 (April 1864): 245; Jones, *Christ in the Camp*, 544.

33. *New York Tablet*, November 8, 1862; *New York Freeman's Journal and Catholic Register*, June 22, 1861, February 27, 1864; Randall Miller, "Catholic Religion, Irish Ethnicity and the Civil War," in Miller et al., *Religion and the American Civil War*, 270–73.

34. *New York Tablet*, November 2, 1861; Germain, *Catholic Military and Naval Chaplains*, 74–77; Tissot, "A Year with the Army of the Potomac," 65–66.

35. Eastman, "Army Chaplain of 1863," 341–42, 347–48; Twichell, *Civil War Letters*, 73, 97–98, 189.

36. Sheeran, *Confederate Chaplain*, 40–41; Upson, *With Sherman to the Sea*, 104–5; Cooney, "War Letters," 158, 223; *Richmond Enquirer*, May 29, 1863.

37. Twichell, *Civil War Letters*, 34, 147, 180; Denison, "A Chaplain's Experience in the Union Army," 449–50; J. J. D. Renfroe, "The Great Revival," Renfroe manuscript sermons, SBHLA; 1862, Tar River Baptist Association (North Carolina) Minute Book, SBHLA.

38. Glatthaar, *General Lee's* Army, 235–36; Thomas, *Robert E. Lee*, 45–46, 152, 160–61; Pryor, *Reading the Man*, 223–35; Lee, *Wartime Washington*, 55–56.

39. Jones, *Personal Reminiscences of Lee*, 415–25, Jones, *Life and Letters of Lee*, 470–73, Taylor, *Lee's Adjutant*, 94; Lee, *Memoirs of William Nelson Pendleton*, 336; Pryor, *Reading the Man*, 235–40; Gary W. Gallagher, "The Idol of His Soldiers and the Hope of His Country: Lee and the Confederate People," in Gallagher, *Lee and His Generals in War and Memory*, 7–8.

40. Robertson, *Stonewall Jackson*, 18–19, 73–74, 133–39; Dabney, *Life and Campaigns of Jackson*, 83–107; Vandiver, *Mighty Stonewall*, 86–87, 109–10.

41. Dabney, *Life and Campaigns of Jackson*, 540–41; D. H. Hill to Robert L. Dabney, June 7, 1863, Dabney Papers, Union Theological Seminary; White, *Sketches of the Life of Captain Hugh A. White*, 124–25; Corsan, *Two Months in the Confederate States*, 100–101; Dabney, *True Courage*, 12–21; Garfield, *Wild Life of the Army*, 173.

42. Royster, *Destructive War*, 69; Douglas, *I Rode with Stonewall*, 91; Jackson, *Life and Letters of Jackson*, 377, 419; Allan, *Life and Letters of Margaret Junkin Preston*, 153; Dabney, *Life and Campaigns of Jackson*, 540–41; Martha White Read to Thomas Griffin Read, June 19–21, 1862, Read Family Correspondence, Notre Dame.

43. Duffield, *The Great Rebellion Thus Far a Failure*, 18; *Evangelist* (New York), December 5, 1861; *German Reformed Messenger* (Chambersburg, Pa.), July 24, October 9, December 18, 1861, March 11, 1863; *New York Times*, September 9, 1861.

44. Cozzens, *This Terrible Sound*, 403–4; Cooney, "War Letters," 164–65, 168–69; Garfield, *Wild Life of the Army*, 226–27, 236, 250.

45. Dunn, "Matthew Andrew Dunn Letters," 119; D. F. Parker to Alonzo Hill, May 4, 1861, Civil War Papers, AAS; *Can I Be Religious While I Am a Soldier?* 1–2; DuBose, *Sermon Addressed to Captain Parkhill's Company*, 5–11; Wyatt-Brown, *Shaping of Southern Culture*, 206–8; "The Revelations of the Crisis," *Monthly Religious Magazine* 28 (July 1862): 52–56; Engs and Brooks, *Their Patriotic Duty*, 118.

46. Trumbull, *Knightly Soldier*, 14–23; *Evangelist* (New York), November 13, 1862; White, *Sketches of the Life of Captain Hugh A. White*, 1–43, 132–39; Thompson, *The Sergeant's Memorial*, 2–242; Bartol, *The Nation's Hour*, 14–25.

47. Rolfs, *No Peace for the Wicked*, 52; Chris C. McKinney to Mary McKinney, February 16, 1862, McKinney Letters, Notre Dame; Dabney, *The Christian Soldier*, 3–8; *German Reformed Messenger* (Chambersburg, Pa.), November 19, 1862.

48. James Branscomb to his sister, July 15, 1862, Branscomb Family Papers, ADAH; Taylor, *Destruction and Reconstruction*, 89–91; Chesnut, *Mary Chesnut's Civil War*, 501–2; Wight, "Church and the Confederate Cause," 371.

49. Perry and Perry, *Widows by the Thousand*, 118; Moxley, *Oh, What a Lonesome Time I Had*, 24; Martha White Read to Thomas Griffin Read, August 7–12, 1861, September 13, 1862, Read Family Correspondence, Notre Dame; Taylor et al., *Leverett Letters*, 333; Joslyn, *Charlotte's Boys*, 5.

50. Snell, *From First to Last*, 58; Billingsley, *From the Flag to the Cross*, 58; Callaway, *Civil War Letters*, 147, 153–54; Macmillan, *Methodist Episcopal Church in Michigan*, 28.

51. Randolph, *Civil War Soldier's Diary*, 10; Rolfs, *No Peace for the Wicked*, 202; *Christian Recorder* (Philadelphia), April 16, 1864; Newton, *A Wisconsin Boy in Dixie*, 73–74; Pettit, *Infantryman Pettit*, 63; MacCauley, *Memories and Memorials*, 600.

52. Geary, *A Politician Goes to War*, 167; Dwight, *Life and Letters of Wilder Dwight*, 271; Squier, *This Wilderness of War*, 3; Smith, *Life and Times of George Foster Pierce*, 440–41; Evans, *Intrepid Warrior*, 470; Sheffey, *Soldier of Southwestern Virginia*, 79; Heg, *Civil War Letters*, 70.

53. Noll, *Civil War as a Theological Crisis*, 84–86; Perry and Perry, *Widows by the Thousand*, 165, 233; Holt, *A Surgeon's Civil War*, 33; *Richmond Daily Dispatch*, November 12, 1862; Manson, *A Spiritual Diary*, 1; Nugent, *My Dear Nellie*, 143.

54. Paludan, *A People's Contest*, 367–68; Faust, *Republic of Suffering*, 174–75; Partin, "Sustaining Faith of an Alabama Soldier," 438; *Soldiers' Letters from Camp, Battle-field and Prison*, 348; Renfroe, *A Model Confederate Soldier*, 9; Willard, *With the 3rd Wisconsin Badgers*, 109–10; Mohr, *Cormany Diaries*, 267–68; *Richmond Daily Dispatch*, December 1, 1862; Shuck, "*Home Sweet Home*"; Richard and Richard, *Defense of Vicksburg*, 267; Turnbull, *Well Done*, 3–19. Drew Faust has perceptively observed how a belief in heaven almost became a "denial of death," an imperfect effort to overcome fear by celebrating the glories of eternal life. Faust, *Republic of Suffering*, 177–80. Mark Schantz has agreed with this point and added the important suggestion that a belief in a literal physical resurrection of the dead helped steel soldiers facing disfigurement and death. Schantz, *Awaiting the Heavenly Country*, 52–62.

55. Robertson, *Soldiers Blue and Gray*, 182; Macmillan, *Methodist Episcopal Church in Michigan*, 30; *Christian Index* (Macon, Ga.), January 26, 1863; *Patriotism Not Piety*; *Jesus, the Soldier's Friend*; Welsh, *Irish Green and Union Blue*, 74; *Independent* (New York), August 4, 1864; Bates, *A Texas Cavalry Officer's Civil War*, 140–41.

56. Baptist Church, Virginia, General Association, *Address of the Baptist General Association of Virginia*, 4–5; *Southern Churchman* (Richmond), January 24, 1862; McMahon, *John T. McMahon's Diary*, 20, 23–24. McMahon did survive the war and became a missionary to India.

57. Penick, *Prodigal Sons*, 1; Pardington, *Dear Sarah*, 11, 40; Clark, *Papers of Walter Clark*, 1:72–73; P. T. Hieronymus to "Cousin Will," March 22, May 22, 1865, Hieronymus Letters, ⟨http://www.district87.org/projects/civilwar/may2265.htm⟩, accessed November 16, 2001.

58. Barber, *Holding the Line*, 100; Hunter, *Sons of Arthur, Children of Lincoln*, 161–62; Silber and Stevens, *Yankee Correspondence*, 89–90; Pender, *General to His Lady*, especially 56–215. Pender was wounded at Gettysburg, an infection set in, and he died at Staunton, Virginia, on July 18, 1863.

59. Upson, *With Sherman to the Sea*, 20–21; Ritner and Ritner, *Love and Valor*, 114–15.

60. Cumming, *Journal of a Confederate Nurse*, 117; Williams, *From That Terrible Field*, 13.

61. Peirce and Peirce, *Dear Catharine, Dear Taylor*, 43–44, 102–6; Melcher, *With a Flash of the Sword*, 207; Willard, *With the Third Wisconsin Badgers*, 118–24; Reinhart, *August Willich's Gallant Dutchmen*, 24; Ritner and Ritner, *Love and Valor*, 58. Perkins, *Three Years a Soldier*, 149; Kamphoefner and Helbich, *Germans in the Civil War*, 114, 281. Worried that soldiers might be attracted to various modern heresies, the attorney general of Virginia wrote a tract defending revealed religion and warning against the diabolical influence of David Hume and other free thinkers. Tucker, *The Bible or Atheism*, 3–30.

62. Lennard, "'Give Yourself No Trouble about Me,'" 25–26; Dunkelman, *War's Relentless Hand*, 175; *A Few Words to the Soldiers of the Confederate States*, 3–24; Norton, *Army Letters*, 142; Mattocks, "*Unspoiled Heart*," 112.

63. Booth and Prentiss, *A Memorial of Lieut. Franklin Butler Crosby*, 9–37; Randolph, *A Civil War Soldier's Diary*, 171.

Chapter 8

1. Bunting, *Our Trust Is In the God of Battles*, 17; *Biblical Recorder* (Raleigh, N.C.), January 29, 1862.

2. *Lieutenant R.; or, the Tract Read in the Theatre*, 1–7; Myers, *Children of Pride*, 835–36; January 27, 1861, Mary Jeffreys Bethell Diary, SHC.

3. February 11, 1862, Alice Ready Diary, SHC; Guerrant, *Bluegrass Confederate*, 47; *Biblical Recorder* (Raleigh, N.C.), March 5, 1862.

4. Davis, *Messages and Papers of Davis*, 1:217–18; *Charleston Mercury*, February 21, 1862; *Southern Christian Advocate* (Charleston), February 27, 1862.

5. March 2, 1862, Sarah Lois Wadley Diary, SHC; *Richmond Daily Dispatch*, March 6, 1862; Taylor, "Diary of Mary W. Taylor," 927; McGuire, *Diary of a Southern Refugee*, 96.

6. Myers, *Children of Pride*, 860; *Southern Churchman* (Richmond), February 21, 1862; Smith, *Life and Times of George Foster Pierce*, 453–54; Beringer et al., *Why the South Lost the Civil War*, 126.

7. Elliott, *New Wine Not to Be Put into Old Bottles*, 5–16; March 10, 1862, Cornelia M. Noble Diary, Center for American History, University of Texas; Lafferty, *A Fast-Day Sermon*, 3–12; J. B. Jeter Notes and Sermons, February 1862 volume, pp. 10–19, VBHS; Wheelwright, *A Discourse Delivered to the Troops*, 5–15; Samuel B. Wilson to William Henry Foote, March 8, 1862, Wilson Papers, PHS-M.

8. *Southern Presbyterian* (Columbia, S.C.), February 22, 1862; Walter W. Lenoir to Rufus Lenoir, February 20, 1862, Lenoir Family Papers, SHC; Fain, *Sanctified Trial*, 34. Burney, *A Southern Soldier's Letter's Home*, 127; Taylor, "Diary of Mary W. Taylor," 926–27; Samuel Barnett to Abner Addison Porter, March 22, 1862, Porter Papers, PHS-M.

9. *OR*, ser. 4, vol. 3, pp. 1102–3; Lincecum, *Gideon Lincecum's Sword*, 247; "Proceedings of the First Congress, Third Session," 175.

10. Lehman and Nolt, *Mennonites, Amish, and Civil War*, 56–64; *OR*, ser. 4, vol. 2, 161, vol. 3, p. 240; Blair, *Virginia's Private War*, 50–51, 57–59, 105–6; Wright, *Conscientious Objectors in the Civil War*, 111–20, 181–82.

11. *OR*, ser. 4, vol. 2, pp. 122, 166; Friends, Virginia Half Yearly Meeting, *Memorial to Legislature of Virginia*, 3–7; Cartland, *Southern Heroes or the Friends in War Time*, 117–28, 139–52; Wright, *Conscientious Objectors in the Civil War*, 91–110.

12. Brunk, *History of Mennonites in Virginia*, 1:156–79; Horst, *Mennonites in the Confederacy*, 23–27, 41–84, 92–94; Lehman and Nolt, *Mennonites, Amish, and Civil War*, 64–71, 184–93; Cartland, *Southern Heroes or the Friends in War Time*, 195–220, 299–326; Janney, *Memoirs of Samuel M. Janney*, 189–94; *An Account of the Sufferings of the Friends of North Carolina Yearly Meeting*, 9–10, 14–15, 17–25.

13. Bunting, *Our Trust Is in the God of Battles*, 41–42; *Christian Observer* (Richmond), March 13, 1862; March 24, 1862, Alice Ready Diary, SHC; Buck, *Shadows on My Heart*, 36–37; Dabney, *Life and Campaigns of Jackson*, 107; Fain, *Sanctified Trial*, 38.

14. May 5, 1862, Mrs. Hill Diary, UVa; May 3, 1862, Cornelia M. Noble Diary, Center for American History, University of Texas; Thornwell, *Our Danger and Our Duty*, 3–14.

15. Baptist Church, Georgia, State Convention, *Minutes of the Fortieth Anniversary*, 12; Cumming, *Journal of a Confederate Nurse*, 35; Richard and Richard, *Defense of Vicksburg*, 17. Georgia volunteer Samuel Burney touched on almost all these themes in an early April letter to his

wife: "This war will do a great deal of good. . . . It will teach us to deny ourselves & sacrifice pleasure for duty. If we conduct ourselves right it will teach us humbly to bow ourselves in resignation to the Providence of God. . . . We should not murmur. God is the cause of this war and He does nothing erring. This war is a blessing—though we cannot see how that is. The Bible tells us that Christ, while on earth, was made perfect through suffering; if so with Him, why not for us. Our sojourn in this wicked world is only for a season; the places that knows us now will soon know us no more. . . . It is wise then to listen to the inviting voice of a loving Savior, who asks us to give Him our hearts. We must die, when we know not, nor where. Let us so live that when that hour of death comes we shall be ready." Burney, *A Southern Soldier's Letters Home*, 148.

16. *Southern Presbyterian* (Columbia, S.C.), May 3, 1862; *Christian Index* (Macon, Ga.), April 22, 1862; *Christian Observer* (Richmond), March 27, 1862; Chambers, *Blood and Sacrifice*, 18; Buck, *Shadows on My Heart*, 39; Annie Sehon to her parents, April 27, 1862, John Kimberly Papers, SHC; Rosen, *Jewish Confederates*, 105.

17. Davis, *Messages and Papers of Davis*, 1:227–28; *Southern Churchman* (Richmond), May 9, 1862; *Religious Herald* (Richmond), May 15, 1862.

18. McGuire, *Diary of a Southern Refugee*, 117; May 16, 1862, Kate S. Carney Diary, SHC; Wooten, "Religious Activities in Civil War Memphis," 142; May 18, 1862, Lyle's Church (Albemarle Association) Minute Book, VBHS; *Southern Christian Advocate* (Charleston), May 22, 1862; Stout, *Upon the Altar of the Nation*, 134–35.

19. *Biblical Recorder* (Raleigh, N.C.), May 27, 1862; Chesebrough, *God Ordained This War*, 229–37; Hildebrand, *A Mennonite Journal*, 11; Cross, *Camp and Field*, 1:32–33; J. B. Jeter, Sermon Psalm 118:6, Jeter Notes and Sermons, VBHS; Robert Lewis Dabney, "Our Ineffectual Prayers," May n.d., 1862, Dabney Papers, Union Theological Seminary.

20. *Independent* (New York), May 29, 1862; Morris, *Christian Life and Character*, 704–10; Carwardine, *Lincoln*, 190; Lincoln, *Collected Works*, 5:212–13, 215–16.

21. Vander Velde, *Presbyterian Churches and Federal Union*, 108–19; McPherson, *Political History of the United States during the Great Rebellion*, 462–63.

22. Dana, *Recollections of the Civil War*, 158; Scott, "'A Visitation of God," 49–50; "The Doctrine of Providence," *Princeton Review* 34 (April 1862): 277–86. For an analysis of the broad and pervasive interpretations of providence during the Civil War, see Noll, *Civil War as a Theological Crisis*, 78–81.

23. Barrows, *Our War and Our Religion, and Their Harmony*, 3–19; Edwards, *Of Singular Genius, Of Singular Grace*, 230; *Evangelist* (New York), February 20, 1862; Stone, *Praise for Victory*, 3–15.

24. Lincoln, *Collected Works*, 5:185–86; Boyd, *Civil War Diary*, 31–32, 38; *New York Herald*, April 17, 1862; Randolph, *Civil War Soldier's Diary*, 72; Mitchell, *Civil War Soldiers*, 187.

25. Phelps, *National Symptoms*, 14–16; Beecher, *Freedom and War*, 248–69; "A Providential View of War," *Universalist Quarterly* 19 (July 1862): 248–57; Wayland, *A Memoir of the Life and Labor of Francis Wayland*, 2:268. For a broader look at the theme of redemption through suffering that raised both painful question and millennial hope, see Frederickson, *Inner Civil War*, 79–85.

26. Phelps, *National Symptoms*, 3–9; Williams, "Letters of General Thomas Williams," 309; *Friend* (Philadelphia), April 12, 1862.

27. Garfield, *Wild Life of the Army*, 100; Bacon, *Conciliation*, 16–20; *New York Tablet*, February 1, March 15, 1862; McGreevy, *Catholicism and American Freedom*, 82–88.

28. Stone, *Emancipation*, 3–28; Stokes, *Church and State in the United States*, 2:205–6; Voegli, *Free but Not Equal*, 138–39.

29. Balme, *American States, Churches and Slavery*, 68–80; Angell, *Henry McNeal Turner*, 41–43; *Ladies' Repository* 22 (February, March 1862): 128, 190.

30. *New York Freeman's Journal and Catholic Register*, May 17, 1862; Wayland, *Memoir of the Life and Labors of Francis Wayland*, 2:267; *Christian Recorder* (Philadelphia), May 17, 1862; Methodist Church, Indiana, North Indiana Conference, *Minutes of the Nineteenth Session*, 31–33; *Friends' Intelligencer* (Philadelphia) April 26, 1862; *Evangelist* (New York), April 24, 1862; *Pittsburgh Catholic*, March 22, 1862.

31. *Liberator* (Boston), May 2, 1862; Heathcote, *Lutheran Church in the Civil War*, 74–83; Beecher, *Freedom and War*, 223–48; Haven, *National Sermons*, 269–90.

32. Palmer, *James Henley Thornwell*, 515–16, 518; Fleet and Fleet, *Green Mount*, 136; *Southern Christian Advocate* (Augusta, Ga.), June 5, 1862; *Biblical Recorder* (Raleigh, N.C.), June 11, 1862; [Cary], "Diary of Miss Harriette Cary," 107, 110, 113.

33. [Cary], "Diary of Miss Harriette Cary," 162, 165; Silver, *Confederate Morale and Church Propaganda*, 50; July 2, 1862, Mary Jeffreys Bethell Diary, SHC; June 30, 1862, Nancy Emerson Diary, UVa; Myers, *Children of Pride*, 922.

34. *Christian Index* (Macon, Ga.), July 15, 1862; *Southern Christian Advocate* (Augusta, Ga.), July 24, August 7, 1862; Hodge, *Life of Charles Hodge*, 475; Fish, *Duty of the Hour*, 6; *Independent* (New York), July 10, September 4, 1862.

35. *Evangelist* (New York), June 26, 1862; Twichell, *Civil War Letters*, 163; Long, *Saints and the Union*, 79.

36. Ridgaway, *Life of Rev. Alfred Cookman*, 250–56; *Evangelist* (New York), July 10, August 7, 1862; Sermon, "These the Beginnings of Sorrow," [104th Pennsylvania], Museum of the Confederacy.

37. *Southern Churchman* (Richmond), July 4, 1862; *Religious Herald* (Richmond), July 10, 1862; *Southern Christian Advocate* (Augusta, Ga.), July 31, 1862.

38. July 4, 1862, Nancy Emerson Diary, UVa; Daniel, *Southern Protestantism in the Confederacy*, 18; Beale, *Journal of Jane Howison Beale*, 98; Towles, *A World Turned Upside Down*, 330; *Southern Churchmen* (Richmond), July 11, 1862; Baptist Church, Texas, Union Baptist Association, *Minutes of the Twenty-third Annual Meeting*, 8.

39. Everson and Simpson, *"Far, Far from Home,"* 136; Hubbs, *Voices from Company D*, 97; Bennett, *Narrative of the Great Revival*, 172–73, 176.

40. Nisbet, *Four Years on the Firing Line*, 42; David Power Conyngham, "Soldiers of the Cross: Nuns and Priests of the Battlefield," chapter 2, Conyngham Papers, Notre Dame; Stuckenberg, *I'm Surrounded by Methodists*, 44; Duke, *Reminiscences of General Basil W. Duke*, 416–18; J. Maxwell Couper to Dora Harper Couper, June 1, 1861, Couper Family Papers, SHC; William Franklin Draper to his wife, January 18, 1863, Draper Papers, LC. In examining the fatalism of the Civil War soldier, I have greatly benefited from the analysis in McPherson, *For Cause and Comrades*, 64–67.

41. Dollar, *Soldiers of the Cross*, 111; Partin, "Sustaining Faith of an Alabama Soldier," 436; Bennett, *Narrative of the Great Revival*, 163; Lee, *Memoirs of William Nelson Pendleton*, 235–36; Holcomb, *Southern Sons, Northern Soldiers*, 46; Henry Brantingham to his wife, Decem-

ber 8, 1862, Brantingham Letters, Joseph Bilby Collection, U.S. Army Military History Institute; Woodworth, *While God Is Marching On*, 33–34.

42. Vaughan, "Diary of Turner Vaughan," 578; Rosen, *Jewish Confederates*, 209–10; Squier, *This Wilderness of War*, 11; Weygant, *One Hundred and Twenty-fourth Regiment, N.Y.*, 242; *Anecdotes for Our Soldiers, No. 1*, 9–10; Perkins, *Three Years a Soldier*, 235; Holt, *A Mississippi Rebel*, 45.

43. Smith, "Confederate Soldier's Diary," 296; Sturtevant, *Josiah Volunteered*, 50; Jones, *Christ in the Camp*, 153; Bean, *Liberty Hall Volunteers*, 186.

44. Cooney, "War Letters of Father Peter Paul Cooney," 68; Shannon, "Archbishop Ireland's Experiences as a Civil War Chaplain," 304–5; Sheeran, *Confederate Chaplain*, 5–6; Clarke, *Lives of the Deceased Bishops of the Catholic Church*, 2:233–34; Corby, *Memoirs of Chaplain Life*, 184, 320–21; Mulholland, *116th Regiment, Pennsylvania Infantry*, 371–72.

45. McPherson, *For Cause and Comrades*, 64; Billingsley, *From the Flag to the Cross*, 202–3; White, *31st Georgia*, 65–66; Newton, *Out of the Briars*, 55–56.

46. Jones, *Christ in the Camp*, 556; Smith, *Incidents of the Christian Commission*, 40; Stuckenberg, *I'm Surrounded by Methodists*, 116.

47. Jordan, "Thomas G. Jordan Family," 135; Neill A. Baker to Emma J. Baker, November 10, 1861, Baker Letter, Lewis Leigh Collection, U.S. Army Military History Institute; Burgwyn, *A Captain's War*, 43; Shepherd, *To Rescue My Native Land*, 151–52, 182–83; Kennett, *Marching through Georgia*, 173; William J. Pegram to Virginia Johnson McIntosh, August 14, 1862, Pegram-Johnson-McIntosh Papers, VHS; Dexter, *Seymour Dexter, Union Army*, 129.

48. Wiley, *Life of Billy Yank*, 73; Stout, *Upon the Altar of the Nation*, 56; Holt, *Mississippi Rebel*, 177–78; Smith, *Incidents of the Christian Commission*, 46.

49. Cumming, *Journal of a Confederate Nurse*, 168; *A Letter to a Son in Camp*, 3–4; December 1, 1861, Myra Smith Diary, Eunice J. Stockwell Papers, Mississippi Department of Archives and History; *Christian Index* (Macon, Ga.), July 29, 1862; *Religious Herald* (Richmond), February 20, March 6, 1862; Stout, *Upon the Altar of the Nation*, 123.

50. Woodworth, *While God Is Marching On*, 104–5, 137–39; Cumming, *Journal of a Confederate Nurse*, 23; Jane S. Tucker to Powhattan Ellis, March 7, 1864, Munford Ellis Papers, Duke University; *Religious Herald* (Richmond), February 13, 1862; Eagleton, "Civil War Diary," 133; Morgan, *Civil War Diary*, 122–23; April 21, 1862, Alice Ready Diary, SHC; Pember, *Southern Woman's Story*, 168.

51. Johnson, *Life and Letters of Robert Lewis Dabney*, 259–60; Glatthaar, *General Lee's Army*, 235; *Southern Presbyterian* (Columbia, S.C.), April 12, 1862; April 8, 1862, Alice Ready Diary, SHC; McPherson, *For Cause and Comrades*, 71–74; Burney, *Southern Soldier's Letters Home*, 169; Bartol, *Remission of Blood*, 3–19.

Chapter 9

1. Clark, *Under the Stars and Bars*, 123–24; Gage, *From Vicksburg to Raleigh*, 234.

2. Chesnut, *Private Mary Chesnut*, 82; Chamberlayne, *Ham Chamberlayne*, 123; Hackett, *Christian Memorials of the War*, 65–66, 166.

3. These scenes and their descriptions were deeply influenced by long-standing notions about what constituted a "good death." In the antebellum decades, many of these ideas had also appeared in sentimental poetry. Schantz, *Awaiting the Heavenly Country*, 96–125.

4. Van Wyck, *A War to Petrify the Heart*, 49; December 11, 1862, Charles S. Granger Diary,

Civil War Miscellaneous Collection, U.S. Army Military History Institute; William M. Sheppard to his wife, December 17, 1862, Sheppard Letter, Fredericksburg and Spotsylvania National Military Park; W. E. D., *A Soldier to His Comrades*; Crumly, *The Soldier's Bible*.

5. Stuckenberg, *I'm Surrounded by Methodists*, 18; Mathis, *In the Land of the Living*, 53; Greene, *Letters from a Sharpshooter*, 27; Amasa Orlando Allen to Agnes Allen, July 3, 1863, Allen Papers, State Historical Society of Iowa, Des Moines.

6. McIntosh, *How Long Have I to Live*; *Are You Ready?*, 1–4; Calvin Diggs to his mother, April 12, 1865, Diggs Letters, ⟨http://indianainthecivilwar.com/letters/84th/diggs.htm⟩; Woodworth, *While God Is Marching On*, 47–50; Bliss, *Sermons Preached at the Funeral of Capt. Lucius H. Bostwick*, 3–16. For common views of death among northern civilians, see Scott, "'A Visitation of God,'" 210–16.

7. Moore, *A Life for the Confederacy*, 24; *Anecdotes for Our Soldiers, No. 1*, 14–15; Lord, *A Discourse in Honor of Capt. Paul Hamilton*, 3–16; McCain, *In Song and Sorrow*, 23.

8. Samary Sherman to Lucretia Silbley, August 26, 1864, Sibley Papers, AAS; Borden, *Legacy of Fannie and Joseph*, 139; J. B. Jeter, Notes and Sermons, May 1862 volume, pp. 74–80, VBHS.

9. Hackett, *Christian Memorials of the War*, 16–17; Billingsley, *From the Flag to the Cross*, 195; Lyle, *Light and Shadows of Army Life*, 57–58, 170; Miller, "Two Civil War Notebooks," 85; Woodworth, *While God Is Marching On*, 46–47; Humphreys, *Field, Camp, Hospital, and Prison*, 247–48.

10. Evans, *Sixteenth Mississippi Infantry*, 268–69; Buck, *Shadows on My Heart*, 226; Mills, *Chronicles of the Twenty-first New York*, 202–3.

11. Tissot, "A Year with the Army of the Potomac," 70; July 4–5, August 8, 1864, Peter P. Cooney Diary and Record Book, Cooney Papers, Notre Dame; *Zion's Herald and Wesleyan Journal* (Boston), April 8, 1863; Cooney, "War Letters," 51–53.

12. Brown, *Army Chaplain*, 29–61; Armstrong, *For Courageous Fighting and Confident Dying*, 52.

13. Billingsley, *From the Flag to the Cross*, 259–61; Twichell, *Civil War Letters*, 143–44; Hartsock, *Soldier of the Cross*, 48–49.

14. Wiatt, *Confederate Chaplain William Edward Wiatt*, 49; *A Word of Comfort for the Sick Soldier*, 1–8; Ware, *A Few Words with the Convalescent*, 3–15; *A Word of Warning for the Sick Soldier*, 1–8; *The Wounded; or, a Time to Think*.

15. Ware, *Wounded in the Hands of the Enemy*, 3–9; Mulholland, *116th Pennsylvania*, 53; Welsh, *Irish Green and Union Blue*, 73; Tillie Foreman to Frank R. Stewart, August 9, 17, 1864, Stewart Papers, Bowling Green State University; Jones, *Christ in the Camp*, 186.

16. Haines, *Fifteenth New Jersey*, 34; Hackett, *Christian Memorials of the War*, 61–65; Faust, *Republic of Suffering*, 22; Bennett, *Narrative of the Great Revival*, 175.

17. United States Christian Commission, *First Annual Report*, 39; Smith, *Incidents of the Christian Commission*, 293, 337; Lane, *"Dear Mother: Don't grieve about me,"* 120.

18. Jones, *Christ in the Camp*, 177, 202; Billingsley, *From the Flag to the Cross*, 142–44, 188–89, 193, 206–7; Hickerson, *Echoes of Happy Valley*, 88.

19. *Southern Churchman* (Richmond), June 13, 1862; Billingsley, *From the Flag to the Cross*, 181–82, 221, 258; Jones, *Christ in the Camp*, 40–41, 205, 474–75, 482; Bennett, *Narrative of the Great Revival*, 78–80; Hackett, *Christian Memorials of the War*, 100–101, 149–50.

20. Hartsock, *Soldier of the Cross*, 16, 33, 35, 54; Weston, *Among the Wounded*, 13.

21. Taylor, *In the Hospital*, 1–6; Ware, *Home to the Hospital*, 3–19; Alcott, *Hospital Sketches*, 31; Imholte, *First Minnesota*, 36–40; Clark, *Thirty-ninth Illinois*, 207–8.

22. *Evangelist* (New York), March 20, 1862; Cross, *Gettysburg and the Christian Commission*, 22–23; Quint, *Potomac and the Rapidan*, 120–21; Trumbull, *War Memories of a Chaplain*, 125–29; Hammond, *Army Chaplain's Manual*, 132–41.

23. *Anecdotes for Our Soldiers No. 1*, 20–21; Cross, *Gettysburg and the Christian Commission*, 24; Mohr, *Cormany Diaries*, 265; *Christian Recorder* (Philadelphia), November 15, 1862; Smith, *Incidents of the Christian Commission*, 47, 50; Bartlett, *Twelfth New Hampshire*, 37; Ropes, *Civil War Nurse*, 101–2.

24. Billingsley, *From the Flag to the Cross*, 254–55; Lane, *"Dear Mother: Don't grieve about me,"* 188; Upson, *With Sherman to the Sea*, 125; Jones, *Christ in the Camp*, 502, 592.

25. Taylor, *Life and Times of James B. Taylor*, 263; Smith, *Incidents of the Christian Commission*, 82; Hoisington, *Gettysburg and the Christian Commission*, 108–9; Jones, *Christ in the Camp*, 565; Hartsock, *Soldier of the Cross*, 88; Wiatt, *Confederate Chaplain William Edward Wiatt*, 15–16.

26. Lyle, *Light and Shadows of Army Life*, 54–56, 133–35; Mills, *Twenty-first New York*, 302–3; Power, *Lee's Miserables*, 193–94; Beaudry, *War Journal*, 121; Smith, *Incidents of the Christian Commission*, 62–63, 219.

27. Hackett, *Christian Memorials of the War*, 235; Smith, *Incidents of the Christian Commission*, 324–25, 463; United States Christian Commission, *Information for Army Meetings* (February 1865): 17–18; Holmes, *Touched with Fire*, 27–29.

28. Billingsley, *From the Flag to the Cross*, 146–47, 187–88, 231; Jones, *Christ in the Camp*, 402, 445; James, *Varieties of Religious Experience*, 47.

29. Smith, *Incidents of the Christian Commission*, 125–26; Eddy, *Sixtieth New York*, 144–45; Paludan, *People's Contest*, 365; *Confederate Hero and His Heroic Father*; Dulles, *Soldier's Friend*, 8; Otto, *Memoirs of a Dutch Mudsill*, 226. See especially the perceptive and penetrating discussion of the "good death" in Faust, *Republic of Suffering*, 6–8. Carrying the argument farther, Mark Schantz points to a range of examples where Americans appeared not only to accept but to embrace and even welcome death. Schantz, *Awaiting the Heavenly Country*, 6–37.

30. Fuller, *Chaplain Fuller*, 267; Hackett, *Christian Memorials of the War*, 40–41, 166–67; Jones, *Christ in the Camp*, 429, 401; Smith, *Incidents of the Christian Commission*, 85.

31. Bennett, *Narrative of the Great Revival*, 182–83; Smith, *Incidents of the Christian Commission*, 100, 174, 184; David Power Conyngham, "Soldiers of the Cross: Nuns and Priests of the Battlefield," chapter 30, Conyngham Papers, Notre Dame; Hackett, *Christian Memorials of the War*, 222–23; Shannon, "Archbishop Ireland's Experiences as a Civil War Chaplain," 303–4; Springer, *Preacher's Tale*, 34–37; Gilbert, *Sermon Delivered in Granby, Conn.*, 17–23.

32. Faust, *Republic of Suffering*, 10–11, 15–16; Brown, *Army Chaplain*, 62–70; Gallagher, *Ramseur*, 165; Smith, *Incidents of the Christian Commission*, 394; Bacot, *Confederate Nurse*, 118; Billingsley, *From the Flag to the Cross*, 206, 252–53.

33. Billingsley, *From the Flag to the Cross*, 140–41, 158–59, 185–86, 198–99, 236, 244–46; Jones, *Christ in the Camp*, 204, 380, 402; Smith, *Incidents of the Christian Commission*, 60–61; Shannon, "Archbishop Ireland's Experiences as a Civil War Chaplain," 305; United States Christian Commission, *Information for Army Meetings* (October 1864): 29; (December 1864), 7.

34. Billingsley, *From the Flag to the Cross*, 248; Hackett, *Christian Memorials of the War*, 234–35; Woodworth, *While God Is Marching On*, 41–46, 52; Bennett, *Narrative of the Great Revival*, 355, 392. For a fuller analysis, see Ted Ownby, "Patriarchy in the World Where There Is No Parting? Power Relations in the Confederate Heaven," in Clinton, *Southern Families at War*, 229–41; Schantz, *Awaiting the Heavenly Country*, 38–69.

35. Hartsock, *Soldier of the Cross*, 53; Stevenson, *78th Ohio*, 116–18; Billingsley, *From the Flag to the Cross*, 241–42; Bennett, *Narrative of the Great Revival*, 161–62.

36. For a thoughtful discussion of this point, see Laderman, *Sacred Remains*, 51–62.

37. For a superb analysis of this "work of death," see Faust, *Republic of Suffering*.

38. Sprague, *13th Connecticut*, 39–40.

39. Weygant, *One Hundred and Twenty-fourth New York*, 76–77; Alcott, *Hospital Sketches*, 80–83; McCain, *In Song and Sorrow*, 92–93; Boyd, *Civil War Diary*, 52; *Soldier's Grave. A Chaplain's Story*, 1–13; McCabe, *Young Mississippian*, 1–12.

40. Quint, *Potomac and Rapidan*, 21–23; Billingsley, *From the Flag to the Cross*, 257, 269; Haydon, *For County, Cause and Leader*, 144; *New York Herald*, April 28, 1862; Fisk, *Hard Marching Every Day*, 183; Betts, *Experience of a Confederate Chaplain*, 22.

41. Cumming, *Journal of a Confederate Nurse*, 99; Blackford, *Memoirs of Life In and Out of the Army in Virginia*, 1:36; November 29, 1862, Sarah Rodgers Espy Diary, ADAH.

42. Towles, *A World Turned Upside Down*, 341, 343, 345; United States Christian Commission, *Information for Army Meetings* (December 1864): 28; Faust, *Republic of Suffering*, 9–10; Smith, *Incidents of the Christian Commission*, 27–28; Borden, *Legacy of Fannie and Joseph*, 139; Faust, *Mothers of Invention*, 188–92.

43. Simkins and Patton, *Women of the Confederacy*, 35, 38; McDonald, *A Woman's Civil War*, 100; Geary, *A Politician Goes to War*, 131, 147; Smith et al., *Mason Smith Family Letters*, 130.

44. Cumming, *Journal of a Confederate Nurse*, 97; Scott, "'A Visitation of God,'" 219–23; Ayers, *In the Presence of Mine Enemies*, 351–52; Skidmore, *Alford Brothers*, 228; Smith, *Incidents of the Christian Commission*, 102–4, 166–67.

45. Smith, *Incidents of the Christian Commission*, 325; June 28, 1862, Elizabeth Collier Diary, SHC; Gratz, *Letters of Rebecca Gratz*, 425; McDannell and Lang, *Heaven, A History*, 228–75.

46. Lee, *Wartime Papers of Robert E. Lee*, 357, 364–65, 379–80; Winters, *Musick of the Mocking Birds*, 30–31; Gray, "Diary of Virginia Davis Gray," 51–52; *Christian Recorder* (Philadelphia), September 27, 1862.

47. Wolosky, *Emily Dickinson: A Voice of War*, 43–98; Child, *Letters from a Civil War Surgeon*, 34, 45–47.

48. Frederickson, *Inner Civil War*, 85–97; Hammond, *Army Chaplain's Manual*, 125–29; November 15, 1863, Anonymous Diary, Natchez, Miss., Mississippi Department of Archives and History; Hickox, *Remarks at the Funeral of Lieut. Percival Leggett*, 3–7; White, *Prison Life among the Rebels*, 26–27; Caruthers, *Frothingham*, 89; *New York Times*, January 17, 1863.

49. *Christian Recorder* (Philadelphia), April 5, 1862; October 6, 1862, Ella Gertrude Clanton Thomas Diary, Duke University; Laderman, *Sacred Remains*, 127–30; Corby, *Memoirs of Chaplain Life*, 161–62.

Chapter 10

1. *Evangelist* (New York), September 4, 1862.

2. Wilson and Davis, *Herndon's Informants*, 107, 233; Browne, *Every-Day Life of Lincoln*, 54; Donald, *Lincoln*, 15, 48–49; Guelzo, *Lincoln: Redeemer President*, 49–51; Lincoln, *Collected Works*, 1:320, 382. For useful discussions of Lincoln's faith, a subject that has generated a vast literature of uneven quality, see Carwardine, *Lincoln*, 32–44; Noll, *One Nation Under God?*, 94–101.

3. Lincoln, *Collected Works*, 1:26, 271–79; Carpenter, *Inner Life of Abraham Lincoln*, 190; Wilson and Douglas, *Herndon's Informants*, 441, 458, 508, 579–80, 588, 602.

4. Wilson and Douglas, *Herndon's Informants*, 358, 464, 547; Temple, *Lincoln: From Skeptic to Prophet*, 38–68; Guelzo, *Abraham Lincoln: Redeemer President*, 148–60.

5. Parrillo, "Lincoln's Calvinist Transformation," 231–37; Miller, *Lincoln's Virtues*, 83–91; Lincoln, *Collected Works*, 2:546–47, 3:204, 445.

6. Temple, *Lincoln: From Skeptic to Prophet*, 119–51; Sprague, *Duty of Sustaining the Government*, 18; White, *Lincoln's Greatest Speech*, 128–51;; Carpenter, *Inner Life of Abraham Lincoln*, 192–94, 282. During this era, a politician's religious views were largely a private matter little known to the public: one New Orleans newspaper reported that Lincoln's family had been Quakers; a British traveler wrote that Lincoln was a Baptist and that McClellan and Stanton were Unitarians! Moore, *Rebellion Record*, 1 (Rumors and Incidents):83; Dicey, *Spectator of America*, 254–59.

7. Wilson and Douglas, *Herndon's Informants*, 156, 167–68; Parrillo, "Lincoln's Calvinist Transformation," 227–31, 237–53; Nicolay, *An Oral History of Lincoln*, 87; Noll, *America's God*, 430–38; Guelzo, *Lincoln: Redeemer President*, 312–14.

8. Holzer, *Dear Mr. Lincoln*, 48; Cole, *Presbyterian Church in Michigan*, 5–6; Carwardine, *Lincoln*, 279.

9. Fleming, "Religious Life of Jefferson Davis," 374–75; Hopley, *Life in the South*, 2:17–19; Myers, *Children of Pride*, 695, 855.

10. Jones, *Rebel War Clerk's Diary*, 1:42, 54, 104, 120, 2:372; *Life and Reminiscences of Jefferson Davis*, 224–41; Cooper, *Jefferson Davis, American*, 262, 387–88; Dirck, *Lincoln and Davis*, 195–99.

11. Elliott, *Extract from a Sermon*, 2; *Religious Herald* (Richmond), November 6, 1862; Baptist Church, South Carolina, Tyger River Baptist Association, *Minutes of the Twenty-ninth Anniversary*, 13; Smith, *Life and Times of George Foster Pierce*, 459.

12. Holcomb, *Southern Sons, Northern Soldiers*, 14; Hartpence, *Our National Crisis*, 1–8; *Pittsburgh Catholic*, August 16, 1862; Morris, *Christian Life and Character*, 726–27; *Christian Recorder* (Philadelphia), October 4, 1862; *Friend* (Philadelphia), August 23, 1862; "God in the Present Contest," *Monthly Religious Magazine* 28 (November 1862): 324–33.

13. *German Reformed Messenger* (Chambersburg, Pa.), October 22, 1862; Fiske, *Mr. Dunn Brown's Experiences in the Army*, 29–31; *Independent* (New York), November 13, 1862; Wimmer, "American Catholic Interpretations of the Civil War," 247; March, *Steadfastness and Preparation in the Day of Adversity*, 5–20.

14. *Charleston Mercury*, December 19, 1862; *Confederate Baptist* (Columbia, S.C.), October 22, 29, 1862.

15. Fain, *Sanctified Trial*, 47; Elliott, *Our Cause in Harmony with the Purposes of Christ Jesus*, 10–22.

16. McLoughlin, *Meaning of Henry Ward Beecher*, 216–20; Beecher, *Freedom and War*, 341–67; March, *Steadfastness and Preparation in the Day of Adversity*, 13.

17. Elliott, *Extract from a Sermon*, 1–4; *Charleston Mercury*, September 18, 1862; Atkinson, *God the Giver of Victory and Peace*, 5–9; J. B. Jeter, Thanksgiving Sermon, September 18, 1862, Jeter Notes and Sermons, May 1862 volume, pp. 57–60, VBHS.

18. Tupper, *A Thanksgiving Discourse*, 10–11; Methodist Episcopal Church, Georgia, *Minutes*

of the Georgia Annual Conference, 1861–1862, 39; Baptist Church, South Carolina, Tyger River Baptist Association, *Minutes of the Twenty-ninth Anniversary*, 15–20; Atkinson, *God the Giver of Victory and Peace*, 12–15.

19. Wimmer, "American Catholic Interpretations of the Civil War," 156–61; *New York Freeman's Journal and Catholic Register*, August 23, 1862; Hughes, *Complete Works*, 2:368–73, 539–42.

20. August 20–21, 1862, Circular Letter, Huntington (Indiana) Baptist Association Minute Book, ABHS; Morris, *Christian Life and Character*, 723–24, 730–32, 743–44, 746–47; September 17, 1862, Methodist Church, Indiana, Indiana Conference, Evangelical Association Minutes (translated from the German), typescript, DePauw.

21. *Christian Observer* (Richmond), July 24, 1862; Stout, *Upon the Altar of the Nation*, 172–73.

22. Burney, *Southern Soldier's Letters Home*, 214–15; *Christian Advocate and Journal* (New York), August 21, 1862; Collier, *Moral Heroism*, 16.

23. Mark E. Neely Jr., "Politics Purified: Religion and the Growth of Antislavery Idealism in Republican Ideology during the Civil War," in Engs and Miller, *Birth of the Grand Old Party*, 112–14; McKivigan, *War against Proslavery Religion*, 188–93; United Brethren in Christ, Indiana, White River Conference, Minutes, August 1862, typescript, DePauw; North Illinois Conference of the Methodist Church to Abraham Lincoln, September 14, 1862, Clarion Association of Baptist Churches to A. G. Curtin, August 23, 1862, Lincoln Papers, LC.

24. Nicolay, *Oral History of Lincoln*, 5; Zoellner, "Negro Colonization: The Climate of Opinion Surrounding Lincoln," 131–50; Guyatt, *Providence and the Invention of the United States*, 282–90; *New York Tablet*, December 21, 1861; *Christian Advocate and Journal* (New York), September 4, 1862.

25. Lincoln, *Collected Works*, 5:278–79, 419–25. The ministers' petition had defined emancipation as a Christian duty and warned that "there is no deliverance from Divine judgments till slavery ceases in the land." The once honorable term "conservative," a New York Presbyterian concluded, has become a hateful epithet against a stiff-necked nation defying God's will. Harwell, *Union Reader*, 150–55; Sloane, *Three Pillars of the Republic*, 8.

26. Chase, *Salmon P. Chase Papers*, 1:394; Welles, *Diary of Gideon Welles*, 1:143; Carwardine, *Lincoln*, 221–28; Welles, "History of Emancipation," 846.

27. Silber and Stevens, *Yankee Correspondence*, 69–70, 85; Justus Gale to his father, September 24, 1862, Gale-Morse Family Papers, Vermont Historical Society, Barre, Vermont; Woodworth, *While God Is Marching On*, 112–15; Peirce and Peirce, *Dear Catharine, Dear Taylor*, 27–28; Campbell, *The Union Must Stand*, 65; November 5, 1862, William N. Jackson Diary, Indiana Historical Society. For a provocative and sophisticated analysis that emphasizes a strong shift of soldier opinion toward emancipation while giving rather short shrift to dissenting voices, see Manning, *What This Cruel War Was Over*, 72–79, 83–102.

28. Prentiss, *Bright Side of Life*, 2:181; Chester County, Pennsylvania, Society of Friends to Abraham Lincoln, October n.d., 1862, Lincoln Papers, LC; Morris, *Christian Life and Character*, 743, 745–46, 748–50; *Presbyter* (Cincinnati), September 25, 1862; *Christian Advocate and Journal* (New York), September 25, October 2, 1862.

29. McPherson, *Political History of the United States*, 499; Morris, *Christian Life and Character*, 750–52; Lawson, *Patriot Fires*, 143–46; Carwardine, *Lincoln*, 279; *Independent* (New York), September 25, 1862; Parish, "Instrument of Providence," 291.

30. Carwardine, *Lincoln*, 276; Stokes, *Church and State in the United States*, 2:206; *Evangelist* (New York), October 30, 1862; Morris, *Christian Life and Character*, 747.

31. Angell, *Henry McNeal Turner*, 43–44; *Christian Inquirer* (New York), November 8, 1862; Morris, *Christian Life and Character*, 725–26; *Presbyter* (Cincinnati), September 11, 1862.

32. Niebuhr, *Faith and History*, 214; E. O. Haven, "The American Crisis," *Methodist Quarterly Review* 44 (October 1862): 657–71; *Christian Advocate and Journal* (New York), November 14, 1861; Shedd, *Union and the War*, 30–40; Duffield, *Humiliation and Hope*, 16–23.

33. Barrows, *War and Slavery*, 3–18; O'Connor, *Fitzpatrick's Boston*, 208–9; *New York Freeman's Journal and Catholic Register*, December 27, 1862; *New York Tablet*, October 4, 18, 1862; "Slavery and the Church," *Brownson's Quarterly Review* 24 (October 1862): 451–87; Hassard, *Life of the Most Reverend John Hughes*, 440.

34. Spalding, "Martin John Spalding's 'Dissertation on the American Civil War,'" 75–82; Richard V. Whelan to James A. McMaster, June 23, 1862, January 29, 1863, O. P. Jarboe and Joseph T. Somerset to McMaster, March 20, 1863, McMaster Papers, Notre Dame; Rice, *Catholic Opinion in the Slavery Controversy*, 146–51.

35. Vander Velde, *Presbyterian Churches and Federal Union*, 141–48, 183–96; Robert J. Breckinridge to Robert W. Landis, June 28, 1862, Landis Papers, PHS-P.

36. Graham, *A Kingdom Not of This World*, 11–40, 90–132, 167–85.

37. *American Annual Cyclopaedia, 1862*, 580–81; Sweet, *Methodist Episcopal Church and Civil War*, 47–55.

38. Sweet, *Methodist Episcopal Church and Civil War*, 56–57; Browder, *Heavens Are Weeping*, 169–71, 175; Coulter, *Civil War and Readjustment in Kentucky*, 394.

39. Sturtevant, *Sermon on Our Duty to Civil Government*, 3–16; Post, *Truman Marcellus Post*, 274–80.

40. Hall, *Presbyterian Conflict and Resolution on Missouri Frontier*, 127–32; Parrish, *History of Missouri*, 62–63, 83–84.

41. Elliott, *South-Western Methodism*, 252–53, 262–65, 267–68, 273–85, 288–89, 325–62; "Methodism in Missouri," *Ladies' Repository* 22 (March 1862): 191.

42. Lewis, *History of Methodism in Missouri*, 17–42, 46–53; Leftwich, *Martyrdom in Missouri*, 1:117–26, 138–62, 167–71, 308–14, 332–34, 417–20; Elliott, *South-Western Methodism*, 363–65.

43. Alonzo Potter to William H. Seward, September 26, 1862, Abraham Lincoln Papers, LC; *Hartford (Conn.) Daily Courant*, November 27, 1862.

44. *Evangelist* (New York), November 27, 1862; Johnson, *Nation's Duty*, 5–15.

45. Hickok, *Mission of Calamity*, 5–8.

46. Leavitt, *God the Protector and Hope of the Nation*, 3–18; Campbell, *Light in the Clouds*, 5–13; Breed, *Faith and Patience*, 3–17; Hickok, *Mission of Calamity*, 28.

47. Paxton, *Nation's Gratitude and Hope*, 5–38; Hickok, *Mission of Calamity*, 8–23; Christian, *Our Present Position*, 5–46; Duffield, *Humiliation and Hope*, 3–16; Wimmer, "American Catholic Interpretations of the Civil War," 287.

48. Gulick, *God, the Author of National Prosperity*, 13–20; Post, *A Thanksgiving Sermon*, 3–15; Spear, *Nation's Blessing in Trial*, 33–39; Clark, *Gold in the Fire*, 3–20; Beecher, *Freedom and War*, 368–95.

49. *Evangelist* (New York), December 4, 1862; *Friends' Intelligencer*, November 6, 1862; *Friend* (Philadelphia), December 13, 1862; Atterbury, *God in Civil Government*, 13–16; Smith, *Our Nation Not Forsaken*, 10–13.

50. Garfield, *Wild Life of the Army*, 200; Mahon, *Winchester Divided*, 72; *Evangelist* (New York), December 25, 1862.

51. Woodworth, *While God Is Marching On*, 135; Thompson, *Presbyterians in the South*, 2:78–79; Myers, *Children of Pride*, 1001; Edmondston, *Journal of a Secesh Lady*, 319; *Charleston Daily Courier*, December 31, 1862, January 3, 21, 1863.

52. Geary, *A Politician Goes to War*, 83; John M. Jackson to his father, December 18, 1862, Jackson Letters, Notre Dame.

Chapter 11

1. Stuckenberg, *I'm Surrounded by Methodists*, 12; McKim, *A Soldier's Recollections*, 60–61; *Christian Observer* (Richmond), July 31, 1862.

2. *Camp Nineveh*; Wiatt, *Confederate Chaplain William Edward Wiatt*, 13–14.

3. Woodworth, *While God Is Marching On*, 196; Bennett, *Narrative of the Great Revival*, 206–7; *Soldier's Hymn Book*; Stillwell, *Stillwell Letters*, 119, 126, 147.

4. Woodworth, *While God Is Marching On*, 210–12; Stillwell, *Stillwell Letters*, 159, 163; Paxton, *Memoir and Memorials*, 90, 92, 94–95.

5. Evans, *Sixteenth Mississippi Infantry*, 124; John Quincy Adams Nadenbousch to Mary Nadenbousch, March 13, 1863, Nadenbousch Letters, Museum of the Confederacy; Nimrod Newton Nash to "Dear Mollie," March 17, 1863, typescript, private collection of Robert K. Krick, Fredericksburg, Virginia; Baptist Church, Virginia, General Association, *Minutes, 1861, 1862, and 1863*, 68–71.

6. Molyneux, *Quill of the Wild Goose*, 78, 81; Beaudry, *War Journal*, 17–18; Adams, *Memorial and Letters of Rev. John R. Adams*, 99.

7. Curtis, *Twenty-fourth Michigan*, 109, 138; Frank M. Guernsey to "Fannie," April 12, 1863, Guernsey Correspondence, Mississippi Valley Collection, University of Memphis; Adams, *Memorial and Letters of Rev. John R. Adams*, 99.

8. Norton, "Revivalism in the Confederate Armies," 410–16; Hieronymus, "For Now and Forever," 268–71; Faust, "Christian Soldiers," 67–68.

9. Jones, *Christ in the Camp*, 468–69; Moore, *A Life for the Confederacy*, 134, 136; Bennett, *Narrative of the Great Revival*, 210–11, 251–52.

10. Bunting, *Our Trust Is in the God of Battles*, 93; Bennett, *Narrative of the Great Revival*, 269–70; Richard and Richard, *Defense of Vicksburg*, 89.

11. Partin, "Sustaining Faith of an Alabama Soldier," 434; Prim, "Southern Methodism in the Confederacy," 244–45; April 11, 1863, William F. Broaddus Diary, Library of Virginia; Brinsfield, *Spirit Divided*, 49–51; *Southern Presbyterian* (Columbia, S.C.), January 8, 1863.

12. Shattuck, *Shield and Hiding Place*, 92. There was apparently much religious indifference in the navy. Bennett, *Union Jacks*, 144–47.

13. Bennett, *Narrative of the Great Revival*, 413; Jones, *Christ in the Camp*, 390; Prim, "Southern Methodism in the Confederacy," 247; Hieronymus, "For Now and Forever," 264–68.

14. Jones, *Christ in the Camp*, 391; Wiley, *Life of Johnny Reb*, 191; Glatthaar, *General Lee's Army*, 236–37, 240–41.

15. *Religious Herald* (Richmond), February 27, 1862; Chester, *Recollections of the War of the Rebellion*, 12; Wiatt, *Confederate Chaplain William Edward Wiatt*, 5, 7–8.

16. *Eternity! Think of It*; *The Great Gathering*; Woodworth, *While God is Marching On*, 60–66; Billingsley, *From the Flag to the Cross*, 200–201. For a skeptical view of whether wartime piety persisted in a society that increasingly emphasized efficiency, practicality, and individualism, see Rose, *Victorian America and the Civil War*, 63–67.

17. *Christian Recorder* (Philadelphia), February 27, 1864; Woodworth, *While God Is Marching On*, 56–60. For a fine discussion of published accounts of conversion and the major themes of these narratives, see Kurt O. Berends, "'Wholesome Reading Purifies and Elevates the Man': The Religious Military Press in the Confederacy," in Miller et al., *Religion and the American Civil War*, 134–42.

18. United States Christian Commission, *Information for Army Meetings* (June and July 1864): 10; ibid. (August 1864): 9; Barclay, *Ted Barclay, Liberty Hall Volunteers*, 60–61, 85. For revealing examples of Christian fathers' concerns for wayward sons, see Scott, "'A Visitation of God,'" 162–66.

19. Billingsley, *From the Flag to the Cross*, 204–5, Wiley C. Tunstall to his mother, August 3, 1862, Tunstall Letters, Fredericksburg and Spotsylvania National Military Park; Humphreys, *Field, Camp, Hospital, and Prison*, 17–18.

20. Jones, *Christ in the Camp*, 36, 40, 184; Pinson, *In Care of the Yellow River*, 108; Gache, *A Frenchman, a Chaplain, a Rebel*, 162.

21. Hammond, *Army Chaplain's Manual*, 122–24; Small, *Road to Richmond*, 48; Hackett, *Christian Memorials of the War*, 48–49; Redkey, "Black Chaplains in the Union Army," 339; Stuckenberg, *I'm Surrounded by Methodists*, 21; Pitts, *Chaplains in Gray*, 8–9, 56–57.

22. Jones, *Christ in the Camp*, 501; Nimrod Newton to "Dear Mollie," March 22, 1863, typescript, Robert K. Krick, Fredericksburg, Va.; Andrew Sydnor Barksdale to "Sister Omis," March 29, 1864, Barksdale Letters, Museum of the Confederacy; Stone, *Wandering to Glory*, 144; December 19, 1863, Mount Olivet (Hanover County) Minute Book, VBHS; March 14, 1864, July 15, 1865, Mars Hill Baptist Church (Summit, Mississippi) Minute Book, SBHLA.

23. *Richmond Enquirer*, April 23, 1861; *Evangelist* (New York), September 26, 1861; Bartol, *Our Sacrifices*, 13; *Christian Advocate and Journal* (New York), March 19, 1863.

24. Schultz, *Women at the Front*, 76; Cumming, *Journal of a Confederate Nurse*, 99; Elmore, *Heritage of Woe*, 20–21.

25. Schultz, *Women at the Front*, 76–77; Maher, *To Bind Up the Wounds*, 70–86; Barton, *Angels of the Battlefield*, 3; Sister Frances Jerome Woods, "Congregations of Religious Women in the Old South," in Miller and Wakelyn, *Catholics in the Old South*, 120–21.

26. Maher, *To Bind Up the Wounds*, 27–40, 99–116; *Dubuque (Iowa) Herald*, April 16, 1862; *Charleston Mercury*, September 21, 1861; Jolly, *Nuns of the Battlefield*, 49.

27. *Charleston Mercury*, August 14, 1861; Healy, *Sisters of Mercy*, 79; David Power Conyngham, "Soldiers of the Cross: Nuns and Priests of the Battlefield," chapter 30, Conyngham Papers, Notre Dame; Jolly, *Nuns of the Battlefield*, 7, 184.

28. Maher, *To Bind Up the Wounds*, 136–49; Greene, *Letters from a Sharpshooter*, 271; Healy, *Sisters of Mercy*, 79.

29. Elder, *Civil War Diary*, 39; Healy, *Sisters of Mercy*, 78; Maher, *To Bind up the Wounds*, 86–93, 116–18.

30. Barton, *Angels of the Battlefield*, 97, 167–68, 233; David Power Conyngham, "Soldiers of the Cross: Nuns and Priests of the Battlefield," chapter 26, Conyngham Papers, Notre Dame; Healy, *Sisters of Mercy*, 136–37; Gache, *A Frenchman, a Chaplain, a Rebel*, 145–49; Mattocks, *"Unspoiled Heart,"* 203.

31. Schultz, *Women at the Front*, 77; Healy, *Sisters of Mercy*, 80; Rothensteiner, *History of the Archdiocese of St. Louis*, 2:214–25.

32. Smith, *Revivalism and Social Reform*, 175–77; Griffin, *Their Brothers' Keepers*, 248–50; Paludan, *People's Contest*, 352.

33. Moss, *Annals of the Christian Commission*, 69–89, 95–110; Brainerd, *Work of the Army Committee*, 5–13, 22–28.

34. Moss, *Annals of the Christian Commission*, 111–35, 162–64, 219–22, 726–34; Raney, "In the Lord's Army," 27–40.

35. Stuart, *Life of George H. Stuart*, 129; United States Christian Commission, *Second Annual Report*, 23–26; United States Christian Commission, *Facts, Principles, and Progress*, 8; Moss, *Annals of the Christian Commission*, 542–50.

36. Henry, "United States Christian Commission," 380; United States Christian Commission, *Information for Army Meetings* (January 1865): 5; Macmillan, *Methodist Episcopal Church in Michigan*, 32; Bristol, *Life of Chaplain McCabe*, 146–68; Gladden, *Recollections*, 140–44; Walker, *Quite Ready to Be Sent Somewhere*, 164.

37. Cannon, "United States Christian Commission," 77; Carter, *Four Brothers in Blue*, 480; Miller, "Two Civil War Notebooks," 77; Peter P. Cooney to E. B. Kilroy, February 18, 1863, Cooney Papers, Notre Dame.

38. Tobie, *First Maine Cavalry*, 377–78; *German Reformed Messenger* (Chambersburg, Pa.), December 30, 1863; Armstrong, *Friend to God's Poor*, 52–59; Moss, *Annals of the Christian Commission*, 212, 337–38.

39. Cannon, "United States Christian Commission," 65–67, 69–70, 74; Stuart, *Instructions to Delegates*, 3–12; United States Christian Commission, *Information for Army Meetings* (September 1864): 11–12; Butterfield, *Christian Commission. A Delegate's Story*. For a very useful discussion of delegate activities, see Woodworth, *While God Is Marching On*, 167–74.

40. Moss, *Annals of the Christian Commission*, 582–83; Cross, *Gettysburg and Christian Commission*, 11–21; Hancock, *South after Gettysburg*, 139; Moss, *Annals of Christian Commission*, 663–684. By 1864 women volunteers were setting up special "diet kitchens" for the sick and wounded, which increased the effectiveness and popularity of the Christian Commission among the troops. United States Christian Commission, *Information for Army Meetings* (February 1865): 11–14; *Christ in the Army*, 84–88.

41. *Christian Recorder* (Philadelphia), September 12, 1863; United States Christian Commission, *Information for Army Meetings* (June and July 1864): 11; United States Christian Commission, *First Annual Report*, 38–39, 58.

42. Moss, *Annals of the Christian Commission*, 362–63, 366; United States Christian Commission, *First Annual Report*, 34–35; White, *Christ in the Army*, 107–8.

43. *Christian Advocate and Journal* (New York), September 1, 1864; [Bacon], *Letters of a Family during the War*, 2:621; Regan, *Lost Civil War Diaries*, 152.

44. Fisk, *Hard Marching Every Day*, 166–67; United States Christian Commission, *Second Annual Report*, 269; United States Christian Commission, *First Annual Report*, 58.

45. Fisk, *Hard Marching Every Day*, 200–1; Moss, *Annals of the Christian Commission*, 546, 586–88; United States Christian Commission, *Information for Army Meetings* (November 1864): 1–3; Bennett, *Union Jacks*, 148–54; *Evangelist* (New York), April 6, 1865.

46. United States Christian Commission, *Third Annual Report*, 100; United States Christian Commission, *Second Annual Report*, 26; *Christian Recorder* (Philadelphia), September 12, 1863; White, *Christ in the Army*, 12, 96–97.

47. Molyneux, *Quill of the Wild Goose*, 157; Poremba, *If I Am Found Dead*, 159, 210–11; *Christian Recorder* (Philadelphia), September 12, 1863; Woodworth, *While God Is Marching On*, 170–74; United States Christian Commission, *First Annual Report*, 35; *Christ in the Army*, 113–15; Fisk, *Hard Marching Every Day*, 213.

48. United States Christian Commission, *Second Annual Report*, 27–31; *Christian Advocate and Journal* (New York), February 5, 1863; David A. Raney, "In the Lord's Army: The United States Christian Commission, Soldiers, and the Union War Effort," in Cimbala and Millers, *Union Soldiers and the Northern Home Front*, 270–73; Quint, *Potomac and the Rapidan*, 243–44. 310–11; Armstrong, *Friend to God's Poor*, 60–70.

49. Moss, *Annals of the Christian Commission*, 315–16; Hackett, *Christian Memorials of the War*, 224–25; White, *Christ in the Army*, 40–41; Stuart, *Life of George H. Stuart*, 138–39; "Soldier's Comforts," *Ladies' Repository* 23 (September 1863): 575; *Ladies' Christian Commissions*, 3–9.

50. White, *Report of the Army Committee*, 3–6; Shattuck, *Shield and Hiding Place*, 24; Paludan, *People's Contest*, 353; United States Christian Commission, *Second Annual Report*, 17–18; Fisk, *Hard Marching Every Day*, 315–16.

51. United States Christian Commission to Abraham Lincoln, February 12, 1863, Lincoln Papers, LC; Welles, *Diary of Gideon Welles*, 1:238; Lincoln, *Collected Works*, 5:67, 6:110, 114–15, 7:394–96.

52. Frederickson, *Inner Civil War*, 98–107; Lawson, *Patriotic Fires*, 17, 30–34; L. P. Brockett, "Philanthropy in Wartime," *Methodist Quarterly Review* 47 (January 1865): 65–81.

53. Cram, *Soldiering with Sherman*, 132; Hackett, *Christian Memorials of the War*, 135–37; Bremner, *Public Good*, 60; Strong, *Diary of George Templeton Strong*, 3:310–11, 589; Maxwell, *Lincoln's Fifth Wheel*, 191–93; McDevitt, "Fighting for the Soul of America," 257; Frederickson, *Inner Civil War*, 107–12.

54. Stout, *Upon the Altar of the Nation*, 391–92; "Western Sanitary Fair—Great Success— Shameful Close," *Ladies' Repository* 24 (February 1864): 128.

Chapter 12

1. December 25, 1862, Ann Wilkinson Penrose Diary, Louisiana State University; Myers, *Children of Pride*, 826; Everson and Simpson, *"Far, Far from Home,"* 168.

2. Bangs, *Autobiography and Journal*, 336; *Christian Advocate and Journal* (New York), January 1, 1863; *Evangelist* (New York), January 1, 1863; William White to Jacob Wead, January 14, 1863, White Letters, Vermont Historical Society, Barre.

3. *Charleston Mercury*, March 18, 1863; Moore, *A Life for the Confederacy*, 80; Williams, *National Renovation*, 3–24; John Buchanan to Sophie Buchanan, January 8, 1863, Buchanan Family Papers, Michigan Historical Collections, Bentley Library, University of Michigan; *Hartford (Conn.) Daily Courant*, January 14, 1863.

4. [Charles Hodge], "The War," *Princeton Review* 35 (January 1863): 140–47; Welsh and Welsh, "Civil War Letters from Two Brothers," 161; Poremba, *If I Am Found Dead*, 81–82; Stewart, *Camp, March and Battlefield*, 290–93.

5. *Confederate Baptist* (Columbia, S.C.), January 7, 1863; Wimmer, "American Catholic Interpretations of the Civil War," 284.

6. [Duncan], *Address to Christians throughout the World*; January 8, 1863, Nancy Emerson Diary, UVa.; Beale, *Journal of Jane Howison Beale*, 100.

7. *Christian Recorder* (Philadelphia), March 14, 1863; *Liberator* (Boston), January 16, 1863; Conway, *Autobiography*, 1:372–74; Franklin, *Emancipation Proclamation*, 93.

8. *Christian Recorder* (Philadelphia), January 3, 1863.

9. Ibid., January 10, 1863; Blight, "Frederick Douglass and the American Apocalypse," 309–28; *Independent* (New York), January 8, 1863; Angell, *Henry McNeal Turner*, 44.

10. Lincoln, *Collected Works*, 6:28–30; Chase, *Salmon P. Chase Papers*, 3:351; N. H., "The Proclamation of Freedom," *Monthly Religious Magazine* 29 (February 1863): 67–77; *Christian Inquirer* (New York), January 17, 1863; Beecher, *Freedom and War*, 420–45; *Independent* (New York), January 1, 1863; *Christian Advocate and Journal* (New York), February 5, 1863.

11. Baptist Church, Indiana, North-Eastern Indiana Baptist Association, *Minutes, 1862*, 5; Strong, *Diary of George Templeton Strong*, 3:286; *Independent* (New York), January 8, 1863; Scott, "'A Visitation of God,'" 115–17; *Zion's Herald and Wesleyan Journal* (Boston), February 4, 1863.

12. *Friend* (Philadelphia) January 10, 1863; *Friends' Review* (Philadelphia) January 10, 1863; Allen, "Slavery Question in Catholic Newspapers," 133–34.

13. Lord, *A Sermon: On the Character and Influence of Washington*, 5–22; [Hopkins], *Life of the Right Reverend John Henry Hopkins*, 330–38; Freidel, *Union Pamphlets on the Civil War*, 2:658–96; Hopkins, *Scriptural, Ecclesiastical, and Historical View of Slavery*, 42–353; Howard, *Religion and Radical Republican Movement*, 64.

14. Bennitt, *"I Hope to Do My Country Service,"* 244; Rolfs, *No Peace for the Wicked*, 162; Long, *Saints and the Union*, 160–61; Haven, *National Sermons*, 361–72; Willson, *Proclamation of Freedom*, 14.

15. *Zion's Herald and Wesleyan Journal* (Boston), March 11, 1863; Deborah B. Lapham Wade to Lester Wade, June 20, 1863, Wade Letters, ABHS; Walker, *Rock in a Weary Land*, 39–43; Fletcher, *Diary of Calvin Fletcher*, 8:6.

16. *Congressional Globe*, 37th Cong., 3rd sess., 994–97.

17. Smith, *God's Honor Man's Ultimate Success*, 11–20; Sturtevant, *Josiah Volunteered*, 114; Fish, *War Record of the First Baptist Church*, 13–18; *German Reformed Messenger* (Chambersburg, Pa.), March 18, April 16, 1863, January 6, October 5, 1864.

18. *Friends' Review* (Philadelphia), May 11, 1861; Morris, *Christian Life and Character*, 773–74; Brock, *Pacifism in the United States*, 715–19; *Friends' Intelligencer* (Philadelphia), November 30, 1861, February 22, March 8, April 19, 1862.

19. Nelson, *Indiana Quakers Confront the Civil War*, 13; *Friends' Review* (Philadelphia), January 2, 1864; *Friend* (Philadelphia), February 15, March 1, 29, 1862.

20. Brock, *Pacifism in the United States*, 344–88, 723–25, 780–95; Isaac Briggs to "Dear James," May 10, 1861, Briggs-Stabler Papers, Maryland Historical Society, Baltimore; Nelson, *Indiana Quakers Confront the Civil War*, 29–43.

21. Geary, *We Need Men*, 36; *Friends' Intelligencer* (Philadelphia), September 6, 1862, March 21, 1863; Wright, *Conscientious Objectors in the Civil War*, 39–40, 48–58; *Friends' Review* (Philadelphia), September 6, November 15, 1862.

22. Nelson, *Indiana Quakers Confront the Civil War*, 90–94; Lincoln, *Collected Works*, 7:535; Wright, *Conscientious Objectors in the Civil War*, 121–38, 192–95; *Friends' Review*, February 27, July 30, 1864; *Friend* (Philadelphia), March 5, 1864. Dunkers and Mennonites adopted a more lenient attitude toward substitution and commutation. For an illuminating discussion of the commutation question and its relationship to Mennonites and Amish in Pennsylvania with

special attention to Thaddeus Stevens and Republican politics, see Lehman and Nolt, *Mennonites, Amish, and Civil War*, 76–90, 143–62.

23. Smith, *118th Pennsylvania*, 292–93; Joseph Scattergood and Joseph Elkington to George G. Meade, August 22, 1863, Abraham Lincoln Papers, LC; Macy, *Jesse Macy: An Autobiography*, 36–49; Pringle, *Record of a Quaker Conscience*, 23–93.

24. *Friends' Review* (Philadelphia), August 31, 1861; Wright, *Conscientious Objectors in the Civil War*, 47–48; Maule, *Transactions and Changes in the Society of Friends*, 220–24, 266–67; Brock, *Pacifism in the United States*, 755–64. Some Quakers were disciplined by monthly meetings for selling horses to the government, joining parades, or even paying taxes that supported the bounty system. Nelson, *Indiana Quakers Confront the Civil War*, 59–69.

25. Nelson, *Indiana Quakers Confront the Civil War*, 15, 18–26; Brock, *Pacifism in the United States*, 727–34; Tyler, *History of the Disciples of Christ*, 286–87; Lehman and Nolt, *Mennonites, Amish, and Civil War*, 90–91, 97–122, 162–83. For Quaker enlistments in one Pennsylvania community, see Harper, *"If Thee Must Fight,"* 19–20, 55, 206.

26. Wright, *Conscientious Objectors Confront the Civil War*, 2; Andreasen, *"'As good a right to pray,'"* 77–110; "The Unchristian Pulpits," *Old Guard* 1 (October–December 1863): 249–50; "The Puritan War," ibid. 1 (March 1863): 58–62; C. Chauncy Burr, "Abolition Preachers versus Christ and the Apostles," ibid. (January 1863): 7–12.

27. Morrow, "Methodists and 'Butternuts,'" 39–40; Hartsock, *Soldier of the Cross*, 129–30, 181–83; Scott, *"'A Visitation of God,'"* 138–39, 178–81; William Adams, "Preaching Politics," *American Presbyterian and Theological Review*, n.s., 1 (January 1863): 122.

28. Andreasen, *"'As good a right to pray,'"* 254–57, 274–310, 354–77; Bryon C. Andreasen, "Civil War Church Trials: Repressing Dissent on the Northern Home Front," in Cimbala and Miller, *An Uncommon Time*, 214–32; Kimbrough, *Reverend Joseph Tarkington*, 134.

29. Andreasen, *"'As good a right to pray,'"* 257–59; 319–38; *New Haven (Conn.) Daily Palladium*, April 21, 1863; Bryon C. Andreasen, "Civil War Church Trials: Repressing Dissent on the Northern Home Front," in Cimbala and Miller, *An Uncommon Time*, 235–42; "An Appeal to Christian and Patriotic Women upon Their Duties in Relation to the War," *Ladies' Repository* 22 (August 1862): 494.

30. Morrow, "Methodists and 'Butternuts," 42–47; Andreasen, *"'As good a right to pray,'"* viii, 384–96, 415–47, 456–81, 488–524, 534–40; Scott, *"'A Visitation of God,'"* 191–93.

31. Sweet, *Methodist Episcopal Church and Civil War*, 73–75; Freidel, *Union Pamphlets on the Civil War*, 1:512–24; Frederickson, *Inner Civil War*, 130–50; Moore, *Rebellion Record*, 6 (Diary of Events):70; *New York Tablet*, March 7, 1863; "Are Catholics Proslavery and Disloyal?" *Brownson's Quarterly Review*, 25 (July 1863): 367–79.

32. Andreasen, *"'As good a right to pray,'"* 148–52; Suydam, *Christian Patriotism*, 5–24; Sweet, *Methodist Episcopal Church and Civil War*, 85; Morris, *Christian Life and Character*, 754; Morrow, "Methodists and 'Butternuts,'" 36–38, 40–41.

33. Morris, *Christian Life and Character*, 753–54, 756; Sweet, *Methodist Episcopal Church and Civil War*, 84–85.

34. Morrow, "Methodists and 'Butternuts,'" 38–39; Scott, *"'A Visitation of God,'"* 200–203; Sweet, *Methodist Episcopal Church and Civil War*, 67, 86.

35. *Christian Advocate and Journal* (New York), November 6, 1862, February 19, 1863; "The Peace Policy: How It Is Urged and What It Means," *Christian Examiner* 74 (January 1863): 113–

32; [Francis Wayland], "No Failure for the North," *Atlantic Monthly* 11 (April 1863): 500–14; *Christian Inquirer* (New York), November 1, 1862. For additional evidence and lay commentary, see Scott, "'A Visitation of God,'" 118–22.

36. Elliott, *"Samson's Riddle,"* 7–14; Davis, *Messages and Papers of Davis*, 1:324–25.

37. Elliott, *"Samson's Riddle,"* 5–7; Norwood, *God and Our Country*, 3–10; Stout, *Upon the Altar of the Nation*, 212; Dalzell, *Thanksgiving to God*.

38. Pierce, *Sermons of Bishop Pierce and Rev. B. M. Palmer*, 16; Burrows, *New Richmond Theater*, 3–16; Norwood, *God and Our Country*, 10–15; Kundahl, *Confederate Engineer*, 116; McDonald, *A Woman's Civil War*, 124; Bonner, *Soldier's Pen*, 102.

39. *OR*, ser. 1, vol. 25, pt. 2, p. 683; Jackson, *Life and Letters of Thomas J. Jackson*, 401; Bennett, *Narrative of the Great Revival*, 259–68, 276; Apperson, *Repairing the "March of Mars*,*"* 395–96; Bunting, *Our Trust Is in the God of Battles*, 151.

40. *Charleston Daily Courier*, March 27, 1863; *Richmond Dispatch*, March 27, 1863; *Chattanooga Daily Rebel*, March 27, 1863; Fain, *Sanctified Trial*, 66; Johnson, *Life and Letters of Benjamin Morgan Palmer*, 267–68; Pierce, *Sermons of Bishop Pierce and Rev. B. M. Palmer*, 3–7, 35–40.

41. *Religious Herald* (Richmond), May 7, 1863; Burns, *Fiddles in the Cumberland*, 189; *Christian Index* (Macon, Ga.), March 2, 1863.

42. Paxton, *Civil War Letters of General Frank "Bull" Paxton*, 82; March 24, 1863, Jason Niles Diary, SHC.

43. Lincoln, *Collected Works*, 6:155–56.

44. Seth Sweetser, Fast Day Sermon, April 2, 1863, Sweetser Papers, AAS; Errett, *Claims of Government*, 7–18; Squier, *This Wilderness of War*, 49.

45. Walker, *Our Nation's Danger*, 3–22; [Horace Bushnell], "The Doctrine of Loyalty," *New Englander* 22 (July 1863): 560–81; Spear, *Duty of the Hour*, 3–16; Cleaveland, *Our Duty in Regard to the Rebellion*, 3–19.

46. Sunderland, *Crisis of the Times*, 23–36; Marshall, *Nation's Inquiry*, 5–24; Henry Augustus Boardman, manuscript sermon, National Fast, April 30, 1863, Boardman Papers, PHS-P; Lewis, *Thoughts of God and Thoughts of Men*, 3–22.

47. Fraser, *Our National Sins*, 3–20; Bellows, *War to End Only When the Rebellion Ceases*, 1–6; Seth Sweetser, Fast Day Sermon, Worcester, April 2, 1863, Sweetser Papers, AAS; *Evangelist* (New York), February 19, 1863.

48. Ide, *Pious Men the Nation's Hope*, 17–30; Weiss, *Northern Strength and Weakness*, 3–23; Rufus Ellis, "The Cause of National Disaster," *Monthly Religious Magazine* 29 (June 1863): 321–30; *Zion's Herald and Wesleyan Journal* (Boston), February 1, May 6, 1863; Wallace, *Fast That God Hath Chosen*, 4; Haven, *National Sermons*, 9–20.

49. J. M. Sherwood, "The Moral Cause of Our National Calamity," *National Preacher and Village Pulpit*, n.s., 6 (June 1863): 137–54; Fuller, *Wrong and Right Dispositions under National Judgments*, 3–27; Brainerd, *Patriotism Aiding Piety*, 5–32; Mitchell, *Civil War Soldiers*, 186.

50. Lamson, *God Hiding Himself in Times of Trouble*, 3–26; Walker, *Fast Day Sermon*, 1–12; Alexander, *Sermon Occasioned by the Death of Edwin Ruthven Keyes*, 3–11.

51. Chase, *Salmon P. Chase Papers*, 4:8; Cleaveland, *Our Duty in Regard to the Rebellion*, 19; [Fitch], *Annals of the Army of the Cumberland*, 324–25.

52. Seth Sweetser, Fast Day Sermon, Worcester, April 2, 1863, Sweetser Papers, AAS;

April 30, 1863, Henry W. Tisdale Diary, ⟨http://www.civilwardiary.net/⟩; Rolfs, *No Peace for the Wicked*, 131, 137; Fisk, *Hard Marching Every Day*, 64–67.

53. Morris, *Christian Life and Character*, 806–10; *Brooklyn Eagle*, May 1, 1863; *Evangelist* (New York), May 7, 1863; Silver, *Confederate Morale and Church Propaganda*, 36; Jenkins, *National Fast*, 21–27.

54. Sunderland, *Crisis of the Times*, 5–11.

Chapter 13

1. Fall session 1863 Narrative, Alton (Illinois) Presbytery Minute Book, PHS-P.

2. Smythe, *Diocese of Ohio*, 316; Congregational Church, Massachusetts, General Association of Massachusetts, *Minutes of the Sixty-second Annual Meeting*, 15–16; *Evangelist* (New York), November 20, 1862; *Christian Advocate and Journal* (New York), November 14, 1861.

3. *Evangelist* (New York), July 16, 1863; Hartsock, *Soldier of the Cross*, 108; Emerson, *Emerson in His Journals*, 508; September 7, 1862, Lucy Larcom Diaries, D. D. Addison Collection, Massachusetts Historical Society; *Christian Recorder* (Philadelphia), October 10, 1863.

4. J. B. Jeter, "The Danger of the Times," April 1863, Jeter Notes and Sermons, VBHS; *Religious Herald* (Richmond), September 22, 1864; Inscoe and McKinney, *Heart of Appalachia*, 70.

5. Baptist Church, North Carolina, Chowan Baptist Association, *Minutes of the Fifty-seventh Annual Session*, 10–11; Baptist Church, Georgia, Columbus Baptist Association, *Minutes of the Thirty-third Annual Session*, 12–13; *Southern Churchman* (Richmond), September 5, 1862; Morgan, "Letters of a North Louisiana Private," 545.

6. Baptist Church, Georgia, Columbus Baptist Association, *Minutes of the Thirty-sixth Annual Session*, 8; Baptist Church, South Carolina, Reedy River Baptist Association, *Minutes, 1862*, 2; Baptist Church, Texas, Little River Association, *Minutes of the Sixth Annual Meeting*, 7–8.

7. Presbyterian Church, General Assembly, *Minutes, 1863*, 291–94; Baptist Church, Georgia, Yellow River Baptist Association, *Minutes of the Thirty-eighth Annual Session*, 4–6; Norton, "Revivalism in the Confederate Armies," 422.

8. *Christian Index* (Macon, Ga.), July 31, 1861; Baptist Church, Mississippi, Chickasaw Baptist Association, *Minutes of the Twenty-third Anniversary*, 8–9; Peck, *Address to the Churches upon the Present Crisis*.

9. Presbyterian Church, Synod of North Carolina, *Minutes of the Forty-eighth Sessions*, 20–23; Jones and Mills, *History of the Presbyterian Church in South Carolina Since 1850*, 112–13; Towles, *A World Turned Upside Down*, 383; Protestant Episcopal Church, Diocese of Virginia, *Journal of the Sixty-eighth Annual Council*, 33–34; September and October 1863, Poplar Spring Baptist Church (Franklin Co., N.C.) Minute Book, SBHLA.

10. Perkins, *Northern Editorials on Secession*, 2:1094; Street, *Sermon Preached in the Presbyterian Church*, 12–14.

11. *Evangelist* (New York), August 21, September 25, 1862; Morris, *Christian Life and Character*, 728; July 29, 1862, Roberts Chapel (Greencastle, Ind.) Church Record, 1847–1876, DePauw.

12. April 1862, Cleveland (Ohio) Presbytery Minute Book, PHS-P; Beardsley, *History of American Revivals*, 241; *Zion's Herald and Wesleyan Journal* (Boston), February 10, 1864; Vander Velde, *Presbyterian Churches and the Union*, 473–74; *American Annual Cyclopaedia, 1862*, 187; ibid., *1863*, 160; Sweet, *Methodism in American History*, 283–88.

13. Stowell, *Rebuilding Zion*, 15–16, 25; *Religious Herald* (Richmond), October 3, 1861; Baptist Church, South Carolina, Charleston Baptist Association, *Minutes of the One Hundred and Tenth Session*, 3–4; Cain, *Methodism in the Mississippi Conference*, 353–55.

14. Protestant Episcopal Church, Diocese of Virginia, *Journal of the Sixty-sixth Annual Convention*, 61–63; June 16, 1861, Annie Darden Diary, North Carolina Department of Archives and History; Stone, *Brokenburn*, 25; Allan, *Life and Letters of Margaret Junkin Preston*, 136; Beale, *Journal of Jane Howison Beale*, 62.

15. Ash, *When the Yankees Came*, 104–5; Sutherland, *Seasons of War*, 107, 211–12; Jones and Mills, *Presbyterian Church in South Carolina since 1850*, 79, 103–7; July 3, 1864, Beaver Dam Baptist Church (Fountain City, Tenn.) Minute Book, SBHLA.

16. Baptist Church, Virginia, Appomattox Baptist Association, *Minutes, 1864*, 10; December 21, 1861, Pungoteague Baptist Church (Accomac County, Va.), Minute Book, SBHLA; Baptist Church, North Carolina, Brown Creek Baptist Association, *Minutes, 1864*, 3.

17. Bennett, *Narrative of the Great Revival*, 34; Baptist Church, Georgia, Sunbury Baptist Association, *Minutes, 1862*, 3; Myers, *Children of Pride*, 1103.

18. March 6, 1864, Samuel Andrew Agnew Diary, SHC; Chesnut, *Mary Chesnut's Civil War*, 313; Baptist Church, Mississippi, Pearl River Baptist Association, *Minutes of the Forty-fifth Annual Meeting*, 2.

19. Baptist Church, South Carolina, Bethel Baptist Association, *Minutes of the Seventy-third Anniversary*, 5; Baptist Church, South Carolina, Fairfield Baptist Association, *Minutes, 1864*, 19–20.

20. Baptist Church, South Carolina, State Convention, *Minutes of the Forty-first Anniversary*, 104; Reid, *Baptists in Alabama*, 108–9; Baptist Church, South Carolina, Tyger River Baptist Association, *Minutes of the Twenty-ninth Anniversary*, 6–7; Baptist Church, North Carolina, Western Baptist Association, *Proceedings of the Seventh Annual Session*, 14–15.

21. Baptist Church, South Carolina, Edgefield Baptist Association, *Minutes of the Fifty-seventh Session*, 5; Protestant Episcopal Church, Diocese of Virginia, *Journal of the Sixty-eighth Annual Council*, 36; Baptist Church, Georgia, Bethel Baptist Association, *Minutes, 1863*, 10.

22. Daniel, *Southern Protestantism in the Confederacy*, 155–57; Stowell, *Rebuilding Zion*, 20–21; Baptist Church, South Carolina, Edgefield Baptist Association, *Minutes of the Fifty-seventh Session*, 6; Protestant Episcopal Church, Diocese of North Carolina, *Journal of the First Annual Council*, 11.

23. Baptist Church, Georgia, Bethel Baptist Association, *Minutes, 1861*, 12–14; ibid., *1862*, 15–16; Finney, *Life and Labors of Enoch Mather Marvin*, 389; June 1864, Eaton's Baptist Church (Mocksville, N.C.) Record Book, SBHLA; Whitaker, *Richard Hooker Wilmer*, 112–13.

24. Belcher, *Religious Denominations in the United States*, 982–86; *Christian Recorder* (Philadelphia), June 7, 1862; Bennitt, *"I Hope to Do My County Service,"* 292–94; *Christian Advocate and Journal* (New York), May 12, June 18, November 26, 1863, January 14, December 29, 1864.

25. Stowell, *Rebuilding Zion*, 24–25; Methodist Episcopal Church, South, Alabama, *Minutes of the Alabama Conference, 1863*, 6; Flynt, *Alabama Baptists*, 130; Bryan, "Churches in Georgia during the Civil War," 294–95; *Christian Index* (Macon, Ga.), October 16, 1863.

26. February 1, 1862, Black Creek Baptist Church (Dovesville, S.C.) Record Book, SBHLA; November 1862, Elizabeth River Parish (Norfolk County) Vestry Book, Library of Virginia; *Christian Observer* (Richmond), March 19, April 2, 1863; Wight, "Pay the Preacher!," 258.

27. January 1864, January 1865, Liberty Baptist Church (Appomattox, Va.), Minute Book,

SBHLA; Cain, *Methodism in the Mississippi Conference*, 390; Chesire, *Church in the Confederate States*, 149–50; September 1864, Zion Hill Baptist Church (Botetourt County) Minute Book, Library of Virginia; *Christian Observer* (Richmond), April 30, May 7, 1863.

28. *Richmond Daily Whig*, November 25, 26, 1862; Bennett, *Narrative of the Great Revival*, 227–29; Kate Burruss to Edward M. Burruss, December 3, 1862, Burruss Family Papers, Louisiana State University; Coulter, *Confederate States of America*, 532.

29. Presbyterian Church, Synod of South Carolina, *Minutes, 1861*, 27–28; Baptist Church, Virginia, Albemarle Baptist Association, *Minutes of the Seventieth Anniversary*, 15; Daniel W. Stowell, "'A Family of Women and Children': The Fains of East Tennessee during Wartime," in Clinton, *Southern Families at War*, 166; Pease and Pease, *Family of Women*, 178–79. The best discussion of women's changing religious role in the family is in Faust, *Mothers of Invention*, 184–87.

30. Morris, *Christian Life and Character*, 794; Scott, "'A Visitation of God,'" 75–86.

31. Gratz, *Letters of Rebecca Gratz*, 430; Miller, "Two Civil War Notebooks," 81–85; April 19, 1864, Galena and Belvidere (Illinois) Presbyteries Minute Book, PHS-P.

32. McColgan, *Century of Charity*, 1:240–42; Korn, *American Jewry and the Civil War*, 98–109; *Christian Advocate and Journal* (New York), May 22, 1862.

33. *Southern Christian Advocate* (Charleston, S.C.), January 9, 1862; Smith, *Life and Times of George Foster Pierce*, 440; Jones, *Rebel War Clerk's Diary*, 2:388.

34. *Southern Christian Advocate* (Charleston, S.C.), February 27, May 29, 1862; William Henry Elder to John Mary Odin, March 16, 1862, Catholic Church, Archdiocese of New Orleans Papers, Notre Dame.

35. Daniel, *Southern Protestantism in the Confederacy*, 148–51; Baptist Church, South Carolina, Charleston Baptist Association, *Minutes of the 111th, 112th and 113th Sessions*, 24; Baptist Church, Alabama, Cahaba Baptist Association, *Minutes of the Forty-fifth Anniversary*, 13; Hundley, *History of Mattaponi Baptist Church*, 416.

36. Williams, *God Timing All National Changes*, 29–46; Baptist Church, Virginia, Appomattox Baptist Association, *Minutes, 1861*, 15; Deborah B. Lapham Wade to her brother, July 11, 1861, Wade Letters, ABHS.

37. June–December 1862, 1864, George Cunningham Hannah Account Book, VHS; Methodist Episcopal Church, Georgia, *Minutes of 1864*, 12–16; Baptist Church, North Carolina, Liberty Baptist Association, *Minutes of the Twenty-ninth Session*, 8.

38. *Friend* (Philadelphia), January 30, 1864; Huggins, *Three Sermons to Young Men*, 86–147; Cole, *Sesquicentennial History of Illinois: Era of the Civil War*, 420–22; *German Reformed Messenger* (Chambersburg, Pa.), November 18, 1863.

39. Flynt, *Alabama Baptists*, 130–31; McDonald, *Address to Chaplains and Missionaries*, 9–12; *Christian Index* (Macon, Ga.), April 1, 1862, January 29, 1864; Taylor et al., *Leverett Letters*, 321; Bryan, *Confederate Georgia*, 240; December 1863, Yeopim Baptist Church (Chowan Co., N.C.) Record Book, SBHLA.

40. Burgwyn, *A Captain's War*, 75; Palmer, *Social Dancing*, 1–4; Fain, *Sanctified Trial*, 148–49, 300; April 15, 1862, Margaret Josephine Miles Gillis Diary, ADAH.

41. *Christian Index* (Macon, Ga.), March 11, 1864; *Religious Herald* (Richmond), April 28, 1864; Bennett, *Narrative of the Great Revival*, 272–73; Hildebrand, *A Mennonite Journal*, 32.

42. October 1864, 1865, Red Grove Baptist Church (Edgefield District, S.C.) Minute Book, SBHLA; February 1865, Yeopim Baptist Church (Chowan Co., N.C.), Record Book, SBHLA;

March 1865, Liberty Baptist Church (Jackson Mississippi) Minute Book, SBHLA; January 14, February 18, March 18, June 17, 1865, Mount Vernon Church (Halifax County) Minute Book, VBHS.

43. Bartol, *Extravagance*, 4; Ritner and Ritner, *Love and Valor*, 387; December 18, 1863, Sarah Rodgers Espy Diary, ADAH.

44. Baptist Church, Virginia, General Association, *Address of the Baptist General Association*, 6; *Southern Presbyterian* (Columbia, S.C.), November 23, 1861; Gache, *A Frenchman, a Chaplain, a Rebel*, 159–61; Mrs. A. P. Acors to Jefferson Davis, March 23, 1862, Letters Received, Confederate Secretary of War, Record Group 109, M437, roll 29, National Archives.

45. Lacy, *Address Delivered at the General Military Hospital*, 3–12; *Southern Presbyterian* (Columbia, S.C.), February 26, 1863; Jones, *Rebel War Clerk's Diary*, 2:79; *Southern Christian Advocate* (Augusta, Ga.), July 3, 1862; Baptist Church, Georgia, Georgia Baptist Association, *Minutes of the Seventy-eighth Anniversary*, 7. For a wide-ranging and cogent discussion of extortion and its relationship to Confederate nationalism, see Faust, *Creation of Confederate Nationalism*, 41–57.

46. *Christian Observer* (Richmond), March 12, 1863; Tucker, *Guilt and Punishment of Extortion*, 5–9, 15–16; Baptist Church, South Carolina, Tyger River Baptist Association, *Minutes of the Thirtieth Anniversary*, 17.

47. Jones, *Rebel War Clerk's Diary*, 1:78; Rosen, *Jewish Confederates*, 265–75; *Religious Herald* (Richmond), November 6, 1862; *Memphis Daily Appeal* (Atlanta), February 6, 1864; *Austin (Tex.) State Gazette*, May 11, 1864; Greenberg, "Ambivalent Relations," 13–29.

48. Michelbacher, *A Sermon Delivered on the Day of Prayer*, 3–14; Michelbacher, *Prayer of the C.S. Soldiers*; *Savannah (Ga.) Republican*, September 15, 1862.

49. *Charleston Mercury*, February 1, 1861, January 9, 1863; Korn, *American Jewry and the Civil War*, xxiii–lxiii.

50. *OR*, ser. 1, vol. 17, pt. 2, pp. 330, 337, 421–22, 424–25. For differing analyses of Grant's motives, see Catton, *Grant Moves South*, 352–56; McFeely, *Grant*, 123–24; Simpson, *Grant*, 163–65; Korn, *American Jewry and the Civil War*, 121–55.

51. *Jewish Record* (New York), January 13, 1863, ⟨http://www.jewish-history.com/civilwar/go11.htm⟩; *OR*, ser. 1, vol. 17, pt. 2, pp. 506, 530, 544, vol. 24, pt. 1, p. 9; Board of Delegates, American Israelites to Abraham Lincoln, January 8, 1863, Lincoln Papers, LC; Korn, *American Jewry and the Civil War*, 121–38.

52. Korn, *American Jewry and the Civil War*, 23–47, 51–52, 170–75.

53. R. A. Mickle to Abner Addison Porter, July 25, 1861, Porter Papers, PHS-M; Daniel, "Virginia Baptists, 1861–1865," 100; Stowell, *Rebuilding Zion*, 58–59.

54. Massey, *Refugee Life in the Confederacy*, 16–17, 161–62; *Religious Herald* (Richmond), April 3, 1862; Protestant Episcopal Church, Diocese of South Carolina, *Journal of the Seventy-fifth Annual Council*, 38, 63.

55. *Religious Herald* (Richmond), October 29, 1863; Lutheran Church, South Carolina Synod, *Minutes, 1863*, 29–30; McDonald, *A Woman's Civil War*, 78; "Proceedings of the Second Congress, Second Session," 268.

56. Stone, *Brokenburn*, 234.

57. Hundley, *History of Mattaponi Baptist Church*, 394–95; Baptist Church, South Carolina, Broad River Baptist Association, *Minutes of the Sixty-third Anniversary*, 5; October 17, 1863, Cove Creek Baptist Church (Ashe Co., N.C.) Minute Books, SBHLA.

58. August 1, 1863, January 16, 1865, Elon Baptist Church (Hanover Co.) Minute Book, VBHS; May 1864 Yeopim Baptist Church (Chowan Co., N.C.) Record Book, SBHLA. For signs of similar reluctance in a northern Baptist congregation, see October 17, 1863, Deer Creek Regular Baptist Church (Miami Co., Ind.) Minute Book, ABHS.

Chapter 14

1. Bennett, *Narrative of the Great Revival*, 285; Stewart, *Camp, March and Battlefield*, 309.

2. Cutrer and Parrish, *Brothers in Gray*, 190–91; Everson and Simpson, *"Far, Far from Home,"* 213–14; Smith, *Life and Times of George Foster Pierce*, 480; Edmondston, *"Journal of a Secesh Lady,"* 388–89.

3. *Zion's Herald and Wesleyan Journal* (Boston), May 13, 1863; Silber and Stevens, *Yankee Correspondence*, 78–79; Thompson, *While My Country Is in Danger*, 63; Wimmer, "American Catholic Interpretations of the Civil War," 249–50.

4. Bartol, *Conditions of Peace*, 3–24; Baptist Church, Pennsylvania, Pittsburgh Regular Baptist Association, *Minutes of the XXIV Anniversary*, 9.

5. McPherson, *Political History of the United States*, 463–65, 470–71; Lincoln, *Collected Works*, 6:244–45.

6. Baptist Church, Virginia, General Association, *Address of the Baptist General Association of Virginia*, 1–3.

7. Brinsfield, *Spirit Divided: Confederacy*, 123; Edmondston, *"Journal of a Secesh Lady,"* 393; Elias Davis to his wife, May 25, 1863, Davis Papers, SHC.

8. Watson, *Sermon Delivered before the Annual Council*, 7–10; Baptist Church, Virginia, General Association, *Address of the Baptist General Association*, 1–2.

9. Wharton, *War Songs and Poems of the Southern Confederacy*, 302–3; Atkinson, *God the Giver of Victory and Peace*, 9–12; Royster, *Destructive War*, 267–69. On problems with Confederate views of providence, see Guyatt, *Providence and the Invention of the United States*, 266–75.

10. Dabney, *Life and Campaigns of Lieut-Gen. Thomas J. Jackson*, 706–10, 713–15, 719, 721–23; Roberston, *Stonewall Jackson*, 740, 748–52.

11. Robertson, *Stonewall Jackson*, 761; Presbyterian Church, Synod of Virginia, *Minutes, 1863*, 332–33; Cumming, *Journal of a Confederate Nurse*, 103.

12. Neely et al., *Confederate Image*, 109; McKivigan, *War against Proslavery Religion*, 187; Quint, *Potomac and the Rapidan*, 205.

13. Presbyterian Church, General Assembly, *Minutes, 1863*, 126; Smith, *Discourse on the Life and Character of Lt. Gen. Thos. J. Jackson*, 3–14; George William White, "On the Death of Stonewall Jackson," White Collection, PHS-M. In analyzing the religious significance of Jackson's life and death, I have greatly benefited from the arguments and evidence presented in Daniel W. Stowell's excellent essay, "Stonewall Jackson and the Providence of God," in Miller et al., *Religion and the American Civil War*, 187–207.

14. Allan, *Life and Letters of Margaret Junkin Preston*, 165; Fain, *Sanctified Glory*, 70–71; William J. Pegram to Mary Evan Pegram, May 11, 1863, Pegram-Johnson-McIntosh Papers, VHS.

15. *Religious Herald* (Richmond), July 9, 1863; *Southern Churchman* (Richmond), May 15, 1863; McGuire, *Diary of a Southern Refugee*, 211–12; Ramsey, *True Eminence Founded on Holiness*, 18–21.

16. Ada Harris to her parents, May 16, 1863, Henry St. George Harris Papers, Duke Univer-

sity; Guerrant, *Bluegrass Confederate*, 276; Apperson, *Repairing the "March of Mars,"* 439; Frobel, *Civil War Diary of Anne S. Frobel*, 183.

17. Cutrer and Parrish, *Brothers in Gray*, 198; Bunting, *Our Trust Is in the God of Battles*, 162.

18. *Southern Churchman* (Richmond), July 3, 1863; Edmondston, *"Journal of a Secesh Lady,"* 415–16; *Christian Index* (Macon, Ga.), June 15, 1863.

19. Daly, *Diary of a Union Lady*, 240; Sweet, *Methodist Episcopal Church and Civil War*, 78; Chase, *Salmon P. Chase Papers*, 4:73.

20. Barber, *Holding the Line*, 101; Walker, *Vicksburg*, 161, 178; Bunting, *Our Trust Is in the God of Battles*, 164; Jones, *Christ in the Camp*, 546.

21. Randall Miller, "Catholic Religion, Irish Ethnicity, and the Civil War," in Miller et al., *Religion and the American Civil War*, 276–82; *New York Freeman's Journal and Catholic Register*, June 13, 1863.

22. Bernstein, *New York City Draft Riots*, 62, 112–13; Hughes, *Complete Works*, 2:544–48; *New York Tablet*, August 1, 1863; *OR*, ser. 1, vol. 27, pt. 2, pp. 893, 938–39.

23. Blied, *Catholics and the Civil War*, 50; Aikman, *Government and Administration*, 1–12; Beecher, *Patriotic Addresses*, 611–12; *Evangelist* (New York), July 16, 1863.

24. Frothingham, *Morality of the New York Riots*, 3–21; Sprague, *God's Purposes in the War*, 25; *Evangelist* (New York), July 23, 1863; *Christian Advocate and Journal* (New York), July 23, 1864.

25. Man, "The Church and New York Draft Riots of 1863," 34–36; *New York Tablet*, July 25, 1863; *New York Freeman's Journal and Catholic Register*, May 2, July 18, 25, August 29, 1863.

26. Lincoln, *Collected Works*, 6:332. For signs of immediate public thanksgiving for the recent victories, see *New York Times*, July 10, 1863.

27. *OR*, ser. 1, vol. 26, pt. 3, p. 519; Kellogg, *Duties of the Hour*, 4; Stout, *Upon the Altar of the Nation*, 242, 248; *New York Tablet*, July 11, 1863.

28. *New York Times*, August 6, 1863; Sprague, *God's Purposes in the War*, 5–12. To Quakers, whose own people sometimes rejoiced over slaughter of the rebels, it seemed particularly appalling that Christian ministers encouraged the prosecution of the war without apparent limits. *Friend* (Philadelphia), July 25, August 15, 1863.

29. Scott, "'A Visitation of God," 149; Kellogg, *Duties of the Hour*, 1–16; Jackson, *The Union—the Constitution—Peace*, 12–23.

30. *New York Times*, August 7, 1863; Wiswell, *Victory Recognized*, 3–14; Gurley, *Man's Prospects and God's Results*, 16; Hay, *Inside Lincoln's White House*, 70. Democratic governor Joel Parker of New Jersey had issued his thanksgiving proclamation that invoked divine blessings for the more conservative war aims and ignored emancipation. *New York Times*, August 3, 1863.

31. *Independent* (New York), July 9, 1863; *Christian Advocate and Journal* (New York), August 20, 1863; *German Reformed Messenger* (Chambersburg, Pa.), August 5, 1863; Cross, *Gettysburg and the Christian Commission*, 3.

32. Hibbard, *A Spiritual Ground of Hope for the Salvation of Our Country*, 4–24; *The Bible on the Present Crisis*, 94–104; Phillips, *American Republic and Human Liberty Foreshadowed in Scripture*, 85–119. See especially the fine discussion about martyrdom and blood in Stout, *Upon the Altar of the Nation*, 248–49. James Moorhead has pointed out the limited appeal of efforts linking wartime events to apocalyptic prophecies but concluded that many Americans embraced general millennial hopes. Moorhead, *American Apocalypse*, 56–65.

33. Gannett, *Ezra Stiles Gannett*, 306; Furness, *Our American Institutions*, 21; *German Reformed Messenger* (Chambersburg, Pa.), July 29, 1863.

34. Baptist Church, Pennsylvania, Pennsylvania Baptist Convention, *Minutes of the Thirty-sixth Anniversary*, 6; Buck, *Civil Ruler as God's Minister*, 22–24; Methodist Church, Indiana, Southeastern Indiana Conference, *Minutes, 1863*, 22–23.

35. Baptist Church, Illinois, Baptist General Association, *Minutes, 1863*, 31; Methodist Church, Indiana, Indiana Conference, *Minutes, 1862–63*, 18–21; Melvin Jameson to Abraham Lincoln, October 19, 1863, Lincoln Papers, LC.

36. Lincoln, *Collected Works*, 6:531, 535–36.

37. David Edwards et al. to Abraham Lincoln, October 3, 10, 1863, J. M. Carpenter to Lincoln, December 8, 1863, Lincoln Papers, LC; *Zion's Herald and Wesleyan Journal* (Boston), November 11, 1863.

38. *Our Triumph*, 1–4; Jones, *Christ in the Camp*, 607; Kingsbury, *The Great Amnesty*; July 29, 1863, Mary Jeffreys Bethell Diary, SHC; Gray, "Diary of Virginia Davis Gray," 51–52; Cutrer and Parrish, *Brothers in Gray*, 206; Stillwell, *Stillwell Letters*, 196–97.

39. Beringer et al., *Why the South Lost the Civil War*, 275–77; Stillwell, *Stillwell Letters*, 201; Wiley, *Scriptural Views of National Trials*, 26, 48.

40. Daniel, "Southern Protestantism—1861 and After," 279; Sheeran, *Confederate Chaplain*, 50–52; Baptist Church, North Carolina, Western Baptist Convention, *Proceedings of the Seventh Annual Session*, 16–17; Cumming, *Journal of a Confederate Nurse*, 135; Lee, *Our Country—Our Dangers—Our Duty*, 13–24.

41. Davis, *Messages and Papers of Davis*, 1:328; Wight, "Church and Confederate Cause," 367; Myers, *Children of Pride*, 1087.

42. Hubbs, *Voices from Company D*, 195; *Contributions to a History of the Richmond Howitzer Battalion*, 221–22; Bunting, *Our Trust Is in the God of Battles*, 190–91.

43. Bunting, *Our Trust Is in the God of Battles*, 192–94; Renfroe, *"The Battle is God's,"* 3–27.

44. Stout, *Upon the Altar of the Nation*, 256–58; Manly, "Diary of Basil Manly," 281; Jones, *Rebel War Clerk's Diary*, 2:21.

45. Buck, *Shadows on My Heart*, 231; J. B. Jeter, Notes and Sermons, June 1863, p. 27, VBHS; Callaway, *Civil War Letters*, 110–11.

46. *Christian Observer* (Richmond), October 15, 1863; *Southern Churchman* (Richmond), August 7, 1863; Heyward, *Confederate Lady Comes of Age*, 22; Cumming, *Journal of a Confederate Nurse*, 133; Landrum, *The Battle Is God's*, 5–12.

47. *Christian Observer* (Richmond), July 9, 1863; *Religious Herald* (Richmond), July 2, 1863; Finley, *The Lord Reigneth*, 11–20; Owen, *Sacred Flame of Love*, 103–4; Beringer et al., *Why the South Lost the Civil War*, 97–98.

48. Lee, *Memoirs of William Nelson Pendleton*, 298–99; Callaway, *Civil War Letters*, 155; Beringer et al., *Why the South Lost the Civil War*, 268–70.

49. July 12, 1863, Sarah Lois Wadley Diary, SHC; Barber, *Holding the Line*, 141; Woodworth, *While God Is Marching On*, 270–73; Walter W. Lenoir to Rufus Lenoir, August 17, 1863, Lenoir Family Papers, SHC; Browder, *Heavens Are Weeping*, 160; Sparks, *On Jordan's Stormy Banks*, 182. For a perceptive general discussion of these problems, see Butterfield, *Christianity and History*, 57–60.

50. Bettersworth, "Mississippi Unionism," 42–48; Holmes, *Diary of Emma Holmes*, 298; Lee, *Our Country—Our Dangers—Our Duty*, 20–21; *Religious Herald* (Richmond), August 13, 1863; Hickerson, *Echoes of Happy Valley*, 74; Galloway, *Dear Old Roswell*, 36–37.

51. Faust, *Mothers of Invention*, 192–94; Richard, *Florence Nightingale of the Southern Army*,

22; Basil Manly Jr. to ?, July 17, 1863, Manly Family Papers, SBHLA; Protestant Episcopal Church, Diocese of Alabama, *Journal of the Thirty-first Annual Convention*, 69.

52. *Biblical Recorder* (Raleigh, N.C.), August 5, 1863; Thompson, *Presbyterians in the South*, 2:80; Baptist Church, Virginia, Middle District Baptist Association, *Minutes of the Eightieth Annual Session*, 8.

53. Baptist Church, North Carolina, State Convention, *Proceedings of the Thirty-fourth Annual Session*, 13–15; *Christian Index* (Macon, Ga.), July 24, 1863.

54. Chesebrough, *God Ordained This War*, 246–62; *Charleston Mercury*, July 15, 1863; July 28, 1863, Anonymous Diary, Mississippi Department of Archives and History.

55. Stillwell, *Stillwell Letters*, 208; Sutherland, *Seasons of War*, 266.

56. Sheffey, *Soldier of Southwestern Virginia*, 175; *Southern Churchman* (Richmond), September 4, 1863; Lee, *Our Country—Our Dangers—Our Duty*, 3–13. For other examples of soldier reasoning on these points, see Manning, *What This Cruel War Was Over*, 141–43.

57. Landrum, *The Battle Is God's*, 12–14; White, *31st Georgia*, 100; Julia Davidson to James M. Davidson, July 17, 1863, Davidson Papers, Emory University; Stiles, *Capt. Thomas E. King*, 49–56; *Southern Churchman* (Richmond), November 20, December 11, 1863.

58. For various texts, see Lincoln, *Collected Works*, 7:17–23. For comparisons of texts and a discussion of the phrase "under God," see the indispensable work on the subject, Boritt, *Gettysburg Gospel*, 119–21, 246–86.

Chapter 15

1. Cumming, *Journal of a Confederate Nurse*, 158; Myers, *Children of Pride*, 1121.

2. Dabney, *Defence of Virginia*, 9; Bond, *Maryland Bride in the Deep South*, 204.

3. Carroll, *History of Texas Baptists*, 332–33; Faust, *Southern Stories*, 25–28; *Christian Index* (Macon, Ga.), May 20, 1864.

4. Renfroe, *"The Battle is God's,"* 17–19; Elliott, *"Samson's Riddle,"* 15–24; Baptist Church, Mississippi, Strong River Baptist Association, *Minutes of the Eleventh Annual Meeting*, 4; Walter W. Lenoir to his brother, July 22, 1863, Lenoir Family Papers, SHC.

5. Fain, *Sanctified Trial*, 10; *Confederate Baptist* (Columbia, S.C.), December 7, 1864; Browder, *Heavens Are Weeping*, 140–41; Smyth, *Complete Works of Rev. Thomas Smyth*, 7:724–26; Methodist Church, South Carolina, *Minutes of the Seventy-fifth Annual Session*, 16–17.

6. Myers, *Children of Pride*, 810; Jones, *Religious Instruction of the Negroes*, 1–25.

7. Wiley, *Southern Negroes*, 98–99; Riley, *History of the Baptists of Alabama*, 300.

8. Carroll, *History of Texas Baptists*, 333–34; Protestant Episcopal Church, Diocese of Virginia, *Journal of the Sixty-eighth Annual Council*, 38; Fain, *Sanctified Trial*, 258.

9. Stone, *Brokenburn*, 41; Myers, *Children of Pride*, 1246; Fain, *Sanctified Trial*, 36–37, 77, 152, 159, 170–71, 242.

10. Chesire, *Church in the Confederate States*, 122–26; Pierce, *Lest Faith Forget*, 78–80; Lazenby, *Methodism in Alabama and West Florida*, 334. 338; May, *First Baptist Church of Nashville*, 111–12; Baptist Church, Virginia, Albemarle Baptist Association, *Minutes of the Seventy-third Anniversary*, 13; Baptist Church, Georgia, Columbus Baptist Association, *Minutes of the Thirty-third Annual Session*, 10.

11. Evans, *History of First Baptist Church, Aberdeen, Mississippi*, 25; Carroll, *History of Texas Baptists*, 335–36; July 14, 1861, Sarah Lois Wadley Diary, SHC.

12. Baptist Church, Virginia, General Association, *Minutes, 1861, 1862, and 1863*, 76–77; Cumming, *Journal of a Confederate Nurse*, 194; Andrews, *Journal of a Georgia Girl*, 69.

13. For state and local estimates of gains and losses, see Protestant Episcopal Church, Diocese of South Carolina, *Journal of the Seventy-fourth Annual Convention*, 21–29; Daniel, "Virginia Baptists, 1861–1865," 109–10; Andrew Witmer, "Race, Religion and Rebellion: Black and White Baptists in Albemarle County, Virginia, during the Civil War," in Ayers et al., *Crucible of the Civil War*, 148–54.

14. Andrews, *Journal of a Georgia Girl*, 71–72; Pierce, *Sermons of Bishop Pierce and Rev. B. M. Palmer*, 7; Presbyterian Church, General Assembly, *Minutes, 1863*, 158.

15. Methodist Church, South Carolina, *Minutes of the Seventy-sixth Annual Session*, 17–20; *OR*, ser. 1, vol. 14, pp. 489–90; Jones, *Christ in the Camp*, 25; Wiley, *Southern Negroes*, 106–7; [Brockenbrough], *A Mother's Parting Words to Her Soldier Boy*, 7–8.

16. Mohr, *On the Threshold of Freedom*, 57; W. B. Allen (Georgia), *Slave Narratives* (CD-ROM); Daniel, *Protestantism in the Confederacy*, 132–33; Baptist Church, Virginia, Albemarle Baptist Association, *Minutes of the Seventy-second Anniversary*, 17.

17. Baptist Church, Virginia, Rappahannock Baptist Association, *Minutes of the Twentieth Annual Meeting*, 22–24; Browder, *Heavens Are Weeping*, 175; Baptist Church, Virginia, Appomattox Baptist Association, *Minutes, 1862 and 1863*, 16.

18. Baptist Church, Virginia, Middle District Baptist Association, *Minutes of the Eightieth Annual Session*, 6; Presbyterian Church, Synod of North Carolina, *Minutes of the Convention of Elders*, 7.

19. *Christian Index* (Macon, Ga.), March 23, September 18, 1863; Chesire, *Church in the Confederate States*, 126; Methodist Episcopal Church, South, Alabama, *Minutes of the Alabama Conference, 1863*, 23; Carroll, *History of Texas Baptists*, 331–32.

20. Tichenor, *Fast-Day Sermon*, 11–12. For fine discussions that raise doubts about whether reforms would have led to abolition, see Faust, *Creation of Confederate Nationalism*, 75–81; Genovese, *A Consuming Fire*, 51–61.

21. Mohr, *On the Threshold of Freedom*, 247–48; Pierce, *Sermons of Bishop Pierce and Rev. B. M. Palmer*, 14–15.

22. McGill, *Faith, the Victory*, 314; Mohr, *On the Threshold of Freedom*, 255–62; *Christian Index* (Macon, Ga.), November 4, 1864.

23. Protestant Episcopal Church, *Pastoral Letter from the Bishops of the Protestant Episcopal Church in the Confederate States*, 11; McGill, *Faith, the Victory*, 313–14; Wiley, *Scriptural Views of National Trials*, 187–200.

24. "A Slave Marriage Law," *Southern Presbyterian Review* 16 (October 1863): 145–63.

25. *Christian Index* (Macon, Ga.), September 9, 30, 1862; Pierce, *Sermons of Bishop Pierce and Rev. B. M. Palmer*, 14–15.

26. *Christian Index* (Macon, Ga.), June 1, 1863; Mohr, *On the Threshold of Freedom*, 249–55; Ringold, *State Legislatures in the Confederacy*, 59.

27. September 19, 1863, Bethesda Baptist Church (Hinds County, Miss.), Minute Book, SBHLA; Hundley, *History of Mattaponi Baptist Church*, 411–12, 414; Sutherland, *Seasons of War*, 212; September 13, 1862, Battle Run Baptist Church (Rappahannock County) Minute Book, Library of Virginia.

28. Baptist Church, Virginia, Rappahannock Baptist Association, *Minutes of the Twenty-*

second *Annual Session*, 10; March and April 1865, Carmel Baptist Church (Caroline Co., Va.) Record Book, SBHLA; Hundley, *History of Mattaponi Baptist Church*, 399. In one Virginia church, the "colored members" met to investigate the behavior of slaves who had been disloyal to their masters and eventually recommended they be excluded from fellowship. Whether this action reflected subtle coercion, sincere conviction, or clever deception is impossible to determine. August 1, 1863, April 3, 1864, Elon Baptist Church (Hanover County) Minute Book, VBHS.

29. *Religious Herald* (Richmond), May 14, 1863; Stowell, *Rebuilding Zion*, 70–73.

30. Haines, *"In the Country of the Enemy,"* 147; Emerson, *Life of Abby Hooper Gibbons*, 318; Wiley, *Life of Billy Yank*, 117; Johnson, *Letters and Diary of Captain Jonathan Huntington Johnson*, 75.

31. Creel, *"A Peculiar People,"* 259–75; Isaac W. Brinckerhoff, "Mission Work among the Freed Negroes," p. 22, ABHS; French, *Slavery in South Carolina*, 131–32.

32. Clarke, *Our Southern Zion*, 218–19; Baptist Church, Mississippi, Choctaw Baptist Association, *Minutes of the Seventy-sixth Annual Session*, 5; Trumbull, *War Memories of a Chaplain*, 389–91.

33. Johnson, *Twenty-eight Years a Slave*, 29–30; Pearson, *Letters from Port Royal*, 50; Wright, *Sixth Iowa*, 169. For excellent discussions of these themes in African American religion, see Raboteau, *Slave Religion*, 301–21; Stowell, *Rebuilding Zion*, 65–70.

34. French, *Slavery in South Carolina*, 133–34; George Washington Bucker (Indiana), *Slave Narratives* (CD-ROM); Litwack, *Been in the Storm So Long*, 455.

35. Katherine L. Dvorak, "After Apocalypse, Moses," in Boles, *Masters and Slaves in the House of the Lord*, 176–78; Haines, *"In the Country of the Enemy,"* 171; *Evangelist* (New York), August 20, 1863; Moore, *Rebellion Record*, 7 (Rumors and Incidents): 21–22; Hawks, *A Woman Doctor's Civil War*, 39–40; Kinsley, *Diary of a Christian Soldier*, 130.

36. Isaac W. Brinckerhoff, "Mission Work among the Freed Negroes," pp. 50–51, ABHS; Haines, *"In the Country of the Enemy,"* 150; Rogers, *War Pictures*, 220–21; Smith, *Incidents of the Christian Commission*, 119–20; *Independent* (New York), July 17, 1862; Fountain, "Christ Unchained," 35–43.

37. Glatthaar, *Forged in Battle*, 15–16, 224–25; Wilson, *Campfires of Freedom*, 130–31, 135–37; Higginson, *Complete Civil War Journal*, 66; Smith, *Incidents of the Christian Commission*, 358, 362–63; Moss, *Annals of the Christian Commission*, 452–53.

38. Richardson, *Christian Reconstruction*, 24–27; *Christian Recorder* (Philadelphia), October 1, 1864; Wilson, *Campfires of Freedom*, 127–43.

39. Hawks, *A Woman Doctor's Civil War*, 70; Higginson, *Complete Civil War Journal*, 180; Wilson, *Campfires of Freedom*, 127–30, 143–44; Bowley, *A Boy Lieutenant*, 70.

40. *Christian Recorder* (Philadelphia), December 12, 1863; Berlin et al., *Freedom, Series II: The Black Military Experience*, 565, 619–20, 626; United States Christian Commission, *Information for Army Meetings* (October 1864): 24; ibid. (November 1864): 15; Billingsley, *From the Flag to the Cross*, 227–28; Smith, *Incidents of the Christian Commission*, 373, 451.

41. Sears, *Camp Nelson, Kentucky*, 131; Berlin et al., *Freedom, Series II: The Black Military Experience*, 623; Billingsley, *From the Flag to the Cross*, 117–18.

42. James C. Owens to Joanna Patterson Moore, July 20, 1865, Alfred S. Williams to Moore, n.d., 1865, Notes from Soldiers of the 56th U.S. Colored Infantry, Helena Arkansas, Moore Papers, ABHS; Wilson, *Campfires of Freedom*, 144; Manning, *What This Cruel War Was Over*,

125-28; Higginson, *Complete Civil War Journal*, 65-66; Grimké, *Journals of Charlotte Forten Grimké*, 404.

43. McPherson, *Political History of the United States*, 481; May 2, 1864, New York Third Presbytery Minute Book, PHS-P. For overviews of denominational efforts, see Smith, *In His Image But*, 218-26; McKivigan, *War against Proslavery Religion*, 196-99.

44. Murray, *Presbyterians and Negro*, 162-81; Vander Velde, *Presbyterian Churches and Federal Union*, 435, 439-46; *Evangelist* (New York), March 17, 1864.

45. Jones, *Sectional Crisis and Northern Methodism*, 112-36; Methodist Church, Indiana, Southeastern Conference, *Minutes, 1864*, 23-25; *Zion's Herald and Wesleyan Journal*, November 4, 1863.

46. Ide, *Freedmen of the War*, 28-29; *Christianity versus Treason and Slavery*, 7-9.

47. Vincent, *Lord of War and of Righteousness*, 36-451; Ide, *Freedmen of the War*, 40-44; Ware, *Danger of To-Day*, 14-15.

48. Ide, *Freedmen of the War*, 3-26; Kinsley, *Diary of a Christian Soldier*, 109; "The Freedmen and Free Labor in the South," *Christian Examiner* 76 (May 1864): 345.

49. Hildebrand, *Times Were Strange and Stirring*, 34-49; Gaines, *African Methodism in the South*, 4-6; Armstrong, *Friend to God's Poor*, 114.

50. Dovorak, *African-American Exodus*, 60, 64-67; *Christian Recorder* (Philadelphia), August 9, 1862, March 4, 1865; Bradley, *History of the A.M.E. Zion Church*, 160-62.

51. *Christian Recorder* (Philadelphia), August 15, 1863.

52. Baptist Church, Illinois, Chicago Baptist Association, *Proceedings, 1863*, 9-10; Baptist Church, Pennsylvania, Philadelphia Baptist Association, *Minutes of the 156th Anniversary*, 20-21; John Wheeler to Abraham Lincoln, September 7, 1863, Lincoln Papers, LC.

53. Howard, *Religion and the Radical Republican Movement*, 65-66; David Edwards to Abraham Lincoln, October 3, 1863, Lincoln Papers, LC; Beidelman, *Civil War Letters*, 190-91.

54. *New York Freeman's Journal and Catholic Register*, October 3, 1863; Hartsock, *Soldier of the Cross*, 117.

55. Jackson, *The Union—the Constitution—Peace*, 11; Baptist Church, Pennsylvania, Central Union Association, *Minutes of the Thirty-first Annual Session*, 19-20; *Friends' Review* (Philadelphia), December 10, 1864; Thome, *Future of the Freed People*, 3-46; *Christian Recorder* (Philadelphia), November 21, 1863.

56. Smith, *God in the War*, 22-23; Phillips, *American Republic and Human Liberty Foreshadowed in Scripture*, especially 232; Bennitt, *"I Hope to Do My Country Service,"* 181.

57. Haley, *Rebel Yell and Yankee Hurrah*, 163; *Christian Advocate and Journal* (New York), January 21, 1864.

Chapter 16

1. Campbell, *The Union Must Stand*, 131.

2. Jones, *Rebel War Clerk's Diary*, 2:45; Myers, *Children of Pride*, 1102; Lane, *"Dear Mother: Don't grieve about me,"* 276.

3. Finney, *Life and Labors of Enoch Mather Martin*, 391; Cumming, *Journal of a Confederate Nurse*, 174; *Biblical Recorder* (Raleigh, N.C.), December 2, 1863.

4. Schenck, *Songs in the Night*, 3-14; Gilmore, *"Hath God Forgotten to Be Gracious,"* 5; Eells, *How and Why We Give Thanks*, 5-7. For an illuminating analysis of the 1863 Thanksgiving sermons, see Stout, *Upon the Altar of the Nation*, 271-74.

5. Lincoln, *Collected Works*, 6:496–97. Yet the proclamation itself won both attention and praise in the press. Scott, "'A Visitation of God,'" 189–90.

6. Morais, *Thanksgiving Sermon*, 3–10; Einhorn, *Sermon Delivered on Thanksgiving Day*, 3–13.

7. *Brooklyn Eagle*, November 27, 1863; Carpenter, *Final Triumph of Equity*, 5–28; Haven, *National Sermons*, 373–74; Goodell, *Thanksgiving Sermon*, 13–15; Vinton, *Mistakes of the Rebellion*, 5–28; Butler, *God with Us*, 15–18; Marshall, *Nation's Changes*, 19–22; Spees, *A New Song*, 11–18.

8. Washburn, *A Sermon Delivered on the Day of National Thanksgiving*, 3–16; Palmer, *The Opening Future*, 3–28; Eells, *How and Why We Give Thanks*, 10–20; Upfold, *God, the Help of the Nation*, 3–24; Kempshall, *A Thanksgiving Sermon*, 3–20.

9. William Bingham to Walter W. Lenoir, December 1, 1863, Lenoir Family Papers, SHC; Fain, *Sanctified Trial*, 143; Chesnut, *Mary Chesnut's Civil War*, 505.

10. Palmer, *A Discourse before the General Assembly of South Carolina*, 3–23; Myers, *Children of Pride*, 1128.

11. Hieronymus, "For Now and Forever," 249–53; Bennett, *Narrative of the Great Revival*, 280–84, 346–47; Bunting, *Our Trust Is in the God of Battles*, 162, 178, 195; Johansson, *Peculiar Honor*, 76–78; M. D. Dewitt, "Tennessee and the Church," in Evans, *Confederate Military History*, 10:279–80; Anderson, *Texas Surgeon in C.S.A.*, 76–77.

12. Brinsfield, *Spirit Divided: Confederacy*, 71–73; Bennett, *Narrative of the Great Revival*, 321–22, 325, 330–31; Fitzpatrick, *Letters to Amanda*, 72; Jones, *Christ in the Camp*, 248–49, 329–30, 335–36; Hugh Denson to Dossie Noble, December 6, 1863, Emily S. York Papers, Special Collections, Auburn University.

13. Dame, *From Rapidan to Richmond*, 49–52; Holt, *Mississippi Rebel in Army of Northern Virginia*, 232–33; J. J. D. Renfroe, "The Great Revival," 1863, Renfroe manuscript sermons, SBHLA; Stone, *Wandering to Glory*, 108–9.

14. Jones, *Christ in the Camp*, 260–61, 333, 381–82, 471–72, 485.

15. Smith, *Incidents of Christian Commission*, 196–97; Fiske, *Mr. Dunn Browne's Experiences in the Army*, 224; Sutherland, *Seasons of War*, 324; Regan, *Lost Civil War Diaries*, 192; Adams, *Memorial and Letters of Rev. John R. Adams*, 143–44.

16. Gage, *From Vicksburg to Raleigh*, 173; Shattuck, *Shield and Hiding Place*, 81–82; Woodworth, *While God Is Marching On*, 227; Hight, *Fifty-Eighth Indiana*, 163–64.

17. United States Christian Commission, *Second Annual Report*, 261; Smith, *Incidents of Christian Commission*, 202–4; Mohr, *Cormany Diaries*, 413–14; Rhodes, *All for the Union*, 123, 133; Poremba, *If I Am Found Dead*, 159–60.

18. Smith, *Smite Them Hip and Thigh!*, 89; Caldwell, *History of a Brigade of South Carolinians*, 112–13; Baptist Church, Georgia, Ebenezer Baptist Association, *Minutes of the Forty-ninth Anniversary*, 17–18.

19. Adams, *Memorial and Letters of Rev. John R. Adams*, 144; Stout, *Upon the Altar of the Nation*, 327; Bennitt, *"I Hope to Do My Country Service,"* 297.

20. Wiley, *Life of Billy Yank*, 274; Muffly, *148th Pennsylvania*, 194–95; Squier, *This Wilderness of War*, 57; *Christian Advocate and Journal* (New York), April 14, May 5, 1864; Gibbs, *Three Years in the Bloody Eleventh*, 244.

21. Daniel, *Soldiering in the Army of Tennessee*, 119–20; Cannon, *Bloody Banners and Barefoot Boys*, 41–42; Wiatt, *Confederate Chaplain William Edward Wiatt*, 71; Jones, *Christ in the Camp*, 329–30, 510–11; Bennett, *Narrative of the Great Revival*, 324, 333–34.

22. Jones, *Life and Letters of Robert Edward Lee*, 466–67; Zwemer, *For Home and the South-*

land, 54; Lee, *Memoirs of William Nelson Pendleton*, 301, 306–7, 336; Chesnut, *Mary Chesnut's Civil War*, 585–86; *Evangelist* (New York), February 4, 1864; Moss, *Annals of Christian Commission*, 401; Jones, *Christ in the Camp*, 329, 378.

23. Krick, *Parker's Virginia Battery*, 108–9; Tripp, *Yankee Town, Southern City*, 131; Sheeran, *Confederate Chaplain*, 53; Day, *A True History of Company I, 49th Regiment, North Carolina Troops*, 45–46.

24. J. J. D. Renfroe, "Sermon for Young Converts," Renfroe manuscript sermons, SBHLA; *Southern Churchman* (Richmond), May 8, 1863; Polk, *Leonidas Polk, Bishop and General*, 2:206–7; Smith, *Life and Letters of James Osgood Andrew*, 490; Daniel, *Southern Protestantism in the Confederacy*, 89–90. The first part of this paragraph closely follows the perceptive analysis in Reid Mitchell, "Christian Soldiers? Perfecting the Confederacy?," in Miller et al., *Religion and the American Civil War*, 305–8.

25. Davis, *Messages and Papers*, 1:412–14; *Charleston Mercury*, April 8, 1864; *Christian Observer* (Richmond), April 7, 1864; *Southern Churchman* (Richmond), April 1, 8, 1864; *Confederate Baptist* (Columbia, S.C.), March 30, 1864.

26. *Richmond Dispatch*, April 11, 1864; Coulter, *Confederate States of America*, 531; Jones, *Christ in the Camp*, 58; Graham, *James A. Graham Papers*, 185; Bennett, *Narrative of the Great Revival*, 372; Hubbs, *Voices from Company D*, 240; Chambers, *Diary of Captain Henry A. Chambers*, 189.

27. Doggett, *War and Its Close*, 5–15; *Religious Herald* (Richmond), April 21, 1864; Caldwell, *A Fast Day Sermon*, 3–14.

28. Dunaway, *A Sermon Delivered by Elder Thomas S. Dunaway*, 3–9; Wilmer, *Future Good— The Explanation of Present Reverses*, 3–13; Elliott, *Gideon's Water-Lappers*, 5–20.

29. Uriah N. Parmelee to his mother, January 8, 1863, Parmelee Papers, Duke University; Thomas Sherman to William Carthell, May 25, 1863, Civil War Papers, AAS; Comey, *A Legacy of Valor*, 150–51; Mears, *Life of Edward Norris Kirk, D.D.*, 299–300.

30. October 1863, Cleveland (Ohio) Presbytery, Minutes, PHS-P; Baptist Church, North Carolina, Liberty Baptist Association, *Minutes of the Thirty-first Annual Session*, 7; Browder, *Heavens Are Weeping*, 143; Lutheran Church, North Carolina Synod, *Minutes of the Sixtieth Meeting*, 5.

31. *Southern Presbyterian* (Columbia, S.C.), October 15, 1863; Jones, *Christ in the Camp*, 343; Carroll, *History of Texas Baptists*, 320.

32. Jones, *Rebel War Clerk's Diary*, 2:64; Edmondston, *"Journal of a Secesh Lady,"* 570.

33. Doyle, *Social Order of a Frontier Community*, 164; Fite, *Social and Industrial Conditions in the North*, 307–10; Dolan, *Catholic Revivalism*, 43.

34. Evans, *Sixteenth Mississippi Infantry*, 242; James Z. Branscomb to his parents, April 19, 1864, Branscom Family Papers, ADAH; Hubbs, *Voices from Company D*, 247.

35. Jones, *Christ in the Camp*, 367, 618–19; Brinsfield, *Spirit Divided: Confederacy*, 80–81; Barclay, *Ted Barclay, Liberty Hall Volunteers*, 136.

36. Ridley, *Battles and Sketches of Army of Tennessee*, 283; Daniel, *Soldiering in the Army of Tennessee*, 122–24; Fitzgerald, *John B. McFerrin*, 275–77; Bennett, *Narrative of the Great Revival*, 359–60; Jones, *Christ in the Camp*, 594.

37. Bennett, *Narrative of the Great Revival*, 314, 338, 368–69; Gay, *Life in Dixie during the War*, 79, 82–86.

38. Quintard, *Doctor Quintard, Chaplain, C.S.A.*, 69–71, 83–84; Fremantle, *Three Months in*

the Southern States, 163–64; McMurry, *John Bell Hood*, 103; Gay, *Life in Dixie during in War*, 79–82.

39. Stillwell, *Stillwell Letters*, 252; Evans, *Sixteenth Mississippi*, 245; Vaughan, "Diary of Turner Vaughan," 593; Jones, *Christ in the Camp*, 356–57, 371–73; Cheshire, *Church in the Confederate States*, 75–76.

40. Ridgaway, *Life of Rev. Alfred Cookman*, 270; McAllister, *Letters of Robert McAllister*, 383, 400, 405; Fleharty, *"Jottings from Dixie,"* 123; Fisk, *Hard Marching Every Day*, 200–1; Perkins, *Three Years a Soldier*, 197–207; Moss, *Annals of Christian Commission*, 301–2. 490–91; Henry, *Turn Them Out to Die Like a Mule*, 351–52; Bennitt, *"I Hope to Do My Country Service,"* 248–49. For a more positive assessment of the revivals, see Woodworth, *While God Is Marching On*, 231–34.

41. September 13, 1863, Henry W. Tisdale Diary, ⟨http://www.civilwardiary.net/⟩; Perkins, *Three Years a Soldier*, 191.

42. Puck, *Sacrifice at Vicksburg*, 57; Remmel, *Like Grass before the Scythe*, 100; Seth Gilbert Evans to his family, February 24, 1864, Evans Letters, Pearce Civil War Collection, Navarro College, Corsicana, Texas; Henry, *Turn Them Out to Die Like a Mule*, 352; Westbrook, *49th Pennsylvania*, 182; Grebner, *Ninth Ohio*, 171.

43. Barber, *Holding the Line*, 167–68; Nugent, *My Dear Nellie*, 179–80; Crawford, *Ashe County's Civil War*, 137; Power, *Lee's Miserables*, 5.

44. Stout, *Upon the Altar of the Nation*, 292; Jones, *Christ in the Camp*, 381; Barber, *Holding the Line*, 173–74; Bennett, *Narrative of the Great Revival*, 365–66.

45. Power, *Lee's Miserables*, 5; Boykin, *The Joyful Tidings*, 1–8; Chambers, *Blood and Sacrifice*, 119–20; Sheeran, *Confederate Chaplain*, 85. For Confederates, signs of internal division and growing demoralization added to the sense of foreboding, but preachers hardly knew what to say. In a sermon delivered after the execution of twenty-two deserters, Methodist chaplain John Paris simply held up Robert E. Lee as a model for emulation and avowed once again, "The true Christian is always a true patriot." Chesebrough, *God Ordained This War*, 263–75.

46. Hubbs, *Voices from Company D*, 235; Bunting, *Our Trust Is in the God of Battles*, 160–61; Lee, *Memoirs of William Nelson Pendleton*, 336.

47. Carmichael, *Last Generation*, 179–88, 197–211; Cutrer and Parrish, *Brothers in Gray*, 224; Barclay, *Ted Barclay, Liberty Hall Volunteers*, 128–29, 144; Rubin, *A Shattered Nation*, 37; Haley, *Rebel Yell and Yankee Hurrah*, 138.

48. Mitchell, *Civil War Soldiers*, 187–88; *Confederate Baptist* (Columbia, S.C.), March 30, 1864; Gary W. Gallagher, "Our Hearts Are Full of Hope: The Army of North Virginia in the Spring of 1864," in Gallagher, *Wilderness Campaign*, 56–57; Brinsfield, *Spirit Divided: Confederacy*, 155; Flynt, *Alabama Baptists*, 114. See the quite useful discussion of how confidence in Confederate arms became linked to confidence in the divine will in Phillips, *Diehard Rebels*, 20–28.

49. Daniel, *Soldiering in the Army of Tennessee*, 122; Sutherland, *Seasons of War*, 274; Sheeran, *Confederate Chaplain*, 85; Barclay, *Ted Barclay, Liberty Hall Volunteers*, 124–25; Nugent, *My Dear Nellie*, 173.

50. *Evangelist* (New York), May 26, 1864; Smith, *Incidents of the Christian Commission*, 244; Beaudry, *War Journal*, 109–10.

51. Adams, *Memorial and Letters of Rev. John R. Adams*, 142; Trumbull, *Desirableness of Active Service*, 3–21; Ritner and Ritner, *Love and Valor*, 275.

Chapter 17

1. Lincoln, *Collected Works*, 7:333.

2. Haven, *National Sermons*, 393–406; *Independent* (New York), May and June 1864; *Pittsburgh Catholic*, May 14, 1864; *New York Freeman's Journal and Catholic Register*, May 21, 1864.

3. *Christian Observer* (Richmond), June 23, 1864; Lutheran Church, Synod of Georgia, *Minutes of the Fourth Annual Convention*, 4–6; *Christian Index* (Macon, Ga.), June 10, 1864; Washington, "Diary of Ella Washington," 20.

4. Schultz, *Women at the Front*, 78; Starr, *The Loyal Soldier*, 7–11.

5. Rhea, *To the North Anna River*, 228; Lyman, *Meade's Army*, 167; Frassanito, *Grant and Lee: The Virginia Campaigns*, 116–21; Hagerty, *Collis' Zouaves*, 287–88.

6. Unless otherwise stated, this account of the McPheeters case rests heavily on Grasty, *Memoir of Rev. Samuel B. McPheeters*; *Complete Correspondence between Union Members of the Pine Street Presbyterian Church and Rev. S. B. McPheeters*; Vander Velde, *Presbyterian Churches and Federal Union*, 305–24; Hall, *Presbyterian Conflict and Resolution on the Missouri Frontier*, 152–65; Gerteis, *Civil War St. Louis*, 183–87.

7. See Curtis's order in McPherson, *Political History of the United States*, 533–34.

8. Jones, *Lincoln and the Preachers*, 148; Lincoln, *Collected Works*, 6:20; Samuel R. Curtis to Abraham Lincoln, December 28, 29, 1862, Apolline Blair to Montgomery Blair, December 29, 1862, Franklin A. Dick to Montgomery Blair, December 29, 1862, Lincoln Papers, LC.

9. Lincoln, *Collected Works*, 6:33–34.

10. Nathan Ranney to Edward Bates, November 9, 1863, John B. Coalter to Bates, December 13, 1863, Oliver D. Filley to Abraham Lincoln, November 9, 1863, John Whitehill et al. to Lincoln, November n.d., 1863, Lincoln Papers, LC; Lincoln, *Collected Works*, 7:85–86.

11. McPheeters, "I acted from principle," 115; *OR*, ser. 1, vol. 15, p. 738; Bettersworth, *Confederate Mississippi*, 288; Hurlburt, *History of the Rebellion in Bradley County, East Tennessee*, 191–96; Wooten, "Religious Activities in Civil War Memphis," 144–49.

12. Butler, *Private and Official Correspondence*, 3:577; Ayers, *Diary of James T. Ayers*, 51; Ash, *When the Yankees Came*, 57; Johnson, *Papers of Andrew Johnson*, 5:447. In Missouri, partisans of the Methodist Episcopal Church, South claimed that squads of Unionist militia or Federal soldiers had shot and even killed several clergy. Leftwich, *Martyrdom in Missouri*, 1:388–91, 429–35, 2:125–30, 133–42, 178–92.

13. Palmer, *Oath of Allegiance*; Browder, *Heavens Are Weeping*, 113–14, 153.

14. *OR*, ser. 1, vol. 34, pt. 3, pp. 348–50; Bates, *Diary of Edward Bates*, 357; Lincoln, *Collected Works*, 7:283–84; Leftwich, *Martyrdom in Missouri*, 2:64–71.

15. William Henry Elder to Francis Xavier Leray, January 10, 1861, Elder to John Mary Odin, July 9, 1863, Catholic Church, Archdiocese of New Orleans Papers, Notre Dame; Elder, *Character-Glimpses of Most Reverend William Henry Elder*, 41–42; Pillar, *Catholic Church in Mississippi*, 294–303.

16. Pillar, *Catholic Church in Mississippi*, 303–38; Elder, *Civil War Diary*, 92–94, 125–26; Mason Brayman to John Mary Odin, July 22, 1864, Catholic Church, Archdiocese of New Orleans Papers, Notre Dame.

17. Elder, *Civil War Diary*, 97–98, 102–4, 125; Elder, *Character-Glimpses of Most Reverend William Henry Elder*, 50–53; Gerow, *Catholicity in Mississippi*, 61–62; Pillar, *Catholic Church in Mississippi*, 332.

18. B. J., Natchez, Miss., to James A. McMaster, August 1, 1864, McMaster Papers, Notre

Dame; *New York Freeman's Journal and Catholic Register*, August 27, September 10, 1864; *Pittsburgh Catholic*, August 20, September 24, 1864; *New York Tablet*, August 27, 1864.

19. *Memphis Bulletin*, September 6, 1863; McPherson, *Political History of United States*, 542–44; Nguyen, "Keeping the Faith," 168–70; *OR*, ser. 1, vol. 17, pt. 2, p. 30; July 10, 1864, William King Diary, SHC.

20. Rhodes, *All for the Union*, 198; Cheshire, *Church in the Confederate States*, 172–73; Perry, *History of American Episcopal Church*, 2:576–78; Marshall, *American Bastille*, 92–96; Ash, *When the Yankees Came*, 89; *OR*, ser. 2, vol. 2, pp. 212–13; Alexandria, Virginia, Episcopalians to Abraham Lincoln, February 9, 1862, Lincoln Papers, LC.

21. *Charleston Mercury*, May 1, 1862; *Southern Christian Advocate* (Charleston), June 19, 1862; Cheshire, *Church in Confederate States*, 167–71; Malone, *Episcopal Church in Georgia*, 106–17; *Southern Churchman* (Richmond), March 14, 1862.

22. Bennitt, *"I Hope to Do My Country Service,"* 192–93; Wooten, "Religious Activities in Civil War Memphis," 255–57; November 2, 1862, William T. Chapman Journals, Bowling Green State University.

23. Browder, *Heavens Are Weeping*, 117–18, 133; Ash, *Middle Tennessee Society Transformed*, 102; March 22, 1862, Alice Ready Diary, SHC.

24. Tyler, *Recollections of the Civil War*, 299; Burton, *Diary of E. P. Burton*, 2; Rhodes, *All for the Union*, 188–89; March 31, 1862, Alice Ready Diary, SHC; Cain, *Methodism in the Mississippi Conference*, 334–45.

25. Locke, *Story of the Regiment*, 63–64; Leftwich, *Martyrdom in Missouri*, 1:285–87, 315–31; McPherson, *Political History of United States*, 537–38.

26. Johnson, *Papers of Andrew Johnson*, 5, 537, 567, 595–96; May, *First Baptist Church of Nashville*, 95–98. Occasionally, arrested ministers were in effect held as hostages either by Confederate or Federal forces. Harrison, *Life of Right Reverend John Barrett Kerfoot*, 1:292–318; Marshall, *American Bastille*, 540–57.

27. Cadwallader C. Washburn to Abraham Lincoln, June 22, 1864, Lincoln Papers, LC; Lincoln, *Collected Works*, 7:247, 339; McPherson, *Political History of the United States*, 543; Davis, *First Baptist Church History, Gadsden, Alabama*, 15–16; Ash, *When the Yankees Came*, 90; Daniel, "Virginia Baptists, 1861–1865," 112.

28. Protestant Episcopal Church, Diocese of South Carolina, *Journal of Seventy-fifth Annual Council*, 46, 57; *Southern Churchman* (Richmond), April 18, 1862, February 19, 1864; May 12, 1862, Kate S. Carney Diary, SHC; Bryan, *Confederate Georgia*, 240.

29. Frobel, *Civil War Diary*, 159; Ryland, *Baptists in Virginia*, 297; Byrdon, "Diocese of Virginia in the Confederacy," 390–95; Gannon, *Rebel Bishop*, 109–14; *OR*, ser. 1, vol. 47, pt. 2, pp. 712, 967–68, pt. 3, pp. 202–4, 566.

30. Downing, *Downing's Civil War Diary*, 145; Elder, *Civil War Diary*, 57; Daniel, *Southern Protestantism in the Confederacy*, 152.

31. *Churches and Institutions of Learning Destroyed during the Civil War*, 5–20; Fleharty, *102d Illinois*, 132; Daniel, *Southern Protestantism in the Confederacy*, 151–52; *New York Herald*, September 16, 1863; Jorantha Semmes to Benedict Joseph Semmes, March 23, 1862, Semmes Papers, SHC; Frobel, *Civil War Diary*, 90.

32. Haydon, *For Country, Cause and Leader*, 126–27; July 12, 1864 Elijah Evan Edwards Diary, DePauw; Elder, *Civil War Diary*, 47; Ash, *Middle Tennessee Society Transformed*, 91; September 13, 1862, Battle Run Baptist Church (Rappahannock County) Minute Book, Library of Vir-

ginia; Cushman, *A Goodly Heritage*, 53; *List of Claims upon Which the Court of Claims Has Made a Report*, 5 ff.; Shaw, *Blue-Eyed Child of Fortune*, 343.

33. December 14, 1862, James Hervey Otey Diary, Otey Papers, SHC; Morgan, *Civil War Diary of Sarah Morgan*, 69; September 20, 1863, Kate D. Foster Diary, Duke University; Browder, *Heavens Are Weeping*, 147; Shepherd, *To Rescue My Native Land*, 304.

34. Blanchard, *I Marched with Sherman*, 59; McDonald, *A Woman's Civil War*, 141; Burton, *Diary of E. P. Burton*, 5; Buck, *Shadows on My Heart*, 55–56; *OR*, ser. 2, vol. 6, p. 776.

35. Jones, *Reminiscences of the Twenty-second Iowa*, 47; Culver, "*Your Affectionate Husband*," 153, 184; Shepherd, *To Rescue My Native Land*, 245–55.

36. Trumbull, *War Memories of a Chaplain*, 17; Haines, *Fifteenth New Jersey*, 104; Hight, *Fifty-Eighth Indiana*, 445; Blanchard, *I Marched with Sherman*, 107; McDonald, *A Woman's Civil War*, 134–35; Chadick, *Incidents of the War*, 255.

37. Bucke et al., *History of American Methodism*, 2:248–50; Clark, *Matthew Simpson*, 230–33; *Christian Advocate and Journal* (New York), December 20, 1863; Clinton B. Fisk to Matthew Simpson, October 29, 1863, Simpson Collection, Methodist Collection, Drew; "Reoccupation of Southern Territory by the Church," *Ladies' Repository* 22 (June 1862): 383–84; "The Church Marching Southward," ibid. 24 (January 1864): 64.

38. Morrow, *Northern Methodism and Reconstruction*, 20–25, 29–32; Sweet, *Methodist Episcopal Church and Civil War*, 96–100.

39. McPherson, *Political History of the United States*, 521, 523–24; Morrow, *Northern Methodism and Reconstruction*, 33–42; December 1863–January 1864, Ames Papers, Drew; Hight, *Fifty-Eighth Indiana*, 275–76; Stowell, *Rebuilding Zion*, 29–30; A. Cummings to Matthew Simpson, April 26, 1864, Simpson Collection, Methodist Collection, Drew.

40. *Evangelist* (New York), December 24, 1863; *Christian Advocate and Journal* (New York), February 11, 1864; Jones, *Sectional Crisis and Northern Methodism*, 44–45; Mordecai J. W. Ambrose to Abraham Lincoln, February 2, 1864, John Hogan to Lincoln, February 13, 1864, Lincoln Papers, LC; Bates, *Diary of Edward Bates*, 351; Lincoln, *Collected Works*, 7:178–79, 182–83.

41. Moss, *Annals of the Christian Commission*, 459, 513; M. J. Cramer to Matthew Simpson, April 25, June 14, July 29, 1864, Samuel D. Baldwin to Andrew Johnson, June 9, 1864, Matthew Simpson Collection, Methodist Collection, Drew; Johnson, *Papers of Andrew Johnson*, 7:369–71, 426–27; Kirby, "McKendree Chapel Affair," 360–70. Three years later Simpson would strongly support Johnson's impeachment.

42. Vander Velde, *Presbyterian Churches and Federal Union*, 458–67; *Evangelist* (New York), July 14, 1864, March 2, 1865.

43. Stowell, *Rebuilding Zion*, 27–28; McPherson, *Political History of the United States*, 521; Baker, *Relations between Northern and Southern Baptists*, 88–89.

44. Smith, *Cross and Flame*, 153–55; Walker, *Rock in a Weary Land*, 43–94; *Christian Advocate and Journal* (New York), April 14, 1864.

45. *Evangelist* (New York), July 30, 1863, December 29, 1864; Kinsley, *Diary of a Christian Soldier*, 153.

46. Lyman Abbott, "Southern Evangelization," *New Englander* 23 (October 1864): 699–708; Armstrong, *Letters from a Pennsylvania Chaplain*, 25; Stowell, *Rebuilding Zion*, 54–57; *American Union Commission*, 5–25.

47. Stone, *Work of New England in the Future of Our Country*, 41–45; Hough, *Our Country's*

Mission, 15–23; *Independent* (New York), December 22, 1864; Marshall, *The Nation's Changes*, 24–25; Hall, *Moral Significance of the Contrasts between Slavery and Freedom*, 15; J. P. Thompson, "The Advancement of Christ's Kingdom by War," *New Englander* 24 (April 1865): 303–18.

Chapter 18

1. Morrow, "Methodists and 'Butternuts,'" 34; Asahel Moore to Abraham Lincoln, April 28, 1864, Lincoln Papers, LC.

2. McPherson, *Political History of the United States*, 497–99.

3. Bucke et al., *History of American Methodism*, 2:214–16; Lincoln, *Collected Works*, 7:350–51; Morrow, *Northern Methodism and Reconstruction*, 15–16.

4. Howard, *Religion and Radical Republican Movement*, 74–75; McPherson, *Political History of the United States*, 465–66, 471–72, 479–80, 493; Street, *Sermon Preached in the Presbyterian Church, York, Pa.*, 3–7; November 26, December 20, 1863, Jonathan Palmer Finley Diary, PHS-P.

5. *New York Freeman's Journal and Catholic Register*, June 18, 1864; B. B. E. to James A. McMaster, May 31, 1864, McMaster Papers, Notre Dame; *New York Tablet*, January 30, 1864; John Purcell to Peter Paul Lefevere, February 19, 1864, Catholic Church Diocese of Detroit Papers, Notre Dame; Haven, *National Sermons*, 439–73; *Independent* (New York), January 28, 1864.

6. Stone, *National Godliness*, 3–8; Boardman, *Sovereignty of God*, 21–25; Stewart, *Southern Rebellion a Failure*, 5–8; Harris and Niflot, *Dear Sister*, 118.

7. Foster, *Moral Reconstruction*, 21–23; Glasgow, *History of the Reformed Presbyterian Church in America*, 130–31; McPherson, *Political History of United States*, 259.

8. Sunderland, *Sermon on the Public Worship of God*, 3–15; *German Reformed Messenger* (Chambersburg, Pa.), December 10, 1862, May 20, 1863; Sloane, *Three Pillars of the Republic*, 13–17; Stout, *Upon the Altar of the Nation*, 373; *Zion's Herald and Wesleyan Journal* (Boston) June 24, 1863; *Christian Recorder* (Philadelphia), November 26, 1864.

9. *Charleston Daily Courier*, November 15, 1864; Owen, *Sacred Flame of Love*, 100–1; Pierce, *Sermons of Bishop Pierce and Rev. B. M. Palmer*, 7–14, 21–35.

10. Downing, *Downing's Civil War Diary*, 201; Ritner and Ritner, *Love and Valor*, 338; Coe, *Mine Eyes Have Seen the Glory*, 131, 154.

11. Harris and Niflot, *Dear Sister*, 139; Geary, *A Politician Goes to War*, 199; Otto, *Memoirs of a Dutch Mudsill*, 283.

12. Bennett, *Narrative of the Great Revival*, 378–79, 383–87, 392; Cate, *Two Soldiers*, 115; Wright, *Sixth Iowa*, 316; Woodworth, *While God Is Marching On*, 242.

13. May 26, June 17, 1864, Zillah Haynie Brandon Diary, ADAH; McClatchey, "A Georgia Woman's Civil War Diary," 204; Baptist Church, Mississippi, Strong River Baptist Association, *Minutes of the Twelfth Annual Meeting*, 4; Beringer et al., *Why The South Lost the Civil War*, 271, 351.

14. Leeke, *A Hundred Days to Richmond*, 170; J. J. D. Renfroe, "The Resurrection of the Confederate Soldier," Renfroe manuscript sermons, SBHLA; *Christian Recorder* (Philadelphia), August 20, 1864; McClatchey, "A Georgia Woman's Civil War Diary," 211.

15. Jones, *Under the Stars and Bars*, 232–33; Baptist Church, South Carolina, State Convention, *Minutes of the 43rd and 44th Anniversaries*, 200–201; Axford, *"To Lochaber Na Mair,"* 133.

16. McKim, *A Soldier's Recollections*, 221; Bennett, *Narrative of the Great Revival*, 414; Turbo, *Twenty-seventh Arkansas*, 208; Johansson, *28th Texas Cavalry*, 133–34. Steven Woodworth has

argued the army revivals were unprecedented and that there was really one large revival rather than a series of revivals. Woodworth emphasizes the relatively large number of converts but even then a vast majority of soldiers may have been largely unaffected by these meetings. Woodworth, *While God Is Marching On*, 245–46.

17. Shattuck, *Shield and Hiding Place*, 88; McAllister, *Letters of Robert McAllister*, 459, 563–64; United States Christian Commission, *Information for Army Meetings* (November 1864): 12–13; Owen, "*Dear Friends at Home*," 71; Adams, *Memorial and Letters of Rev. John R. Adams*, 198, 206–8.

18. Gage, *From Vicksburg to Raleigh*, 249–50; Hight, *Fifty-eighth Indiana*, 404.

19. Adams, *Memorial and Letters of Rev. John R. Adams*, 167; United States Christian Commission, *Information for Army Meetings* (October 1864): 23; Stillwell, *Stillwell Letters*, 271; J. J. D. Renfroe, "Bitter Waters Made Sweet," Renfroe manuscript sermons, SBHLA.

20. Vincent, *Lord of War and Righteousness*, 30–34; Ritner and Ritner, *Love and Valor*, 335; Glatthaar, *March to the Sea and Beyond*, 40, 174.

21. Jones, *Christ in the Camp*, 257–58; Blackburn, *Life Work of John L. Girardeau*, 118; Bennett, *Narrative of the Great Revival*, 389–90.

22. Huckaby and Simpson, *Tulip Evermore*, 45; Wiatt, *Confederate Chaplain William Edward Wiatt*, 206; Bennett, *Narrative of the Great Revival*, 384; November 19, 1864, Nancy Emerson Diary, UVa; Kerby, *Kirby Smith's Confederacy*, 395–96.

23. Osborne, *Jubal*, 385; Lane, "*Dear Mother: Don't grieve about me*," 314–15.

24. Phillips, *Diehard Rebels*, 29–30; Gallagher, *Confederate War*, 50–53; Fellman, *Making of Robert E. Lee*, 177–83; Eggleston, *A Rebel's Recollections*, 177–79.

25. Mitchell, *Civil War Soldiers*, 187; *Christian Recorder* (Philadelphia), September 17, 1864; McCain, *In Song and Sorrow*, 180–81.

26. Lincoln, *Collected Works*, 7:431–32; *Evangelist* (New York), July 28, August 10, 1864; Hill, *Strength in the Time of Trial*, 5–12; *Christian Advocate and Journal* (New York), July 14, August 11, 1864.

27. *New York Tablet*, August 13, 1864; Grimes, *Nation's Last Hope*, 5–20; Hight, *Fifty-eighth Indiana*, 355.

28. Scott, "'A Visitation of God,'" 241–44; Woodworth, *While God Is Marching On*, 261–64; *Friend* (Philadelphia), August 13, October 8, 1864.

29. Nutting, *Three Lessons for the War*, 3–16; Rolfs, *No Peace for the Wicked*, 118; *Christian Recorder* (Philadelphia), July 9, 1864; *Evangelist* (New York), July 7, 1864.

30. *Zion's Herald and Wesleyan Journal* (Boston), August 10, 24, 1864; *Christian Advocate and Journal* (New York), August 25, 1864; Haven, *National Sermons*, 407–20.

31. McGuire, *Diary of a Southern Refugee*, 282–83; Fain, *Sanctified Trial*, 207–8; Welborn Mooney to Sue F. Mooney, December 12, 1864, Mooney Correspondence, in possession of John Grammer, Sewanee, Tennessee. A German Reformed editor, whose Chambersburg printing establishment had been destroyed in the fire, sadly noted that "Providence has changed our locality." *German Reformed Messenger* (Philadelphia), September 7, 1864.

32. Bennett, *Narrative of the Great Revival*, 408; Woodworth, *While God Is Marching On*, 243–44; Ash, *When the Yankees Came*, 221; Elliott, *Funeral Services at the Burial of the Right Rev. Leonidas Polk*, 26; Taylor et al., *Leverett Letters*, 355.

33. Lane, "*Dear Mother: Don't grieve about me*," 312; Breckinridge, *Lucy Breckinridge of Grove Hill*, 188–89; Baptist Church, Georgia, Lower Canoochee Association, *Minutes, 1864*, 4–5.

34. Baptist Church, South Carolina, Charleston Baptist Association, *Minutes of the 111th, 112th and 113th Sessions*, 43–44; Presbyterian Church, Synod of Virginia, *Minutes, 1864*, 361–62; Burrows, *Nationality Insured!*, 7–8; Taylor et al., *Leverett Letters*, 312.

35. Elliott, *Vain Is the Help of Man*, 3–13.

36. United Daughters of the Confederacy, South Carolina Division, *Recollections and Reminiscences*, 2:244; Mallory, *"Fear God and Walk Humbly,"* 340; *Charleston Mercury*, October 11, 1864; *Christian Index* (Macon, Ga.), July 29, 1864.

37. *Charleston Mercury*, November 16, 1864; Minnigerode, *Power: A Sermon Preached at St. Paul's Church, Richmond*, 3–20; Davis, *Messages and Papers of Davis*, 1:564–65.

38. Cate, *Two Soldiers*, 150; Manly, "Diary of Basil Manly," 69; Quintard, *Doctor Quintard, Chaplain, C.S.A.*, 176–77; *Christian Index* (Macon, Ga.), September 16, 1864.

39. United Daughters of the Confederacy, South Carolina Division, *Recollections and Reminiscences*, 2:340; Stowell, *Rebuilding Zion*, 36–7; Cross, *Camp and Field*, 3:156–88; *Christian Observer* (Richmond), August 11, 1864; Whitaker, *Richard Hooker Wilmer*, 119–20; Taylor et al., *Leverett Letters*, 364; Taylor, *Lee's Adjutant*, 171.

40. Green, *Journal of a Milledgeville Girl*, 67; July 22, 1864, William King Diary, SHC; Whites, *Civil War as a Crisis in Gender*, 103.

41. Burrows, *Nationality Insured!*, 3–6; Lutheran Church, North Carolina Synod, *Minutes of the Sixty-first Annual Convention*, 5; Cross, *Camp and Field*, 3:360–90; Lutheran Church, Western Virginia Synod, *Minutes of the 22nd and 23rd Sessions*, 21.

42. Manson, *A Spiritual Diary*, 15; Cate, *Two Soldiers*, 156–57; *Christian Index* (Macon, Ga.), July 8, 1864. For a good discussion of the growing emphasis on spiritual victories, see Shattuck, *Shield and Hiding Place*, 108–9.

43. Marszalek, *Sherman*, 41, 49; Sherman, *Sherman's Civil War*, 267, 624; Fellman, *Citizen Sherman*, 120. I have greatly benefited from the penetrating (albeit contradictory) analyses of Sherman's religious views in Royster, *Destructive War*, 269–71, and Bower, "Theology of the Battlefield," 1005–34.

44. Woodworth, *While God Is Marching On*, 249–52; Geary, *A Politician Goes to War*, 217.

45. October 30, 1864, Zillah Haynie Brandon Diary, ADAH; Burge, *Diary of Dolly Lunt Burge*, 153; Myers, *Children of Pride*, 1227–28, 1233, 1236.

46. McClatchey, "A Georgia Woman's Civil War Diary," 207; Burge, *Diary of Dolly Lunt Burge*, 162; Myers, *Children of Pride*, 1234; Taylor et al., *Leverett Letters*, 376–77; Green, *Journal of a Milledgeville Girl*, 65.

47. Gannon, *Rebel Bishop*, 108; Glatthaar, *March to the Sea and Beyond*, 93; Hight, *Fifty-eighth Indiana*, 443; December 25, 1864, Cornelius C. Platter Diary, University of Georgia. For a provocative interpretation that emphasizes continued defiance, see Campbell, *When Sherman Marched North from the Sea*.

48. Elmore, *Heritage of Woe*, 71.

Chapter 19

1. McPherson, *Political History of the United States*, 502; Lincoln, *Collected Works*, 7:753–54.

2. *Evangelist* (New York), September 8, 1864; Thompson, *Peace through Victory*, 1–6.

3. Howard, *Religion and Radical Republican Movement*, 84–89; Hitchcock, *Thanksgiving for Victories*, 2; Cleaveland, *Patriot's Song of Victory*, 3–14. Even a sermon that repeatedly talked of

"blood" and "blood sacrifice" sounded almost bloodless. "Let us envy them the way of their death," Cyrus Augustus Bartol spoke of the men killed in battle. Bartol, *Purchase by Blood*, 3–12.

4. Lincoln, *Collected Works*, 7:536; *Friend* (Philadelphia), October 22, 1864; Wright, *Conscientious Objectors in the Civil War*, 87–88. Among the Old School Presbyterians there were still some prominent holdouts, such as Henry J. Van Dyke, who deplored the General Assembly's "political" actions while appearing sympathetic to southern slaveholders. Van Dyke, *Spirituality and Independence of the Church*, 4–40.

5. Baptist Church, Indiana, Madison Association, *Minutes of the Thirty-sixth Annual Meeting*, 6; George H. Hepworth to Abraham Lincoln, October 24, 1864, Lincoln Papers, LC.

6. Townsend, *Speech by Dr. S. P. Townsend*, 8–9. I have greatly relied on the excellent treatment of these questions in Carwardine, *Lincoln*, 290–91, 296–98.

7. McPherson, *Political History of the United States*, 481–82; Methodist Church, Indiana, North Indiana Conference, *Minutes of the Twenty-first Session*, 34–35; *Independent* (New York), October 27, 1864.

8. *Christian Inquirer* (New York), October 15, 1864; *Christian Advocate and Journal* (New York), August 25, 1864.

9. Myer S. Isaacs to Abraham Lincoln, October 26, 1864, Timothy F. Neville to Lincoln, June 16, 1864, Lincoln Papers, LC; *New York Tablet*, September 24, November 19, 1864; *New York Freeman's Journal and Catholic Register*, November 5, 1864; *Evangelist* (New York), October 27, 1864.

10. *German Reformed Messenger* (Chambersburg, Pa.), July 27, December 14, 1864; November 8, 1864, Jonathan Palmer Finley Diary, PHS-P; "Ought the War to Go On?," *Monthly Religious Magazine* 32 (October 1864): 205–11; Ewer, *A Rector's Reply to Sundry Requests and Demands for a Political Sermon*, 3–23.

11. This seemingly dramatic endorsement of civil religion and departure from Jeffersonian traditions came at the initiative of Secretary of the Treasury Chase with little discussion or fanfare. ⟨http://www.treas.gov/education/fact-sheets/currency/in-god-we-trust.shtml⟩. There was hardly any editorial comment. One writer did express hope that the change would "augur deliverance from the troubles that beset us, the vindication of outraged laws, the Union of disserved fragments, the return of peace to our distracted land, the integrity of the Republic." "The Esthetics of the Root of All Evil," *Continental Monthly* 6 (December 1864): 684.

12. *Christian Advocate and Journal* (New York), October 13, 1864; Chesebrough, *God Ordained This War*, 103–22; *Evangelist* (New York), October 20, 1864; Boardman, *Civil Government, a Divine Ordinance*, 5–28.

13. Mears, *Life of Edward Norris Kirk*, 307–8; *Independent* (New York), October 20, November 3, 1864; Daly, *Diary of a Union Lady*, 313; Clark, *Life of Matthew Simpson*, 236–43; McKay Edgar Conkling to Matthew Simpson, September 20, 1864, Charles Butlers to Simpson, November 20, 1864, Simpson Collection, Methodist Collection, Drew.

14. *Zion's Herald and Wesleyan Journal* (Boston), September 7, 1864; *Independent* (New York), September 8, 1864; Peck, *Our Country: Its Trials and Its Triumph*, 169–86; *Christian Advocate and Journal* (New York), September 8, 1864; "The Presidential Election," *Ladies' Repository* 24 (November 1864): 702–4.

15. Fletcher, *Diary of Calvin Fletcher*, 8:448; Carey, *Conflict and the Victory*, 3–15.

16. Squier, *This Wilderness of War*, 78–79, 89; Carey, *Conflict and the Victory*, 6; Bennitt, *"I Hope to Do My Country Service,"* 313; August 29, 1864, Francis R. Stewart Diary, Bowling Green State University.

17. *Christian Recorder* (Philadelphia), December 10, 1864; Phelps, *Military Power a Blessing*, 29. For an unusually conciliatory sermon noting "honest and high-souled patriots and Christian men on both sides of this party issue" and calling for a magnanimous southern policy, see Ellis, *Nation's Ballot and Its Decision*, 3–18.

18. Carpenter, *Inner Life of Abraham Lincoln*, 231; *Zion's Herald and Wesleyan Journal* (Boston) November 16, 1864; Stebbins, *The President, the People, and the War*, 5–22.

19. *Christian Advocate and Journal* (New York), November 17, 24, 1864; Aspey, *Causes for National Thanksgiving*, 5–11; Carwardine, *Lincoln*, 307–8.

20. *Newark (Ohio) Advocate*, November 20, 1863; Stout, *Upon the Altar of the Nation*, 387; Lincoln, *Collected Works*, 8:55–56; *Christian Recorder* (Philadelphia), November 26, 1864; Temple, *Abraham Lincoln: From Skeptic to Prophet*, 278, 280.

21. Wilson, *Themes for Thanksgiving*, 3–19; Agnew, *Thanksgiving Sermon, Preached in the Presbyterian Church at Johnstown, Pa.*, 6; Johnson, *Banners of a Free People Set Up in the Name of Their God*, 18–34.

22. West, *Victory and Gratitude*, 3–28; Vincent, *Lord of War and Righteousness*, 5–18.

23. Little, *Relation of the Citizen to the Government*, 3–14; Bingham, *Great Providences toward the Loyal Part of This Nation*, 47.

24. Wadsworth, *War a Discipline*, 22; Smith, *Past Mercies: Present Gratitude: Future Duty*, 15–16; Chesebrough, *God Ordained This War*, 122; Post, *Palingenesy: National Regeneration*, 5–17.

25. Hundley, *Prison Echoes of the Great Rebellion*, 185–87.

26. Chambers, *Diary of Captain Henry A. Chambers*, 235–36; Berkeley, *Four Years in the Confederate Artillery*, 113; Burge, *Diary of Dolly Lunt Burge*, 166–67; Elmore, *Heritage of Woe*, 84–85.

27. Lee, *Memoirs of William Nelson Pendleton*, 384–85; Blitch, *"Thy Kingdom Come,"* 3–15; Huckaby and Simpson, *Tulip Evermore*, 51–52.

28. *Resolutions of Forsberg's Brigade, Wharton's Division*; Berkeley, *Four Years in the Confederate Artillery*, 117; Wiatt, *Confederate Chaplain William Edward Wiatt*, 222.

29. Heartsill, *Fourteen Hundred and 91 Days in the Confederate Army*, 232; McGuire, *Diary of a Southern Refugee*, 332; Phil H. Gully to his son, April 9, 1865, Soldier Letters Collection, Museum of the Confederacy; Spencer, *My Dear Friend*, 172.

30. Elmore, *Heritage of Woe*, 81–82, 99, 103, 106.

31. House, *A Very Violent Rebel*, 149; *Christian Index* (Macon, Ga.), March 30, 1865; Luker, *Southern Tradition in Theology and Social Criticism*, 150–51; Gray, "Diary of Virginia Davis Gray," 165.

32. *Christian Index* (Macon, Ga.), January 12, 26, March 9, 1865; Holmes, *Diary of Emma Holmes*, 406; *Christian Observer* (Richmond), January 12, 1865; John Blair Dabney, sermon, March 10, 1865, Saunders Family Papers, VHS.

33. Bennett, *Narrative of the Great Revival*, 420–21; United Daughters of the Confederacy, South Carolina Division, *Recollections and Reminiscences*, 2:150–51; William J. Pegram to Virginia Johnson McIntosh, March 10, 1865, Pegram-Johnson-McIntosh Papers, VHS; Smith, *Confederate Diary of Robert D. Smith*, 170; Welton, *"My Heart Is So Rebellious,"* 255; John Blair Dabney, sermon, March 10, 1865, Saunders Family Papers, VHS.

34. Chesnut, *Mary Chesnut's Civil War*, 733; Fain, *Sanctified Trial*, 310; John Blair Dabney, sermon, March 10, 1865, Saunders Family Papers, VHS; *Christian Observer* (Richmond), March 30, 1865; Hildebrand, *Times Were Strange and Stirring*, 8; Spencer, *My Dear Friend*, 183; Manson, *Spiritual Diary*, 29; Berkley, *Four Years in the Confederate Artillery*, 116; Elmore, *Heritage of Woe*, 108.

35. J. Williams to H. W. Williams, April 3, 1865, Soldier Letters Collection, Museum of the Confederacy; Clark, *Papers of Walter Clark*, 1:135; Beringer et al., *Why the South Lost the Civil War*, 352; Harris, *Piedmont Farmer*, 355; Mitchell, *Civil War Soldiers*, 188.

36. Edmondston, *"Journal of a Secesh Lady,"* 653; Winter, *Civil War Women*, 75; Silver, *Confederate Morale and Church Propaganda*, 54–55; Alexander, *Fighting for the Confederacy*, 501–2.

37. Phillips, *Diehard Rebels*, 36–39, 160; Beringer et al., *Why the South Lost the Civil War*, 352; Hubbs, *Voices from Company D*, 345.

38. Davis, *Messages and Papers of Davis*, 1:567–68; *Richmond Daily Dispatch*, March 6, 9, 1865; Jones, *Rebel War Clerk's Diary*, 2:444.

39. Chambers, *Blood and Sacrifice*, 206–7; Chambers, *Diary of Henry A. Chambers*, 249; Duke, *Reminiscences of General Basil W. Duke*, 418–19; Dougan, *Confederate Arkansas*, 114.

40. John Blair Dabney, sermon, March 10, 1865, Saunders Family Papers, VHS; *Christian Observer* (Richmond), March 9, 1865; Woodworth, *While God Is Marching On*, 283–84; McKim, *A Soldier's Recollections*, 251–53; Cate, *Two Soldiers*, 200.

41. *Christian Index* (Macon, Ga.), April 13, 1865; April 7, 1865, Mary Hort Journal, South Caroliniana Library.

42. Ingram, *Civil War Letters of George W. and Martha F. Ingram*, 80, 82; Robertson, *Life and Letters of John Albert Broadus*, 211.

43. For a recent overview that presents a damning indictment of Union and Confederate officials, see Sanders, *While in the Hands of the Enemy*.

44. Dunham, *Attitude of Northern Clergy toward the South*, 150–56; Babbitt, *A Sermon on the Death of Walter L. Raymond*, 3–31; Cumming, *Journal of a Confederate Nurse*, 38.

45. A Churchman, *Cruelties of War*, 3–25; Elmore, *Heritage of Woe*, 79–80; *Christian Recorder* (Philadelphia), July 9, 1864.

46. McCain, *In Song and Sorrow*, 56–57; Trumbull, *War Memories of a Chaplain*, 77–79; Sheeran, *Confederate Chaplain*, 112–44; White, *Prison Life among the Rebels*, 55.

47. May 29, June 19, 1864, Henry W. Tisdale Diary, ⟨http://civilwardiary.net⟩; United States Christian Commission, *Information for Army Meetings* (November 1864): 8–9; Genoways and Genoways, *A Perfect Picture of Hell*, 82; Parker, *Twenty-second Massachusetts*, 147.

48. Small, *Road to Richmond*, 262; White, *Prison Life among the Rebels*, 25–26; Marvel, *Andersonville*, 139–40; Gray, *Business of Captivity*, 88, 112. Gerald Linderman has argued that prison life virtually destroyed religious sensibilities, and Steven Woodworth has strongly disagreed. What appears to have been the case was that the entire experience could either strengthen or destroy faith, depending on the men involved and their experiences. In the prisons as in the army camps, the pious were in the minority—albeit a fairly substantial minority. Linderman, *Embattled Courage*, 259; Woodworth, *While God Is Marching On*, 75.

49. Bristol, *Life of Chaplain McCabe*, 80–98, 104; Beaudry, *War Journal*, 58–60; *History of the Thirty-fifth Massachusetts*, 379; Domschcke, *Twenty Months in Captivity*, 44–45; White, *Prison Life among the Rebels*, 24; Cavada, *Libby Life*, 50–51.

50. Kellogg, *Life and Death in Rebel Prisons*, 180–81; *Christian Advocate and Journal* (New York), March 2, 1865; Patterson, *Yankee Rebel*, 151–52.

51. Patterson, *Yankee Rebel*, 162, 165; Inzer, *Diary of a Confederate Soldier*, 63, 65, 66.

52. Domschcke, *Twenty Months in Captivity*, 85; Genoways and Genoways, *A Perfect Picture of Hell*, 72; Adams, *Reminiscences of the Nineteenth Massachusetts*, 118–19.

53. Heffley and Heffley, *Civil War Diaries*, 68; Sheeran, *Confederate Chaplain*, 31, 102–3, 105–6; Domschcke, *Twenty Months in Captivity*, 50–51; Kellogg, *Life and Death in Rebel Prisons*, 163–64; Futch, *History of Andersonville Prison*, 59–60.

54. Futch, *History of Andersonville Prison*, 60–61; *New York Herald*, February 21, 1865; Bennett, *Narrative of the Great Revival*, 409–10.

55. Burgwyn, *A Captain's War*, 157; [Keily], *Prisoner of War*, 95–97; Gray, *Business of Captivity*, 111–13; *OR*, ser. 2, vol. 3, p. 362, vol. 4, p. 423; Levy, *To Die in Chicago*, 39.

56. Patterson, *Yankee Rebel*, 158–59.

Chapter 20

1. Lincoln, *Collected Works*, 5:403–4. Lincoln's secretaries and most Lincoln scholars have maintained that the undated Meditation on the Divine Will was written sometime in the late summer or early fall of 1862, but Douglas Wilson has offered an ingenious and convincing argument for 1864. Wilson, *Lincoln's Sword*, 254–56, 329–30.

2. Lincoln, *Collected Works*, 7:281–82. For penetrating analyses of this letter to Albert G. Hodges, see Wilson, *Lincoln's Sword*, 249–53; White, *Lincoln's Greatest Speech*, 97–99.

3. Lincoln, *Collected Works*, 7:287, 368, 542–43. Lincoln's clerical supporters were far from being on the same theological page. In their view, the Lord would judge the rebels and judge them severely. As one northern Methodist described the capture of Charleston, South Carolina, in February 1865, "Here and now the vial [of wrath] is poured forth on the seat of the beast." Haven, *National Sermons*, 519.

4. Lincoln, *Collected Works*, 7:535. For a most illuminating account of Lincoln's evolving views on these questions, see Wilson, *Lincoln's Sword*, 253–63.

5. The place to begin exploring the "theology" of the second inaugural is the thoughtful, penetrating, and complex treatment in Noll, *America's God*, 426–38. For a fuller and equally valuable analysis, see Miller, *President Lincoln*, 396–416.

6. For the full text, see Lincoln, *Collected Works*, 8:332–33.

7. Douglas Wilson has described the paragraphs that followed as a "prose poem" and emphasizes how Lincoln developed a complex approach to theological questions and one that raised his writing to "successively higher levels." Wilson, *Lincoln's Sword*, 266–76.

8. On the relationship between providence, sovereignty, and judgment, see Niebuhr, *Faith and History*, 102–19; Butterfield, *Christianity and History*, 73; Guelzo, *Abraham Lincoln: Redeemer President*, 414–21.

9. For still useful discussions of the human tendency to confuse human will with divine will, including pretensions to both great knowledge and righteous judgment along with a belief in the ability to control events, see Niebuhr, *Faith and History*, 120–25; Butterfield, *Christianity and History*, 104.

10. In the Second Inaugural, by Ronald C. White's count, Lincoln quoted or paraphrased the Bible four times, referred to God fourteen times, and mentioned prayer three times. "Lin-

coln's Sermon on the Mount: The Second Inaugural," in Miller et al., *Religion and the American Civil War*, 211–12.

11. Lincoln, *Collected Works*, 8:356.

12. Adams, *Memorial and Letters of Rev. John R. Adams*, 210; Scott, "'A Visitation of God,'" 264–65; *Independent* (New York), March 9, 1865. Harry Stout has pointed out that the northern religious press paid more attention to Andrew Johnson's drunken harangue when he had been sworn in as vice president earlier that same day. Stout, *Upon the Altar of the Nation*, 428.

13. White, *Lincoln's Greatest Speech*, 199.

14. Leech, *Reveille in Washington*, 379; Leavitt, *A Sermon Preached April 9, 1865*, 3–18; April 4, 1865, New York Third Presbytery Minute Book, PHS-P; Jones, *Give God the Glory*, 126; April 3, 1865, Philadelphia Presbytery Minute Book, PHS-P.

15. Fletcher, *Diary of Calvin Fletcher*, 9:64; Paludan, *People's Contest*, 363; April 12, 1865, Carlisle (Pennsylvania) Presbytery Minute Book, PHS-P.

16. O'Connor, *Fitzpatrick's Boston*, 225; *German Reformed Messenger* (Philadelphia), April 12, 1865; Beecher, *Patriotic Addresses*, 676–97; Haven, *National Sermons*, 529–550; *Independent* (New York), April 6, 1865.

17. *Christian Advocate and Journal* (New York), April 27, 1865; Laurie, *Three Discourses*, 3–15; Bolster, *James Freeman Clarke*, 283–85.

18. Broadman, *The Peacemakers*, 5–31; Gordon, *Chosen Fast*, 3–12; *Zion's Herald and Wesleyan Journal* (Boston), April 12, 1865.

19. Gordon, *Chosen Fast*, 13.

20. Culver, "*Your Affectionate Husband, J. F. Culver,*" 435; McAllister, *Letters of Robert McAllister*, 611; Scott, "'A Visitation of God,'" 271; Chesebrough, *No Sorrow Like Our Sorrow*, xii–xxii. Chesebrough offers an invaluable guide to the sermon literature on the assassination; on broader public reaction, see Turner, *Beware the People Weeping*.

21. Hathaway, *A Discourse Occasioned by the Death of Lincoln*, 3–14; Sutphen, *Discourse on the Death of Lincoln*, 5–14; Robbins, *Discourse on the Death of Lincoln*, 5–14.

22. *Sermons Preached in Boston*, 251; Burdick, *Two Sermons for the Times*, pp. 3–5; Bush, *Death of President Lincoln*, 3–8; Boardman, *Death of President Lincoln*, 3–4.

23. *Our Martyr President*, 6–7, 86, 241–54; Winn, "Diary of Thomas Harwood," 58–59.

24. Fisk, *Hard Marching Every Day*, 323–24; Bennitt, "*I Hope to Do My Country Service,*" 368–69; Daggett, *Sermon on Death of Lincoln*, 12–16; "The Nation's Joy and Grief," *Ladies' Repository*, 25 (June 1865): 383.

25. Sutphen, *Discourse on the Death of Lincoln*, 16–17; Laurie, *Three Discourses*, 17–27; Tousey, *Discourse on the Death of Lincoln*, 3–15.

26. Silliman, *A New Canaan Private in the Civil War*, 100; *Our Martyr President*, 145–58 278; *Sermons Preached in Boston*, 37–39; Scott, "'A Visitation of God,'" 284–85; Gurley, *Voice of the Rod*, 5–10; Mayo, *Nation's Sacrifice*, 3.

27. Scott, "'A Visitation of God,'" 270–71; Johnston, *Sermon Delivered on Thursday, June 1st 1865*, 4; Johnson, "*God's Ways Unsearchable,*" 4.

28. "President Lincoln," *Princeton Review* 37 (July 1865): 436; *German Reformed Messenger* (Philadelphia), April 19, 1865. This all went a step too far for some ministers who rejected the idea that Booth could have possibly been an instrument of the divine will. As one Methodist true to the Arminian doctrines of his church observed, "There was no providence in his [Lin-

coln's] murder." Salisbury, *Sermon; Preached West Alexandria, Ohio*, 9–11; *Sermons Preached in Boston*, 295–305; Reed, *Discourse Delivered on the Occasion of the Funeral Obsequies of President Lincoln*, 10.

29. Reed, *Discourse Delivered on the Occasion of the Funeral Obsequies of President Lincoln*, 5–10; Booth, *Personal Forgiveness and Public Justice*, 3–23; *Our Martyr President*, 9–32.

30. Eddy, *The Martyr President*, 14–16; Sample, *Curtained Throne*, 17; *Our Martyr President*, 299–300; Steele, *Victory and Mourning*, 13–26.

31. Bogardus, *Sermon on the Death of Our Late President*, 3–16; Atwood, *In Memoriam. Discourses in Commemoration of Lincoln*, 19–31.

32. Eddy, *"The Martyr to Liberty,"* 9–19; Boardman, *Addresses Delivered in the Meeting-House*, 51–64; Glover, *Character of Lincoln*, 3–14; *Sermons Preached in Boston*, 325–34.

33. Baldridge, *The Martyr Prince*, 14; Rankin, *Moses and Joshua*, 10; Hornblower, *Sermon Occasioned by Assassination of Lincoln*, 10–11.

34. Macmillan, *Methodist Episcopal Church in Michigan*, 69; *Our Martyr President*, 66–84, 219–32; Crane, *Sermon on the Death of President Lincoln*, 7–9; Chesebrough, *God Ordained This War*, 137–38; Ray, *A Sermon: Preached before the United Congregations of Wyoming, N.Y.*, 3–18.

35. Yard, *Providential Significance of the Death of Lincoln*, 8; *Evangelist* (New York), April 20, 1865; *Sermons Preached in Boston*, 54–55; White, *Sermon Occasioned by the Assassination of Lincoln*, 11–12.

36. McCauley, *Character and Services of Lincoln*, 7–11; Daggett, *Sermon on Death of Lincoln*, 7–12; E. J. Y., "The Lesson of the Hour," *Monthly Religious Magazine* 33 (May 1865): 298–302; Mayo, *Nation's Sacrifice*, 15–28; Garrison, *Teachings of the Crisis*, 17–18.

37. Quint, *Three Sermons*, 17–18; Rankin, *Moses and Joshua*, 5–7; Korn, *American Jewry and Civil War*, 207–12; Seiss, *Assassinated President*, 3–20; Keeling, *Death of Moses*, 3–16; Blake, *Sermon on Services and Death of Lincoln*, 5–29; Edgar, *Three Sermons*, 9–13; Prime, *Sermon Delivered in Westminster Church*, 3–16. For a few comparisons of Lincoln to Moses in secular newspapers, see *Coshocton (Ohio) Democrat*, May 3, 1865; *Burlington (Iowa) Weekly Hawkeye*, April 22, 29, 1865.

38. Sprague, *President Lincoln's Death*, 6–9; "The Nation's Triumph and Its Sacrifice," *Christian Examiner* 78 (May 1865): 430–43; Hawks, *Woman Doctor's Civil War*, 133–34; Atwood, *In Memoriam. Discourse in Commemoration of Lincoln*, 3–15.

39. Timlow, *Discourse Occasioned by the Death of Lincoln*, 30–32; Billingsley, *From the Flag to the Cross*, 298; Slater, *Nation's Loss*, 11–20; Robbins, *Discourse on Death of Lincoln*, 14. Allen Guelzo has wisely pointed how the people who most wanted to "Christianize" Lincoln never "penetrated to the real heart of Lincoln's personal religious anguish." Guelzo, *Lincoln: Redeemer President*, 446.

40. Steele, *Victory and Mourning*, 5–13; Sutphen, *Discourse on the Death of Lincoln*, 15–16; Robbins, *Discourse on Death of Lincoln*, 14–15; Fowler, *Character and Death of Lincoln*, 11.

41. Brakeman, *A Great Man Fallen*, 5–13; *Sermons Preached in Boston*, 81; Sutphen, *Discourse on the Death of Lincoln*, 14–15; *Friends' Review* (Philadelphia), April 29, 1865; Clark, *Memorial Sermon*, 5.

42. Blum, *Reforging the White Republic*, 21; Everett, *Sermon Preached in Commemoration of Lincoln*, 3–8; *Sermons Preached in Boston*, 91–96, 200–201; Blied, *Catholics and the Civil War*, 142–50; Dix, *Death of Lincoln*, 9–10; Daly, *Diary of a Union Lady*, 354–55.

43. Parker, *Discourse the Day after Reception of the Tidings of the Assassination of Lincoln*, 3;

Post, *Discourse on Assassination of Lincoln*, 2–3; Crane, *Sermon on the Death of Lincoln*, 6; Mooar, *Religion of Loyalty*, 19; Walden, *National Sacrifice*, 11–13, 20; Bushnell, *Vicarious Sacrifice*, especially 46–47, 105–26.

44. Morais, *Address on Death of Lincoln*, 6; Wilson, *Death of President Lincoln*, 22–23; Timlow, *Discourse Occasioned by the Death of Lincoln*, 35–39; *New York Freeman's Journal and Catholic Register*, April 22, 1865; *New York Tablet*, April 29, 1865.

45. Howlett, *Dealings of God with our Nation*, 6; Blackburn, *Crime against the Presidency*, 11–12; Crane, *Sermon on the Death of President Lincoln*, 14–16; Scott, "'A Visitation of God,'" 274–75.

46. Blake, *On Account of the Assassination of Lincoln*, 10; April 26, 1865, New York Second Presbytery (O.S.) Minute Book, PHS-P; Brooks, *Life and Death of Lincoln*, 9; DeNormandie, *The Lord Reigneth*, 4; Hornblower, *Sermon Occasioned by Assassination of Lincoln*, 13–14.

47. Colman, *Assassination of the President*, 5–6; *Our Martyr President*, 139; Duffield, *Nation's Wail*, 14–18. Duffield was referring to the rebellion and plague described in the sixteenth chapter of Numbers.

48. Reed, *Conflict of Truth*, 25–26; *Our Martyr President*, 122; Wentworth, *Discourse on Death of Lincoln*, 22–32; Butler, *Funeral Address on Death of Lincoln*, 25; Hornblower, *Sermon Occasioned by Assassination of Lincoln*, 3–6.

49. Armstrong, *Letters from a Pennsylvania Chaplain*, 28–29; Crane, *Sermon on the Death of President Lincoln*, 28–29; Sutphen, *Discourse on the Death of Lincoln*, 19; *New York Herald*, April 16, 1865; Howard, *Religion and Radical Republican Movement*, 94–95; April 20, 1865, New York Presbytery Minute Book, PHS-P; *Sermons Preached in Boston*, 227–32.

50. Burney, *A Southern Soldier's Letters Home*, 292; *New York Herald*, May 6, 1865; Marcus, *Memoirs of American Jews*, 3:366; Harrell, *When the Bells Tolled for Lincoln*, 36.

51. Burrows, *Palliative and Prejudiced Judgments Condemned*, 3–12; Harrell, *When the Bells Tolled for Lincoln*, 34, 45–46; Blum, *Reforging the White Republic*, 33; Elmore, *Heritage of Woe*, 117.

Epilogue

1. Krick, *Parker's Virginia Battery*, 328; Buck, *Shadows on My Heart*, 319; April 20, 1865, Sarah Lois Wadley Diary, SHC; McClatchey, "A Georgia Woman's Civil War Diary," 213–14; Wiatt, *Confederate Chaplain William Edward Wiatt*, 241–42; Hardin, *Private War of Lizzie Hardin*, 232; Stephens, *Recollections of Alexander H. Stephens*, 262.

2. House, *A Very Violent Rebel*, 162; Burney, *Southern Soldier's Letters Home*, 292; Lefler, "Thomas Atkinson, Third Bishop of North Carolina," 429; Dollar, *Soldiers of the Cross*, 177–223. On the staying power of Confederate civil religion, see Phillips, *Diehard Rebels*, 9–39.

3. Carter, *When the War Was Over*, 90; Jones, *Rebel War Clerk's Diary*, 2:473–74.

4. Green, *Journal of a Milledgeville Girl*, 73–74; Wiatt, *Confederate Chaplain William Edward Wiatt*, 237–38; July 30, 1865, Fannie Page Hume Diary, LC; Hardin, *Private War of Lizzie Hardin*, 242; April 25, 1865, Elizabeth Collier Diary, SHC. Collier's statement anticipated the rise of the Lost Cause that developed important religious themes as it transformed Confederates living and dead into crusading Christian heroes. Familiar notions of providence (though with much less emphasis on war and defeat as punishment for sin) became linked to the celebration of the three primary "martyrs": Lee, Jackson, and Davis. Despite the central importance of ministers such as J. William Jones in crafting this postwar narrative, religion was largely an append-

age to the Lost Cause, even though for some white southerners the Lost Cause itself took on a quasi-religious character. Wilson, *Baptized in Blood*, 7–57, 79–182. For a persuasive argument that deemphasizes the importance of civil religion in the Lost Cause, see Foster, *Ghosts of the Confederacy*, especially 7–8.

5. Schweiger, *Gospel Working Up*, 113; Ann Faulkner to her brother, June 12, 1865, Battle Family Papers, SHC; J. J. D. Renfroe, "Farewell to the Year 1865," Renfroe manuscript sermons, SBHLA; Walker, *Private Journal of Georgiana Gholson Walker*, 122.

6. Ryland, *Baptists in Virginia*, 302; Daniel, *Protestantism in the Confederacy*, 20–21; Mitchell, "Southern Methodist Newspapers during the Civil War," 37.

7. Bushnell, *Building Eras in Religion*, 326.

8. Fish, *Record of the First Baptist Church*, 3–32; Clebsch, *Christian Interpretations of the Civil War*, 11–14. More recently, in an unfailingly stimulating study, Edward J. Blum has shown how religion, and indeed a continuation of both wartime civil religion and millennialism, remained vitally important to public life and shaped debate on many important questions during the Gilded Age. I think there is much more to the story than conservatism, materialism, and "whiteness," but all students of postwar American religious history must wrestle with Blum's arguments. Blum, *Reforging the White Republic*. For more on black millennialism, see Blight, *Race and Reunion*, 319–24.

9. Fain, *Sanctified Trial*, 314, 358–59; Smith, *In His Image But*, 208–16; Genovese, *A Consuming Fire*, 101–4; *American Annual Cyclopaedia 1865*, 706.

10. Genovese, *A Consuming Fire*, 80–98; Fain, *Sanctified Trial*, 322, 344, 350–51.

11. *Christian Recorder* (Philadelphia), April 15, 1865.

12. The story of this complex and at times halting process is best told in Stowell, *Rebuilding Zion*, 80–99. See also Montgomery, *Under Their Own Vine and Fig Tree*, 52–57; Dvorak, *African-American Exodus*, 114–19, 138–43.

13. For an extended and often brilliant analysis of how this "emancipationist" memory was often eclipsed by "reconciliationist" and "Lost Cause" memory, much to the detriment of African Americans, see Blight, *Race and Reunion*.

14. Armstrong, *Friend to God's Poor*, 111–15; Litwack, *Been in the Storm So Long*, 456, 461–62; *Christian Recorder* (Philadelphia), April 8, 1865.

15. April 30, 1865, Carrie Hunter Diary, Cobb and Hunter Family Papers, SHC; Elmore, *Heritage of Woe*, 117–19, 123.

16. Hoge, *Moses Drury Hoge*, 235.

17. May 18, 1865, Abbie Brooks Diary, Atlanta History Center; Cumming, *Journal of a Confederate Nurse*, 307; Elliott, *Sermons*, 476–86; Carroll, *History of Texas Baptists*, 325–26.

18. Maddex, "From Theocracy to Spirituality," 448–53; Harry S. Stout and Christopher Grasso, "Civil War, Religion, and Communications: The Case of Richmond," in Miller et al., *Religion and American Civil War*, 348–49; White, *Rev. William S. White*, 197–98.

19. Jones, *Sectional Crisis and Northern Methodism*, 8–23, 33–44; Carter et al., *Historical Statistics of the United States*, 2:905–6, 909–11. See also *New York Times*, December 6, 1873.

20. Woodworth, *While God Is Marching On*, 294.

21. Bebbington, *Dominance of Evangelicalism*, 267; Cross, *Horace Bushnell*, 134–48; Paludan, *People's Contest*, 366–68; Webb, *Memorial Sermons*, 23–41. For a wide-ranging and penetrating examination of how Americans came to terms with what some termed a "harvest of death" in the Civil War, see Faust, *Republic of Suffering*.

22. Bushnell, *Building Eras in Religion*, 326; C. A. Blauvelt letter, October 15, 1876, Denning House Antiquarian Books, Catalog 291, May 2002; George M. Fredrickson, "The Coming of the Lord: The Northern Protestant Clergy and the Civil War Crisis," in Miller et al., *Religion and American Civil War*, 123–26.

23. For a brilliant and countervailing narrative about how a few intellectuals reacted against the role of fixed ideas and principles in bringing on the Civil War's vast carnage, see Menand, *Metaphysical Club*.

24. Menand, *Metaphysical Club*, 69.

25. Brinsfield, *Spirit Divided: Confederacy*, 271–73.

26. Ellinwood, *Return of the Victors*, 3–10; Thompson, *Memorial Service for Three Hundred Thousand Union Soldiers*, 25.

27. A partial exception is the striking but incomplete use of religion to reinforce the "loss of will" thesis in Beringer et al., *Why the South Lost the Civil War*.

28. Butterfield, *Christianity and History*, 24.

29. Hodgman, *Great Republic Judged*, 7–21.

30. LaSalle Corebell Pickett, "My Soldier," *McClure's Magazine* 30 (March 1908): 569.

BIBLIOGRAPHY

PRIMARY SOURCES

Manuscripts

Alabama Department of Archives and History, Montgomery
    Alabama Presbytery (Tuscaloosa County), Cumberland Presbyterian Church
        Minute Book
    Zillah Haynie Brandon Diary
    Branscomb Family Papers
    Centre Ridge Presbyterian Church (Dallas County) Minute Book
    Newton Davis Letters, Military Records Division
    Sarah R. Espy Diary
    Margaret Josephine Miles Gillis Diary
    Good Hope Baptist Church (Coosa County) Record Book
    Montgomery Station, Methodist Episcopal Church, South, Quarterly
        Conference Record
    Pea River Presbyterian Church (Barbour County) Session Book
    Ramah Baptist Church (Barbour County) Minute Book
    H. C. Reynolds Letters
    Frances Jane (Bestor) Robertson Diary
    James T. Searcy Letters
    James H. Simpson Collection
    Snow Hill Circuit, Methodist Episcopal Church, South, Quarterly
        Conference Minutes
    Thomas Warrick Letters
    Jake Weil Letter
American Antiquarian Society, Worcester, Massachusetts
    Civil War Papers
    John Francis Gleason Papers
    Abijah Marvin Sermons
    Minot Judson Savage Diary
    William Scandlin Diary
    Seth Sweetser Papers
American Baptist Historical Society, Rochester, New York
    Isaac W. Brinckherhoff, "Mission Work among the Freed Negroes. Beaufort,
        S. Carolina, St. Augustine, Florida, Savannah, Georgia, 1862–1874"
    Deer Creek (Miami County, Indiana) Regular Baptist Church Minute Book
    Huntington (Indiana) Baptist Association Minute Book
    Joanna Patterson Moore Papers
    Deborah B. Lapham Wade Letters
Atlanta History Center, Atlanta, Georgia
    Abbie Brooks Diary

Auburn University, Special Collections, Auburn, Alabama
    Emily S. York Papers
Bowling Green State University, Bowling Green, Ohio
    William T. Chapman Journals
    Francis R. Stewart Papers
College of William and Mary, Swem Library, Williamsburg, Virginia
    Cloe Whittle Diary
Connecticut Historical Society, Hartford
    Virgil W. Mattoon Papers
DePauw University, Greencastle, Indiana, Archives of DePauw University and Indiana
       United Methodism
    Elijah Evan Edwards Diary
    Methodist Church, Indiana
        Greencastle, Roberts Chapel Church Record, 1847–1876
        Indiana Conference, Evangelical Association Minutes, translated from German,
          typescripts.
     United Brethren in Christ. Indiana. White River Conference. "White River Annual
       Conference Minutes," August, 1862, August 1863, August 1864. Typescripts.
Drew University, Methodist Collection, Madison, New Jersey
    Edward Raymond Ames Papers
    James M. Campbell Letters
    George W. Farmer Papers
    Funkhouser Family Collection
    John Fletcher Hurst Papers
    Matthew Simpson Collection
Duke University, Special Collections, Perkins Library, Durham, North Carolina
    Alexander Brown Papers
    Clement C. Clay Papers
    John B. S. Dimitry Papers
    Lucy Muse Fletcher Diary
    Kate D. Foster Diary
    John Berkley Grimball Papers
    Henry St. George Harris
    Munford-Ellis Papers
    Samuel and Uriah N. Parmelee Papers
    Presley Person Papers
Emory University, Special Collections, Robert W. Woodruff Library, Atlanta
    Morgan Callaway Papers
    John M. Davidson Papers
    John Dobbins Papers
    Sue Richardson Diary
Fredericksburg and Spotsylvania National Military Park, Fredericksburg, Virginia
    Richard Irby Letters
    James Laird Letter

James T. McElvany Letter

E. P. Miller Diary

William M. Sheppard Letter

Anson B. Shuey Letter

Wiley C. Tunstall Letters

Georgia Department of Archives and History, Atlanta

Civil War Miscellany Collection

Louisa Warren Fletcher Diary

James A. Garrison Letters

Governors' Papers (Joseph E. Brown)

Francis Milton Kennedy Diary, United Daughters of the Confederacy transcripts

Cornelius C. Platter Diary

William R. Stillwell Letters

Historical Society of Pennsylvania, Philadelphia

Andrew Atkinson Humphreys Papers

Indiana Historical Society, Indianapolis

Chapin Family Papers

William N. Jackson Diary

Indiana State Library, Indianapolis

Henry C. Marsh Papers

Library of Congress, Washington, D.C.

William Franklin Draper Papers

Fannie Page Hume Diary

Abraham Lincoln Papers

Library of Virginia, Richmond

Battle Run Baptist Church (Rappahannock County) Minute Book

William F. Broaddus Diary

Buckingham Baptist Church (Buckingham County) Minute Book

George P. Clarke Diary

Elizabeth River Parish (Norfolk County) Vestry Book

Evans-Sibert Family Papers

General Order No. 46, March 23, 1863, Army of Northern Virginia

Governors' Papers (John Letcher)

Hopewell Monthly Meeting (Friends, Frederick County), Record Book

John F. Sale Letters-Diary

Sharon Baptist Church (Buckingham County) Minute Book

Shiloh Baptist Church (Charlotte County) Minute Book

Kate S. Sperry Diary

Mary C. A. Stribling Diary

Upper Gold Mine Baptist Church (Louisa County) Minute Book

Zion Hill Baptist Church (Botetourt County) Minute Book

Louisiana State University, Baton Rouge

John C. Burruss Family Papers

Anna and Sarah Butler Correspondence

Joseph A. Montgomery Papers

Anne Wilkinson Penrose Diary

Micajah Wilkson Papers

Maryland Historical Society, Baltimore

Briggs-Stabler Papers

Massachusetts Historical Society, Boston

Lucy Larcom Diaries, D. D. Addison Collection

Mississippi College, Clinton

Palestine Baptist Church Record, September 1856–June, 1936

Mississippi Department of Archives and History, Jackson

Anonymous Diary, Natchez

Mrs. Calvin Brown Papers

Elizabeth Norton DeHay Papers

Ann Hardeman Diary, Oscar J. E. Stuart Papers

Benjamin G. Humphreys Memoir

Irion-Neilson Papers

Myra Smith Diary, Eunice J. Stockwell Papers

Museum of the Confederacy, Richmond

Andrew Sydnor Barksdale Letters

B. T. Lacy Letter

John Quincy Adams Nadenbousch Letters

William H. Routt Papers

Sermon, "These the Beginnings of Sorrows" copy, William Birch Short Letters

Soldier Letters Collection

National Archives, Washington, D.C.

Letters Received by the Confederate Secretary of War, 1861–65, RG 109, Microcopy M437

North Carolina Department of Archives and History, Raleigh

Annie Darden Diary

Pearce Civil War Collection, Navarro College, Corsicana, Texas

Seth Gilbert Evans Letters

Presbyterian Historical Society, Montreat, North Carolina

Annie G. Baker Diary

Francis Bartlett Converse Papers

George Ewing Eagleton Papers

Hoge Family Papers

Abner Addison Porter Papers

Anna C. Safford Diary, Safford Family Papers

George William White Collection

Samuel B. Wilson Papers

Presbyterian Historical Society, Philadelphia

Alton (Illinois) Presbytery Minute Book

Henry Augustus Boardman Papers

Carlisle (Pennsylvania) Presbytery Minute Book

Cleveland (Ohio) Presbytery Minute Book

Jonathan Palmer Finley Diary
Galena and Belvidere (Illinois) Presbyteries Minute Book
Robert Wharton Landis Diary
New York Fourth Presbytery (N.S) Minute Book
New York Presbytery Minute Book
New York Second Presbytery (O.S.) Minute Book
New York Third Presbytery Minute Book
Philadelphia Presbytery Minute Book
Presbyterian Church in the U.S.A. Board of Missions for Freedmen Records
Princeton University Library, Manuscripts Division, Princeton, New Jersey
    Charles Hodge Papers
South Carolina Historical Society, Charleston
    Alexander Glennie Parish Diary
Southern Baptist Historical Library and Archives, Nashville, Tennessee
    Beaver Dam Baptist Church (Fountain City, Tenn.) Minute Book
    Bethesda Baptist Church (Hinds County, Mississippi) Minute Book
    Black Creek Baptist Church, (Dovesville, S.C.) Record Book
    Brier Creek Baptist Church (Wilkes Co. N.C.) Minutes
    Broadmouth Baptist Church (Abbeville, South Carolina) Minute Book
    Carmel Baptist Church (Caroline Co., Va., Hermon Association) Record Book
    Cashie Baptist Church (Windsor, N.C.) Record Book
    Cove Creek Baptist Church (Sherwood, Ashe County, North Carolina) Minute Book
    Eaton's Baptist Church (Mocksville, N.C.) Record Book
    First Baptist Church (Aiken, South Carolina) Minute Book
    First Baptist Church (Darlington, South Carolina) Minute Book
    First Baptist Church (Rome, Georgia) Minute Book
    First Baptist Church (Whitesburg, Tennessee, Nolachucky Association), Record Book
    Jersey Baptist Church (Liberty Association, Davidson County, North Carolina) Record
        Books
    Una Roberts Lawrence Papers
    Liberty Baptist Church (Appomattox, Va.) Minute Book
    Liberty Baptist Church (Jackson, Mississippi) Minute Book
    Manly Family Papers
    Mars Hill Baptist Church (Summit. Mississippi) Minute Book
    Mountain Creek Baptist Church (Anderson, S.C.), Minutes and Historical Sketch
    Poplar Spring Baptist Church (Franklin Co., N.C.) Record Book
    Pungoteague Baptist Church (Accomac County, Virginia) Minute Book
    Red Grove Baptist Church (Edgefield District, South Carolina) Minute Book
    J. J. D. Renfroe Manuscript Sermons
    Second Baptist Church (Pickens, S.C), Minutes
    Seventy-six United Baptist Church (Albany, Kentucky) Minute Book
    Tar River Baptist Association (North Carolina) Minute Book
    Wake Union Baptist Church (North Carolina) Minute Book
    Yeopim Baptist Church (Chowan County, North Carolina) Record Book

Southern Historical Collection, University of North Carolina, Chapel Hill
  Samuel A. Agnew Diary
  Battle Family Papers
  Calvary Episcopal Church (Edgecombe County, North Carolina), Records
  Kate S. Carney Diary
  Cobb and Hunter Family Papers
  Elizabeth Collier Diary
  Susan Cornwall Book
  Crossroads Primitive Baptist Church (Baywood, Grayson County, Virginia) Record Book
  Elias Davis Letters
  Episcopal Convocation of Edenton Records, Diocese of Eastern North Carolina
  Fries and Shaffner Papers
  Meta Morris Grimball Diary
  George W. F. Harper Papers
  John Kimberly Papers
  William King Diary
  Thomas Butler King Papers
  Henry Champlin Lay Papers
  Lenoir Family Papers
  Emma Mordecai Diary
  Jason Niles Diary
  James Hervey Otey Papers
  John Paris Diary
  William Nelson Pendleton Papers
  James G. M. Ramsey Papers
  Alice Ready Diary
  Sawyers Creek Baptist Church (Camden Co., N.C.) Record Book
  Edmund Kirby Smith Papers
  Sarah Wadley Diary
State Historical Society of Iowa, Des Moines
  Amasa Orlando Allen Papers
State Historical Society of Wisconsin, Madison
  Levi Shell Letters
Stones River National Military Park, Archives Division, Murfreesboro, Tennessee
  Amandus Silsby Correspondence
Tennessee State Library and Archives, Nashville
  Charles Alley Diary
  John Hill Fergusson Diary
  Amanda, McDowell Diary, Curtis McDowell Papers
Union Theological Seminary, Richmond
  Robert Lewis Dabney Papers
  East Hanover Presbytery Minutes
  Lexington Presbytery Minutes
  Montgomery Presbytery Minutes

U.S. Army Military History Institute, Carlisle Barracks, Pennsylvania
   Henry Brantingham Letters, Joseph Bilby Collection
   Civil War Miscellaneous Collection
      Charles S. Granger Diary
      Charles A. Malloy Diary
   Civil War Times Illustrated Collection
      Albert A. Pope Diary
   Lewis Leigh Collection
      Neill A. Baker Letter
      Charles H. Eager Letters
      George E. French Papers
University of Georgia, Athens
   Eviline Harden Jackson Diary
   Shepherd Green Pryor Papers
   Margaret Branch Sexton Papers
University of Memphis, Mississippi Valley Collection, Memphis, Tennessee
   Frank M. Guernsey Correspondence
University of Michigan, Bentley Library, Michigan Historical Collections, Ann Arbor
   Buchanan Family Papers
University of Michigan, Clements Library, Ann Arbor
   Lawrence Hotchkiss Collection
   Schoff Civil War Collection
      Henry Grimes Marshall Papers
   Nathan B. Webb Diary
   James R. Woodworth Diary and Letters
University of Notre Dame, University of Notre Dame Archives, Notre Dame, Indiana
   Benton-Beach Family Correspondence
   Orestes A. Brownson Papers
   Catholic Church
      Archdiocese of Cincinnati Papers
      Archdiocese of New Orleans Papers
      Diocese of Detroit Papers
      Diocese of Hartford Papers
   Civil War Soldiers' and Chaplains' Letters, 1862–1868, Miscellaneous Manuscripts,
      1770–1987
   David Power Conyngham, "Soldiers of the Cross: Nuns and Priests of the Battlefield,"
      David Power Conyngham Papers
   Peter P. Cooney Papers
   William Corby Papers
   John M. Jackson Letters
   Chris C. McKinney Letters
   James A. McMaster Papers
   Samuel T. Reeves Correspondence

University of South Carolina, South Caroliniana Library, Columbia
  Mary Y. Harth Papers
  Mary Hort Journal
University of Texas, Austin, Center for American History
  Margaret Houston Papers
  Cornelia M. Noble Diary
  Pugh Family Papers
  Lizzie Simons Diary
University of Virginia, Special Collections, Alderman Library, Charlottesville
  Lucy Williamson Cocke Diary, Cocke Collection
  Nancy Emerson Diary
  Robert M. T. Hunter Papers
Vermont Historical Society, Barre
  William White Letters
Virginia Baptist Historical Society, University of Richmond
  Beulah Church (King William County) Minute Book
  Bybees Road Church (Fluvanna County) Minute Book
  Colosse Church (King William County) Minute Book
  Elon Baptist Church (Appomattox County) Minute Book
  Elon Baptist Church (Hanover County) Minute Book
  Fork Baptist Church (Fluvanna, County) Minute Book
  Great Fork Church (Nansemond County) Minute Book
  J. B. Jeter Notes and Sermons
  Lyle's Church (Albemarle Association) Minute Book
  Mill Swamp Baptist Church (Isle of Wight County) Minute Book
  Mount Olivet (Hanover County) Minute Book
  Mount Vernon Church (Halifax County) Minute Book
  Red Oak (Appomattox County) Church Minute Book
  C. H. Ryland, Mss. Sermon on Psalm 11:1, 1862
Virginia Historical Society, Richmond
  Barbour Family Papers
  George Cunningham Hannah Account Book, Gravel Hill, Charlotte Co., Penn.
  Jones Family Papers
  Keith Family Papers
  Pegram-Johnson-McIntosh Papers
  Robert E. Lee Letterbook, Lee Family Papers
  Richard Henry Watkins Papers
Virginia Military Institute Archives, Lexington
  Campbell-Varner Family Papers
  Derastus E. W. Myers Letter
Virginia Polytechnic Institute and State University, Special Collections, Blacksburg
  Washington Brown Papers
  Rufus P. Stanick Letter

Western Reserve Historical Society, Cleveland
    E. G. Wood Papers
Yale University, Sterling Library, New Haven, Connecticut
    Charles M. Coit Papers

Auction Catalogs, Private Collections, and Online Manuscripts
B. Behrend, Narrowsburg, Sullivan Co., N.Y., December 4, 1862, to Abraham Lincoln,
    ⟨http://www.geocities.com/Athens/Forum/1867/shabbat.htm⟩
C. A. Blauvelt, Letter, Denning House Antiquarian Books, Catalogue 291, May 2002
Board of Delegates of American Israelites, Office of the Executive Committee, New York,
    December 10, 1861, broadside, Historical Collectible Auctions, September 19, 2002
Joseph Breece Letter, August 7, 1864, ⟨http://www.rootsweb.com/~ncumber/civilwarltr.htm⟩
Circular, HQ, Army of Northern Virginia, January 11, 1864, Document 129 David Zullo Olde
    Soldier Books, Catalogue, No. 204, December 2004
Calvin Diggs Letters, ⟨http://www.indianainthecivilwar.com/letters/84th/diggs.htm⟩.
    In possession of John B. Romeiser
David W. Gillespie Letters, July 23, 25, 1864, Historical Collectible Auction, Limited Edition,
    Catalog, March 14, 2002
Charles S. Goodale Letter, ⟨http://www.geocities.com/TimesSquare/Battlefield/4140/csg1
    .html⟩
Shelby D. Gudgel Letters, ⟨http://www.indianainthecivilwar.com/letters/67th/SHELBYbio
    .htm⟩. In possession of Mia Fleegel
Charles S. Halbert Letter, Gary Hendershott, The Civil War (July 1998, Sale 98)
B. M. Herring Diary, Leslie Hindman Auctioneers, September 22, 2002
Oscar Hinrichs Diary, copy in possession of Robert K. Krick
J. N. Houston Letter, Historical Collections Auctions, September 28, 2000
Robert E. Lee, General Orders No. 83, Profiles in History, Catalog 17, fall 1992
Robert E. Lee Letters, ⟨http://www.jewish-history.com/lee.htm⟩
William C. McGowan Letter, 77th Illinois, Brian and Maria Green Inc. On-line catalog:
    ⟨http://www.bmgcivilwar.com/⟩
Welborn Mooney correspondence, in possession of John Grammer
Alexander Murdock Letter, Historical Collections Auctions, Winter 2001, Item 272
Nimrod Newton Nash Letter, typescript in possession of Robert K. Krick
James Forrester Parrott Letters, 28th Tenn., ⟨http://www.rootsweb.com/~tnoverto/docs/
    CivilWarLettersParrott.html⟩
W. H. Records Letters, ⟨http://www.indianainthecivilwar.com/letters/72nd/Records.htm⟩.
    In possession of Rachel Jordan Jenkins
W. D. Rutherford Letter, July 17, 1864, copy from Robert K. Krick, originals owned by Gerald
    Rutherford
Henry W. Tisdale Diary, ⟨http://www.civilwardiary.net/⟩

Contemporary Periodicals

African Repository

Age (New York)

American Presbyterian Review

American Theological Review

Biblical Recorder (Raleigh, N.C.)

Boston Pilot

Brownson's Quarterly Review

Catholic Telegraph (Cincinnati)

Central Presbyterian (Richmond)

Christian Advocate (Nashville)

Christian Advocate and Journal (New York)

Christian Examiner

Christian Index (Macon, Ga., and Atlanta, Ga.)

Christian Inquirer (New York)

Christian Observer (Philadelphia and Richmond)

Christian Recorder (Philadelphia)

Christian Review (New York)

Christian Watchman and Reflector (Boston)

Confederate Baptist (Columbia, S.C.)

Congregational Quarterly

Continental Monthly

Danville Quarterly Review

Evangelist (New York)

Friend (Philadelphia)

Friends' Intelligencer (Philadelphia)

Friends' Review (Philadelphia)

German Reformed Messenger (Chambersburg, Pa.)

Independent (New York)

Ladies' Repository

Methodist Quarterly Review

Monthly Religious Magazine

National Preacher and Village Pulpit

New Englander

New York Freeman's Journal and Catholic Register

New York Tablet

North Carolina Presbyterian (Fayetteville, N.C.)

Old Guard

Pittsburgh Catholic

Primitive Baptist (Milburnie, N.C.)

Princeton Review

Religious Herald (Richmond)

Southern Christian Advocate (Charleston, S.C., Augusta, Ga., Macon, Ga.)

Southern Churchman (Richmond)

Southern Presbyterian (Milledgeville, Ga., Charleston, S.C. Columbia, S.C.)

Southern Presbyterian Review (Columbia, S.C.)

Universalist Quarterly (Boston)

Western Christian Advocate (Cincinnati)

Zion's Herald and Wesleyan Journal (Boston)

Newspapers

Arkansas True Democrat (Little Rock)

Athens (Ga.) Southern Watchman

Austin (Tex.) State Gazette

Boston Daily Advertiser

Brooklyn Eagle

Burlington (Iowa) Weekly Hawkeye

Charleston Daily Courier

Charleston Mercury

Chattanooga Daily Rebel

Coshocton (Ohio) Democrat

Dubuque (Iowa) Herald

Hartford (Conn.) Daily Courant

Houston Tri-Weekly Telegraph

Jewish Messenger (New York)

Jewish Record (New York)

Liberator (Boston)

Memphis Bulletin

Memphis Daily Appeal

Nashville Dispatch

New Haven (Conn.) Palladium

New York Herald

New York Times

New York Tribune

Newark (Ohio) Advocate

Richmond Daily Whig

Richmond Dispatch

Richmond Enquirer

Northern Church Proceedings

Baptist Church. Illinois. Baptist General Association. *Minutes, 1861*. Elgin, Ill.: H. B. Baldwin, 1861.

————. *Minutes, 1863*. Springfield, Ill.: Johnson and Bradford, 1863.

Baptist Church. Illinois. Carrolton Baptist Association. *Minutes of the Thirty-eighth Anniversary*. Winchester, Ill.: R. B. Dedman, 1865.

Baptist Church. Illinois. Chicago Baptist Association. *Proceedings, 1862*. Elgin, Ill.: Gazette Company, 1862.

————. *Proceedings, 1863*. Elgin, Ill: Gazette Company, 1863.

————. *Minutes of the Thirtieth Anniversary*. Chicago: n.p., 1865.

Baptist Church. Illinois. Springfield Baptist Association. *Minutes of the Twenty-seventh Anniversary*. Springfield, Ill.: E. Paine, 1864.

Baptist Church. Indiana. Madison Association. *Minutes of the Thirty-fifth Annual Meeting*. Madison, Ind.: Courier Steam Printing, 1863.

————. *Minutes of the Thirty-sixth Annual Meeting*. Madison, Ind.: Courier Steam Printing, 1864.

Baptist Church. Indiana. North-Eastern Indiana Baptist Association. *Minutes, 1862*. Coldwater, Mich.: Francis B. Way, 1862.

Baptist Church. Ohio. Cleveland Baptist Association. *Minutes of the Thirtieth Anniversary*. Cleveland: Sanford and Hayward, 1861.

Baptist Church. Ohio. Grand River Baptist Association. *Minutes of the Forty-ninth Annual Meeting*. N.P.: n.p., 1861.

Baptist Church. Ohio. Miami Union Association. *Minutes of the Tenth Anniversary*. Columbus: Glenn, Thrall and Heide, 1863.

Baptist Church. Ohio. State Convention. *Fortieth Annual Report*. Mansfield, Ohio: L. D. Myers, 1866.

Baptist Church. Pennsylvania. Central Union Association. *Minutes of the Thirty-first Annual Session*. Philadelphia: Dickerson and Wagenseller, 1863.

Baptist Church. Pennsylvania. Pennsylvania Baptist Convention. *Minutes of the Thirty-sixth Anniversary*. Philadelphia: J. A. Wagenseller, 1863.

Baptist Church. Pennsylvania. Philadelphia Baptist Association. *Minutes of the 154th Anniversary*. Philadelphia: Dickerson and Wagenseller, 1861.

————. *Minutes of the 155th Anniversary*. Philadelphia: Dickerson and Wagenseller, 1862.

————. *Minutes of the 156th Anniversary*. Philadelphia: J. A. Wagenseller, 1863.

————. *Minutes of the 157th Anniversary*. Philadelphia: J. A. Wagenseller, 1864.

————. *Minutes of the 158th Anniversary*. Philadelphia: J. A. Wagenseller, 1865.

————. *Minutes of the 159th Anniversary*. Philadelphia: J. A. Wagenseller, 1866.

Baptist Church. Pennsylvania. Pittsburgh Regular Baptist Association. *Minutes of the XXII Anniversary*. Pittsburgh: W. S. Haven, 1861.

————. *Minutes of the XXIV Anniversary*. Pittsburgh: W. S. Haven, 1863.

————. *Minutes of the XXV Anniversary*. Pittsburgh: W. S. Haven, 1864.

————. *Minutes of the XXVI Anniversary*. Pittsburgh: Walker and Seibert, 1865.

Congregational Church. Massachusetts. General Association of Massachusetts. *Minutes of the Sixty-second Annual Meeting*. Boston: Crocker and Brewster, 1864.

Methodist Church. Illinois. Illinois Annual Conference. *Minutes of the Thirty-eighth Session.* Quincy, Ill.: Steam Power Press of the Quincy Herald, 1861.

———. *Minutes of the Fortieth Session.* Chicago: Methodist Book Depository, [1863?].

Methodist Church. Indiana. Indiana Conference. *Minutes, 1861.* Cincinnati: Methodist Book Concern, 1861.

———. *Minutes, 1861–62.* Cincinnati: Methodist Book Concern, 1862.

———. *Minutes, 1862–63.* Cincinnati: Methodist Book Concern, 1863.

———. *Minutes, 1863–64.* Cincinnati: Methodist Book Concern, 1864.

Methodist Church. Indiana. North Indiana Conference. *Minutes of the Nineteenth Session.* Cincinnati: Methodist Book Concern, 1862.

———. *Minutes of the Twentieth Session.* Cincinnati: Methodist Book Concern, 1863.

———. *Minutes of the Twenty-first Session.* Cincinnati: Methodist Book Concern, 1864.

———. *Minutes of the Twenty-second Session.* Cincinnati: Methodist Book Concern, 1865.

Methodist Church. Indiana. Northwest Indiana Conference. *Minutes of the Fourteenth Annual Session.* Cincinnati: R. P. Thompson, 1865.

———. *Minutes, 1862.* Lafayette, Ind.: Daily Courier Steam Printing and House and Book Bindery, 1862.

———. *Minutes of the Twelfth Annual Session.* Lafayette, Ind.: Daily Courier Steam Printing House and Book Bindery, 1863.

Methodist Church. Indiana. Southeastern Indiana Conference. *Minutes, 1860–61.* Cincinnati: Methodist Book Concern, 1861.

———. *Minutes, 1863.* Cincinnati: Methodist Book Concern, 1863.

———. *Minutes, 1864.* Cincinnati: Methodist Book Concern, 1864.

Presbyterian Church. *Fourth Annual Report of the General Assembly's Committee on Freedmen.* Pittsburgh: James M'Millin, 1869.

Southern Church Proceedings

Baptist Church. Alabama. Alabama Baptist Association. *Minutes of the Forty-fourth Session.* Montgomery, Ala.: Memphis Appeal Book and Job Printing, 1863.

———. *Minutes of the Forty-fifth Session.* Montgomery, Ala.: Montgomery Advertiser Book and Job Office, 1864.

Baptist Church. Alabama. Cahaba Baptist Association. *Minutes of the Forty-fourth Anniversary.* Marion, Ala.: George C. Rogers, 1861.

———. *Minutes of the Forty-fifth Anniversary.* Marion, Ala.: George C. Rogers, 1862.

Baptist Church. Alabama. Coosa River Baptist Association. *Minutes of the Twenty-eighth Annual Session.* Tuskegee, Ala.: Office of the South Western Baptist, 1861.

Baptist Church. Alabama. Pine Barren Baptist Association. *Minutes of the Thirteenth Annual Session.* Montgomery, Ala.: Montgomery Advertiser Book and Job Office, 1862.

Baptist Church. Georgia. Bethel Baptist Association. *Minutes, 1861.* Atlanta, Ga.: Franklin Printing House, 1861.

———. *Minutes, 1862.* Macon, Ga.: Burke, Boykin and Company, 1862.

———. *Minutes, 1863.* Macon, Ga.: Burke, Boykin, and Company, 1863.

Baptist Church. Georgia. Columbus Baptist Association. *Minutes of the Thirty-third Annual Session.* Columbus, Ga.: Daily Sun Steam Power Press, 1861.

———. *Minutes of the Thirty-sixth Annual Session*. Hamilton, Ga.: Printed at the Office of the Harris County Enterprise, 1864.

Baptist Church. Georgia. Ebenezer Baptist Association. *Minutes of the Forty-ninth Anniversary*. Macon, Ga.: Burke, Boykin and Company, 1863.

———. *Minutes of the Fiftieth Anniversary*. Macon, Ga.: Burke, Boykin and Company, 1864.

Baptist Church. Georgia. Georgia Baptist Association. *Minutes of the Seventy-eighth Anniversary*. Macon, Ga.: Christian Index Office, 1862.

———. *Minutes of the Eightieth Anniversary*. Macon, Ga.: Burke, Boykin, and Company, 1864.

Baptist Church. Georgia. Lower Canoochee Association. *Minutes, 1864*. [Savannah, Ga.?]: n.p., 1864.

Baptist Church. Georgia. Ocmulgee Association. *Minutes, 1862*. Milledgeville, Ga.: Southern Recorder Office, 1862.

Baptist Church. Georgia. State Convention. *Minutes of the Fortieth Anniversary*. Macon, Ga.: John L. Jenkins, 1862.

Baptist Church. Georgia. Sunbury Baptist Association. *Minutes, 1862*. N.p.: n.p., [1862?].

Baptist Church. Georgia. Yellow River Baptist Association. *Minutes of the Thirty-eighth Annual Session*. Atlanta: Office of the Daily Intelligencer, 1862.

———. *Minutes of the Thirty-ninth Annual Session*. Atlanta: Intelligencer Steam Power Press, 1863.

Baptist Church. Mississippi. Aberdeen Baptist Association. *Minutes of the Eighteenth Anniversary*. Greensboro, Miss.: Southern Motive Job Office, 1862.

Baptist Church. Mississippi. Chickasaw Baptist Association. *Minutes of the Twenty-third Anniversary*. Jackson, Miss.: Mississippi Baptist Book and Job Office, 1861.

Baptist Church. Mississippi. Choctaw Baptist Association. *Minutes of the Twenty-third Anniversary*. Jackson, Miss.: Mississippi Baptist Book and Job Office, 1861.

———. *Minutes of the Seventy-sixth Annual Session*. Columbus, Miss.: J. D. Ryan, 1865.

Baptist Church. Mississippi. Mount Pisgah Baptist Association. *Minutes of the Twenty-eighth Annual Session*. Meridian, Miss.: Clarion Book and Job Office, 1864.

Baptist Church. Mississippi. Pearl River Baptist Association. *Minutes of the Forty-fifth Annual Meeting*. Monticello, Miss.: Southern Journal Book and Job Office, 1864.

Baptist Church. Mississippi. Strong River Baptist Association. *Minutes of the Eleventh Annual Meeting*. Brandon, Miss.: Brandon Republican, 1863.

Baptist Church. Mississippi. Strong River Baptist Association.

———. *Minutes of the Twelfth Annual Meeting*. Brandon, Miss.: Brandon Republican Print, 1864.

Baptist Church. Mississippi. Union Baptist Association. *Minutes of the Forty-first [Forty-second] Annual Session*. N.p.: n.p., [1862?].

Baptist Church. North Carolina. Beulah Baptist Association. *Minutes of the Twenty-ninth Annual Session*. Raleigh, N.C.: Biblical Recorder Office, 1862.

Baptist Church. North Carolina. Brown Creek Baptist Association. *Minutes, 1864*. N.p.: n.p. 1864.

Baptist Church. North Carolina. Chowan Baptist Association. *Minutes of the Fifty-seventh Annual Session*. Raleigh, N.C.: Biblical Recorder Office, 1863.

———. *Minutes of the Fifty-eighth Annual Session*. Raleigh, N.C. Biblical Recorder Office, 1864.

Baptist Church. North Carolina. Liberty Baptist Association. *Minutes of the Twenty-ninth Session.* Salisbury, N.C.: J. J. Stewart, 1861.

———. *Minutes of Thirty-first Annual Session.* Raleigh, N.C.: Biblical Recorder Office, 1863.

Baptist Church. North Carolina. Sandy Creek Baptist Association. *Minutes of the One Hundred and Third Session.* Raleigh, N.C.: Biblical Recorder Office, 1861.

Baptist Church. North Carolina. State Convention. *Proceedings of the Thirty-second Annual Session.* Raleigh, N.C.: Biblical Recorder Office, 1861.

———. *Proceedings of the Thirty-fourth Annual Session.* Raleigh, N.C.: Biblical Recorder Office, 1864.

Baptist Church. North Carolina. Union Baptist Association. *Minutes of the Twentieth Annual Session.* Raleigh, N.C.: Biblical Recorder Office, 1864.

Baptist Church. North Carolina. United Baptist Association. *Minutes, 1862.* Marion, N.C.: Enterprise Office, 1862.

Baptist Church. North Carolina. Western Baptist Convention. *Proceedings of the 5th Annual Session.* Henderson, N.C.: Henderson "Times" Print, 1861.

———. *Proceedings of the Seventh Annual Session.* Hendersonville, N.C.: Printed at the "Times" Office, 1863.

Baptist Church. South Carolina. Bethel Baptist Association. *Minutes of the Seventy-third Anniversary.* Spartanburg, S.C.: Henry F. Evans, [1862?].

Baptist Church. South Carolina. Broad River Baptist Association. *Minutes of the Sixty-third Anniversary.* [Spartanburg, S.C.]: Printed at the Spartan Office, 1863.

Baptist Church. South Carolina. Charleston Baptist Association. *Minutes of the One Hundred and Tenth Session.* Charleston: A. J. Burke, 1862.

———. *Minutes of the 111th, 112th and 113th Sessions.* Camden, S.C.: W. K. Rodgers, 1864.

Baptist Church. South Carolina. Edgefield Baptist Association. *Minutes of the Fifty-seventh Session.* Greenville, S.C.: G. E. Elford's Press, 1864.

Baptist Church. South Carolina. Fairfield Baptist Association. *Minutes, 1864.* Columbia, S.C.: Southern Guardian Office, 1864.

Baptist Church. South Carolina. Greenville Baptist Association. *Second Annual Meeting.* [Greenville, S.C.: G. E. Elford, 1862].

Baptist Church. South Carolina. Reedy River Baptist Association. *Minutes, 1862.* N.p.: n.p., [1862?].

Baptist Church. South Carolina. State Convention. *Minutes of the Forty-first Anniversary.* Columbia, S.C.: Southern Guardian Steam Power Press, 1861.

———. *Minutes of the Forty-second Anniversary.* Columbia, S.C.: E. R. Stokes, 1862.

———. *Minutes of the 43rd and 44th Anniversaries.* Columbia, S.C: F. G. DeFontaine, 1864.

Baptist Church. South Carolina. Tyger River Baptist Association. *Minutes of the Twenty-ninth Anniversary.* Columbia, S.C.: E. R. Strokes, 1862.

———. *Minutes of the Thirtieth Anniversary.* Greenville, S.C.: G. E. Elford's Press, 1863.

Baptist Church. South Carolina. Welsh Neck Baptist Association. *Minutes, 1861.* Charleston: A. J. Burke, 1861.

Baptist Church. Southern Baptist Convention. *Proceedings of the Eighth Biennial Session.* Richmond: Macfarlane and Fergusson, 1861.

———. *Proceedings of the Ninth Biennial Session.* Macon, Ga.: Burke, Boykin and Company, 1863.

Baptist Church. Texas. Cherokee Baptist Association. *Minutes, 1863*. Tyler, Tex.: Reporter
    Book and Job Office, 1864.

Baptist Church. Texas. Little River Association. *Minutes of the Sixth Annual Meeting*.
    Cameron, Tex.: Cameron Sentinel Office, 1861.

———. *Minutes of the Ninth Annual Session*. Houston, Tex.: Galveston News Book and Job
    Printing Office, 1863.

Baptist Church. Texas. Trinity River Association. *Minutes of the Sixteenth Annual Session*.
    Crockett, Tex.: Quid Nunc Job Office, 1864.

Baptist Church. Texas. Union Baptist Association. *Minutes of the Twenty-second Annual
    Meeting*. Anderson, Tex.: John H. Wilson, 1861.

———. *Minutes of the Twenty-third Annual Meeting*. Bellville, Tex.: Office of the Bellville
    Countryman, 1862.

Baptist Church. Virginia. Albemarle Baptist Association. *Minutes of the Seventieth
    Anniversary*. Charlottesville, Va.: James Alexander, 1861.

———. *Minutes of the Seventy-first Anniversary*. Richmond: Charles H. Wynne, 1862.

———. *Minutes of the Seventy-second Anniversary*. Richmond: Charles H. Wynne, 1863.

———. *Minutes of the Seventy-third Anniversary*. Charlottesville: James Alexander, 1864.

Baptist Church. Virginia. Appomattox Baptist Association. *Minutes, 1861*. Richmond:
    H. K. Ellyson, 1861.

———. *Minutes, 1862 and 1863*. Petersburg, Va.: Gustavus A. Sykes, 1864.

———. *Minutes, 1864*. Petersburg, Va.: Gustavus A. Sykes, 1864.

Baptist Church. Virginia. Blue Ridge Baptist Association. *Minutes of the Third Annual Session*.
    Richmond: H. K. Ellyson, 1861.

Baptist Church. Virginia. Concord Baptist Association. *Minutes of the Thirty-second Annual
    Session*. Petersburg: John B. Ege, 1863.

Baptist Church. Virginia. Dan River Baptist Association. *Minutes, 1864*. Danville, Va.:
    "Register" Book and Job Office, 1864.

Baptist Church. Virginia. General Association. *Address of the Baptist General Association of
    Virginia, June 4th, 1863*. N.p.: n.p., 1863.

———. *Minutes, 1861, 1862, and 1863*. Richmond: Macfarlane and Fergusson, 1863.

Baptist Church. Virginia. Goshen Baptist Association. *Minutes, 1861*. N.p.: n.p., 1861.

Baptist Church. Virginia. Middle District Baptist Association. *Minutes of the Seventy-ninth
    Annual Session*. Richmond: Macfarlane and Fergusson, 1862.

———. *Minutes of the Eightieth Annual Session*. Richmond: Macfarlane and Fergusson, 1863.

———. *Minutes of the Eighty-first Annual Session*. Richmond: William H. Clemmitt, 1864.

Baptist Church. Virginia. Potomac Baptist Association. *Minutes of the Sixth Annual Meeting*.
    Richmond: H. K. Ellyson, 1861.

Baptist Church. Virginia. Rappahannock Baptist Association. *Minutes of the Seventeenth
    Annual Session*. Richmond: H. K. Ellyson, 1859.

———. *Minutes of the Twentieth Annual Session*. Richmond: Smith, Bailey and Company,
    1863.

———. *Minutes of the Twenty-second Annual Session*. Richmond: Sentinel Job Office, 1864.

———. *Minutes of the Twenty-third Annual Session*. Richmond: Bulletin Job Office, 1865.

Bible Convention of the Confederate States of America. *Proceedings, 1862*. Augusta, Ga.:
    Office of the Constitutionalist, 1862.

Friends, Society of. North Carolina. Yearly Meeting. *Memorial, 1864*. [Greensboro?, N.C.:
    n.p., 1864].

Friends, Society of. Virginia Half Yearly Meeting. *Memorial to Legislature of Virginia*.
    Richmond: George W. Gary, 1863.

Lutheran Church. North Carolina Synod. *Minutes of the Sixtieth Meeting*. Salisbury, N.C.:
    J. J. Bruner, 1863.

———. *Minutes of the Sixty-first Annual Convention*. Salisbury, N.C.: J. J. Bruner, 1864.

Lutheran Church. South Carolina Synod. *Minutes, 1862*. Charleston: Evans and Cogswell,
    1863.

———. *Minutes, 1863*. Columbia, S.C.: Evans and Cogswell, 1864.

Lutheran Church. Synod of Georgia. *Minutes of the Fourth Annual Convention*. Savannah, Ga.:
    George N. Nichols, 1864.

Lutheran Church. Tennessee Synod. *Proceedings of the Forty-second Annual Convention*.
    Greensboro, N.C.: n.p. 1863.

Lutheran Church. Virginia Synod. *Minutes of the Thirty-second Convention*. Singers Glen, Va.,
    Joseph Funk, 1861.

Lutheran Church. Western Virginia Synod. *Minutes of the 22nd and 23rd Sessions*. Lynchburg,
    Va.: Johnson and Schaffter, 1864.

Methodist Episcopal Church. Georgia. *Minutes of the Georgia Annual Conference, 1861–1862*.
    Macon, Ga.: n.p., 1863.

———. *Minutes of 1864*. [Macon, Ga.: n.p., 1865].

Methodist Church. South Carolina. *Minutes of the Seventy-fifth Annual Session*. Charleston:
    Evans and Cogswell, 1863.

———. *Minutes of the Seventy-sixth Annual Session*. Columbia, S.C.: Evans and Cogswell,
    1864.

Methodist Episcopal Church, South. Alabama. *Minutes of the Alabama Conference, 1863*.
    Mobile: John Y. Thompson, 1863.

Presbyterian Church. General Assembly. *Address of the General Assembly of the Presbyterian
    Church in the Confederate States of America, to all the Churches of Jesus Christ throughout
    the Earth*. [Augusta, Ga.: n.p. 1861].

———. *Minutes, 1861*. Augusta, Ga.: Steam Power Press Chronicle and Sentinel, 1861.

———. *Minutes, 1862*. Augusta, Ga.: Chronicle and Sentinel, 1862.

———. *Minutes, 1863*. Columbia, S.C.: Southern Guardian Steam-Power Press, 1863.

———. *Minutes, 1864*. Columbia, S.C.: Evans and Cogswell, 1864.

———. *A Pastoral Letter of the General Assembly of the Presbyterian Church to the Ministers
    and Members of the Congregations in the Confederate Army*. Richmond: Presbyterian
    Committee of Publication, 1862.

Presbyterian Church. Synod of North Carolina. *Minutes of the Convention of Elders and
    Deacons*. Fayetteville, N.C.: Job-Office of the Presbyterian, 1861.

———. *Minutes of the Forty-eighth Sessions*. Fayetteville, N.C.: Presbyterian Office, 1862.

———. *Minutes of the Forty-ninth Sessions*. Fayetteville, N.C.: Presbyterian Office, 1863.

Presbyterian Church. Synod of North Carolina. Fayetteville Presbytery. *Minutes of the One
    Hundredth Sessions*. Fayetteville, N.C.: Presbyterian Office, 1863.

———. *Minutes of the One Hundred and First Sessions*. Fayetteville, N.C.: Presbyterian Office,
    1863.

————. *Minutes of the One Hundred and Second Sessions*. Fayetteville, N.C.: Presbyterian Office, 1864.

————. *Minutes of the One Hundred and Third Sessions*. Fayetteville, N.C.: Presbyterian Office, 1865.

Presbyterian Church. Synod of North Carolina. Orange Presbytery. *Minutes of the One Hundred and Eighty-third Session*. Fayetteville, N.C.: Printed at the Presbyterian Office, 1861.

Presbyterian Church. Synod of South Carolina. *Minutes, 1860*. Charleston: Evans and Cogswell, 1861.

————. *Minutes, 1861*. Charleston: Evans and Cogswell, 1862.

Presbyterian Church. Synod of South Carolina. South Carolina Presbytery. *Minutes, 1864*. Columbia, S.C.: F. G. DeFontaine, 1864.

Presbyterian Church. Synod of Virginia. *Minutes, 1862*. [Richmond: n.p., 1862?].

————. *Minutes, 1863*. [Richmond: n.p., 1863?].

————. *Minutes, 1864*. [Richmond?: n.p., 1864].

Protestant Episcopal Church. *Journal of the Proceedings of an Adjourned Convention of Bishops, Clergymen and Laymen of the Protestant Episcopal Church*. Montgomery, Ala.: Montgomery Advertiser Job Printing Office, 1861.

————. *Pastoral Letter from the Bishops of the Protestant Episcopal Church in the Confederate States*. Augusta, Ga.: Chronicle and Sentinel, 1862.

————. *Proceedings of a Meeting of Bishops, Clergymen, and Laymen*. Montgomery, Ala.: Barrett, Wimbish, 1861.

Protestant Episcopal Church. Diocese of Alabama. *Journal of the Thirty-first Annual Convention*. Montgomery, Ala.: Montgomery Advertiser Book and Job Office, 1863.

————. *Journal of the Thirty-third Annual Council*. Mobile: Farrow and Dennett, 1864.

Protestant Episcopal Church. Diocese of Arkansas. *Pastoral Letter to the Clergy and Members of the Protestant Episcopal Church in the State of Arkansas*. Memphis, Tenn.: Hutton and Freligh, 1861.

Protestant Episcopal Church. Diocese of Georgia. *Journal of the Second Annual Council*. Savannah, Ga.: E. J. Purse, 1864.

————. *To the Clergy of the Diocese of Georgia*. [Savannah, Ga.: n.p., 1861].

Protestant Episcopal Church. Diocese of Louisiana. *Extracts from the Journal of the Twenty-third Annual Convention*. New Orleans: Bulletin Book and Job Office, 1861.

Protestant Episcopal Church. Diocese of Mississippi. *Journal of the Thirty-fifth Annual Convention*. Jackson: Mississippian Book and Job Office, 1861.

Protestant Episcopal Church. Diocese of North Carolina. *Journal of the First Annual Council*. Fayetteville, N.C.: Edward J. Hale, 1863.

Protestant Episcopal Church. Synod of North Carolina. *Journal of the Forty-eighth Annual Council*. Fayetteville, N.C.: Edward J. Hale, 1864.

Protestant Episcopal Church. Diocese of South Carolina. *Journal of the Seventy-fourth Annual Convention*. Charleston: A. E. Miller, 1863.

————. *Journal of the Seventy-fifth Annual Council*. Columbia, S.C. Evans and Cogswell, 1864.

Protestant Episcopal Church. Diocese of Virginia. *Journal of the Sixty-sixth Annual Convention*. Richmond: Charles H. Wynne, 1861.

———. *Journal of the Sixty-eighth Annual Council*. Richmond: Macfarlane and Fergusson, 1863.

State Bible Convention of South Carolina. *Proceedings, 1862*. Columbia, S.C.: Southern Guardian Steam-Power Press, 1862.

Northern Sermons

Adams, E. E. *Government and Rebellion*. Philadelphia: Henry B. Ashmead, 1861.

Adams, William. *Christian Patriotism*. New York: Anson D. F. Randolph, 1863.

———. *Prayer for Rulers; or, Duty of Christian Patriots*. New York: Rudd and Carleton, 1861.

Agnew, B. L. *Thanksgiving Sermon, Preached in the Presbyterian Church at Johnstown, Pa.* [Johnstown, Pa.?: Tribune, 1864].

Aikman, William. *Government and Administration*. Wilmington, Del.: Henry Eckel, 1863.

Alexander, Walter S. *Sermon Occasioned by the Death of Edwin Ruthven Keyes*. Danielsonville, Conn.: Transcript Print, 1863.

Alger, William Rounsville. *Our Civil War, as Seen from the Pulpit*. Boston: Walter, Wise, and Company, 1861.

Anderson, S. J. P. *The Dangers and Duties of the Present Crisis!*. St. Louis, Mo.: Presbyterian of our Union, 1861.

Armitage, Thomas. *The Past, Present, and Future of the United States*. New York: T. Holman, 1862.

Aspey, William S. *Causes for National Thanksgiving*. Bennington, Vt.: J. I. C. Cook, 1864.

Atterbury, John G. *God in Civil Government*. New Albany, Ind.: George R. Beach, 1862.

Atwood, E. S. *In Memoriam. Discourses in Commemoration of Abraham Lincoln*. Salem, Mass.: Office of the Salem Gazette, 1865.

Babbitt, Benjamin B. *A Sermon on the Death of Walter L. Raymond*. Andover, Mass.: W. F. Draper, 1865.

Bacon, Leonard. *Conciliation: A Discourse at a Sunday Evening Service*. New Haven: Peck, White, and Peck, 1862.

Baldridge, S. C. *The Martyr Prince*. Cincinnati: Joseph S. Boyd, 1865.

Barnes, Albert. *The Love of Country*. Philadelphia: C. Sherman and Son, 1861.

———. *The State of the Country*. Philadelphia: Henry B. Ashmead, 1865.

Barrows, William. *Our War and Our Religion, and Their Harmony*. Boston: J. M. Whittemore, 1862.

———. *The War and Slavery; and Their Relations to Each Other*. Boston: John M. Whittemore, 1863.

———. *Conditions of Peace*. Boston: Walker, Wise, 1863.

Bartol, Cyrus Augustus. *The Duty of the Time*. Boston: Walker, Wise, and Company, 1861.

———. *Extravagance: A Sermon for the Times*. Boston: Walker, Wise, and Company, 1864.

———. *The Nation's Hour*. Boston: Walker, Wise and Company, 1862.

———. *Our Sacrifices*. Boston: Ticknor and Fields, 1861.

———. *The Purchase by Blood*. Boston: J. Wilson and Son, 1864.

———. *The Remission of Blood*. Boston: Walker, Wise, and Company, 1862.

Beecher, Henry Ward. *Freedom and War. Discourses on Topics Suggested by the Times*. Boston: Ticknor and Fields, 1863.

———. *Patriotic Addresses in American and England, from 1850 to 1885, on Slavery, the Civil*

War, and the Development of Civil Liberty in the United States New York: Fords, Howard, the Hulburt, 1889.

Bellows, Henry W. *The Advantage of Testing Our Principles, Compensatory of the Evils of Serious Times*. Philadelphia: C. Sherman and Son, 1861.

———. *How We Are to Fulfill Our Lord's Commandment, "Love Your Enemies," in Time of War*. New York: Baker and Godwin, 1861.

———. *The State and the Nation—Sacred to Christian Citizens*. New York: J. Miller, 1861.

———. *The Valley of Decision*. New York: H. B. Price, 1861.

———. *The War to End Only When the Rebellion Ceases*. New York: Anson D. F. Randolph, [1863?].

Beman, I. L. *Thanksgiving Sermon, Delivered in Cortland, N.Y., August 6th, 1863*. Cortland, N.Y.: Charles P. Cole, 1863.

Beman, Nathan S. S. *Our Civil War: The Principles Involved, Its Causes and Cure*. Troy, N.Y.: A. W. Scribner, 1863.

Bingham, Joel F. *Great Providences toward the Loyal Part of This Nation*. Buffalo: Breed and Company, 1864.

Blackburn, William M. *The Crime against the Presidency*. Trenton, N.J.: Murphy and Bechtel, 1865.

Blake, John Falkner. *A Sermon on the Services and Death of Abraham Lincoln*. New York: John F. Trow, 1865.

Blake, Mortimer. *The Issues of the Rebellion*. Taunton, Mass.: Republican Office, 1861.

———. *On Account of the Assassination of President Lincoln*. Champlain, N.Y.: Moorsfield Press, 1925.

Bliss, John C. *Obedience the Fruit of Gratitude. A Sermon Preached on the National Thanksgiving Day, December 7, 1865*. Carlisle, Pa.: Books and Job Office of the "American Volunteer," 1865.

Bliss, Joshua Isham. *Sermons Preached at the Funeral of Capt. Lucius H. Bostwick*. Montpelier, Vt.: E. P. Walton, 1863.

Boardman, George Dana. *Addresses Delivered in the Meeting-House of the First Baptist Church of Philadelphia*. Philadelphia: Sherman and Company, 1865.

———. *Civil Government, a Divine Ordinance*. Philadelphia: Ringwalt and Brown, 1864.

———. *Loyalty to Law, the Duty of the Christian Patriot*. New York: French and Wheat, 1860.

Boardman, George N. *The Death of President Lincoln*. Binghamton, N.Y.: F. N. Chase, 1865.

Boardman, Henry A. *The American Union*. Philadelphia: Lippincott, Grambo, 1851.

———. *Healing and Salvation for Our Country from God Alone*. Philadelphia: William S. and Alfred Martien, 1864.

———. *The Peace We Need, and How to Secure It*. Philadelphia: J. S. Claxton, 1865.

———. *The Peacemakers*. Philadelphia: James S. Claxton, 1865.

———. *The Sovereignty of God, the Sure and Only Stay of the Christian Patriot in Our National Troubles*. Philadelphia: William S. and Alfred Martien, 1862.

Bogardus, W. E. *Sermon on the Death of Our Late President*. New York: Isaac J. Oliver, 1865.

Booth, Robert Russell. *Personal Forgiveness and Public Justice*. New York: Anson D. F. Randolph, 1865.

Booth, Robert Russell, and George Lewis Prentiss. *A Memorial of Lieut. Franklin Butler Crosby, of the Fourth Regiment U.S. Artillery*. New York: A. D. F. Randolph, 1864.

Bosworth, G. W. *The Soldier's Commission against Rebellion*. Portland, Maine: James S. Staples, 1861.

Botsford, A. B. *"The Way of Help."* New York: Edward O. Jenkins, 1862.

Brainerd, Thomas. *Patriotism Aiding Piety*. Philadelphia William F. Geddes, 1863.

Brakeman, N. L. *A Great Man Fallen*. New Orleans: Times Book and Job Office, 1865.

Brantly, William T. *Our National Troubles*. Philadelphia: T. B. Peterson and Brothers, 1860.

Breed, William P. *Faith and Patience*. Philadelphia: J. Alexander, 1863.

———. *The Lights Which God Hath Shewed Us*. Philadelphia: John Alexander, 1861.

———. *The National Nest-Stirring*. Philadelphia: H. B. Ashmead, 1861.

Brooks, Phillips. *The Life and Death of Abraham Lincoln*. Philadelphia: Henry B. Ashmead, 1865.

Buck, D. D. *The Civil Ruler as God's Minister*. Rochester, N.Y.: E. Darrow and Brother, 1863.

Burdick, C. R. *Two Sermons for the Times*. Rochester, N.Y.: Culver, Morey and Company, 1865.

Bush, James S. *Death of President Lincoln*. Orange, N.J.: E. Gardner, 1865.

Bushnell, Horace. *Building Eras in Religion*. New York: Charles Scribner's Sons, 1881.

———. *Reverses Needed*. Hartford: L. E. Hunt, 1861.

Butler, C. M. *Republican Loyalty*. Washington, D.C.: Henry Polkinhorn, 1860.

———. *Funeral Address on the Death of Abraham Lincoln*. Philadelphia: Henry B. Ashmead, 1865.

Butler, J. Glenworth. *God with Us*. Philadelphia: Union League of the Twenty-fourth Ward, 1863.

Campbell, S. M. *The Light in the Clouds*. Utica, N.Y.: Curtiss and White, 1862.

Carey, Isaac E. *The Conflict and the Victory*. Freeport, Ill.: Judson and McCluer, 1864.

———. *The War an Occasion for Thanksgiving*. Keokuk: Iowa: Daily Gate City Print, 1861.

Carpenter, Hugh Smith. *The Final Triumph of Equity*. New York: W. A. Townsend, 1864.

———. *The Relations of Religion to the War*. New York: A. W. Townsend, 1861.

Chaplain, John S. *A True Fast*. Philadelphia: Bryson's Printing Rooms, 1863.

Cheever, George B. *God's Way of Crushing the Rebellion*. New York: n.p., 1861.

Chew, John H. *God's Judgments Teaching Righteousness*. Washington, D.C.: R. A. Waters, 1861.

Christian, Rev. H. L. *Our Present Position*. Philadelphia: William S. and Alfred Martien, 1862.

Clark, Alexander. *Memorial Sermon, Preached on the National Funeral Day of Abraham Lincoln*. Cincinnati: Masonic Review Office, 1865.

Clark, Frederick G. *Gold in the Fire: Our National Position*. New York: John Duyckinck, 1862.

Clarke, James Freeman. *Discourse on the Aspects of the War*. Boston: Walker, Wise, and Company, 1863.

Cleaveland, Elisha Lord. *Love of Country*. New Haven, Conn.: Thomas H. Peace, 1860.

———. *Our Duty in Regard to the Rebellion*. New Haven, Conn.: Thomas H. Pease, 1863.

———. *The Patriot's Song of Victory*. New Haven, Conn.: Thomas H. Pease, 1864.

Collier, Robert Laird. *Moral Heroism: Its Essentialness to the Crisis*. Chicago: Tribune Book and Job Steam Printing Office, 1862.

Collins, Nathaniel G. *The Prospect. The Speech of Rev. N. G. Collins, Chaplain of the 57th Illinois*. Chicago: Church, Goodman, and Cushing, 1863.

Colman, George W. *Assassination of the President*. Boston: S. Chism, 1865.

Coombe, Pennell. *A Sermon on the Divine Origin of Civil Government, and the Sinfulness of Rebellion*. Philadelphia: Barnard and Jones, 1861.

Craig, W. B. *The Lord a Stronghold in the Day of Trouble.* Philadelphia: C. Sherman, 1862.

Craig, Wheelock. *A Sermon on the Fruits of our Bereavement.* New Bedford, Mass.: E. Anthony and Sons, 1865.

Crane, C. B. *Sermon on the Occasion of the Death of President Lincoln.* Hartford, Conn.: Case, Lockwood and Co., 1865.

Cummins, Alexander G. *The Christian's Duty to the Freedmen.* Philadelphia: Sherman and Company, 1865.

Daggett, O. E. *A Sermon on the Death of Abraham Lincoln.* Canandaigua, N.Y.: Milliken, 1865.

Dean, Sidney. *The War: And the Duty of a Loyal People.* Providence: Pierce and Budlong, 1862.

Demerest, James. *Thanksgiving Sermon.* Hackensack, N.J.: Berger County Patriot, 1861.

Demund, Isaac S. *Subordination to Government the Salvation of Our Country.* Lancaster, Pa.: Pearsol and Geist, 1861.

DeNormandie, James. *The Lord Reigneth.* N.p.: n.p., 1865.

Dexter, Henry Martyn. *What Ought to Be Done with the Freedmen and with the Rebels.* Boston: Nichols and Noyes, 1865.

Dix, Morgan. *The Death of President Lincoln.* Cambridge, Mass.: Riverside Press, 1865.

———. *God's Mercies towards the Nation.* New York: F. J. Huntington, 1861.

Duffield, George, Jr. *Courage in a Good Cause.* Philadelphia: Published by request, 1861.

———. *The God of Our Fathers.* Philadelphia: T. B. Pugh, 1861.

———. *The Great Rebellion Thus Far a Failure.* Adrian, Mich.: S. P. Jermain and Company, 1861.

———. *Humiliation and Hope: The Christian Patriot's Duty in the Present Crisis of Our National Affairs.* Detroit: O. S. Gulley, 1862.

———. *The Nation's Wail.* Detroit: Advertiser and Tribune Print, 1865.

———. *Our National Sins to Be Repented of, and the Grounds of Hope for the Preservation of Our Federal Constitution and Union.* Detroit: Free Press Mammoth Book and Job Printing House, 1861.

———. *A Thanksgiving Discourse.* Detroit: Free Press Mammoth Book and Job Printing Office, 1861.

Dunning, H. *The Goodly Heritage and Its Heirs.* Baltimore: Hanzsche and Company, 1860.

Duryea, Joseph T. *Loyalty to the Government: A Divine Command and a Christian Duty.* Troy, N.Y.: A. W. Scribner, 1861.

———. *An Oration Commemorative of the Restoration of the Union.* Philadelphia: McCalla and Staveley, 1866.

Eddy, Daniel C. *Liberty and Union. Our Country: Its Pride and Its Peril.* Boston: John M. Hewes, 1861.

———. *The Martyr President.* Boston: Graves and Young, 1865.

Eddy, Richard. *The Martyr to Liberty.* Philadelphia: H. G. Leisenring, 1865.

Eddy, Zachary. *A Discourse on the War.* Northampton, Mass.: Trumbull and Gere, 1861.

———. *Secession:—Shall It Be Peace or War?* Northampton, Mass.: Trumbull and Gore, 1861.

Edgar, Cornelius H. *God's Help: The Ground of Hope for Our Country.* New York: Baker and Godwin, 1864.

———. *Three Sermons by C. H. Edgar, D.D., Occasioned by the Assassination of President Lincoln.* Easton, Pa.: Free Press Office, 1865.

Eells, W. W. *How and Why We Give Thanks.* Pittsburgh: W. S. Haven, 1864.

Eggleston, Nathaniel H. *Reasons for Thanksgiving*. Pittsfield, Mass.: Henry Chickering, 1861.

Einhorn, David. *Sermon Delivered on Thanksgiving Day, November 26th, 1863*. Philadelphia: Stein and Jones, 1863.

Ellinwood, Frank F. *Return of the Victors*. Rochester, N.Y.: Democrat Steam Printing House, 1865.

Ellis, George Edward. *The Nation's Ballot and Its Decision*. Boston W. V. Spencer, 1864.

———. *"The Preservation of the States United."* Charlestown, Mass.: Abram E. Cutter, 1860.

Errett, Isaac. *The Claims of Civil Government*. Detroit: O. S. Gulley, 1863.

Everett, Charles Carroll. *A Sermon Preached in Commemoration of the Death of Abraham Lincoln*. Bangor, Maine: Benjamin A. Burr, 1865.

Ewer, F. C. *Discourse on the National Crisis Delivered by the Rev. Rev. F. C. Ewer, at St. Ann's Church, New York*. New York: George F. Nesbitt, 1861.

———. *A Rector's Reply to Sundry Requests and Demands for a Political Sermon*. New York: Francis Hart, 1864.

Farquhar, John. *The Claims of God to Recognition in the Assassination of President Lincoln*. Lancaster, Pa.: Pearsol and Geist, 1865.

Farrington, William G. *The Duty of Giving Thanks, and the Blessings for Which to Be Thankful*. New York: R. C. Root, 1863.

Fast Day Sermons; or, The Pulpit on the State of the Country. New York: Rudd and Carleton, 1861.

Fish, Henry Clay. *The Duty of the Hour; or, Lessons from Our Reverses*. New York: Sheldon and Company, 1862.

———. *The Voice of Our Brother's Blood: Its Source and Its Summons*. Newark, N.J.: Douglass and Starbuck, 1856.

———. *War Record of the First Baptist Church, Newark, N.J.* New York: Sheldon and Company, 1865.

Fisher, George P. *National Faults*. New Haven, Conn.: Tuttle, Morehouse, and Taylor, 1860.

———. *Thoughts Proper to the Present Crisis*. New Haven, Conn.: Tuttle, Morehouse and Taylor, 1861.

Fiske, John Orr. *Sermon on the Present National Troubles*. Bath, Maine: Daily Times Office, 1861.

Foss, Cyrus D. *"Songs in the Night": A Thanksgiving Sermon*. New York: N. Tibbals, 1861.

Foster, Eden B. *The Constitution Our Ark in the Storm*. Springfield, Mass.: Samuel Bowles, 1862.

———. *The Rights of the Pulpit, and Perils of Freedom*. Lowell, Mass.: J. J. Judkins, 1854.

Fowler, Henry. *Character and Death of Abraham Lincoln*. Auburn, N.Y.: William J. Moses, 1865.

Fowler, P. H. *National Destruction Threatens Us; Repentance of Sin and Reformation our Hope of Escape*. Utica, N.Y.: Roberts Book and Job Printer, 1861.

Fraser, A. *Our National Sins, the Cause of Our National Calamities, or the "Curse Causeless Shall not Come."* Rochester, N.Y.: A. Strong and Company, 1863.

Frothingham, Octavius Brooks. *Morality of the New York Riots*. New York: David G. Francis, 1864.

Fugitt, James Preston. *A Plea for Peace*. Baltimore: John D. Toy, 1861.

Fuller, Richard. *Mercy Remembered in Wrath*. Baltimore: Henry Taylor, 1861.

———. *Wrong and Right Dispositions under National Judgments*. Baltimore: W. M. Innes, 1863.

Fulton, Justin D. *Radicalism. A Sermon Preached in Tremont Temple*. Boston: J. E. Tilton, 1865.

Furness, William Henry. *The Declaration of Independence*. Philadelphia: C. Sherman and Son, 1862.

———. *A Discourse Delivered on the Occasion of the National Fast*. Philadelphia: T. B. Pugh, 1861.

———. *Our American Institutions*. Philadelphia: T. B. Pugh, 1863.

———. *Put Up Thy Sword*. Boston: E. F. Wallcutt, 1860.

Gannett, Ezra Stiles. *The Relation of the North to Slavery*. Boston: Nichols and Company, 1854.

———. *The State of the Country*. Boston: Crosby, Nichols, and Company, 1856.

Garrison, J. F. *The Teachings of the Crisis*. Camden, N.J.: S. Chew, 1865.

Gilbert, W. H. *Sermon Delivered in Granby, Conn., Jan. 4, 1863, at the Funeral of Roswell Morgan Allen*. Hartford: Charles Montague, 1863.

Gilmore, J. H. "*Hath God Forgotten to Be Gracious.*" Concord, N.H.: P. B. Cogswell, 1864.

Glover, L. M. *The Character of Abraham Lincoln*. Jacksonville, Ill.: Journal Book and Job Office, 1865.

———. *National Sin and Retribution*. Jacksonville, Ill.: Catlin and Company, 1861.

———. *Our Country Vindicated*. Jacksonville, Ill.: Catlin and Company, 1860.

Goodell, C. L. *Thanksgiving Sermon*. Hartford, Conn.: Lockwood and Company, 1863.

Goodrich, William H. *A Sermon on the Christian Necessity of War*. Cleveland: Fairbanks, Benedict and Company, 1861.

Gordon, Adoniram Judson. *The Chosen Fast*. Boston: N. P. Kemp, 1865.

Grimes, J. A. *The Nation's Last Hope*. New Castle, Pa.: E. S. Durban, 1864.

Grimes, J. S. *The National Crisis*. Wrightsville, Pa.: Robert W. Smith, 1861.

Guion, Thomas T. *A Sermon, Preached on the Day of the National Fast*. Brooklyn: I. Van Anden's Print, 1861.

Gulick, J. G. *God, the Author of National Prosperity*. Lodi, N.Y.: Galloup Brothers, 1862.

Gurley, Phineas Densmore. *Man's Projects and God's Results*. Washington, D.C.: W. Ballantyne, 1863.

———. *Voice of the Rod*. Washington, D.C.: William Ballantyne, 1865.

Hall, Charles H. *Our Sins and Duties*. Washington, D.C.: M'Gill and Witherow, 1861.

Hall, Nathaniel. *The Iniquity*. Boston: John L. Wilson, 1859.

———. *The Moral Significance of the Contrasts between Slavery and Freedom*. Boston: Walker, Wise, and Company, 1864.

Hall, Newman. *A Sermon on the Assassination of President Lincoln*. Boston: Bartlett and Halliday, 1865.

Harris, Samuel. *Our Country's Claim*. Bangor, Maine: Wheeler and Lynde, 1861.

Hartpence, A. *Our National Crisis*. Philadelphia: n.p., 1862.

Haskell, T. N. *Christian Patriotism: A Medium of God's Power and Purpose to Bless Our Land*. Boston: Hollis and Gunn, 1863.

Hathaway, Warren. *A Discourse Occasioned by the Death of Abraham Lincoln*. Albany, N.Y.: J. Munsell, 1865.

Haven, Gilbert A. *National Sermons. Sermons, Speeches and Letters on Slavery and Its War*. Boston: Lee and Shepherd, 1869.

Hawley, Silas. *National Reconstruction the Glory and Shame of a Nation*. Cincinnati: Western Tract and Book Society, 1866.

Hedge, Frederic Henry. *The National Weakness*. Boston: Walker, Wise, 1861.

Heywood, J. H. *The Spirit and Duty of Christian Citizenship*. Louisville, Ky.: Maxwell and Company, 1862.

Hibbard, J. R. *A Sermon on the Causes and Uses of the Present Civil War*. Chicago: n.p., 1862.

———. *A Spiritual Ground of Hope for the Salvation of Our Country*. Chicago: Tribune Company's Book and Job Printing Office, 1862.

Hickok, M. J. *The Mission of Calamity*. New York: John F. Trow, 1862.

Hickox, G. H. *Remarks at the Funeral of Lieut. Percival S. Leggett, of Company I, Fifth Regt. Michigan Cavalry*. Detroit: O. S. Gulley, 1863.

Hill, George W. *Strength in the Time of Trial*. Pittsburgh: W. S. Haven, 1864.

Hitchcock, Roswell Dwight. *Our National Sin*. New York: Baker and Goodwin, 1861.

———. *Thanksgiving For Victories*. N.p.: n.p., 1864.

Holmes, John Milton. *The Crisis and Its Claims*. New York: Samuel Booth, 1862.

———. *The Pilgrim Temple-Builders*. New York: Tibbals and Whiting, 1866.

Hornblower, William H. *Sermon Occasioned by the Assassination of President Lincoln*. Paterson, N.J.: Chiswell and Wurts, 1865.

———. *Sermon on the War*. Paterson: A. Mead, 1861.

Hough, Jessie W. *Our Country's Mission*. Burlington, Vt.: Free Press, 1864.

Hovey, Horace C. *The National Fast*. Coldwater, Mich.: Republican Print, 1861.

Howard, Martin S. *The Divine Sanction—The Basis of Human Success*. New Bedford, Mass.: Edmund Anthony, 1862.

Howlett, Thomas Rosling. *The Dealings of God with Our Nation*. Washington, D.C.: Gibson Brothers, 1865.

Huggins, William S. *Three Sermons to Young Men*. Philadelphia: Presbyterian Publication Committee, 1862.

Humphrey, Heman. *Our Nation*. Pittsfield, Mass.: Henry Chickering, 1861.

Ide, George B. *Battle Echoes; or, Lessons from the War*. Boston: Gould and Lincoln, 1866.

———. *The Freedmen of the War*. Philadelphia: American Baptist Publication Society, 1864.

———. *Pious Men the Nation's Hope*. Boston: Gould and Lincoln, 1863.

Jackson, John Walker. *The Sentiments and Conduct Proper to the Present Crisis in Our National Affairs*. Philadelphia: Collins, 1861.

———. *The Union—the Constitution—Peace*. Harrisburg: "Telegraph" Steam Book and Job Office, 1863.

Jenkins, John. *The National Fast. Why It Should Be Kept, and How*. Philadelphia: C. Sherman, 1863.

———. *"Show My People Their Transgressions."* Philadelphia: C. Sherman, 1861.

———. *Thoughts for the Crisis*. Philadelphia: J. B. Lippincott, 1861.

Johnson, Herrick. *The Banners of a Free People Set Up in the Name of Their God*. Pittsburgh: W. S. Haven, 1864.

———. *"God's Ways Unsearchable."* Pittsburgh: W. G. Johnston, 1865.

———. *The Nation's Duty*. Pittsburgh: W. S. Haven, 1862.

Johnston, Elias Schelhammer. *Sermon Delivered on Thursday, June 1st 1865*. Harrisburg: T. F. Scheffer, 1865.

Keeling, R. J. *The Death of Moses*. Washington, D.C.: W. H. and O. H. Morrison, 1865.

Kellogg, Charles D. *The Duties of the Hour*. Wilmington, Del.: Henry Eckel, 1863.

Kempshall, Everard. *A Thanksgiving Sermon*. New York: William C. Martin, 1863.

Lamson, William. *God Hiding Himself in Times of Trouble*. Boston: Gould and Lincoln, 1863.

Larimore, James W. *A Discourse on Our National Dependence on God*. Mount Vernon, Ohio: Knox County Express, 1861.

Laurie, Thomas. *Three Discourses*. Dedham, Mass.: John Cox, Jr., 1865.

Leavitt, W. S. *God the Protector and Hope of the Nation*. Hudson, N.Y.: Bryan and Webb, 1862.

———. *A Sermon Preached April 9, 1865, the Sunday after the Capture of Richmond*. Hudson, N.Y.: Bryan and Webb, 1865.

Leeds, S. P. *Thy Kingdom Come: Thy Will Be Done."* Windsor, Vt.: Bishop and Tracy, 1861.

Levy, Edgar M. *National Thanksgiving*. New York: Holman Book and Job Printer, 1864.

Lewis, Charlton T. *The Thoughts of God and the Thoughts of Men*. Cincinnati: Board of the Union Chapel, 1863.

Little, Charles. *Relation of the Citizen to the Government*. New Haven, Conn.: William H. Stanley, 1864.

Livermore, L. J. *Perseverance in the War, the Interest and Duty of the Nation*. Boston: T. R. Marvin and Son, 1864.

Lord, John C. *Causes and Remedies of the Present Convulsions*. Buffalo, N.Y.: Joseph Warren, 1861.

———. *"The Higher Law," in Its Application to the Fugitive Slave Bill*. New York: Published by Order of the "Union Safety Committee," 1851.

———. *A Sermon: On the Character and Influence of Washington*. Buffalo, N.Y.: A. M. Clapp, 1863.

McCarty, J. H. *The American Union*. Concord, N.H.: Fogg, Hadley and Company, 1862.

McCauley, James A. *Character and Services of Abraham Lincoln*. Baltimore: John D. Toy, 1865.

McDonald, James M. *Prayer for the Country*. New York: John F. Trow, 1860.

McGill, Alexander T. *Sinful but Not Forsaken*. New York: John F. Trow, 1861.

McIlwaine, Charles Pettit. *The Necessity of Religion to the Prosperity of a Nation*. Cincinnati: Bradley and Webb, 1860.

March, Daniel. *The Crisis of Freedom*. Nashua, N.H.: Dodge and Noyes, 1854.

———. *Steadfastness and Preparation in the Day of Adversity*. Philadelphia: C. Sherman and Son, 1862.

Marshall, James. *The Nation's Changes*. Baltimore: John F. Wiley, 1863.

———. *The Nation's Inquiry*. Philadelphia: King and Baird, 1863.

———. *The Nation's Prospects of Peace*. Philadelphia: King and Baird, 1864.

Mayo, A. D. *The Nation's Sacrifice. Abraham Lincoln*. Cincinnati: Robert C. Clarke, 1865.

Mead, Hiram. *Occasions for Gratitude in the Present National Crisis*. Northampton, Mass.: Trumbull and Gere, 1861.

Miller, L. Merrill. *"Perfect through Suffering."* Ogdensburgh, N.Y.: Advance Steam Printing House, 1861.

Mills, Robert C. *The Southern States Hardened until Ruined*. Boston: J. M. Hewes, 1865.

Mooar, George. *The Religion of Loyalty*. San Francisco: Towne and Bacon, 1865.

Moore, Franklin. *Grounds of Humiliation and Hope*. Philadelphia: James H. Bryson, 1863.

Morais, Sabato. *An Address on the Death of Abraham Lincoln*. Philadelphia: Collins, Printer, 1865.

———. *Thanksgiving Sermon*. Philadelphia: Collins, 1863.

Murdock, John N. *Our Civil War: Its Causes and Its Issues*. Boston: Wright and Potter, 1863.

Nadal, B. H. *National Reconstruction*. Washington, D.C.: William H. Moore, 1865.

Nason, Elias. *Our Obligations to Defend the Government of Our Country*. N.p.: n.p., 1861.

———. *A Sermon on the War*. N.p.: n.d.: 1861.

Newton, Richard. *God's Marvelous Doing for the Nation*. Philadelphia: William F. Murphy, 1863.

Niles, William A. *Our Country's Peril and Hope*. Corning, N.Y.: E. E. Robinson, 1861.

Noble, Mason. *Sermon Delivered in the United States Naval Academy*. Newport, R.I.: George T. Hammond, 1865.

Nutting, William J. *Three Lessons for the War, from an Ancient Chronicle*. Ann Arbor, Mich.: C. G. Clark, 1864.

Our Martyr President, Abraham Lincoln. Voices from the Pulpit of New York and Brooklyn. New York: Tibbals and Whiting, 1865.

Oviatt, George A. *A Memorial Address Delivered at the Funeral of Captain Samuel S. Hayden*. Hartford, Conn.: Case, Lockwood, 1863.

Paine, Levi. *Political Lessons of the Rebellion*. Farmington, Conn.: Samuel S. Cowles, 1862.

Palmer, Ray. *The Opening Future; or, The Results of the Present War*. Albany, N.Y.: J. Munsell, 1863.

Parke, Nathan Grier. *The Assassination of the President of the United States Overruled for the Good of Our Country*. Pittston, Pa.: Gazette Office Print, 1865.

Parker, Henry E. *Discourse the Day after the Reception of the Tidings of the Assassination of President Lincoln*. Concord, N.H.: McFarland and Jenks, 1865.

———. *An Election Sermon*. Concord, N.H.: Asa McFarland, 1861.

Patterson, Robert. *A Plea for the Brethren of the Lord*. Chicago: James Barnet, 1864.

Patton, Alfred S. *The Nation's Loss and Its Lessons*. Utica, N.Y.: Curtiss and White, 1865.

Paxton, William M. *The Nation's Gratitude and Hope*. Pittsburgh: W. G. Johnston, 1863.

Peck, David. *Special Reasons for Thanksgiving*. Barre, Mass.: J. Henry Goddard, 1863.

Peck, George. *Our Country: Its Trial and Triumph*. New York: Carlton and Porter, 1865.

Perrin, Lavalette. *The Claims of Caesar*. Hartford, Conn.: Case, Lockwood and Company, 1861.

Phelps, S. D. *Military Power a Blessing*. New Haven: Thomas H. Pease, 1864.

———. *National Symptoms*. New York: Sheldon and Company, 1862.

Plumley, G. S. *Piety Secures the Nation's Prosperity*. New York: F. Somers, 1866.

Post, Henry A. *Sermon Preached in the Presbyterian Church, Warrensburgh, Warren Co., N.Y.* Albany, N.Y.: Weed, Parsons, and Company, 1861.

Post, Jacob. *Discourse on the Assassination of President Lincoln*. Oswego: S. H. Parker, 1865.

Post, M. M. *A Thanksgiving Sermon*. Logansport, Ind.: Dague and Rayhouser, 1862.

Post, Truman M. *Our National Union*. St. Louis: R. P. Studley, 1860.

———. *Palingenesy: National Regeneration*. St. Louis: George Knapp and Co., 1864.

Powell, Edward Payson. *A Sermon on the Recent National Victories, and the National Sorrow*. Adrian, Mich.: Smith and Foster Printers, 1865.

Prime, G. Wendell. *A Sermon Delivered in Westminster Church, Detroit*. Detroit: Advertiser and Tribune, 1865.

Proudfit, John. *The Sanctuary of God, Consulted in the Present Crisis*. 2nd ed. New Brunswick, N.J.: Tribute and Van Anglen, 1861.

Pyne, Smith. *Thanksgiving Sermon*. Washington, D.C.: Chronicle Print, 1863.

Quint, Alonzo. *Christian Patriot's Present Duty*. Boston: Hollis and Gun, 1861.

———. *Three Sermons Preached in the North Congregational Church*. New Bedford, Mass.: Mercury Job Press, 1865.

Rankin, Jeremiah Eames. *Moses and Joshua*. Boston: Dakin and Metcalf, 1865.

———. *A Protest against the Aggressions of Slavery*. Potsdam, N.Y.: Greenleaf and Doty, 1856.

Ray, Charles. *A Sermon: Preached before the United Congregations of Wyoming, N.Y., on the Death of President Lincoln*. Buffalo: A. M. Clapp, 1865.

Reed, S. *A Discourse Delivered on the Occasion of the Funeral Obsequies of President Lincoln*. Boston: George C. Rand and Avery, 1865.

Reed, Villeroy Dibble. *The Conflict of Truth*. Camden, N.J.: S. Chew, 1865.

Relyea, Benjamin J. *The Nation's Mourning*. New York: Jonathan P. Prall, 1865.

Rice. N. L. *Sermon on the Death of Abraham Lincoln*. New York: William C. Bryant, 1865.

Robbins, Frank L. *A Discourse on the Death of Abraham Lincoln*. Philadelphia: Henry B. Ashmead, 1865.

Robinson, James T. *National Anniversary Address*. North Adams, Mass.: W. H. Phillips, 1865.

Rockwell, J. E. *The Day at Hand*. New York: Mission House, 1862.

Rollinson, William. *Sermon Delivered in the Baptist Church, Rahway*. Rahway, N.J.: Rahway Times Office, 1861.

Roset, Joseph. *A Sermon on the Preservation of the Union*. New York: Daly, 1861.

Salisbury, S. *Sermon; Preached West Alexandria, Ohio on the Assassination of Abraham Lincoln*. Eaton, Ohio: Eaton Weekly Register, 1865.

Salter, William. *Our National Sins and Impending Calamities*. Burlington, Iowa: Hawk-Eye Book Office, 1861.

Sample, Robert F. *The Curtained Throne*. Philadelphia: James S. Claxton, 1865.

Schenck, Noah H. *Songs in the Night*. Baltimore: Entz and Bash, 1863.

Sears, Edmund H. *Rebellion or Reform*. Boston: Crosby, Nichols, 1856.

Seiss, Joseph Augustus. *The Assassinated President; or, The Day of National Mourning for Abraham Lincoln*. Philadelphia: n.p., 1865.

———. *The Threatening Ruin; or, Our Times, Our Prospects, and Our Duty*. Philadelphia: Smith, English, 1861.

Sermon in Peterboro May 1, 1865. The National Still Unsaved. Only Repentance Can Save It. Peterboro: n.p., 1865.

Sermons by the Rev. Mr. Weston and the Rev. Byron Sunderland in the House of Representatives, April 28, 1861. Washington, D.C.: Henry Polkinhorn, 1861.

Sermons Preached in Boston on the Death of Abraham Lincoln. Boston: J. E. Tilton and Company, 1865.

Shedd, William G. T. *The Union and the War*. New York: Charles Scribner, 1863.

Simmons, Ichabod. *The Funeral Sermon of Capt. Joseph R. Toy*. Hartford, Conn.: Case, Lockwood, and Company, 1862.

———. *Our Duty in the Crisis*. Hartford, Conn.: Case, Lockwood, and Company, 1861.

Skinner, Thomas H. *Comfort in Tribulation*. New York: Anson D. F. Randolph, 1861.

———. *Light in Darkness*. Stapleton, S.I., [N.Y.]: Gazette Print, 1862.

Slater, Edward C. *The Nation's Loss*. Paducah, Ky.: Blelock, 1865.

Sloane, J. R. W. *Review of Rev. Henry J. Van Dyke's Discourse on "The Character and Influence of Abolitionism."* New York: William Erving, 1861.

———. *The Three Pillars of the Republic.* New York: Phair and Company, 1862.

Smith, Henry. *God in the War.* Buffalo, N.Y.: Wheeler, Matthews and Warren, 1863.

———. *The Religious Sentiments Proper for Our National Crisis.* Buffalo, N.Y.: Matthews and Warren, 1865.

Smith, John Cotton. *Two Discourses on the State of the Country.* New York: John A. Gray, 1861.

Smith, Moses. *God's Honor Man's Ultimate Success.* New Haven, Conn.: Thomas J. Stafford, 1863.

———. *Our Nation Not Forsaken.* Hartford, Conn.: D. E. Moseley, 1863.

———. *Past Mercies: Present Gratitude: Future Duty.* New Haven, Conn.: J. H. Benham, 1865.

Southgate, Horatio. *The Death of Lincoln, April 15th, 1865. Some of the Religious Lessons Which It Teaches.* New York: John W. Amerman, 1865.

Spear, Samuel T. *The Citizen's Duty in the Present Crisis.* New York: N. Tibbals, 1866.

———. *The Duty of the Hour.* New York: Anson D. F. Randolph, 1863.

———. *The Nation's Blessing in Trial.* Brooklyn, N.Y.: William W. Rose, 1862.

———. *Two Sermons for the Times. Obedience to the Civil Authority; and Constitutional Government against Treason.* New York: Nathan Lane, 1861.

Spees, S. G. *A New Song; or, The Marvelous Work of God, in Behalf of the American People.* Dayton, Ohio: Journal Daily and Weekly Book and Job Rooms, 1863.

Sprague, I. N. *The Duty of Sustaining the Government.* Newark, N.J.: Daily Advertiser Office, 1861.

———. *God's Purposes in the War.* Newark, N.J. Daily Advertiser Office, 1863.

———. *President Lincoln's Death.* Newark, N.J.: Daily Advertiser Office, 1865.

Sprague, William B. *Glorifying God in the Fires.* Albany, N.Y.: C. Van Benthuysen, 1861.

Spring, Gardiner. *State Thanksgiving during the Rebellion.* New York: Harper and Brothers, 1862.

Stanton, R. L. *Causes for National Humiliation.* Cincinnati: Moore, Wilstach, Keys and Company, 1861.

———. *Civil Government of God: Obedience a Duty.* Cincinnati: John D. Thorpe, 1860.

Starr, Frederick. *The Loyal Soldier.* Penn-Yan, N.Y.: G. D. M. Bridgman, 1864.

Stearns, Edward J. *The Sword of the Lord.* Baltimore: James S. Waters, 1861.

Stearns, William A. *Necessities of the War and the Conditions of Success in It.* Amherst, Mass.: Henry A. Marsh, 1861.

Stebbins, Horatio. *The President, the People and the War.* San Francisco: Charles F. Robbins, 1864.

Steele, Richard H. *Victory and Mourning.* New Brunswick, N.J.: Terhume and Van Anglen's Press, 1865.

Stevens, Alfred. *The Duty of Christians in Times of National Calamity.* Bellows Falls, Vt.: Phenix Job Office, 1863.

Stewart, William B. *The Southern Rebellion a Failure.* Philadelphia: William S. and Alfred Martien, 1863.

Stone, A. L. *The Divineness of Human Government.* Boston: Hoyt, 1861.

———. *Emancipation.* Boston: Henry Hoyt, 1862.

———. *Fasting and Feasting.* Boston: Henry Hoyt, 1865.

———. *God—the Governor*. Providence, R.I.: Knowles, Anthony and Company, 1861.

———. *National Godliness*. Boston: T. R. Marvin and Son, 1864.

———. *Praise for Victory*. Boston: T. R. Marvin, 1862.

———. *The Work of New England in the Future of Our Country*. Boston: Wright and Potter, 1865.

Street, Thomas. *A Sermon Preached in the Presbyterian Church, York, Pa.* Philadelphia: Henry B. Ashmead, 1863.

Sturtevant, J. M. *A Sermon on Our Duty to Civil Government*. Hannibal, Mo.: Frazee, Ebert, 1862.

Sunderland, Byron. *The Crisis of the Times*. Washington, D.C.: National Banner Press, 1863.

———. *Loyalty versus Copperheadism*. Washington, D.C.: National Union League, 1863.

———. *Sermon on the Public Worship of God*. Washington, D.C.: Chronicle Print, 1864.

Sutphen, Morris C. *Discourse on the Occasion of the Death of Abraham Lincoln*. Philadelphia: James A. Rodgers, 1865.

Suydam, J. Howard. *Christian Patriotism*. [Philadelphia?]: n.p., 1863.

Swain, Leonard. *God in the Strife*. Providence, R.I.: Knowles, Anthony and Company, 1861.

———. *Our Banners Set Up*. Providence, R.I.: Knowles, Anthony and Company, 1861.

Talmage, Goyn. *Admonitions for the Time*. New York: n.p., 1861.

Taylor, A. A. E. *Israel against Benjamin*. Dubuque, Iowa: Upham and Gilmore, 1861.

Thompson, A. C. *Soldier and Christian, Address at the Funeral Robert M. Carson*. [Roxbury, Mass.?: n.p., 1862].

Thompson, Joseph Parrish. *Memorial Service for Three Hundred Thousand Union Soldiers*. New York: Loyal Publication Society, 1866.

———. *No Slavery in Nebraska. The Voice of God against National Crime*. New York: Ivison and Phinney, 1854.

———. *Peace through Victory*. New York: Loyal Publication Society, 1864.

———. *The President's Fast*. New York: Thomas Holman, 1861.

Thompson, M. L. P. *The Sword; a Divine Judgment for Sin*. Cincinnati: Gazette Company Print, 1861.

———. *Thankful for Everything*. Cincinnati: Gazette Company Print, 1861.

Timlow, Heman R. *A Discourse Occasioned by the Death of Abraham Lincoln*. Rhinebeck, N.Y.: Poughkeepsie Telegraph Steam Press, 1865.

———. *A Thanksgiving Discourse*. Poughkeepsie, N.Y.: Platt and Son, 1866.

Tousey, Thomas. *Discourse on the Death of Abraham Lincoln*. Rochester, N.Y.: C. D. Tracy, 1865.

Townsend, S. P. *A Speech by Dr. S. P. Townsend. The Nation Saved by the Interposition of Providence—the Abolitionists—Wm. Lloyd Garrison—Abraham Lincoln—The Financial Question*. [New York?: n.p., 1864].

Trumbull, H. Clay. *Desirableness of Active Service*. Hartford, Conn.: Case, Lockwood, 1864.

———. *Good News! A Sermon to the Veteran Volunteers of the 10th Connecticut Regiment*. Hartford, Conn.: Case, Lockwood, 1864.

Turnbull, Robert. *Well Done. A Funeral Discourse for Captain Albert H. Niles*. Hartford, Conn.: Case, Lockwood, 1863.

Tyler, W. S. *The Law of Sacrifice; or, Death the Only Way to a Higher Life*. New Haven: E. Hayes, 1864.

Tyng, Stephen H. *Christian Loyalty*. New York: John A. Day, 1863.

Upfold, George. *God, the Help of the Nation*. Pittsburgh: W. S. Haven, 1864.

Van Dyke, Henry J. *Giving Thanks for All Things*. New York: G. F. Nesbitt, 1860.

———. *The Spirituality and Independence of the Church*. New York: n.p., 1864.

Vincent, Marvin Richardson. *The Lord of War and of Righteousness*. Troy, N.Y.: A. W. Scribner, 1864.

Vinton, Alexander H. *The Duties of Peace. The Nation's Third Thanksgiving*. New York: John A. Gray, 1865.

———. *God in Government*. Philadelphia: Protestant Episcopal Book Society, 1861.

———. *Mistakes of the Rebellion*. New York: George F. Nesbitt, 1863.

———. *Thanksgiving Sermon, November 29, 1860*. Philadelphia: Protestant Episcopal Church Book Society, 1860.

Vinton, Francis. *The Christian Idea of Civil Government*. New York: George F. Nesbitt, 1861.

Wadsworth, Charles. *American Patriotism*. Philadelphia: J. W. Bradley, 1861.

———. *The Christian Soldier*. Philadelphia: Lindsay and Blakiston, 1861.

———. *God's Culture*. Philadelphia: J. W. Bradley, 1860.

———. *War a Discipline*. San Francisco: H. H. Bancroft, 1864.

Walden, Treadwell. *The National Sacrifice*. Philadelphia: Sherman and Company, 1865.

Walker, George F. *Our Nation's Danger*. Holliston, Mass.: Plimpton and Clark, 1863.

Walker, George Leon. *Fast Day Sermon*. [Portland, Maine?: n.p., 1863].

———. *The Offered National Regeneration*. Portland, Maine: Advertiser Office, 1861.

Walker, James. *A Sermon Delivered before the Executive and Legislative Departments of the Government of Massachusetts*. Boston: Wright and Potter, 1863.

Wallace, C. C. *"A Prince and a Great Man Is Fallen."* Placerville, Calif.: Office of the Tri-Weekly News, 1865.

Wallace, Henry. *The Fast That God Hath Chosen*. Davenport, Iowa: Gazette Steam Book and Job Rooms, 1863.

Ware, John F. W. *The Danger of To-Day*. Baltimore: Cushings and Bailey, 1865.

———. *Our Duty under Reverse; A Sermon Preached in the Church of the "Cambridge Parish," Sunday, 28 July 1861*. Boston: J. Wilson, 1861.

Washburn, Daniel. *A Sermon Delivered on the Day of National Thanksgiving*. Philadelphia: J. S. McCalla, 1863.

Watson, Benjamin. *The Prayer of Asa*. Philadelphia: Collins, 1861.

Watts, Robert. *The Scripture Doctrine of Civil Government Applied to the Present Crisis*. Philadelphia: William S. and Alfred Martien, 1861.

Wayland, Francis. *Dr. Wayland on the Moral and Religious Aspects of the Nebraska Bill*. [Rochester, N.Y.: W. N. Sage, 1854].

Webb, Edwin Bonaparte. *The Christian Religion the Only True Foundation of National Perpetuity*. Augusta, Maine: Stevens and Sayward, 1861.

———. *Memorial Sermons*. Boston: George C. Rand and Avery, 1865.

Weiss, John. *Northern Strength and Weakness*. Boston: Walker, Wise and Company, 1863.

———. *The Political Exigencies of Political Submission*. Boston: Walker, Fuller, and Company, 1865.

Wentworth, J. B. *A Discourse on the Death of Abraham Lincoln*. Buffalo, N.Y.: Matthews and Warren, 1865.

West, Nathaniel. *Sermon Delivered at the Military Encampment, Near Hestonville, West Philadelphia*. Philadelphia: Ringwalt and Brown, 1861.

———. *Victory and Gratitude*. New York: E. B. Clayton's Sons, 1864.

Weston, H. G. *Incentives to Prayer and Hope*. New York: G. P. Putnam, 1861.

Wharton, Francis. *A Willing Reunion Not Impossible*. Boston: E. P. Dutton, 1863.

White, Pliny H. *A Sermon Occasioned by the Assassination of Abraham Lincoln*. Brattleboro, Vt.: Vermont Record Office, 1865.

Williams, Lester, Jr. *Freedom of Speech and Union*. Worcester, Mass.: Charles Hamilton, [1861?].

Williams, William R. *God Timing All National Changes in the Interests of His Christ*. New York: American Tract Society, 1862.

———. *National Renovation: Its Source, Its Channels, and Its Results*. New York: Anson F. D. Randolph, 1863.

Willson, Edmund B. *The Proclamation of Freedom*. Salem, Mass.: T. J. Hutchinson, 1863.

———. *Reasons for Thanksgiving*. Salem, Mass.: Observer, 1862.

Wilson, S. J. *Themes for Thanksgiving*. Pittsburgh: W. S. Haven, 1864.

Wilson, Samuel Ramsey. *The Causes and Remedies of Impending National Calamities. An Address*. Cincinnati: J. B. Elliott, 1860.

Wilson, William. *The Cause of the United States against the Rebel Confederacy, and the Cause of Jehovah Identical*. Cincinnati: B. Frankland, 1861.

Wilson, William T. *The Death of President Lincoln*. Albany, N.Y.: Weed, Parsons, and Company, 1865.

Wiswell, George F. *Victory Recognized*. Wilmington, Del.: Henry Eckel, 1863.

Woodruff, L. M. *The Common Proclamation*. Troy, N.Y.: A. W. Scribner, 1866.

Yard, Robert B. *The Providential Significance of the Death of Abraham Lincoln*. Newark, N.J.: H. Harris, 1865.

Southern and Confederate Sermons

Armstrong, George D. *"The Hand of God upon Us."* Norfolk, Va.: J. D. Gheselin, Jr., 1861.

Atkinson, Joseph M. *God the Giver of Victory and Peace*. [Raleigh?, N.C.: n.p., 1862?].

Atkinson, Thomas. *Extract from the Annual Address of the Rt. Reve. Thomas Atkinson*. [Raleigh, N.C.:] Printed at the Office of the Church Intelligencer, 1861.

———. *"On the Causes of Our National Troubles."* Wilmington, N.C.: Herald Book and Job Office, 1861.

[Barten, O. S.]. *A Sermon Preached in St. James' Church, Warrenton, Va*. Richmond: Enquirer Book and Job Office, 1861.

Blitch, J. L. *"Thy Kingdom Come."* Augusta, Ga.: "Baptist Banner" Press, 1865.

Burrows, John Lansing. *Nationality Insured! Notes of a Sermon*. Augusta, Ga.: James Nathan Ellis, 1864.

———. *The New Richmond Theater*. Richmond: Smith, Bailey and Company, 1863.

———. *Palliative and Prejudiced Judgments Condemned*. Richmond: Office Commercial Bulletin, 1865.

Butler, William C. *Sermon: Preached in St. John's Church, Richmond, Virginia, on the Sunday after the Battle of Manassas, July 21, 1861*. Richmond: Charles H. Wynne, 1861.

Caldwell, John H. *A Fast Day Sermon, Preached in Newman, Ga*. La Grange, Ga.: Daily Bulletin Office, 1864.

———. *Slavery and Southern Methodism: Two Sermons Preached in the Methodist Church in Newman, Georgia*. Newman, Ga.: Printed for the author, 1865.

Dabney, Robert Lewis. *The Christian Soldier: A Sermon Commemorative of the Death of Abram C. Carrington*. Richmond: Presbyterian Committee of Publication, 1863.

———. *True Courage*. Richmond: Presbyterian Committee of Publication of the Confederate States, 1863.

Dalzell, Rev. W. T. D. *Thanksgiving to God*. San Antonio, Tex.: Herald Book and Job Press, [1863?].

Doggett, Rev. D. S. *A Nation's Ebenezer*. Richmond: Enquirer Book and Job Press, 1862.

———. *The War and Its Close*. Richmond: Macfarlane and Fergusson, 1864.

DuBose, John E. *Sermon Addressed to Captain Parkhill's Company, "The Howell Guards."* Tallahassee: Office of the Floridian and Journal, 1861.

Dunaway, Thomas S. *A Sermon Delivered by Elder Thomas S. Dunaway of Lancaster County, Virginia*. Richmond: Enquirer Book and Job Press, [1864?].

Elliott, Rev. J. H. *The Bloodless Victory*. Charleston: A. E. Miller, 1861.

Elliott, Stephen. *Address of the Rt. Rev. Stephen Elliott*. Savannah, Ga.: John M. Cooper and Company, 1861.

———. *Extract from a Sermon Preached by Bishop Elliott*. [Savannah, Ga.?]: n.p., 1862.

———. *Funeral Services at the Burial of the Right Rev. Leonidas Polk*. Columbia, S.C.: Evans and Cogswell, 1864.

———. *Gideon's Water-Lappers*. Macon, Ga.: Burke, Boykin and Company, 1864.

———. *God's Presence with Our Army at Manassas!*. Savannah: W. Thorne Williams, 1861.

———. *God's Presence with the Confederate States*. Savannah, Ga.: W. Thorn Williams, 1861.

———. *How to Renew Our National Strength*. Richmond: McFarlane and Fergusson, 1862.

———. *"New Wine Not to Be Put into Old Bottles."* Savannah, Ga.: John M. Cooper and Company, 1862.

———. *Our Cause in Harmony with the Purposes of God in Christ Jesus*. Savannah, Ga.: John M. Cooper and Company, 1862.

———. *"Samson's Riddle." A Sermon*. Macon, Ga.: Burke, Boykin, and Company, 1863.

———. *Sermons by the Right Reverend Stephen Elliott*. New York: Pott and Amery, 1867.

———. *Vain Is the Help of Man*. Macon, Ga.: Burke, Boykin, and Company, 1864.

Finley, Rev. L. R. *The Lord Reigneth*. Richmond: Soldiers' Tract Association, M.E. Church, South, 1863.

Gregg, Alexander, Bishop of Texas. *Primary Charge, to the Clergy of the Protestant Episcopal Church*. Austin: State Gazette Job Office, 1863.

Handy, Isaac W. K. *Our National Sins*. Portsmouth, Va.: Daily and Weekly Transcript, 1861.

Higgins, S. H. *"The Mountain Moved; or, David upon the Cause and Cure of Public Calamity."* Milledgeville, Ga.: Boughton, Nisbet, Banks and Moore, State Printers, 1863.

Hoge, Moses D. *"The Christian Statesman." A Discourse Delivered at the Funeral of Hon. John Hemphill*. Richmond: Enquirer Book and Job, 1862.

Jacobs, Ferdinand. *The Committing of Our Cause to God*. Charleston: Edward C. Councell, 1851.

Lacy, Drury. *Address Delivered at the General Military Hospital, Wilson, N.C.* Fayetteville, N.C.: Edward J. Hale and Sons, 1863.

Lafferty, R. H. *A Fast-Day Sermon.* Fayetteville, N.C.: Presbyterian Office, 1862.

Lamar, J. S. *A Discourse Delivered in Christian Church.* Augusta, Ga.: Office of the Constitutionalist, 1861.

Landrum, Sylvanus. *The Battle Is God's.* Savannah, Ga.: E. J. Purse, 1863.

Lee, Leroy M. *Our Country—Our Danger—Our Duty.* Richmond: Soldiers' Tract Association, [1863].

Longstreet, Augustus Baldwin. *A Fast-Day Sermon.* Columbia, S.C.: Townsend and North, 1861.

Lord, W. W. *A Discourse, by the Rev. W. W. Lord, D.D. in Honor of Capt. Paul Hamilton.* Vicksburg, Miss.: M. Shannon, 1863.

McDonald, B. W. *Address to the Chaplains and Missionaries.* Petersburg, Va.: Printed at the Register Office, 1863.

Michelbacher, Maximilian J. *A Sermon Delivered on the Day of Prayer at the German Hebrew Synagogue.* Richmond: Macfarlane and Fergusson, 1863.

Miles, James Warley. *God in History.* Charleston: Evans and Cogswell, 1863.

Minnigerode, Charles. *Power: A Sermon Preached at St. Paul's Church, Richmond.* Richmond: W. H. Clemmitt, 1864.

Moore, Thomas Verner. *God Our Refuge and Strength in This War.* Richmond: W. Hargrave White, 1861.

Norwood, William. *God and Our Country.* Richmond: Smith, Bailey and Company, 1863.

Palmer, Benjamin Morgan. *Address Delivered at the Funeral of General Maxcy Gregg.* Columbia, S.C.: Southern Guardian Steam-Power Press, 1863.

———. *A Discourse before the General Assembly of South Carolina.* Columbia, S.C. Charles P. Pelham, 1864.

———. *A Discourse Commemorative of the Life, Character, and Genius of the Late Rev. J. H. Thornwell.* Columbia, S.C.: Southern Guardian Steam-Power Press, 1862.

———. *The Oath of Allegiance to the United States, Discussed in Its Moral and Political Bearings.* Richmond: Mcfarlane and Fergusson, 1863.

Pharr, Walter W. *Funeral Sermon on the Death of Captain A. K. Simonton.* Salisbury, N.C.: J. J. Bruner, 1862.

Pierce, George Foster. *Sermons of Bishop Pierce and Rev. B. M. Palmer, Delivered before the General Assembly at Milledgeville, Ga.* Milledgeville, Ga.: Nisbet and Barnes, 1863.

———. *The Word of God a Nation's Life.* Augusta, Ga.: Office of the Constitutionalist, 1862.

Pinckney, Charles Cotesworth. *Nebuchadnessars's Fault and Fall.* Charleston: A. J. Burke, 1861.

Prentiss, William O. *A Sermon Preached at St. Peter's Church, Charleston.* Charleston: Evans and Cogswell, 1860.

Ramsey, James Beverlin. *True Eminence Founded on Holiness.* Lynchburg, Va.: Water-Power Presses Print, 1863.

Reed, Edward. *A People Saved by the Lord.* Charleston, S.C.: Evans and Cogswell, 1861.

Rees, W. *A Sermon on Divine Providence.* Austin: Texas Almanac Office, 1863.

Renfroe, John J. D. *"The Battle Is God's."* Richmond: Macfarlane and Fergusson, 1863.

Slaughter, P. *Coercion and Conciliation*. [Richmond: Macfarlane and Fergusson, 186?].

Smyth, Thomas. *The Battle of Fort Sumter: His Mystery and Miracle; God's Mastery and Mercy*. Columbia, S.C.: Southern Guardian and Steam-Power Press, 1861.

———. *The Complete Works of Rev. Thomas Smyth*. Edited by J. William Flinn. 10 vols. Columbia, S.C.: R. L. Bryan, 1908–12.

Tichenor, I. T. *Fast-Day Sermon Delivered before the General Assembly of Alabama*. Montgomery, Ala.: Montgomery Advertiser Book and Job Printing Office, 1863.

Tucker, Henry Holcombe. *God in the War*. Milledgeville, Ga.: Boughton, Nisbet, and Barnes, 1861.

Tucker, Joel W. *The Guilt and Punishment of Extortion*. Fayetteville, N.C.: Printed at the Presbyterian Office, 1862.

Tupper, H. A. *A Thanksgiving Discourse, Delivered at Washington, Ga*. Macon, Ga.: Burke, Boykin, and Company, 1862.

Two Sermons on the Times, Preached in St. John's Church, Tallahassee. [Tallahassee, Fla.?: n.p., 186?].

Vedder, C. S. *"Offer unto God Thanksgiving."* Charleston, S.C.: Evans and Cogswell, 1861.

Vernor, W. H. *A Sermon, Delivered before the Marshall Guards No. 1, on Sunday, May 5th, 1861*. Lewisburg, Tenn.: Southern Messenger Office, 1861.

Verot, Augustin. *A Tract for the Times. Slavery and Abolitionism*. [St. Augustine, Fla.?: n.p., 1861?].

Watson, Alfred Augustus. *Sermon Delivered before the Annual Council of the Diocese of North Carolina*. Raleigh, N.C.: Progress Print, 1863.

Wheelwright, William H. *A Discourse Delivered to the Troops. Stationed at Gloucester Point, Va*. Richmond: Charles H. Wynne, 1862.

Wightman, John T. *The Glory of God, the Defence of the South*. Charleston, S.C.: Evans and Cogswell, 1861.

Wilmer, Richard H. *Future Good—The Explanation of Present Reverses*. Charlotte, N.C.: Protestant Episcopal Church Publishing Association, 1864.

Wilson, Joseph Ruggles. *Mutual Relation of Masters and Slaves as Taught in the Bible*. Augusta, Ga.: Chronicle and Sentinel, 1861.

Winkler, Edwin Theodore. *Duties of the Citizen Soldier*. Charleston, S.C.: A. J. Burke, 1861.

Winn, T. S. *The Great Victory at Manassas Junction*. Tuskaloosa, Ala.: J. F. Warren, 1861.

Union Tracts

Dulles, John W. *The Soldier's Friend*. Philadelphia: Chas. S. Luther, 1861.

Tyng, Stephen H. *The Good Soldier of Jesus Christ*. Boston: American Tract Society, 1861.

Ware, John F. W. *A Few Words with the Convalescent*. Boston: American Unitarian Association, 1864.

———. *The Home to the Hospital. Addressed to the Sick and Wounded of the Army of the Union*. Boston: American Unitarian Association, 1862.

———. *On Picket*. Boston: American Unitarian Association, 1863.

———. *The Rebel*. Boston: American Unitarian Association, 1863.

———. *To the Color*. Boston: American Unitarian Association, 1863.

———. *Wounded in the Hands of the Enemy*. Boston: American Unitarian Association, 1863.

Confederate Tracts and Broadsides

Andrews, John Nevins. *Why Do You Swear?*. Raleigh, N.C.: n.p., 186[?].

[Alexander, Archibald]. *Christ's Gracious Invitation*. Raleigh, N.C.: n.p., [1863?].

———. *Love to an Unseen Savior*. Raleigh, N.C.: Raleigh Register, 1863.

Anecdotes for Our Soldiers. No. 1. Charleston: Evans and Cogswell, 186[?].

Anecdotes for Our Soldiers. No. 3. Charleston: Evans and Cogswell, 186[?].

Are You a Soldier?. N.p.: n.p., 186[?].

Are You Prepared?. Raleigh, N.C.: n.p. 186[?].

Are You Ready?. Richmond: Mcfarlane and Ferguson, 186[?].

B., Mrs. L. N. [pseud.]. *The Christian Soldier the True Hero*. Charleston: Evans and Cogswell, 186[?].

Blood upon the Door Posts; or, Means of Safety in the Time of Danger. Petersburg: Evangelical Tract Society, 186[?].

The Bold Blasphemer. A Narrative of Facts. Richmond: Presbyterian Committee of Publication, 186[?].

Boykin, S. *The Joyful Tidings*. Raleigh, N.C.: n.p., 186[?].

[Brockenbrough, Mrs. Frances Blake]. *A Mother's Parting Words to Her Soldier Boy*. Petersburg: n.p., 186[?].

Camp Nineveh. Petersburg, Va.: n.p., 186[?].

Can I Be Religious While I Am a Soldier?. Richmond: Soldiers' Tract Association, 186[?].

Christian, W. H. *The Importance of a Soldier Becoming a Christian*. Richmond: Soldiers' Tract Association, 186[?].

The Confederate Hero and His Heroic Father. Charleston: Evans and Cogswell, [1862?].

Crumly, William W. *The Soldier's Bible by William W. Crumly, Chaplain of Georgia Hospital, Richmond*. Raleigh, N.C.: n.p., 186[?].

[Curry, Jabez L. M.]. *Swearing*. Raleigh: n.p., 186[?].

D., W. E. [pseud.]. *A Soldier to His Comrades*. Richmond: n.p., [1863?].

Dabney, Robert Lewis. *Swear Not*. Petersburg, Va.: n.p., [1863?].

The Day of the Trial. Charleston: Evans and Cogswell, 186[?].

Deems, Charles Force. *Christ in You*. Raleigh, N.C.: n.p., 186[?].

Delay; or, The Accepted Time. Richmond: Presbyterian Committee of Publication, 186[?].

Do Thyself No Harm. Charleston: Evans and Cogswell, 186[?].

[Duncan, James A.]. *Address to Christians throughout the World* [Richmond: n.p., 1863].

Dwight, Timothy. *The Seventh Commandment*. Petersburg, Va.: n.p., [1863?].

[Elford, C. J.]. *The Confederate Sunday School Hymn Book*. Greenville, S.C.: G. E. Elford's Press, 1863.

Eternity! Think of It. Richmond: Soldiers' Tract Association, 186[?].

A Few Words to the Soldiers of the Confederate States. Charleston: Evans and Cogswell, 186[?].

Finley, I. Randolph. *The Broken Vow*. Richmond: Soldiers' Tract Association, 186[?].

The Great Gathering. Raleigh, N.C.: n.p., 186[?].

How Do You Bear Your Trials? The Soldier, Sick, Sorrowful and Dying. Charleston: Evans and Cogswell, 186[?].

How Long Have You Been Sick? The Soldier's Legacy. Charleston: Evans and Cogswell, 186[?].

Jesus, the Soldier's Friend. By a Young Lady of Virginia. Petersburg, Va.: Charles LeRoi, 1862.

Jeter, Jeremiah Bell. *The Evils of Gaming. A Letter to Friend in the Army*. Raleigh, N.C.: n.p., 186[?].

Jones, Delia Wight. *The Christian Regiment Encamped in Every Soul*. Raleigh, N.C.: n.p., 186[?].

A Kind Word to the Officers of Our Army. Charleston: Evans and Cogswell, 186[?].

Kingsbury, Theodore Bryant. *The Great Amnesty*. Raleigh, N.C.: n.p., 186[?].

A Letter to a Son in Camp. Charleston: Evans and Cogswell, 186[?].

Lieutenant R.; or, The Tract Read in the Theatre. Charleston: Evans and Cogswell, 186[?].

Liquor and Lincoln. By a Physician. Petersburg, [Va.?]: n.p., 186[?].

McCabe, John Collins. *The Young Mississippian*. [Richmond: Soldiers' Tract Association, M.E. Church, 1863?].

McGill, John, Bishop of Richmond. *Faith, the Victory; or, A Comprehensive View of the Principal Doctrines of the Christian Religion*. Richmond: J. W. Randolph, 1865.

McGready, James. *An Appeal to the Young*. Raleigh, N.C.: n.p., 186[?].

McIntosh, William H. *How Long Have I to Live?*. Raleigh, N.C.: n.p., 186[?].

Madison, L. B. *The Contrast*. Richmond: Soldiers' Tract Association, M.E. Church, South, 186[?].

Martyrs of the Hospitals. Raleigh, N.C.: n.p., 186[?].

Michelbacher, Maximilian J. *Prayer of the C.S. Soldiers*. Richmond: n.p., 186[?].

[Mott, T. S. W.]. *Catechism, To Be Taught Orally To Those Who Cannot Read: Designed Especially for the Instruction of Slaves, in the Prot. Episcopal Church in the Confederate States*. Raleigh, N.C.: Office of the Church Intelligencer, 1862.

The Muster. Charleston, S.C.: Evans and Cogswell, 186[?].

Now!. Raleigh, N.C.: n.p., 186[?].

Our Triumph. Richmond: Soldiers' Tract Association, 1864.

Our War, Our Cause, and Our Duty. Addressed to the Confederate Soldiers. Charleston, S.C.: Evans and Cogswell, [1861?].

Palmer, Benjamin Morgan. *Social Dancing*. Petersburg, Va.: Evangelical Tract Society, 186[?].

Patriotism Not Piety. Charleston: Evans and Cogwell, 186[?].

Peck, Thomas E. *Address to the Churches, upon the Present Crisis*. Petersburg, Va.: Evangelical Tract Society, 1862.

Penick, Daniel A. *The Captain of Salvation*. Raleigh, N.C.: n.p., 186[?].

———. *Prodigal Sons*. Raleigh, N.C.: n.p., 186[?].

Petheridge, C. W. *The Warfare Ended*. Richmond: Soldiers' Tract Association, [1863?].

Pharr, Walter W. *Funeral Sermon on the Death of Captain A. K. Simonton, of Statesville, N.C.* Salisbury, N.C.: J. J. Bruner, 1862.

Prepare for Battle. Raleigh, N.C.: n.p., 186[?].

Prepare to Meet Thy God. Raleigh, N.C.: n.p., 186[?].

Protestant Episcopal Church. Diocese of Virginia. Diocesan Missionary Society. *Prayer Book for the Camp*. Richmond: McFarland and Ferguson, 1863.

Quintard, C. T. *Balm for the Weary and the Wounded*. Columbia, S.C.: Evans and Cogswell, 1864.

Read, C. H. *National Fast*. Richmond: 1861.

[Royal, William]. *Advice to Soldiers*. Raleigh, N.C.: n.p., 186[?].

The Sentinel. Petersburg, [Va.?]: n.p., [1861?].

Shuck, L. H. *"Home Sweet Home."* Raleigh, N.C.: n.p., 186[?].

The Silly Fish. Columbia, S.C.: Southern Guardian, 186[?].

The Soldier's Grave. A Chaplain's Story. Raleigh, N.C.: n.p., 1863.

The Soldier's Great Want. Petersburg, Va.: Evangelical Tract Society, [1863?].

The Soldier's Hymn Book. Charleston, S.C.: South Carolina Tract Society, 1862.

The Soldier's Pocket Bible. Issued for the Use of the Army of Oliver Cromwell. Charleston, S.C.: Evans and Cogswell, 186[?].

Stiles, Joseph Clay. *Capt. Thomas E. King; or, a Word to the Army and the Country*. Charleston, S.C.: South Carolina Tract Society, 1864.

———. *National Rectitude the Only True Basis of National Prosperity: An Appeal to the Confederate States*. Petersburg, Va.: Evangelical Tract Society, 1863.

Taylor, George B. *In the Hospital*. N.p.: n.p., 186[?].

Teasdale, T. C. *The Season of Divine Mercy*. Raleigh, N.C.: n.p., 186[?].

A Tract for the Soldier. Raleigh, N.C.: n.p., 186[?].

Tucker, John Randolph. *The Bible or Atheism*. Richmond: n.p., 186[?].

A Voice from Heaven. Raleigh, N.C.: Strother and Marcom, 1861.

[Weld, Theodore Dwight]. *Pitching the Tent toward Sodom*. Petersburg, Va.: Evangelical Tract Society, [1863?].

A Word of Comfort for the Sick Soldier. N.p.: n.p., 1861.

A Word of Warning for the Sick Soldier. Raleigh, N.C.: n.p., 186[?].

The Wounded; or, a Time to Think. Richmond: Presbyterian Committee of Publication, 186[?].

Books

Abbott, Henry Livermore. *Fallen Leaves: The Civil War Letters of Major Henry Livermore Abbott*. Edited by Robert Garth Scott. Kent, Ohio: Kent State University Press, 1991.

Abbott, Lyman. *Reminiscences*. Boston: Houghton Mifflin, 1915.

Abbott, Stephen G. *The First Regiment New Hampshire Volunteers in the Great Rebellion*. Keene, N.H.: Sentinel Printing Company, 1890.

An Account of the Sufferings of the Friends of North Carolina Yearly Meeting, in Support of their Testimony against War, from 1861–1865. Baltimore: Peace Association of Friends of America, 1868.

Adams, Nehemiah. *A South-Side View of Slavery; Three Months at the South in 1854*. Boston: T. R. Marvin, 1855.

Adams, John G. B. *Reminiscences of the Nineteenth Massachusetts Regiment*. Boston: Wright and Potter, 1899.

Adams, John Ripley. *Memorial and Letters of Rev. John R. Adams, D.D., Chaplain of the Fifth Maine and One Hundred and Twenty-first New York Regiments during the War of the Rebellion*. [Cambridge, Mass.: University Press, 1890].

Alcott, Louisa May. *Hospital Sketches*. Edited by Bessie Z. Zones. Cambridge, Mass.: Harvard University Press, 1960.

Alexander, Edward Porter. *Fighting for the Confederacy: The Personal Recollections of the General Edward Porter Alexander*. Edited by Gary W. Gallagher. Chapel Hill: University of North Carolina Press, 1989.

Allen, Ujanirtus. *Campaigning with "Old Stonewall": Confederate Captain Ujanirtus Allen's Letters to His Wife.* Edited by Randall Allen and Keith S. Bohannon. Baton Rouge: Louisiana State University Press, 1998.

American Annual Cyclopaedia and Register of Important Events of the Year 1862. New York: D. Appleton, 1872.

American Annual Cyclopaedia and Register of Important Events of the Year 1863. New York: D. Appleton, 1872.

American Annual Cyclopaedia and Register of Important Events of the Year 1864. New York: D. Appleton, 1872.

American Annual Cyclopaedia and Register of Important Events of the Year 1865. New York: D. Appleton, 1872.

The American Union Commission. Speeches of Hon. W. Dennison, Rev. J. P. Thompson, N. G. Taylor, Hon. J. R. Doolittle, Gen. J. A. Garfield, M.C. New York: Sanford, Harroun, and Company, 1865.

Andrews, Eliza Frances. *The War-Time Journal of a Georgia Girl, 1864–1865.* Edited by Spencer Bidwell King Jr. Macon, Ga.: Ardivan Press, 1960.

Andrews, W. H. *Footprints of a Regiment: A Recollection of the 1st Georgia Regulars.* Edited by Richard M. McMurry. Atlanta: Longstreet Press, 1992.

Apperson, John Samuel. *Repairing the "March of Mars": The Civil War Diaries of John Samuel Apperson, Hospital Steward in the Stonewall Brigade, 1861–1865.* Edited by John D. Roper. Macon, Ga.: Mercer University Press, 2001.

Armstrong, Hallock. *Letters from a Pennsylvania Chaplain at the Siege of Petersburg, 1865.* Edited by Hallock F. Raup. Kent, [Ohio?]: n.p., 1961.

Axford, Faye Acton, ed. *"To Lochaber Na Mair": Southerners View the Civil War.* Athens, Ala.: Athens, 1986.

Ayers, James T. *Civil War Diary of James T. Ayers.* Edited by John Hope Franklin. Springfield: Illinois State Historical Society, 1947.

Ayling, Augustus D. *A Yankee at Arms: The Diary of Lieutenant Augustus D. Ayling, 29th Massachusetts Volunteers.* Edited by Charles F. Herberger. Knoxville: University of Tennessee Press, 1999.

[Bacon, Mrs. Georgeanna Muirson]. *Letters of a Family during the War for the Union, 1861–65.* 2 vols. New Haven, Conn.: Tuttle, Morehouse and Taylor, 1899.

Bacot, Ada. *A Confederate Nurse: The Diary of Ada W. Bacot, 1860–1863.* Edited by Jean V. Berlin. Columbia: University of South Carolina Press, 1994.

Bahnson, Charles Frederic. *Bright and Gloomy Days: The Civil War Correspondence of Captain Charles Frederic Bahnson, a Moravian Confederate.* Edited by Sarah Bahnson Chapman. Knoxville: University of Tennessee Press, 2003.

Balme, J. R. *American States, Churches and Slavery.* Edinburgh: Simpkin, Marshall, 1862.

Bangs, Heman. *The Autobiography and Journal of Rev. Heman Bangs.* New York: N. Tibbals and Son, 1874.

Barber, Flavel C. *Holding the Line: The Third Tennessee Infantry, 1861–1864.* Edited by Robert H. Ferrell. Kent, Ohio: Kent State University Press, 1994.

Barclay, Alexander T. *Ted Barclay, Liberty Hall Volunteers: Letters from the Stonewall Brigade (1861–1864).* Edited by Charles W. Turner. Natural Bridge Station, Va.: Rockbridge, 1992.

Barnes, Albert. *An Inquiry into the Scriptural Views of Slavery*. Philadelphia: Parry and McMillan, 1857.

Barnes, Joseph K., *The Medical and Surgical History of the Civil War*. 15 vols. Wilmington, N.C.: Broadfoot, 1990.

Barr, James Michael. *Let Us Meet in Heaven: The Civil War Letters of James Michael Barr, 5th South Carolina Cavalry*. Edited by Thomas D. Mays. Abilene, Tex.: McWhiney Foundation Press, 2001.

Bartlett, Asa W. *History of Twelfth Regiment New Hampshire Volunteers*. Concord, N.H.: Ira C. Evans, 1897.

Bates, Edward. *The Diary of Edward Bates, 1859–1866*. Edited by Howard K. Beale. Washington, D.C.: Government Printing Office, 1933.

Bates, James C. *A Texas Cavalry Officer's Civil War: The Diary and Letters of James C. Bates*. Edited by Richard Lowe. Baton Rouge: Louisiana State University Press, 1999.

Beale, Jane Howison. *The Journal of Jane Howison Beale, Fredericksburg, Virginia, 1850–1862*. Fredericksburg, Va.: Historic Fredericksburg Foundation, 1862.

Beaudry, Louis N. *War Journal of Louis N. Beaudry, Fifth New York Cavalry: The Diary of a Union Chaplain, Commencing February 16, 1863*. Edited by Richard E Beaudry. Jefferson, N.C.: McFarland, 1996.

Beecham, Robert. *As If It Were Glory: Robert Beecham's Civil War from the Iron Brigade to the Black Regiments*. Edited by Michael E. Stevens. Madison, Wisc.: Madison House, 1998.

Beidelman, George Washington. *The Civil War Letters of George Washington Beidelman*. Edited by Catherine H. Vanderslice. New York: Vantage Press, 1978.

Belcher, Joseph. *The Religious Denominations in the United States: Their History, Doctrine, Government and Statistics. With a Preliminary Sketch of Judaism, Paganism and Mohammedanism*. Philadelphia: John E. Porter, 1857.

Bennett, William W. *A Narrative of the Great Revival Which Prevailed in the Southern Armies*. Harrisonburg, Va.: Sprinkle Publications, 1989.

Bennitt, John. *"I Hope to Do My Country Service": The Civil War Letters of John Bennitt, M.D., Surgeon, 19th Michigan Infantry*. Edited by Robert Beasecker. Detroit: Wayne State University Press, 2005.

Berkeley, Henry Robinson. *Four Years in the Confederate Artillery: The Diary of Private Henry Robinson Berkeley*. Edited by William H. Runge. Chapel Hill: University of North Carolina Press, 1961.

Berlin, Ira, et al. *Freedom: A Documentary History of Emancipation*. 4 vols. To date. Cambridge: Cambridge University Press, 1982–.

Betts, Alexander Davis. *Experience of a Confederate Chaplain, 1861–1864*. Edited by W. A. Betts. Greenville, S.C.: n.p., n.d.

Betts, Charles Bowen. *The Civil War Diary of Rev. Charles Bowen Betts, D.D.* Rock Hill, S.C.: privately printed, 1995.

The Bible on the Present Crisis. The Republic of the United States, and Its Counterfeit Presentment: The Slave Power and the Southern Confederacy. . . . New York: Sinclair Tousey, 1863.

Bicknell, George W. *History of the Fifth Regiment Maine Volunteers*. Portland, Maine: Hall L. Davis, 1871.

Billingsley, A. S. *From the Flag to the Cross; or, Scenes and Incidents of Christianity in the War.* Philadelphia: New-World Publishing Company, 1872.

Bishop, Judson W. *The Story of a Regiment: Being a Narrative of the Service of the Second Regiment Minnesota Veteran Volunteer Infantry.* St. Paul, Minn.: n.p., 1890.

Black, Chauncey F. *Essays and Speeches of Jeremiah S. Black. With a Biographical Sketch.* New York: D. Appleton, 1886.

Blackburn, George A., ed. *The Life Work of John L. Girardeau, D.D., LL.D.* Columbia, S.C.: State Company, 1916.

Blackford, Susan Leigh, ed. *Memoirs of Life In and Out of the Army in Virginia during the War between the States.* 2 vols. Lynchburg, Va.: J. P. Bell, 1894.

Blanchard, Ira. *I Marched with Sherman: Civil War Memoirs of the 20th Illinois Volunteer Infantry.* San Francisco: J. D. Huff, 1992.

Bond, Priscilla. *A Maryland Bride in the Deep South: The Civil War Diary of Priscilla Bond.* Edited by Kimberly Harrison. Baton Rouge: Louisiana State University Press, 2006.

Bonner, Robert E. *The Soldier's Pen: Firsthand Impressions of the Civil War.* New York: Hill and Wang, 2006.

Booth, Mary L. *The Uprising of a Great People. The United States in 1861.* Freeport, N.Y.: Books for Libraries Press, 1869.

Borden, Winifred, ed. *The Legacy of Fannie and Joseph.* N.p.: n.p., 1992.

Bowley, Freeman S. *A Boy Lieutenant: The 30th United States Colored Troops.* Edited by Ronald Roy Seagrave. Fredericksburg, Va.: Sergeant Kirkland's Museum and Historical Society, 1997.

Boyd, Cyrus F. *The Civil War Diary of Cyrus F. Boyd: Fifteenth Iowa Infantry, 1861–1863.* Edited by Mildren Thorne. Baton Rouge: Louisiana State University Press, 1998.

Bradley, George S. *The Star Corps; or, Notes of an Army Chaplain, during Sherman's Famous "March to the Sea."* Milwaukee: Jermain and Brightman, 1865.

Bragg, Junius Newport. *Letters of a Confederate Surgeon, 1861–65.* Edited by Helen Bragg Gaughan. Camden, AR: Hurley Company, 1960.

Brainerd, Cephas. *The Work of the Army Committee of the New York Young Men's Christian Association.* New York: J. Medole, 1866.

Brandegee, Charles. *Charlie's Civil War: A Private's Trial by Fire in the 5th New York Volunteers—Duryée Zouaves and 146th New York Volunteer Infantry.* Edited by Charles Brandegee Livingstone. Gettysburg, Pa.: Thomas Publications, 1997.

Breckinridge, Lucy. *Lucy Breckinridge of Grove Hill: The Journal of a Virginia Girl, 1862–1864.* Edited by Mary D. Robertson. Kent, Ohio: Kent State University Press, 1979.

Brevard, Keziah Goodwyn Hopkins. *A Plantation Mistress on the Eve of the Civil War: The Diary of Keziah Hopkins Brevard, 1860–1861.* Edited by John Hammond Moore. Columbia: University of South Carolina Press, 1993.

Brewster, Charles Harvey. *When This Cruel War Is Over: The Civil War Letters of Charles Harvey Brewster.* Edited by David W. Blight. Amherst: University of Massachusetts Press, 1992.

Brinsfield, John Wesley, Jr., ed. *The Spirit Divided: Memoirs of Civil War Chaplains, the Confederacy.* Macon, Ga.: Mercer University Press, 2006.

Brockett, Linus P. *The Philanthropic Results of the War in America.* New York: Sheldon and Company, 1864.

Browder, George Richard. *The Heavens Are Weeping: The Diaries of George Richard Browder, 1852–1886*. Grand Rapids, Mich.: Zondervan, 1987.

Brown, William Young. *The Army Chaplain: His Office, Duties, and Responsibilities, and the Means of Aiding Him*. Philadelphia: William S. and Alfred Martien, 1863.

Browne, Francis Fisher. *The Every-Day Life of Abraham Lincoln*. Minneapolis: Northwestern Publishing Company, 1887.

Brownlow, William G. *Sketches of the Rise, Progress, and Decline of Secession; with a Narrative of Personal Adventures among the Rebels*. Philadelphia: George W. Childs, 1862.

Brunk, H. A., ed. *Life of Peter S. Hartman, with Civil War Reminiscences*. Privately printed, 1937.

Buck, Lucy Rebecca. *Shadows on My Heart: The Civil War Diary of Lucy Rebecca Buck of Virginia*. Edited by Elizabeth R. Baer. Athens: University of Georgia Press, 1997.

Bull, Rice C. *Soldiering: The Civil War Diary of Rice C. Bull, 123rd New York Volunteer Infantry*. San Rafael, Calif.: Presidio Press, 1977.

Bunting, Robert Franklin. *Our Trust Is in the God of Battles: The Civil War Letters of Robert Franklin Bunting, Chaplain, Terry's Texas Rangers, C.S.A.* Edited by Thomas W. Cutrer. Knoxville: University of Tennessee Press, 2006.

Burge, Dolly Lunt. *The Diary of Dolly Lunt Burge, 1848–1879*. Edited by Christine Jacobson Carter. Athens: University of Georgia Press, 1997.

Burgwyn, William H. S. *A Captain's War: The Letters and Diaries of William H. S. Burgwyn, 1861–1865*. Edited by Herbert M. Schiller. Shippensburg, Pa.: White Maine, 1994.

Burney, Samuel A. *A Southern Soldier's Letters Home: The Civil War Letters of Samuel A. Burney, Cobb's Georgia Legion, Army of Northern Virginia*. Edited by Nat S. Turner III. Macon, Ga.: Mercer University Press, 2002.

Burns, Amanda McDowell. *Fiddles in the Cumberland*. Edited Lela McDowell Blankenship. New York: Richard R. Smith, 1943.

Burton, E. P. *Diary of E. P. Burton Surgeon 7th Reg. Ill. 3rd. Brig. 2nd Div. 16A.C.* Des Moines, Iowa: Historical Records Survey, 1939.

Bushnell, Horace. *The Vicarious Sacrifice, Ground in Principles of Universal Obligation*. New York: Charles Scribner, 1866.

Butler, Benjamin F. *Butler's Book: Autobiography and Personal Reminiscences*. Boston: A. M. Thayer, 1892.

———. *Private and Official Correspondence of Gen. Benjamin F. Butler, during the Period of the Civil War*. 5 vols. Norwood, Mass.: Plimpton Press, 1917.

Butterfield, Horatio Quincy. *U.S. Christian Commission: A Delegate's Story*. Philadelphia: n.p., 1863.

Caldwell, J. F. J. *The History of a Brigade of South Carolinians, Known First as "Gregg's," and Subsequently as "McGowan's Brigade."* Philadelphia: King and Baird, 1866.

Callaway, Joshua K. *The Civil War Letters of Joshua K. Callaway*. Edited by Judith Lee Hallock. Athens: University of Georgia Press, 1997.

Campbell, John Quincy Adams. *The Union Must Stand: The Civil War Diary of John Quincy Adams Campbell, Fifth Iowa Volunteer Infantry*. Edited by Mark Grimsley and Todd D. Miller. Knoxville: University of Tennessee Press, 2000.

Cannon, J. P. *Bloody Banners and Barefoot Boys*. Edited by Noel Crowson and John V. Brogden. Shippensburg, Pa.: Burd Street Press, 1997.

Carpenter, Francis B. *The Inner Life of Abraham Lincoln Six Months at the White House.* Boston: Osgood and Company, 1880.

Carter, Robert Goldthwaite. *Four Brothers in Blue; or, Sunshine and Shadows of the War of the Rebellion.* Austin: University of Texas Press, 1978.

Carter, Susan B. et al., eds. *Historical Statistics of the United States.* 5 vols. New York: Cambridge University Press, 2006.

Castleman, Alfred L. *The Army of the Potomac. Behind the Scenes. A Diary of Unwritten History.* Milwaukee: Strickland and Company, 1863.

Cate, Armistead, ed. *Two Soldiers: The Campaign Diaries of Thomas J. Key, C.S.A., December 7, 1863–May 17, 1865 and Robert J. Campbell, U.S.A., January 1, 1864–July 21, 1864.* Chapel Hill: University of North Carolina Press, 1938.

Cavada, F. F. *Libby Life: Experiences of a Prisoner of War in Richmond, Va., 1863–64.* Lanham, Md.: University Press of America, 1985.

Chadick, Mary Jane. *Incidents of the War: The Civil War Journal of Mary Jane Chadick.* Edited by Nancy M. Rohr. Huntsville, Ala.: SilverThreads, 2005.

Chamberlayne, John Hampden. *Ham Chamberlayne—Virginian: Letters and Papers of an Artillery Officer for Southern Independence, 1861–1865.* Edited by C. G. Chamberlayne. Richmond: Dietz Printing, 1932.

Chambers, Henry Alexander. *Diary of Captain Henry A. Chambers.* Edited by T. H. Pearce. Wendell, N.C.: Broadfoot's Bookmark, 1983.

Chambers, William Pitt. *Blood and Sacrifice: The Civil War Journal of a Confederate Soldier.* Edited by Richard A. Baumgartner. Huntington, West Va.: Blue Acorn Press, 1994.

Chase, Salmon P. *The Salmon P. Chase Papers.* 5 vols. Edited by John Niven et al. Kent, Ohio: Kent State University Press, 1993–98.

Cheever, George B. *God against Slavery: And the Freedom and Duty of the Pulpit to Rebuke It, as a Sin against God.* New York: Joseph H. Ladd, 1857.

Chesebrough, David B., ed. *God Ordained This War: Sermons on the Sectional Crisis, 1830–1865.* Columbia: University of South Carolina Press, 1991.

Chesnut, Mary. *Mary Chesnut's Civil War.* Edited by C. Vann Woodward. New Haven, Conn.: Yale University Press, 1981.

———. *The Private Mary Chesnut: The Unpublished Civil War Diaries.* Edited by C. Vann Woodward and Elisabeth Muhlenfeld. New York: Oxford University Press, 1984.

Chester, H. W. *Recollections of the War of the Rebellion: A Story of the 2nd Ohio Volunteer Cavalry, 1861–1865.* Wheaton, Ill.: Wheaton History Center, 1996.

Child, William. *Letters from a Civil War Surgeon: Dr. William Child of the Fifth New Hampshire Volunteers.* Solon, Maine: Polar Bear, 2001.

Chisholm, Daniel. *The Civil War Notebook of Daniel Chisholm: A Chronicle of Daily Life in the Union Army, 1864–1865.* Edited by W. Springer Menge and J. August Shimrak. New York: Orion Books, 1989.

Chittenden, Lucius E. *Invisible Siege: The Journal of Lucius E. Chittenden, April 15, 1861–July 14, 1861.* San Diego, Calif.: Americana Exchange Press, 1969.

Christ in the Army: A Selection of Sketches of the Work of the U.S. Christian Commission. Philadelphia: J. B. Rogers, 1865.

Christ, Mark K., ed. *"Getting Used to Being Shot At": The Spence Family Civil War Letters.* Fayetteville: University of Arkansas Press, 2002.

A Christian Address to the Confederate Soldiers. Winchester, Va.: Printed at the Republican
    Office, 1861.
Christianity versus Treason and Slavery. Religion Rebuking Sedition. [Philadelphia:
    H. B. Ashmead, 1864].
*Churches and Institutions of Learning Destroyed by the United States Military Forces during the
    Civil War, but Not as an Act of Military Necessity, the Materials Having Been Appropriated
    and Used.* Washington, D.C.: Government Printing Office, 1912.
A Churchman. *The Cruelties of War.* Philadelphia: Printed for the Author, 1864.
Clark, Charles M. *History of the Thirty-ninth Regiment Illinois Veteran Volunteer Infantry.*
    Chicago: Veteran Association of the Regiment, 1889.
Clark, Walter. *The Papers of Walter Clark.* Edited by Aubrey Lee Brooks and Hugh Talmage
    Lefler. 2 vols. Chapel Hill: University of North Carolina Press, 1948–50.
————. *Under the Stars and Bars; or, Memoirs of Four Years Service with the Oglethorpes, of
    Augusta, Georgia.* Augusta, Ga.: Chronicle Printing, 1900.
Clarke, James Freeman. *Secession, Concession, or Self-Possession: Which?.* Boston: Walker,
    Wise, 1861.
Coe, Hamlin Alexander. *Mine Eyes Have Seen the Glory: Combat Diaries of Union Sergeant
    Hamlin Alexander Coe.* Edited by David Coe. Rutherford, N.J.: Fairleigh Dickinson
    University Press, 1975.
Coles, R. T. *From Huntsville to Appomattox: R. T. Coles's History of 4th Regiment,
    Alabama Volunteer Infantry, C.S.A., Army of Northern Virginia.* Edited by Jeffrey D. Stoker.
    Knoxville: University of Tennessee Press, 1996.
Colyer, Vincent. *Report of the Christian Mission to the United States Army.* New York:
    G. A. Whitehorne, [1862?].
Comey, Henry Newton. *A Legacy of Valor: The Memoirs and Letters of Captain Henry Newton
    Comey, 2nd Massachusetts Infantry.* Edited by Lyman Richard Comey. Knoxville:
    University of Tennessee Press, 2004.
*The Complete Correspondence between Union Members of Pine Street Presbyterian Church and
    Their Pastor, Rev. S. B. McPheeters, D.D., upon the Subject of Loyalty to the Government.* St.
    Louis, Mo.: printed for the use of the members of that church and congregation, 1862.
Contributions to a History of the Richmond Howitzer Battalion. Edited by Lee A. Wallace Jr.
    Baltimore: Butternut and Blue, 2000.
Conway, Moncure Daniel. *Autobiography: Memories and Experiences of Moncure Daniel
    Conway.* 2 vols. Boston: Houghton, Mifflin, 1904.
Corby, William. *Memoirs of Chaplain Life: Three Years with the Irish Brigade in the Army of the
    Potomac.* Edited by Lawrence Frederick Kohl. New York: Fordham University Press,
    1992.
Corsan, W. C. *Two Months in the Confederate States: An Englishman's Travels through the South.*
    Edited by Benjamin H. Trask. Baton Rouge: Louisiana State University Press, 1996.
Cram, George F. *Soldiering with Sherman: Civil War Letters of George F. Cram.* Edited by
    Jennifer Cain Bohrnstedt. DeKalb: Northern Illinois University Press, 2000.
Cross, Andrew Boyd. *The Battle of Gettysburg and the Christian Commission.* [Baltimore?: n.p.,
    1865].
Cross, Joseph. *Camp and Field. Papers from the Portfolio of an Army Chaplain.* 4 vols. Macon,
    Ga.: Burke, Boykin and Company, 1864.

Culver, J. F. *"Your Affectionate Husband, J. F. Culver": Letters Written during the Civil War.* Edited by Leslie W. Dunlap. Iowa City: Friends of the University of Iowa Libraries, 1978.

Cumming, Kate. *Kate: The Journal of a Confederate Nurse.* Edited by Richard Barksdale. Baton Rouge: Louisiana State University Press, 1959.

Curtis, Newton Martin. *From Bull Run to Chancellorsville: The Story of the Sixteenth New York Infantry Together with Personal Reminiscences.* New York: G. P. Putnam's Sons, 1906.

Curtis, Orson Blair. *History of the Twenty-fourth Michigan of the Iron Brigade, Known as the Detroit and Wayne County Regiment.* Detroit: Winn and Hammond, 1891.

Cutrer, Thomas W., and T. Michael Parrish, eds. *Brothers in Gray: The Civil War Letters of the Pierson Family.* Baton Rouge: Louisiana State University Press, 1997.

Dabney, Robert Lewis. *A Defence of Virginia, [and through Her of the South], in Recent and Pending Contests against the Sectional Party.* New York: E. J. Hale, 1867.

———. *Life and Campaigns of Lieut.-Gen. Thomas J. Jackson.* New York: Blelock and Company, 1866.

Daly, Maria Lydig. *Diary of a Union Lady.* Edited by Harold Earl Hammond. New York: Funk and Wagnalls, 1962.

Dame, William Butler. *From the Rapidan to Richmond and the Spotsylvania Campaign: A Sketch in Personal Narrative of the Scenes a Soldier Saw.* Baltimore: Green-Lucas, 1920.

Dana, Charles A. *Recollections of the Civil War: With the Leaders at Washington and in the Field in the Sixties.* New York: D. Appleton, 1898.

Davis, Charles E. *Three Years in the Army. The Story of the Thirteenth Massachusetts Volunteers from July 16, 1861, to August 1, 1864.* Boston: Estes and Lauriat, 1894.

Davis, Jefferson. *The Messages and Papers of Jefferson Davis and Confederacy Including Diplomatic Correspondence, 1861–1865.* Edited by James D. Richardson. 2 vols. New York: Chelsea House-Robert Hector, 1966.

Davis, Nicholas A. *Chaplain Davis and Hood's Texas Brigade.* Edited by Donald E. Everett. Baton Rouge: Louisiana State University Press, 1999.

Davis, William. *The Civil War Journal of Billy Davis From Hopewell, Indiana to Port Republic, Virginia.* Edited by Richard S. Skidmore. Greencastle, Ind.: Nuggett Publishers, 1989.

Day, W. A. *A True History of Company I, 49th Regiment, North Carolina Troops, in the Great Civil War, between the North and South.* Newton, N.C.: Enterprise Job Office, 1893.

Denison, Frederic. *Shot and Shell: The Third Rhode Island Heavy Artillery Regiment in the Rebellion, 1861–1865.* Providence, R.I.: J. A. and R. A. Reid, 1879.

Dexter, Seymour. *Seymour Dexter, Union Army: Journal and Letters of Civil War Service in Company K, 23rd New York Volunteer Regiment of Elmira.* Edited by Carl A. Morrell. Jefferson, N.C.: McFarland, 1996.

Dicey, Edward. *The Spectator of America.* Edited by Herbert Mitang. Athens: University of Georgia Press, 1989.

Dimond, E. Grey, and Herman Hattaway, eds. *Letters from Forest Place: A Plantation Family's Correspondence, 1846–1881.* Jackson: University Press of Mississippi, 1993.

Domestic Slavery Considered as a Scriptural Institution: In a Correspondence between the Rev. Richard Fuller, of Beaufort, S.C., and Rev. Francis Wayland of Providence, R.I. New York: Lewis Colby, 1845.

Domschcke, Bernhard. *Twenty Months in Captivity: The Memoirs of a Union Officer in*

Confederate Prisons. Edited and translated by Frederic Trautman. Rutherford, N.J.: Fairleigh Dickinson University Press, 1987.

Dooley, John Edward. *John Dooley, Confederate Soldier: His War Journal*. Edited by Joseph T. Durkin. Notre Dame, Ind.: University of Notre Dame Press, 1983.

Douglas, Henry Kyd. *I Rode with Stonewall*. Chapel Hill: University of North Carolina Press, 1940.

Downing, Alexander G. *Downing's Civil War Diary*. Edited by Olynthis B. Clark. Des Moines, Iowa: Historical Department of Iowa, 1916.

Duke, Basil W. *Reminiscences of General Basil W. Duke, C.S.A.* Garden City, N.Y.: Doubleday, Page, 1911.

Dunham, Albertus A., and Charles LaForest Dunham. *Through the South with a Union Soldier*. Edited by Arthur H. DeRosier Jr. Johnson City: East Tennessee State University, 1969.

Dwight, Elizabeth A. *Life and Letters of Wilder Dwight, Lieut-Col. Second Mass. Inf. Vols.* Boston: Ticknor and Fields, 1868.

Eagleton, Davis F. *A Memorial Sketch of Rev. George Eagleton: The Record of a Busy Life*. Richmond: Whittet and Shepperson, 1900.

Eaton, John. *Grant, Lincoln, and the Freedmen*. New York: Longmans, Green, 1907.

Eddy, Richard. *History of the Sixtieth Regiment New York State Volunteers*. Philadelphia: Eddy, 1864.

Edmondson, Belle. *A Lost Heroine of the Confederacy: The Diaries and Letters of Belle Edmondson*. Jackson: University Press of Mississippi, 1990.

Edmondston, Catherine Ann Devereux. *"Journal of a Secesh Lady": The Diary of Catherine Ann Devereux Edmondston, 1860–1866*. Edited by Beth G. Crabtree and James W. Patton. Raleigh, N.C.: Division of Archives and History, 1979.

Eggleston, George Carry. *A Rebel's Recollections*. Edited by David Donald. Bloomington: Indiana University Press, 1959.

Elder, Bishop William Henry. *Civil War Diary (1862–1865) of Bishop William Henry Elder, Bishop of Natchez*. [Natchez?, Miss.?]: R. O. Geron, 1960.

Elliott, Charles. *South-Western Methodism, a History of the M.E. Church in the South-West from 1844 to 1864*. Cincinnati: Poe and Hitchcock, 1868.

Elmore, Grace Brown. *A Heritage of Woe: The Civil War Diary of Grace Brown Elmore, 1861–1868*. Edited by Marli F. Weiner. Athens: University of Georgia Press, 1997.

Emerson, Ralph Waldo. *Emerson in His Journals*. Edited by Joe Porte. Cambridge, Mass.: Harvard University Press, 1982.

Emerson, Sarah Hopper, ed. *Life of Abby Hopper Gibbons: Told Chiefly through Her Correspondence*. New York: G. P. Putnam's Sons, 1897.

English Combatant. *Battle-Fields of the South, from Bull Run to Fredericksburgh; With Sketches of Confederate Commanders, and Gossip of the Camps*. New York: John Bradburn, 1864.

Engs, Robert F., and Corey M. Brooks, ed. *Their Patriotic Duty: The Civil War Letters of the Evans Family of Brown County, Ohio*. New York: Fordham University Press, 2007.

Evans, Clement Anselm. *Confederate Military History Extended Edition*. 17 vols. Wilmington, N.C.: Broadfoot, 1987.

———. *Intrepid Warrior: Clement Anselm Evans, Confederate General from Georgia, Life, Letters, and Diaries of the War Years*. Edited by Robert Grier Stephens Jr. Dayton, Ohio: Morningside, 1992.

Evans, Robert G., ed. *The Sixteenth Mississippi Infantry: Civil War Letters and Reminiscences*. Jackson: University Press of Mississippi, 2002.

Everson, Guy R., and Edward H. Simpson Jr., eds. *"Far, Far from Home": The Wartime Letters of Dick and Tally Simpson, Third South Carolina Volunteers*. New York: Oxford University Press, 1994.

Fain, Eliza Rhea Anderson. *Sanctified Trial: The Diary of Eliza Rhea Anderson Fain, a Confederate Woman in East Tennessee*. Edited by John N. Fain. Knoxville: University of Tennessee Press, 2004.

Fay, Edwin H. *"This Infernal War": The Confederate Letters of Sgt. Edwin H. Fay*. Austin: University Texas Press, 1958.

Fee, John Gregg. *Autobiography of John G. Fee, Berea, Kentucky*. Chicago: National Christian Association, 1891.

Ferebee, L. R. *A Brief History of the Slave Life of Rev. L. R. Ferebee, and the Battle of Life, and Years of His Ministerial Life*. Raleigh: Edwards, Broughton and Company, 1882.

Fehrenbacher, Don E., and Virginia Fehrenbacher, eds. *Recollected Words of Abraham Lincoln*. Stanford, Calif.: Stanford University Press, 1996.

Fisk, Wilbur. *Hard Marching Every Day: The Civil War Letters of Private Wilbur Fisk, 1861–1865*. Edited Emil Rosenblatt and Ruth Rosenblatt. Lawrence: University Press of Kansas, 1992.

Fiske, Samuel W. *Mr. Dunn Browne's Experiences in the Army: The Civil War Letters of Samuel W. Fiske*. Edited by Stephen W. Sears. New York: Fordham University Press, 1998.

[Fitch, John Alton]. *Annals of the Army of the Cumberland*. Philadelphia: J. B. Lippincott, 1863.

Fitzpatrick, Marion Hill. *Letters to Amanda: The Civil War Letters of Marion Hill Fitzpatrick, Army of Northern Virginia*. Edited by Jeffrey C. Lowe and Sam Hodges. Macon, Ga.: Mercer University Press, 1998.

Fleet, Betsey, and John D. P. Fuller, eds. *Green Mount: A Virginia Plantation Family during the Civil War*. Lexington: University Press of Kentucky, 1962.

Fleharty, Stephen F. *"Jottings from Dixie": The Civil War Dispatches of Sergeant Major Stephen F. Fleharty, U.S.A.* Edited by Philip J. Reyburn and Terry L. Wilson. Baton Rouge: Louisiana State University Press, 1999.

————. *Our Regiment. A History of the 102d Illinois Infantry Volunteers, with Sketches of the Atlanta Campaign, the Georgia Raid, and the Campaign of the Carolinas*. Chicago: Brewster and Hanscom, 1865.

Fleming, Robert. *The Elementary Spelling Book, Revised and Adapted to the Youth of the Southern Confederacy, Interpreted with Bible Readings on Domestic Slavery*. Atlanta: J. J. Toon, 1863.

Fleming, Walter L., ed. *Documentary History of Reconstruction*. 2 vols. Arthur H. Clark, 1906.

Fletcher, Calvin. *The Diary of Calvin Fletcher*. 9 vols. Edited by Gayle Thornbrough et al. Indianapolis: Indiana Historical Society, 1972–83.

Floyd, David Bittle. *History of the Seventy-fifth Regiment of Indiana Infantry Volunteers*. Philadelphia: Lutheran Publication Society, 1893.

Foster, Stephen S. *The Brotherhood of Thieves; or, a True Picture of the American Church and Clergy*. New London, Conn.: William Bolles, 1843.

Freidel, Frank, ed. *Union Pamphlets of the Civil War, 1861–1865*. 2 vols. Cambridge, Mass.: Harvard University Press, 1967.

Fremantle, Arthur J. L. *Three Months in the Southern States: April–June 1863*. New York: John Bradburn, 1864.

French, Mrs. A. M. *Slavery in South Carolina and the Ex-slaves; The Port Royal Mission*. New York: Winchell M. French, 1862.

Frobel, Anne S. *The Civil War Diary of Anne S. Frobel*. Edited by Mary H. and Dallas M. Lancaster. McLean, Va.: EPM, 1992.

Frueauff, John Frederick. *Freddy's War: The Civil War Letters of John Frederick Frueauff*. Edited by Daniel R. Gilbert Sr. Bethlehem, Pa.: Moravian College, 2006.

Fuller, Richard F. *Chaplain Fuller: Being a Life Sketch of a New England Clergyman and Army Chaplain*. Boston: Walker, Wise, 1864.

Furman, Richard. *Rev. Dr. Richard Furman's Exposition of the Views of the Baptists Relative to the Colored Population*. 2nd ed. Charleston: A. E. Miller, 1838.

Gache, Pere Louis-Hippolyte. *A Frenchman, a Chaplain, a Rebel: The War Letters of Pere Louis-Hippolyte Gache, S.J.* Translated by Cornelius M. Buckley. Chicago: Loyola University Press, 1981.

Gage, Moses D. *From Vicksburg to Raleigh; or, A Complete History of the Twelfth Regiment Indiana Volunteer Infantry*. Chicago: Clarke and Company, 1865.

Gaines, Wesley J. *African Methodism in the South; or, Twenty-five Years of Freedom*. Atlanta: Franklin Publishing House, 1890.

Galloway, Tammy Harden, ed. *Dear Old Roswell: The Civil War Letters of the King Family of Roswell, Georgia*. Macon, Ga.: Mercer University Press, 2003.

Gannett, William C. *Ezra Stiles Gannett: Unitarian Minister in Boston, 1824–1871; A Memoir*. Port Washington, N.Y.: Kennikat Press, 1971.

Garey, Joseph. *A Keystone Rebel: The Civil War Diary of Joseph Garey, Hudson's Battery, Mississippi Volunteers*. Gettysburg, Pa.: Thomas Publications, 1996.

Garfield, James A. *The Wild Life of the Army: Civil War Letters of James A. Garfield*. Edited by Frederick D. Williams. East Lansing: Michigan State University Press, 1964.

Gates, Theodore B. *The Civil War Diaries of Col. Theodore B. Gates, 20th New York State Militia*. Edited by Seward R. Osborne. Hightstown, N.J.: Longstreet House, 1991.

Gay, Mary A. H. *Life in Dixie during the War*. Atlanta: Darby Printing, 1979.

Geary, John White. *A Politician Goes to War: The Civil War Letters of John White Geary*. Edited by William Alan Blair. University Park: Pennsylvania State University Press, 1995.

Genoways, Ted, and Hugh H. Genoways, eds. *A Perfect Picture of Hell: Accounts by Civil War Prisoners from the 12th Iowa*. Iowa City: University of Iowa Press, 2001.

Gladden, Washington. *Recollections*. Boston: Houghton Mifflin, 1909.

Goodell, William. *Come-Outerism. The Duty of Secession from a Corrupt Church*. New York: American Anti-Slavery Society, 1845.

Goodwin, Daniel R. *Southern Slavery in Its Present Aspects: Containing a Reply to a Late Work of the Bishop of Vermont on Slavery*. Philadelphia: J. B. Lippincott, 1864.

Gorgas, Josiah. *The Journals of Josiah Gorgas, 1857–1878*. Edited by Sarah Woolfolk Wiggins. Tuscaloosa: University of Alabama Press, 1995.

Gould, John Mead. *The Civil War Journals of John Mead Gould, 1861–1865*. Edited by William B. Jordan. Baltimore: Butternut and Blue, 1997.

Graham, James A. *The James A. Graham Papers, 1861–1884*. Edited H. M. Wagstaff. Chapel Hill: University of North Carolina Press, 1928.

Grasty, John S. *Memoir of Rev. Samuel B. McPheeters, D.D.* Saint Louis: Southwestern Book and Publishing Company, 1871.

Gratz, Rebecca. *Letters of Rebecca Gratz.* Edited by David Philipson. Philadelphia: Jewish Publication Society of America, 1929.

Grebner, Constantine. *A History of the Ninth Regiment, Ohio Volunteer Infantry, April 17, 1861, to June 7, 1864.* Edited by Frederic Trautmann. Kent, Ohio: Kent State University Press, 1987.

Green, Anna Maria. *The Journal of a Milledgeville Girl, 1861–1867.* Edited by James C. Bonner. Athens: University of Georgia Press, 1964.

Green, William Mercer. *Memoir of Rt. Rev. James Hervey Otey, D.D., LL.D., The First Bishop of Tennessee.* New York: James Pott, 1885.

Greene, William B. *Letters from a Sharpshooter: The Civil War Letters of Private William B. Greene, Co. G 2nd United States Sharpshooters.* Edited by William H. Hastings. Belleville, Wisc.: Historical Publications, 1993.

Grimké, Charlotte Forten. *The Journals of Charlotte Forten Grimké.* Edited by Brenda Stevenson. New York: Oxford University Press, 1988.

Guerrant, Edward O. *Bluegrass Confederate: The Headquarters Diary of Edward O. Guerrant.* Edited by William C. Davis and Meredith L. Swentor. Baton Rouge: Louisiana State University Press, 1999.

Hackett, Horatio B. *Christian Memorials of the War; or, Scenes and Incidents Illustrative of Religious Faith and Principle, Patriotism and Bravery of Our Army, with Historical Notes.* Boston: Gould and Lincoln, 1864.

Haines, Alanson A. *History of the Fifteenth Regiment New Jersey Volunteers.* New York: Jenkins and Thomas, 1883.

Haines, Zenas T. *"In the Country of the Enemy": The Civil War Reports of a Massachusetts Corporal.* Edited by William C. Harris. Gainesville: University Press of Florida, 1999.

Haley, John. *The Rebel Yell and the Yankee Hurrah: The Civil War Journal of Maine Volunteer.* Edited by Ruth L. Silliker. Camden, Maine: Down East Books, 1985.

[Hallock, Charles]. *A Complete Biographical Sketch of "Stonewall" Jackson.* Augusta, Ga.: Steam Power Press Chronicle and Sentinel, 1863.

Halsey, Edmund. *Brother against Brother: The Lost Civil War Diary of Lt. Edmund Halsey.* Edited by Bruce Chadwick. Secaucus, N.J.: Birch Lane Press, 2001.

Hammond, J. Pinkney. *The Army Chaplain's Manual, Designed as a Help to Chaplains in the Discharge of Their Various Duties, Both Temporal and Spiritual.* Philadelphia: J. B. Lippincott, 1863.

Hancock, Cornelia. *South after Gettysburg: Letters of Cornelia Hancock, 1863–1868.* Edited by Henrietta Stratton Jaquette. New York: Thomas Y. Crowell, 1956.

Hardin, Elizabeth Pendleton. *The Private War of Lizzie Hardin: A Kentucky Confederate Girl's Diary of the Civil War in Kentucky, Virginia, Tennessee, Alabama, and Georgia.* Edited by G. Glenn Clift. Frankfort: Kentucky Historical Society, 1963.

Harris, David Golightly. *Piedmont Farmer: The Journals of David Golightly Harris, 1855–1870.* Edited by Philip N. Racine. Knoxville: University of Tennessee Press, 1990.

Harris, Robert F., and John Niflot, eds. *Dear Sister: The Civil War Letters of the Brothers Gould.* Westport, Conn.: Praeger, 1998.

Harrison, William Pope, ed. *The Gospel among the Slaves: A Short Account of Missionary*

Operations among the African Slaves of the Southern States. Nashville, Tenn.: Publishing
House of the Methodist Episcopal Church, South, 1893.

Hartsock, Andrew Jackson. *Soldier of the Cross: The Civil War Diary and Correspondence of
Rev. Andrew Jackson Hartsock*. Manhattan, Kan.: Military Affairs/Aerospace Historian
Publishing, 1979.

Hartwell, John F. L. *To My Beloved Wife and Boy at Home: The Letters and Diaries of Orderly
Sergeant John F. L. Hartwell*. Edited by Ann Hartwell Britton and Thomas J. Reed.
Madison, N.J.: Fairleigh Dickinson University Press, 1997.

Harwell, Richard B., ed. *The Union Reader: As the North Saw the War*. New York: Dover
Publications, 1996.

Hawks, Esther Hill. *A Woman Doctor's Civil War: Esther Hill Hawks' Diary*. Edited by Gerald
Schwartz. Columbia: University of South Carolina Press, 1989.

Hay, John. *Inside Lincoln's White House: The Complete Civil War Diary of John Hay*. Carbondale:
Southern Illinois University Press, 1997.

Haydon, Charles B. [2nd Lt., Co. I, 2nd Michigan]. *For Country, Cause and Leader: The Civil
War Journal of Charles B. Haydon*. Edited by Stephen W. Sears. New York: Tichnor and
Fields, 1993.

Hays, Alexander. *Life and Letters of Alexander Hays*. Edited by George Thornton Fleming.
Pittsburgh: privately printed, 1919.

Healy, Kathleen, ed. *Sisters of Mercy: Spirituality in America, 1843–1900*. New York: Paulist
Press, 1992.

Heartsill, W. W. *Fourteen Hundred and 91 Days in the Confederate Army: A Journal Kept by W. W.
Heartsill for Four Years, One Month and One Day or Camp Life: Day by Day, of the W. P. Lane
Rangers, from April 19, 1861 to May 20, 1865*. Edited by Bell Irvin Wiley. Wilmington, N.C.:
Broadfoot, 1992.

Heffley, Albert, and Cyrus P. Heffley. *Civil War Diaries of Capt. Albert Heffley and Lt. Cyrus P.
Heffley, Company F-142nd Regt. Penna. Vol., Army of the Potomac*. Apollo, Pa.: Closson Press,
2000.

Heg, Hans Christian. *The Civil War Letters of Colonel Hans Christian Heg*. Edited by
Theodore C. Blegen. Northfield, Minn.: Norwegian-American Historical Association,
1936.

Henry, John N. *Turn Them Out to Die Like a Mule: The Civil War Letters of John N. Henry, 49th
New York, 1861–1865*. Edited by John Michael Priest. Leesburg, Va.: Gauley Mount Press,
1995.

Hepworth, George H. *The Whip, Hoe, and Sword; or, the Gulf-Department in '63*. Boston:
Walker, Wise, and Company, 1864.

Heyward, Pauline DeCaradeuc. *A Confederate Lady Comes of Age: The Journal of Pauline
DeCaradeuc Heyward, 1863–1888*. Edited by Mary D. Robertson. Columbia: University of
South Carolina Press, 1992.

Hickerson, Thomas Felix. *Echoes of Happy Valley: Letters and Diaries, Family Life in the South,
Civil War History*. Chapel Hill: Bull's Head Bookshop, 1962.

Higginson, Thomas Wentworth. *The Complete Civil War Journal and Selected Letters of Thomas
Wentworth Higginson*. Edited by Christopher Looby. Chicago: University of Chicago Press,
2000.

Hight, John J. *History of the Fifty-eighth Regiment of Indiana Volunteer Infantry*. Compiled by Gilbert R. Stormont. Princeton, Ind.: Press of the Clarion, 1895.

Hildebrand, Jacob R. *A Mennonite Journal, 1862–1865: A Father's Account of the Civil War in the Shenandoah Valley*. Edited by John R. Hildebrand. Shippensburg, Pa.: Burd Street Press, 1996.

History of the Thirty-fifth Regiment Massachusetts Volunteers, 1862–1865. Boston: Mills, Knight, 1884.

History of the One Hundred and Twenty-fifth Regiment Pennsylvania Volunteers, 1862–1863. Philadelphia: J. B. Lippincott, 1906.

Hodge, Alexander A. *The Life of Charles Hodge, D.D*. London: T. Nelson, 1881.

Hodgman, Stephen Alexander. *The Great Republic Judged, but not Destroyed; or the Beginning of the End of Slavery, and the Justice of God Displayed in the Doom of Slaveholders*. New York: Robert Craighead, 1865.

Hoge, William J. *Sketch of Dabney Carr Harrison, Minister of the Gospel and Captain in the Army of the Confederate States of America*. Richmond: Presbyterian Committee of Publication of the Confederate States, 1862.

Hoge, Peyton Harrison. *Moses Drury Hoge: Life and Letters*. Richmond: Presbyterian Committee Publication, 1899.

Hoisington, Daniel J. *Gettysburg and the Christian Commission*. Roseville, Minn.: Edinborough Press, 2002.

Holcomb, Julie, ed. *Southern Sons, Northern Soldiers: The Civil War Letters of the Remley Brothers, 22nd Iowa Infantry*. DeKalb: Northern Illinois University Press, 2004.

Holmes, Emma. *The Diary of Miss Emma Holmes, 1861–1866*. Edited by John F. Marszalek. Baton Rouge: Louisiana State University Press, 1979.

Holmes, Oliver Wendell. *Touched with Fire: Civil War Letters and Diary of Oliver Wendell Holmes, Jr., 1861–1864*. Edited by Mark De Wolfe Howe. Cambridge, Mass.: Harvard University Press, 1946.

Holt, Daniel M. *A Surgeon's Civil War: The Letters and Diary of Daniel M. Holt*. Edited by James M. Greiner, Janet L. Coryell, and James R. Smither. Kent, Ohio: Kent State University Press, 1994.

Holt, David. *A Mississippi Rebel in the Army of Northern Virginia: The Civil War Memoirs of Private David Holt*. Edited by Thomas D. Cockrell and Michael B. Ballard. Baton Rouge: Louisiana State University Press, 1995.

Holzer, Harold, ed. *Dear Mr. Lincoln: Letters to the President*. Reading, Mass.: Addison-Wesley, 1995.

———, ed. *The Lincoln Mailbag: America Writes to the President, 1861–1865*. Carbondale: Southern Illinois University Press, 1998.

Hopkins, John Henry. *Letter from the Right Rev. John H. Hopkins, D.D., LL.D., Bishop of Vermont, on the Bible View of Slavery*. New York: W. F. Kost, 1861.

———. *A Scriptural, Ecclesiastical, and Historical View of Slavery*. New York: W. L. Pooley, 1864.

Hopley, Catherine C. *Life in the South; from the Commencement of the War*. 2 vols. London: Chapman and Hall, 1863.

Horrocks, James. *My Dear Parents: The Civil War as Seen by an English Union Soldier*. Edited by A. S. Lewis. New York: Harcourt Brace, 1982.

House, Ellen Renshaw. *A Very Violent Rebel: The Civil War Diary of Ellen Rensahw House*. Edited by Daniel E. Sutherland. Knoxville: University of Tennessee Press, 1996.

Howard, Oliver Otis. *Major-General Howard's Address at the Second Anniversary of the U.S. Christian Commission*. Philadelphia: Caxton Press, 1864.

Howard, R. L. *History of the 124th Regiment Illinois Infantry Volunteers*. Springfield, Ill.: H. K. Hokker, 1880.

Howe, Julia Ward. *Reminiscences, 1819–1899*. Boston: Houghton, Mifflin, 1899.

Hubbs, G. Ward, ed. *Voices from Company D: Diaries by the Greensboro Guards, Fifth Alabama Infantry Regiment, Army of Northern Virginia*. Athens: University of Georgia Press, 2003.

Huckaby, Elizabeth Paisley, and Ethel C. Simpson, eds. *Tulip Evermore: Emma Butler and William Paisley, Their Lives in Letters, 1857–1887*. Fayetteville: University of Arkansas Press, 1985.

Hughes, John. *Complete Works of the Most Reverend John Hughes, D.D.* Edited by Lawrence Kehoe. 2 vols. New York: Catholic Publication House, 1865.

Humphreys, Charles A. *Field, Camp, Hospital, and Prison in the Civil War*. Boston: George H. Ellis, 1918.

Hundley, Daniel R. *Prison Echoes of the Great Rebellion*. New York: S. W. Green, 1874.

Hurlburt, J. S. *History of the Rebellion in Bradley County, East Tennessee*. Indianapolis: n.p., 1866.

Ingram, George W. *Civil War Letters of George W. and Martha F. Ingram, 1861–1865*. Compiled by Henry L. Ingram. College Station: Printed at Texas A&M University, 1973.

Inman, Myra. *Myra Inman: A Diary of the Civil War in East Tennessee*. Edited by William R. Snell. Macon, Ga.: Mercer University Press, 2000.

Inzer, John Washington. *The Diary of a Confederate Soldier: John Washington Inzer, 1834–1928*. Edited by Mattie Lou Teague Crow. Huntsville, Ala.: Strode Publishers, 1977.

Jackson, Mary Anna Morrison. *Life and Letters of General Thomas J. Jackson (Stonewall Jackson)*. New York: Harper & Brothers, 1891.

Janney, Samuel H. *Memoirs of Samuel M. Janney*. Philadelphia: Friends' Book Association, 1881.

Johns, John. *A Memoir of the Life of the Right Rev. William Meade, D.D., Bishop of the Protestant Episcopal Church in the Diocese of Richmond*. Baltimore: Innes, 1867.

Johnson, Andrew. *The Papers of Andrew Johnson*. Edited by Leroy P. Graf et al. 16 vols. Knoxville: University of Tennessee Press, 1967–2000.

Johnson, Jonathan Huntington. *The Letters and Diary of Captain Jonathan Huntington Johnson*. Compiled by Alden Chase Brett. N.p.: Alden Chase Brett, 1961.

Johnson, Thomas Lewis. *Twenty-eight Years a Slave; or, The Story of My Life in Three Continents*. Bournemouth, Eng.: W. Mate and Sons, 1909.

Jones, Benjamin Washington. *Under the Stars and Bars: A History of the Surry Light Artillery; Recollections of a Private Soldier in the War between the States*. Dayton, Ohio: Morningside Bookshop, 1975.

Jones, Charles Colcock. *Religious Instruction of the Negroes*. Richmond: Presbyterian Committee of Publication, [1862?].

———. *The Religious Instruction of the Negroes. In the United States*. Savannah: Thomas Purse, 1842.

Jones, J. William. *Christ in the Camp or Religion in the Confederate Army*. Atlanta: Martin and Hoyt, 1904.

———. *Life and Letters of Robert Edward Lee: Soldier and Man*. New York: Neale, 1906.

———. *Personal Reminiscences of General Robert E. Lee*. Richmond: United States Historical Society Press, 1989.

Jones, John B. *A Rebel War Clerk's Diary at the Confederate States Capital*. 2 vols. Philadelphia: J. B. Lippincott, 1866.

Jones, Katharine M., ed. *Ladies of Richmond, Confederate Capital*. Indianapolis: Bobbs-Merrill, 1962.

Jones, Melvin, ed. *Give God the Glory: Memoirs of a Civil War Soldier*. Grand Rapids, Mich.: Paris Press, 1979.

Jones, Samuel Calvin. *Reminiscences of the Twenty-second Iowa Volunteer Infantry . . . As Taken from the Diary of Lieutenant S.C. Jones of Company A*. Iowa City, Iowa: 1907.

Joslyn, Mauriel Phillips. *Charlotte's Boys: Civil War Letters of the Branch Family of Savannah*. Berryville, Va.: Rockbridge Publishing Company, 1996.

Journal of the Congress of the Confederate States of America, 1861–1865. 7 vols. Washington, D.C.: Government Printing Office, 1904.

Junkin, D. X. *The Reverend George Junkin, D.D., LL.D. A Historical Biography*. Philadelphia: J. B. Lippincott, 1871.

Kamphoefner, Walter D., and Wolfgang Helbich, eds. *Germans in the Civil War: The Letters They Wrote Home*. Translated by Susan Carter Vogel. Chapel Hill: University of North Carolina Press, 2006.

Kauffman, Henry. *The Civil War Letters (1862–1865) of Private Henry Kauffman: The Harmony Boys Are All Well*. Edited by David McCordick. Lewiston, N.Y.: Edwin Mellen Press, 1991.

[Keily, Anthony M.]. *Prisoner of War; or, Five Months among the Yankees*. Richmond: West and Johnson, [1865].

Kellogg, Robert H. *Life and Death in Rebel Prisons*. Hartford, Conn.: L. Stebbins, 1865.

Kinsley, Rufus. *Diary of a Christian Soldier: Rufus Kinsley and the Civil War*. Edited by David C. Rankin. Cambridge: Cambridge University Press, 2004.

Kircher, Henry A. *A German in the Yankee Fatherland: The Civil War Letters of Henry A. Kircher*. Edited by Earl J. Hess. Kent, Ohio: Kent State University Press, 1983.

Kirk, Edward Norris. *Mustered Out. The Country's Welcome to the Heroes and Defenders Returning to Their Homes*. Boston: American Tract Society, 1865.

Ladies' Christian Commissions: Auxiliary to the U.S. Christian Commission. Philadelphia: C. Sherman, 1864.

Landers, Eli Pinson. *In Care of the Yellow River: The Complete Civil War Letters of Pvt. Eli Pinson Landers to His Mother*. Edited by Elizabeth Whiley Roberson. Gretna, La.: Pelican, 1997.

Lane, Miles, ed. *"Dear Mother: Don't grieve about me. If I get killed, I'll only be dead." Letters from Georgia Soldiers in the Civil War*. Savannah, Ga.: Beehive Press, 1977.

Lauderdale, John Vance. *The Wounded River: The Civil War Letters of John Vance Lauderdale, M.D.* Edited by Peter Josyph. East Lansing: Michigan State University Press, 1993.

Lee, Elizabeth Blair. *Wartime Washington: The Civil War Letters of Elizabeth Blair Lee*. Edited by Virginia Jean Laas. Urbana: University of Illinois Press, 1991.

Lee, Robert E. *The Wartime Papers of R. E. Lee*. Edited by Clifford Dowdey and Louis H. Manarin. New York: Bramhill House, 1961.

Lee, Susan P. *Memoirs of William Nelson Pendleton, D.D.* Philadelphia: J. B. Lippincott, 1893.

Leeke, Jim, ed. *A Hundred Days to Richmond: Ohio's "Hundred Days" Men in the Civil War.* Bloomington: Indiana University Press, 1999.

Leftwich, W. M. *Martyrdom in Missouri, a History of the Religious Proscription, the Seizure of Churches, and the Persecution of Ministers of the Gospel, in the State of Missouri during the Late Civil War and under the "Test Oath" of the Constitution.* 2 vols. St. Louis: Southwestern Book and Publishing Company, 1870.

Ley, John C. *Fifty-two Years in Florida.* Nashville, Tenn.: Publishing House of Methodist Episcopal Church, South, 1899.

Life and Reminiscences of Jefferson Davis by Distinguished Men of His Time. Baltimore: R. H. Woodward, 1890.

Lincoln, Abraham. *The Collected Works of Abraham Lincoln.* Edited by Roy P. Basler. 8 vols. New Brunswick, N.J.: Rutgers University Press, 1953.

Lincecum, Gideon. *Gideon Lincecum's Sword: Civil War Letters from the Texas Home Front.* Edited by Jerry Bryan Lincecum, Edward Hake Phillips, and Peggy A. Redshaw. Denton: University of North Texas Press, 2001.

Lines, Amelia Akehurst. *To Raise Myself a Little: The Diaries and Letters of Jennie, a Georgia Teacher, 1861–1886.* Edited by Thomas Dyer. Athens: University of Georgia Press, 1982.

List of Claims upon Which the Court of Claims Has Made a Report, but Which Are Not Included in H. R. 19115. Washington, D.C.: Government Printing Office, 1912.

List of War Claims, Confined Entirely to Claims for Use and Occupation or Rent of Church Buildings, College Buildings, and Other Public Buildings, by the Military Forces of the United States during the War, Coupled in Some Cases with a Claim for Damages Done to the Building during the Occupancy with Statement of Each Case Compiled for Examination of H. R. 19115. Washington, D.C.: Government Printing Office, 1912.

List of War Claims Including a Few Exceptional Cases for Churches; Also List of Other Claims to Which Objections Appear, Such as Latches, No Proof of Loyalty, Insufficient Evidence as to Fasts, Evidence of Payment and Statutory Bars, with a Statement of Each Case Compiled for the Convenience of Members of the Senate Committee on Claims in Connection with an Examination of H.R. 19115. Washington, D.C.: Government Printing Office, 1912.

Locke, William Henry [Chaplain]. *The Story of the Regiment* [11th Pennsylvania Infantry]. Philadelphia: J. B. Lippincott, 1868.

Logan, David Jackson. *"A Rising Star of Promise": The Civil War Odyssey of David Jackson Logan, 17th South Carolina Volunteers, 1861–1864.* Edited by Samuel N. Thomas Jr. and Jason H. Silverman. Campbell, Calif.: Savas, 1998.

Long, A. L. *Memoirs of Robert E. Lee: His Military and Personal History Embracing a Large Amount of Information Hitherto Unpublished.* Secaucus, N.J.: Blue and Grey Press, 1983.

Lusk, William Thompson. *War Letters of William Thompson Lusk.* New York: privately printed, 1911.

Lyle, William W. *Light and Shadows of Army Life; or, Pen Pictures from the Battlefield, the Camp, and the Hospital.* Cincinnati: R. W. Carroll, 1865.

Lyman, Theodore. *Meade's Army: The Private Notebooks of Lt. Col. Theodore Lyman.* Edited by David W. Lowe. Kent, Ohio: Kent State University Press, 2007.

McAllister, Robert. *The Civil War Letters of General Robert McAllister.* Edited by James I. Robertson Jr. New Brunswick, N.J.: Rutgers University Press, 1965.

McCain, Thomas Hart Benton. *In Song and Sorrow: The Daily Journal of Thomas Hart Benton McCain of the Eighty-sixth Indiana Volunteer Infantry*. Edited Richard K. Rue and Geraldine M. Rue. Carmel, Ind.: Guild Press, 1998.

MacCauley, Clay. *Memories and Memorials: Gatherings from an Eventful Life*. Tokyo: Fukuin Printing, 1914.

McClellan, George B. *The Civil War Papers of General George B. McClellan: Selected Correspondence, 1860–1865*. Edited by Stephen W. Sears. New York: Ticknor and Fields, 1989.

McDonald, Cornelia Peake. *A Woman's Civil War: A Diary with Reminiscences of the War, from March 1862*. Edited by Minrose C. Gwin. Madison: University of Wisconsin Press, 1992.

McDonald, James Madison, and Charles Hodge. *On Praying and Giving Thanks for Victories; A Correspondence between Rev. J. M. McDonald, and the Rev. Dr. Hodge*. Princeton, N.J.: n.p., 1864.

McGuire, Judith W. *Diary of a Southern Refugee during the War, by a Lady of Virginia*. New York: E. J. Hale, 1867.

McJunkin, Milton. *The Bloody 85th: The Letters of Milton McJunkin, a Western Pennsylvania Soldier in the Civil War*. Edited by Richard Sauers. Lynchburg, Va.: Shroeder Publications, 2002.

McKim, Randolph Harrison. *A Soldier's Recollections: Leaves from the Diary of a Young Confederate*. New York: Longmans, Green, 1918.

McKinley, Emilie Riley. *From the Pen of a She-Rebel: The Civil War Diary of Emilie Riley McKinley*. Edited by Gordon A. Cotton. Columbia: University of South Carolina Press, 2001.

McMahon, John T. *John T. McMahon's Diary of the 136th New York, 1861–1864*. Edited by John Michael Priest. Shippensburg, Pa.: White Mane, 1993.

McMillan, Malcolm C., ed. *The Alabama Confederate Reader*. Tuscaloosa: University of Alabama Press, 1963.

McPheeters, William M. *"I acted from principle": The Civil War Diary of Dr. William M. McPheeters, Confederate Surgeon in the Trans-Mississippi*. Edited by Cynthia Dehaven Pitcock and Bill J. Gurley. Fayetteville: University of Arkansas Press, 2002.

McPherson, Edward, ed. *The Political History of the United States of America, during the Great Rebellion*. 2nd ed. Washington, D.C.: Philip and Solomons, 1865.

Macy, Jesse. *Jesse Macy: An Autobiography*. Edited by Katharine Macy Jones. Springfield, Ill.: Charles C. Thomas, 1933.

Magee, B. F. *History of the 72d Indiana Volunteer Infantry of the Mounted Lightning Brigade*. LaFayette, Ind.: S. Vater, 1882.

Mahon, Michael G., ed. *Winchester Divided: The Civil War Diaries of Julia Chase and Laura Lee*. Mechanicsburg, Pa.: Stackpole Books, 2002.

Mallory, James. *"Fear God and Walk Humbly": The Agricultural Journal of James Mallory, 1843–1877*. Edited by Grady McWhiney, Warner O. Moore Jr., and Robert F. Pace. Tuscaloosa: University of Alabama Press, 1997.

Manson, Joseph Richard. *A Spiritual Diary*. Havertown, Pa.: William T. Zielinski, 1992.

Marcus, Jacob Rader, ed. *Memoirs of American Jews, 1776–1865*. 3 vols. Philadelphia: Jewish Publication Society of America, 1954–55.

Marks, J. J. *The Peninsula Campaign in Virginia or Incidents and Scenes on the Battlefield and in Richmond*. Philadelphia: J. B. Lippincott, 1863.

Marshall, John A. *American Bastille. A History of the Illegal Arrests and Imprisonment of American Citizens during the Late Civil War*. Philadelphia: Thomas W. Hartley, 1878.

Maryniak, Benedict R., and John Wesley Brinsfield Jr., eds. *The Spirit Divided: Memoirs of Civil Chaplains; The Union*. Macon, Ga.: Mercer University Press, 2007.

Mathis, Ray, ed. *In the Land of the Living: Wartime Letters by Confederates from the Chattahoochee Valley of Alabama and Georgia*. Troy, Ala.: Troy State University Press, 1981.

Matlack, Lucius C. *The Antislavery Struggle and Triumph in the Methodist Episcopal Church*. New York: Phillips and Hunt, 1881.

Matthews, James M., ed. *The Statutes at Large of the Provisional Government of the Confederate States of America*. Richmond: R. M. Smith, Printer to Congress, 1864.

Mattocks, Charles. *"Unspoiled Heart": The Journal of Charles Mattocks of the 17th Maine*. Edited by Philip N. Racine. Knoxville: University of Tennessee Press, 1994.

Maule, Joshua. *Transactions and Changes in the Society of Friends, and Incidents in the Life of Joshua Maule*. Philadelphia: J. B. Lippincott, 1886.

Meade, George. *The Life and Letters of George Gordon Meade, Major-General United States Army*. 2 vols. New York: Charles Scribner's Sons, 1913.

Means, Alexander. *Diary for 1861*. Edited by Ross H. McLean. Atlanta: The Library, Emory University, 1949.

Mears, David O. *Life of Edward Norris Kirk, D.D.* Boston: D. Lothrop And Company, 1877.

Melcher, Holman S. *With a Flash of His Sword: The Writings of Major Holman S. Melcher, 20th Maine Infantry*. Edited by William B. Styple. Kearny, N.J.: Belle Grove, 1994.

Memorials of Methodism in Macon, Georgia, from 1828 to 1878. Macon, Ga.: J. W. Burke, 1879.

Milburn, William Henry. *Ten Years of Preacher-Life: Chapters from an Autobiography*. New York: Derby and Jackson, 1859.

Miller, James T. *Bound to Be a Soldier: The Letters of Private James T. Miller, 111th Pennsylvania Infantry, 1861–1864*. Edited by Jedediah Mannis and Galen R. Wilson. Knoxville: University of Tennessee Press, 2001.

Miller, William Bluffton. *Fighting for Liberty and Right: The Civil War Diary of William Bluffton Miller, First Sergeant, Company K, Seventy-fifth Indiana Volunteer Infantry*. Edited by Jeffrey J. Patrick and Robert J. Willey. Knoxville: University of Tennessee Press, 2005.

Mills, John Harrison. *Chronicles of the Twenty-first Regiment, New York State Volunteers*. Buffalo: 21st Reg't Veteran Association of Buffalo, 1887.

Mitchell, J. C. *A Bible Defense of Slavery, and the Unity of Mankind*. Mobile: J. Y. Thompson, 1861.

Mohr, James C., ed. *The Cormany Diaries: A Northern Family in the Civil War*. Pittsburgh: University of Pittsburgh Press, 1982.

Molyneux, Joel. *Quill of the Wild Goose: Civil War Letters and Diaries of Private Joel Molyneux, 141st P.V.* Edited by Kermit Molyneux Bird. Shippensburg, Pa.: Burd Street Press, 1996.

Moore, Frank A., ed. *The Rebellion Record: A Diary of American Events*. 12 vols. New York: Arno Press, 1977.

Moore, Robert A. *A Life for the Confederacy as Recorded in the Pocket Diaries of Pvt. Robert A. Moore, Co. G, 17th Mississippi Regiment, Confederate Guards*. Edited by James W. Silver. Jackson, Tenn.: McCowat-Mercer Press, 1959.

Morgan, Sarah. *The Civil War Diary of Sarah Morgan*. Edited by Charles East. Athens: University of Georgia Press, 1991.

Morris, Benjamin Franklin. *Christian Life and Character of the Civil Institutions of the United States Developed in the Official and Historical Annals of the Republic.* Philadelphia: George W. Childs, 1864.

Moss, Lemuel. *Annals of the United States Christian Commission.* Philadelphia: J. B. Lippincott, 1868.

Moxley, William Morel. *Oh, What a Loansome Time I Had: The Civil War Letters of Major William Morel Moxley, Eighteenth Alabama Infantry, and Emily Beck Moxley.* Edited by Thomas W. Cutrer. Tuscaloosa: University of Alabama Press, 2002.

Muffly, J. W., ed. *The Story of Our Regiment: A History of the 148th Pennsylvania Vols.* Des Moines: Kenyon Printing and Manufacturing, 1904.

Mulholland, St. Clair Augustine. *The Story of the 116th Regiment, Pennsylvania Infantry: War of Secession, 1862–1865.* Philadelphia: F. McManus, Jr. and Company Printers, 1903.

Myers, Robert Manson, ed. *The Children of Pride: A True Story of Georgia and the Civil War.* New Haven, Conn.: Yale University Press, 1972.

Nash, Eugene Arus. *A History of the Forty-fourth Regiment New York Volunteer Infantry in the Civil War, 1861–1865.* Chicago: R. R. Donnelley, 1910.

Neese, George M. *Three Years in the Confederate Horse Artillery.* Dayton, Ohio: Morningside, 1988.

Newell, Joseph Keith. *"Ours." Annals of the 10th Regiment Massachusetts Volunteers, in the Rebellion.* Springfield, Mass.: C. A. Nichols and Company, 1875.

The New Texas Primary Reader. Designed for the Use of Schools in Texas. Houston: E. H. Cushing, 1863.

Newton, A. H. *Out of the Briars: An Autobiography and Sketch of the Twenty-ninth Regiment Connecticut Volunteers.* Philadelphia: A.M.E. Book Concern, 1910.

Newton, James K. *A Wisconsin Boy in Dixie: Civil War Letters of James K. Newton.* Edited by Stephen E. Ambrose. Madison: University of Wisconsin Press, 1961.

New York Sabbath Committee. *Plea for the Sabbath in War.* [New York: Sabbath Committee, 1861].

Nicolay, John G. *An Oral History of Abraham Lincoln: John G. Nicolay's Interviews and Essays.* Edited by Michael Burlingame. Carbondale: Southern Illinois University Press, 1996.

Nisbet, James Cooper. *Four Years on the Firing Line.* Edited by Bell Irvin Wiley. Jackson, Tenn.: McCowat-Mercer Press, 1963.

Norton, Oliver Willcox. *Army Letters, 1861–1865.* Dayton, Ohio: Morningside, 1990.

Norwood, Frederick A., ed. *Sourcebook of American Methodism.* Nashville: Abingdon, 1982.

Nugent, William Lewis. *My Dear Nellie: The Civil War Letters of William L. Nugent to Eleanor Smith Nugent.* Edited by William M. Cash and Lucy Somerville Howorth. Jackson: University Press of Mississippi, 1977.

Official Records of the Union and Confederate Navies in the War of the Rebellion. 31 vols. Washington, D.C.: Government Printing Office, 1894–1922.

Olds, Edson B. *Arbitrary Arrests. Speech of Hon. Edson B. Olds, for Which He Was Arrested, and His Reception Speeches on His Return from the Bastille.* Circleville, [Ohio?]: n.p., 1862.

Otto, John Henry. *Memoirs of a Dutch Mudsill: The "War Memories of John Henry Otto, Captain, Company D, 21st Regiment Wisconsin Volunteer Infantry.* Edited by David Gould and James B. Kennedy. Kent, Ohio: Kent State University Press, 2004.

Owen, Thomas James. *"Dear Friends at Home . . .": The Letter and Diary of Thomas James Owen,*

Fiftieth New York Volunteer Engineer Regiment, during the Civil War. Edited by Dale E. Floyd. Washington, D.C.: Historical Division, Office of Administrative Services, Office of the Chief of Engineers, 1985.

Owen, William Miller. *In Camp and Battle with the Washington Artillery of New Orleans*. Boston: Ticknor and Company, 1885.

Palmer, Benjamin Morgan. *The Life and Letters of James Henley Thornwell*. Richmond: Whittet and Shepperson, 1875.

Pardington, John H. *Dear Sarah: Letters Home from a Soldier of the Iron Brigade*. Edited by Coralou Peel Lassen. Bloomington: Indiana University Press, 1999.

Parker, John L. *Henry Wilson's Regiment: History of the Twenty-Second Massachusetts Infantry, the Second Company Sharpshooters, and the Third Light Battery, in the War of the Rebellion*. Boston: Rand Avery, 1887.

Patterson, Edmund DeWitt. *Yankee Rebel: The Civil War Journal of Edmund DeWitt Patterson*. Edited by John G. Barrett. Chapel Hill: University of North Carolina, 1996.

Paxton, Elisha Franklin. *Memoir and Memorials: Elisha Franklin Paxton*. New York: De Vinne, 1905.

Paxton, John Gallatin, ed. *The Civil War Letters of General Frank "Bull" Paxton, C.S.A.* Hillsboro, Tex.: Hill Jr. College Press, 1978.

Pearne, Thomas H. *Sixty-one Years of Itinerant Christian Life in Church and State*. Cincinnati, Ohio: Curts and Jennings, 1899.

Pearson, Elizabeth Ware, ed. *Letters from Port Royal, 1862–1868*. Boston: W. B. Clarke, 1906.

Peirce, Taylor, and Catharine Peirce. *Dear Catharine, Dear Taylor: The Civil War Letters of a Union Soldier and His Wife*. Edited by Richard L. Kiper. Lawrence: University Press of Kansas, 2002.

Pember, Phoebe Yates. *A Southern Woman's Story: Life in Confederate Richmond*. Edited by Bell Irvin Wiley. Jackson, Tenn.: McCowat-Mercer Press, 1959.

Pender, William Dorsey. *The General to His Lady: The Civil War Letters of William Dorsey Pender to Fanny Pender*. Edited by William W. Hassler. Chapel Hill: University of North Carolina Press, 1965.

Pepper, George W. *Personal Recollections of Sherman's Campaigns, in Georgia and the Carolinas*. Zanesville, Ohio: H. Dunne, 1866.

Perkins, George. *Three Years a Soldier: The Diary and Newspaper Correspondence of Private George Perkins, Sixth New York Independent Battery, 1861–1864*. Edited by Richard N. Griffin. Knoxville: University of Tennessee Press, 2006.

Perkins, Howard Cecil, ed. *Northern Editorials on Secession*. 2 vols. Gloucester, Mass.: Peter Smith, 1964.

Perry, Henry Fales. *History of the Thirty-eighth Regiment Indiana Volunteer Infantry*. Palo Alto, Calif.: F. A. Stuart, 1906.

Perry, Theophilus, and Harriet Perry. *Widows by the Thousand: The Civil War Letters of Theophilus and Harriet Perry, 1862–1864*. Edited by M. Jane Johansson. Fayetteville: University of Arkansas Press, 2000.

Peter, Frances. *A Union Woman in Civil War Kentucky: The Diary of Frances Peter*. Edited by John David Smith and William Cooper Jr. Lexington: University Press of Kentucky, 2000.

Pettit, Frederick. *Infantryman Pettit: The Civil War Letters of Corporal Frederick Pettit*. Edited by William Gilfallan Gavin. Shippensburg, Pa.: White Mane, 1990.

Phillips, George C. *The American Republic and Human Liberty Foreshadowed in Scripture*. Cincinnati: Poe and Hitchcock, 1864.

Polley, J. B. *A Soldier's Letters to Charming Nellie*. New York: Neale, 1908.

Poremba, David Lee, ed. *If I Am Found Dead: Michigan Voices from the Civil War*. Ann Arbor: Ann Arbor Media Group, 2006.

Post, Lydia M., ed. *Soldiers' Letters, from Camp, Battle-field and Prison*. New York: Bunce and Huntington, 1865.

Post, Truman A. *Truman Marcellus Post, D.D., a Biography, Personal and Literary*. Boston: Congregational Sunday-School and Publishing Society, 1891.

Prentiss, George L. *The Bright Side of Life: Glimpses of It through Four-score Years*. 2 vols. N.p.: privately printed, 1901.

Price, Vina Chandler, ed. *Records of the Prince William Primitive Baptist Church, 1812–1912, Hampton County, South Carolina*. Hamilton, Ala.: n.p., 1979.

Price, William Newton. *One Year in the Civil War: A Diary of the Events April 1st, 1864, to April 1st, 1865*. N.p.: n.p., n.d.

Pringle, Cyrus Guernsey. *The Record of a Quaker Conscience: Cyrus Pringle's Diary*. New York: Macmillan, 1918.

Providential Aspect and Salutary Tendency of the Existing Crisis. New Orleans: Picayune Office Print, 1861.

Pryor, Mrs. Roger A. *Reminiscences of Peace and War*. New York: Macmillan, 1924.

Puck, Susan T., ed. *Sacrifice at Vicksburg: Letters from the Front*. Shippensburg, Pa.: Burd Street Press, 1997.

Quint, Alonzo. *The Potomac and the Rapidan. Army Notes from the Failure at Winchester to the Reinforcement of Rosecrans, 1861–3*. Boston: Crosby and Nichols, 1864.

Quintard, Charles Todd. *Doctor Quintard, Chaplain, C.S.A. and Second Bishop of Tennessee: The Memoir and Civil War Diary of Charles Todd Quintard*. Edited by Sam Davis Elliott. Baton Rouge: Louisiana State University Press, 2003.

Randolph, Valentine C. *A Civil War Soldier's Diary: Valentine C. Randolph, 39th Illinois Regiment*. Edited by David D. Roe. DeKalb: Northern Illinois University Press, 2006.

Read, Hollis. *The Coming Crisis of the World; or, The Great Battle and the Golden Age. The Signs of the Times Indicating the Approach of the Great Crisis, and the Duty of the Church*. Columbus, Ohio: Follett, Foster and Company, 1861.

Regan, Timothy J. *The Lost Civil War Diaries: The Diaries of Timothy J. Regan*. Edited by David C. Newton and Kenneth J. Pluskat. Victoria, British Columbia: Trafford, 2003.

Reid, Harvey. *Uncommon Soldiers: Harvey Reid and the 22nd Wisconsin March with Sherman*. Edited by Frank L. Byrne. Knoxville: University of Tennessee Press, 2001.

Reinhart, Joseph R., ed. *August Willich's Gallant Dutchmen: Civil War Letters from the 32nd Indiana Infantry*. Kent, Ohio: Kent State University Press, 2006.

Remmel, William. *Like Grass before the Scythe: The Life and Death of Sgt. William Remmel, 121st New York Infantry*. Edited by Robert Patrick Bender. Tuscaloosa: University of Alabama Press, 2007.

Renfroe, Rev. J. J. D. *A Model Confederate Soldier, Being a Brief Sketch of the Rev. Nathaniel D. Renfroe*. N.p.: n.p., 1863.

Resolutions of Forsberg's Brigade, Wharton's Division. [Richmond: n.p., 1865].

Rhodes, Elisha Hunt. *All for the Union: The Civil War Diary and Letters of Elisha Hunt Rhodes*. Edited by Robert Hunt Rhodes. New York: Orion Books, 1985.

Richard, Allen C., Jr., and Mary Margaret Higginbotham Richard, eds. *The Defense of Vicksburg: A Louisiana Chronicle*. College Station: Texas A&M University Press, 2004.

Richard, J. Fraise, ed. *The Florence Nightingale of the Southern Army: Experiences of Ella K. Newsom, Confederate Nurse in the Great War of 1861–1865*. New York: Broadway, 1914.

Ridley, Bromfield L. *Battles and Sketches of the Army of Tennessee*. Mexico, Mo.: Missouri Publishing Company, 1906.

Ritner, Jacob, and Emeline Ritner. *Love and Valor: Intimate Civil War Letters between Captain Jacob and Emeline Ritner*. Edited by Charles F. Larimer. Western Springs, Ill.: Sigourney Press, 2000.

Robbins, Gilbert. *The Christian Patriot, a Biography of James E. McClellan*. Worcester, Mass.: Grout and Bigelow, 1865.

Robinson, William A. *The Civil War Letters of William A. Robinson and Story of the Eighty-ninth New York Volunteer Infantry*. Edited by Robert J. Taylor. Bowie, Md.: Heritage Books, 2000.

Rogers, James B. *War Pictures. Experiences and Observations of a Chaplain in the U.S. Army in the War of the Southern Rebellion*. Chicago: Church and Graham, 1863.

Ropes, Hannah. *Civil War Nurse: The Diary and Letters of Hannah Ropes*. Edited by John R. Brumgardt. Knoxville: University of Tennessee Press, 1980.

Royse, Isaac Henry Clay. *History of the 115th Regiment Illinois Volunteer Infantry*. Terre Haute, Ind.: published by the author, 1900.

Ruffin, Edmund. *The Diary of Edmund Ruffin*. 3 vols. Edited by William Kauffman Scarborough. Baton Rouge: Louisiana State University Press, 1972–89,

Schaff, Philip. *America. A Sketch of the Political, Social, and Religious Character of the United States of North America*. New York: C. Scribner, 1855.

Sears, Richard D. *Camp Nelson, Kentucky: A Civil War History*. Lexington: University Press of Kentucky, 2002.

Seat, W. H. *The Confederate States in Prophecy*. Nashville: Southern Methodist Publishing House, 1861.

Sernett, Milton C., ed. *Afro-American Religious History: A Documentary Witness*. Durham, N.C.: Duke University Press, 1985.

The Services of the Protestant Episcopal Church in the United States of America as Ordered by the Bishops, during the Civil War. Brooklyn: Hatch and Company, 1864.

Shaw, James. *Twelve Years in America*. London: Hamilton, Adams, 1867.

Shaw, Robert Gould. *Blue-Eyed Child of Fortune: The Civil War Letters of Colonel Robert Gould Shaw*. Edited by Russell Duncan. Athens: University of Georgia Press, 1992.

Sheeran, James B. *Confederate Chaplain: A War Journal of Rev. James B. Sheeran, c.ss.r., 14th Louisiana, C.S.A.* Edited by Joseph T. Durkin. Milwaukee: Bruce, 1960.

Sheffey, John Preston. *Soldier of Southwestern Virginia: The Civil War Letters of Captain John Preston Sheffey*. Edited by James I. Robertson Jr. Baton Rouge: Louisiana State University Press, 2004.

Shepherd, William T. *To Rescue My Native Land: The Civil War Letters of William T. Shepherd, First Illinois Light Artillery*. Edited by Kurt H. Hackemer. Knoxville: University of Tennessee Press, 2005.

Sherman, William T. *Sherman's Civil War: Selected Correspondence of William T. Sherman, 1860–1865*. Edited by Brooks D. Simpson and Jean V. Berlin. Chapel Hill: University of North Carolina Press, 1999.

Silber, Nina, and Mary Beth Stevens, eds. *Yankee Correspondence: Civil War Letters between New England Soldiers and the Home Front*. Charlottesville: University Press of Virginia, 1996.

Silliman, Justus M. *A New Canaan Private in the Civil War: Letters of Justus M. Silliman, 17th Connecticut Volunteers*. Edited by Edward Marcus. New Canaan, Conn.: New Canaan Historical Society, 1984.

Simpson, John Hemphill. *Echoes of Mercy—Whispers of Love: Diaries of John Hemphill Simpson*. Edited by Michael J. Miller. Greenville, S.C.: Associate Reformed Presbyterian Foundation, 2001.

Skidmore, Richard S., ed. *The Alford Brothers: "We All Must Dye Sooner or Later."* Hanover, Ind.: Nugget Publishers, 1995.

Slaughter, Rev. Philip. *A Sketch of the Life of Randolph Fairfax, a Private in the Ranks of the Rockbridge Artillery, Attached to the "Stonewall Brigade."* Richmond: Tyler, Allegre, and McDaniel, Enquirer Job Office, 1864.

Slave Narratives. CD-ROM. Orem, Utah: MyFamily.com, 2000.

Small, Abner R. *The Road to Richmond: The Civil War Memoirs of Major Abner R. Small of Sixteenth Maine Regiment*. Edited by Harold Adams Small. Berkeley: University of California Press, 1939.

Smith, Abram P. *History of the Seventy-sixth Regiment New York Volunteers*. Cortland, N.Y.: Truair, Smith and Miles, 1867.

Smith, Daniel E. Huger, Alice E. Huger Smith, and Arney R. Childs, eds. *Mason Smith Family Letters, 1860–1868*. Columbia: University of South Carolina Press, 1950.

Smith, Edward P. *Incidents of the United States Christian Commission*. Philadelphia: J. B. Lippincott, 1869.

Smith, Francis H. *Discourse on the Life and Character of Lt. Gen. Thos. J. Jackson, (C.S.A.), Late Professor of Natural and Experimental Philosophy in the Virginia Military Institute*. Richmond: Ritchie and Dunnavant, 1863.

Smith, George Winston, and Charles Judah, eds. *Life in the North during the Civil War: A Source History*. Albuquerque: University of New Mexico Press, 1966.

Smith, John L. *History of the 118th Pennsylvania Volunteers, Corn Exchange Regiment, from Their First Engagement at Antietam to Appomattox*. Philadelphia: J. L. Smith, 1905.

Smith, Robert D. *Confederate Diary of Robert D. Smith*. Edited Virginia W. Alexander and Elaine W. Davidson. Columbia, Tenn.: Captain James Madison Sparkman Chapter, UDC, 1997.

Smith, Thomas C. *Here's Your Mule: The Diary of Thomas C. Smith, 3rd Sergeant, Company "G," Wood's Regiment, 32nd Texas Cavalry, C.S.A., March 30, 1862–December 31, 1862*. Waco: Little Texan Press, 1958.

Smith, W. A. *The Anson Guards: Company C, Fourteenth Regiment North Carolina Volunteers, 1861–1865*. Charlotte, N.C.: Stone, 1914.

Spencer, Alva Benjamin. *My Dear Friend: The Civil War Letters of Alva Benjamin Spencer, 3rd Georgia Regiment, Company C*. Edited by Clyde G. Wiggins III. Macon, Ga.: Mercer University Press, 2007.

Spiegel, Marcus. *Your True Marcus: The Civil War Letters of a Jewish Colonel*. Edited by
    Frank L. Byrne and Jean Powers Soman. Kent, Ohio: Kent State University Press, 1985.
Sprague, Homer B. *History of the 13th Infantry Regiment of Connecticut Volunteers, during the
    Great Rebellion*. Hartford, Conn.: Case, Lockwood, 1867.
———. *Lights and Shadows in Confederate Prisons: A Personal Experience, 1864–5*. New York:
    G. P. Putnam's Sons, 1915.
Spring, Gardiner. *Personal Reminiscences of the Life and Times of Gardiner Spring*. 2 vols. New
    York: C. Scribner, 1866.
Springer, Francis. *The Preacher's Tale: The Civil War Journal of Rev. Francis Springer, Chaplain,
    U.S. Army of the Frontier*. Edited by William Furry. Fayetteville: University of Arkansas
    Press, 2001.
Squier, George W. *This Wilderness of War: The Civil War Letters of George W. Squier,
    Hoosier Volunteer*. Edited by Julie A. Doyle, John David Smith, and Richard M. McMurry.
    Knoxville: University of Tennessee Press, 1998.
Stanton, Robert Livingston. *The Church and the Rebellion*. New York: Derby and Miller, 1864.
Stephens, Alexander H. *Recollections of Alexander H. Stephens*. Edited by Myrta Lockett Avary.
    New York: Doubleday, Page, 1910.
Stephenson, Philip Daingerfield. *The Civil War Memoir of Philip Daingerfield Stephenson, D.D.*
    Edited by Nathaniel Cheairs Hughes, Jr. Baton Rouge: Louisiana State University Press,
    1998.
Sterling, Richard. *Our Own Third Reader: For the Use of Schools and Families*. Greensboro, N.C.:
    Sterling, Campbell and Albright, 1862.
Stevens, C. A. *Berdan's United States Sharpshooters in the Army of the Potomac, 1861–1865*.
    Dayton, Ohio: Morningside, 1984.
Stevens, George T. *Three Years in the Sixth Corps*. Albany, N.Y.: S. R. Gray, 1866.
Stevenson, Thomas. *History of the 78th O.V.V.I., from Its 'Muster-in' to Its 'Muster-out';
    Comprising Its Organization, Marches, Campaigns, Battles and Skirmishes*. Zanesville, Ohio:
    Hugh Dunne, 1865.
Stewart, Alexander Morrison. *Camp, March and Battlefield; or, Three Years and a Half with the
    Army of the Potomac*. Philadelphia: J. B. Rodgers, 1865.
Stiles, Joseph C. *Modern Reform Examined; or, the Union of North and South on the Subject of
    Slavery*. Philadelphia: J. B. Lippincott, 1857.
———. *National Rectitude the Only True Basis of National Prosperity: An Appeal to the
    Confederate States*. Petersburg, Va.: Evangelical Tract Society, 1863.
Stiles, Robert. *Four Years under Marse Robert*. New York: Neale, 1903.
Stillwell, William R. *The Stillwell Letters: A Georgian in Longstreet's Corps, Army of
    Northern Virginia*. Edited by Ronald H. Moseley. Macon, Ga.: Mercer University Press, 2002.
Stone, DeWitt Boyd, Jr., ed. *Wandering to Glory: Confederate Veterans Remember Evans'
    Brigade*. Columbia: University of South Carolina Press, 2002.
Stone, Kate. *Brokenburn: The Journal of Kate Stone, 1861–1868*. Edited by John Q. Anderson.
    Baton Rouge: Louisiana State University Press, 1955.
Story of the Fifty-fifth Regiment Illinois Volunteer Infantry in the Civil War, 1861–1865. Clinton:
    Mass: W. J. Coulter, 1887.
Strong, George Templeton. *The Diary of George Templeton Strong*. 4 vols. Edited by Allan
    Nevins and Milton Halsey Thomas. New York: Macmillan, 1952.

Strother, David Hunter. *A Virginia Yankee in the Civil War: The Diaries of David Hunter Strother.* Edited by Cecil D. Eby Jr. Chapel Hill: University of North Carolina Press, 1961.

Stuart, George H. *Instructions to Delegates of the U.S. Christian Commission.* Philadelphia: n.p., 1862.

———. *The Life of George H. Stuart, Written by Himself.* Edited by Robert Ellis Thompson. Philadelphia: J. M. Stoddart, 1890.

Stuckenberg, John H. W. *I'm Surrounded by Methodists. . . . Diary of John H. W. Stuckenberg Chaplain of the 145th Pennsylvania Volunteer Infantry.* Edited by David T. Hedrick and Gordon Barry Davis Jr. Gettysburg, Pa.: Thomas Publications, 1995.

Sturtevant, Arnold H., ed. *Josiah Volunteered: A Collection of Diaries, Letters, and Photographs of Josiah H. Sturtevant, His Wife, Helen, and His Four Children.* Farmington, Maine: Knowlton & McLeary, 1977.

Sullins, David. *Recollections of an Old Man: Seventy Years in Dixie, 1827–1897.* Bristol, Tenn.: King Printing Company, 1910.

Sumner, Charles. *Selected Letters of Charles Sumner.* Edited by Beverly Wilson Palmer. 2 vols. Boston: Northeastern University Press, 1990.

Swint, Henry L., ed. *Dear Ones at Home: Letters from Contraband Camps.* Nashville: Vanderbilt University Press, 1966.

Tarbox, Increase N. *The Curse; or, The Position in the World's History Occupied by the Race of Ham.* Boston: American Tract Society, 1864.

Taylor, Benjamin F. *Mission Ridge and Lookout Mountain with Pictures of Life in Camp and Field.* New York: D. Appleton, 1872.

Taylor, Frances Wallace, Caroline Taylor Matthews, and J. Tracy Power, eds. *The Leverett Letters: Correspondence of a South Carolina Family, 1851–1868.* Columbia: University of South Carolina Press, 2000.

Taylor, George B. *Life and Times of James B. Taylor.* Philadelphia: Bible and Publication Society, 1872.

Taylor, Richard. *Destruction and Reconstruction: Personal Experiences of the Late Civil War.* Edited by Richard B. Harwell. New York: Longmans, Green, 1955.

Taylor, Walter Herron. *Lee's Adjutant: The Wartime Letters of Colonel Walter Herron Taylor, 1862–1865.* Edited by R. Lockwood Tower. Columbia: University of South Carolina Press, 1995.

Thomas, Alfred A. *Correspondence of Thomas Ebenezer Thomas, Mainly Relating to the Anti-Slavery Conflict in Ohio, especially in the Presbyterian Church.* N.p.: n.p., 1909.

Thomas, Ella Gertrude Clanton. *The Secret Eye: The Journal of Ella Gertrude Clanton Thomas, 1848–1889.* Edited by Virginia Ingraham Burr. Chapel Hill: University of North Carolina Press, 1990.

Thome, James. *The Future of the Freed People.* Cincinnati: American Reform and Tract and Book Society, 1863.

Thompson, Joseph Parrish. *The Sergeant's Memorial.* New York: Anson D. F. Randolph, 1863.

Thompson, Richard S. *While My Country Is in Danger: The Life and Letters of Lieutenant Colonel Richard S. Thompson, Twelfth New Jersey Volunteers.* Edited by Gerry Harder Poriss and Ralph G. Porriss. Hamilton, N.Y.: Edmonston, 1994.

Thornwell, James Henley. *Our Danger and Our Duty*. Columbia, S.C.: Southern Guardian Press, 1862.

Tobie, Edward P. *History of the First Maine Cavalry, 1861–1865*. Boston: Emery & Hughes, 1887.

Tocqueville, Alexis de. *Democracy in America*. 2 vols. Translated by Henry Reeve. New York: Schocken Books, 1961.

Tourgée, Albion Winegar. *The Story of a Thousand: Being a History of the Services of the 105th Ohio Volunteer Infantry, in the War for the Union from August 21, 1862 to June 6, 1865*. Buffalo: S. McGerald, 1896.

Towles, Louis P., ed. *A World Turned Upside Down: The Palmers of South Santee, 1818–1881*. Columbia: University of South Carolina Press, 1996.

Trueheart, Charles, and Henry Trueheart. *Rebel Brothers: The Civil War Letters of the Truehearts*. Edited by Edward B. Williams. College Station: Texas A&M University Press, 1995.

Truesdale, John. *The Blue Coats, and How They Lived, Fought and Died for the Union. With Scenes and Incidents of the Great Rebellion*. Philadelphia: National Publishing, 1867.

Trumbull, H. Clay. *The Knightly Soldier: A Biography of Major Henry Ward Camp, Tenth Conn. Vols*. 6th ed., rev. Boston: Noyes, Holmes, 1871.

————. *War Memories of a Chaplain*. Philadelphia: J. D. Wattles, 1898.

Tucker, John Randolph. *The Bible or Atheism*. N.p., Va.: n.p., 186[?].

Turner, Charles W., ed. *The Allen Family of Amherst Virginia: Civil War Letters*. Berryville, Va.: Rockbridge, 1995.

Turner, Henry McNeal. *Respect Black: The Writings and Speeches of Henry McNeal Turner*. Edited by Edwin S. Redkey. New York: Arno Press, 1971.

Tuttle, Russell M. *The Civil War Journal of Lt. Russell M. Tuttle, New York Volunteer Infantry*. Edited by George H. Tappan. Jefferson, N.C.: McFarland, 2006.

Twichell, Joseph Hopkins. *The Civil War Letters of Joseph Hopkins Twichell: A Chaplain's Story*. Edited by Peter Messent and Steve Courtney. Athens: University of Georgia Press, 2006.

Tyler, Mason Whiting. *Recollections of the Civil War: With Many Original Diary Entries and Letters Written from the Seat of War, and with Annotated References*. Edited by William S. Tyler. New York: G. P. Putnam's Sons, 1912.

United Daughters of the Confederacy, South Carolina Division. *Recollections and Reminiscences, 1861–1865 through World War I*. 12 vols. [S.C.]: South Carolina Division, United Daughters of the Confederacy, 1990–2002.

United States Christian Commission. *Facts, Principles, and Progress: January 1864*. Philadelphia: W. S. and A. Martien, 1864.

————. *First Annual Report*. Philadelphia: n.p., 1863.

————. *Information for Army Meetings* (June 1864–March 1865). Philadelphia: James B. Rodgers, n.d.

————. *Second Annual Report*. Philadelphia: n.p., 1864.

————. *Third Annual Report*. Philadelphia: n.p., 1864.

United States Congress. *Report of the Joint Committee on Reconstruction at the First Session Thirty-ninth Congress*. Washington, D.C.: Government Printing Office, 1866.

————. *Report of the Joint Committee on the Conduct of the War*. 8 vols. Wilmington, N.C.: Broadfoot, 1999–2002.

Upson, Theodore F. *With Sherman to the Sea: The Journal of Theodore F. Upson*. Edited by Oscar Osburn Winther. Baton Rouge: Louisiana State University Press, 1943.

Van Wyck, Richard T. *A War to Petrify the Heart: The Civil War Letters of a Dutchess County, N.Y. Volunteer*. Edited by Virginia Hughes Kaminsky. Hensonville, N.Y.: Black Dome Press, 1997.

The Victory Won: A Memorial of the Rev. William J. Hoge, D.D., Late Pastor of the Tabb Street Presbyterian Church. Petersburg, Va.: Presbyterian Committee of Publications, 1864.

Wakelyn, Jon L., ed. *Southern Pamphlets on Secession, November 1860–April 1861*. Chapel Hill: University of North Carolina Press, 1996.

Walker, Aldace F. *Quite Ready to Be Sent Somewhere: The Civil War Letters of Aldace Freeman Walker*. Edited by Tom Ledoux. Victoria, British Columbia: Trafford, 2002.

Walker, David. *Walker's Appeal in Four Articles*. New York: Arno Press, 1969.

Walker, Georgiana. *The Private Journal of Georgiana Gholson Walker, 1862–1865, with Selections from the Post-War Years, 1865–1876*. Edited by Dwight Franklin Henderson. Tuscaloosa, Ala.: Confederate, 1963.

War of the Rebellion: A Compilation of the Official Records of the Union and Confederate Armies. 128 vols. Washington, D.C.: Government Printing Office, 1880–1901.

Washburn, George H. *A Complete History and Record of the 108th Regiment N.Y. Vols. from the 1862 to 1894*. Rochester, N.Y.: Press of E. R. Andrews, 1894.

Watford, Christopher M., ed. *The Civil War in North Carolina, Soldiers' and Civilians' Letters and Diaries, 1861–1865*, vol. 1: *The Piedmont*. Jefferson, N.C.: McFarland, 2003.

Watkins, Sam R. *"Co. Atych," Maury Grays, First Tennessee Regiment; or, A Side Show of the Big Show*. Edited by Bell Irvin Wiley. Jackson, Tenn.: McCowat-Mercer Press, 1952.

Wayland, Francis, Jr., and H. L Wayland. *A Memoir of the Life and Labors of Francis Wayland, D.D., L.L.D.* 2 vols. New York: Sheldon and Company, 1867.

Weddle, Robert S. *Plow-Horse Cavalry: The Caney Creek Boys of the Thirty-fourth Texas*. Austin, Tex.: Madrona Press, 1974.

Welles, Gideon. *Diary of Gideon Welles: Secretary of the Navy under Lincoln and Johnson*. Edited by Howard K. Beale. 3 vols. New York: W. W. Norton, 1960.

Welsh, Peter. *Irish Green and Union Blue: The Civil War Letters of Peter Welsh, Color Sergeant, 28th Regiment Massachusetts Volunteers*. Edited by Lawrence Frederick Kohl and Margaret Cossé Richard. New York: Fordham University Press, 1986.

Welton, J. Michael, ed. *"My Heart Is So Rebellious": The Caldwell Letters, 1861–1865*. Warrenton, Va.: Fauquier National Bank, n.d.

Weston, David. *Among the Wounded: U.S. Christian Commission; Experiences of a Delegate*. Philadelphia: J. B. Rodgers, 1864.

Weygant, Charles H. *History of the One Hundred and Twenty-fourth Regiment, N.Y.S.V.* Newburgh, N.Y.: Journal Printing House, 1877.

Wharton, H. M. *War Songs and Poems of the Southern Confederacy, 1861–1865*. Edison, N.J.: Castle Books, 2000.

Wheeler, William. *Letters of William Wheeler of the Class of 1855, Y.C.* Cambridge, Mass.: H. O. Houghton, 1875.

White, Andrew Dickson. *Christ in the Army: A Selection of Sketches of the Work U.S. Christian Commission*. [Philadelphia?: Ladies Christian Commission, 1865].

———. *Report of the Army Committee of U.S. Christian Commission, Pittsburgh, Pa.* [Pittsburgh, Pa.: Johnstons], 1861.

White, Henry S. *Prison Life among the Rebels: Recollections of a Union Chaplain.* Edited by Edward D. Jervey. Kent, Ohio: Kent State University Press, 1990.

White, William S. *Rev. William S. White, D.D., and His Times: An Autobiography.* Edited by H. M. White. Richmond: Whittet and Sheperson, 1891.

———. *Sketches of the Life of Captain Hugh A. White of the Stonewall Brigade.* Columbia: South Carolina Steam Press, 1864.

Wiatt, William Edward. *Confederate Chaplain William Edward Wiatt: An Annotated Diary.* Edited by Alex L. Wiatt. Lynchburg, Va.: H. E. Howard, 1994.

Wickman, Donald H., ed. *Letters to Vermont: From Her Civil War Soldier Correspondents to the Home Press.* 2 vols. Bennington, Vt.: Images from the Past, 1998.

Wightman, Edward King. *From Antietam to Fort Fisher: The Civil War Letters of Edward King Wightman, 1862–1865.* Edited by Edward G. Longacre. Cranbury, N.J.: Fairleigh Dickinson University Press, 1985.

Wiley, Calvin Henderson. *Scriptural Views of National Trials; or, The True Road to the Independence and Peace of the Confederate States of America.* Greensboro, N.C.: Sterling, Campbell and Albright, 1863.

Willard, Van R. *With the 3rd Wisconsin Badgers: The Living Experience of the Civil War through the Journals of Van R. Willard.* Edited by Steven S. Raab. Mechanicsburg, Pa.: Stackpole Books, 1999.

Willett, Alfred C. *A Union Soldier Returns South: The Civil War Letters and Diary of Alfred C. Willett, 113th Ohio Volunteer Infantry.* Edited by Charles E. Willett. Johnson City, Tenn.: Overmountain Press, 1994.

Williams, James M. *From That Terrible Field: Civil War Letters of James M. Williams, Twenty-first Alabama Infantry Volunteers.* Edited by John Kent Folmar. Tuscaloosa: University of Alabama Press, 1981.

Wilson, Douglas L., and Rodney O. Davis. *Herndon's Informants: Letters, Interviews, and Statements about Abraham Lincoln.* Urbana: University of Illinois Press, 1998.

Winter, Robert M., ed. *Civil War Women: The Diaries of Belle Strickland and Cora Harris Watson, Holly Springs, Mississippi, July 25, 1864–June 22, 1868.* Lafayette, Calif.: Thomas Berryhill Press, 2001.

Winters, William. *The Musick of the Mocking Birds, the Roar of the Cannon: The Civil War Diary and Letters of William Winters.* Edited by Steven E. Woodworth. Lincoln: University of Nebraska Press, 1998.

Worley, Ted R., ed. *At Home in Confederate Arkansas: Letters to and from Pulaski Countians, 1861–1865.* Little Rock, Ark.: Pulaski County Historical Society, 1955.

Worsham, W. J. *The Old Nineteenth Tennessee Regiment, C.S.A., June, 1861–April, 1865.* Oxford, Miss.: Guild Bindery Press, 1992.

Wright, Henry H. *A History of the Sixth Iowa Infantry.* Iowa City: State Historical Society of Iowa, 1923.

Yearns, W. Buck, and John G. Barrett, eds. *North Carolina Civil War Documentary.* Chapel Hill: University of North Carolina Press, 1980.

Articles

Bettersworth, John K., ed. "Mississippi Unionism: The Case of the Reverend James A. Lyon."
    Journal of Mississippi History 1 (January 1939): 37–52.

Boots, E. N. "Civil War Letters of E. N. Boots from New Bern and Plymouth." Edited by
    Wilfred W. Black. *North Carolina Historical Review* 36 (April 1959): 205–23.

Boyle, Francis Atherton. "The Prison Diary of Adjutant Francis Atherton Boyle, C.S.A." Edited
    by Mary Lindsay Thornton. *North Carolina Historical Review* 39 (Winter 1962): 58–84.

Bradford, James H. "The Chaplains in the Volunteer Army." In *War Papers Being Papers Read
    before the Commandery of the District of Columbia, Military Order of the Loyal Legion of the
    United States*, edited by E. P. Halstead, 1:153–67. Wilmington, N.C.: Broadfoot, 1993.

Cable, George Washington, ed. "War Diary of a Union Woman in the South." *Century
    Magazine* 38 (October 1889): 931–46.

[Cary, Harriette]. "Diary of Miss Harriette Cary, Kept by Her from May 6, 1862, to July 24,
    1862." *Tyler's Quarterly Historical and Genealogical Magazine* 9 (October 1927): 104–15;
    12 (January 1931): 160–73.

Chaffin, Nora C. "A Southern Advocate of Methodist Unification in 1865." *North Carolina
    Historical Review* 18 (January 1941): 38–47.

Clark, William Allen. "'Please Send Stamps': The Civil War Letters of William Allen Clark."
    Indiana Magazine of History 91 (March–December 1995): 81–108, 197–224, 288–319,
    407–36.

Cooney, Peter Paul. "The War Letters of Father Peter Paul Cooney of the Congregation of the
    Holy Cross." Edited by Thomas McAvoy. *Records of the American Catholic Historical Society*
    44 (1933): 47–69, 151–69, 220–37.

Couture, Richard T. "The Bolling-Cabell Letters—1861: The Early Letters of Julia (Juliet)
    Calvert Bolling to Philip Barrand Cabell, Part. III." *Goochland County Historical Society
    Magazine* 14 (1982): 20–33.

Denison, Frederic. "A Chaplain's Experience in the Union Army." In *Personal Narratives of
    Events in the War of the Rebellion, Being Papers Read before the Rhode Island Soldiers and
    Sailors Historical Society*, 7:435–77. Wilmington, N.C.: Broadfoot, 1993.

Duffield, George. "The Diary of George Duffield." *Mississippi Valley Historical Review* 24 (June
    1937): 21–34.

Dunn, Mathew Andrew. "Mathew Andrew Dunn Letters." Edited by Weymouth T. Jordan.
    Journal of Mississippi History 1 (April 1939): 110–27.

Eagleton, Ethie M. Foute. "'Stray Thoughts': The Civil War Diary of Ethie M. Foute Eagleton."
    Edited by Elvie Eagleton Skipper and Ruth Gove. *East Tennessee Historical Society's
    Publications* 40–41 (1968–69): 128–37, 116–28.

Eastman, William R. "The Army Chaplain of 1863." *Personal Recollections of the War of the
    Rebellion: Addresses Delivered before the Commandery of the State of New York, Military
    Order of the Loyal Legion of the United States*, 4:338–50. Wilmington, N.C.: Broadfoot,
    1994.

Frear, Sara S. "'You My Brother Will be Glad with Me': The Letters of Augusta Jane Evans
    to Walter Clopton Harriss, January 29, 1856, to October 29, 185[8?]." *Alabama Review*,
    60 (April 2007): 111–41.

Gray, Virginia Davis. "Life in Confederate Arkansas: The Diary of Virginia Davis Gray, 1863–

1865," parts I and II. Edited by Carl H. Moneyhon. *Arkansas Historical Quarterly* 42 (Spring–Summer 1983): 47–85, 134–69.

Heffelfinger, Jacob. "'Dear Sister Jennie' 'Dear Brother Jacob': Correspondence between a Northern Soldiers and His Sister." Edited by Florence C. McLaughlin. *Western Pennsylvania Historical Magazine* 60 (April, July 1977): 109–43, 203–40.

Ingraham, Elizabeth Mary Meade. "The Vicksburg Diary of Mrs. Alfred Ingraham." Edited by W. Maury Darst. *Journal of Mississippi History* 64 (May 1982): 148–79.

Jordan, Thomas G. "The Thomas G. Jordan Family during the War between the States." *Georgia Historical Quarterly* 59 (Supplement 1975): 134–40.

Kollock, Susan M., ed. "Letters of the Kollock and Allied Families, 1826–1884." *Georgia Historical Quarterly* 34 (June, September, December 1950): 126–57, 227–57, 313–27.

Lacy, B. T. "An Address of the Chaplains of the Second Corps ('Stonewall' Jackson's), Army of Northern Virginia, to the Churches of the Confederate States." *Southern Historical Society Papers* 14 (1886): 348–56.

Law, J. G. "Diary of Rev. J. G. Law." *Southern Historical Society Papers* 10 (1882): 564–69.

Lay, Henry C. "Sherman in Georgia." *Atlantic Monthly* 149 (February 1932): 166–72.

Lennard, George W. Z "'Give Yourself No Trouble about Me': The Shiloh Letters of George W. Lennard." Edited by Paul Hubbard and Christine Lews. *Indiana Magazine of History* 76 (March 1980): 21–53.

Manly, Basil. "The Diary of Dr. Basil Manly, 1858–1867," parts 1–5. Edited by W. Stanley Hoole. *Alabama Review* 4–5 (April 1951, July, October 1951; January and April 1952): 127–49, 221–36, 270–89, 61–74, 142–55.

McClatchey, Minerva Leah Rowles. "A Georgia Woman's Civil War Diary: The Journal of Minerva Leah Rowles McClatchey, 1864–65." *Georgia Historical Quarterly* 51 (June 1967): 197–216.

McKinley, William. "A Civil War Diary of William McKinley." Edited by H. Wayne Morgan. *Ohio Historical Quarterly* 69 (January 1960): 272–90.

Miller, James Russell. "Two Civil War Notebooks of James Russell Miller." *Journal of the Presbyterian Historical Society* 37 (June 1959): 65–90.

Morgan, Harry T. "Letters of a North Louisiana Private to His Wife, 1862–1865." *Mississippi Valley Historical Review* 30 (March 1944): 533–50.

Pressley, John G. "Extracts from the Diary of Lieutenant-Colonel John G. Pressley, of the Twenty-fifth South Carolina Volunteers." *Southern Historical Society Papers* 14 (1886): 35–62.

"Proceedings of the First Congress, Third Session." *Southern Historical Society Papers* 47 (1930).

"Proceedings of the Second Congress, Second Session." *Southern Historical Society Papers* 52 (1959).

Shannon, James P., ed. "Archbishop Ireland's Experiences as a Civil War Chaplain." *Catholic Historical Review* 39 (October 1953): 298–305.

Smith, James West. "A Confederate Soldier's Diary." *Southwest Review* 28 (Spring 1943): 293–327.

Spalding, Martin John. "Martin John Spalding's 'Dissertation on the American Civil War.'" Edited by David Spalding. *Catholic Historical Review* 52 (January 1966): 66–85.

Taylor, Mary W. "The Diary of Mary W. Taylor, 1860–1864." *Virginia Baptist Register* 19 (1980): 916–38.

Tissot, Reverend Father. "A Year with the Army of the Potomac: Diary of the Reverend Father Tissot, S.J., Military Chaplain." United States Catholic Historical Society, *Historical Records and Studies* 3 (1908), pt. 1: 42–87.

Vander Velde, L. G., ed. "Notes from the Diary of George Duffield." *Mississippi Valley Historical Review* 24 (January 1937): 53–67.

Vaughan, Turner. "Diary of Turner Vaughan, Co. 'C,' 4th Alabama Regiment, C.S.A., Commenced March 4th, 1863, and Ending February 12, 1864." *Alabama Historical Quarterly* 18 (1956): 573–604.

Walmsley, James Elliott. "The Change of Secession Sentiment in Virginia in 1861." *American Historical Review* 31 (October 1925): 82–101.

Waring, Martha Gallaudet, and Mary Alston Waring, eds. "Some Observations of the Years, 1860 and 1861 as Revealed in a Packet of Old Letters." *Georgia Historical Quarterly* 15 (September 1931): 272–92.

Washington, Ella. "'An Army of Devils: The Diary of Ella Washington." Edited by James O. Hall. *Civil War Times Illustrated* 16 (February 1978): 18–25.

Welles, Gideon. "The History of Emancipation." *Galaxy* 14 (December 1872): 838–51.

Welsh, George Wilson, and Philip Rudsil Welsh. "Civil War Letters from Two Brothers." *Yale Review* 18 (September 1928): 148–61.

Wight, Willard E., ed. "Pay the Preacher! Two Letters from Louisiana, 1864." *Louisiana History* 1 (Summer 1960): 251–59.

———, ed. "Some Wartime Letters of Bishop Lynch." *Catholic Historical Review* 43 (April 1957): 20–37.

———, ed. "War Letters of the Bishop of Richmond." *Virginia Magazine of History and Biography* 67 (July 1959): 259–70.

Williams, Sarah Frances Hicks. "Plantation Experiences of a New York Woman." Edited by James C. Bonner. *North Carolina Historical Review* 33 (July, October 1956): 384–411, 529–45.

Williams, Thomas. "Letters of General Thomas Williams, 1862." *American Historical Review* 14 (January 1909): 304–28.

SECONDARY SOURCES
Books

Aamodt, Terrie Dopp. *Righteous Armies, Holy Cause: Apocalyptic Imagery and the Civil War.* Macon, Ga.: Mercer University Press, 2002.

Ahlstrom, Sydney E. *A Religious History of the American People.* New Haven: Yale University Press, 1972.

Allan, Elizabeth Preston. *The Life and Letters of Margaret Junkin Preston.* Boston: Houghton, Mifflin., 1903.

Anderson, John Q. *A Texas Surgeon in the C.S.A.* Tuscaloosa, Ala.: Confederate, 1957.

Angell, Stephen Ward. *Bishop Henry McNeal Turner and African-American Religion in the South.* Knoxville: University of Tennessee Press, 1992.

Armstrong, Warren B. *For Courageous Fighting and Confident Dying: Union Chaplains in the Civil War.* Lawrence: University Press of Kansas, 1998.

Armstrong, William H. *A Friend to God's Poor: Edward Parmelee Smith*. Athens: University of Georgia Press, 1993.

Ash, Stephen V. *Middle Tennessee Society Transformed, 1860–1870*. Baton Rouge: Louisiana State University Press, 1988.

———. *When the Yankees Came: Conflict and Chaos in the Occupied South, 1861–1865*. Chapel Hill: University of North Carolina Press, 1995.

Auer, J. Jeffrey. *Antislavery and Disunion, 1858–1861: Studies in the Rhetoric of Compromise and Conflict*. New York: Harper and Row, 1963.

Ayers, Edward L. *In the Presence of Mine Enemies: War in the Heart of America, 1859–1863*. New York: W. W. Norton, 2003.

———. *What Caused the Civil War? Reflections on the South and Southern History*. New York: W. W. Norton, 2005.

Ayers, Edward L., Gary W. Gallagher, and Andrew J. Torget, eds. *Crucible of the Civil War: Virginia from Secession to Commemoration*. Charlottesville: University of Virginia Press, 2006.

Bacon, Leonard W. *A History of American Christianity*. New York: Christian Literature, 1897.

Bacon, Theodore T. *Leonard Bacon: A Statesman in the Church*. New Haven: Yale University Press, 1931.

Bailey, David T. *Shadow on the Church: Southwestern Evangelical and the Issue of Slavery, 1783–1860*. Ithaca, N.Y.: Cornell University Press, 1985.

Baker, Robert Andrew. *Relations between Northern and Southern Baptists*. New York: Arno Press, 1980.

Barclay, Wade Crawford. *History of Methodist Missions*. 4 vols. New York: Board of Mission of the Methodist Church, 1957.

Barton, George. *Angels of the Battlefield: A History of the Labors of the Catholic Sisterhoods in the Civil War*. Philadelphia: Catholic Art Publishing Company, 1897.

Baum, Dale. *The Shattering of Texas Unionism: Politics in the Lone Star State during the Civil War Era*. Baton Rouge: Louisiana State University Press, 1998.

Bean, W. G. *The Liberty Hall Volunteers: Stonewall's College Boys*. Charlottesville: University Press of Virginia, 1964.

Beard, Augustus Field. *A Crusade of Brotherhood: A History of the American Missionary Association*. Boston: Pilgrim Press, 1909.

Beardsley, Frank Grenville. *A History of American Revivals*. 3rd ed. New York: American Tract Society, 1912.

Bebbington, David W. *The Dominance of Evangelicalism: The Age of Spurgeon and Moody*. Downers Grove, Ill.: InterVarsity Press, 2005.

Bennett, P. S., and James Lawson. *History of Methodism in Wisconsin*. Cincinnati: Cranston and Stowe, 1890.

Bennett, Michael J. *Union Jacks: Yankee Sailors in the Civil War*. Chapel Hill: University of North Carolina Press, 2004.

Beringer, Richard E., et al. *Why the South Lost the Civil War*. Athens: University of Georgia Press, 1986.

Bernstein, Iver. *The New York City Draft Riots: Their Significance for American Society and the Politics in the Age of the Civil War*. New York: Oxford University Press, 1990.

Bettersworth, John K. *Confederate Mississippi: The People and Policies of a Cotton State in Wartime*. Baton Rouge: Louisiana State University Press, 1943.

Blair, William. *Virginia's Private War: Feeding Body and Soul in the Confederacy, 1861–1865*. New York: Oxford University Press, 1998.

Blied, Benjamin. *Catholics and the Civil War*. Milwaukee: privately printed, 1945.

Blight, David W. *Race and Reunion: The Civil War in American Memory*. Cambridge, Mass.: Harvard University Press, 2001.

Blum, Edward J. *Reforging the White Republic: Race, Religion, and American Nationalism, 1865–1898*. Baton Rouge: Louisiana State University Press, 2005.

Blum, Edward J., and W. Scott Poole, eds. *Vale of Tears: New Essays on Religion and Reconstruction*. Macon, Ga.: Mercer University Press, 2005.

Boles, John B. *Black Southerners, 1619–1869*. Lexington: University Press of Kentucky, 1984.

———. *The Great Revival, 1787–1805: The Origins of the Southern Evangelical Mind*. Lexington: University of Kentucky Press, 1972.

———, ed. *Masters and Slaves in the House of the Lord: Race and Religion in the American South, 1740–1870*. Lexington: University Press of Kentucky, 1988.

Bolster, Arthur S., Jr. *James Freeman Clarke: Disciple to Advancing Truth*. Boston: Beacon Press, 1954.

Bonner, Robert E. *Colors and Blood: Flag Passions of the Confederate South*. Princeton: Princeton University Press, 2002.

———. *Mastering America: Southern Slaveholders and the Crisis of American Nationhood*. Cambridge: Cambridge University Press, 2009.

Boritt, Gabor. *The Gettysburg Gospel: The Lincoln Speech That Nobody Knows*. New York: Simon and Schuster, 2006.

Bowden, Haygood S. *History of Savannah Methodism from John Wesley to Silas Johnson*. Macon, Ga.: J. W. Burke, 1929.

Boyd, Jesse Laney. *A Popular History of the Baptists in Mississippi*. Jackson, Miss.: Baptist Press, 1930.

Boylan, Anne. *Sunday School: The Formation of an American Institution, 1790–1880*. New Haven, Conn.: Yale University Press, 1988.

Bozeman, Theodore Dwight. *Protestants in an Age of Science: The Baconian Ideal and Antebellum American Religious Thought*. Chapel Hill: University of North Carolina Press, 1977.

Bradley, David Henry, Sr. *History of the A.M.E. Zion Church, 1796–1872*. Nashville: Parthenon Press, 1956.

Brandt, Dennis W. *From Home Guards to Heroes: The 87th Pennsylvania and Its Civil War Community*. Columbia: University of Missouri Press, 2006.

Bremner, Robert H. *The Public Good: Philanthropy and Welfare in the Civil War Era*. New York: Alfred A. Knopf, 1980.

Brinsfield, John W., et al., eds. *Faith in the Fight: Civil War Chaplains*. Mechanicsburg, Pa.: Stackpole Books, 2003.

Bristol, Frank Milton. *The Life of Chaplain McCabe: Bishop of the Methodist Episcopal Church*. Cincinnati: Jennings and Graham, 1908.

Brock, Peter. *Pacifism in the United States: From the Colonial Era to the First World War*. Princeton, N.J.: Princeton University Press, 1968.

Bruce, Dickson D. *And They All Sang Hallelujah: Plain-Folk Camp-Meeting Religion, 1800–1845*. Knoxville: University of Tennessee Press, 1974.

Brunk, Harry Anthony. *History of the Mennonites in Virginia, 1727–1900*. 2 vols. Staunton, Va.: McClure Printing, 1959.

Bryan, T. Conn. *Confederate Georgia*. Athens: University of Georgia Press, 1953.

Bucke, Emory Stephens, et al. *The History of American Methodism*. 3 vols. New York: Abington Press, 1964.

Buckley, James M. *A History of Methodism in the United States*. 2 vols. New York: Harper and Brothers, 1898.

Burton, Orville Vernon. *In My Father's House Are Many Mansions: Family and Community in Edgefield, South Carolina*. Chapel Hill: University of North Carolina Press, 1985.

Butler, Diana Hochstedt. *Standing against the Whirlwind: Evangelical Episcopalians in Nineteenth-Century America*. New York: Oxford University Press, 1995.

Butler, Jon. *Awash in a Sea of Faith: Christianizing the American People*. Cambridge, Mass.: Harvard University Press, 1990.

Butterfield, Herbert. *Christianity and History*. New York: Scribner, 1950.

Cain, John Buford. *Methodism in the Mississippi Conference, 1846–1870*. Jackson, Miss.: Hawkins Foundation, 1939.

Calhoon, Robert M. *Evangelicals and Conservatives in the Early South, 1740–1861*. Columbia: University of South Carolina Press, 1988.

Campbell, Jacqueline Glass. *When Sherman Marched North from the Sea: Resistance on the Confederate Home Front*. Chapel Hill: University of North Carolina Press, 2003.

Carmichael, Peter S. *The Last Generation: Young Virginians in Peace, War, and Reunion*. Chapel Hill: University of North Carolina Press, 2005.

———. *Lee's Young Artillerist: William R. J. Pegram*. Charlottesville: University Press of Virginia, 1995.

Carroll, J. M. *A History of Texas Baptists; Comprising a Detailed Account of Their Activities, Their Progress, and Their Achievements*. Edited by J. B. Cranfill. Dallas, Tex.: Baptist Standard, 1923.

Carter, Dan T. *When the War Was Over: The Failure of Self-Reconstruction in the South, 1865–1867*. Baton Rouge: Louisiana State University Press, 1982.

Caruthers, J. Wade. *Octavius Brooks Frothingham, Gentle Radical*. University: University of Alabama Press, 1977.

Cartland, Fernando G. *Southern Heroes or the Friends in War Time*. Cambridge, Mass.: Riverside Press, 1895.

Carwardine, Richard J. *Evangelicals and Politics in Antebellum America*. New Haven, Conn.: Yale University Press, 1993.

———. *Lincoln: A Life of Purpose and Power*. New York: Alfred A. Knopf, 2006.

Cashin, Joan E., ed. *The War Was You and Me: Civilians in the American Civil War*. Princeton, N.J.: Princeton University Press, 2002.

Catton, Bruce. *Grant Moves South*. Boston: Little, Brown, 1960.

[Cheney, Mary Bushnell]. *Life and Letters of Horace Bushnell*. New York: Charles Scribner's Sons, 1903.

Chesebrough, David B. *Clergy Dissent in the Old South, 1830–1865*. Carbondale: Southern Illinois University Press, 1996.

———. "No Sorrow like Our Sorrow": Northern Protestant Ministers and the Assassination of Lincoln. Kent, Ohio: Kent State University Press, 1994.

Cheshire, Joseph Blount. The Church in the Confederate States: A History of the Protestant Episcopal Church in the Confederate States. New York: Longmans, Green, 1912.

Christian, John T. History of the Baptists of Louisiana. Shreveport: Executive Board of the Louisiana Baptist Convention, 1923.

Cimbala, Paul A., and Randall M. Miller, eds. An Uncommon Time: The Civil War and the Northern Home Front. New York: Fordham University Press, 2002.

———, eds. Union Soldiers and the Northern Home Front: Wartime Experiences, Postwar Adjustments. New York: Fordham University Press, 2002.

Clark, Robert D. The Life of Matthew Simpson. New York: Macmillan, 1956.

Clarke, Erskine. Our Southern Zion: A History of Calvinism in the South Carolina Low Country, 1690–1990. Tuscaloosa: University of Alabama Press, 1996.

Clarke, Richard H. Lives of the Deceased Bishops of the Catholic Church in the United States. 3 vols. New York: Richard H. Clarke, 1888.

Clebsch, William A. Christian Interpretations of the Civil War. Philadelphia: Fortress Press, 1969.

Clinton, Catherine, ed. Southern Families at War: Loyalty and Conflict in the Civil War South. New York: Oxford University Press, 2000.

Coffman, Edward M. The Old Army: A Portrait of the American Army in Peacetime, 1784–1898. New York: Oxford University Press, 1986.

Cohen, Patricia Cline. A Calculating People: The Spread of Numeracy in Early America. Chicago: University of Chicago Press, 1982.

Cole, Arthur Charles. The Sesquicentennial History of Illinois, vol. 3: The Era of the Civil War, 1848–1870. Urbana: University of Illinois Press, 1987.

Cole, Charles C., Jr. The Social Ideas of the Northern Evangelists, 1826–1860. New York: Columbia University Press, 1954.

Cole, Maurice F. The Impact of the Civil War on the Presbyterian Church in Michigan. Lansing: Michigan Civil War Centennial Observance Commission, 1965.

Cooke, George Willis. Unitarianism in America: A History of Its Origins and Development. Boston: American Unitarian Association, 1902.

Cooper, William J., Jr. Jefferson Davis, American. New York: Alfred A. Knopf, 2000.

Cornelius, Janet Duitsman. Slave Missions and the Black Church in the Antebellum South. Columbia: University of South Carolina Press, 1999.

———. "When I Can Read My Title Clear": Literacy, Slavery, and Religion in the Antebellum South. Columbia: University of South Carolina Press, 1991.

Cott, Nancy F. The Bonds of Womanhood: "Woman's Sphere" in New England, 1780–1835. New Haven, Conn.: Yale University Press, 1977.

Cotton, Gordon A. Of Primitive Faith and Order: A History of the Mississippi Primitive Baptist Church, 1780–1974. Raymond, Miss.: Keith Press, 1974.

Coulter, E. Merton. Civil War and Readjustment in Kentucky. Chapel Hill: University of North Carolina Press, 1926.

———. The Confederate States of America, 1861–1865. Baton Rouge: Louisiana State University Press, 1948.

Cozzens, Peters. *This Terrible Sound: The Battle of Chickamauga*. Urbana: University of Illinois Press, 1992.

Crawford, Martin. *Ashe County's Civil War: Community and Society in the Appalachian South.* Charlottesville: University Press of Virginia, 2001.

Creel, Margaret Washington. *"A Peculiar People": Slave Religion and Community-Culture Among the Gullahs.* New York: New York University Press, 1988.

Cross, Barbara. *Horace Bushnell: Minister to a Changing America.* Chicago: University of Chicago Press, 1958.

Crowther, Edward R. *Southern Evangelicals and the Coming of the Civil War.* Lewiston, N.Y.: Edward Mellen Press, 2000.

Culver, Dwight W. *Negro Segregation in the Methodist Church.* New Haven, Conn.: Yale University Press, 1953.

Current, Richard N. *The History of Wisconsin*, vol. 2: *The Civil War Era, 1848–1873.* Madison: State Historical Society of Wisconsin, 1976.

Curry, Daniel. *Life-Story of Rev. Davis Wasgatt Clark, Bishop of the Methodist Episcopal Church.* New York: Nelson and Phillips, 1874.

Cushman, Joseph D. *A Goodly Heritage: The Episcopal Church in Florida, 1821–1892.* Gainesville: University of Florida Press, 1965.

Cuthbert, James H. *Life of Richard Fuller, D.D.* New York: Sheldon and Company, 1879.

Daniel, Larry J. *Soldiering in the Army of Tennessee: A Portrait of Life in a Confederate Army.* Chapel Hill: University of North Carolina Press, 1991.

Daniel, W. Harrison. *Southern Protestantism in the Confederacy.* Bedford, Va.: Print Shop, 1989.

Davenport, Frederick M. *Primitive Traits in Religious Revivals.* New York: Gordon Press, 1905.

Davis, J. Treadwell. *Relations between the Northern and Southern Presbyterian Churches, 1861–1888.* Nashville, Tenn.: Joint Universities Libraries, 1951.

Davis, Oscar Adams. *First Baptist Church History, Gadsden, Alabama, 1855–1985.* Tallahassee, Fla.: Father and Son Publishing, 1987.

Dean, Eric. *Shook over Hell: Post-Traumatic Stress, Vietnam, and the Civil War.* Cambridge, Mass.: Harvard University Press, 1977.

Dillon, Merton L. *The Abolitionists: The Growth of a Dissenting Minority.* New York: W. W. Norton, 1974.

Dirck, Brian. *Lincoln and Davis: Imagining America, 1809–1865.* Lawrence: University Press of Kansas, 2001.

Dolan, Jay P. *Catholic Revivalism: The American Experience, 1830–1900.* Notre Dame, Ind.: University of Notre Dame Press, 1978.

———. *Immigrant Church: New York's Irish and German Catholics, 1815–1865.* Baltimore: Johns Hopkins University Press, 1975.

Dollar, Kent T. *Soldiers of the Cross: Confederate Soldier-Christians and the Impact of War on Their Faith.* Macon, Ga.: Mercer University Press, 2005.

Donald, David Herbert. *Lincoln.* New York: Simon and Schuster, 1995.

Dougan, Michael B. *Confederate Arkansas: The People and Politics of a Frontier State in Wartime.* University: University of Alabama Press, 1976.

Doyle, Don Harrison. *The Social Order of a Frontier Community: Jacksonville, Illinois, 1825–1870*. Urbana: University of Illinois Press, 1978.

Dunham, Chester Forrester. *The Attitude of the Northern Clergy toward the South, 1861–1865*. Toledo, Ohio: Gray, 1942.

Dunkelman, Mark H. *Brothers One and All: Esprit de Corps in a Civil War Regiment*. Baton Rouge: Louisiana State University Press, 2004.

———. *War's Relentless Hand: Twelve Tales of Civil War Soldiers*. Baton Rouge: Louisiana State University Press, 2006.

Durkin, Joseph T. *Confederate Navy Chief: Stephen R. Mallory*. Chapel Hill: University of North Carolina Press, 1954.

Dvorak, Katherine L. *An African-American Exodus: The Segregation of the Southern Churches*. Brooklyn, N.Y.: Carlson, 1991.

Eaton, Grace M. *A Heroine of the Cross: Sketches of the Life and Work of Miss Joanna P. Moore*. N.p.: n.p., 1934.

Eckert, Ralph Lowell. *John Brown Gordon: Soldier, Southerner, American*. Baton Rouge: Louisiana State University Press, 1989.

Edwards, Robert. *Of Singular Genius, Of Singular Grace: A Biography of Horace Bushnell*. Cleveland: Pilgrim Press, 1992.

Eighmy, John Lee. *Churches in Cultural Captivity: A History of the Social Attitudes of Southern Baptists*. Knoxville: University of Tennessee Press, 1972.

Elder, William Henry. *Character-Glimpses of Most Reverend William Henry Elder, D.D., Second Archbishop of Cincinnati*. Ratisbon, N.Y.: Frederick Pustet, 1911.

Engs, Robert F., and Randall M. Miller, eds. *The Birth of the Grand Old Party: Republicans' First Generation*. Philadelphia: University of Pennsylvania Press, 2002.

Escott, Paul D. *Many Excellent People: Power and Privilege in North Carolina, 1850–1900*. Chapel Hill: University of North Carolina Press, 1985.

Evans, W. A. *A History of the First Baptist Church, Aberdeen, Mississippi, 1837 to 1945*. Aberdeen, Miss. First Baptist Church, 1945.

Fallows, Alice Katherine. *Everybody's Bishop: Being the Life and Times of Right Reverend Samuel Fallows, D. D.* New York: J. H. Sears, 1927.

Farish, Hunter Dickinson. *The Circuit Rider Dismounts: A Social History of Southern Methodism, 1865–1900*. Richmond: Dietz Press, 1938.

Farmer, James O. *The Metaphysical Confederacy: James Henley Thornwell and the Synthesis of Southern Values*. Macon, Ga.: Mercer University Press, 1986.

Faust, Drew Gilpin. *The Creation of Confederate Nationalism: Ideology and Identity in the Civil War South*. Baton Rouge: Louisiana State University Press, 1988.

———. *Mothers of Invention: Women of the Slaveholding South in the American Civil War*. Chapel Hill: University of North Carolina Press, 1996.

———. *The Republic of Suffering: Death and the American Civil War*. New York: Alfred A. Knopf, 2008.

———. *Southern Stories: Slaveholders in Peace and War*. Columbia: University of Missouri Press, 1992.

Fellman, Michael. *Citizen Sherman: A Life of William Tecumseh Sherman*. New York: Random House, 1995.

———. *Inside War: The Guerrilla Conflict in Missouri during the American Civil War*. New York: Oxford University Press, 1989.

———. *The Making of Robert E. Lee*. New York: Random House, 2000.

Finke, Roger, and Rodney Stark. *The Churching of America, 1776–1990: Winners and Losers in Our Religious Economy*. New Brunswick, N.J.: Rutgers University Press, 1992.

Finney, Thomas M. *Life and Labors of Enoch Mather Marvin, Late Bishop of the Methodist Episcopal Church, South*. St. Louis: James H. Chambers, 1880.

Fite, Emerson David. *Social and Industrial Conditions in the North during the Civil War*. New York: Macmillan, 1910.

Fitzgerald, O. P. *John B. McFerrin: A Biography*. Nashville: Publishing House of the M.E. Church, South, 1889.

Fleming, John Kerr. *History of the Third Creek Presbyterian Church, Cleveland, North Carolina, 1787–1966*. Raleigh: Synod of North Carolina, 1967.

Fleming, Walter L. *Civil War and Reconstruction in Alabama*. New York: Columbia University Press, 1905.

Flynt, Wayne. *Alabama Baptists: Southern Baptists in the Heart of Dixie*. Tuscaloosa: University of Alabama Press, 1998.

Fordham, Monroe. *Major Themes in Northern Black Religious Thought, 1800–1860*. Hicksville, N.Y.: Exposition Press, 1975.

Foster, Gaines M. *Ghosts of the Confederacy: Defeat, the Lost Cause, and the Emergence of the New South*. New York: Oxford University Press, 1987.

———. *Moral Reconstruction: Christian Lobbyists and the Federal Legislation of Morality, 1865–1920*. Chapel Hill: University of North Carolina Press, 2002.

Fox-Genovese, Elizabeth, and Eugene Genovese. *The Mind of the Master Class: History and Faith in the Southern Slaveholders' Worldview*. Cambridge: Cambridge University Press, 2005.

Franklin, John Hope. *The Emancipation Proclamation*. Garden City, N.Y.: Doubleday, 1963.

Frassanito, William A. *Grant and Lee: The Virginia Campaigns, 1864–1865*. New York: Charles Scribner's Sons, 1983.

Frederickson, George. *The Inner Civil War: Northern Intellectuals and the Crisis of the Union*. New York: Harper and Row, 1965.

Freehling, William W. *The Road to Disunion*, vol. 2: *Secessionists Triumphant, 1854–1861*. New York: Oxford University Press, 2007.

Freeman, Douglas Southall. *Lee's Lieutenants*. 3 vols. New York: Charles Scribner's Sons, 1942–44.

———. *R. E. Lee, a Biography*. 4 vols. New York: Charles Scribner's Sons, 1934–35.

Fuller, A. James. *Chaplain to the Confederacy: Basily Manly and Baptist Life in the Old South*. Baton Rouge: Louisiana State University Press, 2000.

Funk, Benjamin. *Life and Labors of Edler John Kline the Martyr Missionary*. Elgin, Ill.: Brethren Publishing House, 1900.

Futch, Ovid L. *History of Andersonville Prison*. Gainesville: University of Florida Press, 1968.

Gallagher, Gary W. *The Confederate War*. Cambridge, Mass.: Harvard University Press, 1997.

———. *Lee and His Generals in War and Memory*. Baton Rouge: Louisiana State University Press, 1998.

———. *Stephen Dodson Ramseur: Lee's Gallant General*. Chapel Hill: University of North Carolina Press, 1985.

———, ed. *The Wilderness Campaign*. Chapel Hill: University of North Carolina Press, 1997.

Gaines, Wesley J. *African Methodism in the South; or, Twenty-Five Years of Freedom*. Atlanta: Franklin, 1890.

Gannon, Michael V. *Rebel Bishop: The Life and Era of Augustin Verot*. Milwaukee: Bruce, 1964.

Gardner, Robert G. *A Decade of Debate and Division: Georgia Baptists and the Formation of the Southern Baptist Convention*. Macon, Ga.: Mercer University Press, 1995.

Gardner, Robert G., et al. *A History of the Georgia Baptist Association, 1784–1984*. Atlanta: Georgia Baptist Historical Society, 1988.

Gaustad, Edwin. *Historical Atlas of Religion in America*. Rev. ed. New York: Harper and Row, 1976.

Gavin, William Gilfillan. *Campaigning with the Roundheads: The History of the Hundredth Pennsylvania Veteran Volunteer Infantry Regiment in the American Civil War, 1861–1865*. Dayton, Ohio: Morningside, 1989.

Geary, James W. *We Need Men: The Union Draft in the Civil War*. DeKalb: Northern Illinois University Press, 1991.

Genovese, Eugene D. *A Consuming Fire: The Fall of the Confederacy in the Mind of the White Christian South*. Athens: University of Georgia Press, 1998.

———. *Roll, Jordan, Roll: The World the Slaves Made*. New York: Pantheon Books, 1974.

Germain, Aidan Henry. *Catholic Military and Naval Chaplains, 1776–1917*. Washington, D.C.: Catholic University Press, 1929.

Gerow, Richard O., ed. *Catholicity in Mississippi*. Marrero, La.: Hope Haven Press, 1939.

———. *Cradle Days of St. Mary's at Natchez*. Marrero, La.: Hope Haven Press, 1941.

Gerteis, Louis S. *Civil War St. Louis*. Lawrence: University Press of Kansas, 2001.

Gibbs, Joseph. *Three Years in the Bloody Eleventh: The Campaigns of a Pennsylvania Reserves Regiment*. University Park: Pennsylvania State University Press, 2002.

Glasgow, W. Melancthon. *History of the Reformed Presbyterian Church in America*. Baltimore: Hill and Harvery, 1888.

Glatthaar, Joseph T. *Forged in Battle: The Civil War Alliance of Black Soldiers and White Officers*. New York: Free Press, 1990.

———. *General Lee's Army: From Victory to Collapse*. New York: Free Press, 2008.

———. *The March to the Sea and Beyond: Sherman's Troops in the Savannah and Carolinas Campaigns*. New York: New York University Press, 1986.

Goen, C. C. *Broken Churches, Broken Nation: Denominational Schisms and the Coming of the Civil War*. Macon, Ga.: Mercer University Press, 1985.

Graham, Preston D., Jr. *A Kingdom Not of This World: Stuart Robinson's Struggle to Distinguish the Sacred from the Secular during the Civil War*. Macon, Ga.: Mercer University Press, 2002.

Gravely, William B. *Gilbert Haven: Methodist Abolitionist: A Study in Race, Religion, and Reform, 1850–1880*. Nashville, Tenn.: Abindgon Press, 1971.

Gray, Michael P. *The Business of Captivity: Elmira and Its Civil War Prison*. Kent, Ohio: Kent State University Press, 2001.

Griffin, Clifford S. *Their Brothers' Keepers: Moral Stewardship in the United States, 1800–1865*. New Brunswick, N.J.: Rutgers University Press, 1960.

Guelzo, Allen C. *Abraham Lincoln: Redeemer President*. Grand Rapids, Mich.: William B. Eerdmans, 1999.

———. *Lincoln's Emancipation Proclamation: The End of Slavery in America*. New York: Simon and Schuster, 2004.

Guyatt, Nicholas. *Providence and the Invention of the United States, 1607–1876*. New York: Cambridge University Press, 2007.

Hagerty, Edward J. *Collis' Zouaves: The 114th Pennsylvania Volunteers in the Civil War*. Baton Rouge: Louisiana State University Press, 1997.

Hall, David D. *Worlds of Wonder, Days of Judgment: Popular Religious Belief in Early New England*. New York: Alfred A. Knopf, 1989.

Hall, James W. *A History of First Presbyterian Church of Mocksville, North Carolina*. N.p.: n.p., 1963.

Hall, Joseph H. *Presbyterian Conflict and Resolution on the Missouri Frontier*. Lewiston, N.Y.: Edwin Mellen Press, 1987.

Hanley, Mark Y. *Beyond a Christian Commonwealth: The Protestant Quarrel with the American Republic, 1830–1860*. Chapel Hill: University of North Carolina Press, 1994.

Harper, Douglas R. *"If Thee Must Fight": A Civil War History of Chester County, Pennsylvania*. West Chester, Pa.: Chester County Historical Society, 1990.

Harrell, Carolyn L. *When the Bells Tolled for Lincoln: Southern Reaction to the Assassination*. Macon, Ga.: Mercer University Press, 1997.

Harrell, David E. *A Social History of the Disciples of Christ*. 2 vols. Nashville: Disciples of Christ Historical Society, 1966–73.

Harrison, Hall. *The Life of Right Reverend John Barrett Kerfoot, D.D., LL.D., First Bishop of Pittsburgh*. 2 vols. New York: James Pott, 1886.

Hassard, John Rose Greene. *Life of the Most Reverend John Hughes, D.D., First Archbishop of New York. With Extracts from his Private Correspondence*. New York: D. Appleton, 1866.

Hatch, Nathan. *The Democratization of American Christianity*. New Haven, Conn.: Yale University Press, 1989.

Hatch, Nathan O., and Mark A. Noll, eds. *The Bible in America: Essays in Cultural History*. New York: Oxford University Press, 1982.

Hawthorne, Frank W. *Episcopal Church in Michigan during the Civil War*. Lansing: Michigan Civil War Centennial Observance Commission, 1966.

Haynes, Stephen R. *Noah's Curse: The Biblical Justification of American Slavery*. New York: Oxford University Press, 2002.

Heathcote, Charles William. *The Lutheran Church in the Civil War*. New York: Fleming H. Revell, 1919.

Herek, Raymond J. *These Men Have Seen Hard Service: The First Michigan Sharpshooters in the Civil War*. Detroit: Wayne State University Press, 1998.

Hess, Earl J. *The Union Soldier in Battle: Enduring the Ordeal of Combat*. Lawrence: University Press of Kansas, 1997.

Heyrman, Christine Leigh. *Southern Cross: The Beginnings of the Bible Belt*. New York: Alfred A. Knopf, 1997.

Hildebrand, Reginald F. *The Times Were Strange and Stirring: Methodist Preachers and the Crisis of Emancipation.* Durham, N.C.: Duke University Press, 1995.

History of the Baptist Denomination in Georgia: With Biographical Compendium and Portrait Gallery of Baptist Ministers and Other Georgia Baptists. Atlanta: James P. Harrison, 1881.

Holder, Ray. *William Winans: Methodist Leader in Antebellum Mississippi.* Jackson: University Press of Mississippi, 1977.

Holifield, E. Brooks. *The Gentleman Theologians: American Theology in Southern Culture, 1795–1860.* Durham, N.C.: Duke University Press, 1978.

———. *Theology in America: Christian Thought from the Age of the Puritans to the Civil War.* New Haven, Conn.: Yale University Press, 2003.

Holland, J. G. *J. G. Holland's Life of Abraham Lincoln.* Lincoln: University of Nebraska Press, 1988.

Hood, James W. *One Hundred Years of the African Methodist Episcopal Zion Church: The Centennial of African Methodism.* New York: AME Zion Book Concern, 1895.

[Hopkins, John Henry, Jr.]. *The Life of Right Reverend John Henry Hopkins, First Bishop of Vermont and Seventh Presiding Bishop, by One of His Sons.* New York: Huntington, 1873.

Horst, Samuel. *Mennonites in the Confederacy: A Study in Civil War Pacifism.* Scottsdale, Pa.: Herald Press, 1967.

Howard, Philip E. *The Life Story of Henry Clay Trumbull: Missionary, Army Chaplain, Editor and Author.* Philadelphia: Sunday School Times, 1905.

Howard, Victor B. *Conscience and Slavery: The Evangelistic Calvinist Domestic Missions, 1837–1861.* Kent, Ohio: Kent State University Press, 1990.

———. *Religion and the Radical Republican Movement, 1860–1870.* Lexington: University Press of Kentucky, 1990.

Howe, Daniel Walker. *The Unitarian Conscience: Harvard Moral Philosophy, 1805–1861.* Cambridge, Mass.: Harvard University Press, 1970.

Hundley, William T. *History of Mattaponi Baptist Church, King and Queen County, Virginia.* Richmond: Appeals Press, 1928.

Hunter, Jerry. *Sons of Arthur, Children of Lincoln, Welsh Writings from the American Civil War.* Cardiff: University Wales Press, 2007.

Hutchinson, William T. *Cyrus Hall McCormick.* 2 vols. New York: D. Appleton-Century, 1930–35.

Imholte, John Quinn. *The First Volunteers: History of the First Minnesota Volunteer Regiment, 1861–1865.* Minneapolis: Ross and Haines, 1963.

Inscoe, John C., and Gordon B. McKinney. *The Heart of Appalachia: Western North Carolina in the Civil War.* Chapel Hill: University of North Carolina Press, 2000.

Iobst, Richard W. *Civil War Macon: The History of a Confederate City.* Macon, Ga.: Mercer University Press, 1999.

James, William. *The Varieties of Religious Experience: A Study in Human Nature.* New York: Penguin Books, 1982.

Jenkins, William Sumner. *Pro-Slavery Thought in the Old South.* Chapel Hill: University of North Carolina Press, 1935.

Johansson, M. Jane. *Peculiar Honor: A History of the 28th Texas Cavalry, 1862–1865.* Fayetteville: University of Arkansas Press, 1998.

Johnson, Curtis D. *Redeeming America: Evangelicals and the Road to Civil War.* Chicago: Ivan R. Dee, 1993.

Johnson, James Turner. *Just War Tradition and the Restraint of War: A Moral and Historical Inquiry.* Princeton, N.J.: Princeton University Press, 1981.

Johnson, Thomas Cary. *The Life and Letters of Robert Lewis Dabney.* Richmond: Presbyterian Committee of Publication, 1903.

———. *The Life and Letters of Benjamin Morgan Palmer.* Richmond: Presbyterian Committee of Publication, 1906.

Jolly, Ellen Ryan. *Nuns of the Battlefield.* Providence, R.I.: Providence Visitor Press, 1927.

Jones, Donald G. *The Sectional Crisis and Northern Methodism: A Study in Piety, Political Ethics and Civil Religion.* Metuchen, N.J.: Scarecrow Press, 1979.

Jones, Edgar De Witt. *Lincoln and the Preachers.* New York: Harper, 1948.

Jones, F. D., and W. H. Mills, eds. *History of the Presbyterian Church in South Carolina since 1850.* Columbia: R. L. Bryan, 1926.

Jordan, Ervin L., Jr. *Black Confederates and Afro-Yankees in Civil War Virginia.* Charlottesville: University Press of Virginia, 1995.

Jordan, Ryan P. *Slavery and the Meeting House: The Quakers and the Abolitionist Dilemma, 1820–1865.* Bloomington: Indiana University Press, 2007.

Kendall, W. Fred. *A History of the Tennessee Baptist Convention.* Brentwood: Executive Board of the Tennessee Baptist Convention, 1974.

Kennett, Lee. *Marching through Georgia: The Story of Soldiers and Civilians during Sherman's Campaign.* New York: HarperCollins, 1995.

Kerby, Robert L. *Kirby Smith's Confederacy: The Trans-Mississippi South, 1863–1865.* New York: Columbia University Press, 1972.

Kimbrough, David L. *Reverend Joseph Tarkington, Methodist Circuit Rider: From Frontier Evangelism to Refined Religion.* Knoxville: University of Tennessee Press, 1997.

Korn, Bertram. *American Jewry and the Civil War.* Philadelphia: Jewish Publication Society of America, 1961.

Krick, Robert K. *Parker's Virginia Battery C.S.A.* 2nd ed. Rev. Wilmington, N.C.: Broadfoot, 1989.

Kundahl, George G. *Confederate Engineer: Training and Campaigning with John Morris Wampler.* Knoxville: University of Tennessee Press, 2000.

Lacy, Benjamin Rice. *Revivals in the Midst of Years.* Richmond: John Knox Press, 1943.

Laderman, Gary. *The Sacred Remains: American Attitudes toward Death, 1799–1883.* New Haven, Conn.: Yale University Press, 1996.

Lakey, Othal Hawthorne. *The History of the CME Church.* Memphis, Tenn.: CME Publishing, 1996.

Lawson, Melinda. *Patriot Fires: Forging a New American Nationalism in the Civil War North.* Lawrence: University Press of Kansas, 2002.

Lazenby, Marion Elias. *History of Methodism in Alabama and West Florida.* N.p.: North Alabama Conference and Alabama-West Florida Conference, 1960.

Lebsock, Suzanne. *The Free Women of Petersburg: Status and Culture in a Southern Town, 1784–1860.* New York: W. W. Norton, 1984.

Leech, Margaret. *Reveille in Washington, 1860–1865.* New York: Harper and Brothers, 1941.

Lehman, James O., and Stephen M. Nolt. *Mennonites, Amish, and the American Civil War*. Baltimore: Johns Hopkins University Press, 2007.

Lehrman, Lewis E. *Lincoln at Peoria: The Turning Point*. Mechanicsburg, Pa.: Stackpole Books, 2008.

Levy, George. *To Die in Chicago: Confederate Prisoners at Camp Douglas, 1862–1865*. Evanston, Ill.: Evanston Publishing, 1994.

Lewis, W. H. *The History of Methodism in Missouri for a Decade of Years, from 1860 to 1870*. Nashville: Methodist Episcopal Church, South, 1890.

Linderman, Gerald F. *Embattled Courage: The Experience of Combat in the American Civil War*. New York: Free Press, 1987.

Litwack, Leon F. *Been in the Storm So Long: The Aftermath of Slavery*. New York: Alfred A. Knopf, 1979.

———. *North of Slavery: The Negro in the Free States, 1790–1860*. Chicago: University of Chicago Press, 1961.

Logan, John R. *Sketches, Biographical and Historical of the Broad River and King's Mountain Baptist Associations from 1800–1882*. Shelby, N.C.: Babington Roberts, 1887.

Long, E. B. *The Saints and the Union: Utah Territory during the Civil War*. Urbana: University of Illinois Press, 1981.

Long, Kathryn Teresa. *The Revival of 1857–58: Interpreting an American Religious Awakening*. New York: Oxford University Press, 1998.

Lord, Francis A. *They Fought for the Union*. Harrisburg, Pa.: Stackpole, 1960.

Loveland, Anne C. *Southern Evangelicals and the Social Order, 1800–1860*. Baton Rouge: Louisiana State University Press, 1980.

Lowe, Richard. *Walker's Texas Division, C.S.A.: Greyhounds of the Trans-Mississippi*. Baton Rouge: Louisiana State University Press, 2004.

Luker, Ralph E. *A Southern Tradition in Theology and Social Criticism, 1830–1930: The Religious Liberalism and Social Conservatism of James Warley Miles, William Porcher DuBose and Edgar Gardner Murphy*. New York: Edwin Mellen Press, 1984.

McCardell, John. *The Idea of a Southern Nation: Southern Nationalists and Southern Nationalism, 1830–1860*. New York: W. W. Norton, 1979.

McCash, William B. *Thomas R. R. Cobb (1823–1862): The Making of a Southern Nationalist*. Macon, Ga.: Mercer University Press, 1983.

McCaslin, Richard B. *Lee in the Shadow of Washington*. Baton Rouge: Louisiana State University Press, 2001.

McCaslin, Robert H. *Presbyterianism in Memphis*. Memphis: Adams Printing, n.d.

McColgan, Daniel T. *A Century of Charity: The First Hundred Years of the Society of St. Vincent De Paul in the United States*. 2 vols. Milwaukee: Bruce, 1951.

McCurry, Stephanie. *Masters of Small Worlds: Yeomen Households, Gender Relations, and the Political Culture of the Antebellum South Carolina Low Country*. New York: Oxford University Press, 1995.

McDannell, Colleen, and Bernhard Lang. *Heaven, A History*. New Haven, Conn.: Yale University Press, 1988.

McDonald, W., and John E. Searles. *The Life of Rev. John S. Inskip, President of the National Association for the Promotion of Holiness*. Boston: McDonald and Gill, 1885.

McFeely, William S. *Grant, a Biography*. New York: W. W. Norton, 1981.

McGreevy, John T. *Catholicism and American Freedom, a History*. New York: W. W. Norton, 2003.

McKivigan, John R. *The War against Proslavery Religion: Abolitionism and the Northern Churches, 1830–1865*. Ithaca, N.Y.: Cornell University Press, 1984.

McKivigan, John R., and Mitchell Snay, eds. *Religion and the Antebellum Debate over Slavery*. Athens: University of Georgia Press, 1998.

McLoughlin, William G. *The Meaning of Henry Ward Beecher*. New York: Alfred A. Knopf, 1970.

———. *Revivals, Awakenings, and Reform: An Essay on Religion and Social Change in America, 1607–1977*. Chicago: University of Chicago Press, 1978.

Macmillan, Margaret. *The Methodist Episcopal Church in Michigan during the Civil War*. Lansing: Michigan Civil War Centennial Observance Commission, 1965.

McMurry, Richard M. *John Bell Hood and the War for Southern Independence*. Lexington: University Press of Kentucky, 1982.

McPherson, James M. *For Cause and Comrades: Why Men Fought in the Civil War*. New York: Oxford University Press, 1997.

Maher, Sister Mary Denis. *To Bind Up the Wounds: Catholic Sister Nurses in the U.S. Civil War*. New York: Greenwood Press, 1989.

Malone, Henry Thompson. *The Episcopal Church in Georgia, 1733–1957*. Atlanta: Protestant Episcopal Church, 1960.

Manning, Chandra. *What This Cruel War Was Over: Soldiers, Slavery, and the Civil War*. New York: Alfred A. Knopf, 2007.

Marlay, John F. *The Life of Rev. Thomas A. Morris, D.D., Late Senior Bishop of the Methodist Episcopal Church*. Cincinnati: Hitchcock and Walden, 1875.

Marsden, George M. *The Evangelical Mind and the New School Presbyterian Experience: A Case Study of Thought and Theology in Nineteenth-Century America*. New Haven, Conn.: Yale University Press, 1970.

Marszalek, John F. *Sherman: A Soldier's Passion for Order*. New York: Free Press, 1993.

Marvel, William. *Andersonville: The Last Depot*. Chapel Hill: University of North Carolina Press, 1994.

Massey, Mary Elizabeth. *Refugee Life in the Confederacy*. Baton Rouge: Louisiana State University Press, 1964.

Mathews, Donald G. *Religion in the Old South*. Chicago: University of Chicago Press, 1977.

———. *Slavery and Methodism: A Chapter in American Morality, 1780–1845*. Princeton, N.J.: Princeton University Press, 1965.

Maxwell, William Quentin. *Lincoln's Fifth Wheel: The Political History of the United States Sanitary Commission*. New York: Longmans, Green, 1956.

May, Lynn E., Jr. *The First Baptist Church of Nashville, Tennessee, 1820–1970*. Nashville: First Baptist Church, Nashville, Tennessee, 1970.

Menand, Louis. *The Metaphysical Club*. New York: Farrar, Straus and Giroux, 2001.

Miller, Gene Ramsey. *A History of North Mississippi Methodism, 1820–1900*. Nashville, Tenn.: Parthenon Press, 1966.

Miller, Perry. *The Life of the Mind in America: From the Revolution to the Civil War*. New York: Harcourt, Brace and World, 1965.

Miller, Randall M., Harry S. Stout, and Charles Reagan Wilson, eds. *Religion and the American Civil War*. New York: Oxford University Press, 1998.

Miller, Randall, and Jon L. Wakelyn. *Catholics in the Old South: Essays on Church and Culture.* Macon, Ga.: Mercer University Press, 1983.

Miller, Robert J. *Both Prayed to the Same God: Religion and Faith in the American Civil War.* Lanham, Md.: Lexington Books, 2007.

Miller, William Lee. *Lincoln's Virtues: An Ethical Biography.* New York: Alfred A. Knopf, 2002.

———. *President Lincoln: The Duty of a Statesman.* New York: Alfred A. Knopf, 2008.

Mitchell, Reid. *Civil War Soldiers: Their Expectations and Their Experiences.* New York: Viking, 1988.

———. *The Vacant Chair: The Northern Soldier Leaves Home.* New York: Oxford University Press, 1993.

Mohr, Clarence L. *On the Threshold of Freedom: Masters and Slaves in Civil War Georgia.* Athens: University of Georgia Press, 1986.

Moe, Richard. *The Last Full Measure: The Life and Death of the First Minnesota Volunteers.* New York: Henry Holt, 1993.

Montgomery, William E. *Under Their Own Vine and Fig Tree: The African-American Church in the South, 1865–1900.* Baton Rouge: Louisiana State University, 1993.

Moorhead, James H. *American Apocalypse: Yankee Protestants and the Civil War, 1860–1869.* New Haven, Conn.: Yale University Press, 1978.

Morel, Lucas E. *Lincoln's Sacred Effort: Defining Religion's Role in American Self-Government.* Lanham, Md.: Lexington Books, 2000.

Morrow, Ralph E. *Northern Methodism and Reconstruction.* East Lansing: Michigan State University Press, 1956.

Mullin, Robert Bruce. *The Puritan as Yankee: A Life of Horace Bushnell.* Grand Rapids, Mich.: William B. Erdmans, 2002.

Murphy, DuBose. *A Short History of the Protestant Episcopal Church in Texas.* Dallas: Turner Company, 1935.

Murray, Andrew E. *Presbyterians and the Negro—A History.* Philadelphia: Presbyterian Historical Society, 1966.

Neely, Mark E., Jr. *Southern Rights: Political Prisoners and the Myth of Confederate Constitutionalism.* Charlottesville: University Press of Virginia, 1999.

Neely, Mark E., Jr., Harold Holzer, and Gabor Boritt. *The Confederate Image: Prints of the Lost Cause.* Chapel Hill: University of North Carolina Press, 1987.

Nelson, Jacquelyn S. *Indiana Quakers Confront the Civil War.* Indianapolis: Indiana Historical Society, 1991.

Niebuhr, H. Richard. *Christ and Culture.* New York: Harper and Brothers, 1951.

———. *The Kingdom of God in America.* New York: Harper and Brothers, 1937.

Niebuhr, Reinhold. *Faith and History: A Comparison of Christian and Modern Views of History.* New York: Charles Scribner's Sons, 1949.

Niven, John. *Connecticut for the Union: The Role of the State in the Civil War.* New Haven, Conn.: Yale University Press, 1965.

Noll, Mark A. *America's God: From Jonathan Edwards to Abraham Lincoln.* New York: Oxford University Press, 2002.

———. *The Civil War as a Theological Crisis.* Chapel Hill: University of North Carolina Press, 2006.

————. *One Nation under God? Christian Faith and Political Action in America*. New York: Harper and Row, 1988.

O'Brien, Michael. *Conjectures of Order: Intellectual Life and the Antebellum South, 1810–1860*. 2 vols. Chapel Hill: University of North Carolina Press, 2004.

O'Connor, Thomas H. *Fitzpatrick's Boston: 1846–1866; John Bernard Fitzpatrick, Third Bishop of Boston*. Boston: Northeastern University Press, 1984.

Osborne, Charles C. *Jubal: The Life and Times of General Jubal A. Early, CSA, Defender of the Lost Cause*. Chapel Hill, N.C.: Algonquin Books, 1992.

Owen, Christopher H. *The Sacred Flame of Love: Methodism and Society in Nineteenth-Century Georgia*. Athens: University of Georgia Press, 1998.

Paludan, Phillip Shaw. *"A People's Contest": The Union and Civil War, 1861–1865*. New York: Harper and Row, 1988.

Paradis, James M. *Strike the Blow for Freedom: The 6th United States Colored Infantry in the United States*. Shippensburg, Pa.: White Mane, 1998.

Parker, Harold M., Jr. *The United Synod of the South: The Southern New School Presbyterian Church*. Westport, Conn.: Greenwood Press, 1988.

Parrish, William E. *A History of Missouri*, vol. 3: *1860–1875*. Columbia: University of Missouri Press, 1973.

Pease, Jane H., and William H. Pease. *A Family of Women: The Carolina Petigrus in Peace and War*. Chapel Hill: University of North Carolina Press, 1999.

Perry, Lewis, and Michael Fellman, eds. *Antislavery Reconsidered: New Perspectives on the Abolitionists*. Baton Rouge: Louisiana State University Press, 1979.

Perry, William Stevens. *The History of the American Episcopal Church: 1587–1883*. 2 vols. Boston: James R. Osgood, 1885.

Peterson, Merrill D. *Lincoln in American Memory*. New York: Oxford University Press, 1994.

Pfanz, Harry W. *Gettysburg: The Second Day*. Chapel Hill: University of North Carolina Press, 1987.

Phelan, Macum. *A History of Early Methodism in Texas, 1817–1866*. Nashville, Tenn.: Cokesbury Press, 1924.

Phillips, C. H. *The History of the Colored Methodist Episcopal Church in America: Comprising Its Organization, Subsequent Development and Present Status*. 3rd ed. Jackson, Tenn.: Publishing House C.M.E. Church, 1925.

Phillips, Jason. *Diehard Rebels: The Confederate Culture of Invincibility*. Athens: University of Georgia Press, 2007.

Pierce, Alfred Mann. *Lest Faith Forget: The Story of Methodism in Georgia*. Atlanta: North and South Georgia Annual Conferences, 1951.

Pillar, James J. *The Catholic Church in Mississippi, 1837–1865*. New Orleans: Hauser Press, 1964.

Piston, William Garrett, and Richard W. Hatcher III. *Wilson's Creek: The Second Battle of the Civil War and the Men Who Fought It*. Chapel Hill: University of North Carolina Press, 2000.

Pitts, Charles F. *Chaplains in Gray: The Confederate Chaplains' Story*. Nashville: Broadman Press, 1957.

Polk, William M. *Leonidas Polk Bishop and General*. 2 vols. Longmans, Green, 1893.

Posey, Walter Brownlow. *Frontier Mission: A History of Religion West of the Southern Appalachians to 1861*. Lexington: University Press of Kentucky, 1966.

Power, J. Tracy. *Lee's Miserables: Life in the Army of Northern Virginia from the Wilderness to Appomattox*. Chapel Hill: University of North Carolina Press, 1998.

Pryor, Elizabeth Brown. *Reading the Man: A Portrait of Robert E. Lee through His Private Letters*. New York: Viking, 2007.

Quarles, Benjamin. *The Negro in the Civil War*. Boston: Little, Brown, 1963.

Rable, George C. *The Confederate Republic: A Revolution against Politics*. Chapel Hill: University of North Carolina Press, 1994.

Raboteau, Albert J. *Slave Religion: The "Invisible Institution" in the Antebellum South*. New York: Oxford University Press, 1978.

Raus, Edmund J., Jr. *Banners South: A Northern Community at War*. Kent, Ohio: Kent State University Press, 2005.

Red, William Stuart. *A History of the Presbyterian Church in Texas*. Austin, Texas: Steck, 1936.

Reid, Avery Hamilton. *Baptists in Alabama: Their Organization and Witness*. Montgomery: Alabama Baptist State Convention, 1967.

Reidy, Joseph P. *From Slavery to Agrarian Capitalism in the Cotton Plantation South: Central Georgia, 1800–1880*. Chapel Hill: University of North Carolina Press, 1992.

Reynolds, Donald E. *Editors Make War: Southern Newspapers in the Secession Crisis*. Nashville: Vanderbilt University Press, 1970.

———. *Texas Terror: The Slave Insurrection Panic of 1860 and the Secession of the Lower South*. Baton Rouge: Louisiana State University Press, 2007.

Rhea, Gordon C. *To the North Anna River: Grant and Lee, May 13–25, 1864*. Baton Rouge: Louisiana State University Press, 2000.

Rice, Madeleine Hook. *American Catholic Opinion in the Slavery Controversy*. New York: Columbia University Press, 1944.

Richardson, Joe M. *Christian Reconstruction: The American Missionary Association and Southern Blacks, 1861–1890*. Athens: University of Georgia Press, 1986.

Richey, Russell E. *The Methodist Conference in America, A History*. Nashville, Tenn.: Kingwood Books, 1996.

Ridgaway, Henry B. *The Life of the Rev. Alfred Cookman with Some Account of His Father, the Rev. George Grimston Cookman*. New York: Harper and Brothers, 1873.

Riley, B. F. *History of the Baptists of Alabama from the Time of Their First Occupation of Alabama in 1808, until 1894*. Birmingham: Roberts and Son, 1896.

Ringold, May Spencer. *The Role of the State Legislatures in the Confederacy*. Athens: University of Georgia Press, 1966.

Rivers, R. H. *The Life of Robert Paine D.D., Bishop of the Methodist Episcopal Church, South*. Nashville, Tenn.: Publishing House of the M.E. Church, South, 1916.

Robertson, A. T. *Life and Letters of John Albert Broadus*. Philadelphia: American Baptist Publication Society, 1901.

Robertson, James I., Jr. *Soldiers Blue and Gray*. Columbia: University of South Carolina Press, 1988.

———. *Stonewall Jackson*. New York: Macmillan, 1997.

Robinson, David. *The Unitarians and the Universalists*. Westport, Conn.: Greenwood Press, 1985.

Roland, Charles P. *Louisiana Sugar Plantations during the Civil War*. Leiden: E. J. Brill, 1957.

Rolfs, David. *No Peace for the Wicked: Northern Protestant Soldiers and the American Civil War*. Knoxville: University of Tennessee Press, 2009.

Romero, Sidney J. *Religion in the Rebel Ranks*. Lanham, Md.: University Press of America, 1983.

Rose, Anne C. *Victorian America and the Civil War*. Cambridge: Cambridge University Press, 1992.

Rosen, Robert N. *The Jewish Confederates*. Columbia: University of South Carolina Press, 2000.

Rothensteiner, John. *History of the Archdiocese of St. Louis*. 2 vols. St. Louis: Blackwell Wielandy, 1928.

Rowland, Thomas J. *George B. McClellan and Civil War History: In the Shadow of Grant and Sherman*. Kent, Ohio: Kent State University Press, 1998.

Royster, Charles. *The Destructive War: William Tecumseh Sherman, Stonewall Jackson, and the Americans*. New York: Alfred A. Knopf, 1991.

Rubin, Anne Sarah. *A Shattered Nation: The Rise and Fall of the Confederacy, 1861–1868*. Chapel Hill: University of North Carolina Press, 2005.

Ryland, Garnett. *The Baptists in Virginia, 1609–1926*. Richmond: Baptist Board of Mission and Education, 1955.

Sandeen, Ernest R. *The Roots of Fundamentalism: British and American Millenarianism, 1800–1930*. Chicago: University of Chicago Press, 1970.

Sanders, Charles W., Jr. *While in the Hands of the Enemy: Military Prisons of the Civil War*. Baton Rouge: Louisiana State University Press, 2005.

Sarris, Jonathan. *A Separate Civil War: Communities in Conflict in the Mountain South*. Charlottesville: University of Virginia Press, 2006.

Saum, Lewis O. *The Popular Mood of Pre–Civil War America*. Westport, Conn.: Greenwood Press, 1980.

Schantz, Mark S. *Awaiting the Heavenly Country: The Civil War and America's Culture of Death*. Ithaca, N.Y.: Cornell University Press, 2008.

Schultz, Jane E. *Women at the Front: Hospital Workers in Civil War America*. Chapel Hill: University of North Carolina Press, 2004.

Schweiger, Beth Barton. *The Gospel Working Up: Progress and the Pulpit in Nineteenth-Century Virginia*. New York: Oxford University Press, 2000.

Scott, Donald M. *From Office to Profession: The New England Ministry, 1750–1850*. Philadelphia: University of Pennsylvania Press, 1978.

Sears, Stephen W. *George B. McClellan: The Young Napoleon*. New York: Ticknor and Fields, 1988.

Sellers, James B. *The First Methodist Church of Tuscaloosa, Alabama 1818–1968*. Tuscaloosa, Ala.: Weatherford Printing, 1968.

Sernett, Milton C. *Black Religion and American Evangelicalism: White Protestants, Plantation Missions, and the Flowering of Negro Christianity, 1787–1865*. Metuchen, N.J.: Scarecrow Press, 1975.

Shackelford, Josephus. *History of the Muscle Shoals Baptist Association from 1820 to 1890, a Period of Years, with a History of the Churches of the Same and a Biographical Sketch of Its Ministers*. Trinity, Ala.: Published by the author, 1891.

Shannon, Fred Albert. *The Organization and Administration of the Union Army, 1861–1865.* 2 vols. Cleveland: Arthur H. Clark, 1928.

Shattuck, Gardner H. *A Shield and Hiding Place: The Religious Life of the Civil War Armies.* Macon, Ga.: Mercer University Press, 1987.

Shaw, Richard. *Dagger John: The Unquiet Life and Times of Archbishop John Hughes of New York.* New York: Paulist Press, 1977.

Sheehan-Dean, Aaron, ed. *View from the Ground: Experiences of Civil War Soldiers.* Lexington: University Press of Kentucky, 2007.

Shenk, Charlotte Forgey, and Donald Hugh Shenk. *History of the First Presbyterian Church, Huntsville, Alabama: Sesquicentennial Observance, 1818–1968.* Montgomery, Ala.: Paragon Press, 1968.

Shipp, Albert M. *The History of Methodism in South Carolina.* Nashville: Southern Methodist Publishing House, 1883.

Siegel, Alan A. *For the Glory of the Union: Myth, Reality, and the Media in Civil War New Jersey.* Rutherford, N.J.: Fairleigh Dickinson University Press, 1984.

Silver, James W. *Confederate Morale and Church Propaganda.* Tuscaloosa, Ala.: Confederate, 1957.

Simkins, Francis Butler, and James Welch Patton. *The Women of the Confederacy.* Richmond: Garrett and Massie, 1936.

Simpson, Brooks D. *Ulysses S. Grant: Triumph over Adversity, 1822–1865.* Boston: Houghton Mifflin, 2000.

Simpson, John Wells. *History of the First Presbyterian Church of Greensboro, North Carolina.* N.p.: n.p., n.d.

Smith, George G. *The History of Georgia Methodism from 1786 to 1866.* Atlanta: A. B. Caldwell, 1913.

———. *The Life and Letters of James Osgood Andrew, Bishop of the Methodist Episcopal Church South. With Glances at His Contemporaries and at Events in Church History.* Nashville: Southern Methodist Publishing House, 1883.

———. *The Life and Times of George Foster Pierce.* Sparta, Ga.: Hancock Publishing Company, 1888.

Smith, Gerald J. *Smite Them Hip and Thigh! Georgia Methodist Ministers in the Confederate Military.* Murfreesboro, Tenn.: Ambassador Press, 1993.

Smith, H. Shelton. *In His Image But . . . Racism in Southern Religion, 1780–1910.* Durham, N.C.: Duke University Press, 1972.

Smith, John Abernathy. *Cross and Flame: Two Centuries of United Methodism in Middle Tennessee.* Nashville: Commission on Archives and History of the Tennessee Conference, 1984.

Smith, John David, ed. *Black Soldiers in Blue: African American Troops in the Civil War Era.* Chapel Hill: University of North Carolina Press, 2002.

Smith, T. E. *History of the Washington Baptist Association of Georgia.* Milledgeville, Ga.: Doyle Middlebrooks, 1979.

Smith, Timothy L. *Revivalism and Social Reform in Mid-Nineteenth Century America.* Nashville: Abingdon, 1957.

Smith, William Alexander. *The Anson Guards, Company C, Fourteenth Regiment North Carolina Volunteers, 1861–1865.* Charlotte, N.C.: Stone, 1914.

Smythe, George Franklin. *A History of the Diocese of Ohio until the Year 1918*. Cleveland: Horace Carr, 1931.

Snay, Mitchell. *Gospel of Disunion: Religion and Separatism in the Antebellum South*. New York: Cambridge University Press, 1993.

Snell, Mark A. *From First to Last: The Life of Major General William B. Franklin*. New York: Fordham University Press, 2002.

Sobel, Mechal. *Trabelin' On: The Slave Journey to an Afro-Baptist Faith*. Princeton, N.J.: Princeton University Press, 1988.

Spain, Rufus B. *At Ease in Zion: A Social History of Southern Baptists, 1865–1900*. Nashville, Tenn.: Vanderbilt University Press, 1967.

Sparks, Randy J. *On Jordan's Stormy Banks: Evangelicalism in Mississippi, 1773–1876*. Athens: University of Georgia Press, 1994.

Stacy, James. *History of the Midway Congregational Church, Liberty County, Georgia*. Newman, Ga.: S. W. Murray, [1951].

Startup, Kenneth Moore. *The Root of All Evil: The Protestant Clergy and the Economic Mind of the Old South*. Athens: University of Georgia Press, 1997.

Staudenraus, P. J. *The African Colonization Movement, 1816–1865*. New York: Columbia University Press, 1961.

Stewart, James Brewer. *Holy Warriors: The Abolitionists and American Slavery*. New York: Hill and Wang, 1976.

Stokes, Anson Phelps. *Church and State in the United States*. 3 vols. New York: Harper and Brothers, 1950.

Stout, Harry S. *Upon the Altar of the Nation: A Moral History of the Civil War*. New York: Viking, 2006.

Stowell, Daniel W. *Rebuilding Zion: The Religious Reconstruction of the South, 1863–1877*. New York: Oxford University Press, 1998.

Strong, Douglas M. *Perfectionist Politics: Abolitionism and the Religious Tensions of American Democracy*. Syracuse, N.Y.: Syracuse University Press, 1999.

Stroupe, Henry Smith. *The Religious Press in the South Atlantic States, 1802–1865*. Durham, N.C.: Duke University Press, 1956.

Strout, Cushing. *The New Heavens and New Earth: Political Religion in America*. New York: Harper and Row, 1974.

Sutherland, Daniel E. *The Expansion of Everyday Life, 1860–1876*. New York: Harper and Row, 1989.

———. *Seasons of War: The Ordeal of a Confederate Community*. New York: Free Press, 1995.

Sutton, William R. *Journeymen for Jesus: Evangelical Artisans Confront Capitalism in Jacksonian Baltimore*. University Park: Pennsylvania State University Press, 1998.

Swaney, Charles Baumer. *Episcopal Methodism and Slavery: With Sidelights on Ecclesiastical Politics*. New York: Negro Universities Press, 1969.

Sweet, William Warren. *Methodism in American History*. New York: Methodist Book Concern, 1912.

———. *The Methodist Episcopal Church and the Civil War*. Cincinnati: Methodist Book Concern Press, 1912.

Taylor, George Braxton. *Life and Letters of George Boardman Taylor, D.D.* Lynchburg, Va.: J. P. Bell, 1908.

Temple, Wayne C. *Abraham Lincoln: From Skeptic to Prophet*. Mahomet, Ill.: Mayhaven, 1995.

Thomas, Emory M. *The Confederate State of Richmond: A Biography of the Capital*. Austin: University of Texas Press, 1971.

———. *Robert E. Lee, a Biography*. New York: W. W. Norton, 1995.

Thompson, Ernest Trice. *Presbyterians in the South*. 3 vols. Richmond: John Knox Press, 1963–73.

———. *The Spirituality of the Church: A Distinctive Doctrine of the Presbyterian Church in the United States*. Richmond: John Knox Press, 1961.

Thornbrough, Emma Lou. *Indiana in the Civil War Era, 1850–1880*. Indianapolis: Indianapolis Historical Bureau & Indiana Historical Society, 1965.

Tise, Larry. *Proslavery: A History of the Defense of Slavery in America*. Athens: University of Georgia Press, 1987.

Tripp, Steven Elliott. *Yankee Town, Southern City: Race and Class Relations in Civil War Lynchburg*. New York: New York University Press, 1997.

Trumbull, H. Clay. *The Knightly Soldier: A Biography of Major Henry Ward Camp, Tenth Conn. Vols*. 6th ed. Rev. Boston: Noyes, Holmes, 1871.

Tucker, Phillip Thomas. *The Confederacy's Fighting Chaplain: Father John B. Bannon*. Tuscaloosa: University of Alabama Press, 1992.

Turbo, Silas Claborn. *History of the Twenty-seventh Arkansas Confederate Infantry*. Conway: Arkansas Research, 1988.

Turner, Thomas Reed. *Beware the People Weeping: Public Opinion and the Assassination of Abraham Lincoln*. Baton Rouge: Louisiana State University Press, 1982.

Tuveson, Ernest Lee. *Redeemer Nation: The Idea of America's Millennial Role*. Chicago: University of Chicago Press, 1968.

Tyler, B. B. *History of the Disciples of Christ*. New York: Christian Literature, 1894.

Vander Velde, Lewis G. *The Presbyterian Churches and the Federal Union, 1861–1869*. Cambridge, Mass.: Harvard University Press, 1932.

Vandiver, Frank E. *Mighty Stonewall*. New York: Macmillan, 1957.

Voegli, V. Jacque. *Free but Not Equal: The Midwest and the Negro during the Civil War*. Chicago: University of Chicago Press, 1967.

Wade, John D. *Augustus Baldwin Longstreet: A Study of the Development of Culture in the South*. New York: Macmillan, 1924.

Walker, Clarence E. *A Rock in a Weary Land: The African Methodist Episcopal Church during the Civil War and Reconstruction*. Baton Rouge: Louisiana State University Press, 1982.

Walker, Peter F. *Vicksburg: A People at War, 1860–1865*. Chapel Hill: University of North Carolina Press, 1960.

Walters, Ronald G. *The Antislavery Appeal: American Abolitionism after 1830*. Baltimore: Johns Hopkins University Press, 1976.

Walzer, Michael. *Just and Unjust Wars: A Moral Argument with Historical Illustrations*. New York: Basic Books, 1977.

Washington, James Melvin. *Frustrated Fellowship: The Black Baptist Quest for Social Power*. Macon, Ga.: Mercer University Press, 1986.

Washington, Versalle F. *Eagles on Their Buttons: A Black Infantry Regiment in the Civil War*. Columbia: University of Missouri Press, 1999.

Wayne, Michael. *The Reshaping of Plantation Society: The Natchez District, 1860–1880*. Baton Rouge: Louisiana State University Press, 1983.

Weeks, Louis B. *Kentucky Presbyterians*. Atlanta: John Knox Press, 1973.

Weeks, Stephen B. *Southern Quakers and Slavery*. Baltimore: Johns Hopkins University Press, 1896.

Weiss, John. *Life and Correspondence of Theodore Parker, Minister of the Twenty-eighth Congregational Society, Boston*. 2 vols. New York: D. Appleton and Company, 1864.

Welter, Rush. *The Mind of America, 1820–1860*. New York: Columbia University Press, 1975.

West, Anson. *A History of Methodism in Alabama*. Nashville, Tenn.: Publishing House, Methodist Episcopal Church, South, 1893.

Westbrook, Robert S. *History of the 49th Pennsylvania Volunteers*. Altoona, Pa.: Altoona Times Print, 1898.

Wetherington, Mark V. *Plain Folk's Fight: The Civil War and Reconstruction in Piney Woods Georgia*. Chapel Hill: University of North Carolina Press, 2005.

Whitaker, Walter C. *Richard Hooker Wilmer: Second Bishop of Alabama, a Biography*. Philadelphia: George W. Jacobs, 1907.

White, Gregory C. *A History of the 31st Georgia Volunteer Infantry*. Baltimore: Butternut and Blue, 1997.

White, Ronald C. *Lincoln's Greatest Speech: The Second Inaugural*. New York: Simon and Schuster, 2002.

Whites, LeeAnn. *The Civil War as a Crisis in Gender: Augusta, Georgia, 1860–1890*. Athens: University of Georgia Press, 1995.

Wiley, Bell Irvin. *The Life of Billy Yank: The Common Soldiers of the Union*. Indianapolis: Bobbs-Merrill, 1952.

———. *The Life of Johnny Reb: The Common Soldier of the Confederacy*. Indianapolis: Bobbs-Merrill, 1943.

———. *Southern Negroes, 1861–1865*. New Haven, Conn.: Yale University Press, 1938.

Wilkinson, Warren, and Steven E. Woodworth. *A Scythe of Fire: A Civil War Story of the Eighth Georgia Infantry Regiment*. New York: William Morrow, 2002.

Williamson, B. B., Jr. *History of Livingston First Baptist Church: Sesquicentennial, 1834–1884*. Livingston, Ala.: Sumter Graphics, 1984.

Wills, Gary. *Lincoln at Gettysburg: The Words That Remade America*. New York: Simon and Schuster, 1992.

Wills, Gregory A. *Democratic Religion: Freedom, Authority, and Church Discipline in the Baptist South, 1785–1900*. New York: Oxford University Press, 1997.

Wilson, Charles Reagan. *Baptized in Blood: The Religion of the Lost Cause, 1865–1920*. Athens: University of Georgia Press, 1980.

Wilson, Douglas L. *Lincoln's Sword: The Presidency and the Power of Words*. New York: Alfred A. Knopf, 2006.

Wilson, Edmund. *Patriotic Gore: Studies in the Literature of the American Civil War*. New York: Oxford University Press, 1962.

Wilson, Kenneth P. *Campfires of Freedom: The Camp Life of Black Soldiers during the Civil War*. Kent, Ohio: Kent State University Press, 2002.

Wolf, William J. *The Almost Chosen People: A Study of the Religion of Abraham Lincoln*. Garden City, N.Y.: Doubleday, 1959.

Wolosky, Shira. *Emily Dickinson: A Voice of War*. New Haven, Conn.: Yale University Press, 1984.

Wood, Forrest G. *The Arrogance of Faith: Christianity and Race in America from the Colonial Era to the Twentieth Century*. New York: Alfred A. Knopf, 1990.

Woodworth, Steven E. *While God Is Marching On: The Religious World of Civil War Soldiers*. Lawrence: University Press of Kansas, 2001.

Wooster, Ralph A. *The Secession Conventions of the South*. Princeton, N.J.: Princeton University Press, 1962.

Wright, Edward Needles. *Conscientious Objectors in the Civil War*. Philadelphia: University of Pennsylvania Press, 1931.

Wright, Mary Emily. *The Missionary Work of the Southern Baptist Convention*. Philadelphia: American Baptist Publication Society, 1902.

Wyatt-Brown, Bertram. *The Shaping of Southern Culture: Honor, Grace and War, 1760s–1890s*. Chapel Hill: University of North Carolina Press, 2001.

York, Robert M. *George B. Cheever, Religious and Social Reformer, 1807–1890*. Orono: University of Maine Press, 1955.

Zwemer, John. *For Home and the Southland: A History of the 48th Georgia Infantry Regiment*. Baltimore: Butternut and Blue, 1999.

Articles

Allen, Cuthbert E. "The Slavery Question in Catholic Newspapers, 1850–1865." United States Catholic Historical Society, *Historical Records and Studies* 26 (1936): 99–169.

Andrews, Reba M. "Slavery Views of a Northern Prelate." *Church History* 3 (March 1934): 60–78.

Angrosino, Michael. "Civil Religion Redux." *Anthropological Quarterly* 75 (Spring 2002): 239–67.

Bailey, Kenneth K. "The Post–Civil War Racial Separations in Southern Protestantism: Another Look." *Church History* 46 (December 1977): 453–77.

Barnes, Howard A. "The Idea That Caused a War: Horace Bushnell versus Thomas Jefferson." *Journal of Church and State* 16 (1974): 73–83.

Bartour, Ron. "American Views on 'Biblical Slavery': 1835–1865, a Comparative Study." *Slavery and Abolition* 4 (May 1983): 41–55.

Blight, David W. "Frederick Douglass and the American Apocalypse." *Civil War History* 31 (December 1985): 309–28.

Bower, Stephen E. "The Theology of the Battlefield: William Tecumseh Sherman and the U.S. Civil War." *Journal of Military History* 64 (October 2000): 1005–34.

Brown, Bruce T. "Grace Church, Galesburg, Illinois, 1864–1866: The Supposed Neutrality of the Episcopal Church during the Years of the Civil War." *Historical Magazine of the Protestant Episcopal Church* 46 (June 1977): 187–208.

Bryan, T. Conn. "Churches in Georgia during the Civil War." *Georgia Historical Quarterly* 33 (December 1949): 283–302.

Budd, Richard M. "Ohio Army Chaplains and the Professionalization of Military Chaplaincy in the Civil War." *Ohio History* 102 (Winter–Spring, 1993): 5–19.

Burger, Nash Kerr. "The Diocese of Mississippi in the Confederacy." *Historical Magazine of the Protestant Episcopal Church* 9 (March 1940): 52–77.

Byrdon, G. MacLaren. "Diocese of Virginia in the Southern Confederacy." *Historical Magazine of the Protest Episcopal Church* 17 (December 1948): 384–410.

Cannon, M. Hamlin. "The United States Christian Commission." *Mississippi Valley Historical Review* 38 (June 1951): 61–80.

Carwardine, Richard J. "Lincoln, Evangelical Religion, and American Political Culture in the Era of the Civil War." *Journal of the Abraham Lincoln Association* 18 (Winter 1997): 27–55.

———. "Methodists, Politics, and the Coming of the American Civil War." *Church History* 69 (September 2000): 578–609.

Chrisman, Richard. "'For God and Country': Illinois Methodist Church Support for President Lincoln during the Civil War." *Lincoln Herald* 80 (Summer 1997): 80–89.

Clarke, T. Erskine. "An Experiment in Paternalism: Presbyterian and Slaves in Charleston, South Carolina." *Journal of Presbyterian History* 53 (Fall 1975): 223–38.

Cole, Charles C., Jr. "Horace Bushnell and the Slavery Question." *New England Quarterly* 23 (March 1950): 19–30.

Connor, Charles P. "The Northern Catholic Position on Slavery and the Civil War: Archbishop Hughes as a Test Case." *Records of the American Catholic Historical Society of Philadelphia* 96 (1986): 35–48.

Crowther, Edward R. "'Jacob's Ladder: The Religious Views of Andrew Johnson." *Journal of East Tennessee History* 65 (December 1993): 53–69.

Daniel, W. Harrison. "An Aspect of Church and State Relations in the Confederacy: Southern Protestantism and the Office of Army Chaplain." *North Carolina Historical Review* 36 (January 1959): 47–52.

———. "Bible Publication and Procurement in the Confederacy." *Journal of Southern History* 24 (May 1958): 191–201.

———. "A Brief Account of the Methodist Episcopal Church, South in the Confederacy." *Methodist History* 6 (January 1968): 27–41.

———. "Southern Protestantism—1861 and After." *Civil War History* 5 (September 1959): 276–82.

———. "Southern Protestantism and Army Missions in the Confederacy." *Mississippi Quarterly* 17 (Fall 1964): 179–91.

———. "Southern Protestantism and the Negro, 1860–1865." *North Carolina Historical Review* 41 (July 1964): 338–59.

———. "Virginia Baptists, 1861–1865." *Virginia Magazine of History and Biography* 72 (January 1964): 94–114.

"Father Joseph O'Hagan." *Woodstock Letters* 8 (1879): 173–83.

Faust, Drew Gilpin. "Christian Soldiers: The Meaning of Revivalism in the Confederate Army." *Journal of Southern History* 53 (February 1987): 63–90.

———. "The Civil War Soldier and the Art of Dying." *Journal of Southern History* 67 (February 2001): 3–38.

Fleming, Walter L. "The Religious Life of Jefferson Davis." *Confederate Veteran*, 35 (October, November 1927): 374–76, 420–21.

Fletcher, Jessie C. "A History of the Foreign Mission Board of the Southern Baptist Convention during the Civil War." *Baptist History and Heritage* 10 (October 1975): 204–19, 232, 255.

Fortenbaugh, Robert. "American Lutheran Synods and Slavery, 1830–1860." *Journal of Religion* 13 (January 1933): 72–92.

Fountain, Dan. "Christ Unchained: African American Conversions during the Civil War Era." *Ohio Valley History* 3 (Summer 2003): 31–46.

Freehling, William W. "James Henley Thornwell's Mysterious Antislavery Moment." *Journal of Southern History* 57 (August 1991): 383–406.

Frese, Joseph R. "The Hierarchy and Peace in the War of Secession." *Thought* 18 (June 1943): 293–305.

Genovese, Eugene D. "King Solomon's Dilemma—and the Confederacy's." *Southern Cultures* 10 (October 2004): 55–75.

Greenberg, Mark I. "Ambivalent Relations: Acceptance and Anti-Semitism in Confederate Thomasville." *American Jewish Archives* 45 (1993): 13–29.

Henry, Joseph O. "The United States Christian Commission in the Civil War." *Civil War History* 6 (1960): 374–88.

Hitchcock, James. "Race, Religion, and Rebellion: Hilary Tucker and the Civil War." *Catholic Historical Review* 80 (July 1994): 497–517.

Holifield, E. Brooks. "The Penurious Preacher? Nineteenth Century Clerical Wealth, North and South." *Journal of the American Academy of Religion* 58 (Spring 1990): 17–36.

Kirby, James E. "The McKendree Chapel Affair." *Tennessee Historical Quarterly* 25 (Winter 1966): 360–70.

Lefler, Hugh T. "Thomas Atkinson, Third Bishop of North Carolina." *Historical Magazine of the Protest Episcopal Church* 17 (December 1948): 422–34.

Lipscomb, Oscar Hugh. "The Administration of John Quinlan, Second Bishop of Mobile, 1859–1883." *Records of the American Catholic Historical Society of Philadelphia* 78 (1967): 3–145.

Loveland, Anne C. "Evangelicalism and 'Immediate Emancipation' in American Antislavery Thought." *Journal of Southern History* 32 (May 1966): 172–88.

Luker, Ralph E. "Bushnell in Black and White: Evidences of the 'Racism' of Horace Bushnell." *New England Quarterly* 45 (September 1972): 408–16.

Maddex, Jack P., Jr. "From Theocracy to Spirituality: The Southern Presbyterian Reversal on Church and State." *Journal of Presbyterian History* 54 (Winter 1976): 438–57.

———. "Proslavery Millennialism: Social Eschatology in Antebellum Southern Calvinism." *American Quarterly* 31 (Spring 1979): 46–62.

Man, Albon P., Jr. "The Church and the New York Draft Riots of 1863." *Records of the American Catholic Historical Society* 62 (1951): 33–50.

Mathews, Donald G. "Charles Colcock Jones and the Southern Evangelical Crusade to Form a Biracial Community." *Journal of Southern History* 41 (August 1975): 299–320.

Mitchell, Joseph. "Southern Methodist Newspapers during the Civil War." *Methodist History* 11 (January 1973): 20–39.

Monroe, Haskell. "Bishop Palmer's Thanksgiving Day Address." *Louisiana History* 4 (Spring 1963): 105–18.

Moore, Margaret DesChamps. "Religion in Mississippi in 1860." *Journal of Mississippi History* 22 (October 1960): 223–38.

Moorhead, James H. "Between Progress and Apocalypse: A Reassessment of Millennialism in American Religious Thought, 1800–1880." *Journal of American History* 71 (December 1984): 524–42.

Morrow, Ralph E. "Methodists and 'Butternuts' in the Old Northwest." *Journal of Illinois State Historical Society* 49 (Spring 1956): 34–47.

Murphy, DuBose. "The Spirit of a Primitive Fellowship: The Reunion of the Church." *Historical Magazine of the Protest Episcopal Church* 17 (December 1948): 435–48.

Murphy, Robert J. "The Catholic Church in the United States during the Civil War Period (1852–1866)." *Records of the American Catholic Historical Society* 39 (December 1928): 271–346.

Nguyen, Julia Huston. "Keeping the Faith: The Political Significance of Religious Services in Civil War Louisiana, 1860–1865." *Louisiana History* 44 (Spring 2003): 165–83.

Norton, Herman. "Revivalism in the Confederate Armies." *Civil War History* 6 (December 1960): 410–24.

Norton, Wesley. "The Methodist Episcopal Church and the Civil Disturbances in North Texas in 1859 and 1860." *Southwestern Historical Quarterly* 68 (January 1965): 317–41.

———. "The Role of a Religious Newspaper in Georgia during the Civil War." *Georgia Historical Quarterly* 48 (June 1964): 125–46.

Parish, Peter J. "The Instrument of Providence: Slavery, Civil War and the American Churches." *Studies in Church History* 20 (1987): 291–320.

Parrillo, Nicholas. "Lincoln's Calvinist Transformation: Emancipation and War." *Civil War History* 46 (September 2000): 227–53.

Partin, Robert. "The Sustaining Faith of an Alabama Soldier." *Civil War History* 6 (December 1960): 425–38.

Perkins, Haven P. "Religion for Slaves: Difficulties and Methods." *Church History* 10 (September 1941): 228–45.

Prim, G. Clinton. "Revivals in the Armies of Mississippi during the Civil War." *Journal of Mississippi History* 44 (August 1982): 227–34.

———. "Southern Methodism in the Confederacy." *Methodist History* 23 (July 1985): 240–49.

Purifoy, Lewis M. "The Southern Methodist Church and the Proslavery Argument." *Journal of Southern History* 32 (August 1966): 325–41.

Quimby, Rollin W. "The Chaplains' Predicament." *Civil War History* 8 (March 1962): 25–37.

———. "Congress and the Civil War Chaplaincy." *Civil War History* 10 (1964): 246–59.

———. "Recurrent Themes and Purposes in the Sermons of the Union Army Chaplains." *Speech Monographs* 31 (November 1964): 425–36.

Redkey, Edwin S. "Black Chaplains in the Union Army." *Civil War History* 33 (December 1987): 331–50.

Riforgiato, Leonard R. "Bishop Timon, Buffalo, and the Civil War." *Catholic Historical Review* 73 (January 1987): 62–80.

Romero, Sidney J. "Louisiana Clergy and the Confederate Army." *Louisiana History* 2 (Summer 1961): 277–300.

Sabine, David. "The Fifth Wheel." *Civil War Times Illustrated* 19 (May 1980): 14–23.

Sandlund, Vivien. "Robert Breckinridge, Presbyterian Antislavery Conservative." *Journal of Presbyterian History* 78 (Summer 2000): 145–54.

Shanks, Caroline L. "The Biblical Anti-Slavery Argument of the Decade, 1830–1840." *Journal of Negro History* 16 (April 1931): 132–57.

Sharrow, Walter G. "John Hughes and a Catholic Response to Slavery in Antebellum America." *Journal of Negro History* 57 (July 1972): 254–69.

Smith, Elwyn A. "The Role of the South in the Presbyterian Schism of 1837–38." *Church History* 29 (March 1960): 44–63.

Smith, Timothy L. "Righteousness and Hope: Christian Holiness and the Millennial Vision in America, 1800–1900." *American Quarterly* 31 (Spring 1979): 21–45.

Snay, Mitchell. "American Thought and Southern Distinctiveness: The Southern Clergy and the Sanctification of Slavery." *Civil War History* 35 (December 1989): 311–28.

Snyder, Edward D. "The Biblical Background of the Battle Hymn of the Republic." *New England Quarterly* 24 (June 1951): 231–38.

Sweet, William W. "Methodist Church Influence in Southern Politics." *Mississippi Valley Historical Review* 1 (March 1915): 546–60.

Urwin, Gregory J. W. "'The Lord Has Not Forsaken Me and I Won't Forsake Him': Religion in Frederick Steele's Union Army, 1863–1864." *Arkansas Historical Quarterly* 52 (Autumn 1993): 318–40.

Weber, Jennifer L. "'If Ever War Was Holy': Quaker Soldiers and the Union Army." *North and South* 5 (April 2002): 66–67.

Wight, Willard E. "Bishop Elder and the Civil War." *Catholic Historical Review* 44 (1958): 290–306.

———. "The Church and the Confederate Cause." *Civil War History* 6 (December 1960): 361–73.

Wiley, Bell Irvin. "'Holy Joes' of the Sixties: A Study of Civil War Chaplains." *Huntington Library Quarterly* 16 (May 1953): 287–304.

Wooten, Fred T., Jr. "Religious Activities in Civil War Memphis." *Tennessee Historical Quarterly* 3 (June–September 1944): 131–49, 360–68.

Zoellner, Robert H. "Negro Colonization: The Climate of Opinion Surrounding Lincoln, 1860–65." *Mid-America* 42 (July 1960): 131–50.

Dissertations

Andreasen, Bryon C. "'As good a right to pray': Copperhead Christians on the Northern Civil War Home Front." Ph.D. dissertation, University of Illinois, Urbana-Campaign, 1998.

Hieronymus, Frank L. "For Now and Forever: The Chaplains of the Confederate States Army." Ph.D. dissertation, University of California, Los Angeles, 1964.

McCann, Mary Agnes. "Archbishop Purcell and the Archdiocese of Cincinnati." Ph.D. Dissertation, Catholic University, 1918.

McDevitt, Theresa Rose. "Fighting for the Soul of America: A History of the United States Christian Commission." Ph.D. dissertation, Kent State University, 1997.

Norton, Herman. "The Organization and Function of the Confederate Chaplaincy, 1861–1865." Ph.D. dissertation, Vanderbilt University, 1956.

Overy, David Henry. "Robert Lewis Dabney: Apostle of the Old South." Ph.D. Dissertation, University of Wisconsin, 1967.

Porch, Luther Quentin. "The First Baptist Church, Tuscaloosa, Alabama, 1818–1871." M.A. thesis, University of Alabama, 1965.

Raney, David Alan. "In the Lord's Army: The United States Christian Commission in the Civil War." Ph.D. dissertation, University of Illinois, 2001.

Rolfs, David Wayne. "No Peace for the Wicked: How Northern Christians Justified Their Participation in the American Civil War." Ph.D. dissertation, Florida State University, 2002.

Scott, Sean Andrew. "'A Visitation of God': Northern Civilians Interpret the Civil War." Ph.D. dissertation, Purdue University, 2008.

Wimmer, Judith Conrad. "American Catholic Interpretations of the Civil War." Ph.D. dissertation, Drew University, 1980.

Winn, Robert Howard. "The Diary of Thomas Harwood: A Personal Perspective of the Northern Chaplaincy during the Civil War." M.T. Thesis, Dallas Theological Seminary, 1981.

ACKNOWLEDGMENTS

This project began in the late spring of 1997 with a phone call from Gary Gallagher and an invitation to write a volume for the Littlefield History of the Civil War era. Gary and the other series editor T. Michael Parrish enthusiastically accepted the idea of a volume on the role of religion during the war. There seemed to be little work being done on the subject, though that has changed dramatically in recent years, and I am deeply indebted to many fellow toilers in the field.

Archivists across the country were unfailingly helpful in identifying important sources and granting access to their collections. Several deserve special mention. Betsey K. Dunbar at the American Baptist Historical Society, Rochester, New York, and Darlene Slater at the Virginia Baptist Historical Society in Richmond searched out useful denominational and congregational records. John Coski at the Museum of the Confederacy in Richmond provided his usual help and encouragement laced with his trademark wry humor. L. Dale Patterson at the General Commission on Archives and History, United Methodist Church, Drew University; Reverend Kenneth J. Ross at the Presbyterian Historical Society, Philadelphia; Paula Skreslet at Union Theological Seminary in Richmond; and Bill Summers at the Southern Baptist Historical Library and Archives, Nashville, all helped me navigate their important collections.

Closer to home in the Gorgas Library at the University of Alabama, Pat Causey tirelessly responded to innumerable interlibrary loan requests. Pat's cheerful assistance was truly extraordinary. Brett Spencer assiduously and enthusiastically supports the addition of historical material to the collections while keeping students and faculty up to date on the latest databases and web resources.

During this book's long gestation period three different History Department chairs, Howard Jones, Larry Clayton, and Michael Mendle have all offered much support and encouragement. In addition, Michael called my attention to a Civil War era edition of Oliver Cromwell's famous *Soldier's Pocket Bible*. And Howard served as a friendly (though tricky!) competitor as we each labored away on our Littlefield volumes. Financial support from the Summersell Fund in Southern History helped defray the expenses of several research trips.

A number of individuals supplied useful information from a range of sources. The late Reverend Emmet Gribbin of Tuscaloosa, Alabama, shared some notes, sources, and microfilm on southern Episcopalians. A longtime friend Phil Lambooy provided valuable citations to several religious periodicals. Rosalind Tedards of Greenville, South Carolina, thoughtfully sent along material from the *Anderson (S.C). Intelligencer*. Budge Weidman generously supplied the service record of Garland H. White. John Grammer of Sewanee, Tennessee, granted permission to quote from the Welborn Mooney correspondence in his possession. Carol Reardon and Lesley Gordon helped answer questions about the closing Pickett quotation. Sean Scott kindly emailed me his excellent (and soon to be published) dissertation on the religious views of northern civilians.

Over many years, Robert Krick, William Marvel, and Mike Parrish have been filling my mailbox (or inbox) with research suggestions, notes, and copies of obscure documents. They will find much of that material scattered through the text and notes in this volume, and their generous assistance is much appreciated. Invitations from William Blair at Pennsylvania State University, Gary Gallagher at the University of Virginia, and Kurt Piehler at the University of Tennessee presented wonderful opportunities to test some early ideas about this project with their graduate students and faculty colleagues. Special thanks are due to William Freehling, whose probing questions on a drive to the Birmingham airport helped break an interpretative logjam.

At the University of North Carolina Press, Brian MacDonald expertly copyedited the manuscript. Once again, Ron Maner has managed the editing and production details with good humor and remarkable efficiency. Thanks to David Perry for his steady support and sage counsel for yet another hefty manuscript.

A friend and former colleague, Merle Strege, read an early draft of the manuscript and tendered some good advice. Harry Stout kindly agreed to read a substantially longer version and, at the last minute, a revised, shorter one, making some astute recommendations on both occasions. Skip generously shared research notes and offered timely support and warm encouragement at some critical moments. An anonymous reader for the University of North Carolina Press crafted a pointed, detailed, and invaluable critique that led to a good deal of revising. Likewise, series editors Gary Gallagher and Mike Parrish made many shrewd suggestions on matters large and small, offering much needed support along the way. Mike pointed out some important problems and added fine suggestions on how to fix them, and Gary came up with an excellent solution for bringing the story to a close.

——— .

Friends and family are among the greatest of God's blessings and have contributed mightily to the completion of this book. Longtime "bro" Tom Schott read some early chapters with his keen editorial eye. He, along with rest of what has occasionally been dubbed the "LSU mafia," has been a fast and true friend for many, many years. The Wednesday morning "Cracker Barrel Club"—Ian Brown, John Hall, Guy Hubbs, and Jim Stovall—offered stimulating conversation and bantering humor. The Fellowship class at Forest Lake United Methodist Church—despite on occasion being a "stiff-necked" group—has taught me a great deal about faith and friendship. Larry Kohl has no doubt heard more than enough about this project in many lunch conversations, but I have greatly appreciated his probing questions, suggestions on Roman Catholic materials, and unfailing friendship. Each year Marius Carriere, Chip Dawson, Frank Wetta, and I meet at the Southern Historical Association, an annual reunion that I anticipate eagerly and cherish deeply. A. Wilson "Coach" Greene and I have known each other for more years than we would prefer to recall, but Will's dedication to public history, frequent letters, and more importantly his deep and abiding friendship continue to inform my work and warm my heart.

While this project was underway, daughters Anne and Katie graduated from high school and from college. Their accomplishments and personal strengths never cease to amaze their proud parents. In 2005, Anne married David Bernath, who has proved to be a fine son-in-law despite his highly questionable sports loyalties. From Bloomington, Indiana, to Auburn, Alabama, to Chandler, Arizona, I have enjoyed following Katie, Anne, and Dave's activities while phone calls and visits have kept the bonds of love strong. And what can be said of my wife Kay? Many wonderful things, but above all she has taught me to appreciate each day of our life together.

INDEX

Abolitionists, and antebellum religion, 12–14

Adger, John, 21, 59

African American chaplains, 421–22 (n. 11)

African American churches, 20–21. *See also* African American religion

African American ministers, 20. *See also* African American religion

African American religion: in antebellum period, 18–21; during war, 286–94; after war, 392–93

African Americans: and push for emancipation, 156; and Emancipation Proclamation, 195, 224–25; and northern missionaries, 291–94

African American soldiers, and religion, 289–90

African Methodist Episcopal Church, 20–21, 294–95, 333, 392

African Methodist Episcopal Zion Church, 294, 333

Alcohol, 78, 100–103, 118

Alexander, Edward Porter, 8, 363

Allen, Richard, 20

Allen, W. B., 283

American Baptist Home Mission Society, 334, 371

American Bible Society, 130, 132

American Board of Commissioners for Foreign Missions, 196

American Missionary Association, 290, 292

American (Know Nothing) Party, 29–30

American Standard (Jersey City), 242

American Tract Society, 132–33

Ames, Edward R., 331

Anderson, Galusha, 199

Anderson, Robert, 51–52

Andrew, James Osgood, 23, 45, 251, 307, 391

Andrews, Eliza Frances, 281–82

Anti-Catholicism, 28–29

Antietam, battle of, 163, 182, 194, 204

Anti-Semitism, 253–55

Apocalyptic thinking, 3–4

Aspey, William, 357

Atkinson, Joseph, 191

Atkinson, Thomas, 41

Atlanta, capture of, 338–39

Bacon, Leonard, 26, 155

Baldwin, Samuel, 332

Balfour, Emma, 265–66

Ball's Bluff, battle of, 175

Bangs, Heman, 35, 222

Bannon, John B., 116, 121

Baptism, 209, 311

Baptists: and slavery, 23–24; and alcohol, 101–2; and army missions, 108; and southern missions, 292–93; and southern churches, 334

Barber, Lorenzo, 116

Barksdale, William, 205

Barrows, William, 154

Barten, O. S., 62

Bartol, Cyrus Augustus, 56, 164, 251–52, 259

Bates, Edward, 321, 323, 331–32

Battle Hymn of the Republic, 89

Beaurdry, Louis, 101

Bebbington, David, 394–95

Beecher, Henry Ward: and politics, 26, 29; on John Brown, 30; on sin during secession crisis, 43; and patriotic preaching, 70; on Lincoln and slavery, 157; on democracy and religion, 190–91; and emancipation, 202; and Emancipation Proclamation, 225; on Stonewall Jackson, 262; on New York draft riots, 266; and 1864 election, 356; on war's end, 375

Beecher, Thomas K., 368

Beidelman, George Washington, 295

Corinth, siege of, 179
Cramer, M. J., 332
Crosby, Franklin Butler, 145
Crummell, Alexander, 26
Cumming, Kate, 179–80, 181, 210, 261, 278,
    281, 300, 365
Curtis, Samuel R., 320–21

Dabney, Robert Lewis: on providence, 2, 4;
    on Bible and slavery, 14, 17; and seces-
    sion, 38, 48; and confidence in Confeder-
    ate arms, 68; speaking to troops, 69, 73;
    and fast day observance, 74; on swear-
    ing, 99; and conversion message, 133; on
    Christian soldiers, 140; and fast day ser-
    mon, 153; and proslavery argument, 278
Daly, Maria Lydig, 264, 384
Dancing, 251
Daniel, John M., 152–53
Danville Quarterly Review, 198
Davis, Jefferson: and days of fasting, hu-
    miliation, and prayer, 73, 148, 152–53,
    232–33, 271, 307, 348, 363–64, and con-
    scription, 149; and Quakers, 150; and
    religion, 188; and war's end, 375; and
    Lincoln's assassination, 386
Death: and providence, 77; pervasiveness
    of, 166–67; fear of, 167–68; and religious
    faith, 167–69; preparation for, 168–71;
    and chaplains, 169–70; soldiers facing,
    174–76; and final words, 176–78; idea
    of good, 176–78, 433 (n. 3), 435 (n. 29);
    funerals and burial after, 179–80; news
    of, at home, 179–82; meaning of, in war,
    182–84; and evangelism, 208
Denominationalism, in the army, 134–36
Deseret News, 54
Deserters, and churches, 256. 451 (n. 58)
Dicey, Edward, 12
Dickinson, Alfred E., 131
Dickinson, Emily, 182
Doggett, Daniel S., 1–2
Douglas, Stephen A., 27, 34
Douglass, Frederick, 195, 225, 374

Draper, William Franklin, 160
Duffield, George, Jr., 36, 128, 197, 201, 385

Eastman, William R., 135
Eddy, Thomas, 335
Eddy, Zachary, 49, 52
Edmondston, Catherine Ann Devereaux, 310
Elder, William Henry, 46, 61, 211, 249, 323–
    25
Election of 1860, 34–37
Election of 1864, 354–57, 468 (n. 17)
Elliott, Stephen: and secession, 47, 59; fast
    day sermon of, 74, 347–48; and criti-
    cism of northern civil religion, 76; on
    providence in battle, 77; on Confederate
    strategy, 82–83; on soldier religion, 91;
    on democracy, 148; and confidence in
    Confederacy, 188; and slavery, 190; and
    talk of peace, 232–33; and Confederate
    fast, 275; and civilian disaffection, 309;
    and baptism of Braxton Bragg, 311; on
    death of Leonidas Polk, 346; and postwar
    religious faith, 394
Elmore, Grace Brown, 210, 360–61, 363, 365,
    387, 393
Emancipation: and thanksgiving, 201–2,
    301; and providence, 376–77, 391–93
Emancipation Proclamation, 224–27
Emerson, Nancy, 130, 224
Emerson, Ralph Waldo, 241
Episcopalians: and defense of slavery, 14;
    and secession, 40, 48; and beginning of
    war, 59–60; and prayers for those in au-
    thority, 325; and slavery, 336
Epsy, Sarah Rodgers, 180, 252
Evangelism, in armies, 208–10. *See also*
    Revivalism
Evans, Augusta, 274
Evans, Clement, 142
Ewell, Richard S., 138
Extortion, 252–55

Fain, Eliza, 67, 73, 248, 263, 280–81, 302,
    346, 392

Holmes, Oliver Wendell, Jr., 175, 395

Holt, David, 163

Home Missionary Society, 24

Hood, John Bell, 131, 311

Hooker, Joseph, 258, 267

Hopkins, John Henry, 226, 295

Hopley, Catherine, 74

Hornblower, William, 386

Hort, Mary, 364

Hospitals, 170–73, 210–13

House, Ellen Renshaw, 361

Howard, Oliver Otis, 99, 112, 139

Howe, Julia Ward, 88

Hoyt, Thomas A., 42

Hughes, John: and slavery, 28, 86; and anti-Catholicism, 29; and 1860 election, 34; and loyalty to government, 61; and reaction to First Bull Run, 78; and support for Union, 192; and emancipation, 197; and nation's sins, 259; and New York draft riots, 265–66

Humphrey, Heman, 42

Hundley, Daniel R., 359

Hunter, Robert M. T., 302, 363

Ide, George, 65, 87, 236, 292–93

Independent: on biblical prophecies, 4–5; on John Brown, 30; on election of 1860, 34; on day of fasting, humiliation, and prayer, 41; on secession, 49; on bloodshed and war, 67; on soldiers and prayer, 94; on temperance, 103; on chaplains, 111; on war deaths, 143; and criticism of Lincoln administration, 158; on providence, 189; on Emancipation Proclamation, 225–26; on southern mission work, 334; on Catholics and loyalty, 336; on election of 1864, 354; on Lincoln's Second Inaugural, 374; on capture of Richmond, 375

Jackson, Thomas J.: and secession, 38; and chaplains, 108; and soldiers' spiritual welfare, 112; as Christian soldier, 137–38,

140; on trust in God, 151; and fast days, 233; death of, 261–64, 451 (n. 13)

James, William, 175–76

Janney, Samuel M., 130

Jeremiad, 80–81, 87, 153, 234–39, 275, 280, 400–401 (n. 17)

Jeter, Jeremiah Bell, 63, 133, 168

Jewish chaplains, 421–22 (n. 11)

Jews: and defense of slavery, 14; and anti-Semitism, 253–55; and camp worship, 424 (n. 48)

Johnson, Andrew, 322, 326, 332, 386, 471 (n. 12)

Johnson, Edmund, 177

Johnson, Thomas Lewis, 288

Johnston, Joseph E., 311

Jones, Charles Colcock, 18, 222, 280

Jones, J. William, 207

Jones, John B., 253, 272, 299, 310, 390

Jones, Mary, 302

Jones, Peter, 209

Jones, W. G. H., 114

Just war theory, 53, 409 (n. 8)

Kansas-Nebraska Act, 27–28

Kennesaw Mountain, battle of, 166

Kenrick, Peter Richard, 56

Kentucky, church divisions in, 197–88

Lacy, B. T., 108

Ladies' Hebrew Association, 249

Ladies' Repository, 377

Lamson, William, 237

Larned, Benjamin, 111

Lawrence, Evan, 166

Lee, George L., 69

Lee, Robert E.: on Sabbath observance, 95; and gambling, 105; as Christian soldier, 136–37, 360; and deaths at home, 181; and fast day, 233; and Chancellorsville, 258; and army revivals, 306; and days of fasting, humiliation, and prayer, 308; and Confederate revivals, 343; surrender of, 375–76, 389

and beginning of war, 55–56; and war, 88; and emancipation, 196, 295, 297; and thanksgiving, 201, 301; in African American religion, 287–88; and southern mission work, 334; and election of 1864, 358–59

Miller, James Russell, 169

Mill Springs, battle of, 147

Ministers: and southern social order, 35; and secession, 35–41; and Buchanan's proclamation, 41–44; as volunteer soldiers, 107–8; effects of war on, 246–47; arrest of, 326, 462 (n. 26)

Minnigerode, Charles, 188, 348

Missionaries: for army, 108; war's effect on, 249–50; in southern states, 291–94; and southern churches, 330–34

Missouri: church divisions in, 199–200; church troubles in, 319–23, 331–32, 461 (n. 12)

Moody, Dwight L., 332, 368

Moody, Granville, 232

Moore, Robert A., 125, 206

Moorhead, James, 452 (n. 32)

Morale, and religious faith, 359–65

Morality: in the army, 70–72, 92–94; war's impact on, 250–52

Morgan, Sarah, 329

Mormons, and Civil War, 53–54

Mudd, Samuel A., 417 (n. 51)

Music, 128–29

Nason, Elias, 53

National Reform Association, 337

New Orleans, 35

New York Bible Society, 130

New York draft riots, 265–66

New York Freeman's Journal and Catholic Register, 86

New York Herald, 386

New York Irish-American, 266

New York Tablet, 122

New York Times, 52, 268

Niebuhr, Reinhold, 88, 196

Noll, Mark, 402 (n. 13), 407 (n. 32)

Northern Christian Advocate, 132

Nugent, William L., 142

Oaths, and southern ministers, 322–23

Officers: religious influence of, 91, 95; and chaplains, 112–13

O'Hagan, James B., 135–36

O'Keefe, Camilla, 212

O'Sullivan, Timothy, 319

Otey, James, 48, 52

Otto, John Henry, 339

Palfrey, William T., 80

Palmer, Benjamin Morgan: on secession, 35–36, 48–49; and civil religion, 63; fast day sermon of, 73–74, 234; and fasting, humiliation, and prayer, 271; and Confederate defeats, 302; on loyalty oaths, 323

Palmer, Sarah, 180

Pardington, John, 143

Paris, John, 460 (n. 45)

Parker, Theodore, 15, 26

Patrick, Marsena, 169

Patriotism, and religion, 65, 67

Patterson, Edmund DeWitt, 367–69

Paxton, Frank, 234

Payne, Daniel, 334

Payne, James H., 290

Peace, talk of, 356

Peace Democrats. *See* Copperheads

Pegram, William R. J., 162, 263, 362

Pember, Phoebe, 164

Pender, William Dorsey, 144

Pendleton, William Nelson, 31, 137, 273, 306, 314, 360

Peninsula Campaign, 152, 157–59

Perry, Theophilus, 142

Petersburg campaign, 215, 340

Phelps, Elizabeth Stuart, 181

Phillips, George C., 297

Pickett, George E., 397

Pierce, George Foster: on Confederate constitution and civil religion, 62–64, 338; on Confederate defeats, 148; on providence, 188–89; fast day sermon of, 234; on slavery, 282, 284; on Confederate constitution, 338

Pierce, Taylor, 145

Pierson, Reuben Allen, 258

Pliant, George, 163

Political preaching, 34–35, 44

Polk, Leonidas, 48, 59–60, 311, 307, 346

Post, Truman, 359

Potter, Alonzo, 226

Prayer: and battle, 1; in Episcopal churches, 59–60; early in war, 72–73; for those in authority, 323–26

Prayer meetings, 129, 366–67

Presbyterian Church in the Confederate States of America, 59

Presbyterians: and schism, 15–16; and slavery, 15–16, 27, 84, 155, 336; and secession, 35–37, 39–40, 45; and beginning of war, 56–59; and civil religion, 63, 467 (n. 4); and army missions, 108; and support for war, 153, 259–60; in border states, 198–99; and thanksgiving, 201; and southern missions, 292; in Missouri, 319–22; and southern churches, 332–33

Preston, Margaret Junkin, 263

Price, Sterling, 320

Princeton Review, 40

Pringle, Cyrus, 229

Prisoners, and religious faith, 365–69, 469 (n. 48)

Protestant Episcopal Church in the Confederate States of America, 60

Providence: and Civil War, 1–3, 8, 9; and secession, 7, 47; in daily life, 24–25; and course of war, 54–55, 82, 147–48, 153–54, 299, 345–46, 349–50, 431–32 (n. 15); and battles, 74–80, 202–3, 258–61, 268–69, 318; and soldiers' faith, 142, 154, 338–40; and Union victories, 154–56, 358; and defeat in battle, 189, 270–76, 308–9, 389–92; and emancipation, 195–98, 225,

294–95, 376–77; and divine chastisement, 222–24; and Stonewall Jackson's death, 261; and fate of Confederacy, 313–15, 460 (n. 48); and end of war, 363–64, 396–97; and war's continuation, 370–74, 470 (n. 3); and Lincoln's assassination, 377–87, 471–72 (n. 28)

Purcell, John Baptist, 61, 192

Purvis, Robert, 26

Quakers: and war, 66; and conscription, 150, 228–30, 445 (n. 24); and emancipation, 226, 353–54; and Lincoln, 353–54

Quinn, William Paul, 21

Quint, Alonzo, 111

Quintard, Charles Todd, 59–60, 311, 348–49

Racial attitudes, and churches, 237, 295–97

Randolph, Valentine, 145–46, 154

Raphall, Morris, 254

Reed, Edward, 76

Reed, Villeroy, 385

Refugees, 255–56

Religious character of Americans, 11–12

Religious education, 245–46

Religious Herald, 116, 253

Religious instruction of slaves, 17–21, 280–84

Religious press, 55

Religious services: become warlike, 55–56; early in war, 70–72; in camp, 119–30; and Christian Commission, 217–18; in prisons, 366–69. *See also* Revivalism

Religious skepticism, 144–45, 429 (n. 61)

Renfroe, J. J. D., 124, 272, 279, 339–40, 342

Revivalism: in Confederate armies, 204–7, 303–7, 310–15, 339–44, 360–62; in Union armies, 205, 304–6, 312–13; and number of converts, 207–8, 440 (n. 12)

Richardson, Marvin, 293

Richmond, capture by Union forces, 374–75

Richmond bread riot, 252

Richmond Dispatch, 77, 364

Richmond Enquirer, 17

Stringfellow, Thornton, 279

Strobel, P. A., 216

Strong, George P., 320

Strong, George Templeton, 30–31, 56, 220

Stuart, George H., 213. 219–20

Stuart, James Ewell Brown, 114

Stuckenberg, John H., 135, 200

Sumner, Charles, 29

Sunday schools, 244–45

Sunderland, Byron, 337

Swain, Leonard, 55, 67

Swearing, 78, 98–100

Taylor, Walter H., 90, 119

Texas, religious troubles in, 33

Thanksgiving, days of, 35, 80–83, 87–88,
    154–55, 200–202, 266–70, 301–2, 353–54,
    357–59, 415 (n. 33), 452 (n. 30)

Thome, James, 296

Thompson, Joseph Parrish, 27, 42, 396

Thornwell, James Henley: and defense of
    slavery, 13–14; and secession, 27, 36, 45;
    on southern Presbyterians, 59; and civil
    religion, 63; on patriotism, 151; on de-
    fense of Richmond, 157

Tichenor, Isaac Taylor, 116, 283–84

Tise, Larry, 402 (n. 14)

Tissot, Peter, 118, 120, 135

Tocqueville, Alexis de, 25, 210

Tracts, 132–34

True Presbyterian, 58–59

Trumbull, Henry Clay, 123

Tucker, J. W., 253

Turner, Henry McNeal, 79–80, 156, 196, 344,
    365

Tuttle, James, 324

Twichell, Joseph Hopkins, 112, 125, 135–36,
    170

Unionists: in Confederacy, 255; persecuted
    in southern churches, 322

Union League, 354

Unitarians: and slavery, 15; and secession,
    40

United States Christian Commission, 131–
    32, 169, 213–19, 442 (n. 40)

United States Sanitary Commission, 219–20

Universalist Quarterly, 155

Vallandigham, Clement L., 231, 295

Van Dorn, Earl, 116

Van Dyke, Henry J., 37, 45, 467 (n. 4)

Vengeance, 346

Verot, Augustin, 41, 327–28

Vicksburg, campaign of, 264–65

Virginia Bible Society, 130

Wade, Deborah B. Lapham, 250

Wadley, Sarah Lois, 40, 273, 281

Wadsworth, Charles, 42, 66, 359–60

Walker, Leroy P., 109

Walthall, Edward C., 362

Ware, John F. W., 133, 293

Watkins, William H., 326

Wayland, Francis, 23, 27–28, 155, 156, 232

Weed, Thurlow, 374

Welles, Gideon, 194

Wesley, John, 22

Whelan, Peter, 368

Whelan, Richard V., 61

White, Garland H., 340

White, Ronald C., 470–71 (n. 10)

White, William S., 137, 261

Whitman, Lafayette, 256

Wiatt, William Edward, 113–14, 117

Wigfall, Louis T., 247

Wightman, Edward King, 125

Wilderness, battle of, 317

Wiley, Bell, 207

Williams, James, 144–45

Williams, Thomas, 155

Williams, William R., 249–50, 380

Willson, Edmund, 227

Wilmer, Richard H., 246, 308, 349

Wilson, Douglas, 470 (nn. 1, 7)

Wilson, Henry, 227

Wilson's Creek, battle of, 181

Wirz, Henry, 368

MIX
Paper from
responsible sources
FSC® C013483
www.fsc.org